# 2026 새 교과서에 맞춘 16차 개정판

# 중학영문법 3800제 1학년

**발행** 16차 개정판 3쇄 (2026년 1월 31일)

**교재 개발 책임** 서은숙　**교재 개발 진행** 박상우, 이혜빈, 최민정, 최은조, 김현수, 이윤정, 도예원

**문제편 집필** 김경미(강남 대치) 선생님, 김은미(대구 달서구) 선생님, 소피아(김규은 경기 분당) 선생님, 최은조, 남현정, 서연서, 이윤정, 이옥현, 양진희, 홍성경, 고미라(서울 상경중) 선생님, 김현, 김주현, 김혜진, 박혜미, 김다영, 서은숙, 박상우, 이혜빈, 최민정

**교재 검토** 김경미(강남 대치) 선생님, 윤미선(서울 하계) 선생님, 조현정(서울 중계) 선생님, 최은조(경기 안양) 선생님, 김미경(서울 동작) 선생님, 김미옥(강남 일원) 선생님, 김은미(대구 달서구) 선생님, 이은혜(경기 일산) 선생님, 소피아(김규은 경기 분당) 선생님, 양원석(서울 서초) 선생님, 송수아(충남 보령) 선생님

**교정** 김경미(강남 대치) 선생님, 김현수, 최은조, 박상우, 신소미, 이혜빈, 최민정, 신준기, 정은주, 홍지민, 신진실, 도예원, 조수성, 서연서, 이윤정, 윤수경, 양진희, 성은혜, 홍성경, 오정훈, 하은옥, 이은영, 유지원, 김다영

**감수** 김유경(서울 목동) 선생님, 이용희(서울 서초) 선생님, 고민정(경기 하남) 선생님, 이태규(서울 대치) 선생님

**영문 감수** Kathryn O' Handley　**디자인** 김연실, 양은선　**삽화** 정제욱, 박주혜, 이혜승, 백승헌, 이유진, 이순웅, 정재환

**단어장 녹음** 손정은, Janet Lee, 최석환　**녹음 편집** 와이알 미디어　**인디자인 편집** 박경아

**제작** 이주영　**발행인** 문숙영　**발행처** 마더텅(Mother Tongue Co., Ltd.)

**주소** 서울시 금천구 가마산로 96, 708호(가산동, 대륭테크노타운 8차)

**팩스** 02-3142-9126　**홈페이지** www.toptutor.co.kr　**등록번호** 제 1-2423호




**마더텅 교재를 풀면서 궁금한 점이 생기셨나요?**

교재 관련 내용 문의나 오류신고 사항이 있으면 아래 문의처로 보내 주세요!
문의하신 내용에 대해 성심성의껏 답변해 드리겠습니다.
또한 교재의 **내용 오류** 또는 **오·탈자, 그 외 수정이 필요한 사항**에 대해
가장 먼저 신고해 주신 분께는 감사의 마음을 담아

네이버페이 포인트 1천 원 을 보내 드립니다!

*기한: 2026년 10월 31일
*오류신고 이벤트는 당사 사정에 따라 조기 종료될 수 있습니다.
*홈페이지에 게시된 정오표 기준으로 최초 신고된 오류에 한하여
　상품권을 보내 드립니다.

💬 **카카오톡** mothertongue　📷 **이메일** mothert1004@toptutor.co.kr
🏠 **홈페이지** www.toptutor.co.kr　📋 **교재Q&A게시판**　🎧 **고객센터 전화** 1661-1064(07:00~22:00)
✉ **문자** 010-6640-1064(문자수신전용)

# 차례

## 1. 규칙 변화형

|  | 원급 | 비교급 | 최상급 |
|---|---|---|---|
| 대부분의 경우: -er/-est | tall | tall**er** | tall**est** |
| -e로 끝나는 경우: -r/-st | nice | nic**er** | nic**est** |
| 단모음 + 단자음으로 끝나는 경우<br>: 마지막 자음 하나 더 쓰고 -er/-est | fat | fat**ter** | fat**test** |
| 자음 +y로 끝나는 경우<br>: y를 i로 바꾸고 -er/-est | pretty | prett**ier** | prett**iest** |
| 대부분의 2음절 이상 형용사 | useful | **more** useful | **most** useful |
| | famous | **more** famous | **most** famous |
| 분사 형태 형용사 | excited | **more** excited | **most** excited |
| [형용사 + ly] 형태의 부사 | quickly | **more** quickly | **most** quickly |

## 2. 불규칙 변화형

| 원급 | 비교급 | 최상급 |
|---|---|---|
| good / well | better | best |
| bad / badly / ill | worse | worst |
| many / much | more | most |
| little | less | least |
| old | older (나이 든) | oldest |
| | elder (연상의) | eldest |
| late | later (늦은) | latest |
| | latter (나중인) | last |
| far | farther (먼) | farthest |
| | further (더욱) | furthest |

# 일반동사의 불규칙 변화형 CHAPTER 2 PSS 2-4

## 1. AAA형 (원형, 과거형, 과거분사형이 같은 형)

| 원형 | 과거형 | 과거분사형 | 뜻 |
|---|---|---|---|
| cost | cost | cost | 비용이 들다 |
| hit | hit | hit | 치다 |
| let | let | let | ～하게 하다 |
| put | put | put | 놓다 |
| read [riːd] | read [red] | read [red] | 읽다 |
| set | set | set | 놓다 |

## 2. ABB형 (과거형과 과거분사형이 같은 형)

| 원형 | 과거형 | 과거분사형 | 뜻 |
|---|---|---|---|
| bring | brought | brought | 가져오다 |
| build | built | built | 짓다 |
| buy | bought | bought | 사다 |
| catch | caught | caught | 잡다 |
| feel | felt | felt | 느끼다 |
| fight | fought | fought | 싸우다 |
| find | found | found | 발견하다 |
| get | got | got(ten) | 얻다 |
| have | had | had | 가지다, 먹다 |
| hear | heard [həːrd] | heard [həːrd] | 듣다 |
| hold | held | held | 지니다 |
| keep | kept | kept | 유지하다 |
| lead | led | led | 인도하다 |
| leave | left | left | 떠나다 |
| lose | lost | lost | 잃어버리다 |
| make | made | made | 만들다 |
| meet | met | met | 만나다 |
| pay | paid | paid | 지불하다 |
| say | said [sed] | said [sed] | 말하다 |
| sell | sold | sold | 팔다 |
| send | sent | sent | 보내다 |
| sit | sat | sat | 앉다 |

| | | | |
|---|---|---|---|
| spend | spent | spent | 소비하다 |
| teach | taught | taught | 가르치다 |
| tell | told | told | 말하다 |
| think | thought | thought | 생각하다 |
| understand | understood | understood | 이해하다 |
| win | won | won | 이기다 |

## 3. ABC형 (원형, 과거형, 과거분사형이 다른 형)

| 원형 | 과거형 | 과거분사형 | 뜻 |
|---|---|---|---|
| be | was / were | been | ～이다, 있다 |
| begin | began | begun | 시작하다 |
| break | broke | broken | 깨뜨리다 |
| choose | chose | chosen | 선택하다 |
| do | did | done | 하다 |
| drive | drove | driven | 운전하다 |
| eat | ate | eaten | 먹다 |
| fall | fell | fallen | 떨어지다 |
| forget | forgot | forgotten | 잊다 |
| give | gave | given | 주다 |
| go | went | gone | 가다 |
| know | knew | known | 알다 |
| see | saw | seen | 보다 |
| sing | sang | sung | 노래하다 |
| speak | spoke | spoken | 말하다 |
| swim | swam | swum | 수영하다 |
| take | took | taken | 가지고 가다 |
| throw | threw | thrown | 던지다 |
| wear | wore | worn | 입다 |
| write | wrote | written | 쓰다 |

## 4. ABA형 (원형과 과거분사형이 같은 형)

| 원형 | 과거형 | 과거분사형 | 뜻 |
|---|---|---|---|
| become | became | become | 되다 |
| come | came | come | 오다 |
| run | ran | run | 달리다 |

## 인칭대명사 CHAPTER 1 **PSS 1** & CHAPTER 6 **PSS 1**

| 수 | 인칭 | 주격 | 소유격 | 목적격 | 소유대명사 |
|---|---|---|---|---|---|
| 단수 | 1 | I | my | me | mine |
| | 2 | you | your | you | yours |
| | 3 | he | his | him | his |
| | 3 | she | her | her | hers |
| | | it | its | it | – |
| 복수 | 1 | we | our | us | ours |
| | 2 | you | your | you | yours |
| | 3 | they | their | them | theirs |

## 명사의 복수형 CHAPTER 5 **PSS 2**

| 규칙 복수형 I | 대부분의 경우 | -s | pencil – pencils, sport – sports |
|---|---|---|---|
| | -s, -x, -ch, -sh로 끝날 때 | -es | bus - buses, box - boxes, church - churches, dish - dishes |
| | 자음 +o로 끝날 때 | -es | potato - potatoes, tomato - tomatoes *cf.* piano - pianos, photo - photos |
| | 모음 +o로 끝날 때 | -s | radio - radios, audio - audios |
| 규칙 복수형 II | 자음 +y로 끝날 때 | y를 i로 바꾸고 -es | candy - candies , country - countries |
| | 모음 +y로 끝날 때 | -s | day - days, boy - boys |
| | -f, -fe로 끝날 때 | f / fe를 v로 바꾸고 -es | leaf - leaves, wolf - wolves knife - knives *cf.* roof - roofs |
| 불규칙 복수형 | 단수형과 복수형이 같은 명사 | | deer - deer, fish - fish, sheep - sheep |
| | 그 밖의 명사의 불규칙 복수형 | | foot - feet, tooth - teeth, man - men, woman - women, goose - geese, mouse - mice |

# 중학영문법 3800제 열공 학습진도표 1학년

## CHAPTER 1 문장의 기초

| PSS | | 체크 | 학습날짜 |
|---|---|---|---|
| PSS 1 | 1-1 | ☐ | / |
| | 1-2 | ☐ | / |
| | 1-3 | ☐ | / |
| | 1-4 | ☐ | / |
| | 1-5 | ☐ | / |
| | 1-6 | ☐ | / |
| | 1-7 | ☐ | / |
| | 1-8 | ☐ | / |
| | 1-9 | ☐ | / |
| | 1-10 | ☐ | / |
| | 1-11 | ☐ | / |
| | 1-12 | ☐ | / |
| | 1-13 | ☐ | / |
| PSS 2 | 2-1 | ☐ | / |
| | 2-2 | ☐ | / |
| | 2-3 | ☐ | / |
| | 2-4 | ☐ | / |
| | 2-5 | ☐ | / |
| 중간·기말 대비 | | ☐ | / |

## CHAPTER 2 시제

| PSS | | 체크 | 학습날짜 |
|---|---|---|---|
| PSS 1 | 1-1 | ☐ | / |
| | 1-2 | ☐ | / |
| | 1-3 | ☐ | / |
| | 1-4 | ☐ | / |
| PSS 2 | 2-1 | ☐ | / |
| | 2-2 | ☐ | / |
| | 2-3 | ☐ | / |
| | 2-4 | ☐ | / |
| | 2-5 | ☐ | / |
| PSS 3 | | ☐ | / |
| PSS 4 | 4-1 | ☐ | / |
| | 4-2 | ☐ | / |
| | 4-3 | ☐ | / |
| | 4-4 | ☐ | / |
| PSS 5 | 5-1 | ☐ | / |
| | 5-2 | ☐ | / |
| 중간·기말 대비 | | ☐ | / |

## CHAPTER 3 조동사

| PSS | | 체크 | 학습날짜 |
|---|---|---|---|
| PSS 1 | | ☐ | / |
| PSS 2 | | ☐ | / |
| PSS 3 | | ☐ | / |
| PSS 4 | 4-1 | ☐ | / |
| | 4-2 | ☐ | / |
| | 4-3 | ☐ | / |
| | 4-4 | ☐ | / |
| | 4-5 | ☐ | / |
| | 4-6 | ☐ | / |
| | 4-7 | ☐ | / |
| | 4-8 | ☐ | / |
| | 4-9 | ☐ | / |
| | 4-10 | ☐ | / |
| 중간·기밀 대비 | | ☐ | / |

## CHAPTER 4 수동태

| PSS | | 체크 | 학습날짜 |
|---|---|---|---|
| PSS 1 | | ☐ | / |
| PSS 2 | | ☐ | / |
| PSS 3 | | ☐ | / |
| PSS 4 | | ☐ | / |
| PSS 5 | | ☐ | / |
| PSS 6 | | ☐ | / |
| 중간·기말 대비 | | ☐ | / |

## CHAPTER 5 명사와 관사

| PSS | | 체크 | 학습날짜 |
|---|---|---|---|
| PSS 1 | | ☐ | / |
| PSS 2 | 2-1 | ☐ | / |
| | 2-2 | ☐ | / |
| | 2-3 | ☐ | / |
| PSS 3 | | ☐ | / |
| PSS 4 | | ☐ | / |
| PSS 5 | | ☐ | / |
| PSS 6 | | ☐ | / |
| PSS 7 | | ☐ | / |
| PSS 8 | | ☐ | / |
| PSS 9 | | ☐ | / |
| PSS 10 | | ☐ | / |
| PSS 11 | | ☐ | / |
| 중간·기말 대비 | | ☐ | / |

## CHAPTER 6 대명사

| PSS | | 체크 | 학습날짜 |
|---|---|---|---|
| PSS 1 | | ☐ | / |
| PSS 2 | | ☐ | / |
| PSS 3 | | ☐ | / |
| PSS 4 | | ☐ | / |
| PSS 5 | 5-1 | ☐ | / |
| | 5-2 | ☐ | / |
| | 5-3 | ☐ | / |
| PSS 6 | 6-1 | ☐ | / |
| | 6-2 | ☐ | / |
| PSS 7 | | ☐ | / |
| 중간·기말 대비 | | ☐ | / |

중학영문법 3800제 열공 학습진도표 1학년

## CHAPTER 7 부정사

| PSS | | 체크 | 학습날짜 |
|---|---|---|---|
| PSS 1 | 1-1 | ☐ | / |
| | 1-2 | ☐ | / |
| PSS 2 | | ☐ | / |
| PSS 3 | | ☐ | / |
| PSS 4 | 4-1 | ☐ | / |
| | 4-2 | ☐ | / |
| 중간·기말 대비 | | ☐ | / |

## CHAPTER 8 동명사

| PSS | | 체크 | 학습날짜 |
|---|---|---|---|
| PSS 1 | | ☐ | / |
| PSS 2 | | ☐ | / |
| PSS 3 | 3-1 | ☐ | / |
| | 3-2 | ☐ | / |
| | 3-3 | ☐ | / |
| 중간·기말 대비 | | ☐ | / |

## CHAPTER 9 분사

| PSS | 체크 | 학습날짜 |
|---|---|---|
| PSS 1 | ☐ | / |
| PSS 2 | ☐ | / |
| PSS 3 | ☐ | / |
| PSS 4 | ☐ | / |
| PSS 5 | ☐ | / |
| 중간·기말 대비 | ☐ | / |

## CHAPTER 10 형용사

| PSS | | 체크 | 학습날짜 |
|---|---|---|---|
| PSS 1 | | ☐ | / |
| PSS 2 | | ☐ | / |
| PSS 3 | | ☐ | / |
| PSS 4 | 4-1 | ☐ | / |
| | 4-2 | ☐ | / |
| | 4-3 | ☐ | / |
| | 4-4 | ☐ | / |
| | 4-5 | ☐ | / |
| | 4-6 | ☐ | / |
| | 4-7 | ☐ | / |
| | 4-8 | ☐ | / |
| | 4-9 | ☐ | / |
| PSS 5 | 5-1 | ☐ | / |
| | 5-2 | ☐ | / |
| PSS 6 | 6-1 | ☐ | / |
| | 6-2 | ☐ | / |
| | 6-3 | ☐ | / |
| | 6-4 | ☐ | / |
| 중간·기말 대비 | | ☐ | / |

## CHAPTER 11 부사

| PSS | | 체크 | 학습날짜 |
|---|---|---|---|
| PSS 1 | 1-1 | ☐ | / |
| | 1-2 | ☐ | / |
| PSS 2 | 2-1 | ☐ | / |
| | 2-2 | ☐ | / |
| PSS 3 | | ☐ | / |
| PSS 4 | | ☐ | / |
| PSS 5 | 5-1 | ☐ | / |
| | 5-2 | ☐ | / |
| PSS 6 | 6-1 | ☐ | / |
| | 6-2 | ☐ | / |
| 중간·기말 대비 | | ☐ | / |

## CHAPTER 12 비교구문

| PSS | | 체크 | 학습날짜 |
|---|---|---|---|
| PSS 1 | 1-1 | ☐ | / |
| | 1-2 | ☐ | / |
| | 1-3 | ☐ | / |
| | 1-4 | ☐ | / |
| PSS 2 | | ☐ | / |
| PSS 3 | 3-1 | ☐ | / |
| | 3-2 | ☐ | / |
| | 3-3 | ☐ | / |
| PSS 4 | 4-1 | ☐ | / |
| | 4-2 | ☐ | / |
| 중간·기말 대비 | | ☐ | / |

## CHAPTER 13 접속사

| PSS | 체크 | 학습날짜 |
|---|---|---|
| PSS 1 | ☐ | / |
| PSS 2 | ☐ | / |
| PSS 3 | ☐ | / |
| PSS 4 | ☐ | / |
| PSS 5 | ☐ | / |
| PSS 6 | ☐ | / |
| PSS 7 | ☐ | / |
| 중간·기말 대비 | ☐ | / |

## CHAPTER 14 전치사 & 속담

| PSS | | 체크 | 학습날짜 |
|---|---|---|---|
| PSS 1 | 1-1 | ☐ | / |
| | 1-2 | ☐ | / |
| | 1-3 | ☐ | / |
| | 1-4 | ☐ | / |
| PSS 2 | 2-1 | ☐ | / |
| | 2-2 | ☐ | / |
| | 2-3 | ☐ | / |
| | 2-4 | ☐ | / |
| PSS 3 | 3-1 | ☐ | / |
| | 3-2 | ☐ | / |
| | 3-3 | ☐ | / |
| PSS 4 | | ☐ | / |
| PSS 5 | | ☐ | / |
| PSS 6 | 6-1 | ☐ | / |
| | 6-2 | ☐ | / |
| PSS 7 | | ☐ | / |
| 중간·기말 대비 | | ☐ | / |

PROBLEM SOLVING SKILL

www.toptutor.co.kr

# CHAPTER 1
# 문장의 기초

# PSS 1 문장의 종류



## PSS 1-1 명사의 인칭 구분

인칭대명사는 사람, 사물의 이름을 대신하여 쓰는 명사이다. 말하는 사람은 1인칭, 듣는 사람은 2인칭, 그 밖의 사람/사물은 3인칭이라고 한다. 한 명은 단수로 나타내지만, 여러 명은 복수로 나타낸다.

| he (3인칭 단수) | she (3인칭 단수) | it (3인칭 단수) |
|---|---|---|
| Mike | Jane | a car |
| Mr. Lee | Ms. Kim | the book |
| an uncle | an aunt | my school |
| my father | my mother | this dog |
| a boy | a girl | that box |
| the man | the woman | Seoul |

| we (1인칭 복수) | you (2인칭 복수) | they (3인칭 복수) |
|---|---|---|
| you and I | you and Ann | Tom and Sue |
| Jack and I | you and your friends | these pens |
| my friends and I | you and Jake | those children |
| you, my brother and I | you and her sister | teachers |

정답 p.0

## PRACTICE 1

다음을 인칭대명사(he, she, it, we, you, they)로 바꾸어 쓰세요.

1 your bicycle ➡ _______________
2 my friends ➡ _______________
3 you and my friend ➡ _______________
4 his brother ➡ _______________
5 the apples ➡ _______________
6 his bag ➡ _______________
7 she and I ➡ _______________
8 Tom and Jane ➡ _______________
9 a tall man ➡ _______________
10 you and I ➡ _______________
11 that pretty girl ➡ _______________
12 you and your teacher ➡ _______________
13 computers ➡ _______________
14 these children ➡ _______________

## PSS 1-2 인칭대명사와 be동사

| 현재형 | | | 과거형 | |
|---|---|---|---|---|
| I | **am** | (= I'm) | I | **was** |
| he<br>she<br>it | **is** | (= he's)<br>(= she's)<br>(= it's) | he<br>she<br>it | **was** |
| we<br>you<br>they | **are** | (= we're)<br>(= you're)<br>(= they're) | we<br>you<br>they | **were** |

***cf.*** it's와 it의 소유격 its는 헷갈리기 쉬우므로 주의해야 한다.

**It's** his book. 그것은 그의 책이다.

**Its** mouth is big. 그것의 입은 크다.

정답 p.0

## PRACTICE 2

다음 우리말 해석과 뜻이 통하도록 빈칸에 알맞은 be동사를 쓰세요.

**1** 나는 작년에 12살이었다.

➡ I _________ 12 years old last year.

**2** 어젯밤은 추웠다.

➡ It _________ cold last night.

**3** Mike와 Andy는 학생이다.

➡ Mike and Andy _________ students.

**4** 그녀의 양손은 사탕으로 가득했다.

➡ Her hands _________ full of candies.

**5** 너는 한국인이다.

➡ You _________ Korean.

**6** 나는 캐나다 출신이다.

➡ I _________ from Canada.

정답 p.0

## PRACTICE 3

다음 우리말 해석과 뜻이 통하도록 밑줄 친 부분을 고쳐 쓰세요. (단, 틀린 곳이 없으면 O표시할 것.)

**1** 그녀는 선생님이다.

➡ She <u>are</u> a teacher. _________

**2** 그것은 잠자리이다.

➡ It <u>is</u> a dragonfly. _________

**3** 너와 나는 친구이다.

➡ You and I <u>am</u> friends. _________

**4** Peter와 David는 형제이다.

➡ Peter and David <u>is</u> brothers. _________

**5** 우리는 버스를 타고 있다.

➡ We <u>are</u> on the bus. _________

**6** 나는 행복하다.

➡ I <u>was</u> happy. _________

**7** 그들은 도서관에 있었다.

➡ They <u>was</u> at the library. _________

**8** 그는 피곤했다.

➡ He <u>were</u> tired. _________

# PSS 1-3 be동사의 부정문

| 현재형 – am/is/are+not | | 과거형 – was/were+not | |
|---|---|---|---|
| I **am not** | (= I'm not) | I **was not** | (= I wasn't) |
| he | (= he's not / he isn't) | he | (= he wasn't) |
| she **is not** | (= she's not / she isn't) | she **was not** | (= she wasn't) |
| it | (= it's not / it isn't) | it | (= it wasn't) |
| we | (= we're not / we aren't) | we | (= we weren't) |
| you **are not** | (= you're not / you aren't) | you **were not** | (= you weren't) |
| they | (= they're not / they aren't) | they | (= they weren't) |

***cf.*** 주어와 be동사의 과거형은 줄여 쓸 수 없다. He was → He's (X)

정답 p.0

## PRACTICE 4

다음 문장의 밑줄 친 부분을 줄여서 다시 쓰세요.

**1** You are not 15 years old.
➡ _You're not[You aren't]_ 15 years old.

**2** He is at home.
➡ ____________ at home.

**3** I am not happy.
➡ ____________ happy.

**4** She is not angry.
➡ ____________ angry.

**5** We are not thirsty.
➡ ____________ thirsty.

**6** You were not a visitor.
➡ ____________ a visitor.

**7** They are Korean.
➡ ____________ Korean.

**8** It is not warm.
➡ ____________ warm.

**9** I was not in Busan.
➡ ____________ in Busan.

**10** She was not busy.
➡ ____________ busy.

**11** We were not ready.
➡ ____________ ready.

**12** It was not her dog.
➡ ____________ her dog.

**13** He was not small.
➡ ____________ small.

**14** They are not students.
➡ ____________ students.

**15** You are not late.
➡ ____________ late.

**16** He is not my friend.
➡ ____________ my friend.

## PRACTICE 5

다음 문장을 부정문으로 바꾸어 쓰세요.

**1** He is my uncle.
➡ He is not[He's not/He isn't] my uncle.

**2** The boy was very friendly.
➡ _______________________

**3** I am thirteen years old.
➡ _______________________

**4** This towel was wet.
➡ _______________________

**5** You were afraid of dogs.
➡ _______________________

**6** The flowers are very pretty.
➡ _______________________

**7** She is from London.
➡ _______________________

**8** We are late.
➡ _______________________

**9** I was in the school band.
➡ _______________________

**10** We were happy with the news.
➡ _______________________

# PSS 1-4 일반동사의 긍정문/부정문

일반동사는 be동사와 조동사를 제외한 모든 동사를 말하며, 주어의 동작이나 상태를 나타낸다.

### 1. 긍정문

| 주어＋동사원형 | | 주어＋동사원형＋-(e)s | |
|---|---|---|---|
| I<br>we<br>you<br>they | play<br>like ~<br>work | he<br>she<br>it | plays<br>likes ~<br>works |

*cf.* 주어가 he, she, it과 같은 3인칭 단수이고 현재시제일 때는 동사원형에 -(e)s를 붙인다.

### 2. 부정문

| 현재형 – do/does＋not＋동사원형 | | | 과거형 – did＋not＋동사원형 | | |
|---|---|---|---|---|---|
| I **do not** (= I don't) | | | I **did not** (= I didn't) | | |
| he (= he doesn't)<br>she **does not** (= she doesn't)<br>it (= it doesn't) | play<br>like ~<br>work | | he (= he didn't)<br>she **did not** (= she didn't)<br>it (= it didn't) | play<br>like ~<br>work | |
| we (= we don't)<br>you **do not** (= you don't)<br>they (= they don't) | | | we (= we didn't)<br>you **did not** (= you didn't)<br>they (= they didn't) | | |

## PRACTICE 6

다음 문장을 부정문으로 바꾸어 쓰세요.

**1** She likes me.
➡ _____She does not[doesn't] like me._____

**2** It rained a lot.
➡ _______________________

**3** You drink coffee.
➡ _______________________

**4** I want a pet.
➡ _______________________

**5** We bought a newspaper.
➡ _______________________

**6** It happens very often.
➡ _______________________

**7** They work very hard.
➡ _______________________

**8** He looks like a good player.
➡ _______________________

**9** Mike went to the cinema.
➡ _______________________

**10** He watches TV in the morning.
➡ _______________________



## PRACTICE 7

우리말과 같은 뜻이 되도록 빈칸에 알맞은 단어를 쓰세요. (단, 부정문의 경우 축약형으로 쓰세요.)

**1** 지나는 춤을 추지 않았다. = Jina ___didn't___ ___dance___ .

**2** 그들은 우유를 좋아한다. = They ___________ milk.

**3** 그는 초콜릿을 만든다. = He ___________ chocolate.

**4** 형과 나는 싸우지 않는다. = My brother and I ___________ ___________ .

**5** 한 소녀가 스마트폰을 산다. = A girl ___________ a smartphone.

**6** 그것은 꼬리를 가지고 있지 않다. = It ___________ ___________ a tail.

**7** 우리는 우리의 아버지를 사랑한다. = We ___________ our father.

**8** 그녀는 수영을 잘하지 않는다. = She ___________ well.

**9** 너는 영어를 공부하지 않았다. = You ___________ English.

**10** 나는 책을 읽지 않는다. = I ___________ ___________ books.

의문사로 시작되지 않는 의문문은 Yes나 No로 대답한다.

### 1. be동사가 있는 의문문

> 「Be동사+주어 ~?」 – Yes, 주어+be동사. / No, 주어+be동사+not.

She is happy. 그녀는 행복하다.

**Is she** happy? 그녀는 행복하니?

– **Yes**, she is. / **No**, she isn't.
응, 행복해. / 아니, 행복하지 않아.

**Is it** your dog?
그것은 너의 개니?

– **Yes**, it is. / **No**, it isn't.
응, 내 개야. / 아니, 내 개가 아니야.

**Was Sumi** late?
수미가 늦었니?

– **Yes**, she was. / **No**, she wasn't.
응, 늦었어. / 아니, 늦지 않았어.

**Were they** kind? – **Yes**, they were. / **No**, they weren't.
그들은 친절했니?　　　응, 친절했어. / 아니, 친절하지 않았어.

### 2. 일반동사가 있는 의문문

> 「Do[Does, Did]+주어+동사원형 ~?」
> – Yes, 주어+do[does, did]. / No, 주어+do[does, did]+not.

You like music. 너는 음악을 좋아한다.

**Do you like** music? 너는 음악을 좋아하니?

– **Yes**, I do. / **No**, I don't. 응, 좋아해. / 아니, 좋아하지 않아.

**Does he love** dogs? – **Yes**, he does. / **No**, he doesn't.
그는 개를 좋아하니?　　　응, 좋아해. / 아니, 좋아하지 않아.

**Did they have** breakfast? – **Yes**, they did. / **No**, they didn't.
그들은 아침을 먹었니?　　　응, 먹었어. / 아니, 먹지 않았어.

## PRACTICE 8

다음 문장을 의문문으로 바꾸어 쓰세요.

**1** Sue is hungry.
➡ _______Is Sue hungry?_______

**2** You are in this class.
➡ _______________________

**3** Mary likes cats.
➡ _______________________

**4** You live near here.
➡ _______________________

**5** He took photographs.
➡ _______________________

**6** Tom's father was in hospital.
➡ _______________________

**7** They enjoy a rock concert.
➡ _______________________

**8** She has big blue eyes.
➡ _______________________

**9** These books were very interesting.
➡ _______________________

**10** This is the Empire State Building.
➡ _______________________

---

## PSS 1-6 부정의문문

부정어가 들어가 있는 의문문을 부정의문문이라 하며, 대답은 질문의 긍정/부정 형태와 관계 없이 대답의 내용이 긍정이면 Yes, 부정이면 No로 답한다. 이때 Yes, No는 우리말의 '네', '아니오'와는 반대이므로 주의해야 한다.

**Don't you** know Tom? 너는 Tom을 알지 않니?

 – **Yes**, I do. (= Yes, I know Tom.) 아니요, 압니다.

 – **No**, I don't. (= No, I don't know Tom.) 네, 모릅니다.

Isn't she American? – **Yes**, she is. / **No**, she isn't.

그녀는 미국인이지 않니?　　아니, 미국인이야. / 응, 미국인이 아니야.

**Aren't you** hungry? – **Yes**, I am. / **No**, I'm not.

너 배고프지 않니?　　아니, 배고파. / 응, 배고프지 않아.

**Weren't these shoes** dirty? – **Yes**, they were. / **No**, they weren't.

이 신발은 더럽지 않았니?　　아니, 더러웠어. / 응, 더럽지 않았어.

**Doesn't he** like soccer? – **Yes**, he does. / **No**, he doesn't.

그는 축구를 좋아하지 않니?　　아니, 좋아해. / 응, 좋아하지 않아.

**Didn't you** use the Internet? – **Yes**, I did. / **No**, I didn't.

너는 인터넷을 사용하지 않았니?　　아니, 사용했어. / 응, 사용하지 않았어.

정답 p.0

## PRACTICE 9

〈보기〉와 같이 주어진 질문에 대한 알맞은 대답을 빈칸에 쓰세요.

> 보 기
> *A*: Isn't she an English teacher?
> *B*: <u>Yes, she is.</u> (She is an English teacher.)

**1** *A*: Isn't he married?

   *B*: _________________ (He isn't married.)

**2** *A*: Don't you speak Spanish?

   *B*: _________________ (We speak Spanish.)

**3** *A*: Does Tim enjoy Korean food?

   *B*: _________________ (Tim enjoys Korean food.)

**4** *A*: Weren't they here?

   *B*: _________________ (They were here.)

**5** *A*: Is your room cold?

   *B*: _________________ (My room isn't cold.)

**6** *A*: Did they draw a picture?

   *B*: _________________ (They didn't draw a picture.)

**7** *A*: Aren't you Becky?

   *B*: _________________ (I'm not Becky.)

**8** *A*: Was Cathy free this morning?

   *B*: _________________ (Cathy was free this morning.)

9  *A*: Didn't Sena find her watch?

   *B*: ___________________ (Sena found her watch.)

10 *A*: Do you want some bread?

   *B*: ___________________ (I don't want any bread.)

## PSS 1-7 의문사로 시작하는 의문문

의문사로 시작하는 의문문은 Yes나 No로 대답하지 않는다. be동사가 있는 의문문은 「의문사+be동사+주어 ~?」로, 일반동사가 있는 의문문은 일반적으로 「의문사+do[does, did]+주어+동사원형 ~?」의 어순으로 쓴다.

**Who** is she? — **She is my sister.**

그녀는 누구니? 그녀는 내 여동생이야.

**What** did you do last night? — **I went to a concert.**

너는 어젯밤에 무엇을 했니? 나는 콘서트에 갔어.

**Where** was she yesterday? — **She was at home.**

그녀는 어제 어디에 있었니? 그녀는 집에 있었어.

**When** did you go jogging? — **I went jogging this morning.**

너는 언제 조깅하러 갔니? 오늘 아침에 조깅하러 갔어.

**How** was your trip? — **It was wonderful.**

너의 여행은 어땠니? 매우 좋았어.

**Why** is he absent today? — **Because he is ill.**

그는 오늘 왜 결석을 하는 것이니? 왜냐하면 그는 아프기 때문이야.

**PRACTICE 10**

다음 대답을 보고, 괄호 안에 주어진 말을 바르게 배열하여 의문문을 완성하세요.

1  _______________________________________  – My name is Amy.
   (your, is, what, name)

2  _______________________________________  – He is my brother.
   (is, who, boy, that)

3  _______________________________________  – I'm from Canada.
   (where, from, you, are)

4  _______________________________________  – It was great.
   (was, vacation, your, how)

5  _______________________________________  – I bought it last year.
   (it, did, you, when, buy)

6  _______________________________________  – Because I got a good grade on my test.
   (you, are, so happy, why)

7  _______________________________________  – She is a writer.
   (what, do, does, she)

8  _______________________________________  – It's just around the corner.
   (the, is, bank, where)

9  _______________________________________  – I go to school by bus.
   (how, go, you, do, to school)

10  _______________________________________  – It is tomorrow night.
   (the, when, party, is)

---

# PSS 1-8 선택의문문

**선택의문문은 둘 중에 하나를 선택하여 대답**하는 의문문이므로 Yes나 No로 대답하지 않는다.

Which do you like better, **summer or winter**?  – **I like winter better.**
너는 여름과 겨울 중 어느 것이 더 좋니?  나는 겨울이 더 좋아.

Who cleaned the room, **Tom or Bob**?  – **Tom cleaned it.**
Tom과 Bob 중 누가 그 방을 청소했니?  Tom이 그곳을 청소했어.

Did you go there **by bus or by train**?  – **I went there by train.**
너는 거기에 버스를 타고 갔니, 기차를 타고 갔니?  나는 거기에 기차를 타고 갔어.

Is she **a nurse or a doctor**?  – **She is a doctor.**
그녀는 간호사인가요, 의사인가요?  그녀는 의사예요.

## PRACTICE 11

다음 그림을 보고, 빈칸에 알맞은 단어를 쓰세요.

1  **A**: _________________ do you want, milk _________________ juice?
   **B**: _________________, please.

2  **A**: _________________ is your sister, Kate _________________ Liza?
   **B**: _________________ is my sister. She is tall.

3  **A**: Do you have a cat _________________ a dog?
   **B**: I have a _________________.

4  **A**: Did you order a hamburger _________________ a salad?
   **B**: I ordered a _________________.

5  **A**: Did you eat oranges _________________ apples?
   **B**: I ate _________________.

6  **A**: _________________ do you like better, red _________________ blue?
   **B**: I like _________________ better.

7  **A**: _________________ is holding the bag, the man _________________ the woman?
   **B**: The _________________ is holding the bag.

8  **A**: _________________ the cat black _________________ white?
   **B**: The cat is _________________.

## PSS 1-9 부가의문문

상대방에게 확인이나 동의를 구하기 위해 문장 맨 끝에 짧게 덧붙이는 의문문으로 **긍정문 뒤에는 부정의 부가의문문**이, **부정문 뒤에는 긍정의 부가의문문**이 온다. **부가의문문의 주어는** 앞의 주어를 받아 그에 맞는 **인칭대명사**를 써야 한다.

1. 주어+동사의 긍정형, be/do/조동사의 부정형+인칭대명사?

    **be동사** He **is** a teacher, **isn't he?** 그는 선생님이야, 그렇지 않니?

    **일반동사** You **like** Tom, **don't you?** 너는 Tom을 좋아해, 그렇지 않니?

    **조동사** Jane **will** meet her friend, **won't she?** Jane은 그녀의 친구를 만날 거야, 그렇지 않니?

    ***cf.*** 부가의문문의 부정형은 반드시 축약형으로 써야 한다.

    　　She is smart, **isn't she?** (○)　She is smart, is not she? (×)

2. 주어+동사의 부정형, be/do/조동사의 긍정형+인칭대명사?

    You **aren't** tired, **are you?** 너는 피곤하지 않아, 그렇지?

    He **doesn't** speak French, **does he?** 그는 프랑스어를 하지 못해, 그렇지?

    The students **didn't** study hard, **did they?** 그 학생들은 열심히 공부하지 않았어, 그렇지?

    We **can't** play soccer, **can we?** 우리는 축구를 할 수 없어, 그렇지?

    You **couldn't** finish your homework, **could you?** 너는 너의 과제를 끝내지 못했어, 그렇지?

정답 p.1

## PRACTICE 12

다음 문장의 빈칸에 알맞은 부가의문문을 쓰세요.

1　He can't swim well, _______________________?

2　The room isn't clean, _______________________?

3　Isu and I are in the same class, _______________________?

4　They won't go to the gym, _______________________?

5　My mother doesn't know him, _______________________?

6　Computers can work fast, _______________________?

7　James plays the violin, _______________________?

8　You like sports, _______________________?

9　Mrs. Brown didn't sleep well last night, _______________________?

10　You and Brian are on vacation, _______________________?

# PSS 1-10 명령문

1. **명령문**은 주어 없이 **동사원형으로 시작**하는 문장으로 '**～해라**'의 뜻을 나타낸다. 명령문이어도 공손하게 지시하는 상황일 경우 please를 붙이기도 한다.
   be동사 am, is, are에 대한 동사원형은 be이다.

You are quiet. 너는 조용하다.

<u>Be</u> quiet. 조용히 해라. / <u>Be</u> quiet, please. [Please, <u>be</u> quiet.] 조용히 해 주세요.

You are kind to others. ➡ **Be** kind to others.
너는 다른 사람들에게 친절하다.   다른 사람들에게 친절해라.
You clean the classroom. ➡ **Clean** the classroom.
너는 교실을 청소한다.                교실을 청소해라.

2. **부정명령문**은 「Don't+동사원형」의 형태로, '～하지 마라'의 뜻을 나타낸다.

You make a noise. 너는 시끄럽게 한다.

Don't make a noise. 시끄럽게 하지 마라.

You close the door. ➡ **Don't close** the door.
너는 문을 닫는다.          문을 닫지 말아라.

   ***cf.*** Don't 대신 Never를 사용해 의미가 강조된 부정명령문을 만들 수 있다.
     **Never talk** to strangers. 절대 낯선 사람과 이야기하지 마.

## PRACTICE 13

다음 문장을 괄호 안의 지시에 따라 바꾸어 쓰세요.

**1** You wear a helmet. ➡ _________________________ (긍정명령문으로)

**2** You are afraid of snakes. ➡ _________________________ (부정명령문으로)

**3** You take a bus or a taxi. ➡ _________________________ (긍정명령문으로)

**4** You are late again. ➡ _________________________ (부정명령문으로)

**5** You enter my room. ➡ _________________________ (긍정명령문으로)

**6** You worry about the test. ➡ _________________________ (부정명령문으로)

**7** You are careful. ➡ _________________________ (긍정명령문으로)

**8** You are upset. ➡ _________________________ (부정명령문으로)

**9** You are ready to go. ➡ _________________________ (긍정명령문으로)

**10** You turn on the TV. ➡ _________________________ (부정명령문으로)

**11** You are prepared for anything. ➡ _________________________ (긍정명령문으로)

**12** You tell her the truth. ➡ _________________________ (부정명령문으로)

---

# PSS 1-11 Let's로 시작하는 청유문

Let's로 시작하는 **청유문**은 「Let's+동사원형」의 형태로 권유나 제안을 할 때 쓴다. '~하자' 의 뜻을 나타내며 '~할까?' 혹은 '~하는 게 어때?'라는 의미의 Shall we ~?, Why don't we ~?와 바꿔 쓸 수 있다. Let's는 Let us의 줄임말이다. 부정형은 「Let's not+동사원형」 으로 '~하지 말자'의 뜻을 나타낸다.

**Let's play** soccer. 축구하자.
**Let's not fight.** 싸우지 말자.

***cf.*** 「Let me+동사원형 ~」은 '제가 ~하도록 (허락)해주세요, ~하겠습니다'의 뜻을 나타낸다.

**Let me introduce** myself.
제 소개를 하겠습니다.
**Let me open** the door.
제가 문을 열게요.

## PRACTICE 14

우리말과 같은 뜻이 되도록 괄호 안에 주어진 단어를 사용하여 빈칸을 바르게 채우세요.

**1** 계속 연락합시다. = _________________________ in touch. (keep)

**2** 잠시 쉬자. = _________________________ a break. (take)

**3** 영화 보러 가자. = _________________________ to a movie. (go)

**4** 제가 도와드릴게요. = _________________________ you. (help)

**5** 서두르지 말자. = _________________________ . (hurry)

**6** 제가 그것에 대해 이야기해 드릴게요. = _________________________ you about it. (tell)

**7** 지금부터 영어 공부하자. = _________________________ English from now on. (study)

**8** 문을 열지 말자. = _________________________ the door. (open)

**9** 여기서 시끄럽게 하지 말자. = _________________________ a noise here. (make)

**10** 이 동아리에 가입하자. = _________________________ this club. (join)

---

# PSS 1-12 주의해야 할 부가의문문

앞 문장의 내용이 긍정형이든 부정형이든 상관없이 **명령문의 부가의문문**은 항상 **will you?**
로, Let's로 시작하는 **청유문의 부가의문문**은 **shall we?**로 쓴다.

### 1. 명령문, will you?

| | | | |
|---|---|---|---|
| **Be** | quiet, | | 조용히 해, 알겠니? |
| **Close** | the door, | **will you?** | 문을 닫아라, 알겠니? |
| **Don't be** | late, | | 늦지 마, 알겠니? |
| **Don't ride** | a bicycle, | | 자전거를 타지 말아라, 알겠니? |

### 2. Let's ~, shall we?

| | | | |
|---|---|---|---|
| **Let's** | go climbing, | **shall we?** | 등산 가자, 어떠니? |
| **Let's not** | watch TV, | | TV 보지 말자, 어떠니? |

정답 p.1

## PRACTICE 15 [1-12]

다음 문장의 빈칸에 알맞은 부가의문문을 쓰세요.

**1** Let's listen to music, _________________ ?

**2** Go to bed early, _________________ ?

3 She played the piano, _______________?

4 Don't cry, _______________?

5 This bag is so small, _______________?

6 You can ride a bicycle, _______________?

7 Mr. Lee has a son and two daughters, _______________?

8 Let's not play computer games, _______________?

9 These stories are interesting, _______________?

10 Nami doesn't want hamburgers, _______________?

11 Be on time, _______________?

12 Tom didn't lose the game, _______________?

## PSS 1-13 감탄문

how나 what을 사용하여 '정말 ~하구나!'라는 감탄의 의미를 표현할 수 있다. 주어와 동사는 생략이 가능하며 문장의 맨 끝에는 감탄부호(!)를 붙인다.

1. **How** + **형용사/부사** (+주어+동사)!

You are very kind. ➡ **How** kind (you are)!
너는 매우 친절하다.    (너는) 정말 친절하구나!
She runs very fast. ➡ **How** fast (she runs)!
그녀는 아주 빨리 달려.    (그녀는) 정말 빠르게 달리는구나!

2.  [ What ]  (+a/an) +  [ 형용사 ]  +  [ 명사 ]  (+주어+동사)!

She has a really beautiful flower. 그녀는 정말 아름다운 꽃을 가지고 있다.
➡ **What** a beautiful flower (she has)! (그녀는) 정말 아름다운 꽃을 가지고 있구나!

***cf.*** 감탄의 대상이 되는 명사가 복수일 때는 「What+형용사+복수명사(+주어+동사)!」의 형태로 쓴다.

These are very amazing stories. ➡ **What** amazing stories (these are)!
이것들은 매우 놀라운 이야기들이다.        (이것들은) 정말 놀라운 이야기들이구나!

***cf.*** 감탄문을 쓸 때는 very, really, so와 같은 강조 표현은 같이 쓰지 않는다.

How <u>very</u> kind of him! (X)        What a <u>really</u> cute baby she is! (X)

정답 p.1

## PRACTICE 16

괄호 안의 단어를 바르게 배열하여 감탄문을 완성하세요.

**1** (beautiful, is, garden, this, how)!
➡ How beautiful this garden is!

**2** (she, how, is, pretty)!
➡ _______________________

**3** (eyes, big, what, have, you)!
➡ _______________________

**4** (waterfall, huge, what, a)!
➡ _______________________

**5** (he, is, how, handsome)!
➡ _______________________

**6** (fast, move, can, how, the, robots)!
➡ _______________________

**7** (you, what, are, a, liar, big)!
➡ _______________________

**8** (those, are, cute, mascots, what)!
➡ _______________________

**9** (mountain, a, what, high)!
➡ _______________________

**10** (what, museum, nice, a)!
➡ _______________________

**11** (you, dictionary, have, a, what, small)!
➡ _______________________

**12** (I, happy, how, am)!
➡ _______________________

# PSS 2  품사/문장의 요소/문장의 5형식

## PSS 2-1 영어의 8품사

| 명사 | 명사는 **이름을 나타내는 말**이다. 문장 내에서 **주어, 목적어, 보어**로 쓰인다.<br>**Birds** sing. 새들이 노래한다. (주어)<br>Mary likes **dogs**. Mary는 개를 좋아한다. (목적어)<br>Tom is a **teacher**. Tom은 선생님이다. (보어) |
|---|---|
| 대명사 | 대명사는 **명사를 대신하는 말**이다. 명사의 반복을 피하기 위해 쓴다. 문장 내에서 **주어, 목적어, 보어**로 쓰인다.<br>**This** is a yellow book. 이것은 노란 책이다. (주어)<br>Do you know **him**? 너는 그를 아니? (목적어)<br>The farm is **theirs**. 그 농장은 그들의 것이다. (보어) |
| 동사 | 동사는 **상태나 행동을 나타내는 말**로 '～다'로 해석된다. 동사에는 be동사와 일반동사가 있다.<br>I **am** a student. 나는 학생이다. (be동사)<br>My mother **loves** me. 나의 어머니는 나를 사랑하신다. (일반동사) |
| 형용사 | 형용사는 명사, 대명사의 **성질, 상태 등을 나타내거나 보충 설명하는 말**이다. 문장 내에서 **수식어** 또는 **보어**로 쓰인다.<br>There is a **tall** tree. 키 큰 나무가 있다. (수식어)<br>I was **sick** yesterday. 나는 어제 아팠다. (보어) |
| 부사 | 부사는 **시간, 장소, 정도, 빈도, 방법** 등을 나타내는 말이다. 문장 내에서 **형용사, 동사, 다른 부사, 문장 전체를 수식하는 수식어**로 쓰인다.<br>She sings **well**. 그녀는 노래를 잘한다. (수식어 – 동사 수식) |
| 전치사 | 전치사는 **명사, 대명사의 앞에서 시간, 장소, 방향, 위치를 나타내는 말**이다.<br>There are no classes **on** Saturday. 토요일에는 수업이 없다. (시간)<br>Look at the moon **in** the sky. 하늘에 있는 달을 봐. (장소) |
| 접속사 | 접속사는 **단어와 단어, 구와 구, 절과 절을 연결하는 말**이다.<br>He is old **but** healthy. 그는 늙었지만 건강하다. (단어 연결)<br>I will clean my room **and** wash the dishes.<br>나는 내 방을 청소하고, 설거지를 할 것이다. (구 연결)<br>I was tired, **so** I went to bed early. 나는 피곤해서 일찍 잠자리에 들었다. (절 연결) |
| 감탄사 | 감탄사는 **감정을 표현하는 말**이다.<br>**Wow**, it smells good! 와, 그것은 좋은 냄새가 나! |

## PRACTICE **17**

**다음 밑줄 친 단어의 품사를 쓰세요.**

**1** Your classmates study <u>hard</u>.　　　　　[　　　　]

**2** Did you make them <u>or</u> buy them?　　　[　　　　]

**3** She <u>looks</u> good today.　　　　　　　　[　　　　]

**4** I will give <u>you</u> some advice.　　　　　[　　　　]

**5** Economics is very <u>difficult</u>.　　　　　[　　　　]

**6** James opened the <u>door</u> quietly.　　　　[　　　　]

**7** <u>Oh, no</u>! We took the wrong bus.　　　　[　　　　]

**8** We took a walk <u>along</u> the river.　　　　[　　　　]

**9** My cat <u>was</u> sick yesterday.　　　　　　[　　　　]

**10** Sally saw something <u>strange</u>.　　　　　[　　　　]



## PRACTICE **18**

**괄호 안에 주어진 단어 중 알맞은 것을 고르세요.**

**1** Rock climbing is quite (dangerous, danger).

**2** That magic was (amaze, amazing).

**3** I (arrival, arrived) in Los Angeles on Christmas Day.

**4** The Internet provides us with a lot of (information, inform).

**5** Is Tim a teacher (or, on) an office worker?

**6** Let me (introduction, introduce) my best friend.

**7** You look (happy, happily) today.

**8** She told us a (scare, scary) story.

**9** Exercising makes you (health, healthy).

**10** Why is Belle so (busy, business) today?

**11** He always (helps, helpful) his classmates.

**12** This box is too (heavily, heavy) for me.

**13** He is a (care, careful) student.

영어 문장은 네 가지 주요 성분(주어, 동사, 목적어, 보어)과 수식어로 이뤄진다.

**1. 주어** – 동작이나 상태의 주체로 우리말 '~은, 는, 이, 가'에 해당한다.

> **John** played basketball. John은 농구를 했다.

**2. 동사** – 상태나 동작을 나타내는 말로 우리말 '~(하)다'에 해당한다.

> He **wrote** a letter to her. 그는 그녀에게 편지를 썼다.
> It **is** cold today. 오늘 (날씨가) 춥다.

**3. 목적어** – 동사가 의미하는 동작의 대상이 되는 말로 우리말 '~을, 를'에 해당한다.

> My father wears **glasses**. 나의 아버지는 안경을 쓰신다.
> ***cf.*** 전치사의 목적어: 전치사는 목적어를 취할 수 없는 자동사나 형용사가 목적어를 취할 수 있게 해 준다.
> She looks **after them**. 그녀는 그들을 돌본다.　I am afraid **of bugs**. 나는 벌레를 두려워한다.

**4. 보어** – 동사만으로는 문장의 의미를 명확하게 나타낼 수 없기에 그 뜻을 보충해 주는 말로 주어를 설명해주는 것을 주격 보어, 목적어를 설명해주는 것을 목적격 보어라고 한다.

> My dog is **cute**. 나의 개는 귀엽다.
> She became **a teacher**. 그녀는 선생님이 되었다.
> I found the book **difficult**. 나는 그 책이 어렵다는 것을 알았다.
> We saw him **painting**. 우리는 그가 페인트칠하고 있는 것을 보았다.

**5. 수식어** – 문장의 주요 성분을 부연 설명하는 역할을 하며 생략해도 문법적인 오류를 일으키지 않는다.

> You walk **too fast**. 너는 너무 빠르게 걷는다.
> 주어 동사　수식어
> Audrey enjoys going shopping **with her mother**. Audrey는 그녀의 엄마와 쇼핑하러 가는 것을 즐긴다.
> 　주어　　동사　　목적어　　　　수식어

정답 p.1

## PRACTICE 19

다음 문장의 주어에는 ○, 동사에는 △표시를 하세요.

**1**　Her cap is red.

**2**　They went camping last Saturday.

**3**　She keeps a diary every day.

**4**　My favorite subject is music.

**5**　Tony sat on the bench.

**6**　Her family lives in Seoul.

## PRACTICE 20

다음 문장의 목적어에 밑줄을 그으세요.

**1** My family planted some trees.

**2** She heard his voice.

**3** I don't know them.

**4** We watch TV after dinner.

**5** I bought a notebook.

**6** They play tennis.



## PRACTICE 21

다음 문장의 보어에 밑줄을 그으세요.

**1** He is Mr. Brown.

**2** We felt cold.

**3** I find it interesting.

**4** She heard the birds sing.

**5** The game is exciting.

**6** He became a cook.



## PRACTICE 22

다음 문장의 수식어에 밑줄을 그으세요.

**1** I am so happy.

**2** You can meet her next time.

**3** It will rain heavily tomorrow.

**4** I took a class about computer science.

**5** The class ends late.

**6** In my opinion, you are wrong.



## PRACTICE 23

괄호 안에 주어진 말을 바르게 배열하여 문장을 완성하세요.

**1** _________________________________________ (he, happy, is)

**2** _________________________________________ (winter, we, love)

**3** _________________________________________ (small, are, these shirts)

**4** _________________________________________ (live, New York, her parents, in)

**5** _________________________________________ (teaches, the teacher, math)

**6** _________________________________________ (my mother, the dishes, washed)

# PSS 2-3 문장의 5형식

## 1. 목적어를 가지지 않는 문장

① 1형식     The stars   twinkle   in the darkness. 별들이 어둠 속에서 반짝거린다.
               [주어]     [동사]     [(수식어)]

               The sun   shines   in the blue sky. 해가 푸른 하늘에서 빛난다.
               [주어]     [동사]     [(수식어)]

***cf.*** 「주어+동사」 뒤에는 부사(구) 또는 전치사구 같은 수식어가 올 수 있지만 문장의 형식에는 영향을 주지 않는다.

② 2형식     주격 보어로는 형용사나 명사가 온다.

               He   looks   happy. 그는 행복해 보인다.
               [주어]   [동사]   [주격 보어]

               My brother   is   an actor. 나의 오빠는 배우이다.
               [주어]   [동사]   [주격 보어]

## 2. 목적어를 가지는 문장

① 3형식     Amy   likes   her teacher. Amy는 그녀의 선생님을 좋아한다.
               [주어]   [동사]   [목적어]

               I   ate   lunch   with my friends. 난 내 친구들과 점심을 먹었다.
               [주어]   [동사]   [목적어]   [(수식어)]

② 4형식     She   gave   me   a book. 그녀는 나에게 책을 주었다.
               [주어]   [동사]   [간접목적어(사람)]   [직접목적어(사물)]

               I   bought   my sister   a doll. 난 내 여동생에게 인형을 사주었다.
               [주어]   [동사]   [간접목적어(사람)]   [직접목적어(사물)]

③ 5형식     Music   makes   me   happy. 음악은 나를 행복하게 한다.
               [주어]   [동사]   [목적어]   [목적격 보어]

               My family   called   the dog   Lucy. 우리 가족은 그 개를 Lucy라고 불렀다.
               [주어]   [동사]   [목적어]   [목적격 보어]

***cf.*** 4형식과 5형식의 구분 방법

5형식은 목적어와 목적격 보어가 동격이거나 주술 관계를 가지지만, 4형식은 그렇지 않다.

Mom made me a sweater. (4형식) 엄마께서는 나에게 스웨터를 만들어 주셨다.
           [간접목적어]   [직접목적어]
              └──── ≠ ────┘

She made her son a doctor. (5형식) 그녀는 그녀의 아들을 의사로 만들었다.
           [목적어]   [목적격 보어]
              └──── = ────┘

## PRACTICE 24

〈보기〉와 같이 주어진 문장의 문장 형식과 밑줄 친 부분에 해당하는 각각의 문장 성분을 쓰세요.

<table>
<tr><td>보 기</td><td>I cleaned my room. [ 3형식 ]<br>주어 동사 목적어</td></tr>
</table>

1 The wind blows through the trees. [ 형식 ]

2 The man is strong. [ 형식 ]

3 Mary found the article interesting. [ 형식 ]

4 I opened the door. [ 형식 ]

5 He gave her the ring. [ 형식 ]

6 John has a brother. [ 형식 ]

7 The movie made me sad. [ 형식 ]

8 The baby cried loudly. [ 형식 ]

9 He became an engineer. [ 형식 ]

10 We gave him a big hug. [ 형식 ]

11 Leaves turn red and yellow. [ 형식 ]

12 She bought her baby a new toy. [ 형식 ]

13 I woke up late in the morning. [ 형식 ]

14 I kept my room clean. [ 형식 ]

15 I became popular after the school festival. [ 형식 ]

16 Sometimes I go to work by car. [ 형식 ]

17 Vegetables make you healthy. [ 형식 ]

18 Are you ready? [ 형식 ]

19 Did she tell you the secret? [ 형식 ]

20 I found him smart. [ 형식 ]

21 She smiled at me. [ 형식 ]

22 Pass me the salt, please. [ 형식 ]

23 I arrived at the airport early. [ 형식 ]

24 Swimming is a good hobby. [ 형식 ]

25 The soup tastes salty. [ 형식 ]

26 Mom plays the cello very well. [ 형식 ]

27 He baked me an apple pie. [ 형식 ]

28 Sound travels more slowly than light. [ 형식 ]

29 I sold my toys last Friday. [ 형식 ]

30 My parents named my sister Annie. [ 형식 ]

## PSS 2-4 감각동사 + 주격 보어(형용사)

look, feel, sound, smell, taste와 같은 감각동사 뒤에는 보어로 형용사가 온다.

주어 +
| |
|---|
| look '~하게 보이다' |
| feel '~하게 느끼다' |
| sound '~하게 들리다' |
| smell '~한 냄새가 나다' |
| taste '~한 맛이 나다' |
+ 형용사

You **look kind**. 너는 친절해 보인다.
I **feel happy**. 나는 행복하게 느낀다.
That **sounds great**. 그 말은 좋게 들린다.
It **smells good**. 그것은 좋은 냄새가 난다.
The candy **tastes sweet**.
그 사탕은 달콤한 맛이 난다.

*cf.* 「감각동사 like+명사」 '~처럼 …하다'
The baby **looks like a small doll**. 그 아기는 작은 인형처럼 보인다.
It **sounds like a great plan**. 그것은 훌륭한 계획처럼 들린다.
This candy **tastes like peaches**. 이 사탕은 복숭아 맛이 난다.

정답 p.3

## PRACTICE 25

〈보기〉에서 알맞은 단어를 골라 빈칸에 쓰세요.

| 보 기 | terrible ghost sadly beautiful beautifully soap<br>strangely strange delicious hungry soft softly |
|---|---|

1   너는 아름답게 보인다.   ➡ You look _______________.

2   그 파이는 맛있는 냄새가 난다.   ➡ The pie smells _______________.

3   이것은 이상하게 들린다.   ➡ This sounds _______________.

4   그들은 방을 아름답게 꾸몄다.   ➡ They decorated the room _______________.

5   그는 배고프게 느낀다.   ➡ He feels _______________.

6   그것은 유령처럼 보인다.   ➡ It looks like a _______________.

7   그녀는 슬프게 고개를 가로저었다.   ➡ She shook her head _______________.

8   저것은 끔찍한 맛이 난다.   ➡ That tastes _______________.

9   그녀의 목소리는 부드럽게 들렸다.   ➡ Her voice sounded _______________.

10   그녀는 이상하게 차분했고
한편 그는 겁에 질려 있었다.   ➡ She was _______________ calm
while he was panicking.

11   그 수건들은 비누 같은 냄새가 났다.   ➡ The towels smelled like _______________.

12   그는 나를 부드럽게 포옹했다.   ➡ He hugged me _______________.

## PSS 2-5 4형식에서 3형식으로의 전환

두 개의 목적어를 필요로 하는 4형식 문장을 3형식으로 전환할 때는 간접목적어와 직접목적어의 위치를 바꾸고 간접목적어 앞에 to, for, of 중 해당하는 전치사를 넣는다.

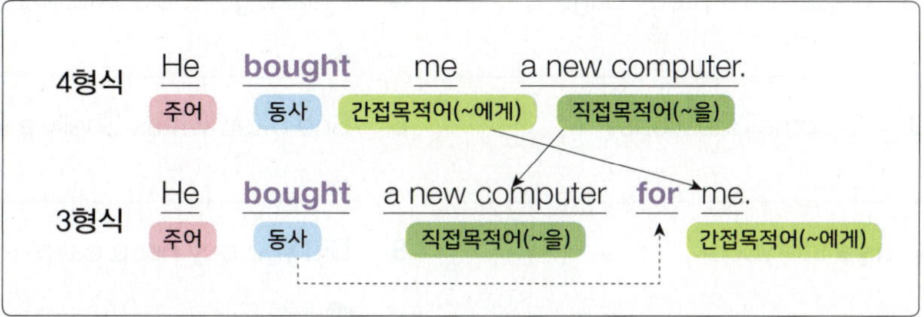


1. **to를 쓰는 동사** – give, send, pass, show, teach, tell, write, read

   My parents **gave** me a present. 나의 부모님이 나에게 선물을 주셨다.
   ➡ My parents **gave** a present **to** me.

2. **for를 쓰는 동사** – buy, cook, find, get, make, build

   She **made** us some cookies. 그녀가 우리에게 쿠키를 만들어 주었다.
   ➡ She **made** some cookies **for** us.

3. **of를 쓰는 동사** – ask

   The girl **asked** him a favor. 그 소녀는 그에게 부탁을 하나 했다.
   ➡ The girl **asked** a favor **of** him.

정답 p.3

## PRACTICE 26

괄호 안에 주어진 단어 중 알맞은 것을 고르세요.

1　She made a scarf (to, for) me.

2　He gave roses (to, of) the woman.

3　Andy bought the camera (to, for) me.

4　She told the secret (to, for) her friend.

5　May I ask a favor (to, of) you?

6　I showed my heart (to, for) you.

7　Jane sent some books (to, of) her cousin.

8　Mrs. Smith cooked dinner (to, for) us.

9　I got two tickets (to, for) my parents.

10　Mike taught math (to, of) his brothers.

## PRACTICE 27

다음 4형식 문장을 3형식으로 바꾸어 쓰세요.

**1** Mary told him the news.

➡ _______________

**2** Mr. Kim teaches them English.

➡ _______________

**3** My mother made me a pretty bag.

➡ _______________

**4** Please get me some water.

➡ _______________

**5** Can I ask you some questions?

➡ _______________

**6** She often writes Shelly a letter.

➡ _______________

**7** He found us a storybook.

➡ _______________

**8** Did you buy her a cake?

➡ _______________

**9** Will you show me your album?

➡ _______________

**10** The Internet gives us a lot of information.

➡ _______________

**11** Please tell me the real reason.

➡ _______________

**12** Will you pass me the salt?

➡ _______________

**13** Vivien sent me some flowers.

➡ _______________

**14** We built the family a new house.

➡ _______________

**15** My dad cooked me spaghetti.

➡ _______________

**16** I read senior citizens a newspaper.

➡ _______________

**17** Can I ask you a favor?

➡ _______________

**18** Homework gives us too much stress.

➡ _______________

**19** I sent you a birthday gift.

➡ _______________

**20** My friend made me a birthday cake.

➡ _______________

**21** Will you give me another chance?

➡ _______________

**22** Can you get me that book?

➡ _______________

**23** He bought us a box of chocolates.

➡ _______________

**24** Olivia teaches students Korean history.

➡ _______________

**25** Evan built his children a treehouse.

➡ _______________

**26** Mom often cooks me noodles.

➡ _______________

**27** She often reads her son a fairy tale.

➡ _______________

**28** He showed his father his report card.

➡ _______________

**29** The police officer found me the car key.

➡ _______________

**30** Dominic made his son a big sand castle.

➡ _______________

**1** (A)~(E)의 빈칸에 들어갈 말이 나머지 넷과 <u>다른</u> 것은?

(A) It ____________ a rainy day, isn't it?
(B) The Han River ____________ in Seoul.
(C) ____________ Somi late?
(D) ____________ your father a farmer?
(E) Minsoo ____________ the dishes after dinner.

① (A)　② (B)　③ (C)　④ (D)　⑤ (E)

**2** 다음 중 축약형이 <u>잘못된</u> 것의 개수는?

| | | | |
|---|---|---|---|
| He's | We're | I amn't | They'r |
| This's | That's | You're | She're |

① 1개　② 2개　③ 3개　④ 4개　⑤ 5개

**3** 다음 빈칸에 들어갈 알맞은 부가의문문은?

Jack practices the violin, ____________?

① did he
② didn't he
③ doesn't he
④ does he
⑤ doesn't Jack

**4** 다음 중 어법상 바른 것은?

① Don't shy, will you?
② The movie made me happily.
③ This juice tastes like strawberry.
④ How tall boy you are!
⑤ Does your father likes to go fishing?

**5** 다음 문장에서 틀린 곳을 찾아 그 번호를 쓰고, 바르게 고치세요.

He doesn't has a letter for me today.
　①　　②　　③　　④　　　⑤

(　　) ____________ ➡ ____________

**6** (a)~(e) 중 어법상 옳은 것을 <u>있는</u> 대로 고른 것은?

My family goes to the park near our house. There (a) <u>is</u> a big pond and many tall trees. Some ducks (b) <u>are</u> swimming in the pond. There (c) <u>is</u> a bench next to the pond. My father asks me, "(d) <u>Are</u> you want to sit on the bench?" The bench is wet. I (e) <u>do not</u> want to sit on the bench.

① (a), (b), (c)　　② (a), (c), (d)
③ (b), (c), (e)　　④ (b), (d), (e)
⑤ (c), (d), (e)

**7** 다음 중 축약형이 바른 것은?

① I do not - I'd not
② It is - Its
③ I am not - I amn't
④ Jane does not - Jane's not
⑤ They are - They're

**8** 우리말과 같은 뜻이 되도록 빈칸에 알맞은 단어를 쓰세요.

• 절대 다시는 늦지 마라.
　= Never ____________ late again.

**9** 다음은 소연의 자기소개입니다. 빈칸에 알맞은 말을 쓰세요.

Hello, everyone. My name __________ Soyeon. I __________ a middle school student. My favorite subjects __________ English and math. My hobby __________ listening to pop songs. My father __________ a good cook and I love his food.

**10** 두 단어의 관계가 나머지와 <u>다른</u> 것은?

① happy : happiness
② humorous : humor
③ beautiful : beauty
④ create : creation
⑤ strong : strength

**11** 다음 밑줄 친 부분 중 옳지 <u>않은</u> 것은?

Hi, my name ①<u>is</u> Kate. I ②<u>am</u> from L.A. ③<u>I</u> have a sister. ④<u>She</u> is 13 years old. I like baseball, but she doesn't ⑤<u>likes</u> it.

**12** A에 대한 B의 대답을 지시대로 쓰세요. (단, 부정문은 축약형으로 쓸 것.)

A: Didn't you enjoy the movie?
B: (1) 긍정의 대답 → __________
　 (2) 부정의 대답 → __________

**13** 빈칸을 채워 다음을 의문문으로 바꾸세요.

(1) She reads books in the evening.
➡ __________ she __________ books in the evening?

(2) My brother is watching TV.
➡ __________ __________ __________ watching TV?

(3) Yumi met him last week.
➡ __________ Yumi __________ him last week?

**14** 다음 감탄문 중에서 어법에 맞는 것은?

① What beautiful lady she is!
② How nice!
③ How a kind boy!
④ How boring books they are!
⑤ What a very wonderful world!

**15** 다음 중 어법상 빈칸에 알맞지 <u>않은</u> 것은?

A: Did you __________ him the bag?
B: Yes, I did.

① bring　　　② give　　　③ send
④ help　　　⑤ show

**16** 다음 〈조건〉에 맞게 주어진 단어를 사용하여 문장을 완성하세요.

조건1. What을 사용할 것.
조건2. 6단어로 영작할 것.
조건3. 문장부호를 꼭 쓸 것.
• 그것은 정말 작은 원숭이구나! (small, monkey)
= __________

## 17 다음 중 평서문을 부정문으로 바르게 고친 것은?

① My friends are angry.

   ➡ My friends don't angry.

② Bob likes action movies.

   ➡ Bob doesn't likes action movies.

③ It was my 14th birthday.

   ➡ It isn't my 14th birthday.

④ I had five classes on Tuesday.

   ➡ I didn't have five classes on Tuesday.

⑤ I called Maria yesterday.

   ➡ I didn't called Maria yesterday.

## 18 (a)~(f) 중 어법상 바른 것을 있는 대로 고른 것은?

> (a) Sarah and I am classmates.
> (b) The dog barks loudly at night.
> (c) My little sister isn't likes carrots.
> (d) I am reading a book in my room.
> (e) The children run in the park every day.
> (f) Lisa and Jenny walks to school together.

① (a), (b), (c)      ② (a), (b), (e)

③ (b), (d), (e)      ④ (c), (e), (f)

⑤ (d), (e), (f)

## 19 빈칸에 들어갈 단어가 순서대로 짝지어진 것은?

> • Sally bought a cake __________ him.
> • Linda showed her birthday photos __________ him.
> • Rachel teaches English __________ us.

① for – to – for

② for – for – to

③ for – to – to

④ to – for – to

⑤ to – for – for

## 20 의문문으로 고친 것 중 바른 것을 고르세요.

① My brother bought some flowers.

   ➡ Did my brother bought any flowers?

② Susan goes to high school.

   ➡ Does Susan go to high school?

③ You have a cell phone.

   ➡ Does you have a cell phone?

④ They have a big house.

   ➡ Do they has a big house?

⑤ She likes movies.

   ➡ Do she like movies?

## 21 다음 빈칸에 들어갈 알맞은 문장을 고르세요.

> A: _________________________
> B: No, they don't.

① Don't you go to the bookstore?

② Aren't you American?

③ Does Eric ride a bicycle?

④ Do Kevin and Jim play badminton?

⑤ Are you students?

## 22 질문에 대한 대답이 적절하지 못한 것은?

① Do you walk to school?

   – Yes, I do.

② Didn't you study for the test yesterday?

   – No, I didn't.

③ Are you from India?

   – Yes, I am.

④ Aren't they washing their hands?

   – No, they aren't.

⑤ Is he fourteen years old?

   – No, he is.

## 23 다음 중 어법상 옳은 문장을 <u>모두</u> 고른 것은?

ⓐ What delicious cookies this is!
ⓑ The insect looks like a dead leaf.
ⓒ The dress makes me look nicely.
ⓓ It's an expensive but useful machine.
ⓔ She sang very good today.
ⓕ Show your ticket to the woman at the gate.
ⓖ Alex cleaned the room with a vacuum, doesn't he?

① ⓐ, ⓑ, ⓔ
② ⓑ, ⓓ, ⓕ
③ ⓒ, ⓔ, ⓖ
④ ⓑ, ⓓ, ⓕ, ⓖ
⑤ ⓒ, ⓔ, ⓕ, ⓖ

## 24 대화의 밑줄 친 부분과 바꾸어 쓸 수 있는 것은?

A: Did you have fun at the party?
B: <u>Sure.</u> I met lots of friends there.

① Yes, you did.　　② Yes, I did.
③ Yes, we were.　　④ No, I didn't.
⑤ No, we didn't.

## 25 다음 질문의 빈칸에 들어갈 표현이 <u>아닌</u> 것은?

㉠ ___________ does she usually get up?
㉡ ___________ are you feeling these days?
㉢ ___________ did the boys do last night?
㉣ ___________ will you be coming back?
㉤ ___________ are you going now?

① What　　② Where　　③ When
④ Who　　⑤ How

## 26 다음 표를 설명하는 문장 중에서 어법상 오류 없이 내용과 일치하는 것을 고르세요.

|  | Tommy | Jane | Somi | Mark |
|---|---|---|---|---|
| English | 😊 | 😊 | 😊 | 😊 |
| Science | ☹ | ☹ | ☹ | ☹ |
| Math | 😊 | 😊 | ☹ | ☹ |

① Tommy like science.
② Jane do not like science.
③ Somi and Mark likes math.
④ All students like English.
⑤ Mark doesn't likes math.

## 27 다음 대화의 빈칸에 들어갈 말로 알맞은 것은?

A: ___________ like grapes?
B: No, I don't. I don't like fruit.

① Does Cathy　　② Does Jack
③ Do you　　④ Do they
⑤ Do I

## 28 어법상 어색한 곳을 하나씩 찾아 바르게 고쳐 쓰세요.

(가) Please let me knowing if you cannot attend my class.
(나) Her voice sounds sweetly.

〈잘못된 곳〉　　〈바르게 고친 것〉

(가) ___________ ➡ ___________

(나) ___________ ➡ ___________

**29** 밑줄 친 부분의 쓰임이 <u>잘못된</u> 문장을 고르세요.

① <u>Do</u> they play table tennis?

② <u>Do</u> you have a pet?

③ What <u>does</u> Eric do?

④ <u>Do</u> Insu and Sumin study hard?

⑤ <u>Does</u> Kevin's parents get up early?

**30** 그림의 내용과 일치하도록 빈칸에 들어갈 말을 〈조건〉에 맞게 영어로 쓰세요.

| 조 건 | • 어법에 맞도록 구성하세요.<br>• 반드시 give를 포함한 4단어로 완성하세요. |
| --- | --- |

➡ Sam _______ _______ _______ _______ Lisa.

**31** 다음 빈칸에 들어갈 알맞은 말은?

Jane has dogs, but she ___________ cats.

① isn't have

② doesn't has

③ don't have

④ doesn't have

⑤ does have

**32** 다음 빈칸에 들어갈 말로 알맞지 <u>않은</u> 것은?

It ___________ good.

① sees

② feels

③ looks

④ smells

⑤ sounds

**33** 다음 질문에 대한 알맞은 대답을 빈칸에 쓰세요.

*A*: Mary played badminton with Emily, didn't she?

*B*: ___________, ___________ ___________.
She was sick, so she stayed at home.

**34** 빈칸에 들어갈 단어가 나머지 넷과 <u>다른</u> 하나는?

① ___________ a nice car you have!

② ___________ a handsome boy he is!

③ ___________ a beautiful hat it is!

④ ___________ wonderful it is!

⑤ ___________ exciting stories these are!

**35** 다음 빈칸에 들어갈 수 <u>없는</u> 것은?

Susan is ___________.

① from Canada

② runs fast

③ at home

④ my classmate

⑤ very kind

## 36 다음 빈칸에 들어갈 말이 바르게 짝지어진 것은?

> *A*: You can't swim well, _____________?
> *B*: No, __________.

① can you   – I'm not
② can't you – you can't
③ can you   – I can't
④ can't you – I can't
⑤ are you   – I can

## 37 다음 중 어법상 옳은 것을 <u>모두</u> 고른 것은?

> ⓐ Be nice to your friends!
> ⓑ Doesn't jump here!
> ⓒ Let me introduce myself.
> ⓓ Jimin looks like happy.
> ⓔ My mother makes a cake to me.

① ⓐ,ⓑ              ② ⓑ,ⓔ
③ ⓐ,ⓒ              ④ ⓑ,ⓒ,ⓓ
⑤ ⓐ,ⓒ,ⓔ

## 38 밑줄 친 부분의 쓰임이 나머지 넷과 <u>다른</u> 것은?

① You <u>made</u> me angry.
② Rain sometimes <u>makes</u> people sad.
③ Linda <u>made</u> her mother orange juice.
④ The homework <u>made</u> him tired.
⑤ This music always <u>makes</u> me happy.

## 39 다음 밑줄 친 부분의 오류를 가장 적절하게 고친 학생은?

> 너는 가게에서 야채가 필요했어, 그렇지 않니?
> ➡ You needed vegetables at the store, <u>do you</u>?

① 연수: 앞에 나온 동사가 과거형이니까 뒤에는 did you?로 써야 해.
② 보근: 긍정문 뒤에는 부정의 부가의문문이 오는데 동사가 과거시제이므로 didn't you?를 써야 해.
③ 혜리: 부가의문문은 be동사를 사용해야 해서 are you?를 쓰는 것이 옳아.
④ 민지: 부가의문문은 be동사를 써서 만들지만 부정의 형태를 가져야 해서 aren't you?를 써야 해.
⑤ 영호: 부가의문문은 앞의 동사와 같은 것을 사용해야 해서 need you?를 써야 해.

## 40 대화의 빈칸에 들어갈 내용으로 가장 적절한 것은?

> *G*: Brian, what are you doing?
> *B*: I'm looking for a new backpack online.
> *G*: What kind of backpack do you want?
> *B*: __________________ What do you think of this one?
> *G*: Yeah, it looks really nice.

① I already have a backpack.
② I want one that's light and big.
③ I'm not buying anything today.
④ I am looking for a pair of shoes.
⑤ I don't feel like going shopping.

## 41 다음 대화의 빈칸에 들어갈 알맞은 말을 고르세요.

A: Let's have dinner.
B: No, I'll just drink water.
A: Aren't you hungry?
B: ___________ But I'm on a diet now.

① No, I'm not.　　② Yes, I am.
③ No, I am.　　④ Yes, it is.
⑤ Yes, I don't.

## 42 우리말과 같은 뜻이 되도록 빈칸에 알맞은 말을 넣어 대화를 완성하세요.

A: Lunch time's almost over.
B: ___________ run to the classroom.
(교실까지 뛰어가자.)

## 43 다음 중 빈칸에 들어갈 전치사가 다른 하나는?

① Mom gave a book _________ me.
② Mom made a sweater _________ me.
③ Mom teaches cooking _________ me.
④ Mom told a funny story _________ me.
⑤ Mom showed her pictures _________ me.

## 44 다음 글에서 ⓐ~ⓔ에 들어갈 말이 나머지 넷과 다른 것은?

Yesterday ⓐ Mike's birthday. I ⓑ at his birthday party and many friends ⓒ there, too. My present for him ⓓ a soccer ball. The party ⓔ really fun.

① ⓐ　② ⓑ　③ ⓒ　④ ⓓ　⑤ ⓔ

## 45 다음 밑줄 친 부분의 쓰임이 잘못된 것은?

① It's very sunny today, isn't it?
② You can't play the guitar, can you?
③ Sumi likes dancing, isn't she?
④ You are a driver, aren't you?
⑤ He doesn't study very hard, does he?

## 46 평서문을 감탄문으로 바꾼 것 중 바른 것을 고르세요.

① You are so handsome.
➡ How handsome you are!
② This is a really wonderful gift.
➡ What wonderful gift this is!
③ These are very nice pants.
➡ What very nice pants these are!
④ Your dog is very smart.
➡ How smart is your dog!
⑤ It's a very cloudy day.
➡ What cloudy day it is!

## 47 ⓐ~ⓔ 중 밑줄 친 단어의 쓰임이 옳은 것을 있는 대로 고른 것은?

ⓐ That song makes me sadly.
ⓑ Are you ready for a fun trip?
ⓒ Joanne wants to seat beside me.
ⓓ He sings perfect in front of everyone.
ⓔ This food tastes delicious.

① ⓐⓑ　　② ⓑⓓ　　③ ⓒⓔ
④ ⓑⓔ　　⑤ ⓐⓑⓔ

## 48 다음 밑줄 친 부분이 잘못 쓰인 것을 모두 고르세요.

① You look lovely today.
② The cookies taste greatly.
③ Don't you feel happy now?
④ That sounds good.
⑤ This soup smells very badly.

## 49 다음 중 문장의 전환이 바르지 않은 것을 고르세요.

① He teaches students English.
   ➡ He teaches English to students.
② Tommy sent me a card.
   ➡ Tommy sent a card to me.
③ They made me some soup.
   ➡ They made some soup to me.
④ He gave me some boxes.
   ➡ He gave some boxes to me.
⑤ My father bought me a new coat.
   ➡ My father bought a new coat for me.

## 50 어법상 바른 문장은?

① Not talk nonsense.
② My father gave the guitar me.
③ You aren't Korean, aren't you?
④ Do you play the guitar?
⑤ He don't look good today.

## 51 대화가 어법적으로 옳은 것끼리 짝지어진 것은?

① A: Is the cat sleep on the bed?
   B: No, it isn't. It is sleeping on the sofa.
② A: Are there any cookies for us?
   B: No, there are only some breads left.
③ A: Is your sister reading a book now?
   B: Yes, she is. She loves reading books.
④ A: What are you doing with your friends?
   B: We do playing soccer on the playground.
⑤ A: Is she doing her homework now?
   B: Yes, she does. She wants to finish it
      before dinner.

## 52 (a)～(e) 중 어법상 옳은 문장은?

| | |
|---|---|
| Ms. Park: | Students! (a) What have you on your desk at home? |
| Jaeho: | A small plant! I look at the plant. (b) It grow every day just like me. |
| Sumin: | I keep many colorful pens. I use them. (c) They make writing more fun. |
| Angie: | A calendar! My mom gave it to me. (d) She don't want me to forget important dates. |
| Nick: | I have a desk lamp. It brightens my space during late-night studying. |
| Ms. Park: | Thank you for sharing. (e) Let's keeping useful things on your desk. |

① (a)　② (b)　③ (c)　④ (d)　⑤ (e)

# CHAPTER 2
# 시제

# PSS 1  현재시제

## PSS 1-1 일반동사의 3인칭 현재 단수형 I

주어가 3인칭 단수(he/she/it/Mike/Jane/a car)일 때, 일반동사의 현재형은
「동사원형+(e)s」로 나타낸다.

| 대부분의 경우 | -s | get – get**s**<br>know – know**s** | like – like**s**<br>walk – walk**s** |
|---|---|---|---|
| -o, -s, -x, -ch, -sh로<br>끝나는 경우 | -es | do – do**es**<br>mix – mix**es**<br>finish – finish**es** | pass – pass**es**<br>watch – watch**es** |

정답 p.8

### PRACTICE 1

다음 동사의 3인칭 현재 단수형을 쓰세요.

1  stand   – _______________

2  reach   – _______________

3  impress – _______________

4  read    – _______________

5  begin   – _______________

6  wish    – _______________

7  push    – _______________

8  spend – _______________

9  send    – _______________

10  miss   – _______________

11  wake   – _______________

12  meet   – _______________

13  teach  – _______________

14  solve  – _______________

15  wear   – _______________

16  catch  – _______________

17  sound  – _______________

18  go     – _______________

19  mix    – _______________

20  find   – _______________

21  pass   – _______________

22  finish – _______________

23  ride   – _______________

24  watch – _______________

25  wash   – _______________

26  sit    – _______________

27  throw  – _______________

28  burn   – _______________

29  climb  – _______________

30  cross  – _______________

## PSS 1-2 일반동사의 3인칭 현재 단수형 Ⅱ

| 자음+y로 끝나는 경우 | y를 i로 바꾸고 -es | copy – cop**ies**   cry – cr**ies** <br> study – stud**ies**   try – tr**ies** |
| --- | --- | --- |
| 모음+y로 끝나는 경우 | -s | buy – buy**s**   enjoy – enjoy**s** <br> pay – pay**s**   say – say**s** |

***cf.*** 불규칙 동사 have – ha**s**

정답 p.8

### PRACTICE 2 [1-60]

다음 동사의 3인칭 현재 단수형을 쓰세요.

1 drink – _______________  2 buy – _______________

3 study – _______________  4 hurry – _______________

5 discuss – _______________  6 draw – _______________

7 lay – _______________  8 sell – _______________

9 have – _______________  10 pay – _______________

11 say – _______________  12 cry – _______________

13 copy – _______________  14 put – _______________

15 close – _______________  16 enjoy – _______________

17 touch – _______________  18 try – _______________

19 believe – _______________  20 lose – _______________

21 tell – _______________  22 carry – _______________

23 repeat – _______________  24 grow – _______________

25 play – _______________  26 make – _______________

27 cost – _______________  28 judge – _______________

29 cheer – _______________  30 use – _______________

31 bring – _______________  32 think – _______________

33 mean – _______________  34 break – _______________

35 show – _______________  36 fly – _______________

37 visit – _______________  38 feel – _______________

39 sing – _______________  40 turn – _______________

| 41 | harm | – _______________ | 42 | win | – _______________ |
| 43 | fall | – _______________ | 44 | build | – _______________ |
| 45 | stay | – _______________ | 46 | set | – _______________ |
| 47 | see | – _______________ | 48 | envy | – _______________ |
| 49 | dream | – _______________ | 50 | speak | – _______________ |
| 51 | eat | – _______________ | 52 | leave | – _______________ |
| 53 | get | – _______________ | 54 | understand | – _______________ |
| 55 | worry | – _______________ | 56 | keep | – _______________ |
| 57 | give | – _______________ | 58 | laugh | – _______________ |
| 59 | hold | – _______________ | 60 | hear | – _______________ |

원어민 발음 들어보기 ▶

## PSS 1-3 3인칭 현재 단수형의 '-(e)s' 발음

| 발음 | 용법 |
|---|---|
| [s] | [s, ʃ, tʃ]음을 제외한 무성음으로 끝나는 경우<br>➡ stop**s**, forget**s**, cook**s**, laugh**s** |
| [z] | [z, dʒ]음을 제외한 유성음으로 끝나는 경우<br>➡ lend**s**, hug**s**, arrive**s**, seem**s**, find**s**, sing**s**, tell**s**, wear**s**, agree**s** |
| [iz] | [s, z, ʃ, tʃ, dʒ]음으로 끝나는 경우<br>➡ mix**es**, lose**s**, touch**es**, change**s** |

***cf.*** 무성음: 성대가 울리지 않는 소리 ex) [p], [t], [k] 등

유성음: 성대가 울리는 소리 ex) [b], [d], [g] 등

정답 p.8

## PRACTICE 3

〈보기〉와 같이 주어진 단어의 밑줄 친 부분의 발음으로 알맞은 것을 [s], [z], [iz] 중에서 골라 쓰세요.

원어민 발음 들어보기 ▶ 

보 기    wishe<u>s</u> [ iz ]    trie<u>s</u> [ z ]    put<u>s</u> [ s ]

| 1 | watche<u>s</u> [ ] | 2 | call<u>s</u> [ ] | 3 | hide<u>s</u> [ ] |
| 4 | hug<u>s</u> [ ] | 5 | stay<u>s</u> [ ] | 6 | write<u>s</u> [ ] |
| 7 | use<u>s</u> [ ] | 8 | set<u>s</u> [ ] | 9 | dream<u>s</u> [ ] |
| 10 | pick<u>s</u> [ ] | 11 | misse<u>s</u> [ ] | 12 | check<u>s</u> [ ] |
| 13 | live<u>s</u> [ ] | 14 | decorate<u>s</u> [ ] | 15 | judge<u>s</u> [ ] |

| | | |
|---|---|---|
| **16** orders [ ] | **17** seems [ ] | **18** beats [ ] |
| **19** attacks [ ] | **20** wears [ ] | **21** visits [ ] |
| **22** sneezes [ ] | **23** impresses [ ] | **24** suggests [ ] |
| **25** worries [ ] | **26** pushes [ ] | **27** meets [ ] |
| **28** places [ ] | **29** tells [ ] | **30** feels [ ] |
| **31** guesses [ ] | **32** camps [ ] | **33** teaches [ ] |
| **34** blesses [ ] | **35** escapes [ ] | **36** touches [ ] |
| **37** runs [ ] | **38** raises [ ] | **39** brushes [ ] |
| **40** carries [ ] | **41** repeats [ ] | **42** recycles [ ] |
| **43** thanks [ ] | **44** causes [ ] | **45** likes [ ] |

## PSS 1-4 현재시제의 쓰임

현재의 상태나 습관, 일반적 사실, 속담 등을 나타내며 주어의 인칭과 수에 따라 동사의 모양이 변한다.

### 1. 현재의 상태

She **is** a teacher.
그녀는 선생님이다.
Alice **looks** happy **now**.
Alice는 지금 행복해 보인다.

### 2. 습관, 반복적인 일

He **always drinks** milk **every morning**.
그는 매일 아침 항상 우유를 마신다.
She **keeps** a diary **every day**.
그녀는 매일 일기를 쓴다.

### 3. 일반적인 사실, 진리

Three and one **is** four. 3 더하기 1은 4이다.
Water **freezes** at 0°C. 물은 0도에서 언다.

### 4. 속담, 격언

A rolling stone **gathers** no moss.
구르는 돌에는 이끼가 끼지 않는다.
Time **is** gold. 시간은 금이다.

## PRACTICE 4

괄호 안의 단어를 현재시제의 쓰임에 맞게 바꾸어 빈칸에 쓰세요.

1  I _________________ a painter. (be)

2  She _________________ tennis. (play)

3  Mina usually _________________ for school at 8. (leave)

4  You _________________ sick. (be)

5  The Earth _________________ around the Sun. (go)

6  We _________________ from Korea. (be)

7  Minsu _________________ football. (like)

8  The weather _________________ nice today. (be)

9  You and Mina _________________ very happy. (look)

10  My brothers _________________ very tall. (be)

11  Bill _________________ TV after dinner. (watch)

12  They _________________ hungry. (be)

13  He _________________ very hard. (study)

14  Tokyo _________________ the capital of Japan. (be)

15  The Sun _________________ in the east. (rise)

16  Grandmother always _________________ up early. (get)

17  Seoul _________________ many beautiful mountains. (have)

18  My father _________________ the newspaper in the morning. (read)

19  Many hands _________________ light work. (make)

## PSS 2  과거시제



### PSS 2-1  일반동사의 규칙 변화형 I

| | | | |
|---|---|---|---|
| 대부분의 경우 | -ed | finish – finish**ed**<br>play – play**ed** | pass – pass**ed**<br>walk – walk**ed** |
| -e로 끝나는 경우 | -d | dance – danc**ed**<br>move – mov**ed** | like – lik**ed**<br>save – sav**ed** |

| 단모음+단자음으로<br>끝나는 경우 | 마지막 자음을<br>하나 더 쓰고 -ed | drop – drop**ped**   plan – plan**ned**<br>shop – shop**ped**   stop – stop**ped**<br><br>***cf.*** 강세가 앞에 오는 2음절 동사의 경우<br>enter – enter**ed**   visit – visit**ed** |
| --- | --- | --- |



정답 p.9

## PRACTICE 5

다음 동사의 과거형을 쓰세요.

| | | | | |
| --- | --- | --- | --- | --- |
| **1** | shop | – __________ | **2** | agree | – __________ |
| **3** | call | – __________ | **4** | wish | – __________ |
| **5** | invent | – __________ | **6** | believe | – __________ |
| **7** | cross | – __________ | **8** | rain | – __________ |
| **9** | save | – __________ | **10** | work | – __________ |
| **11** | start | – __________ | **12** | turn | – __________ |
| **13** | live | – __________ | **14** | plan | – __________ |
| **15** | raise | – __________ | **16** | happen | – __________ |
| **17** | want | – __________ | **18** | move | – __________ |
| **19** | improve | – __________ | **20** | love | – __________ |
| **21** | walk | – __________ | **22** | jump | – __________ |
| **23** | visit | – __________ | **24** | arrive | – __________ |
| **25** | push | – __________ | **26** | cover | – __________ |
| **27** | place | – __________ | **28** | stop | – __________ |
| **29** | learn | – __________ | **30** | open | – __________ |

## PSS 2-2 일반동사의 규칙 변화형 Ⅱ

| 자음+y로 끝나는 경우 | y를 i로<br>바꾸고 -ed | cry – cr**ied**   study – stud**ied**<br>try – tr**ied**   worry – worr**ied** |
| --- | --- | --- |
| 모음+y로 끝나는 경우 | -ed | enjoy – enjoy**ed**   obey – obey**ed**<br>play – play**ed**   stay – stay**ed** |

## PRACTICE 6

다음 동사의 과거형을 쓰세요.

| | | | |
|---|---|---|---|
| **1** close – ______ | | **2** guide – ______ | |
| **3** worry – ______ | | **4** use – ______ | |
| **5** repeat – ______ | | **6** wait – ______ | |
| **7** stay – ______ | | **8** join – ______ | |
| **9** wonder – ______ | | **10** end – ______ | |
| **11** study – ______ | | **12** surprise – ______ | |
| **13** add – ______ | | **14** connect – ______ | |
| **15** drop – ______ | | **16** play – ______ | |
| **17** try – ______ | | **18** spoil – ______ | |
| **19** bake – ______ | | **20** suggest – ______ | |
| **21** roll – ______ | | **22** tie – ______ | |
| **23** collect – ______ | | **24** carry – ______ | |
| **25** enter – ______ | | **26** obey – ______ | |
| **27** discuss – ______ | | **28** answer – ______ | |
| **29** touch – ______ | | **30** solve – ______ | |
| **31** enjoy – ______ | | **32** help – ______ | |
| **33** marry – ______ | | **34** serve – ______ | |
| **35** listen – ______ | | **36** waste – ______ | |
| **37** watch – ______ | | **38** sound – ______ | |
| **39** share – ______ | | **40** train – ______ | |
| **41** hurry – ______ | | **42** pour – ______ | |
| **43** cheer – ______ | | **44** dance – ______ | |
| **45** return – ______ | | **46** miss – ______ | |
| **47** lock – ______ | | **48** laugh – ______ | |
| **49** hate – ______ | | **50** type – ______ | |
| **51** seem – ______ | | **52** fail – ______ | |
| **53** look – ______ | | **54** decide – ______ | |
| **55** practice – ______ | | **56** kick – ______ | |
| **57** guess – ______ | | **58** change – ______ | |
| **59** reach – ______ | | **60** swallow – ______ | |

## PSS 2-3 규칙 변화 과거형의 '-(e)d' 발음

| 발음 | 용법 |
| --- | --- |
| [t] | [t]음을 제외한 무성음으로 끝나는 경우<br>➡ stopp**ed**, talk**ed**, laugh**ed**, miss**ed**, push**ed**, watch**ed** |
| [d] | [d]음을 제외한 유성음으로 끝나는 경우<br>➡ liv**ed**, harm**ed**, clean**ed**, call**ed**, cheer**ed**, rais**ed**, enjoy**ed** |
| [id] | [t, d]음으로 끝나는 경우<br>➡ want**ed**, visit**ed**, add**ed**, end**ed** |

정답 p.9

## PRACTICE 7

〈보기〉와 같이 규칙 변화 과거형 동사의 -(e)d의 발음으로 알맞은 것을 [t], [d], [id] 중에서 골라 쓰세요.



| 보 기 | cried [ d ] | picked [ t ] | visited [ id ] |
| --- | --- | --- | --- |

| | | | | | |
| --- | --- | --- | --- | --- | --- |
| 1 talked [ ] | | 2 stayed [ ] | | 3 worked [ ] | |
| 4 called [ ] | | 5 looked [ ] | | 6 collected [ ] | |
| 7 rained [ ] | | 8 explained [ ] | | 9 wanted [ ] | |
| 10 showed [ ] | | 11 shouted [ ] | | 12 answered [ ] | |
| 13 touched [ ] | | 14 cleaned [ ] | | 15 stopped [ ] | |
| 16 lived [ ] | | 17 arrived [ ] | | 18 walked [ ] | |
| 19 started [ ] | | 20 enjoyed [ ] | | 21 helped [ ] | |
| 22 harmed [ ] | | 23 learned [ ] | | 24 thanked [ ] | |
| 25 played [ ] | | 26 asked [ ] | | 27 added [ ] | |
| 28 laughed [ ] | | 29 kicked [ ] | | 30 decided [ ] | |
| 31 spelled [ ] | | 32 cheered [ ] | | 33 missed [ ] | |
| 34 watched [ ] | | 35 ended [ ] | | 36 typed [ ] | |
| 37 spoiled [ ] | | 38 saved [ ] | | 39 attacked [ ] | |
| 40 connected [ ] | | 41 pushed [ ] | | 42 turned [ ] | |
| 43 moved [ ] | | 44 invented [ ] | | 45 happened [ ] | |

# PSS 2-4 일반동사의 불규칙 변화형

## 1. AAA형(원형, 과거형, 과거분사형이 같은 형)

| 원형 | 과거형 | 과거분사형 | 뜻 |
|---|---|---|---|
| cost | cost | cost | 비용이 들다 |
| hit | hit | hit | 치다 |
| hurt | hurt | hurt | 다치게 하다 |
| let | let | let | ~하게 하다 |
| put | put | put | 놓다 |
| read[riːd] | read[red] | read[red] | 읽다 |
| set | set | set | 놓다 |
| shut | shut | shut | 닫다 |
| spread | spread | spread | 퍼지다 |

## 2. ABB형(과거형과 과거분사형이 같은 형)

| 원형 | 과거형 | 과거분사형 | 뜻 |
|---|---|---|---|
| bring | brought | brought | 가져오다 |
| build | built | built | 짓다 |
| burn | burned / burnt | burned / burnt | 타다 |
| buy | bought | bought | 사다 |
| catch | caught | caught | 잡다 |
| dream | dreamed / dreamt | dreamed / dreamt | 꿈꾸다 |
| feed | fed | fed | 먹이다 |
| feel | felt | felt | 느끼다 |
| fight | fought | fought | 싸우다 |
| find | found | found | 발견하다 |
| get | got | got(ten) | 얻다 |

| 원형 | 과거형 | 과거분사형 | 뜻 |
| --- | --- | --- | --- |
| have | had | had | 가지다, 먹다 |
| hear | heard[həːrd] | heard[həːrd] | 듣다 |
| hold | held | held | 지니다 |
| keep | kept | kept | 유지하다 |
| lay | laid | laid | 놓다, 낳다 |
| lead | led | led | 인도하다 |
| leave | left | left | 떠나다 |
| lend | lent | lent | 빌려주다 |
| lose | lost | lost | 잃어버리다 |
| make | made | made | 만들다 |
| mean | meant[ment] | meant[ment] | 의미하다 |
| meet | met | met | 만나다 |
| pay | paid | paid | 지불하다 |
| say | said[sed] | said[sed] | 말하다 |
| sell | sold | sold | 팔다 |
| send | sent | sent | 보내다 |
| sit | sat | sat | 앉다 |
| sleep | slept | slept | 자다 |
| slide | slid | slid | 미끄러지다 |
| smell | smelled / smelt | smelled / smelt | 냄새 맡다 |
| spend | spent | spent | 소비하다 |
| stand | stood | stood | 서다 |
| teach | taught | taught | 가르치다 |
| tell | told | told | 말하다 |
| think | thought | thought | 생각하다 |
| understand | understood | understood | 이해하다 |
| win | won | won | 이기다 |

## 3. ABC형(원형, 과거형, 과거분사형이 다른 형)

| 원형 | 과거형 | 과거분사형 | 뜻 |
|---|---|---|---|
| be | was / were | been | ～이다, 있다 |
| bear | bore | borne/born | 낳다, 견디다 |
| begin | began | begun | 시작하다 |
| bite | bit | bitten | 물다 |
| blow | blew | blown | 불다 |
| break | broke | broken | 깨뜨리다 |
| choose | chose | chosen | 선택하다 |
| do | did | done | 하다 |
| draw | drew | drawn | 그리다 |
| drink | drank | drunk | 마시다 |
| drive | drove | driven | 운전하다 |
| eat | ate | eaten | 먹다 |
| fall | fell | fallen | 떨어지다 |
| forget | forgot | forgotten | 잊다 |
| fly | flew | flown | 날다 |
| give | gave | given | 주다 |
| go | went | gone | 가다 |
| grow | grew | grown | 자라다 |
| know | knew | known | 알다 |
| ride | rode | ridden | 타다 |
| ring | rang | rung | 울리다 |
| rise [raɪz] | rose [róuz] | risen [rízn] | 오르다 |
| see | saw | seen | 보다 |
| sing | sang | sung | 노래하다 |
| show | showed | shown | 보여주다 |
| speak | spoke | spoken | 말하다 |
| swim | swam | swum | 수영하다 |
| 원형 | 과거형 | 과거분사형 | 뜻 |

| 원형 | 과거형 | 과거분사형 | 뜻 |
|---|---|---|---|
| take | took | taken | 가지고 가다 |
| throw | threw | thrown | 던지다 |
| wake | woke | woken | 깨다 |
| wear | wore | worn | 입다 |
| write | wrote | written | 쓰다 |

## 4. ABA형(원형과 과거분사형이 같은 형)



| 원형 | 과거형 | 과거분사형 | 뜻 |
|---|---|---|---|
| become | became | become | 되다 |
| come | came | come | 오다 |
| run | ran | run | 달리다 |

정답 p.9

## PRACTICE 8 [1-90]

다음 동사의 과거형과 과거분사형을 쓰세요.



| | | | | |
|---|---|---|---|---|
| 1 set – ___ – ___ | 2 hold – ___ – ___ |
| 3 become – ___ – ___ | 4 smell – ___ – ___ |
| 5 bear – ___ – ___ | 6 break – ___ – ___ |
| 7 cost – ___ – ___ | 8 mean – ___ – ___ |
| 9 stay – ___ – ___ | 10 dream – ___ – ___ |
| 11 run – ___ – ___ | 12 blow – ___ – ___ |
| 13 feed – ___ – ___ | 14 drive – ___ – ___ |
| 15 put – ___ – ___ | 16 understand – ___ – ___ |
| 17 come – ___ – ___ | 18 choose – ___ – ___ |
| 19 drink – ___ – ___ | 20 draw – ___ – ___ |
| 21 read – ___ – ___ | 22 shop – ___ – ___ |
| 23 fight – ___ – ___ | 24 stand – ___ – ___ |
| 25 wear – ___ – ___ | 26 bite – ___ – ___ |
| 27 sing – ___ – ___ | 28 let – ___ – ___ |

| 29 | win | – ________ – ________ | 30 | hit | – ________ – ________ |
| 31 | tell | – ________ – ________ | 32 | write | – ________ – ________ |
| 33 | sell | – ________ – ________ | 34 | slide | – ________ – ________ |
| 35 | take | – ________ – ________ | 36 | wake | – ________ – ________ |
| 37 | fly | – ________ – ________ | 38 | carry | – ________ – ________ |
| 39 | try | – ________ – ________ | 40 | swim | – ________ – ________ |
| 41 | feel | – ________ – ________ | 42 | show | – ________ – ________ |
| 43 | burn | – ________ – ________ | 44 | keep | – ________ – ________ |
| 45 | forget | – ________ – ________ | 46 | ring | – ________ – ________ |
| 47 | send | – ________ – ________ | 48 | hear | – ________ – ________ |
| 49 | build | – ________ – ________ | 50 | hurt | – ________ – ________ |
| 51 | rise | – ________ – ________ | 52 | catch | – ________ – ________ |
| 53 | bring | – ________ – ________ | 54 | spread | – ________ – ________ |
| 55 | lend | – ________ – ________ | 56 | grow | – ________ – ________ |
| 57 | begin | – ________ – ________ | 58 | throw | – ________ – ________ |
| 59 | buy | – ________ – ________ | 60 | enjoy | – ________ – ________ |
| 61 | sit | – ________ – ________ | 62 | be | – ________ – ________ |
| 63 | play | – ________ – ________ | 64 | find | – ________ – ________ |
| 65 | go | – ________ – ________ | 66 | give | – ________ – ________ |
| 67 | plan | – ________ – ________ | 68 | eat | – ________ – ________ |
| 69 | ride | – ________ – ________ | 70 | know | – ________ – ________ |
| 71 | spend | – ________ – ________ | 72 | close | – ________ – ________ |
| 73 | speak | – ________ – ________ | 74 | get | – ________ – ________ |
| 75 | teach | – ________ – ________ | 76 | see | – ________ – ________ |
| 77 | lead | – ________ – ________ | 78 | study | – ________ – ________ |
| 79 | make | – ________ – ________ | 80 | have | – ________ – ________ |
| 81 | fall | – ________ – ________ | 82 | say | – ________ – ________ |
| 83 | lose | – ________ – ________ | 84 | leave | – ________ – ________ |
| 85 | sleep | – ________ – ________ | 86 | do | – ________ – ________ |
| 87 | meet | – ________ – ________ | 88 | think | – ________ – ________ |
| 89 | lay | – ________ – ________ | 90 | pay | – ________ – ________ |

## PSS 2-5 과거시제의 쓰임

**과거시제는 과거에 이미 끝난 동작이나 상태, 역사적 사실을 나타낼 때 쓰인다.**

It **was** sunny **yesterday**.
어제는 화창했다.
We **saw** a movie **last weekend**.
우리는 지난 주말에 영화를 보았다.
The Korean War **broke** out **in 1950**.
한국전쟁은 1950년에 일어났다.

I **went** to the beach **two days ago**. 나는 이틀 전에 해변에 갔다.

정답 p.10

### PRACTICE 9

괄호 안에 주어진 단어 중 알맞은 것을 고르세요.

1  It (is, was) cold yesterday, but it is warm today.

2  I (am, was) 10 years old this year.

3  I am tall, but I (wasn't, weren't) tall last year.

4  My cat (was, were) sick yesterday afternoon.

5  Barbara and I (are, were) at a restaurant last night.

6  They (are, were) in Japan last weekend.

7  We (aren't, weren't) good at snowboarding two years ago.

8  Ms. Kim (is, was) a teacher. She teaches us English.

9  You were a driver two years ago, but you (are, were) an engineer now.

10  Minho and I are often late for class, but we (aren't, weren't) late yesterday.

정답 p.10

### PRACTICE 10  [1-10]

괄호 안의 단어를 알맞은 형태로 바꾸어 빈칸에 쓰세요.

1  Yesterday was his birthday. We ________________ a T-shirt for him. (buy)

2  I usually ________________ breakfast, but this morning I skipped it. (eat)

**3** He ________________ to bed early because he was very tired. (go)

**4** My grandma ________________ glasses when she reads a book. (wear)

**5** She ________________ a sand castle on the beach yesterday. (build)

**6** It ________________ to rain last night. (begin)

**7** Seho ________________ this novel a month ago. (read)

**8** She ________________ her lost wallet yesterday. (find)

**9** They ________________ the picture an hour ago. (finish)

**10** Namsu always ________________ the violin when he stays home. (practice)

## PSS 3   미래시제 – will과 be going to

I **will** carry it for you.
제가 그것을 들어드릴게요.

I**'m going to** play soccer after school.
나는 방과 후에 축구를 하려고 한다.

will이나 be going to를 사용하여 미래시제를 표현할 수 있다.

| 주어 | will/be going to | 동사원형 |
|---|---|---|
| I | will<br>am going to | be at home. |
| He / She / It | will<br>is going to | |
| We / You / They | will<br>are going to | |

1. 미래에 대한 추측이나 의지를 나타낼 때 – will '~일 것이다, ~할 것이다'

**I'll** show you my album. 네게 내 사진첩을 보여줄게.

It **will** rain **next Sunday**. 다음 주 일요일에는 비가 올 것이다.

**weather forecast**

| MON | TUE | WED | THU | FRI | SAT | SUN |
|-----|-----|-----|-----|-----|-----|-----|

*cf.* 추측을 나타낼 경우 be going to로도 쓸 수 있다.

It **is going to** rain **next Sunday**. 다음 주 일요일에는 비가 올 것이다.

2. 미래의 계획이나 예정을 나타낼 때 – be going to '~하려고 하다'

He **is going to** have a date with Jane **tomorrow**.

그는 내일 Jane과 데이트를 하려고 한다.

What **are** they **going to** do **this weekend**? – They**'re going to** have a party.

그들은 이번 주말에 무엇을 하려고 하니?                그들은 파티를 열 거야.



정답 p.10

## PRACTICE 11

〈보기〉와 같이 짝지어진 두 문장의 의미가 같도록 빈칸을 채우세요.

| 보 기 | It will snow this afternoon.<br>= It <u>is going to snow</u> this afternoon. |
|---|---|

**1**  Jack will pass the exam.

= Jack ________________________ the exam.

**2**  They will go to the museum.

= They ________________________ to the museum.

**3**  We will get there tomorrow morning.

= We ________________________ there tomorrow morning.

**4**  He will visit his grandparents.

= He ________________________ his grandparents.

**5**  She will make dinner for us.

= She ________________________ dinner for us.

**6**  You and Eric will do a science project together.

= You and Eric ________________________ a science project together.

## PRACTICE 12

괄호 안에 주어진 말 중 알맞은 것을 고르세요.

1   I'm going to (help, helps) my grandpa with shopping.

2   (Is, Will) he going to play tennis?

3   We (are, will) be fourteen years old next year.

4   He (went, will go) to the market yesterday.

5   They will (make, makes) time for their family.

6   (Are, Will) you be there tonight?

7   Mary will (be, is) a singer someday.

8   Ted always (get, gets) up at six.

9   Tom (studied, will study) math last night.

10   How long (will, are) you going to stay there?



## PRACTICE 13

그림을 보고, 〈보기〉에서 알맞은 동사를 골라 B의 대답을 완성하세요.

| 보 기 | travel   buy   study   paint   have |
| --- | --- |

| 1 | 2 | 3 | 4 | 5 |
| --- | --- | --- | --- | --- |

1   A: What are you going to do this Saturday?   B: I _________________ my house.

2   A: What will he do during his next vacation?   B: He _________________ to Egypt.

3   A: What is Kelly going to do today?   B: She _________________ at the library.

4   A: What will you do this weekend?   B: We _________________ a party.

5   A: What are they going to do?   B: They _________________ some flowers.

# PSS 4  진행시제

## PSS 4 - 1  동사의 -ing형 Ⅰ

| 대부분의 경우 | -ing | call – call**ing**<br>start – start**ing** | sing – sing**ing**<br>teach – teach**ing** |
|---|---|---|---|
| 자음+e로 끝나는 경우 | e를 빼고 -ing | come – com**ing**<br>make – mak**ing** | give – giv**ing**<br>ride – rid**ing** |

정답 p.10

## PRACTICE 14

다음 동사의 -ing형을 쓰세요.

**1** live – ___________

**2** leave – ___________

**3** sleep – ___________

**4** hold – ___________

**5** draw – ___________

**6** play – ___________

**7** carry – ___________

**8** believe – ___________

**9** write – ___________

**10** say – ___________

**11** buy – ___________

**12** spend – ___________

**13** lose – ___________

**14** wake – ___________

**15** check – ___________

**16** bring – ___________

**17** look – ___________

**18** dive – ___________

**19** join – ___________

**20** smoke – ___________

**21** do – ___________

**22** blow – ___________

**23** make – ___________

**24** choose – ___________

**25** add – ___________

**26** sell – ___________

**27** give – ___________

**28** have – ___________

**29** take – ___________

**30** meet – ___________

## PSS 4-2 동사의 -ing형 Ⅱ

| -ie로 끝나는 경우 | ie를 y로 바꾸고 -ing | lie – lying    tie – tying |
|---|---|---|
| 단모음+단자음으로 끝나는 경우 | 마지막 자음을 하나 더 쓰고 -ing | run – running    get – getting<br>put – putting    begin – beginning<br>*cf.* 강세가 앞에 오는 2음절 동사의 경우<br>enter – entering    visit – visiting |

정답 p.10

### PRACTICE 15

다음 동사의 -ing형을 쓰세요.

| | | | | | |
|---|---|---|---|---|---|
| **1** | get | – __________ | **2** | lie | – __________ |
| **3** | change | – __________ | **4** | open | – __________ |
| **5** | park | – __________ | **6** | push | – __________ |
| **7** | read | – __________ | **8** | wear | – __________ |
| **9** | put | – __________ | **10** | call | – __________ |
| **11** | find | – __________ | **12** | bike | – __________ |
| **13** | burn | – __________ | **14** | set | – __________ |
| **15** | come | – __________ | **16** | respect | – __________ |
| **17** | win | – __________ | **18** | see | – __________ |
| **19** | close | – __________ | **20** | begin | – __________ |
| **21** | tie | – __________ | **22** | grow | – __________ |
| **23** | keep | – __________ | **24** | drink | – __________ |
| **25** | swim | – __________ | **26** | help | – __________ |
| **27** | climb | – __________ | **28** | enter | – __________ |
| **29** | sing | – __________ | **30** | go | – __________ |
| **31** | jump | – __________ | **32** | shop | – __________ |
| **33** | lend | – __________ | **34** | catch | – __________ |
| **35** | collect | – __________ | **36** | send | – __________ |

| | | | | | | |
|---|---|---|---|---|---|---|
| **37** | stay | – ___________ | | **38** | ride | – ___________ |
| **39** | fall | – ___________ | | **40** | fly | – ___________ |
| **41** | teach | – ___________ | | **42** | dream | – ___________ |
| **43** | sit | – ___________ | | **44** | drive | – ___________ |
| **45** | plant | – ___________ | | **46** | turn | – ___________ |
| **47** | stand | – ___________ | | **48** | start | – ___________ |
| **49** | float | – ___________ | | **50** | break | – ___________ |
| **51** | tell | – ___________ | | **52** | eat | – ___________ |
| **53** | speak | – ___________ | | **54** | run | – ___________ |
| **55** | arrive | – ___________ | | **56** | build | – ___________ |
| **57** | ask | – ___________ | | **58** | camp | – ___________ |
| **59** | cheer | – ___________ | | **60** | walk | – ___________ |

## PSS 4-3 현재진행시제와 과거진행시제

<Now>

My father **is sleeping** now.

나의 아버지는 지금 주무시고 계신다.

1. 현재진행 – 「am / is / are +-ing」
   '～하고 있다'

   Ted **is listening** to pop songs.

   Ted는 대중 가요를 듣고 있다.

   Insu and Suji **are having** lunch together.

   인수와 수지는 함께 점심을 먹고 있다.

<Last night>

My father **was working** last night.

나의 아버지는 어젯밤에 일하고 계셨다.

2. 과거진행 – 「was / were +-ing」
   '～하고 있었다'

   Ted **was listening** to pop songs.

   Ted는 대중 가요를 듣고 있었다.

   Insu and Suji **were having** lunch together.

   인수와 수지는 함께 점심을 먹고 있었다.

## PRACTICE 16

〈보기〉와 같이 주어진 문장을 진행시제의 문장으로 바꾸어 쓰세요.

> 보 기
> Tom reads a book.
> ➡ Tom is reading a book.

**1** It snows.
➡ ___________________________

**2** I clean my room.
➡ ___________________________

**3** Sumi makes a card.
➡ ___________________________

**4** He wears blue jeans.
➡ ___________________________

**5** It flew over the tree.
➡ ___________________________

**6** We enjoyed the holiday.
➡ ___________________________

**7** They do their homework.
➡ ___________________________

**8** My grandparents smiled at us.
➡ ___________________________

**9** A man stood in front of the door.
➡ ___________________________

**10** I played basketball with my friends.
➡ ___________________________

---

## PSS 4-4 미래를 나타내는 현재진행시제

1. **현재진행형**으로 **가까운 미래의 계획**을 나타낼 수 있다. 주로 **왕래발착**을 나타내는 동사인 **go, come, start, leave, arrive**와 함께 쓰이지만, 다른 동사들도 미래를 나타내는 부사나 부사구와 함께 현재진행형으로 미래를 나타낼 수 있다.

   We **are going** camping **this weekend**. 우리는 이번 주말에 캠핑을 갈 것이다.
   He **is coming** here **soon**. 그는 곧 여기로 올 것이다.
   **I'm leaving** **tomorrow morning**. 나는 내일 아침에 떠날 것이다.

2. '진행'을 나타내는 현재진행형과 '미래'를 나타내는 현재진행형의 비교

   What **are** you **doing now**?  – **I'm studying** math.
   너는 지금 무엇을 하고 있니?  나는 수학을 공부하고 있어.

   What **are** you **doing tomorrow**?  – **I'm studying** in the library **tomorrow**.
   너는 내일 무엇을 할 거니?  나는 내일 도서관에서 공부할 거야.

   (= **I'm going to study** in the library **tomorrow**.)

## PRACTICE 17

**괄호 안의 말을 이용하여 현재진행형으로 B의 대답을 완성하세요.**

**1** A: What is Junho doing tomorrow morning?

　　B: He ___is cleaning the house___ tomorrow morning. (clean, the house)

**2** A: What are you doing this evening?

　　B: I ________________________ this evening. (read, a book)

**3** A: What is Liza doing next vacation?

　　B: She ________________________ next vacation. (visit, her aunt)

**4** A: What are they doing next Saturday?

　　B: They ________________________ next Saturday. (eat out, with their family)

**5** A: What are you doing this Sunday?

　　B: We ________________________ this Sunday. (go, to church)



## PRACTICE 18

**그림을 보고, 〈보기〉에서 알맞은 동사를 골라 B의 대답을 완성하세요.**

| 보 기 | walk　bake　go　take　paint |
| --- | --- |

**1** A: What is Nari doing now?　　　　　　　B: She ________________ a selfie.

**2** A: What did you guys do yesterday?　　　B: We ________________ to the movies.

**3** A: What are you going to do tomorrow?　B: I ________________ a cake for the party.

**4** A: What will Jinho do at home?　　　　　B: He ________________ a picture.

**5** A: What was she doing at 7 a.m.?　　　　B: She ________________ her dog.

# PSS 5  현재완료시제

## PSS 5-1  현재완료시제의 쓰임

현재완료시제는 「have/has+과거분사」의 형태로 과거에 일어난 일을 현재와 연관지어 나타낼 때 쓴다. 의문문은 「Have(Has)+주어+과거분사~?」의 형태로 쓴다.

| 주어 | have/has | 과거분사 |
|---|---|---|
| I/You/We/They | **have**<br>**have not** (= haven't) | **been** ill since last week. |
| He/She/It | **has**<br>**has not** (= hasn't) | |

He began to live in Paris six years ago. He lives in Paris now.

그는 6년 전에 파리에서 살기 시작했다. 그는 지금 파리에 산다.

➡ He **has lived** in Paris for six years. 그는 6년째 파리에서 살고 있다.

<6 years ago>    <Now>

**Have** you ever **been** to Canada? – Yes, I have. / No, I haven't.

너는 캐나다에 가본 적이 있니?          응, 가봤어. / 아니, 가보지 않았어.

## PRACTICE 19

괄호 안의 단어를 현재완료시제로 바꾸어 빈칸에 쓰세요.

1  They ___*have built*___ the bridge since last year. (build)

2  She _______________ a sports car for four months. (drive)

3  I _______________ anything about him. (not, hear)

4  _______________ Bill _______________ Cathy? (meet)

5  Hana _______________ a bicycle since last week. (have)

6  _______________ you ever _______________ New York? (visit)

7  My brother and I _______________ the sunrise. (not, see)

8  Ms. Song _______________ math for a long time. (teach)

9  _______________ you _______________ in the library before? (study)



## PRACTICE 20

다음 밑줄 친 부분이 현재완료시제가 되도록 어법에 맞게 고쳐 쓰세요.

1  Sujin <u>have played</u> the violin since 2023.
   ➡ ___*has played*___

2  <u>Has she watch</u> a soccer game before?
   ➡ _______________

3  They <u>haven't leaved</u> the building yet.
   ➡ _______________

4  I <u>have feeded</u> a lost dog for 2 weeks.
   ➡ _______________

5  Seyeon <u>had</u> the cell phone since last year.
   ➡ _______________

6  He <u>hasn't did</u> his homework yet.
   ➡ _______________

7  She <u>has founded</u> her lost keys in the room.
   ➡ _______________

8  How long <u>have he been</u> in that seat?
   ➡ _______________

9  I <u>never read</u> a fantasy novel in my life.
   ➡ _______________

10  Seungjun <u>has grew</u> 20cm since last year.
   ➡ _______________

| 현재완료 | 과거 |
|---|---|
| 과거 ────▶ 현재 | 과거 ● 현재 |

**현재완료**

1. **과거부터 현재까지 계속되는 동작이나 상태**를 나타낸다.

   Steve **has stayed** in Japan for two months. Steve는 두 달 동안 일본에 있었다. (현재 일본에 계속 있다는 의미)

2. **기간을 나타내는 부사(구)**와 함께 쓸 수 있다. since는 '과거의 어느 시점부터 (현재까지)'란 뜻을 가지며 주로 현재완료시제와 잘 쓰인다.

   She **has played** the piano **since last year**. 그녀는 작년부터 피아노를 쳤다.

**과거**

1. **과거에 이미 끝난 동작이나 상태**를 나타낸다.

   Steve **stayed** in Japan for two months. Steve는 두 달 동안 일본에 있었다. (현재 일본에 있지 않다는 의미)

2. yesterday, 'last+명사', ago, 'in+과거 연도'와 같은 **명백한 과거 시점을 나타내는 부사(구)**와 함께 쓸 수 있다.

   She **played** the piano **a few days ago**. 그녀는 며칠 전에 피아노를 쳤다.

*cf.* 의문사 when은 현재완료시제와 함께 쓰일 수 없다.

   **When did** you **clean** your room? 너는 방을 언제 청소했니?

정답 p.11

## PRACTICE 21

괄호 안에 주어진 표현 중 알맞은 것을 고르세요.

1  (Have, Did) you ever seen that movie?

2  He (lived, has lived) in Seoul since 2023.

3  Last night he (brushed, has brushed) his teeth.

4  When (did, has) he go there?

**5** He (left, has left) Korea last year.

**6** They (have been, are) married for ten years.

**7** I have (know, known) her for a long time.

**8** Mina has (plays, played) the violin for five years.

**9** She (met, has met) her friends last night.

**10** He (has, was) been sick for the last few days.

**11** We (have studied, studied) English since 2020.

**12** Sally (watched, has watched) the movie a week ago.

**13** My uncle (has worked, worked) in a bank since this summer.

**14** He (went, has gone) to work by car yesterday.

**15** The party (ended, has ended) at midnight.

**16** It (rained, has rained) since last night.

**17** We (had, have had) his birthday party last weekend.

**18** She has (listens, listened) to music for an hour.

**19** He (threw, has thrown) away the bottles a moment ago.

**20** They have (make, made) carpets for 50 years.

**21** (Have, Did) you finish your homework?

**22** She (won, has won) the first prize in the art competition last month.

**23** We (have visited, visited) New York 2 years ago.

**24** The actor (played, has played) the role since last year.

**25** It (has snowed, snowed) heavily two hours ago.

**26** (Have, Did) you ever been to London?

**27** I (have been, was) with Suji last Friday.

# 중간·기말고사 대비문제

**1** 다음 중 밑줄 친 부분이 <u>어색한</u> 것을 고르세요.

> This ① <u>is</u> my best friend, Jack. He ② <u>lives</u> across the street. He ③ <u>has</u> a rabbit. He ④ <u>go</u> to English academy every day. He ⑤ <u>plays</u> computer games with me. We are good friends.

**2** 빈칸에 들어갈 표현으로 가장 알맞은 것은?

> Isabella is interested in K-pop and Korean dramas. She is eager to deeply understand Korean culture. So, she started to learn Korean two years ago. Since she ___________ Korean for two years, she can now watch Korean dramas without English subtitles.
>
> *subtitle 자막

① study
② studies
③ has studied
④ had studied
⑤ have studied

**3** 다음 밑줄 친 부분 중 어법상 바른 것은?

① <u>Does</u> it snow heavily yesterday?
② He <u>is moving</u> to Seoul next month.
③ She <u>had</u> the house since last year.
④ I have already <u>finish</u> my homework.
⑤ The woman <u>was walking</u> by the post office now.

**4** 다음 글에서 어법상 <u>틀린</u> 곳을 찾아 바르게 고쳐 쓰세요.

> David liked to grow tropical plants. He builded a small greenhouse for himself. It cost a lot of money.

___________ ➡ ___________

**5** 빈칸에 들어갈 말로 알맞지 <u>않은</u> 것은?

> ___________ go to the library.

① We
② Women
③ Sue and John
④ People
⑤ My aunt

**6** 다음 문장을 〈보기〉와 같이 바꾸어 쓰세요.

> 보 기 ｜ I have lunch at noon.
> ➡ He <u>has</u> lunch at noon.

· I do the cooking in the evening.
➡ She ___________ the cooking in the evening.

**7** 주어진 우리말을 영어로 가장 바르게 영작한 학생은?

> 우리는 탁구를 치고 있는 중이었다.

① 수혁 : We were playing table tennis.
② 서진 : We are going to play table tennis.
③ 민주 : We are playing table tennis.
④ 승준 : We played table tennis.
⑤ 윤서 : We was playing table tennis.

**8** 다음 대화의 빈칸에 공통으로 들어갈 단어를 쓰세요.

> *A*: How ___________ the weather there yesterday?
> *B*: It ___________ cloudy.

**9** 다음 우리말을 참조하여 빈칸에 알맞은 말을 쓰세요. (단, 주어진 동사를 사용하고, 필요한 경우 동사의 형태를 변형할 것)

> 그는 내일 그 도시를 떠날 것이다. (be, leave)
> ➡ He _______ _______ the town tomorrow.

**10** 괄호 안의 단어를 현재시제로 바꾸어 빈칸에 쓰세요.

> Yuri ⓐ ___________ (go) to school at 9:00.
> She ⓑ ___________ (have) lunch at 12:30.
> After lunch, she ⓒ ___________ (read) books with her friends. School ⓓ ___________ (end) at 3:00.

**11** 빈칸에 들어갈 수 있는 것을 <u>두 개</u> 고르면?

| 동사원형 | 과거형 | 과거분사형 |
|---|---|---|
| ride | r□de | ridden |
| draw | drew | dr□wn |
| bear | b□re | b□rn |
| begin | beg□n | begun |

① a ② e ③ i
④ o ⑤ u

**12** 다음 Amy의 시험 일정에 대한 글에서 어법상 옳은 문장은?

> Today is June thirteenth. ① The final exam was next Friday. ② I finish studying math yesterday. ③ I will reviews it again next Wednesday. ④ Now I am study English. ⑤ I am going to study science next week.

**13** 다음 빈칸에 들어갈 수 <u>없는</u> 말은?

> Where did you go ___________________?

① last winter ② yesterday
③ this afternoon ④ three days ago
⑤ next Saturday

**14** ⓐ~ⓔ 중 어법상 옳은 것을 <u>있는 대로</u> 고른 것은?

> ⓐ Is Alex fixing his computer?
> ⓑ I amn't painting a beautiful picture.
> ⓒ My mom does cooking dinner now.
> ⓓ Mike is swiming in the pool with friends.
> ⓔ They are doing their homework in the library.

① ⓐⓒ ② ⓐⓔ ③ ⓑⓓ
④ ⓒⓓ ⑤ ⓓⓔ

**15** 다음 질문에 대한 대답으로 알맞은 것은?

> *A*: What are you going to do?
> *B*: ___________________

① Yes, I am.
② I'm going to do my homework.
③ I'm good at swimming.
④ Yes, I have to go now.
⑤ I went home.

## 16 다음 밑줄 친 부분의 쓰임이 <u>다른</u> 하나는?

① I'm <u>going to</u> the zoo now.
② I'm <u>going to</u> write a letter.
③ I'm <u>going to</u> have a party tonight.
④ I'm <u>going to</u> make a plan.
⑤ I'm <u>going to</u> go to London.

## 17 다음 대화의 빈칸에 들어갈 단어로 알맞게 짝지어진 것은?

> *A*: ___________ he and his family visited here?
> *B*: Yes, they ___________.

① Has  – have
② Has  – has
③ Has  – had
④ Have – has
⑤ Have – have

## 18 다음 밑줄 친 동사의 형태가 <u>잘못된</u> 것은?

① Mary <u>takes</u> a bus.
② She <u>plaies</u> the violin with her mother.
③ Your father <u>has</u> a nice car.
④ He <u>studies</u> English very hard.
⑤ Mike <u>gets</u> up early in the morning.

## 19 다음 빈칸에 들어갈 말로 알맞은 것을 <u>모두</u> 고르세요.

> Alice ___________ shopping next weekend.

① go
② went
③ will go
④ is going
⑤ has gone

## 20 우리말과 의미가 같도록 괄호 안의 말을 배열할 때 <u>세 번째</u>로 오는 것은?

> • 나는 여기에 7일째 머무르고 있다.
>  (seven, stayed, for, I, days, have, here)

① here
② seven
③ have
④ stayed
⑤ for

## 21 다음 중 어법상 옳은 문장의 개수는?

> ⓐ This's your cell phone.
> ⓑ She will makes it in time.
> ⓒ He read the book last week.
> ⓓ Mr. and Mrs. Cheney are my good neighbors.
> ⓔ Jane and I am talking about the homework.

① 1개
② 2개
③ 3개
④ 4개
⑤ 5개

## 22 밑줄 친 동사의 알맞은 형태를 고르세요.

> A few years ago, her father <u>make</u> kites for her.

① makes
② made
③ making
④ has made
⑤ is making

## 23 다음 문장을 〈보기〉와 같이 바꾸어 쓰세요.

> 보 기 | Do you clean your room?
> ➡ <u>Are you cleaning your room?</u>

Does she water the plant?

➡ ___________________________

## 24 다음 밑줄 친 현재진행형 중 쓰임이 옳은 것의 개수는?

> Minho is standing at the bus stop. He ⓐ is carrying a heavy backpack and is waiting for his friends. They ⓑ are riding their bikes to school today. A bus is stopping in front of the stop, and some students ⓒ are geting off. One of them ⓓ is smileing at Minho. His teacher is ⓔ coming down the street to greet the students.

① 1개　　② 2개　　③ 3개　　④ 4개　　⑤ 5개

## 25 다음 중 밑줄 친 부분의 쓰임이 나머지 넷과 다른 하나는?

① My dad is going fishing tomorrow.
② Mr. Smith is coming soon.
③ Are you meeting Alex next week?
④ We are having a barbecue this Friday.
⑤ What are you doing now?

## 26 다음 문장의 밑줄 친 부분과 쓰임이 같은 문장으로 짝지어진 것은?

> What are we going to do there?

> ⓐ I am going to clean my room.
> ⓑ He is going to a concert with Evan.
> ⓒ We are going to go to Jeju-do for a family trip.
> ⓓ She is going to the science museum.
> ⓔ Jina is going to wear a new dress.

① ⓐ,ⓑ　　　② ⓐ,ⓒ,ⓔ　　　③ ⓐ,ⓓ,ⓔ
④ ⓑ,ⓓ　　　⑤ ⓑ,ⓓ,ⓔ

## 27 다음 두 문장을 한 문장으로 알맞게 바꿔 쓴 것은?

> • Cathy started to work at this company two years ago. She still works at this company.

① Cathy has started to work at this company since two years ago.
② Cathy has started to work at this company for two years ago.
③ Cathy was working at this company for two years.
④ Cathy has worked at this company since two years.
⑤ Cathy has worked at this company for two years.

## 28 아래의 그림을 보고 주어진 물음에 답하세요.

(1) What is Bomi doing?

➡ _______________________________

(2) What are Peter and John doing?

➡ _______________________________

## 29 어법상 옳은 문장은?

① Is your mom cooks dinner now?
② He is listening not to the radio.
③ She is tie a ribbon around the gift.
④ Do they having a good time at the mall?
⑤ Our baking club is looking for new members.

**30** 다음 문장을 괄호 안의 조건대로 옮긴 것 중 잘못된 것은?

> She plays the piano.

① (현재완료로) → She has played the piano.
② (현재진행형으로) → She is playing the piano.
③ (미래시제로) → She will plays the piano.
④ (과거시제로) → She played the piano.
⑤ (과거진행형으로) → She was playing the piano.

**31** 다음 〈보기〉의 두 문장을 〈조건〉에 맞게 하나의 문장으로 완성하세요.

| 조 건 | 반드시 for를 사용해서 Susan을 제외한 7단어로 답안을 작성해야 함. |
|---|---|

| 보 기 | • Susan moved to Busan five years ago.<br>• She still lives in Busan. |
|---|---|

➡ Susan _________________________________ .

**32** 다음 세미의 일정표를 보고 be going to를 이용하여 질문에 알맞은 답을 쓰세요.

| Tuesday | buy some books |
|---|---|
| Wednesday | make cookies |
| Thursday | go swimming |
| Friday | go to the movies |

Q: What is Semi going to do on Thursday?
A: She _______________________________ .

**33** 다음 중 동사의 변화형이 잘못된 것을 고르세요.

① feel – felt – felt
② know – knew – known
③ give – gave – given
④ make – made – maden
⑤ come – came – come

**34** 다음 중 어법상 옳은 것을 2개 고르세요.

① The Korean War began in 1950 and ended in 1953.
② We meeting our teacher after class today.
③ She have lived in this town since 2015.
④ I have visited the art gallery three times.
⑤ I am liking the taste of this new drink.

**35** 다음 가게의 영업 시간표를 보고 괄호 안의 단어를 활용하여 문장을 완성하세요.

| <Open> Daily 9:30 a.m. |
|---|
| <Break Time> 2:00~3:00 p.m. |
| <Close> 6 p.m. |

➡ It __________ (open) at 9:30 a.m. every day.
➡ It __________ (have) a break time from 2 p.m. to 3 p.m.
➡ It __________ (close) at 6 p.m.

**36** 다음 중 어법상 어색한 문장을 모두 고르세요.

① How are you doing?
② I go to Mt. Halla last week.
③ It was great.
④ I made new friends.
⑤ She's name is Sumin.

## 37 다음 빈칸에 순서대로 들어갈 be동사의 알맞은 형태는?

- I ___________ 13 years old last year.
- I ___________ 14 years old now.
- I ___________ 15 years old next year.

① am – was – will be
② was – am – will be
③ will be – was – am
④ am – will be – was
⑤ was – will be – am

## 38 다음 문장에서 잘못된 두 군데를 찾아 바르게 고쳐 쓰세요.

He get up early and go jogging every morning.

➡ ___________________

➡ ___________________

## 39 다음 중 현재진행형으로 고친 문장이 바르지 않은 것은?

① You study math.
　➡ You are studying math.
② She lies on the floor.
　➡ She is lieing on the floor.
③ The class begins.
　➡ The class is beginning.
④ I do exercises.
　➡ I am doing exercises.
⑤ He plays the piano.
　➡ He is playing the piano.

## 40 다음 @~ⓒ에 들어갈 말을 알맞게 짝지은 것은?

On Sunday morning, Bora ___@___ taking a walk. Then, she saw two foreigners. They ___ⓑ___ Bora for help. They were ___ⓒ___ for a bus stop.  Bora showed them the way to the bus stop.

|     | @ | ⓑ | ⓒ |
|-----|------|--------|---------|
| ① | was | asked | look |
| ② | was | ask | looking |
| ③ | was | asked | looking |
| ④ | were | asked | looking |
| ⑤ | were | ask | look |

## 41 빈칸에 들어갈 알맞은 말은?

Who am I ___________ to, please?

① talk　　② talks　　③ can talk
④ talking　　⑤ will talk

## 42 다음 중 밑줄 친 부분의 형태가 잘못된 것은?

① We cleanned our house.
② He washed his clothes.
③ I made some food for my parents.
④ We had dinner together.
⑤ My sister came back home at eight.

## 43  다음 중 어법상 올바른 문장을 고르세요.

① I will a good designer.
② I will did the laundry tomorrow.
③ Cathy is having lunch now.
④ Mr. Park was busy tomorrow.
⑤ He was playing not basketball this morning.


## 44  다음 빈칸에 들어갈 알맞은 말은?

*A*: You look tired, Susan.
*B*: I didn't sleep well last night.
*A*: What happened?
*B*: _______________________

① I will study English tonight.
② A man is walking down the hall.
③ He looks tired.
④ I am going to go fishing.
⑤ My baby sister cried all night.


## 45  다음 문장에서 틀린 곳을 올바르게 고치지 <u>않은</u> 것은?

① Minsu sing very well. → Minsu sings very well.
② She have a lovely cat. → She has a lovely cat.
③ He need little help. → He needs little help.
④ John play the violin. → John plays the violin.
⑤ He fly to many countries. → He flys to many countries.


## 46  밑줄 친 단어를 알맞은 형태로 바꾸어 쓰세요.

*A*: What time did you eat lunch yesterday?
*B*: I <u>eat</u> lunch at 12:30.

➡ _______________________________


## 47  다음 중 빈칸에 go를 쓸 수 <u>없는</u> 문장은?

① Minji will ___________ to Busan.
② I sometimes ___________ to Jane's house.
③ What time does he ___________ to school?
④ Minho ___________ hiking with his friends.
⑤ My parents ___________ to bed early every night.


## 48  다음 글을 읽고 어법상 <u>어색한</u> 문장을 고르세요.

① Mike is going to busy next week. ② He is planning to wash his father's car on Monday. ③ He is going to study in the library on Wednesday. ④ He will play basketball with his friends on Friday. ⑤ He will go swimming on Saturday.


## 49  다음 중 주어진 문장의 내용을 <u>잘못</u> 파악한 사람은?

*A*. Lisa has worked as a lawyer for 2 years.
*B*. Sunny and her aunt have just had lunch.
*C*. Kate and Mina have lived in Seoul since they were babies.
*D*. Jiah has gone to Australia with her family.
*E*. Junho has liked this cartoon since he was seven years old.

① 보람: Lisa는 2년째 변호사로 일하고 있어.
② 하늘: Sunny와 그녀의 이모는 지금 점심을 먹고 있어.
③ 민아: Kate와 Mina는 아기였을 때부터 쭉 서울에 살고 있어.
④ 상호: Jiah와 그녀의 가족은 호주로 가버렸고, 지금 이곳에 없어.
⑤ 현진: Junho는 7살 때부터 지금까지 이 만화를 좋아하고 있어.

## 50 다음 중 어법상 옳은 문장은?

① We were playing soccer now.
② Sue and Mary are talking about him.
③ They learned an important lesson tomorrow.
④ He will finish his homework a few minutes ago.
⑤ We're going to have a field trip last week.

## 51 다음 글의 밑줄 친 부분 중 쓰임이 <u>어색한</u> 것은?

Dear Jane,

How are you ①doing? I am fine. I ②went to Mt. Bukhan on a picnic last week. My mother ③makes lunch for me. It was delicious.
I have new friends. They ④are Sejin and Yumi. I ⑤like to go to school these days.
How is your school?

Your friend,
*Minji*

## 52 다음 중 어법상 <u>어색한</u> 문장은?

① I will call you tonight.
② When will she leave for New York?
③ Will you going to visit Paris this summer?
④ I am going to play soccer after school.
⑤ She is going to take a dance lesson on Tuesday.

## 53 다음 표는 학급 친구들이 내일 방과 후에 할 일입니다. 〈보기〉와 같이 빈칸을 완성하세요.

| 이름 | 할 일 |
| --- | --- |
| Jaemin | listen to music |
| Mina and Suji | play the guitar |
| Jieun | make spaghetti |

보 기 | Jaemin <u>is going to listen to music.</u>

(1) Mina and Suji ______________________________
______________________________.

(2) Jieun ______________________________
______________________________.

## 54 다음 괄호 속의 동사를 문맥에 맞게 고친 것은?

㉠ They (study) Chinese since last year.
㉡ Tony (visit) his parents last weekend.
㉢ She (teach) English in this school for the past 3 years.

|  | ㉠ | ㉡ | ㉢ |
| --- | --- | --- | --- |
| ① | studied | visited | taught |
| ② | studied | has visited | taught |
| ③ | have studied | visited | has taught |
| ④ | have studied | has visited | has taught |
| ⑤ | have studied | visited | is teaching |

**55** 〈보기〉에서 가장 적절한 말을 골라 빈칸을 완성하세요.

| 보 기 | play / draw / take / read |
|---|---|

| 조 건 | 1) 필요시, 〈보기〉의 단어를 적절히 변형할 것.<br>2) 〈보기〉의 단어를 한 번씩만 사용할 것. |
|---|---|

(1) They visited the museum and ___________ many pictures together.
(2) She is good at ___________ pictures of animals.
(3) I have just ___________ a new comic book.
(4) We ___________ soccer yesterday.

**56** 대화의 빈칸에 들어갈 말로 적절한 것은?

> A: _____________________________
> B: I am planning to visit my grandparents this Saturday.

① How will you visit your grandparents?
② Do you visit your grandparents every week?
③ What are you visiting your grandparents for?
④ Why did you plan to visit your grandparents?
⑤ What are you planning to do this Saturday?

**57** 다음 대화의 밑줄 친 read와 같은 소리로 발음되는 것을 모두 고르시오.

> B: Have you watched the movie, *The Big Choice*?
> G: Yes, I have. I've read the book, too.
> B: Do you recommend reading the book?
> G: Of course! You should read it.

① Does he know how to read?
② Have you read the email from our teacher?
③ Did you read the homework assignment?
④ Mr. Kim told me to read the sign before entering.
⑤ When I was a child, my mom read bedtime stories to me.

**58** 다음 글 전체의 시제와 일치하지 <u>않는</u> 동사 3개를 찾아 바르게 고쳐 쓰세요.

> Yesterday, my family had a party because it was my mom's birthday. I prepared a birthday cake, and my sister decorates our house with balloons. My dad bought some pretty roses for my mom. My grandparents also come to our house to celebrate mom's birthday. We sing a birthday song together and my mom cut the cake. It was the best birthday party ever!

ⓐ ___________ ➡ ___________
ⓑ ___________ ➡ ___________
ⓒ ___________ ➡ ___________

# CHAPTER 3
# 조동사

# 조동사

조동사는 be동사와 일반동사를 도와주며 의미(능력, 허가, 요청, 추측, 제안, 의무, 충고 등)를 더하는 동사이다. 조동사 뒤에는 항상 동사원형이 온다.

## PSS 1  조동사 + 동사원형



| 주어 | 조동사 | 동사원형 |
|---|---|---|
|  | can |  |
|  | could |  |
|  | may | be |
| I | might | park |
| He / She / It | will | come   ~ |
| We / You / They | would | do |
|  | must | make |
|  | should |  |
|  | had better |  |

*cf.* 조동사는 겹쳐 쓰지 않는다.

He **will can** buy the ticket. ( × )  He **will** buy the ticket. ( ○ )

## PRACTICE 1

괄호 안에 주어진 단어 중 알맞은 것을 고르세요.

**1** You should (watch, watched) the ball.

**2** Minho can (swim, swims) in the sea.

**3** He will (can, be able to) stay with us.

**4** You had better (see, saw) a doctor.

**5** She always (leave, leaves) for work early.

**6** He may (come, comes) to class.

**7** We must (be, been) ready for the rainy weather.

**8** Seho really (want, wants) something to eat.

**9** I could (wash, washed) my dirty hands in that place.

**10** She thought she would (have, has) a cup of coffee.

**11** Tony often (write, writes) letters to your sister.

**12** That dog might (bite, bitten) you.

---

# PSS 2 조동사의 부정형과 축약형

PROBLEM
SOLVING
SKILL

| 조동사+not | 축약형 | 예문 |
|---|---|---|
| cannot | can't | She **cannot[can't]** drive. 그녀는 운전을 하지 못한다. |
| could not | couldn't | I **couldn't** find him. 나는 그를 찾을 수 없었다. |
| may not | — | You **may not** be right. 네가 옳지 않을지도 모른다. |
| might not | mightn't | We **mightn't** win the match.<br>우리가 그 시합에서 이기지 못할지도 모른다. |
| will not | won't | They **won't** meet him. 그들은 그를 만나지 않을 것이다.<br>= They**'ll not** meet him. |
| would not | wouldn't | She said she **wouldn't** be late. 그녀는 늦지 않을 거라고 말했다. |
| must not | mustn't | He **mustn't** be late. 그는 늦어서는 안 된다. |
| should not | shouldn't | We **shouldn't** break off the branches.<br>우리는 나뭇가지를 꺾어서는 안 된다. |
| had better not | — | You **had better not** go there. 너는 그곳에 가지 않는 게 낫다.<br>= You**'d better not** go there. |

## PRACTICE 2

〈보기〉와 같이 주어진 문장의 조동사에 not을 붙여 부정문으로 바꾸어 쓰세요.

> 보 기     Alex could sleep well last night.
> ➡ <u>Alex could not[couldn't] sleep well last night.</u>

**1** Jane will use your desk.

➡ _______________________________

**2** You must take this ball.

➡ _______________________________

**3** She can play the guitar.

➡ _______________________________

**4** He should break the promise.

➡ _______________________________

**5** It might be true.

➡ _______________________________

**6** Minsu could dance last night.

➡ _______________________________

**7** I knew she would come here.

➡ _______________________________

**8** You may like the movie.

➡ _______________________________

**9** You had better stay here.

➡ _______________________________

# PSS 3   조동사로 시작하는 의문문

PROBLEM SOLVING SKILL

「조동사+주어+동사원형 ～?」의 어순으로 의문문을 만든다.

> You can speak English. 너는 영어를 말할 수 있다.
>
> **Can you** speak English? 너는 영어를 말할 수 있니?
>
> - **Yes**, I can. / **No**, I can't.
>   응, 할 수 있어. / 아니, 할 수 없어.

**Will he** be at home?   – **Yes**, he will. / **No**, he won't.

그가 집에 있을까?     응, 있을 거야. / 아니, 없을 거야.

**Should I** leave here?   – **Yes**, you should. / **No**, you shouldn't.

내가 여기를 떠나야 하니?     응, 그래야 해. / 아니, 그래서는 안 돼.

## PRACTICE 3

〈보기〉와 같이 주어진 문장을 의문문으로 바꾸어 쓰세요.

> 보 기   You can change a ten-dollar bill.
> ➡ <u>Can you change a ten-dollar bill?</u>

**1** They will get there by subway.
➡ _______________________________

**2** We should take a bus.
➡ _______________________________

**3** He can play the violin.
➡ _______________________________

**4** Jenny will move to London.
➡ _______________________________

**5** I should buy this shirt.
➡ _______________________________

**6** Minsu can cook Chinese food.
➡ _______________________________

**7** The movie will start at 11:20.
➡ _______________________________

**8** This elephant can draw pictures.
➡ _______________________________



## PRACTICE 4

우리말과 같은 뜻이 되도록 괄호 안에 주어진 말을 바르게 배열하세요.

**1** 너는 젓가락을 사용할 수 있니?
= _______________________________
(chopsticks, use, you, can)

**2** 커피 좀 마실래요?
= _______________________________
(like, some coffee, you, would)

**3** 내가 민수를 저녁식사에 초대해야 해?
= _______________________________
(invite, should, Minsu, to dinner, I)

**4** 당신의 전화기를 써도 될까요?
= _______________________________
(I, your phone, may, use)

**5** 제 가방을 들어 주시겠어요?
= _______________________________
(my bag, could, you, carry)

**6** 나와 함께 거기에 갈래?
= _______________________________
(will, go there, you, with me)

**7** 이 병들을 재활용해야 합니까?
= _______________________________
(I, recycle, must, these bottles)

**8** Bill과 통화할 수 있을까요?
= _______________________________
(speak, Bill, may, I, to)

# PSS 4 조동사의 종류



## PSS 4-1 can Ⅰ

He **can** swim.
그는 수영할 수 있다.

**능력**

1. '~할 수 있다'의 뜻으로 능력을 나타낼 때는 be able to로 바꾸어 쓸 수 있다.

    I **can** drive a car. 나는 차를 운전할 수 있다.

    = I **am able to** drive a car.

    She **can't** drive a car. 그녀는 차를 운전할 수 없다.

    = She **isn't able to** drive a car.

    **Can** you drive a car? 너는 차를 운전할 수 있니?

    = **Are** you **able to** drive a car?

2. can의 과거형은 could로 '~할 수 있었다'의 뜻을 나타낸다.

    Mark **couldn't** drive a car. Mark는 차를 운전할 수 없었다.

    = Mark **wasn't able to** drive a car.

정답 p.16

## PRACTICE 5

〈보기〉와 같이 밑줄 친 부분을 be able to를 이용하여 바꾸어 쓰세요.

> 보 기
>
> Jenny <u>couldn't</u> say a word for a while.
>
> ➡ Jenny <u>wasn't able to</u> say a word for a while.

**1** She <u>can</u> take a picture well.

  ➡ She ________________ take a picture well.

**2** I <u>can't</u> understand his lecture.

  ➡ I ________________ understand his lecture.

**3** <u>Can</u> you make it at six?

  ➡ ________________ you ________________ make it at six?

**4** He <u>could</u> get a new bike on Christmas Day.

  ➡ He ________________ get a new bike on Christmas Day.

**5** We <u>couldn't</u> find an exit in that store.

  ➡ We ________________ find an exit in that store.

**6** <u>Can</u> you find this word in a dictionary?

  ➡ ________________ you ________________ find this word in a dictionary?

# PSS 4-2 can Ⅱ

| | |
|---|---|
| 허가 | '~해도 된다'라는 뜻이며, 이때의 can을 **부정형인 cannot[can't]**으로 쓰면 '**~해서는 안 된다**'라는 금지의 뜻을 가진다.<br><br>You **can** open the window. 너는 창문을 열어도 된다.<br>He **can't** open the window. 그는 창문을 열어서는 안 된다.<br>**Can I** open the window? 내가 창문을 열어도 될까?<br>**Could I** open the window? 제가 창문을 열어도 될까요?<br>***cf.*** Could I ~?는 Can I ~?보다 정중한 표현으로 이때의 could는 can의 과거형이 아니다. |
| 요청 | **Can you ~?** 또는 **Could you ~?**의 형태로 쓰이며, '**~해주겠니?**'라는 뜻을 가진다.<br><br>**Can you** send these packages for me? 네가 나 대신 이 택배물들을 보내주겠니?<br>**Could you** send these packages for me?<br>당신이 저 대신 이 택배물들을 보내주시겠어요?<br>***cf.*** Could you ~?는 Can you ~?보다 정중한 표현으로 이때의 could는 can의 과거형이 아니다. |

정답 p.16

## PRACTICE 6

다음 문장의 빈칸에 can, could, can't 중 알맞은 것을 넣으세요.

**1** You look thirsty. You _______________ drink juice there.

**2** You _______________ go out alone at night. It's dangerous.

**3** Jane, _______________ I borrow your pen?

**4** _______________ you come down a little?

**5** Hello, _______________ I speak to Tom, please?

**6** She loves him, but she _______________ marry him.

**7** _______________ you give me a hand?

**8** You _______________ park here. Please move your car.

**9** _______________ you do me a favor?

**10** Do your homework first. Then, you _______________ watch TV.

# PSS 4-3 may

| | |
|---|---|
| 추측 | '~일지도 모른다'라는 뜻으로 **약한 추측**을 나타낸다.<br>She **may** go out. 그녀는 외출할지도 모른다.<br>She **may not** go out. 그녀는 외출하지 않을지도 모른다. |
| 허가 | '~해도 좋다'라는 뜻이며, 이때의 may를 **부정형인 may not**으로 쓰면 '~해서는 안 된다'라는 금지의 뜻을 가진다.<br>You **may** sit here. 너는 여기에 앉아도 좋다.<br>You **may not** sit here.<br>너는 여기에 앉아서는 안 된다.<br>**May** I sit here? 제가 여기에 앉아도 될까요? |



정답 p.16

## PRACTICE 7

밑줄 친 부분이 추측과 허가 중 어떤 의미를 지니는지 구분하여 쓰세요.

1  Hi, <u>may</u> I help you? [          ]

2  You <u>may</u> use my pencil. [          ]

3  She <u>may</u> not be sick. [          ]

4  It <u>may</u> be true. [          ]

5  They <u>may</u> be busy. [          ]

6  <u>May</u> I ask a question? [          ]

7  Hello, <u>may</u> I speak to Mr. Smith? [          ]

8  She <u>may</u> not want to see us. [          ]

9  The bus <u>may</u> come in five minutes. [          ]

10  Jenny <u>may</u> be thirsty. [          ]

11  You <u>may</u> bring it back tomorrow. [          ]

12  She <u>may</u> be 42 years old. [          ]

13  <u>May</u> I borrow the car? [          ]

14  You <u>may</u> have a seat. [          ]

| 승낙 | 거절 |
|---|---|
| Yes, you may. 응, 그래도 돼.<br>Yes, you can. 응, 그래도 돼.<br>Sure. 그럼.<br>Of course. 물론이지.<br>Why not? 왜 안 되겠니?<br>Okay. 알았어. | No, you may not. 아니, 안 돼.<br>No, you must not. 아니, 절대 안 돼.<br>Sorry, you can't. 미안하지만, 안 돼.<br>I'm afraid not. 그럴 수는 없을 것 같아. |

정답 p.17

## PRACTICE 8

빈칸에 알맞은 단어를 넣어 대화를 완성하세요.

1  *A*: May I sit here?
   *B*: Yes, you ________________ .

2  *A*: May I have some coffee?
   *B*: Sure, why ________________ ?

3  *A*: May I go out?
   *B*: I'm sorry, but ________________ can't.

4  *A*: May I take your message?
   *B*: Of ________________ .

5  *A*: May I use your computer?
   *B*: I am afraid ________________ .

6  *A*: May I try this shirt on?
   *B*: ________________ .

7  *A*: May I come in?
   *B*: No, you ________________ not.

8  *A*: May I have a sandwich for dinner?
   *B*: ________________ not?

| 요청 |
| --- |
| Will you ~?나 Would you ~?의 형태로 쓰이며, '~해줄래요?'라는 뜻을 가진다. Will you ~?보다는 Would you ~?가 보다 정중한 표현이다.<br>**Will you** please be quiet? 좀 조용히 해줄래요?<br>**Would you** please be quiet?<br>좀 조용히 해주시겠어요?<br>**Will you** close the window? 창문을 닫아 줄래요?<br>**Would you** close the window?<br>창문을 닫아 주시겠어요? |

정답 p.17

## PRACTICE 9

우리말과 같은 뜻이 되도록 괄호 안에 주어진 말을 바르게 배열하세요.

**1** 여기서 머무를래요? (you, will, stay, here)

= ________________________________________

**2** 저 좀 도와주시겠습니까? (help, you, would, me)

= ________________________________________

**3** 음악(소리) 좀 줄여 주시겠어요? (would, the music, you, turn down)

= ________________________________________

**4** 저한테 이메일 좀 보내줄래요? (you, send, will, an email, me)

= ________________________________________

**5** 내일 아침 7시에 깨워줄래요? (will, at 7 a.m. tomorrow, you, wake me up)

= ________________________________________

**6** 당신의 전화번호를 말씀해주시겠습니까? (you, me, would, tell, your phone number)

= ________________________________________

**7** 당신의 신분증을 보여주시겠습니까? (you, would, me, show, your ID card)

= ________________________________________

| would like+(대)명사 | would like to+동사원형 |
|---|---|
| would like는 '~을 원하다'라는 뜻으로 want와 같은 의미이다.<br><br>**Would** you **like** some ice cream?<br>너는 아이스크림을 좀 원하니?<br>= **Do you want** some ice cream?<br>**I'd like a bigger room.**<br>나는 더 큰 방을 원해요.<br>She **would like** some water.<br>그녀는 물을 좀 원해요. | would like to는 '~하고 싶다'라는 뜻으로 want to와 같은 의미이다.<br><br>**I'd like to go** to sleep.<br>나는 자고 싶다.<br>= I **want to go** to sleep.<br>We**'d like to go** to the park.<br>우리는 공원에 가고 싶다.<br>He**'d like to play** basketball.<br>그는 농구를 하고 싶다. |

정답 p.17

## PRACTICE 10

빈칸에 would like 또는 would like to를 넣어 대화를 완성하세요.

**1** A: I ________________ two hamburgers and a small coke.
  B: OK. For here or to go?

**2** A: ________________ you ________________ join our team?
  B: Yes, I'd love to.

**3** A: Which color would you like to try on?
  B: I ________________ try on the blue one.

**4** A: What would you like to do tonight?
  B: I ________________ watch TV tonight.

**5** A: ________________ you ________________ some bread?
  B: No, thank you.

**6** A: Where ________________ you ________________ go?
  B: I ________________ visit the Louvre Museum.

정답 p.17

## PRACTICE 11 [1-8]

우리말과 같은 뜻이 되도록 괄호 안에 주어진 말 중 알맞은 것을 고르세요.

**1** 이것을 입어 봐도 될까요?
  = (Could, Would) I try this on?

**2** Tom은 마지막 문제를 풀지 못했다.

= Tom (can, could) not solve the last problem.

**3** 너는 기타를 칠 수 있니?

= (Can, May) you play the guitar?

**4** Sarah는 내일까지 그 일을 끝낼 것이다.

= Sarah (will, would) finish the work by tomorrow.

**5** 더러운 물은 우리를 병에 걸리게 할지도 모른다.

= Dirty water (would like to, may) make us sick.

**6** 주스 좀 더 드시겠어요?

= (Will, Would) you like more juice?

**7** 그것에 대해 말해 줄래요?

= (May, Will) you tell me about it?

**8** 방과 후에 내게 전화해주겠니?

= (Can, May) you call me after school?

## PSS 4-7 must I

| | |
|---|---|
| 의무 | **'～해야 한다'**라는 뜻으로 **의무**를 나타낸다.<br>You **must** get there by 10. 너는 10시까지 그곳에 도착해야 한다.<br>I **must** wait for Becky. 나는 Becky를 기다려야 한다. |
| 강한 추측 | **'～임에 틀림없다'**라는 뜻으로 **강한 추측**을 나타낸다.<br>That restaurant **must** be very good. 그 음식점은 아주 훌륭할 것임에 틀림없다.<br>He **must** be at home. 그는 집에 있을 것임에 틀림없다. |

정답 p.17

### PRACTICE 12

밑줄 친 부분이 의무와 강한 추측 중 어떤 의미를 지니는지 구분하여 쓰세요.

**1** Cars go very fast on this street. We <u>must</u> be careful.  [          ]

**2** She hasn't eaten anything all day. She <u>must</u> be hungry.  [          ]

**3** Students <u>must</u> wear uniforms. They cannot wear casual clothes.  [          ]

**4** I have a test tomorrow. I <u>must</u> study hard.  [          ]

**5** Sorry. I <u>must</u> have the wrong number.  [          ]

**6** The baby is crying. She <u>must</u> be sleepy.  [          ]

**7** Don't say anything about it. You <u>must</u> keep it secret.  [          ]

**8** There is a fire. We <u>must</u> call the fire station.  [          ]

**9** Nari wears pink every day. She <u>must</u> like that color.  [          ]

**10** Minho looks young. He <u>must</u> be a student.  [          ]

**11** I can't go out. I <u>must</u> help Mom at home.  [          ]

**12** He studied until late at night. He <u>must</u> be tired.  [          ]



## PSS 4-8 must Ⅱ

| | | |
|---|---|---|
| 의무 | 현재 | must가 '~해야 한다'는 뜻의 의무를 나타낼 때는 have[has] to로 바꾸어 쓸 수 있다.<br>We **must** go to Seoul now. 우리는 지금 서울에 가야 한다.<br>= We **have to** go to Seoul now.<br>She **must** go to Seoul now. 그녀는 지금 서울에 가야 한다.<br>= She **has to** go to Seoul now. |
| | 과거 | must는 쓸 수 없고 had to로 쓴다.<br>We **had to** go to Seoul yesterday. 우리는 어제 서울에 가야 했다. |

*cf.* have to는 조동사가 아니므로 의문문에서 주어 앞으로 이동하지 않고, 「Do[Does/Did]+주어 +have to ~?」의 어순으로 의문문을 만든다.

**Do we have to** go to the party? 우리는 파티에 가야 하니?

**Does he have to** get up early tomorrow? 그는 내일 일찍 일어나야 하니?

**Did you have to** wear a uniform in your school? 너는 학교에서 교복을 입어야 했니?

정답 p.17

### PRACTICE 13

〈보기〉와 같이 짝지어진 두 문장의 의미가 같도록 빈칸을 채우세요.

| 보 기 | They must go to school.<br>= They _have to_ go to school. |
|---|---|

**1** People must follow the law.

= People _________________ follow the law.

**2** Jeff must pass this exam.

= Jeff _________________ pass this exam.

**3** She must get up early.

= She _________________ get up early.

**4** I must be in good shape.

= I _________________ be in good shape.

**5** You must do your homework.

= You _________________ do your homework.

**6** We must wait for the train.

= We _________________ wait for the train.

## PRACTICE 14

빈칸에 have[has] to 또는 had to를 넣어 문장을 완성하세요.

1  It was late. We _______________ take a taxi.

2  He is very hungry. He _______________ eat some food.

3  It is very cold outside. You _______________ wear a coat.

4  We missed the bus last night. We _______________ walk home.

5  I _______________ sleep now. I want to get up early tomorrow.

6  Bob's room isn't clean. He _______________ clean it right now.

7  I broke my glasses. I _______________ buy a new pair last week.

8  Tomorrow is Parents' Day. We _______________ buy carnations now.

9  I met Ted. I _______________ borrow the book from him yesterday.

10  She broke her arm. She _______________ go to the hospital an hour ago.

---

## PSS 4-9  must not, don't have to

| | |
|---|---|
| must not | '~해서는 안 된다'라는 뜻으로 **금지**를 나타낸다.<br>You **must not** be late for school. 너는 학교에 지각해서는 안 된다.<br>She **must not** go out now. 그녀는 지금 외출해서는 안 된다. |
| don't have to | '~할 필요가 없다'라는 뜻으로 **불필요**를 나타낸다.<br>They **don't have to** hurry. 그들은 서두를 필요가 없다.<br>Jinsu **doesn't have to** move to Suwon. 진수는 수원으로 이사할 필요가 없다. |



## PRACTICE 15

그림을 보고, must not 또는 don't[doesn't] have to를 넣어 문장을 완성하세요.

1

2

3

**1** Sujin _______________ get up early. She doesn't work today.

**2** You _______________ drink and drive.

**3** Here's the elevator. You _______________ climb the stairs.

**4** Don't make a noise. We _______________ wake the baby.

**5** You _______________ bring food in this room. It should be kept clean.

**6** You _______________ wash the dishes. I'll take care of it.

## PSS 4-10 should, had better

| should | '~해야 한다'의 뜻으로 **의무나 당연**을 나타낸다. |
| --- | --- |
| | I **should** call her tonight. 나는 오늘 밤에 그녀에게 전화해야 한다. |
| | He **should not** sit here. 그는 여기에 앉지 말아야 한다. |
| had better | '~하는 게 낫다'의 뜻으로 **강한 충고나 권유**를 나타낸다. |
| | You **had better** go to the dentist. 너는 치과 의사에게 가는 게 낫다. |
| | We**'d better not** take a bus. 우리는 버스를 타지 않는 게 낫다. |

## PRACTICE 16

〈보기〉에서 알맞은 단어를 골라 should나 had better를 사용하여 문장을 완성하세요.

| 보 기 | wear make walk go play stay put throw change copy |
| --- | --- |

**1** 너는 학급 친구들에게 좋은 인상을 주어야 한다.

= You ________________________________ a good impression on your classmates.

**2** 나는 감기에 걸렸다. 나는 이 코트를 입는 게 낫겠다.

= I got a cold. I ________________________________ on this coat.

**3** 너는 창문 밖으로 쓰레기를 던져서는 안 된다.

= You ________________________________ waste out of the window.

**4** 네 눈을 보호하기 위해서 선글라스를 끼는 게 좋겠다.

= You ________________________________ sunglasses to protect your eyes.

**5** 너는 컴퓨터 게임을 너무 많이 해서는 안 된다.

= You ________________________________ computer games too much.

**6** 비가 아주 많이 내리고 있다. 우리는 나가지 않는 게 좋겠다.

= It's raining heavily. We ________________________________ outside.

**7** 너는 옷을 갈아입어야 한다.

= You ________________________________ your clothes.

**8** 너는 역까지 걸어가지 않는 게 좋겠다. 그곳은 여기에서 매우 멀다.

= You ________________________________ to the station. It's very far from here.

**9** 너는 다른 사람의 숙제를 베껴서는 안 된다.

= You ________________________________ others' homework.

**10** 그녀는 햇볕 속에 너무 오래 나가있지 않는 게 좋겠다.

= She ________________________________ out in the sun for too long.



## PRACTICE 17

우리말과 같은 뜻이 되도록 괄호 안에 주어진 말 중 알맞은 것을 고르세요.

**1** 그가 또다시 거짓말을 하고 있음에 틀림없다.

= He (must, can) be telling a lie again.

**2** 너는 그것에 대해 걱정할 필요가 없다.

= You (don't have to, must not) worry about that.

**3** 나무가 없다면, 우리는 깨끗한 공기를 얻을 수 없다.

= Without trees, we (should not, cannot) get clean air.

**4** 소금 좀 건네주시겠어요?

= (Would, Should) you pass me the salt?

**5** 지난밤 나는 보름달을 볼 수 있었다.

= Last night I (should, could) see the full moon.

**6** 그녀는 거실에 있을지도 모른다.

= She (may, must) be in the living room.

**7** 비가 올지도 모른다. 우산을 챙기는 게 좋겠다.

= It (may, had better) rain. You (can, had better) take an umbrella.

**8** 나는 숙제로 내가 가장 좋아하는 동물을 그려야 한다.

= I (have to, will) draw my favorite animal for homework.

**9** 뭐 마실 것 좀 드릴까요?

= (Will, Would) you like something to drink?

**10** 영화 보는 동안 시끄럽게 해서는 안 된다.

= You (don't have to, should not) make a noise during the movie.

**11** 오늘 밤에 여기서 묵어도 될까요?

= (Can, Will) I stay here tonight?

**12** 우리는 건강을 위해 운동을 시작해야 한다.

= We (should, had to) start exercising for our health.

**13** 너는 곧장 가서는 안 된다.

= You (don't have to, must not) go straight.

**14** 나는 너무 늦게까지 깨어 있지 않는 게 낫겠다.

= I (must, had better) not stay up too late.

**15** 상자를 열어주시겠어요?

= (Could, May) you open the box?

**16** 너는 노는 데 많은 시간을 보내서는 안 된다.

= You (don't have to, should not) spend a lot of time playing.

**17** 그들은 신발을 벗어야 했다.

= They (must, had to) take off their shoes.

**18** 그는 설거지를 하지 않을 것이다.

= He (will, must) not wash the dishes.

**1** 다음 중 어법상 옳은 것은?

① I can't began to tell you how happy I am.
② He willn't go to the park tomorrow.
③ My friend could dances beautifully.
④ She may be at the library right now.
⑤ He should studied harder for the test.

**2** 다음 밑줄 친 부분과 바꾸어 쓸 수 있는 말을 고르세요.

You <u>must</u> take care of your little sister.

① have to　② has to　③ can
④ are going to　⑤ had better

**3** 다음 밑줄 친 표현과 바꿔 쓸 수 있는 말을 세 단어로 쓰세요.

• 그녀는 인터넷에서 무엇이든 살 수 있습니다.
= She <u>can</u> buy anything on the Internet.

= She ＿＿＿＿ ＿＿＿＿ ＿＿＿＿
buy anything on the Internet.

**4** 다음 밑줄 친 부분이 어떤 조동사와 함께 축약된 것인지를 고르세요.

<u>I'd</u> like to buy a nice car.

① I did　② I had　③ I would
④ I should　⑤ I could

**5** 다음 질문에 대한 대답으로 알맞은 것은?

A: Can John run fast?
B: ＿＿＿＿＿＿＿＿＿

① Yes, he can't.　② Yes, he cans.
③ Sure, he can't.　④ No, John can.
⑤ No, he can't.

**6** 다음 우리말과 같은 뜻이 되도록 빈칸에 알맞은 말을 쓰세요.

• 우리는 다음 달의 계획을 세우는 게 좋겠다.
= We ＿＿＿＿＿＿ ＿＿＿＿＿＿ make
plans for next month.

**7** 다음 문장에서 어법상 틀린 부분을 찾아 바르게 고쳐 쓰세요.

(1) You will are a good teacher.
＿＿＿＿＿＿＿＿ ➡ ＿＿＿＿＿＿＿＿

(2) Can I borrowing your umbrella?
＿＿＿＿＿＿＿＿ ➡ ＿＿＿＿＿＿＿＿

**8** 빈칸에 들어갈 말로 알맞은 것을 고르세요.

We can get anything with money. But we
＿＿＿＿＿＿ get health with it.

① do　② should　③ shouldn't
④ can　⑤ can't

**9** 다음 빈칸에 들어갈 말로 알맞은 것을 고르세요.

> *A*: May I park my car here?
> *B*: ___________________________ There's a
>    sign that says, 'No parking.'

① Yes, you may.　　② Yes, you should.

③ No, you could not.　④ No, you must not.

⑤ No, you don't have to.

---

**10** 우리말과 같은 뜻이 되도록 주어진 단어들을 바르게 배열하세요.

> • 제가 지금 집에 가야만 하나요?
>
>  = ___________________________
>
>  (have, I, home, do, go, to, now)

---

**11** 다음 두 문장이 같은 뜻이 되도록 빈칸에 들어갈 알맞은 말을 쓰세요.

> • Humans can change the world.
>   = Humans ___________ ___________
>   ___________ change the world.

---

**12** 다음 빈칸에 알맞은 말은?

> She is always late for school.
> She ___________ be lazy.

① will　　② has to　　③ had better

④ must　　⑤ should

---

**13** 다음 우리말과 같은 의미가 되도록 〈조건〉에 맞게 영작하세요.

> 그는 내일 그의 친구들을 만날 것인가?
>
> 조건1 – meet 동사를 포함시킬 것.
> 조건2 – 6단어로 쓸 것.
> 조건3 – 문장 부호를 반드시 삽입할 것.

➡ ___________________________

---

**14** 의미상 다음의 빈칸에 들어갈 수 <u>없는</u> 말은?

> You ___________________________ in the
> classroom.

① must not run

② have to be quiet

③ must listen to your teacher

④ don't have to study hard

⑤ should not fight

---

**15** 다음 그림 표지판과 같은 뜻이 되도록 빈칸을 채울 때 알맞지 <u>않은</u> 것은?

> You ___________ take a picture here.

① cannot　　　　② must not

③ don't have to　④ should not

⑤ may not

**16** 조동사 will과 괄호 안의 말을 사용하여 아래 두 문장을 우리말에 맞게 쓰세요. (단, 필요시 단어를 변형 및 추가할 것.)

(1) 그녀는 대중가요를 듣지 않을 것이다.
　( pop songs, to, she, listen )

　➡ ＿＿＿＿＿＿＿＿＿＿＿＿＿＿

　　 ＿＿＿＿＿＿＿＿＿＿＿＿＿＿

(2) 도서관에서 조용히 해주실래요?
　( the, quiet, library, are, in, you )

　➡ ＿＿＿＿＿＿＿＿＿＿＿＿＿＿

　　 ＿＿＿＿＿＿＿＿＿＿＿＿＿＿


**17** 다음 두 문장의 뜻이 같도록 빈칸에 들어갈 알맞은 단어를 고르세요.

- I would like to know about your country.
  = I ＿＿＿＿＿ to know about your country.

① have　　　② plan　　　③ want
④ think　　　⑤ begin


**18** 다음 밑줄 친 부분의 쓰임이 <u>어색한</u> 것은?

① It <u>may not</u> rain this afternoon.
② <u>Can</u> you bring me an umbrella?
③ He <u>won't</u> arrive here in time.
④ You <u>should</u> make a noise in the library.
⑤ You <u>must</u> turn off your cell phone in the theater.


**19** 다음 글의 빈칸에 들어갈 말로 알맞은 것은?

If you fall asleep with the window open, you ＿＿＿＿＿ catch a cold.

① may　　　② must not　　　③ had better
④ cannot　　　⑤ have to


**20** 다음 중 밑줄 친 <u>can</u>의 쓰임이 같은 것끼리 묶인 것은?

ⓐ <u>Can</u> I park my car here?
ⓑ He <u>can</u> understand Spanish well.
ⓒ <u>Can</u> you play the guitar?
ⓓ <u>Can</u> I help you?
ⓔ Come on. You <u>can</u> do it.

① (ⓐ),(ⓑⓒⓓⓔ)　　② (ⓐⓑ),(ⓒⓓⓔ)
③ (ⓐⓓ),(ⓑⓒⓔ)　　④ (ⓐⓒⓓ),(ⓑⓔ)
⑤ (ⓐⓑⓒⓔ),(ⓓ)


**21** 다음 질문에 대한 대답으로 알맞은 것은?

A: Can I have some hamburgers?
B: ＿＿＿＿＿＿＿＿＿＿＿

① Sure, here you are.
② I don't like hamburgers.
③ I like spaghetti very much.
④ No, thanks. I'm full.
⑤ Wow! It's delicious.


**22** 다음 대화의 빈칸에 들어갈 단어로 알맞게 짝지어진 것은?

A: Mom, ＿＿＿＿＿ I play baseball with my friends?
B: No! You ＿＿＿＿＿ finish your homework first.

① can　– can　　　② should – will
③ may　– must　　④ may　– can
⑤ must – will

## 23 다음 중 문장의 전환이 옳지 않은 것은?

① She can make delicious *bulgogi*. (의문문)
➡ Can she make delicious *bulgogi*?
② The story may be true. (부정문)
➡ The story may not be true.
③ Robert has to wear glasses. (의문문)
➡ Has Robert to wear glasses?
④ We should recycle cans and bottles. (의문문)
➡ Should we recycle cans and bottles?
⑤ He will move to Incheon. (부정문)
➡ He won't move to Incheon.

## 24 다음 질문에 대한 대답으로 알맞지 않은 것은?

> A: Can you join our club?
> B: _______________________

① I'm afraid not.　　② I'm sorry, I can't.
③ Sure.　　④ Yes, you can.
⑤ Of course.

## 25 다음 중 어법상 어색한 문장은?

① They will not stay at home.
② He is going to go to the museum next Sunday.
③ She had better go home now.
④ Can he play soccer?
⑤ David can will swim well.

## 26 주어진 문장을 must를 이용하여 금지를 나타내는 말로 바꾸어 쓰세요.

> • You have to carry a balloon here.
> ➡ _______________________
> _______________________

## 27 밑줄 친 may의 쓰임이 다른 하나는?

① It may be fine tomorrow.
② She may win the contest.
③ It may be difficult for you.
④ May I take your order?
⑤ She may come, or she may not.

## 28 어법상 옳은 문장을 고르세요.

① Birds cans fly.
② I can speaks Chinese.
③ Penguins not can fly.
④ Bears cannot see well at night.
⑤ Tom cans rides a bike very well.

## 29 주어진 대답에 적절한 질문을 〈조건〉에 맞추어 쓰세요.

> 질문: _______________________
> 대답: No, you may not. It is dangerous to
> swim in this river.

> 조 건
> 1. 6단어로 쓸 것.
> 2. 대소문자와 문장부호 규칙을 준수하며 한 문장으로 쓸 것.

➡ _______________________

## 30 다음 빈칸에 공통으로 들어갈 알맞은 말은?

> • You ___________ wear a swimming cap.
> • You ___________ be kind to other people.

① are　　② would like　　③ were
④ need　　⑤ should

# 31

다음 대화의 빈칸에 들어갈 표현으로 <u>어색한</u> 것을 고르세요.

> A: May I go to the movies tonight?
> B: _______________

① Yes, you may.　② Yes, you can.
③ Yes, I would.　④ No, you can't.
⑤ No, you should not.

# 32

다음 대화의 빈칸에 들어갈 알맞은 말은?

> A: I'm going to the post office. Will you come with me?
> B: _______________ I have to do my homework.

① I'm sorry, I can't.　② Sure.
③ Of course.　④ Yes, I will.
⑤ Why not?

# 33

다음 주어진 문장들 중 어법상 옳은 것의 개수는?

> • Birds can fly with their wings.
> • This work may easy for you.
> • You have not to bring your library card.
> • You shouldn't talk or eat loudly here.
> • He musts practice English every day.

① 1개　② 2개　③ 3개
④ 4개　⑤ 5개

# 34

다음 중 밑줄 친 부분의 쓰임이 <u>어색한</u> 것을 고르세요.

① You <u>cannot</u> sit here.
② Study hard, or you <u>willn't</u> succeed in life.
③ Junsu <u>doesn't</u> like his name.
④ You <u>don't</u> have to go to the bank.
⑤ He <u>couldn't</u> find the book.

# 35

밑줄 친 부분이 어법상 <u>잘못된</u> 것은?

① He <u>had to</u> help his mother.
② Mr. Brown <u>have to</u> stay home today.
③ My parents <u>had to</u> visit my school.
④ I <u>have to</u> see a doctor.
⑤ We <u>have to</u> throw trash in a trash can.

# 36

우리말과 같은 뜻이 되도록 할 때 빈칸에 들어갈 알맞은 말은?

> • 상호는 그곳에서 수영을 하고 놀 수 있었다.
>   = Sangho _______________ swim and play there.

① could　② can　③ couldn't
④ cannot　⑤ should

# 37

다음 빈칸에 공통으로 들어갈 알맞은 단어는?

> • _______________ I help you?
>   – Yes. I'm looking for a shirt.
> • _______________ I speak to Alex?
>   – This is Alex speaking. Who's calling, please?

① Would　② Should　③ Must
④ Do　⑤ May

## 38 다음 대화의 빈칸에 들어갈 알맞은 것은?

A: It's very cold here, isn't it?
B: Yes, it is.
A: ______________________________
B: No problem.

① Will you close the door?
② Why are you closing the door?
③ Must you close the door?
④ May you close the door?
⑤ Do I have to close the door?

## 39 빈칸에 들어갈 말들이 바르게 짝지어진 것은?

Bob: Would you like ___________ to the
     movies tonight?
Sarah: Sure, sounds good.
Bob: What time shall we ___________?
Sarah: How about six?
Bob: OK. Let's meet at six.

① to go – meet     ② going – meeting
③ go    – meet     ④ go     – meeting
⑤ to go – to meet

## 40 다음 빈칸에 공통으로 들어갈 알맞은 말은?

• I ___________ go home now.
• You ___________ get there before dark.
• She ___________ buy a new book.

① must     ② have to     ③ has to
④ need     ⑤ do

## 41 다음 밑줄 친 우리말을 영어로 바르게 옮긴 것은?

A: Why didn't you come to my house?
B: 나는 내 방을 청소해야 했어.

① I must clean up my room.
② I did must clean up my room.
③ I have to clean up my room.
④ I had to clean up my room.
⑤ I had had to clean up my room.

## 42 다음 대화를 읽고 빈칸에 들어갈 알맞은 말을 고르세요.

A: You look sick. What's the matter?
B: I have a toothache.
A: That's too bad. I think you ___________
   see a dentist.

① will     ② have     ③ has to
④ should     ⑤ able to

## 43 괄호 안의 단어를 알맞게 배열하여 문장을 완성하세요.

Mom: ___________________________________
     (better, go, bed, you, to, had) early
     tonight. You don't want to be late for
     school, do you?
Mary: I know. Would you wake me up at 6?

## 44 다음 괄호 안의 단어들로 문장을 만들 때 다섯 번째로 올 단어는?

(for, to, would, lunch, what, you, like, eat)?

① for      ② to      ③ like
④ eat      ⑤ lunch

## 45 다음 중 밑줄 친 may의 쓰임이 다른 하나는?

① She <u>may</u> be angry about your lie.
② You <u>may</u> not bring outside food in here.
③ He <u>may</u> be sick. He doesn't look well.
④ It snows a lot. She <u>may</u> be late.
⑤ People <u>may</u> see squirrels here.

## 46 다음과 같이 말하는 아이에게 해줄 수 있는 충고로 적절하지 <u>않은</u> 것을 고르세요.

I want to be healthy. What should I do?

① You should exercise every day.
② You should not eat junk food.
③ You should skip meals.
④ You shouldn't go to bed late.
⑤ You should eat a lot of vegetables.

## 47 다음 표지판을 보고 〈조건〉에 맞게 쓰세요.

〈표지판〉

① 내용: 휴대전화 사용 금지
   장소: on the bus

② 내용: 음식물 반입 금지
   장소: into the classroom

③ 내용: 사진 촬영 가능
   장소: at the festival

조 건

1. ①~③의 표지판에 대해 설명하는 글을 '내용'과 '장소'를 모두 포함하여 각 1문장씩, 총 3문장 쓸 것.
2. 모든 문장은 You로 시작하고, 조동사 may를 사용할 것.
3. 대소문자와 문장부호 규칙을 준수할 것.

① ______________________________
② ______________________________
③ ______________________________

## 48 짝지어진 두 문장의 의미가 같지 <u>않은</u> 것은?

① May I speak to Minhee?
= Can I speak to Minhee?
② You must not make noise here.
= You don't have to make noise here.
③ You must come to school early tomorrow.
= You have to come to school early tomorrow.
④ Can you wash the dishes for me?
= Could you wash the dishes for me?
⑤ He is able to read and write in French.
= He can read and write in French.

# CHAPTER 4
# 수동태

**태(voice)는 주어와 동사의 관계를 나타낸다.**

① 능동태(active voice)는 주어가 동사의 동작을 하는 경우에 쓴다.

She opened the door. 그녀는 문을 열었다.
주어　동사
└─ 능동관계

② 수동태(passive voice)는 주어가 동사의 동작을 받을 때 쓴다.

The door was opened by her. 문은 그녀에 의해 열어졌다.
주어　동사
└─ 수동관계 ─┘

# PSS 1 격 변화 – 주격과 목적격

| 주격(~은, 는) | I | you | he | she | it | we | they |
| --- | --- | --- | --- | --- | --- | --- | --- |
| 목적격(~을, 를) | me | you | him | her | it | us | them |

인칭대명사만이 격 변화가 있고, 명사(Tom/this book/my parents)는 주격과 목적격의 형태가 같다.

**I** love you. You love **me**. 나는 너를 사랑한다. 너는 나를 사랑한다.

**Tom** loves you. You love **Tom**. Tom은 너를 사랑한다. 너는 Tom을 사랑한다.

정답 p.20

## PRACTICE 1

주어진 말을 알맞은 형태로 바꾸어 빈칸에 쓰세요.

**1** he
① My dog likes ___________ .
② ___________ likes my dog.

**2** they
① ___________ visited their aunt.
② Their aunt visited ___________ .

**3** Sumi
① They invited ___________ .
② ___________ invited them.

**4** it
① ___________ changed him.
② He changed ___________ .

**5** we
① ___________ called her.
② She called ___________ .

**6** my family
① Mr. Kim knows ___________ .
② ___________ knows Mr. Kim.

**7** I
① ___________ met her.
② She met ___________ .

**8** you
① ___________ can understand them.
② They can understand ___________ .

**9** the bird
① ___________ is looking at me.
② I'm looking at ___________ .

**10** she
① I told ___________ about it.
② ___________ told me about it.

**11** your brother
① ___________ taught me.
② I taught ___________ .

**12** their parents
① ___________ help them.
② They help ___________ .

# PSS 2  수동태에 많이 쓰이는 불규칙동사

| 원형 | 과거형 | 과거분사형 | 원형 | 과거형 | 과거분사형 |
|---|---|---|---|---|---|
| be | was/were | been | lose | lost | lost |
| bear | bore | borne/born | make | made | made |
| bite | bit | bitten | read[ri:d] | read[red] | read[red] |
| blow | blew | blown | ride | rode | ridden |
| break | broke | broken | say[sei] | said[sed] | said[sed] |
| bring | brought | brought | see | saw | seen |
| build | built | built | set | set | set |
| buy | bought | bought | sell | sold | sold |
| catch | caught | caught | send | sent | sent |
| do | did | done | sing | sang | sung |
| draw | drew | drawn | speak | spoke | spoken |
| drink | drank | drunk | spend | spent | spent |
| eat | ate | eaten | steal | stole | stolen |
| find | found | found | take | took | taken |
| fly | flew | flown | teach | taught | taught |
| forget | forgot | forgotten | tell | told | told |
| get | got | got(ten) | think | thought | thought |
| give | gave | given | throw | threw | thrown |
| hold | held | held | understand | understood | understood |
| keep | kept | kept | wake | woke | woken |
| know | knew | known | wear | wore | worn |
| lay | laid | laid | write | wrote | written |

정답 p.20

## PRACTICE 2  [1-60]

다음 동사의 과거형과 과거분사형을 쓰세요.

**1** throw – __________ – __________

**2** cook – __________ – __________

**3** make – __________ – __________

**4** bring – __________ – __________

| **5** begin | – _________ – _________ | **6** call | – _________ – _________ |
| --- | --- | --- | --- |
| **7** invent | – _________ – _________ | **8** hold | – _________ – _________ |
| **9** wear | – _________ – _________ | **10** blow | – _________ – _________ |
| **11** read | – _________ – _________ | **12** build | – _________ – _________ |
| **13** fly | – _________ – _________ | **14** kill | – _________ – _________ |
| **15** lose | – _________ – _________ | **16** wake | – _________ – _________ |
| **17** take | – _________ – _________ | **18** clean | – _________ – _________ |
| **19** bear | – _________ – _________ | **20** say | – _________ – _________ |
| **21** answer | – _________ – _________ | **22** find | – _________ – _________ |
| **23** catch | – _________ – _________ | **24** know | – _________ – _________ |
| **25** invite | – _________ – _________ | **26** steal | – _________ – _________ |
| **27** think | – _________ – _________ | **28** write | – _________ – _________ |
| **29** ride | – _________ – _________ | **30** open | – _________ – _________ |
| **31** spend | – _________ – _________ | **32** be | – _________ – _________ |
| **33** buy | – _________ – _________ | **34** stop | – _________ – _________ |
| **35** use | – _________ – _________ | **36** speak | – _________ – _________ |
| **37** bite | – _________ – _________ | **38** put | – _________ – _________ |
| **39** get | – _________ – _________ | **40** do | – _________ – _________ |
| **41** collect | – _________ – _________ | **42** lay | – _________ – _________ |
| **43** understand | – _________ – _________ | **44** drink | – _________ – _________ |
| **45** break | – _________ – _________ | **46** keep | – _________ – _________ |
| **47** sell | – _________ – _________ | **48** forget | – _________ – _________ |
| **49** carry | – _________ – _________ | **50** eat | – _________ – _________ |
| **51** send | – _________ – _________ | **52** see | – _________ – _________ |
| **53** sing | – _________ – _________ | **54** set | – _________ – _________ |
| **55** try | – _________ – _________ | **56** draw | – _________ – _________ |
| **57** give | – _________ – _________ | **58** tell | – _________ – _________ |
| **59** drop | – _________ – _________ | **60** teach | – _________ – _________ |

# PSS 3  수동태 문장 만드는 법



주어가 동작을 행하는 형식의 문장을 능동태, **주어가 동작의 대상이 되는 형식의 문장을 수동 태**라고 한다. 능동태 문장은 '〜가 …을 하다'로, **수동태 문장은 '〜가 …되어지다'**로 해석한다.

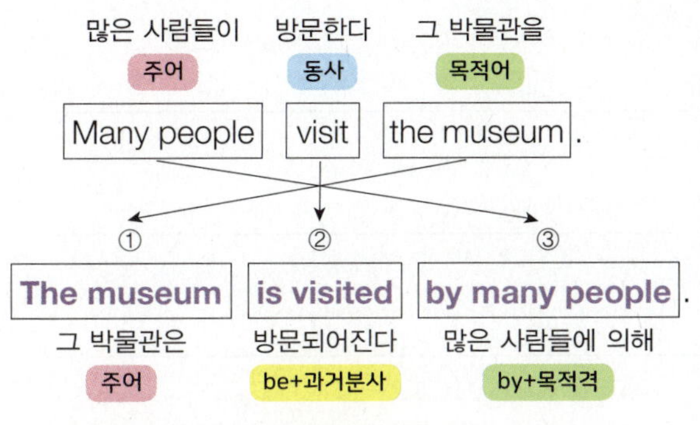

① **능동태의 목적어**를 **수동태의 주어**로 한다.

the museum ➡ The museum

② **능동태의 동사**를 「be동사+과거분사」의 형태로 바꾼다.

이때, **be동사**는 바뀐 주어의 **인칭과 수**, 원래 능동태 문장의 **동사의 시제**에 일치시킨다.

visit ➡ is visited

③ **능동태의 주어**를 「by+목적격」의 형태로 바꾼다.

Many people ➡ by many people

My parents love me. 나의 부모님은 나를 사랑하신다.

➡ I **am loved by** my parents. 나는 나의 부모님에 의해 사랑 받는다.

Ann always locks the doors. Ann은 항상 문을 잠근다.

➡ The doors **are** always **locked by** Ann. 문은 항상 Ann에 의해 잠긴다.

정답 p.21

## PRACTICE 3 [1-13]

다음 문장의 밑줄 친 부분을 주어로 하는 수동태 문장으로 바꾸어 써 보세요.

**1**  David writes a letter.

➡ _______________________________________________

**2**  I send an e-mail.

➡ _______________________________________________

**3**  Chickens lay eggs.

➡ _______________________________________________

**4** I collect <u>foreign coins</u>.

➡ ______________________________________________

**5** My mother cooks <u>the steaks</u>.

➡ ______________________________________________

**6** Their father teaches <u>them</u>.

➡ ______________________________________________

**7** My brother reads <u>the book</u>.

➡ ______________________________________________

**8** Most people use <u>this expression</u>.

➡ ______________________________________________

**9** The principal calls <u>them</u>.

➡ ______________________________________________

**10** She makes <u>these bags</u>.

➡ ______________________________________________

**11** She paints <u>those pictures</u>.

➡ ______________________________________________

**12** The teacher answers <u>the questions</u>.

➡ ______________________________________________

**13** Jacob picks up <u>the trash in the river</u>.

➡ ______________________________________________

## PSS 4 현재시제와 과거시제의 수동태



현재시제의 수동태는 「am/is/are+과거분사」의 형태로, 과거시제의 수동태는 「was/were+과거분사」의 형태로 쓴다.

I **clean** my room. ➡ My room **is cleaned** by me.
나는 내 방을 청소한다. 내 방은 나에 의해 청소된다.

I **cleaned** my room. ➡ My room **was cleaned** by me.
나는 내 방을 청소했다. 내 방은 나에 의해 청소되었다.

## PRACTICE 4

다음 문장을 수동태로 바꿀 때, 빈칸에 알맞은 말을 쓰세요.

1 She opened the boxes. ➡ The boxes _______________ by her.

2 Ms. Song plays the piano. ➡ The piano _______________ by Ms. Song.

3 Giho broke my glasses. ➡ My glasses _______________ by Giho.

4 Mina uses the computer. ➡ The computer _______________ by Mina.

5 My mother washes the dishes. ➡ The dishes _______________ by my mother.

6 The dog bit my sister. ➡ My sister _______________ by the dog.

7 The students sing this song. ➡ This song _______________ by the students.

8 Bell invented the telephone. ➡ The telephone _______________ by Bell.

9 My grandfather grows potatoes. ➡ Potatoes _______________ by my grandfather.

10 The president delivered the speech. ➡ The speech _______________ by the president.

# PSS 5 「by + 목적격」의 생략



**능동태의 주어**가 people 또는 you, we, they로 **일반 사람**을 나타낼 경우 「**by+목적격**」을 **대체로 생략**한다. 또 **행위자가 분명하지 않거나 나타낼 필요가 없을 때에도 생략**할 수 있다.

**People** speak English all over the world. 사람들은 전 세계적으로 영어를 쓴다.
➡ English **is spoken** all over the world. 영어는 전 세계적으로 쓰인다.
**Someone** broke the vase. 누군가가 꽃병을 깨뜨렸다.
➡ The vase **was broken** (**by someone**). 꽃병이 (누군가에 의해) 깨졌다.



## PRACTICE 5 [1-10]

다음 능동태 문장을 수동태 문장으로 바꾸어 쓰세요.

1 We write a lot of letters.

➡ _______________

2 People buy groceries here.

➡ _______________

**3** You wear shorts in summer.

➡ _______________________________

**5** We use smartphones every day.

➡ _______________________________

**7** People forgot the memories.

➡ _______________________________

**9** We sell fresh fruit in the store.

➡ _______________________________

**4** They found the lost dog yesterday.

➡ _______________________________

**6** Someone stole my bicycle.

➡ _______________________________

**8** Someone made this wine in 1970.

➡ _______________________________

**10** They built these buildings 20 years ago.

➡ _______________________________

## PSS 6  5형식 문장의 수동태 전환

The movie makes them sad. 그 영화는 그들을 슬프게 만든다.

➡ They **are made** sad by the movie. 그들은 그 영화에 의해 슬퍼진다.

A refrigerator keeps food fresh. 냉장고는 음식을 신선하게 유지시킨다.

➡ Food **is kept** fresh by a refrigerator. 음식은 냉장고에 의해 신선하게 유지된다.

## PRACTICE 6

다음 능동태 문장을 수동태 문장으로 바꾸어 쓰세요.

**1** Some readers find the story interesting.
➡ ______________________________________

**2** We elected him president.
➡ ______________________________________

**3** People call a lion the king of the jungle.
➡ ______________________________________

**4** Good paintings make people happy.
➡ ______________________________________

**5** Mira found the rabbit dead.
➡ ______________________________________

**6** My parents called me a princess.
➡ ______________________________________



## PRACTICE 7

다음 능동태 문장을 수동태 문장으로 바꾸어 쓰세요.

**1** Her children respect her.
➡ ______________________________________

**2** He made his sister angry.
➡ ______________________________________

**3** The teacher helped us.
➡ ______________________________________

**4** They keep their village clean.
➡ ______________________________________

**5** A famous fashion designer designed those dresses.
➡ ______________________________________

**6** Ms. Smith finished this work.
➡ ______________________________________

**7** We speak many languages in Switzerland.
➡ ______________________________________

**8** A lot of teenagers watch TV programs.
➡ ______________________________________

**9** We call Mozart and Beethoven great musicians.
➡ ______________________________________

**10** The company published the magazine in 2023.
➡ ______________________________________

**1** 다음 우리말과 같은 뜻이 되도록 빈칸에 들어갈 알맞은 말을 고르세요.

> • 꿀은 일벌에 의해 만들어진다.
> = Honey ____________ by worker bees.

① makes ② made
③ is made ④ are made
⑤ is making

**2** 두 문장이 같은 뜻이 되도록 빈칸에 들어갈 알맞은 단어를 쓰세요.

> • They often invite us for dinner.
> = ____________ are often ____________ for dinner by them.

**3** 다음 문장에서 생략해도 되는 부분을 찾아 쓰세요.

> The letter was delivered yesterday by someone.

➡ ____________________________________

**4** 다음 밑줄 친 단어를 알맞은 형태로 바꾼 것을 고르세요.

> The World Cup is <u>hold</u> every four years.

① hold ② held
③ holding ④ holds
⑤ holded

**5** 다음 두 문장이 같은 뜻이 되도록 빈칸에 들어갈 알맞은 말을 고르세요.

> • Peter broke the window.
> = The window ____________ by Peter.

① breaks ② broke ③ broken
④ is broken ⑤ was broken

**6** 다음 문장에서 밑줄 친 단어를 바르게 고친 것을 고르세요.

> A long time ago, *gimchi* was <u>calling</u> 'Dimchae'.

① called ② calls ③ be called
④ is calling ⑤ call

**7** 다음 괄호 안의 단어를 사용하여 문장과 뜻이 일치하도록 영작하세요.

(1) 이 방은 매일 청소된다. (clean)
= ____________________________________ every day.

(2) 그 상자는 창고에 보관된다. (keep)
= ____________________________________ in the warehouse.

(3) 그 이메일은 당신이 버튼을 클릭한 후 즉시 전송된다. (send)
= ____________________________________ immediately after you click the button.

## 8 다음 주어진 문장의 밑줄 친 부분을 바르게 고쳐 쓰세요.

> *Romeo and Juliet* <u>wrote</u> by Shakespeare.

➡ ___________________________________

## 9 다음 두 문장이 같은 뜻이 되도록 빈칸에 알맞은 말을 쓰세요.

> • The music makes me happy.
> = I ___________ ___________
> ___________ by the music.

## 10 다음 중 어법상 바르지 <u>않은</u> 문장은?

① Vegetables are sold in markets.
② Those potatoes are grown by my mom.
③ My bicycle was fix by Tom.
④ These were drawn by my little sister.
⑤ The school was founded in 2020.

## 11 다음 빈칸에 한 번이라도 들어갈 수 <u>없는</u> 것을 고르시오.

> • She was ___________ a large box.
> • The exhibition is ___________ annually.
> • He ___________ the world record for the 100 meters.
> • The meeting will ___________ in the community center.

① hold  　② holds  　③ holding
④ be held  　⑤ held

## 12 주어진 문장을 수동태 문장으로 옳게 바꾼 것은?

① He writes a new book.
　= A new book written by him.
② He prepares a special dish.
　= A special dish was prepared by him.
③ My mom waters the plants.
　= The plants is watered by my mom.
④ They named the dog Max.
　= Max was named the dog by them.
⑤ The coach made the team strong.
　= The team was made strong by the coach.



## 13 〈보기〉의 말을 사용하여 주어진 우리말을 영작하세요. (단, 필요시 어법에 맞게 형태를 바꾸어야 함)

(1)

| 보 기 | teach, Mr. Kim, be, English, by |
|---|---|

영어는 김 선생님에 의해 가르쳐진다.

➡ ___________________________________

(2)

| 보 기 | be, her handbag, by, steal, the thief |
|---|---|

그녀의 핸드백은 도둑에 의해 도난당했다.

➡ ___________________________________

## 14 다음을 수동태 문장으로 바르게 바꾼 것은?

> People call her Big Mouth.

① Big Mouth is called by her.
② Big Mouth was called by her.
③ People are called by Big Mouth.
④ She is called Big Mouth.
⑤ She was called Big Mouth.

**15** 우리말에 맞게 영작한 문장으로 어법상 옳지 <u>않은</u> 것은?

① 이 옷은 유명한 디자이너에 의해 디자인되었다.
  ➡ This clothing was designed by a famous designer.
② 김선생님께서 우리에게 강의를 해주시고 있다.
  ➡ Mr. Kim is giving us a lecture.
③ 그녀는 피겨 스케이팅의 여왕이라고 불린다.
  ➡ She is called the queen of figure skating.
④ 그들은 우리에게 음식을 주었고 우리는 그들에게 감사했다.
  ➡ They gave us food and we were grateful to them.
⑤ 거울은 조심스럽게 다뤄져야 한다.
  ➡ Mirrors should handle carefully.

**16** 우리말과 같은 뜻이 되도록 주어진 단어를 바르게 배열하세요. (단, 필요시 어형을 바꿀 것)

- 그 집은 나의 할아버지에 의해 지어졌다.
  = ______________________________________
  (my, the, be, build, grandfather, house, by)

**17** 다음 두 문장이 같은 뜻이 되도록 빈칸에 들어갈 알맞은 말을 쓰세요.

- My brother makes the bed.
  = The bed _________ _________ by my brother.

**18** 다음 대화의 빈칸에 들어갈 알맞은 말은?

A: This is a very good picture.
B: I think so, too. It __________ in Paris.

① takes　　　② is taken　　　③ was taken
④ took　　　⑤ taken

**19** 다음 문장에서 <u>어색한</u> 부분을 찾아 그 번호를 쓰고, 바르게 고치세요.

①<u>My</u> bicycle ②<u>is</u> ③<u>stolen</u> ④<u>a week</u> ago by ⑤<u>somebody</u>.

(　　) ______________ ➡ ______________

**20** 다음 중 어법상 바르지 <u>않은</u> 문장은?

① The office is cleaned once a week.
② Rice is grown in Asia.
③ He was bite by my dog.
④ English is spoken all over the world.
⑤ The letter was sent by her.

**21** 다음 중 어법상 옳은 문장의 개수를 고르세요.

- These flowers were planted by my father.
- Some cookies were maden by her.
- The baby was left alone.
- The cartoons were drawing by us.
- French is not spoken in this country.

① 1개　　　② 2개　　　③ 3개
④ 4개　　　⑤ 5개

**22** 주어진 두 문장의 내용이 같도록 빈칸에 적절한 표현을 쓰세요.

(1) Jake bought the wallet.
  = The wallet ______________________.
(2) The desk was broken by my brother.
  = My brother ______________________.

# CHAPTER 5
# 명사와 관사

# PSS 1  명사의 종류

| 셀 수 있는 명사 | a(n)을 붙이거나 복수형으로 쓸 수 있다.<br><br>1. **보통명사** – 사람이나 사물을 나타낸다.<br> car, banana, father, egg, flower, girl, city, job, sister, house, bird<br><br>2. **집합명사** – 사람이나 사물이 모여 집합체를 나타낸다.<br> class, family, audience, band, team, club |
|---|---|
| 셀 수 없는 명사 | a(n)을 붙일 수 없고 복수형으로도 쓸 수 없다.<br><br>1. **고유명사** – 사람의 이름, 지명과 같이 고유한 이름을 말하며 첫 글자를 항상 대문자로 표기한다.<br> Mike, Emily, Mt. Everest, the Nile, America<br><br>2. **추상명사** – 형태 없이 단순히 개념이나 감정을 나타낸다.<br> hope, life, kindness, beauty, truth, freedom, love, peace, advice<br><br>3. **물질명사** – 물이나 공기처럼 일정한 형태가 없는 것을 말한다.<br> paper, sugar, gas, snow, hair, water, bread, butter, rice, flour, air |

정답 p.24

## PRACTICE 1

다음 중 단어의 성격이 나머지 넷과 <u>다른</u> 것을 고르세요.

| | | | | | |
|---|---|---|---|---|---|
| **1** | ① eye | ② newspaper | ③ coffee | ④ coin | ⑤ book |
| **2** | ① subway | ② Becky | ③ village | ④ tree | ⑤ kite |
| **3** | ① group | ② audience | ③ band | ④ team | ⑤ dictionary |
| **4** | ① England | ② Busan | ③ Niagara Falls | ④ club | ⑤ China |
| **5** | ① wealth | ② dish | ③ kindness | ④ pity | ⑤ science |
| **6** | ① class | ② rain | ③ meat | ④ fire | ⑤ iron |
| **7** | ① pleasure | ② luck | ③ health | ④ life | ⑤ family |
| **8** | ① paper | ② Mt. Halla | ③ cheese | ④ money | ⑤ hair |
| **9** | ① animal | ② lesson | ③ smoke | ④ girl | ⑤ job |
| **10** | ① information | ② happiness | ③ hope | ④ snow | ⑤ truth |

**PRACTICE 2**

괄호 안에 주어진 표현 중 알맞은 것을 고르세요.

1  (A water, Water) always changes its form.

2  We brought (a child, child) with us.

3  Her (family, families) is now in New York.

4  I put (sugar, a sugar) in my coffee.

5  (A Korea, Korea) has four seasons.

6  (A friendship, Friendship) is very important to me.

7  My favorite (class, classes) is music.

8  We want to enjoy (a freedom, freedom).

9  (A Mike, Mike) has a nice car.

10  She drew (a flower, flower) on the paper.

11  Spread (butter, a butter) inside the bread.

12  (A love, Love) can change the world.

# PSS 2  명사의 복수형

PROBLEM<br>SOLVING<br>SKILL

## PSS 2-1  명사의 규칙 복수형 I

| | | | |
|---|---|---|---|
| 대부분의 경우 | -s | map – map**s**<br>pencil – pencil**s** | star – star**s**<br>sport – sport**s** |
| -s, -x, -ch, -sh로<br>끝나는 경우 | -es | bus – bus**es**<br>church – church**es** | box – box**es**<br>dish – dish**es** |
| 자음+o로 끝나는 경우 | -es | potato – potato**es**<br>*cf.* piano – piano**s**<br>mosquito – mosquito**(e)s** | tomato – tomato**es**<br>photo – photo**s** |
| 모음+o로 끝나는 경우 | -s | radio – radio**s**<br>video – video**s** | audio – audio**s**<br>zoo – zoo**s** |

## PRACTICE 3

다음 명사의 복수형을 쓰세요.

| | | | | |
|---|---|---|---|---|
| 1 | egg ➡ _______ | 2 | bus ➡ _______ |
| 3 | address ➡ _______ | 4 | star ➡ _______ |
| 5 | day ➡ _______ | 6 | present ➡ _______ |
| 7 | photo ➡ _______ | 8 | umbrella ➡ _______ |
| 9 | sport ➡ _______ | 10 | cup ➡ _______ |
| 11 | beach ➡ _______ | 12 | friend ➡ _______ |
| 13 | cat ➡ _______ | 14 | problem ➡ _______ |
| 15 | tomato ➡ _______ | 16 | shirt ➡ _______ |
| 17 | box ➡ _______ | 18 | map ➡ _______ |
| 19 | zoo ➡ _______ | 20 | bath ➡ _______ |
| 21 | cookie ➡ _______ | 22 | boat ➡ _______ |
| 23 | flower ➡ _______ | 24 | watch ➡ _______ |
| 25 | radio ➡ _______ | 26 | mosquito ➡ _______ |
| 27 | passport ➡ _______ | 28 | test ➡ _______ |
| 29 | brush ➡ _______ | 30 | potato ➡ _______ |

## PSS 2-2 명사의 규칙 복수형 Ⅱ

| | | | |
|---|---|---|---|
| 자음+y로 끝나는 경우 | y를 i로 바꾸고 -es | city – cit**ies**<br>candy – cand**ies** | baby – bab**ies**<br>country – countr**ies** |
| 모음+y로 끝나는 경우 | -s | boy – boy**s**<br>monkey – monkey**s** | day – day**s**<br>toy – toy**s** |
| -f, -fe로 끝나는 경우 | f/fe를 v로 바꾸고 -es | leaf – lea**ves**<br>knife – kni**ves**<br>**cf.** roof – roof**s** | wolf – wol**ves**<br>wife – wi**ves**<br>safe – safe**s** |

## PRACTICE 4

**다음 명사의 복수형을 쓰세요.**

| | | | | |
|---|---|---|---|---|
| **1** candy ➡ __________ | | **2** song ➡ __________ |
| **3** day ➡ __________ | | **4** idea ➡ __________ |
| **5** knife ➡ __________ | | **6** body ➡ __________ |
| **7** cow ➡ __________ | | **8** class ➡ __________ |
| **9** shelf ➡ __________ | | **10** factory ➡ __________ |
| **11** wife ➡ __________ | | **12** lady ➡ __________ |
| **13** building ➡ __________ | | **14** animal ➡ __________ |
| **15** mistake ➡ __________ | | **16** door ➡ __________ |
| **17** family ➡ __________ | | **18** safe ➡ __________ |
| **19** pencil ➡ __________ | | **20** story ➡ __________ |
| **21** dish ➡ __________ | | **22** picture ➡ __________ |
| **23** audio ➡ __________ | | **24** doll ➡ __________ |
| **25** toy ➡ __________ | | **26** key ➡ __________ |
| **27** wolf ➡ __________ | | **28** fox ➡ __________ |
| **29** boy ➡ __________ | | **30** sandwich ➡ __________ |
| **31** ship ➡ __________ | | **32** video ➡ __________ |
| **33** monkey ➡ __________ | | **34** leaf ➡ __________ |
| **35** letter ➡ __________ | | **36** banana ➡ __________ |
| **37** piano ➡ __________ | | **38** computer ➡ __________ |
| **39** baby ➡ __________ | | **40** note ➡ __________ |
| **41** town ➡ __________ | | **42** party ➡ __________ |
| **43** blouse ➡ __________ | | **44** question ➡ __________ |
| **45** pig ➡ __________ | | **46** doughnut ➡ __________ |
| **47** card ➡ __________ | | **48** holiday ➡ __________ |
| **49** city ➡ __________ | | **50** farmer ➡ __________ |
| **51** headache ➡ __________ | | **52** bottle ➡ __________ |
| **53** house ➡ __________ | | **54** country ➡ __________ |
| **55** poster ➡ __________ | | **56** roof ➡ __________ |
| **57** block ➡ __________ | | **58** diary ➡ __________ |
| **59** church ➡ __________ | | **60** self ➡ __________ |

CH 5 명사와 관사

## 1. 단수형과 복수형이 같은 명사

deer – deer          fish – fish          sheep – sheep

***cf.*** fish의 복수형은 같은 종류의 물고기가 여럿 있을 때는 fish, 서로 다른 종류의 물고기가 여럿 있을 때는 fishes로 쓴다.

## 2. 그 밖의 명사의 불규칙 복수형

foot – feet          tooth – teeth          goose – geese
man – men          woman – women          mouse – mice
child – children          ox – oxen

정답 p.25

## PRACTICE 5

다음 명사의 복수형을 쓰세요.

| | | | | |
|---|---|---|---|---|
| 1 | duck ➡ _________ | | 2 | hobby ➡ _________ |
| 3 | ox ➡ _________ | | 4 | festival ➡ _________ |
| 5 | scarf ➡ _________ | | 6 | deer ➡ _________ |
| 7 | room ➡ _________ | | 8 | student ➡ _________ |
| 9 | sheep ➡ _________ | | 10 | man ➡ _________ |
| 11 | candle ➡ _________ | | 12 | month ➡ _________ |
| 13 | mouse ➡ _________ | | 14 | foot ➡ _________ |
| 15 | team ➡ _________ | | 16 | subject ➡ _________ |
| 17 | snowman ➡ _________ | | 18 | neighbor ➡ _________ |
| 19 | goose ➡ _________ | | 20 | hour ➡ _________ |
| 21 | fish ➡ _________ | | 22 | woman ➡ _________ |
| 23 | sweater ➡ _________ | | 24 | bag ➡ _________ |
| 25 | child ➡ _________ | | 26 | seat ➡ _________ |
| 27 | bench ➡ _________ | | 28 | habit ➡ _________ |
| 29 | tooth ➡ _________ | | 30 | thief ➡ _________ |

## PRACTICE 6

〈보기〉와 같이 괄호 안의 명사를 알맞은 형태로 바꾸어 빈칸에 쓰세요.

> 보 기　　He has ten <u>geese</u> on his farm. (goose)

1　Could you sharpen these two ________________ for me? (knife)

2　________________ eat everything around the house. (mouse)

3　There is a ________________ in the city. (church)

4　Some ________________ are making snowmen outside. (child)

5　I need a ________________ for my test. (pencil)

6　My ________________ are about nine inches long. (foot)

7　The ________________ change colors in autumn. (leaf)

8　The ________________ in the fishbowl are goldfish. (fish)

9　I want to make good movies about ________________. (woman)

10　My grandfather raises a lot of ________________. (sheep)

11　Two ________________ are pulling the wagon. (ox)

12　How do ________________ protect themselves? (deer)

13　Don't forget to brush your ________________. (tooth)

14　Kate enjoys reading as one of her favorite ________________. (hobby)

# PSS 3　단위명사의 쓰임

PROBLEM SOLVING SKILL

**a piece of** cheese
치즈 한 조각

**two cups of** coffee
커피 두 잔

**a glass of** water
물 한 잔

**three slices of** bread
빵 세 조각

1. 셀 수 없는 물질명사의 경우, 그 모양이나 담는 그릇을 나타내는 말을 이용하여 수량을 나타낸다. 복수형으로 쓰일 때에는 물질명사는 그대로 두고 단위를 나타내는 명사에 -(e)s를 붙인다.

| a piece of | bread[cake, cheese, pizza, paper, chalk]<br>advice[information, news] / furniture<br><br>***cf.*** advice, information, news는 추상명사이고, furniture는 의미상<br>으로는 집합명사에 가깝지만 수량 표현 시 piece를 사용한다. |
|---|---|
| a cup of | coffee[tea] |
| a glass of | water[milk, juice, beer] |
| a slice of | bread[meat, cheese, pizza] |
| a pound of | sugar[meat]<br>*pound 영어권 국가에서 사용하는 무게 단위 (1 파운드 = 약 453g) |
| a bottle of | beer[ink, juice, milk] |

Do you want **a slice of** **pizza**? 피자 한 조각을 원하니?
Please give me **two pieces of** **paper**. 제게 종이 두 장을 주세요.
I'd like **three glasses of** **grape juice**. 포도 주스 세 잔을 원해요.

2. 두 개의 짝으로 이루어져 복수형으로 쓰는 명사인 glasses(안경), scissors, pants, jeans의 수량을 나타낼 때에는 a pair of, two pairs of …의 형태를 이용한다.

He bought **a** new **pair of** **pants**. 그는 새 바지 한 벌을 샀다.

정답 p.25

## PRACTICE 7

〈보기〉와 같이 주어진 말을 알맞은 형태로 바꾸어 빈칸에 쓰세요.

| 보 기 | a piece of cake ➡ three *pieces of cake* |
|---|---|

**1** a glass of milk ➡ two ________________

**2** a piece of furniture ➡ six ________________

**3** a bottle of juice ➡ three ________________

**4** a piece of chalk ➡ ten ________________

**5** a glass of water ➡ some ________________

**6** a slice of bread ➡ four ________________

**7** a pair of scissors ➡ two ________________

**8** a pound of sugar ➡ three ________________

**9** a cup of tea ➡ five ________________

**10** a piece of news ➡ four ________________

**11** a slice of pizza     ➡ eight ________________________________________

**12** a pair of socks     ➡ seven ________________________________________

**13** a piece of paper     ➡ ten ________________________________________

**14** a bottle of ink     ➡ two ________________________________________

**15** a pound of flour     ➡ six ________________________________________

정답 p.25

## PRACTICE **8**

〈보기〉에 주어진 단어를 알맞게 활용하여 빈칸에 쓰세요.

| 보 기 | pair   glass   cup   bottle   piece   slice   pound |
| --- | --- |

**1** Do you have a _______________ of scissors?

**2** He bought a _______________ of jeans today.

**3** They ate a _______________ of cake after dinner.

**4** Five _______________ of bread are on the table.

**5** I drink a _______________ of milk every morning.

**6** Mr. Kim drinks four _______________ of coffee every day.

**7** He got a new _______________ of glasses.

**8** We ate two _______________ of meat.

**9** Mike carried three _______________ of beer with him.

**10** He gave a _______________ of chalk to his teacher.

## PSS 4 명사의 소유격



1. **사람이나 동물**을 나타내는 **명사**는 **'(s)**를 이용하여 **소유격**을 만든다.

① 단수 명사+'s
Sora**'s** brother 소라의 남동생
an elephant**'s** nose 코끼리의 코
② -s로 끝나는 복수 명사+'
the boys**'** bags 그 소년들의 가방들

③ -s로 끝나지 않는 복수 명사+'s

    a women**'s** university 여자대학교

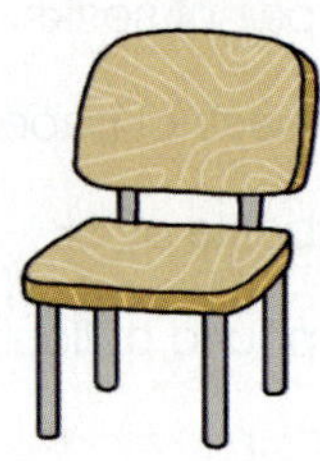

2. **무생물을 나타내는 명사는 of**를 이용하여 소유격을 만든다.

the window **of** this room 이 방의 창문

students **of** our school 우리 학교의 학생들

the legs **of** the chair
의자의 다리들

3. **명사가 반복**되거나 공공건물, 집, 상점 등의 **명사가 소유격 뒤에 오면 그 명사는 생략이 가능**하다.

This camera is **Sumi's** (camera). 이 카메라는 수미의 것이다.

I stayed at my **uncle's** (house). 나는 삼촌 댁에 머물렀다.

정답 p.25

## PRACTICE 9

괄호 안의 말과 어퍼스트로피(')를 사용하여 문장을 완성하세요.

**1** Where is ___Kelly's house___ ? (Kelly, house)

**2** I go to a _______________________ . (boys, middle school)

**3** Tomorrow is _______________________ . (Ted, birthday)

**4** What is your _______________________ ? (dog, name)

**5** It is a famous _______________________ . (women, university)

**6** She is in the _______________________ . (teachers, room)

**7** He is _______________________ . (Mr. Kim, son)

**8** It is my _______________________ . (parents, photo album)

**9** We should respect other _______________________ . (people, ideas)

**10** Is there a _______________________ around here? (children, bookstore)

**11** I have to clean out the _______________________ . (dogs, houses)

**12** _______________________ is best known for its seafood dishes. (Ana and Hailey, restaurant)

**13** What is _______________________ ? (Andy, job)

**14** _______________________ is amazing. (Richard, voice)

## PRACTICE 10

괄호 안의 말과 of를 사용하여 문장을 완성하세요.

**1** Seoul is _____the capital of Korea_____. (Korea, the capital)

**2** Here is _______________________. (this city, the end)

**3** Can you open _______________________? (the door, the room)

**4** A dog has a good _______________________. (smell, sense)

**5** _______________________ had a special party. (the people, the village)

**6** What is _______________________? (the color, your shoes)

**7** Here is _______________________. (the classes, the list)

**8** We put candles in _______________________. (the middle, the table)

**9** _______________________ are quiet. (this class, the students)

**10** We remember _______________________. (the mountain, the name)



## PRACTICE 11

〈보기〉와 같이 짝지어진 두 문장의 의미가 같도록 빈칸을 채우세요.

| 보 기 | This is my father's car.<br>= This <u>car</u> is <u>my father's</u>. |
| --- | --- |

**1** That is Mira's umbrella.
= That _________ is _________.

**2** It is my daughter's voice.
= The _________ is _________.

**3** This is her brother's puppy.
= This _________ is _________.

**4** Which is Mr. Felini's house?
= Which _________ is _________?

**5** These are Peter's books.
= These _________ are _________.

**6** That is a robot's arm.
= That _________ is _________.

**7** It is Mr. Smith's painting.
= The _________ is _________.

**8** This is Yumi's room.
= This _________ is _________.

**9** That is my friend's jacket.
= That _________ is _________.

**10** Those are the children's toys.
= Those _________ are _________.

# PSS 5 주의해야 할 명사의 수



숫자와 명사가 하이픈(–)으로 연결되어 뒤에 오는 명사를 꾸며주는 형용사처럼 쓰일 때는
「숫자-단수 명사」의 형태를 취한다.

a **fifty**-**year**-old man 50세의 남자
a **two**-**week** vacation 2주일의 방학
two **four**-**leaf** clovers 네 잎 클로버 2장

This house has **three stories**. 이 집은 3층이다.
= This is a **three-story** house. 이것은 3층짜리 집이다.
I have two brothers. They are **four years old**. 나는 남동생 2명이 있다. 그들은 4살이다.
= I have two **four-year-old** brothers. 나에게는 4살짜리 남동생 2명이 있다.

정답 p.26

## PRACTICE 12

〈보기〉와 같이 짝지어진 두 문장의 의미가 같도록 빈칸을 채우세요.

> 보 기
> Tom is six years old.
> = Tom is a six-year-old boy.

**1** This clover has four leaves.

= This is a ________________ clover.

**2** Our vacation is five weeks.

= We have a ________________ vacation.

**3** This book has one hundred pages.

= This is a ________________ book.

**4** She has a son. He is three years old.

= She has a ________________ son.

**5** Those buildings have ten stories.

= Those are ________________ buildings.

**6** Ethan and Luke are twin brothers. They are eight years old.

= Ethan and Luke are ________________ twin brothers.

**7** They planned a trip. It was two months.

= They planned a ________________ trip.

**8** I saw three fish. They were two meters long.

= I saw three _________________________ fish.

**9** I have a bill. It is five dollars.

= I have a _________________ bill.

**10** The break is ten minutes.

= There is a _________________ break.



## PSS 6 부정관사 a(n)의 쓰임

She had **a** banana and **an** apple.
그녀는 바나나와 사과를 먹었다.

셀 수 있는 단수 명사 앞에 a(n)를 쓴다.
a(n)는 많은 것들 중 막연한 하나를 나타내며,
대부분의 경우 해석하지 않는다.

| 첫소리가 자음인 단어 앞에는 a | 첫소리가 모음인 단어 앞에는 an |
|---|---|
| **1. a+명사**<br>**a** pencil, **a** desk, **a** house, **a** taxi, **a** farmer | **1. an+명사**<br>**an** artist, **an** engineer, **an** umbrella, **an** egg |
| **2. a+형용사+명사**<br>**a** special day, **a** new student | **2. an+형용사+명사**<br>**an** interesting story, **an** old book |
| *cf.* 철자가 모음이지만 발음이 자음으로 시작하는 경우에는 a를 쓴다.<br>**a** uniform, **a** university | *cf.* 철자가 자음이지만 발음이 모음으로 시작하는 경우에는 an을 쓴다.<br>**an** hour, **an** honest boy |

정답 p.26

## PRACTICE 13 [1-20]

다음 문장의 빈칸에 a나 an 중 알맞은 것을 쓰세요.

**1** She is ________ English teacher.

**2** A computer is _________ useful tool.

**3** I want to be _________ animal doctor.

**4** The student didn't wear _________ uniform.

**5** I met _________ European during my travels.

**6** Jinho lent me _________ umbrella.

**7** My mother found _________ old dress in her box.

**8** He saw _________ picture on the wall.

**9** He looks like _________ honest person.

**10** I decided to go to _________ university abroad.

**11** Mike is _________ elementary school student.

**12** She had _________ busy day yesterday.

**13** The book has _________ interesting story in it.

**14** John drove for _________ hour.

**15** I will open _________ hospital for sick people.

**16** Do you have _________ idea about this?

**17** We had _________ wonderful time last weekend.

**18** I'm staying here for _________ year.

**19** Wait _________ minute, please.

**20** We learned _________ important lesson from this story.

## PSS 7  a(n)의 의미 구별



| 용법 | 예문 |
|---|---|
| one 하나의 | **A** year has twelve months. 1년은 열두 달이다. |
| per ~마다 | I go to the gym twice **a** week. 나는 일주일에 두 번 체육관에 간다. |
| 종족 전체를 대표 | **A** cow is a useful animal. 소는 유용한 동물이다. |

## PRACTICE 14

밑줄 친 a(n)의 용법과 같은 것을 〈보기〉에서 골라 그 번호를 쓰세요.

| 보 기 |
| --- |
| ① He has <u>a</u> son and two daughters. |
| ② I met him once <u>a</u> month. |
| ③ <u>A</u> fish cannot live without water. |

**1** They were running for <u>an</u> hour. [    ]

**2** <u>A</u> crane has long legs. [    ]

**3** She has only three classes <u>a</u> week. [    ]

**4** We need eleven players for <u>a</u> team. [    ]

**5** I usually study eight hours <u>a</u> day. [    ]

**6** <u>A</u> snake sleeps during the winter. [    ]

**7** <u>An</u> elephant has a long nose. [    ]

**8** Rome wasn't built in <u>a</u> day. [    ]

**9** Minsu visits his grandparents twice <u>a</u> year. [    ]



# PSS 8 정관사 the의 쓰임

PROBLEM SOLVING SKILL

He is reading **a** book.

그는 책을 읽고 있다.

She is reading a book. **The** book is interesting.

그녀는 책을 읽고 있다. 그 책은 재미있다.

**특정한 것을 가리킬 때 the**를 쓰며, 단수 명사와 복수 명사 앞에 모두 쓰인다.

| 용법 | 예문 |
| --- | --- |
| 앞에 나온 명사가 다시 반복될 때 | I have **a doll**. **The doll** is very cute.<br>나에게는 인형이 있다. 그 인형은 매우 귀엽다. |
| 문맥이나 상황으로 보아 무엇을 가리키는지 알 수 있을 때 | Would you please open **the** window?<br>그 창문 좀 열어주실래요? |

| 용법 | 예문 |
| --- | --- |
| 구나 절에 의해 수식을 받아 가리키는 대상이 분명할 때 | **The** key **on the table** isn't mine.<br>탁자 위의 열쇠는 내 것이 아니다. |
| 일반적으로 유일한 것을 말할 때 | **The Earth** goes around **the Sun**.<br>지구는 태양 주위를 돈다. |
| 서수, 최상급, last, only, same, very 앞 | She lives on **the third** floor.<br>그녀는 3층에 산다. |
| 악기 이름 앞 | She can play **the piano**.<br>그녀는 피아노를 칠 수 있다. |
| 종족 전체를 대표 | **The dog** is a friendly animal.<br>개는 다정한 동물이다. |

정답 p.26

## PRACTICE 15

밑줄 친 the의 용법과 같은 것을 〈보기〉에서 골라 그 번호를 쓰세요.

> 보 기
> ① They took a trip. The trip was great.
> ② Please pass me the salt.
> ③ The rooms in the house are small.
> ④ The sky is clear and blue.
> ⑤ It is the tallest building in Korea.
> ⑥ I play the violin every day.
> ⑦ The chicken cannot fly.

1  Can you imagine a trip to the Moon? [      ]

2  A bee is one of the most useful insects to people. [      ]

3  The Jindo dog is very faithful. [      ]

4  Paris is the capital of France. [      ]

5  Minho practiced the piano. [      ]

6  It was a book about space. I liked the book. [      ]

7  Excuse me. Where is the post office? [      ]

**PRACTICE 16**

괄호 안에 주어진 단어 중 알맞은 것을 고르세요.

1  He is learning to play (a, the) violin.

2  It's (a, the) third Sunday in June.

3  Look at (a, the) traffic light.

4  They spend 9 hours (a, the) day at school.

5  (A, The) Sun rises in the east.

6  (A, The) week has seven days.

7  She walks for (an, the) hour in the morning.

8  They are all in (a, the) same class.

9  She needs 25 hours in (a, the) day.

10  (A, The) restrooms of the station are clean.

11  She pointed at (the, a) hole in the door.

12  They got on (a, the) last airplane.

13  A boy is playing at the beach. (A, The) boy looks happy.

---

## PSS 9 관사를 쓰지 않는 경우



1. **식사, 운동, 질병 이름 앞에**

I had **breakfast**. 나는 아침을 먹었다.
We are playing **baseball**. 우리는 야구를 하고 있다.
My grandmother had **cancer**. 나의 할머니는 암에 걸리셨다.

2. **건물, 기구가 본래의 목적으로 쓰일 때**

go to **school** (공부하러) 학교에 가다
go to **church** (예배 드리러) 교회에 가다
go to **bed** 잠자리에 들다

*cf.* I went to the school. – 여기서의 school은 '학교 건물'을 의미하며, 정규 수업을 받기 위해서가 아니라 다른 목적으로 학교에 간 상황을 나타낸다.
I went to **the** school to see my son's English teacher.
나는 나의 아들의 영어 선생님을 뵈러 학교에 갔다.

## PRACTICE 17

다음 문장의 빈칸에 a(n)나 the 중 알맞은 것을 쓰고, 필요 없는 곳에는 ×표 하세요.

**1** I got _________ F on the test.

**2** She has _________ breakfast at seven thirty.

**3** Sally is _________ tallest student in her class.

**4** We go to _________ school from Monday to Friday.

**5** He often plays _________ tennis.

**6** I went to _________ school to pick up my daughter after her soccer practice.

**7** He is playing _________ guitar.

**8** I am _________ middle school student.

**9** He died of _________ cancer.

**10** My parents go to _________ church every Sunday.

**11** Mike wears _________ same shirt every day.

**12** Shall we meet after _________ lunch?

**13** I come here three times _________ month.

**14** Go to _________ bed early tonight.

**15** Will you close _________ door?

---

# PSS 10 There is/are



There is/are는 '~가 있다'의 뜻으로 주어는 be동사 뒤에 오며, 이때 There은 별도로 해석하지 않는다. there is 뒤에는 단수 명사가 오고, there are 뒤에는 복수 명사가 온다.

| | |
|---|---|
| There is+단수 명사<br>주어 | **There is a book** on the desk.<br>책상 위에 책 한 권이 있다.<br>**Is there a book** on the desk?<br>책상 위에 책 한 권이 있니?<br>– Yes, there is. / No, there isn't.<br>응, 있어. / 아니, 없어.<br>**There was a book** on the desk.<br>책상 위에 책 한 권이 있었다. |

*cf.* 셀 수 없는 명사는 단수 취급하므로 there is를 쓴다.

**There is** some **milk** in the bottle. 병 안에 약간의 우유가 있다.

**There are books** on the desk.
책상 위에 책들이 있다.
**Are there books** on the desk?
책상 위에 책들이 있니?
– Yes, there are. / No, there aren't.
응, 있어. / 아니, 없어.
**There were books** on the desk.
책상 위에 책들이 있었다.

There are+복수 명사
주어

*cf.* '~가 몇 개 있니?'의 표현으로는 How many ~ are there?를 쓴다.
**How many festivals are there** in Korea?
한국에는 몇 개의 축제가 있니?

'~가 얼마나 있니?'의 표현으로는 How much ~ is there?를 쓴다.
**How much money is there** in your pocket?
네 주머니 속에 돈이 얼마나 있니?



## PRACTICE 18

다음 문장의 빈칸에 is 또는 are를 넣어 문장을 완성하세요.

**1** There __________ another key in my bag.

**2** __________ there a lot of seats in the theater?

**3** There __________ some money in my pocket.

**4** __________ there apples in the box?

**5** __________ there a soccer game today?

**6** There __________ many famous buildings in the city.

**7** There __________ some children in the park.

**8** __________ there any sugar in the bowl?

**9** There __________ three toys in his room.

**10** There __________ water in my ears.

## PRACTICE 19

그림을 보고, 빈칸에 알맞은 말을 쓰세요.

1   Is there an orange on the table? – Yes, ________________.

2   ________________ an accident yesterday? – Yes, there was.

3   How many desks ________________ in the classroom? – There are 25 desks.

4   Were there a lot of people in the park? – No, ________________.

5   ________________ students are there on the playground?
    – ________________ five students on the playground.

6   ________________ there many stores on the street? – Yes, ________________.

7   How many armchairs are there in the room? – ________________ 2 armchairs.

8   ________________ there a dog on the sofa? – Yes, ________________.

9   ________________ milk is there in your mug?
    – ________________ about 200ml of milk in my mug.

# PSS 11 동격

명사나 대명사를 보충 설명하기 위해 **그 뒤에 콤마(,)를 덧붙여 다른 명사(구)**를 쓸 수 있는 데 이런 관계를 동격이라 한다.

This is **my friend, Mariah**.

이 사람은 내 친구인 Mariah입니다.

I like **Junwoo, the boy in the blue shirt**.

난 파란 셔츠를 입고 있는 소년인 준우를 좋아해.

**Jason, the most popular boy in my school**, talked to me.

우리 학교에서 가장 인기가 많은 소년인 Jason이 나에게 말을 걸었다.

**The Moon, a satellite of the Earth**, goes around the Earth.

지구의 위성인 달은 지구의 주위를 돈다.

정답 p.27

## PRACTICE 20

밑줄 친 부분이 동격을 나타내면 ○, 동격을 나타내지 않으면 ×를 쓰세요.

1   After dark, the children returned to their home. [      ]

2   Yesterday was a hot, humid and airless day. [      ]

3   My favorite writer is Shakespeare, the writer of *Romeo and Juliet*. [      ]

4   My sister entered London University, a top medical school. [      ]

5   They came soon, and solved the problem. [      ]

6   My mom cooked a big American bird, turkey. [      ]

7   If you study hard, you will succeed. [      ]

8   We visited Abuja, the capital of Nigeria. [      ]

9   She was tired, hungry and sleepy. [      ]

10   He didn't say anything to me, so I know nothing about the plan. [      ]

11   My favorite place, the English building, is on 4th Street. [      ]

12   When he came into the room, I didn't recognize him. [      ]

13   I'd like to introduce my sister, Suji. [      ]

14   After I ran for an hour, I took a break for ten minutes. [      ]

**1** Which is NOT a correct answer for the blank?

> This is a ___________.

① computer
② water
③ picture
④ book
⑤ desk

**2** 다음 빈칸에 들어갈 단어로 알맞은 것은?

> There are many ___________.

① butter
② baby
③ sheep
④ man
⑤ child

**3** Which is the correct answer for the blank?

> This is ___________ umbrella.

① a
② an
③ lots of
④ many
⑤ much

**4** 다음 중 셀 수 <u>없는</u> 명사를 <u>모두</u> 고르세요.

| 보 기 | air | tooth | furniture |
|---|---|---|---|
| | money | milk | doll |

➡ ___________________________

**5** 다음 글의 밑줄 친 부분과 쓰임이 같은 것은?

> Hello, my name is Joey. I'm in the first grade at Seoul middle school. I live with my grandparents. My grandmother's job is a writer. She writes children's books. She's a good story-teller.

① He's my English teacher.
② John's dad wakes him up.
③ Where's her bag?
④ What's your favorite kind of music?
⑤ It's twenty minutes' walk to the station.

**6** 다음 대화의 빈칸에 들어갈 알맞은 말을 고르세요.

> A: Is there a book on the desk?
> B: Yes, ___________.

① it isn't
② it is
③ there are
④ there isn't
⑤ there is

**7** 다음 빈칸에 들어갈 수 <u>없는</u> 단어는?

> I have five ___________.

① candies
② milk
③ mice
④ deer
⑤ fish

**8** 다음 문장에서 어법상 <u>잘못된</u> 것을 고르세요.

> ①There ②is five ③beds and two ④desks ⑤in the room.

## 9 다음 밑줄 친 부분을 바르게 고쳐 쓰세요.

> • There are a lot of ⓐ<u>deers</u> in the park.
> • My ⓑ<u>foot</u> are about seven inches long.
> • ⓒ<u>Man</u> are cooking in the kitchen.

ⓐ _________ ⓑ _________ ⓒ _________

## 10 다음 밑줄 친 부분의 쓰임이 바른 것을 고르세요.

① It takes <u>an</u> hour.
② This is <u>an</u> spoon.
③ That is <u>a</u> interesting story.
④ He is <u>a</u> office worker.
⑤ I have to buy <u>an</u> uniform.

## 11 짝지어진 두 문장이 같은 뜻이 되도록 빈칸에 알맞은 말을 쓰세요.

(1) This jacket is Jane's.
　= This is _________ _________.

(2) The building is my father's.
　= It is my _________ _________.

(3) That is my friend's cell phone.
　= That cell phone is _________ _________.

## 12 다음 문장 중에서 어법상 올바른 것은?

① Gooses can make great pets.
② She saves many people's lifes.
③ How many child are there in the picture?
④ There are three cookies on the plate.
⑤ What are the coolest hobbys?

## 13 다음 빈칸에 들어갈 알맞은 말을 쓰세요.

> • There ⓐ _________ many beautiful trees in the park.
> 　공원에 많은 아름다운 나무들이 있다.
> • ⓑ _________ there any salt in the bowl?
> 　그릇에 소금이 있나요?
> • There ⓒ _________ some juice in the glass.
> 　유리잔에 약간의 주스가 있다.

ⓐ _________ ⓑ _________ ⓒ _________

## 14 다음 그림을 묘사한 것 중 어법이 올바르지 <u>않은</u> 것을 세 개 고르세요.

① There are eight desks in the classroom.
② There are two doors in the classroom.
③ There is two plants in the classroom.
④ There is a women in the classroom.
⑤ There are a blackboard in the classroom.

## 15 다음 밑줄 친 문장 중 어법상 틀린 문장을 찾아 그 기호를 쓰고, 올바르게 고쳐 쓰세요.

> ⓐ<u>I am playing the basketball with my friends.</u> I am a member of the school basketball club. ⓑ<u>I'm the tallest student in our team.</u> ⓒ<u>We practice after school twice a week.</u> We will have a big match soon. I am doing my best.

➡ ( 　 ) _________________________

## 16 다음 주어진 두 문장을 하나의 문장으로 바르게 만든 것은?

> • She made me chocolate cake.
> • Chocolate cake is my favorite dessert.

① She made, chocolate cake, my favorite
  dessert, me.
② She made my favorite dessert, me,
  chocolate cake.
③ She made me my favorite dessert's
  chocolate cake.
④ She made me chocolate cake of my favorite
  dessert.
⑤ She made me my favorite dessert, chocolate
  cake.

## 17 밑줄 친 부분의 쓰임이 잘못된 것은?

① There <u>are</u> a book and two pencils.
② There <u>is</u> a gym in my school.
③ There <u>are</u> seven days in a week.
④ There <u>is</u> not enough water.
⑤ There <u>are</u> a lot of juice in the bottle.

## 18 다음 중 밑줄 친 a[an]의 의미가 <u>다른</u> 하나를 고르세요.

① We eat out twice <u>a</u> month.
② I brush my teeth three times <u>a</u> day.
③ It took <u>an</u> hour to fix it.
④ He goes shopping twice <u>a</u> week.
⑤ They meet together once <u>a</u> year.

## 19 다음 중 어법상 <u>어색한</u> 문장을 고르세요.

① He is taking pictures.
② He is listening to music.
③ He is watching movies.
④ He is playing guitar.
⑤ He is drawing pictures.

## 20 빈칸에 들어갈 단어가 나머지 넷과 <u>다른</u> 하나는?

① There ____________ a girl next to a baby.
② There ____________ some people in the park.
③ ____________ there many books in the library?
④ There ____________ pencils on my desk.
⑤ There ____________ pretty birds on the tree.

## 21 빈칸에 들어갈 단어가 바르게 짝지어진 것은?

> • I found your post ____________ useful
>   read.
> • Mr. Lee is ____________ office worker.

① a – a      ② an – an      ③ a – an
④ an – a      ⑤ the – a

## 22 빈칸에 들어갈 단어가 순서대로 바르게 짝지어진 것은?

> • There ____________ some shoes on the
>   shelves.
> • There ____________ jeans on the bed.
> • There ____________ a clock on the wall.

① is – is – are      ② are – is – is
③ is – are – is      ④ are – are – is
⑤ are – is – are

## 23 다음 대화의 밑줄 친 부분 중 **틀린** 것을 고르세요.

> A: How ① many ② childrens do you ③ have?
> B: I have three ④ sons and two ⑤ daughters.

## 24 다음 빈칸에 들어갈 알맞은 말을 고르세요.

> There are ＿＿＿＿＿＿＿ in the field.

① three sheep
② two mouses
③ four wolfs
④ three benchs
⑤ five foxs

## 25 다음 지문을 읽고, ⓐ, ⓑ, ⓒ에 들어갈 알맞은 관사를 골라 쓰세요.

> Minsu always gets up at 6 o'clock. As soon as he wakes up, he watches the morning news to decide whether or not to bring ⓐ ( a / an ) umbrella. Then, he has breakfast and takes a shower. He usually goes to school ⓑ ( a / an ) hour before the first class begins. He takes ⓒ ( a / an ) university entrance exam two months later. So, he tries to go to school early and do self-studying.

ⓐ: ＿＿＿＿＿＿    ⓑ: ＿＿＿＿＿＿    ⓒ: ＿＿＿＿＿＿

## 26 다음 중 어법상 바르게 쓰인 문장은?

① We had nice dinner.
② I will see you at the noon.
③ My father is a very fat.
④ Do you play piano?
⑤ Is she a teacher, too?

## 27 밑줄 친 우리말을 영어로 바르게 옮긴 것끼리 짝 지어진 것은?

> We bought 피자 세 조각 and 콜라 두 병.

① three slice of pizza    – two bottle of coke
② three slices of pizza   – two bottles of coke
③ three pieces of pizza – two bottle of coke
④ three piece of pizzas – two bottle of cokes
⑤ three slices of pizzas – two bottles of cokes

## 28 다음 두 문장의 뜻이 같도록 빈칸에 들어갈 알맞은 말을 고르세요.

> • Korea has many old buildings.
>   = ＿＿＿＿＿＿ many old buildings in Korea.

① Here is
② It is
③ They are
④ There is
⑤ There are

## 29 다음 글에서 **틀린** 부분을 고르세요.

> Jessica has ① small ears, a small nose, and ② a big mouth. She also has ③ big blue eyes, ④ long legs, and ⑤ red hairs.

## 30 우리말과 같은 뜻이 되도록 빈칸에 알맞은 단어를 쓰세요.

> A: Is this pen yours?
> B: No. It's my ＿＿＿＿＿＿ pen.
>    (아니요. 그건 제 삼촌의 펜이에요.)

**31** 다음 중 밑줄 친 부분의 쓰임이 바른 것을 고르세요.

① She likes to wear <u>an</u> uniform.
② I am <u>an</u> middle school student.
③ Your father is <u>an</u> taxi driver.
④ He's <u>an</u> engineer.
⑤ Are you <u>an</u> nurse?

**32** 다음 우리말과 같은 뜻이 되도록 빈칸에 들어갈 알맞은 말을 쓰세요.

> • 나의 가족은 지구를 위해 좋은 일을 하려고 노력한다.
> = My family tries to do good things
>   for ________________________.

**33** 다음 괄호 안의 말을 이용하여 알맞은 문장을 쓰세요.

> A: (1) ________________________
>    ________________________
>    (how)
> B: There are four books on the desk.
> A: Whose books are they?
> B: (2) ________________________
>    (Jane)

**34** 다음 문장의 밑줄 친 <u>a</u>와 쓰임이 같은 것을 고르세요.

> I watch TV several times <u>a</u> week.

① We studied for <u>an</u> hour.
② <u>A</u> cat is an independent animal.
③ There is <u>a</u> park in my town.
④ I eat out twice <u>a</u> month.
⑤ It is <u>a</u> wonderful day.

**35** 다음 그림을 보고 〈예시〉처럼 There is/are를 이용하여 괄호 안의 주어진 단어를 가지고 말을 만드세요.

> | 예 시 | There is a chair in front of the desk.<br>(chair, in front of the desk) |
> |---|---|

(1) ________________________
   (cat, on the bed)
(2) ________________________
   (ball, on the floor)

**36** 다음 중 어법상 옳은 문장을 고르세요.

① I'd like to buy a pairs of shoes.
② Can I drink two glass of water?
③ She ate a slice of cheese.
④ My mother bought two bottle of juices.
⑤ He needs three pieces of papers.

**37** 빈칸에 들어갈 단어가 바르게 짝지어진 것은?

> • We work eight hours ___________ day.
> • March is ___________ third month of the year.

① a – the      ② the – a
③ a – a      ④ the – the
⑤ an – the

**38** 다음 중 어법상 옳은 문장을 고르세요.

① Is John student?
② Suji is a newspaper reporter.
③ Today is a second day of school.
④ My homeroom teacher is math teacher.
⑤ She looks a very honest.

**39** 다음 중 어법상 바르지 <u>않은</u> 문장을 고르세요.

① The boy's name is James.
② I like your sister's bag.
③ This is Mr. Kim's daughter.
④ The door's color is yellow.
⑤ It's Yongsu's dog.

**40** 다음 밑줄 친 부분의 쓰임이 <u>어색한</u> 것은?

① The sun sets in <u>the</u> west.
② Could you open <u>the</u> door?
③ We can play <u>the</u> soccer after school.
④ I'm <u>the</u> youngest girl in my class.
⑤ Look at <u>the</u> Chinese boy.

**41** 다음 중 밑줄 친 부분의 쓰임이 <u>잘못된</u> 것을 고르세요.

We ① <u>went</u> sightseeing in New York last summer. There ② <u>were</u> many famous places to visit in the city. We visited the Empire State Building. It was once ③ <u>the</u> tallest building in the world. We enjoyed ④ <u>plays</u> and concerts on Broadway. We took lots of ⑤ <u>photoes</u> together.

**42** 다음 중 어법상 올바른 문장을 고르세요.

① I'm wearing glass.
② What kind of pant do you want?
③ She wants to buy red shoes.
④ Miki likes these jean.
⑤ Did you find your scissor?

**43** 다음을 읽고 <u>틀린</u> 부분을 찾아서 바르게 고쳐 쓰세요.

Sora always goes to the school at eight o'clock. She usually has six classes a day. She has ten-minutes breaks between classes. She has the lunch at twelve o'clock.

(1) ________________ ➡ ________________

(2) ________________ ➡ ________________

(3) ________________ ➡ ________________

**44** 다음 빈칸에 들어갈 수 <u>없는</u> 것은?

Andy is looking for a pair of ____________.

① jeans
② shoes
③ scissors
④ notebooks
⑤ glasses

**45** 다음 빈칸에 들어갈 단어로 알맞지 <u>않은</u> 것은?

A: Can I help you?
B: Yes, I'd like ____________. How much is it?
A: It is 2 dollars and 40 cents.

① sugar
② bread
③ cheese
④ coffee
⑤ tomatoes

**46** 다음 두 문장을 〈보기〉처럼 하나의 문장으로 바꿔 쓰세요.

보 기

- Grandma is a great cook.
- She prepared the tasty soup.

➡ <u>Grandma, a great cook, prepared the</u>
<u>tasty soup.</u>

- Sungmin is the leader of our volunteer club.
- He is kind to everyone.

➡ _______________________________________

_______________________________________


**47** 빈칸에 들어갈 말이 바르게 짝지어진 것은?

*A*: How many oranges ___________ in the basket?

*B*: ___________ only one orange in the basket.

① is there   – There are
② are there – There is
③ are they   – They are
④ is there   – They are
⑤ are there – This is


**48** 다음 중 〈보기〉의 밑줄 친 부분과 쓰임이 <u>다른</u> 것은?

보 기 | My brother<u>'s</u> name is Minsu.

① What is your teacher<u>'s</u> name?
② Tom<u>'s</u> mom likes us.
③ I want to write children<u>'s</u> books.
④ He is my father<u>'s</u> friend.
⑤ She<u>'s</u> having dinner with us.


**49** 다음 밑줄 친 부분의 뜻이 나머지와 <u>다른</u> 하나는?

① Are <u>there</u> many children in the playground?
② They go <u>there</u> with my brother.
③ <u>There</u> are eight buildings on this street.
④ Is <u>there</u> a desk in your room?
⑤ <u>There</u> is an elephant in the zoo.


**50** 다음 대화의 빈칸에 들어갈 알맞은 말을 고르세요.

*A*: There's ___________________.

*B*: Really? Where?

*A*: Over there. It's under the oak tree.

*B*: Keep it. It will bring you good luck.

① a four leaf clovers
② four leaves clover
③ a four-leaf clover
④ four-leaves clovers
⑤ a four leaves clovers


**51** 다음 중 어법상 바르지 <u>않은</u> 것을 고르세요.

When I have some ①<u>questions</u> or ②<u>problems</u>, I ask my sister for some ③<u>help</u>. She always gives me good ④<u>advices</u> and helpful ⑤<u>information</u>.

**52** 다음 중 밑줄 친 부분의 쓰임이 나머지와 <u>다른</u> 것은?

① He drank coffee, his favorite drink, every morning.
② We, human beings, should love each other.
③ She bought a skirt, a blouse, and a jacket.
④ Do you like *bibimbap*, a Korean dish?
⑤ Ms. Lee, my English teacher, is very kind to me.

# CHAPTER 6
# 대명사

# PSS 1 인칭대명사

| 수 | 인칭 | 주격<br>(~은, 는, 이, 가) | 소유격<br>(~의) | 목적격<br>(~을, 를, 에게) | 소유대명사<br>(~의 것) |
|---|---|---|---|---|---|
| 단수 | 1 | I | my | me | mine |
| | 2 | you | your | you | yours |
| | 3 | he | his | him | his |
| | | she | her | her | hers |
| | | it | its | it | — |
| 복수 | 1 | we | our | us | ours |
| | 2 | you | your | you | yours |
| | 3 | they | their | them | theirs |

1. 주격과 목적격 – 주격 대명사는 주어로, 목적격 대명사는 목적어로 쓰인다.

**Minho** likes **milk**. ➡ **He** likes **it**.

민호는 우유를 좋아한다.  그는 그것을 좋아한다.

**Sumi** likes **books**. ➡ **She** likes **them**.

수미는 책을 좋아한다.   그녀는 그것들을 좋아한다.

**Sumi and Minho** like **their house**. ➡ **They** like **it**.

수미와 민호는 그들의 집을 좋아한다.       그들은 그것을 좋아한다.

2. 소유격과 소유대명사 – 소유격 뒤에는 명사가 오지만, 소유대명사 뒤에는 명사가 오지 않는다.

This is **my dog**. ➡ This dog is **mine**.

이것은 나의 개이다.   이 개는 나의 것이다.

That is **our car**. ➡ That car is **ours**.

저것은 우리의 차이다.   저 차는 우리의 것이다.

These are **your shoes**. ➡ These shoes are **yours**.

이것들은 너의 신발이다.     이 신발은 너의 것이다.

3. 전치사 뒤에는 주로 목적격 인칭대명사가 온다.

Babies are curious about everything **around** **them**.

아기들은 그들 주변의 모든 것에 대하여 궁금해한다.

## PRACTICE 1

〈보기〉와 같이 밑줄 친 부분을 알맞은 인칭대명사로 바꾸어 쓰세요.

| 보 기 | I don't want grapes. ➡ I don't want _them._ |
|---|---|

**1** That is his room.
➡ That room is ___________.

**2** The cat is brown.
➡ ___________ is brown.

**3** That is my present.
➡ That present is ___________.

**4** This is my grandparents' farm.
➡ This farm is ___________.

**5** The girl works at a bakery.
➡ ___________ works at a bakery.

**6** Is this her photo album?
➡ Is this photo album ___________?

**7** My brother and I got there by bus.
➡ ___________ got there by bus.

**8** Junho rested with his family.
➡ ___________ rested with his family.

**9** The dog's tail is very long.
➡ ___________ tail is very long.

**10** She welcomed my brother and me.
➡ She welcomed ___________.

**11** Minsu's and my hometown isn't far.
➡ ___________ hometown isn't far.

**12** TV helps me learn a lot of things.
➡ ___________ helps me learn a lot of things.

**13** Inho showed his new shirt to Susan.
➡ Inho showed his new shirt to ___________.

**14** You should wash your hands very often.
➡ You should wash ___________ very often.

**15** Tom and his friends' journey was very tough.
➡ ___________ journey was very tough.

**16** Those are your glasses.
➡ Those glasses are ___________.



## PRACTICE 2 [1-20]

괄호 안에 주어진 단어를 알맞은 형태로 바꾸어 빈칸에 쓰세요.

**1** What's ___________ name? (you)

**2** We made some food for ___________. (they)

**3** This prize is ___________. (he)

**4** Please help ___________ with my English. (I)

**5** Mike just returned from ___________ trip. (he)

**6** Our culture is similar to ___________. (you)

**7** I often play tennis in ___________ free time. (I)

**8** ___________ room is full of books. (she)

**9** It is because of ___________. (he)



CH
6
대명사

**10** This classroom is ___________. (we)

**11** ___________ is my notebook. (it)

**12** The house is ___________. (they)

**13** She gave ___________ a lot of food. (we)

**14** He may give ___________ some advice. (you)

**15** Food is very important for ___________ lives. (we)

**16** I made ___________ a cold drink. (she)

**17** I don't like ___________ color. (it)

**18** That old textbook isn't ___________. (I)

**19** This yellow blouse is ___________. (she)

**20** They usually wear shoes in ___________ homes. (they)

## PSS 2 재귀대명사

| 단수 | 복수 |
|---|---|
| I ➡ **myself** | we ➡ **ourselves** |
| you ➡ **yourself** | you ➡ **yourselves** |
| he ➡ **himself** | |
| she ➡ **herself** | they ➡ **themselves** |
| it ➡ **itself** | |

**She** is looking at **herself** in the mirror. 그녀는 거울에 비친 자신의 모습을 보고 있다.

1. **재귀 용법** – **문장의 주어와 목적어가 같을 때** 동사 또는 전치사의 목적어로 재귀대명사를 쓴다.

   **He** loves **himself**. 그는 그 자신을 사랑한다.
   **They** enjoyed **themselves** at the party. 그들은 파티에서 신나게 즐겼다.
   **You** should be proud of **yourself**. 너는 스스로를 자랑스러워해야 한다.

2. **강조 용법** – **주어나 목적어, 보어를 강조할 때** 강조되는 말 바로 뒤나 문장 맨 끝에 재귀대명사를 쓴다. 이때의 재귀대명사는 **생략이 가능**하다.

   **My father** (**himself**) designed that building. 아버지가 직접 그 건물을 설계하셨다.
   = **My father** designed that building (**himself**).

## PRACTICE 3

괄호 안에 주어진 단어 중 알맞은 것을 고르세요.

**1** I feel proud of (me, myself).

**2** They (yourselves, themselves) got very tired.

**3** The cat cleaned (itself, themselves).

**4** Let me introduce (myself, ourselves).

**5** Namsu (him, himself) sent an e-mail to me.

**6** Did you make the salad (you, yourself)?

**7** He thought to (myself, himself), 'No way.'

**8** The weather (it, itself) doesn't matter.

**9** Sometimes Susan talks to (yourself, herself).

**10** Many people enjoyed (ourselves, themselves) in the park.

**11** I was angry with (myself, himself).

**12** Feel free to make (yourself, you) at home.

**13** Help (you, yourself) to some *bibimbap*.

**14** Mike likes (himself, itself) in a cap.

**15** A lot of people don't know about (itself, themselves).



## PRACTICE 4

밑줄 친 부분을 생략할 수 있으면 ○표, 생략할 수 없으면 ×표 하세요.

**1** I decided to go there <u>myself</u>. [     ]

**2** He had a whole pizza to <u>himself</u>. [     ]

**3** She paid for <u>herself</u> at the restaurant. [     ]

**4** Computers <u>themselves</u> help us study alone. [     ]

**5** Mike's father likes playing football <u>himself</u>. [     ]

**6** The dinner <u>itself</u> was really delicious. [     ]

**7** Can you imagine <u>yourself</u> in ten years? [     ]

**8** History repeats <u>itself</u>. [     ]

**9** She caught a cold <u>herself</u>. [     ]

**10** I said to <u>myself</u>, "Is it true?" [     ]

# PSS 3 비인칭 주어 it

비인칭 주어 it은 시간, 날짜, 요일, 계절, 날씨, 거리, 명암을 나타낼 때 쓰인다. 이 때의 it은 가리키는 대상이 없고, 특별한 의미를 갖지 않으므로 해석하지 않는다.

① 시간 : What time is **it**? – **It** is eight o'clock. 지금 몇 시니? – 8시야.

② 날짜 : What date is **it** today? – **It**'s May 24th. 오늘은 며칠이니? – 5월 24일이야.

③ 요일 : What day is **it** today? – **It** is Friday. 오늘은 무슨 요일이니? – 금요일이야.

④ 계절 : **It** is winter now. 지금은 겨울이다.

⑤ 날씨 : **It** was cold yesterday. 어제는 추웠다.

⑥ 거리 : How far is **it** from here to the museum? 여기서 박물관까지 얼마나 머니?

　　　　 – **It** is about three miles. 약 3마일이야.

⑦ 명암 : **It**'s dark outside. 밖이 어둡다.

***cf.*** 대명사 it은 '그것'이라고 해석한다.

There is **a pencil** on the desk. **It** (= The pencil) is hers.

책상 위에 연필이 한 자루 있다. 그것은 그녀의 것이다.

정답 p.30

## PRACTICE 5

다음 문장의 밑줄 친 it의 용법이 〈보기〉의 A와 같으면 A를, B와 같으면 B를 쓰세요.

| 보 기 | A. It is Saturday. |
| | B. I'll bring it tomorrow. |

**1** What does it mean? [　　]

**2** It's three thirty. [　　]

**3** It was a summer day. [　　]

**4** What a huge turtle it is! [　　]

**5** It takes ten minutes by bus. [　　]

**6** It is Wednesday. [　　]

**7** It is still spring. [　　]

**8** It is hot today. [　　]

**9** It helps me save time. [　　]

**10** It is November 9th. [　　]

**11** It is getting dark. [　　]

**12** It is my brother's umbrella. [　　]

**13** What time is it now? [　　]

**14** It is between the bank and the store. [　　]

**15** It isn't your fault. [　　]

**16** How many miles is it from Seoul to Daegu? [　　]

# PSS 4  지시대명사

1. this / these – 가까이에 있는 사람이나 사물을 가리킬 때 쓰인다.

   **This** is my bag. 이것은 나의 가방이다.　　　**These** are my bags.  이것들은 나의 가방들이다.

2. that / those – 멀리 있는 사람이나 사물을 가리킬 때 쓰인다.

   **That** is my watch. 저것은 내 시계이다.　　　**Those** are my watches. 저것들은 내 시계들이다.

*cf.* this / these와 that / those는 지시형용사로서 명사 앞에 쓰여 명사를 꾸며주기도 한다.
   **This cake** is very delicious. 이 케이크는 매우 맛있다.
   **Those notebooks** are mine. 저 공책들은 내 것이다.

3. 누군가를 소개할 때나 전화상에서 전화를 건 사람과 받는 사람을 가리킬 때는 this를 쓴다.

   Tim, **this** is Jane. Jane, **this** is Tim. Tim, 얘는 Jane이야. Jane, 얘는 Tim이야.
   Hello, **this** is Sumi. Is **this** Mike? 여보세요, 나 수미인데. Mike니?

## PRACTICE 6

그림을 보고, 빈칸에 this/these 또는 that/those를 넣어 문장을 완성하세요.

1 ________________ is my dog, Sandy.

2 Who is ________________ girl?

3 Are ________________ pine trees?

4 ________________ is Mary speaking. Who's calling, please?

5 How about ____________ shoes?

6 ____________ is my house.

7 Are ____________ your glasses on the table?

8 ____________ are my family's pictures.

## PSS 5 부정대명사



### PSS 5-1 one

1. **앞에서 언급한 명사와 종류는 같지만, 특정하지 않은 막연한 대상에 대해 말할 때는 one**을 쓴다.

   My computer is too old. I want a new **one**. (one = computer)
   내 컴퓨터는 너무 오래됐다. 나는 새것을 원한다.

   ***cf.*** 앞에서 언급한 특정한 명사를 가리킬 때는 it을 쓴다.
   My computer is too old. I don't like **it**. (it = my computer)
   내 컴퓨터는 너무 오래됐다. 나는 그것을 좋아하지 않는다.

2. **앞에서 언급한 명사가 복수형일 때는 one 대신 ones**를 쓴다.

   My shoes are too old. I want new **ones**. (ones = shoes)
   내 신발은 너무 낡았다. 나는 새것들을 원한다.

## PRACTICE 7

다음 문장의 빈칸에 one, ones 또는 it을 넣어 문장을 완성하세요.

1 She bought some meal kits. I want to buy the same ______________.

2 Don't throw paper away. We can use ______________ again.

3 Where is an umbrella? – There is ______________ in my room.

4 I went to London. ______________ is a very beautiful city.

5 I lost my bag. I need a new ______________.

6 I don't like yellow roses. I will buy red ______________.



---

# PSS 5-2 another, others, the other(s)

일부를 뺀 나머지에 대해 말할 때는 another, others, the other(s)를 사용할 수 있다. 특정한 것을 가리킬 때는 the를 붙인다.

**1. another '또 다른 하나'**

I don't like this color. Can you show me **another**?
나는 이 색깔을 좋아하지 않아요. 저에게 또 다른 것을 보여줄래요?

**2. One ~ the other … '하나는 ~, 다른 사람[것]〈나머지 하나〉은 …'**

She has two flowers. **One** is a rose and **the other** is a lily.
그녀는 두 송이의 꽃을 가지고 있다. 하나는 장미이고 다른 하나는 백합이다.

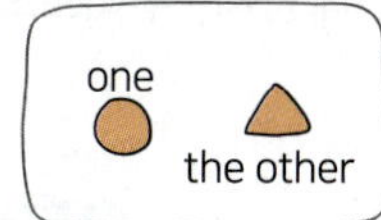


**3. Some ~ others … '몇몇은 ~, 다른 사람[것]들〈나머지 일부〉은 …'**

**Some students** like English. **Others** don't like it.
몇몇 학생들은 영어를 좋아한다. 다른 학생들은 그것을 좋아하지 않는다.
= Some students like English. Other students don't like it.

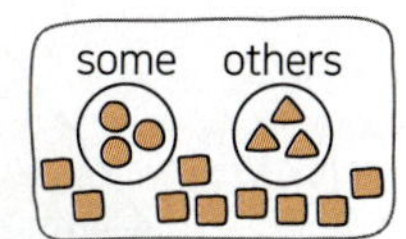


**4. Some ~ the others … '몇몇은 ~, 다른 사람[것]들〈나머지 전부〉은 …'**

**Some cats** are white. **The others** are brown.
몇몇 고양이들은 털이 하얗다. 다른 고양이들은 털이 갈색이다.
= Some cats are white. The other cats are brown.

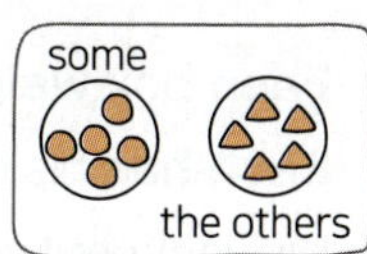


***cf.*** another와 other는 「another+단수 명사」와 「other+복수 명사」의 형태로 명사를 수식하는 형용사로 쓰인다.

Can you show me **another shirt**? 저에게 또 다른 셔츠를 보여줄래요?
Can you show me **other shirts**? 저에게 다른 셔츠들을 보여줄래요?

## PRACTICE 8

괄호 안에 주어진 표현 중 알맞은 것을 고르세요.

1 Some people are honest, but (other, others) are dishonest.

2 He wants to read (another, other) book.

3 She has a lot of fruits. (Some, They) of them are oranges, and the others are apples.

4 Ingyu's mother made two doughnuts. One is Ingyu's, and (another, the other) is hers.

5 They did well in some courses, but they didn't do well in (other, others) courses.

6 This is (another, other) good example.

7 I have two brothers. One is tall, and (another, the other) is short.

8 Some of the dresses are clean, but (other, the others) are not.

9 There are two coats. (It, One) is blue, and the other is black.

10 This pen is broken. Do you have (another, other)?

---

# PSS 5-3 each, every

1. **each** – '각자, 각기, 각각의'의 뜻으로 **단수 명사를 수식**하고 **단수 취급**한다. each는 대명사, 부사로도 쓰인다.

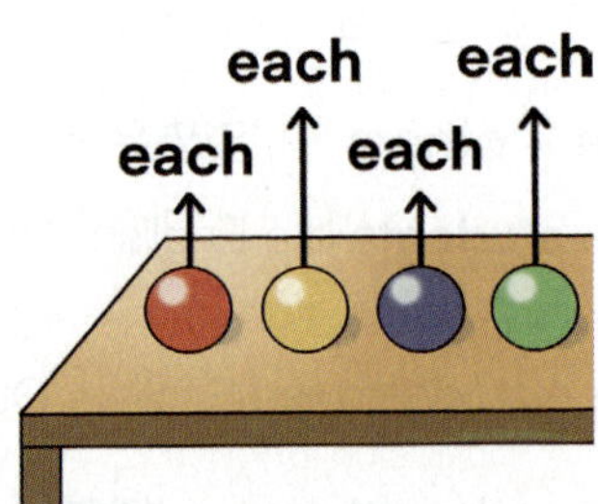


**Each** box **weighs** 200 pounds. 각각의 상자는 무게가 200파운드이다. (형용사)
**Each has** his own opinion. 각자 자기만의 의견을 가지고 있다. (대명사)
I gave them five cards **each**. 나는 그들에게 각각 카드 다섯 장씩 주었다. (부사)

2. **every** – '모든'의 뜻으로 **단수 명사를 수식**하고 **단수 취급**한다.

I want to make **every child** happy. 나는 모든 아이들을 행복하게 만들고 싶다.
every people (X)　　　　　every children (X)

*cf.* everyone, everybody, everything도 단수 취급한다.
　　**Everyone likes** watching movies. 모든 사람들이 영화를 보는 것을 좋아한다.

## PRACTICE 9

괄호 안에 주어진 단어 중 알맞은 것을 고르세요.

**1**  What will each (men, man) have for lunch?

**2**  He wrapped each (present, presents).

**3**  Every dog (has, have) his day.

**4**  Everything (is, are) going to be all right.

**5**  How does each (students, student) go to school?

## PSS 6  의문대명사



### PSS 6-1  who

사람의 이름이나 관계 등을 물을 때 쓴다.

**1.  주격**

**Who** is she?　　　　　　– She is **my aunt**.

그녀는 누구니?　　　　　　그녀는 우리 이모야.

**2.  소유격**

**Whose** car is this?　　– It's **my father's**.

이것은 누구의 차니?　　　그것은 우리 아빠의 것이야.

**cf.** 「whose+명사」에서 whose는 who의 소유격으로 '누구의'라는 의미를 나타내지만, whose가
명사 없이 단독으로 쓰일 경우에는 소유대명사로서 '누구의 것'이라는 의미이다.

**Whose** is this car? 이 차는 누구의 것이니?

**3.  목적격**

**Whom** did you meet yesterday?　　– I met **Minho**.

너는 어제 누구를 만났니?　　　　　　나는 민호를 만났어.

**cf.** 구어체에서는 whom보다 who를 쓰는 경향이 많다.



## PRACTICE 10

다음 문장의 빈칸에 who, whose, whom 중 알맞은 것을 쓰세요. (단, who와 whom이 모두 가능할 경우에는
whom을 쓸 것)

**1**  ______________ did they help?

**2**  ______________ teaches science?

**3**  ______________ is this watch?

**4**  ______________ is your favorite singer?

**5**  ______________ did he visit?

**6**  ______________ does she talk to?

**7**  ______________ book is that?

**8**  ______________ is your homeroom teacher?

**9**  ______________ are those clothes?

**10**  ______________ makes you sad?

# PSS 6-2 what, which

1. **what** – 동물이나 사물, 그리고 사람의 직업이나 신분을 물을 때 쓴다.

   **What** did Mary buy?　　　　　　– She bought **some clothes**.

   Mary가 무엇을 샀니?　　　　　　　그녀는 옷을 몇 벌 샀어.

   **What** does your father do?　　　– He is **a teacher**.

   너의 아버지는 무엇을 하시니?　　　그는 선생님이셔.

   ***cf.*** what은 「what+명사」의 형태로 명사를 수식하는 의문형용사로도 쓰인다.

   　　**What food** do you like? 너는 어떤 음식을 좋아하니?

2. **which** – 동물이나 사물을 가리킬 때 쓴다. 단, 제한된 선택의 범위 내에서 '어느 것'인지를 물을 때 쓴다.

   **Which** is cheaper, meat **or** fish? 고기와 생선 중 어느 것이 더 값이 싸니?

   **Which** do you want, tea **or** coffee? 차와 커피 중 어느 것을 원하니?

   ***cf.*** which는 「which+명사」의 형태로 명사를 수식하는 의문형용사로도 쓰인다.

   　　**Which season** do you like, summer **or** winter? 여름과 겨울 중 어느 계절을 좋아하니?

## PRACTICE 11

**괄호 안에 주어진 단어 중 알맞은 것을 고르세요.**

1 (What, Who) is your favorite song?

2 (Whom, Whose) did he meet last night?

3 (Who, Whose) violin is this?

4 (What, Who) is this baby in the photo?

5 (What, Who) size do you wear?

6 (Who, Whose) book did you borrow?

7 (What, Which) is bigger, Canada or Australia?

8 (What, Which) pet do you like better, a dog or a cat?

9 (Whose, Whom) phone is ringing now?

10 (Whose, Who) did you invite to the party?

11 (Who, Which) of them is your uncle?

12 (What, Whose) made you laugh so hard?



## PRACTICE 12

**다음 질문에 알맞은 응답을 찾아 그 기호를 쓰세요.**

**[A]**

1 Which team is stronger? [     ]　　　ⓐ It's mine.

2 Whose book is that? [     ]　　　ⓑ How about five o'clock?

3 Who is this man? [     ]　　　ⓒ He is my father.

4 What time shall we make it? [     ]　　　ⓓ The Spanish team is stronger.

**[B]**

5 Who's calling, please? [     ]　　　ⓔ I'm hanging out with Tom.

6 What did you get at Christmas? [     ]　　　ⓕ This is Susan.

7 Whom are you hanging out with? [     ]　　　ⓖ A subway, of course.

8 Which is faster, a taxi or a subway? [     ]　　　ⓗ A backpack.

# PSS 7  so, same, such



| | |
|---|---|
| **so** | '**그렇게**'라는 뜻으로 think, suppose, believe, expect, hope, say, tell의 목적어로 쓰이며 **앞에 나온 긍정의 문장을 대신한다.**<br>She will be safe. – I hope **so**. 그녀는 안전할 것이다. – 나도 그러길 바란다. |
| **same** | '**같은**'이라는 뜻으로 **항상 정관사 the와 함께 쓴다.**<br>The prices are **the same**. 그 가격들은 같다.<br><br>***cf.*** A is/are the same as B 'A는 B와 같다'<br>The password **is the same as** the username.<br>비밀번호는 사용자 명과 동일하다.<br><br>**same은 형용사로도 쓰인다.**<br>Jaewon and Minsu go to **the same** school. 재원이와 민수는 같은 학교에 다닌다.<br><br>***cf.*** the same ~ as … '…와 같은 ~'<br>I bought **the same** umbrella **as** Jenny. 나는 Jenny와 같은 우산을 샀다.<br>Do you like **the same** music **as** Kevin? 너는 Kevin과 같은 음악을 좋아하니? |
| **such** | '**그러한 것**'이라는 뜻으로 **앞에 나온 단어, 구, 절을 받는다.**<br>**Such** was his answer. 그의 대답은 그러했다.<br><br>***cf.*** such as ~ '~와 같은 그런'<br>I like team sports **such as** soccer. 나는 축구와 같은 그런 단체 운동을 좋아한다. |

## PRACTICE 13

**우리말과 일치하도록 괄호 안에 주어진 단어를 바르게 배열하세요.**

**1** 그녀는 부지런하다. – 나는 그렇게 생각하지 않아.

= She is diligent. – ________________________________ (I, so, think, don't)

**2** 그것들은 같아 보이지 않는다.

= ________________________________ (don't, look, they, the, same)

**3** 그는 너와 같은 의견을 가지고 있다.

= ________________________________ (has, the, as, same, he, you, opinion)

**4** 나는 노란색과 같은 밝은 색을 좋아한다.

= ________________________________ (such, I, like, yellow, as, bright, colors)

**5** 이 신발들은 사이즈가 같다.

= ________________________________ (shoes, these, the, same, are, size)

**6** 그가 이번 웅변 대회에서 우승할거야. – 나도 그렇게 믿어.

= He will win this speech contest. – ________________________________ (so, I, believe)

**7** 그와 나는 같은 시간에 도착했다.

= ________________________________ (time, I, at, arrived, same, he, the, and)

**8** 내 여동생은 초콜릿과 같은 단 것을 좋아한다.

= ________________________________

(sweets, chocolate, sister, as, likes, such, my)

**9** 오늘의 날씨는 어제의 날씨와 같다.

= ________________________________

(same, yesterday's, weather, today's, is, as, the)

**10** 그는 정말 좋은 사람이구나!

= ________________________________ (such, nice, he, guy, a, is)

**11** 너는 그러한 문제들을 어떻게 풀었니?

= ________________________________ (problems, solve, how, such, did, you)

**12** 그 꽃들의 색은 같다.

= ________________________________ (the, are, colors, same, the, flowers')

**1** 다음 대화의 빈칸에 들어갈 알맞은 단어는?

> *Jane*: Do you like pop songs, Ted?
> *Ted*: Yes, I like ___________ very much.

① this ② that ③ it
④ they ⑤ them

**2** 빈칸에 공통으로 들어갈 알맞은 단어를 쓰세요.

> • Look at ___________ picture.
>   – Wow, it's beautiful.
> • May I speak to Nick, please?
>   – Oh, ___________ is Nick.

**3** 다음 대화의 빈칸에 들어갈 알맞은 단어는?

> A: ___________ camera is this?
> B: It's my father's.

① What ② Who ③ Whose
④ Which ⑤ When

**4** 다음 빈칸에 알맞은 말을 쓰세요.

> Olivia likes watching movies. She is going to watch two different movies this week.
> (1) ___________ is science fiction and
> (2) ___________ is horror.

**5** 다음 빈칸에 들어갈 말이 차례대로 짝지어진 것은?

> Hi, everyone! My name is Codi. ___________ am from Canada. My friends and I like to play baseball. ___________ team often plays baseball after school. My uniform number is nine. ___________ is my favorite baseball player's number.

① I – Their – It ② We – Their – It
③ I – Our – He ④ I – Our – It
⑤ We – My – He

**6** 대화의 ⓐ~ⓒ에 들어갈 알맞은 말을 순서대로 연결한 것은?

> A: Are you ready for our picnic today, Brian?
> B: Eunjung, didn't you check the weather forecast?
> A: ___ⓐ___. What did it say?
> B: It's going to rain all day.
> A: Oh, no. Rain might spoil our picnic.
> B: Yeah, I'm worried about the weather.
> A: We can go on ___ⓑ___ day.
> B: You're right. I'll tell ___ⓒ___ friends right now.
> A: Perfect.

|   | ⓐ | ⓑ | ⓒ |
|---|---|---|---|
| ① | Yes, I did. | another | the other |
| ② | Yes, I didn't. | the other | another |
| ③ | No, I did. | another | the other |
| ④ | No, I didn't. | the other | another |
| ⑤ | No, I didn't. | another | the other |

## 7 다음 대화의 빈칸에 들어갈 알맞은 단어를 쓰세요.

*A*: _____________ do you want, a chocolate cake or a cheesecake?

*B*: A chocolate cake.

## 8 다음 빈칸 ⓐ~ⓓ에 들어가지 <u>않는</u> 것은?

- I don't like the red one. Show me __________ⓐ__________.
- There are 30 strawberries in the basket. __________ⓑ__________ of them are rotten.
- Yumi has two dogs. __________ⓒ__________ is black, and __________ⓓ__________ is white.

① some  ② one  ③ the other

④ the others  ⑤ another

## 9 빈칸에 공통으로 들어갈 알맞은 단어는?

- _____________ time is it?
- _____________'s the weather like?

## 10 우리말을 영어로 표현할 때 ⓐ에 들어갈 단어는?

- 소라는 진희와 똑같은 가방을 가지고 있다.
  = Sora __________ __________ __________ⓐ__________ __________ __________ Jinhee.

① same  ② the  ③ has  ④ bag  ⑤ as

## 11 다음의 빈칸 어디에도 들어갈 수 <u>없는</u> 것은?

- This house is _____________.
- This house belongs to _____________.
- _____________ own this house.

① mine  ② you  ③ he  ④ us  ⑤ theirs

## 12 주어진 두 문장을 한 문장으로 바꿀 때 바르게 쓰인 것을 고르세요.

Minjun is a student. I am a student, too.

① He is a student.

② You are students.

③ We are students.

④ They are students.

⑤ She and I are students.

## 13 (a)~(e)가 가리키는 것이 바르지 <u>않은</u> 것은?

Hello, everyone! I'm Ji-a. Today, it is my turn to tell you a little about myself. So, I want to show you some of my favorite things in my bedroom. First, this is a picture of my teddy bear. I hug (a) it when I go to bed. Next, I have a big world map on my wall. I look at (b) it and think about other countries. I want to visit (c) them someday. Lastly, I have a small whiteboard. I draw on (d) it. I also write fun messages to myself. (e) They make me smile.

① (a): my teddy bear

② (b): my wall

③ (c): other countries

④ (d): a small whiteboard

⑤ (e): fun messages

## 14 다음 우리말과 같은 뜻이 되도록 빈칸에 들어갈 알맞은 단어를 쓰세요.

- 그는 그 자신을 자랑스럽게 여겼다.
  = He felt proud of _____________.

## 15 다음 대화에서 밑줄 친 부분의 어법이 틀린 것은?

A: I don't have a pen. I have to buy ①one.
B: I have two pens. You can use the red one.
A: Thank you. Where is ②it?
B: Oh, I put ③one in my pencil case, but I can't find ④it.
A: Oh, then never mind. I can borrow ⑤one from Paul.

## 16 다음 빈칸에 들어갈 단어가 순서대로 바르게 짝 지어진 것은?

• ___________'s your favorite book?
• ___________'s your favorite writer?

① What  – Who　　　② Who  – When
③ When – Why　　　④ What – What
⑤ Who  – What

## 17 다음 중 어법상 어색한 문장은?

① Helen and Jack love their son.
② What is your favorite season?
③ This is our house.
④ I have a pig. It's tail is short.
⑤ These are my pictures.

## 18 다음 빈칸에 공통으로 들어갈 재귀대명사를 쓰세요.

• She blamed ___________ for the mistake.
• My mom made this cake ___________.
• She said to ___________, "It will be okay."

## 19 다음 중 보기의 밑줄 친 it과 쓰임이 같은 문장은?

보 기 | It's fall here. It's getting cold.

ⓐ It's raining now.
ⓑ She bought it for my birthday.
ⓒ How far is it from here to the library?
ⓓ It's my favorite food.
ⓔ It's five o'clock.

① ⓐⓑ　　　② ⓐⓑⓒ　　　③ ⓐⓒⓔ
④ ⓑⓓⓔ　　　⑤ ⓒⓓⓔ

## 20 다음 글에서 밑줄 친 ⓐ를 괄호 안의 단어를 이용하여 영어로 바르게 옮겨 쓰세요.

The penguin and the *ostrich are birds. ⓐ하지만, 펭귄은 타조와 같지 않다. Its neck and legs are very short. It can't run fast, but can swim well.

*ostrich 타조

➡ But, the penguin is ___________________

___________________________________.

(same, as)

## 21 다음 중 밑줄 친 부분이 틀린 것은?

A: How do you like these beautiful fish?
B: ①They are good, but I can't hold them in ②my arms. I like pets with fur.
A: Then how about ③this hamster?
B: Oh, ④its perfect! It has fur, and I can hold ⑤it!

**22** 다음 대화에서 우리말과 같은 뜻이 되도록 빈칸에 들어갈 알맞은 말을 쓰세요.

> A: Hello, may I speak to Mr. Brown?
> B: Who's calling, please?
> A: ______________ ______________ John.
> (저는 John이에요.)

**23** 다음 글의 빈칸에 들어갈 단어가 순서대로 바르게 짝지어진 것은?

> ______________ people buy all their needs on the Internet. ______________ people don't want to buy them on the Internet.

① Some – Others     ② Some – Other
③ One    – The others   ④ One    – Others
⑤ One    – Another

**24** 다음 대화에서 밑줄 친 부분 대신에 쓸 수 있는 단어는?

> A: Can I help you?
> B: Yes, please. Do you have a backpack?
> A: Yes, we do. What color do you want?
> B: A yellow <u>backpack</u>.

① this      ② that      ③ one
④ it      ⑤ else

**25** 다음 대화의 빈칸에 들어갈 가장 알맞은 문장을 고르세요.

> A: ______________________
> B: He is a fashion designer.

① What does he do?
② What does he like?
③ How is he?
④ How is he doing?
⑤ What will he do?

**26** 다음 중 밑줄 친 부분을 생략할 수 <u>없는</u> 것을 고르세요.

① Let me introduce <u>myself</u>.
② I <u>myself</u> went there.
③ Did you cook this meal <u>yourself</u>?
④ John would like to make music <u>himself</u>.
⑤ The cute girl was Sujin <u>herself</u>.

**27** 다음 글에서 빈칸에 들어갈 적절한 단어는?

> Everyone in this club ______________ a musical instrument.

① play          ② plays
③ playing     ④ were playing
⑤ are playing

**28** 다음 밑줄 친 우리말을 괄호 안의 단어를 이용하여 영어로 바르게 옮겨 쓰세요.

> *Reporter* : You're a famous painter. <u>모든 사람이 당신의 그림을 좋아하나요?</u>
> *Monet*: Of course. My paintings make people happy.

→ ______________________________

(everybody)

**29** 다음 밑줄 친 It의 쓰임이 나머지와 <u>다른</u> 하나는?

① <u>It</u> takes 15 minutes on foot.
② <u>It</u> is eight thirty.
③ <u>It</u>'s March 17th.
④ <u>It</u>'s a very big clock.
⑤ <u>It</u>'s Tuesday today.

**30** 괄호 안의 단어를 우리말에 맞게 배열하여 문장을 완성하세요.

> • 너는 아침에 몇 시에 학교에 가니?
>
> = __________________________
>
>  in the morning? (do, what, go, you, time, school, to)

**31** 다음 대화의 빈칸에 들어갈 알맞은 단어는?

> A: How do I get to Gyeongbokgung?
> B: You can take the subway.
> A: __________ line?
> B: Line 3.

① Who  ② Which  ③ How
④ Where  ⑤ Whose

**32** 다음 빈칸에 알맞은 것은?

> A: She is good at science. I think she will
>   be a great scientist someday.
> B: I think __________, too.

① so  ② same  ③ as
④ such  ⑤ either

**33** 다음 밑줄 친 부분을 소유대명사로 바꾼 것 중 잘못된 것을 고르세요.

① That is his computer.
  = That computer is his.
② This is her hat.
  = This hat is hers.
③ Those are their bags.
  = Those bags are theirs.
④ This is our car.
  = This car is us.
⑤ This is your pencil case.
  = This pencil case is yours.

**34** 다음 중 어법상 바르지 않은 것을 모두 고르세요.

① Every baby is cute.
② Cut each apple with a knife.
③ He loves every children.
④ Each class is about 35 minutes.
⑤ Everything look beautiful.

**35** 다음 글의 빈칸에 들어갈 단어가 순서대로 바르게 짝지어진 것은?

> I have two sons. __________ is a teacher, and __________ is a pilot.

① One  – the other  ② One  – other
③ Some – other  ④ Some – the other
⑤ Some – the others

**36** 다음 밑줄 친 부분을 대명사로 바꾼 것 중 잘못된 것을 고르세요.

① She met Mr. Han. (➡ him)
② I know Sally. (➡ her)
③ He studies English and science. (➡ it)
④ We helped Jason and Cathy. (➡ them)
⑤ They visited Mrs. Lopez. (➡ her)

**37** 다음 빈칸에 들어갈 단어가 순서대로 짝지어진 것은?

> • I don't like desserts ________ as pudding.
> • They stayed at the ________ hotel.

① such – so  ② such – same
③ so  – such  ④ so  – same
⑤ same – such

# CHAPTER 7
# 부정사

# PSS 1 명사처럼 쓰이는 to부정사

## PSS 1-1 주어와 보어로 쓰이는 to부정사

「to+동사원형」의 형태로 **동사의 의미나 성질을 가지면서** 동시에 **명사, 형용사, 부사의 역할**을 하는 것을 to부정사라고 한다. **to부정사가 명사처럼 쓰일 때**는 문장 안에서 **주어, 목적어, 보어의 역할**을 하며 '**~하는 것**'으로 풀이된다.

| | | |
|---|---|---|
| **swim** '수영하다' | ➡ | **to swim** '수영하는 것' |
| **play the guitar** '기타를 치다' | ➡ | **to play the guitar** '기타를 치는 것' |
| **study English** '영어를 공부하다' | ➡ | **to study English** '영어를 공부하는 것' |

### 1. 주어

**To use** chopsticks isn't easy. = **It** isn't easy **to use** chopsticks.
젓가락을 사용하는 것은 쉽지 않다.

**To play** the piano is a lot of fun. = **It** is a lot of fun **to play** the piano.
피아노를 치는 것은 아주 재미있다.

***cf.*** to부정사가 주어인 경우에는 **주어 자리에 it**을 쓰고 **to부정사를 뒤로 보낼 수 있다**. to부정사로 시작하는 문장보다 「It ~ to부정사」 구문이 보다 자연스러운 문장이다. **이때 쓰인 it**을 **가주어**라고 하고, **to부정사구**를 **진주어**라고 한다.

### 2. 보어

My hobby is **to read** books. 나의 취미는 책을 읽는 것이다.
My goal is **to lose** five kilograms. 나의 목표는 5킬로그램을 감량하는 것이다.

정답 p.34

## PRACTICE 1

〈보기〉와 같이 주어진 문장을 바꾸어 쓰세요.

| 보 기 | To send an e-mail is simple. ➡ It is simple to send an e-mail. |
|---|---|
| | To find your house was difficult. ➡ It was difficult to find your house. |

**1** To visit a historic place is interesting.
➡ It is interesting ___________________________________.

**2** To raise cows is a farmer's work.
➡ ___________________________________ to raise cows.

**3** To make good friends is helpful to your life.
➡ It is helpful to your life ___________________________________.

**4** To stay here for a week was my plan.

➡ ___________________________________________ to stay here for a week.

**5** To get enough sleep is good for your health.

➡ It is good for your health ___________________________________________ .

**6** To get lost in these woods was very dangerous.

➡ ___________________________________________ to get lost in these woods.

정답 p.34

## PRACTICE 2

주어진 동사를 동사원형 또는 to부정사 중 알맞은 형태를 골라 빈칸에 쓰세요.

**1** sing
(1) My dream is ______________ in front of people.
(2) Do you think I should ______________ in front of people?

**2** read
(1) My homework is ______________ a newspaper.
(2) I ______________ a book in my free time.

**3** visit
(1) My hope is ______________ New York.
(2) I ______________ my grandparents' house every weekend.

---

## PSS 1-2 목적어로 쓰이는 to부정사

1. **to부정사를 목적어로 쓰는 동사**들은 다음과 같다.

| begin | decide | expect | hope | like | love |
|---|---|---|---|---|---|
| need | plan | start | try | want | would like |

\+ to부정사

I **hope to be** a famous scientist. 나는 유명한 과학자가 되기를 바란다.

I **like to study** the stars. 나는 별을 연구하는 것을 좋아한다.

We **decided to give** Jim a birthday party. 우리는 Jim에게 생일 파티를 열어주기로 결정했다.

2. 「**의문사+to부정사**」는 문장 안에서 **주로 목적어 역할**을 한다.

I don't know **how to drive** a car. 나는 차를 운전하는 방법을 모른다.

We haven't decided **when to meet**. 우리는 언제 만날지 결정하지 않았다.

Do you know **what to do** in an emergency? 너는 응급상황에 무엇을 해야 하는지 아니?

I'm not sure **where to visit** in Spain. 나는 스페인에서 어디를 방문해야 할지 모르겠다.

## PRACTICE 3

〈보기〉에서 알맞은 동사를 골라 to부정사의 형태로 바꾸어 빈칸에 쓰세요.

| 보 기 | buy   meet   watch   live   come   start |
| --- | --- |

**1** We planned ________________ jogging next week.

**2** Ingyu needs ______________ a book.

**3** I want ______________ in a peaceful world.

**4** I hope ______________ the president.

**5** She loves ______________ the stars in the sky.

**6** Would you like ______________ to dinner?



## PRACTICE 4

우리말과 같은 뜻이 되도록 괄호 안에 주어진 단어를 바르게 배열하세요.

**1** 비가 오기 시작했다.
= Rain _______________________________________. (fall, to, began)

**2** 그들은 그 호텔에서 머무르기를 기대했다.
= They _______________________________ at the hotel. (to, stay, expected)

**3** 나는 이 기계를 어떻게 쓰는지 모른다.
= I have no idea _______________________________ this machine. (use, to, how)

**4** 그의 친구들은 그를 그곳에서 만나기로 결정했다.
= His friends _______________________________ there. (meet, to, decided, him)

**5** 나는 토마토를 재배하기 시작했다.
= I _______________________________. (tomatoes, grow, started, to)

**6** 너는 나에게 마트에서 무엇을 살지 말해줄 수 있니?
= Can you tell me _______________________________ at the market? (to, what, buy)

**7** 그녀는 매일 일기를 쓰려고 노력한다.
= She _______________________________ a diary every day. (keep, tries, to)

**8** 저에게 시청에 가는 방법을 알려주시겠어요?
= Could you tell me _______________________________ to City Hall? (get, how, to)

# PSS 2 형용사처럼 쓰이는 to부정사

to부정사가 명사나 대명사를 뒤에서 꾸며주는 형용사의 역할을 할 때는 '~할, ~해야 할'로 풀이된다.

She has many interesting **books** **to read**. 그녀는 읽을 많은 재미있는 책을 가지고 있다.

They looked for **something** **to eat**. 그들은 먹을 것을 찾았다.

*cf.* 형용사는 보통 수식하는 명사 앞에 쓰이지만, to부정사는 명사 뒤에서 수식한다.

I need **cold water**. 나는 차가운 물이 필요하다.

I need **water** **to drink**. 나는 마실 물이 필요하다.

전치사의 목적어 자리에 오는 명사가 to부정사의 수식을 받을 때, 반드시 to부정사 뒤에 전치사를 써야 한다.

Could you give me **a chair** **to sit on**? 앉을 의자를 저에게 주실 수 있나요?

She has no **friend** **to play with**. 그녀는 같이 놀 친구가 없다.

정답 p.35

## PRACTICE 5

괄호 안에 주어진 말 중 알맞은 것을 고르세요.

**1** I have a lot of (to do homework, homework to do).

**2** It was your (turn to introduce, introduce to turn) your family.

**3** The museum is a good (place to visit, visit to place).

**4** We had no (to talk chance, chance to talk) together.

**5** My family doesn't have any (time to exercise, to exercise time).

**6** He wants a pen (to write, to write with).

**7** She is asking for (something to put on, to put on something).

**8** It's (time say to, time to say) good-bye.

**9** Is there a sofa (to lie, to lie on)?

**10** Is there (anything to read, to read anything) here?

정답 p.35

## PRACTICE 6 [1-6]

우리말과 일치하도록 괄호 안에 주어진 단어를 활용하여 빈칸에 알맞은 말을 쓰세요.

**1** 돌아갈 시간이다.

= It is ___________________________________. (go back, time)

**2** 우리는 먹을 것을 살 필요가 있다.

= We need to buy ___________________________________. (eat, something)

**3** 경주는 방문하기에 멋진 도시였다.

= Gyeongju was a nice ___________________________________. (city, visit)

**4** 아버지는 입을 셔츠를 찾지 못했다.

= My father didn't find a ___________________________________. (shirt, wear)

**5** 인호는 다음 주 금요일에 치를 시험이 있다.

= Inho has a ___________________________________ next Friday. (take, test)

**6** 그녀는 지불해야 할 치과 의사의 청구서를 받았다.

= She got the dentist's ___________________________________. (bill, pay)

## PSS 3   부사처럼 쓰이는 to부정사 PROBLEM SOLVING SKILL

**to부정사는 부사처럼 동사, 형용사 등을 꾸며주는 역할을 한다.**

1. **목적 '~하기 위해서'**

   He **used** science **to help** many people. 그는 많은 사람들을 돕기 위해서 과학을 이용했다.

   I **went** to the store **to buy** a backpack. 나는 배낭을 사기 위해서 가게에 갔다.

2. **형용사 수식 '~하기에'**

   This problem is **difficult to solve**. 이 문제는 풀기에 어렵다.

   The books are **hard to understand**. 그 책들은 이해하기에 어렵다.

3. **감정의 원인 '~하니, ~하게 되어'**

   | glad | happy | pleased | sad | sorry | surprised |
   |------|-------|---------|-----|-------|-----------|

   I'm **glad to see** you. 나는 당신을 보니 기쁘다.

   He was **surprised to learn** that she was deaf. 그는 그녀가 귀가 멀었다는 것을 알게 되어 놀랐다.

4. **결과 '~해서 (결국) …하다'**

   My grandfather **lived to be** 80 years old. 나의 할아버지는 80세까지 사셨다.

   She **grew up to be** a doctor. 그녀는 자라서 결국 의사가 되었다.

## PRACTICE 7

〈보기〉에서 알맞은 표현을 골라 to부정사의 형태로 바꾸어 빈칸에 쓰세요.

| 보 기 | make cookies | play soccer | be 100 years old |
|---|---|---|---|
| | watch with children | be a famous painter | hear the bad news |
| | find a new cure | understand without a dictionary | |

1  He grew up ________________________________.

2  I am sorry ________________________________.

3  She used flour ________________________________.

4  The old man lived ________________________________.

5  The doctors are happy ________________________________.

6  The movie is not good ________________________________.

7  The word isn't easy ________________________________.

8  How many players do you need ________________________________?

정답 p.35

## PRACTICE 8

다음 문장을 밑줄 친 to부정사의 사용에 유의하여 우리말로 해석하세요.

1  What do you want <u>to buy</u>?

➡ ________________________________

2  It is important <u>to set</u> goals.

➡ ________________________________

3  It's time <u>to go</u> to school.

➡ ________________________________

4  We cut down trees <u>to make</u> paper.

➡ ________________________________

5  What can we do <u>to lose</u> weight?

➡ ________________________________

6  His novel was easy <u>to read</u>.

➡ ________________________________

7  To see is <u>to believe</u>.

➡ ________________________________

8  He grew up <u>to be</u> a great father.

➡ ________________________________

# PSS 4  to가 없는 원형부정사



## PSS 4-1  사역동사(let, have, make)＋목적어＋원형부정사

**원형부정사**는 to부정사와 형태상으로 비교해 볼 때 **to 없이 동사원형만**으로 이루어져 있다. **사역동사의 목적격 보어**로 쓰인다.

사역동사 + 목적어 + 원형부정사 '～가 …하게 하다'

|  | | | |
|---|---|---|---|
| • | **Let** | **me** | **show** | you an example. 내가 네게 하나의 예를 보여줄게. |
| • He | **had** | **us** | **clean** | our classroom. 그는 우리가 우리의 교실을 청소하게 했다. |
| • She | **makes** | **her son** | **keep** | a diary every day. 그녀는 그녀의 아들이 매일 일기를 쓰게 한다. |

***cf.*** 준사역동사인 help는 목적격 보어로 **원형부정사 대신 to부정사를 쓰기도 한다.**
I **helped** him (**to**) **do** his homework. 나는 그가 그의 숙제를 하는 것을 도와주었다.

정답 p.36

## PRACTICE 9

〈보기〉와 같이 우리말과 같은 뜻이 되도록 주어진 단어를 순서대로 배열하세요.

> 보 기   나의 학창 시절에 대해 이야기해줄게. (tell, you, me, let)
>
> = <u>Let me tell you</u> about my school days.

1  내가 네 가방을 들어줄게. (hold, let, me)
= ＿＿＿＿＿＿＿＿＿＿＿＿＿＿ your bag.

2  꽃은 사람들을 기분 좋게 만든다. (good, make, people, feel)
= Flowers ＿＿＿＿＿＿＿＿＿＿＿＿＿＿＿＿＿＿ .

3  주의를 기울여 듣는 것은 당신이 사람들을 더 잘 이해하도록 돕는다. (better, helps, understand, you, people)
= Listening carefully ＿＿＿＿＿＿＿＿＿＿＿＿＿＿＿＿＿＿＿ .

**4** 화학 약품은 잡초를 죽게 한다. (weeds, die, make)

= Chemicals ________________________________________.

**5** 그들은 내가 여름 내내 머물도록 해줄 것이다. (me, let, stay)

= They'll _____________________ for the whole summer.

**6** 나는 내 여동생에게 매일 책을 읽게 했다. (read, my, books, had, sister)

= I _________________________________ every day.



## PSS 4-2 지각동사(hear, see, watch, feel)＋목적어＋원형부정사

I **heard** **Mary** **sing**.
나는 Mary가 노래하는 걸 들었다.

He **saw** **them** **cross** the road.
그는 그들이 길을 건너는 것을 보았다.

**지각동사의 목적격 보어로 원형부정사가 쓰인다.**

지각동사 ＋ 목적어 ＋ 원형부정사 '～가 …하는 것을 듣다/보다/느끼다'

| | 지각동사 | 목적어 | 원형부정사 | |
|---|---|---|---|---|
| • I | **heard** | **her** | **play** | the violin. 나는 그녀가 바이올린을 연주하는 것을 들었다. |
| • They | **saw** | **Jack** | **go** | out. 그들은 Jack이 외출하는 것을 보았다. |
| • She | **watched** | **him** | **cook** | dinner. 그녀는 그가 저녁 요리하는 것을 지켜봤다. |
| • We | **felt** | **the house** | **shake** | . 우리는 집이 흔들리는 것을 느꼈다. |

*cf.* 동작이 진행 중임을 강조할 때는 지각동사의 **목적격 보어로 현재분사(-ing)**를 쓰기도 한다.

I **heard** her **playing** the violin. 나는 그녀가 바이올린을 연주하고 있는 것을 들었다.

정답 p.36

### PRACTICE 10 [1-10]

**괄호 안에 주어진 표현 중 알맞은 것을 고르세요.**

**1** She helped us (solving, to solve) this problem.

**2** They saw him (play, to play) football.

**3** We felt the storm (comes, coming).

**4** Tim watched his brother (feed, feeds) the dog.

**5**  Let me (show, to show) you something.

**6**  Mr. Smith made his son (cleans, clean) his room.

**7**  I saw the girl (sells, selling) flowers.

**8**  My mother had me (do, to do) my homework.

**9**  She heard him (calling, called) her name.

**10**  My teacher let me (go, going) home early.

정답 p.36

## PRACTICE 11

〈보기〉에서 알맞은 단어를 골라 빈칸에 쓰세요.

| 보 기 | run   wait   go   shout   bring   swim |
| --- | --- |

**1**  They watched me ________________ out.

**2**  He had his son ________________ a glass of water.

**3**  They heard her ________________ .

**4**  The man made us ________________ for an hour.

**5**  I saw the dog ________________ after me.

**6**  Her parents didn't let her ________________ in the sea.

정답 p.36

## PRACTICE 12

괄호 안에 주어진 표현 중 알맞은 것을 고르세요.

**1**  Let me (write, to write) it down.

**2**  Have you ever learned how (swim, to swim)?

**3**  Did you let him (go, to go) home?

**4**  He made his son (study, to study) abroad.

**5**  Mr. Han had Linda (wait, to wait) for him.

**6**  Have you ever seen a chicken (fly, to fly)?

**7**  I can't hear him (talk, to talk).

**8**  His words make her (to feel, feel) special.

**9**  Can I help you (find, finding) the website?

**10**  I saw a blind man (to walk, walking) on the street.

**11**  I could feel someone (to look, looking) at me.

**12**  I watched the children (play, to play) in the park.

# 중간·기말고사 대비문제

## 1 다음 빈칸에 들어갈 말로 알맞은 것은?

I hope to hear from you soon and ___________ some volunteer work there.

① done
② doing
③ to do
④ to doing
⑤ is doing

## 2 밑줄 친 부분 중 잘못 쓰인 것을 고르세요.

①My hobby is ②go for a ③walk ④In the park ⑤every morning.

## 3 다음 주어진 단어를 우리말에 맞게 배열한 문장은?

• 그들은 그에게 무엇을 사주길 원하니?
= What (want, they, do, buy, to) for him?

① What they want to do buy for him?
② What to want buy do they for him?
③ What they want buy to do for him?
④ What do they want to buy for him?
⑤ What buy they want do to for him?

## 4 다음 중 어법상 어색한 문장을 고르세요.

① We want to live in a world with no war.
② He went to the store to buy a present.
③ I love go shopping with my sister.
④ She likes to wear a skirt.
⑤ They hope to see her soon.

## 5 다음 빈칸에 들어갈 알맞은 말을 쓰세요.

• 그들은 해야 할 많은 숙제가 있다.
= They have a lot of ___________ ___________ ___________.

## 6 주어진 문장의 밑줄 친 부분과 쓰임이 같은 것은?

It is important to focus on your teacher in class.

① It is dark outside.
② It is October 5th.
③ It is used to make cookies.
④ It is not mine. It's Jinu's.
⑤ It is easy to get there by bus.

## 7 다음 중 어법상 옳은 문장의 개수는?

(a) He taught me how to play guitar.
(b) To exercise regularly is good for your health.
(c) My parents don't allow to me stay out late.
(d) Do you know to study a good place?
(e) She was surprised to hear the news.
(f) I had my friend to open the window.

① 2개　② 3개　③ 4개　④ 5개　⑤ 6개

## 8 다음 주어진 문장에서 잘못된 부분을 찾아 바르게 고쳐 쓰세요.

We decided inviting you to the party.

___________ ➡ ___________

**9** 다음 그림을 보고 빈칸에 들어갈 알맞은 말을 써서 대화를 완성하세요.

(1)
Q: Do you know ___________ ___________ ___________ a bike?
A: No, I don't.

(2)
Q: Do you know ___________ ___________ ___________ to the library?
A: Sure. Go straight and turn right. It's on your left.

(1) 자전거를 타는 방법

➡ ___________ ___________ ___________ a bike

(2) 도서관에 가는 방법

➡ ___________ ___________ ___________ to the library

**10** 주어진 문장의 밑줄 친 부분과 쓰임이 같은 것은?

Joining a club also gives you a chance to work as a team and take on responsibilities.

① I hope to visit Paris someday.
② He needs something to write with.
③ She studies hard to get good grades.
④ His dream is to become a scientist.
⑤ Is it possible to finish on time?

**11** 빈칸에 들어갈 동사의 알맞은 형태를 고르세요.

He made me ___________ the house.

① paint  ② paints  ③ painted
④ to paint  ⑤ painting

**12** 주어진 단어를 반드시 사용하여 우리말을 영작하세요.

나는 그녀에게 누구를 초대해야 하는지 물었다. (to / invite)
➡ I ___________________________________.

**13** 빈칸에 들어갈 알맞은 말을 두 개 고르세요.

• 나는 그녀가 수영장에서 수영하는 것을 보았다.
  = I saw her ___________ in the pool.

① swim  ② swims  ③ swam
④ swimming  ⑤ to swim

**14** 주어진 문장의 밑줄 친 부분과 용법이 같은 것은?

We went there to help him.

① Kids love to play with toys.
② I cut down these trees to make a boat.
③ I want something to eat.
④ He started to run fast.
⑤ To read a book is very interesting.

**15** 다음 빈칸에 들어갈 수 없는 것을 모두 고르세요.

She ___________ me to clean the table.

① asked  ② made  ③ told
④ wanted  ⑤ saw

**16** 그림의 내용과 일치하도록 빈칸에 들어갈 말을 〈조건〉에 맞게 영어로 쓰세요.

| 조 건 | • 사역동사를 포함하여 3단어로 쓰세요.<br>• 어법에 맞게 쓰세요.<br>• 우리말 해석: Sam은 Jenny가 그의 전화기를 사용하게 해 주었다. |
| --- | --- |

➡ Sam ＿＿＿ ＿＿＿ ＿＿＿ his phone.

**17** 다음 주어진 문장의 밑줄 친 부분과 용법이 <u>다른</u> 하나를 고르세요.

> They have no chance <u>to talk</u> together.

① We like <u>to play</u> cards.
② Please give me something <u>to drink</u>.
③ They have no money <u>to buy</u> a house.
④ Sumi has many friends <u>to help</u> her.
⑤ He doesn't have any time <u>to exercise</u>.

**18** 다음 우리말과 같은 뜻이 되도록 주어진 말을 알맞게 배열하세요.

> • 밤에 혼자 걷는 것은 위험하다.
> (to, it, alone, walk, at night, is, dangerous)

➡ ＿＿＿＿＿＿＿＿＿＿＿＿＿＿

**19** 다음 주어진 문장의 밑줄 친 부분과 쓰임이 같은 것을 고르세요.

> She plans <u>to</u> visit her grandparents.

① Ann went <u>to</u> the library to study.
② She gave a pencil case <u>to</u> her friend.
③ Jack invited Maria <u>to</u> the party at his home.
④ A dog moves its tail from side <u>to</u> side.
⑤ I took a bus <u>to</u> go there.

**20** 다음 빈칸에 들어갈 알맞은 말을 고르세요.

> He can't decide ＿＿＿＿＿＿＿＿.
> He hopes to find a place with good reviews.

① what to stay          ② how to stay
③ way to stay           ④ where to stay
⑤ when to stay

**21** 다음 중 어법상 옳은 것은?

① Let me to show you my new shoes.
② Scott didn't want going to the party.
③ Mike heard a dog to bark late at night.
④ I decided to staying in Canada for a while.
⑤ The book helps me understand math well.

**22** 다음 밑줄 친 부분의 쓰임이 나머지와 <u>다른</u> 하나를 고르세요.

① She likes <u>to</u> change clothes every morning.
② I want <u>to</u> help poor children in the world.
③ How many players do you need <u>to</u> play soccer?
④ They went there <u>to</u> take part in the recycling campaign.
⑤ Many people went <u>to</u> the park and enjoyed the sun.

## 23 다음 밑줄 친 부분의 쓰임이 <u>잘못된</u> 것을 고르세요.

A: This room is very cold.
       ①        ②
B: Let me closes the window.
   ③      ④        ⑤

## 24 다음 ⓐ, ⓑ에 들어갈 말을 〈조건〉에 알맞게 배열하세요.

John: Every time I see you, you're reading a book.
Betty: Yes, I love reading books. ⓐ(new, interesting, it, characters, meet, be, to)
John: Is reading helpful to you?
Betty: Of course. ⓑ(vocabulary, help, my, to, it, me, increase)

조 건
• 필요시 단어의 형태를 바꿀 것.
• ⓐ, ⓑ에 각각 제시된 단어들은 모두 한 번씩 사용할 것.

ⓐ: ___________________________________

___________________________________

ⓑ: ___________________________________

___________________________________

## 25 다음 문장의 밑줄 친 부분과 바꾸어 쓸 수 있는 것은?

Could you let me know <u>how to produce</u> a map?

① how producing
② how I produced
③ how I should produce
④ how it is produced
⑤ how it has to produce

## 26 밑줄 친 부분과 쓰임이 같은 것은?

Dear Diary,
Today our class talked about our volunteer work in nursing homes. My best friend, Inho sang and danced for elderly people. I played games and served lunch. I was glad <u>to see</u> my friend enjoy doing volunteer work.

① Eric hopes <u>to be</u> a movie star.
② She learned <u>to speak</u> Chinese.
③ He needs water <u>to drink</u>.
④ It is not easy <u>to find</u> a quiet place.
⑤ I go to the supermarket <u>to buy</u> some food.

## 27 다음 그림을 보고 Jim이 지난주에 한 일의 목적을 괄호 안의 단어를 이용하여 〈보기〉와 같이 쓰세요.

보 기
Jim went to the bakery <u>to buy some bread</u>. (buy)

(1) Jim went to the library

___________________________________. (borrow)

(2) Jim went to the post office

___________________________________. (send)

# CHAPTER 8
# 동명사

| Problem Solving Skill | 페이지 | 성취도 | | | | |
|---|---|---|---|---|---|---|
| | | 100% | 99~75% | 74~50% | 49~25% | 24~0% |
| PSS 1 동명사의 역할 | 174 | | | | | |
| PSS 2 동명사를 목적어로 쓰는 동사와<br>동명사와 to부정사 모두를 목적어로<br>쓰는 동사 | 176 | | | | | |

| PSS 3 동명사의 관용 표현 | 페이지 | 성취도 | | | | |
|---|---|---|---|---|---|---|
| | | 100% | 99~75% | 74~50% | 49~25% | 24~0% |
| PSS 3-1 go+-ing | 177 | | | | | |
| PSS 3-2 How[What] about+-ing? | 179 | | | | | |
| PSS 3-3 그 외 관용 표현 | 180 | | | | | |
| 중간·기말고사 대비문제 | 182 | | | | | |

# PSS 1  동명사의 역할

「동사원형+-ing」의 형태로 동사의 의미나 성질을 가지면서 명사 역할을 하는 것을 동명사라고 한다.

| | |
|---|---|
| cook '요리하다' | ➡ cooking '요리하는 것' |
| sing a song '노래를 부르다' | ➡ singing a song '노래를 부르는 것' |
| ride a horse '말을 타다' | ➡ riding a horse '말을 타는 것' |

동명사는 문장에서 주어, 목적어, 보어의 역할을 하고 부정형은 「not[never]+~ing」로 쓴다.

1. 주어

   **Sending** an e-mail is fast. 이메일을 보내는 것은 빠르다.
   **Seeing** is believing. 보는 것이 믿는 것이다.

   *cf.* 동명사 주어는 단수 취급한다.
   **Raising pets is** good for children. 애완동물들을 키우는 것은 아이들에게 좋다.

2. 보어

   Her hobby is **knitting** scarves.
   그녀의 취미는 목도리를 뜨는 것이다.
   My favorite activity is **drawing** pictures.
   내가 가장 좋아하는 활동은 그림을 그리는 것이다.

3. 타동사의 목적어

   We **enjoyed talking** about Korea and America. 우리는 한국과 미국에 대해 이야기하는 것을 즐겼다.
   I think we should **start exercising**. 나는 우리가 운동하는 것을 시작해야 한다고 생각한다.

4. 전치사의 목적어

   I learned a lot **about farming**. 나는 농사짓는 것에 대해 많이 배웠다.
   Thank you **for inviting** me. 나를 초대해줘서 고마워.

정답 p.38

## PRACTICE 1

〈보기〉에서 알맞은 동사를 골라 동명사의 형태로 바꾸어 빈칸에 쓰세요.

| 보 기 | take | draw | play | become | come |
|---|---|---|---|---|---|
| | buy | keep | exercise | join | do |

1 Nari finished ________________ her homework.

**2** Her good habit is _______________ a diary every day.

**3** _______________ regularly is good for our health.

**4** Thank you for _______________ to see me.

**5** Hana is good at _______________ the piano.

**6** Do you mind _______________ the subway?

**7** I like _______________ cartoons.

**8** They talked about _______________ a science club.

**9** My dream is _______________ a teacher.

**10** _______________ a book through the Internet is easy.

정답 p.38

## PRACTICE 2

밑줄 친 동명사의 쓰임과 같은 것을 〈보기〉에서 골라 그 번호를 쓰세요.

보 기
① <u>Talking</u> with him is boring.
② Our goal is <u>winning</u> a prize.
③ She finished <u>writing</u> the report.
④ Cats are good at <u>climbing</u>.

**1** <u>Riding</u> a bicycle is fun. [     ]

**2** I love <u>studying</u> wild flowers and plants. [     ]

**3** <u>Recycling</u> paper is a good idea. [     ]

**4** I'm sorry for <u>being</u> late. [     ]

**5** Her job is <u>selling</u> flowers. [     ]

**6** They didn't practice <u>dancing</u>. [     ]

**7** His hobby is <u>listening</u> to classical music. [     ]

**8** She really enjoys <u>helping</u> others. [     ]

**9** Are you interested in <u>working</u> with children? [     ]

**10** <u>Flying</u> the model airplane is a lot of fun. [     ]

**11** We need clean water for <u>drinking</u>. [     ]

**12** Mike's plan is <u>studying</u> abroad. [     ]

## PSS 2 동명사를 목적어로 쓰는 동사와 동명사와 to부정사 모두를 목적어로 쓰는 동사

---

### 1. 동명사만을 목적어로 쓰는 동사들

| enjoy | finish | give up |
| mind | practice | stop |

+ 동명사

He **enjoys** **visiting** other countries. 그는 다른 나라를 방문하는 것을 즐긴다.

My mother **finished** **cleaning** the kitchen. 나의 어머니는 부엌을 청소하는 것을 끝내셨다.

I don't **mind** **waiting**.

나는 기다리는 것을 꺼려하지 않는다.

Jack **stopped** **eating**.

Jack은 먹는 것을 멈추었다.

***cf.*** Jack stopped **to eat**.

Jack은 먹기 위해서 멈추었다.

stop **eating**

stop **to eat**

여기서 to eat은 '~하기 위해서'라는 뜻의 목적을 나타내는 to부정사의 부사적 용법으로 쓰였다.

### 2. 동명사와 to부정사 모두를 목적어로 쓰는 동사들

| begin | start | continue |
| like | love | prefer | hate |

+ 동명사/to부정사

It **started** **raining**. = It **started** **to rain**. 비가 내리기 시작했다.

She **loves** **reading** a book. = She **loves** **to read** a book. 그녀는 책을 읽는 것을 좋아한다.

---

정답 p.38

## PRACTICE 3

괄호 안의 단어를 알맞은 형태로 바꾸어 빈칸에 쓰세요. (단, 답이 두 개인 경우 둘 다 쓰세요.)

1  He loves ___________________________ abroad. (travel)

2  I don't mind ___________________________ the door. (open)

3  They continue ___________________________ English. (study)

4  We would like ___________________________ a movie. (watch)

5  Kitty kept ___________________________ for her brother. (wait)

6  We decided ___________________________ to the beach. (go)

7 He will not give up ________________________ it. (try)

8 The baby started ________________________ asleep. (fall)

9 Did people finish ________________________ their dinner? (eat)

10 I hope ________________________ Jejudo some day. (visit)

11 I enjoy ________________________ for a walk. (go)

12 I must have a cold. I can't stop ________________________ . (sneeze)

13 Jim expected ________________________ in New York. (stay)

14 I would like ________________________ with you. (exercise)

15 Linda began ________________________ the dishes. (wash)

16 People need ________________________ the rules. (obey)

17 I hate ________________________ the dentist. (see)

18 I practice ________________________ every day. (sing)

19 Cathy likes ________________________ with children. (play)

20 He wants ________________________ a car. (drive)

21 She prefers ________________________ her school uniform. (wear)

22 I plan ________________________ for New York tomorrow. (leave)

## PSS 3 동명사의 관용 표현



### PSS 3-1 go + -ing

go -ing는 '〜하러 가다'라는 의미를 나타낸다.

- go shopping '쇼핑하러 가다'
- go surfing '서핑하러 가다'
- go swimming '수영하러 가다'
- go skating '스케이트 타러 가다'
- go skiing '스키 타러 가다'
- go fishing '낚시하러 가다'
- go camping '야영하러 가다'
- go hiking '하이킹하러 가다'

## PRACTICE 4

〈보기〉와 같이 우리말과 같은 뜻이 되도록 괄호 안의 단어를 알맞은 형태로 바꾸어 빈칸에 쓰세요.

| 보 기 | 그는 어제 야영하러 갔다.<br>= He <u>went camping</u> yesterday. (camp) |
| --- | --- |

**1** 내일 나는 수영하러 갈 것이다.
= Tomorrow, I'll _______________________. (swim)

**2** 우리는 지난 겨울에 스케이트를 타러 갔다.
= We _______________________ last winter. (skate)

**3** 그는 딸과 낚시하러 갈 것이다.
= He will _______________________ with his daughter. (fish)

**4** Alex는 여름마다 서핑하러 간다.
= Alex _______________________ every summer. (surf)

**5** 그들은 새 상점에 쇼핑하러 갔다.
= They _______________________ at a new store. (shop)

**6** 많은 사람들이 그 산에 스키를 타러 간다.
= A lot of people _______________________ on the mountain. (ski)

**7** Paul은 친구와 함께 배를 타러 갔다.
= Paul _______________________ with his friend. (sail)

**8** John은 하이킹 가는 것을 좋아한다.
= John loves to _______________________. (hike)

**9** 우리는 저녁식사 후에 드라이브를 하러 갈 것이다.
= We will _______________________ after dinner. (drive)

**10** 우리는 Kelly의 파티에 춤추러 갔다.
= We _______________________ at Kelly's party. (dance)

**11** 나미는 승마하러 갈 계획을 세웠다.
= Nami planned to _______________________. (ride)

**12** 그 남자들은 함께 사냥하러 갔다.
= The men _______________________ together. (hunt)

**13** 그녀는 아침에 조깅하러 갔다.
= She _______________________ in the morning. (jog)

# PSS 3-2 How[What] about+-ing?

**How about taking** some pictures?
사진을 좀 찍는 것이 어떠니?



**How[What] about -ing?는 '~하는 것이 어떠니?'라는 의미를 나타낸다.**

**How about writing** a letter to her? 그녀에게 편지를 쓰는 것이 어떠니?
= **What about writing** a letter to her?
**How about using** the Internet? 인터넷을 사용하는 것이 어떠니?
= **What about using** the Internet?
**How about going** shopping? 쇼핑하러 가는 것이 어떠니?
= **What about going** shopping?

***cf.*** How[What] about -ing?는 「Let's+동사원형」으로 바꾸어 쓸 수 있다.
**How[What] about going** on a picnic? ➡ **Let's go** on a picnic.
소풍 가는 것이 어떠니?　　　　　　　　　　소풍 가자.

정답 p.38

## PRACTICE 5 [1-10]

〈보기〉와 같이 주어진 문장을 바꾸어 쓰세요.

> 보 기　　　Let's go by bus.
> ➡ How[What] about going by bus?

**1**　Let's help each other.　➡ _______________

**2**　Let's get some rest.　➡ _______________

**3**　Let's keep the promise.　➡ _______________

**4**　Let's have lunch together.　➡ _______________

**5**　Let's play basketball tomorrow.　➡ _______________

**6**　Let's drink a cup of coffee.　➡ _______________

**7** Let's study Spanish.   ➡ ___________________________________________

**8** Let's read the newspaper.   ➡ ___________________________________________

**9** Let's buy some fruit.   ➡ ___________________________________________

**10** Let's sit down on the bench.   ➡ ___________________________________________

정답 p.38

## PRACTICE 6

〈보기〉에서 알맞은 동사를 골라 동명사의 형태로 바꾸어 빈칸에 쓰세요.

| 보 기 | try | eat | play | stay | do | go | visit | write | take | talk |
|---|---|---|---|---|---|---|---|---|---|---|

**1** How about _______________ at Minsu's house?

**2** How about _______________ Mt. Halla?

**3** What about _______________ a picture?

**4** How about _______________ to the movie theater?

**5** What about _______________ a letter to your mom?

**6** What about _______________ about your family?

**7** How about _______________ on this skirt?

**8** How about _______________ your homework?

**9** What about _______________ basketball?

**10** How about _______________ pizza for lunch?

---

## PSS 3-3 그 외 관용 표현

1. **keep[stop]** ··· **from ~ing** '···가 ~하는 것을 막다[방지하다]'

    Heavy snow **kept[stopped]** him **from visiting** his hometown.
    폭설이 그가 그의 고향을 방문하는 것을 막았다.

2. **spend** ··· **~ing** '~하는 데 ···를 소비하다'

    My children **spend** too much time **playing** computer games.
    나의 자녀들은 컴퓨터 게임을 하는 데 너무 많은 시간을 소비한다.

## PRACTICE 7

〈보기〉와 같이 우리말과 같은 뜻이 되도록 괄호 안의 단어를 알맞은 형태로 바꾸어 빈칸에 쓰세요.

> 보 기  그는 파티를 여는 데 많은 돈을 쓴다.
> = He <u>spends</u> a lot of money <u>having</u> a party. (spend, have)

**1** 빗소리는 그녀가 자는 것을 방해했다.
= The noise of rain ___________ her ___________ ___________. (stop, from, sleep)

**2** 그녀는 그 옷을 사는 데 300달러를 썼다.
= She ___________ $300 ___________ the dress. (spend, buy)

**3** 폭설로 나는 외출하지 못했다.
= The heavy snow ___________ me ___________ ___________ ___________.
(keep, from, go out)

**4** Mary는 그녀의 친구들과 이야기하는 데 시간을 보내고 있는 중이다.
= Mary ___________ ___________ time ___________ with her friends. (spend, talk)

**5** 그들은 외식하는 데 50달러를 썼다.
= They ___________ $50 ___________ ___________. (spend, eat out)

**6** 우리는 그가 떠나는 것을 막을 수 없었다.
= We couldn't ___________ him ___________ ___________. (keep, from, leave)

**7** 그는 그 두 소년이 싸우지 못하게 막았다.
= He ___________ the two boys ___________ ___________. (stop, from, fight)

**8** 나는 눈물이 나오는 것을 막을 수 없었다.
= I couldn't ___________ tears ___________ ___________ ___________. (keep, from, come out)

**9** 그는 샤워하는 데 많은 시간을 보내지 않는다.
= He doesn't ___________ much time ___________ a shower. (spend, take)

**10** 나는 그 개가 누구도 물지 못하게 막았다.
= I ___________ the dog ___________ ___________ anyone. (stop, from, bite)

**11** 공을 차는 것은 대부분의 아이들이 뚱뚱해지는 것을 방지할 수 있다.
= Kicking a ball can ___________ most children ___________ ___________ fat.
(keep, from, become)

**12** 나는 매일 두 시간을 내 휴대폰을 사용하는 데 보낸다.
= I ___________ two hours ___________ my cell phone every day. (spend, use)

# 중간·기말고사 대비문제



**1** 밑줄 친 ⓐ~ⓔ 중 바르게 쓰인 표현의 개수는?

Jerry likes ⓐ <u>travelling</u> to foreign countries. He plans ⓑ <u>to visit</u> France this summer. He enjoys ⓒ <u>talk</u> with people from different countries. So, he has been practicing ⓓ <u>speak</u> French these days. Also, he will visit the Louvre and ⓔ <u>seeing</u> the Mona Lisa.

① 1개　② 2개　③ 3개　④ 4개　⑤ 5개

**2** 다음 우리말과 같은 뜻이 되도록 빈칸에 알맞은 단어를 쓰세요.

- Nami는 일주일에 한 번씩 수영을 하러 간다.
  = Nami goes ___________ once a week.

**3** 다음 빈칸에 알맞지 <u>않은</u> 것을 고르세요.

Julie ___________ reading books.

① began　② wanted　③ loved
④ liked　⑤ hated

**4** 다음 중 밑줄 친 부분이 바르게 쓰인 것을 고르세요.

① She kept <u>to draw</u> cartoons.
② <u>Protect</u> nature is important.
③ Thank you for <u>take</u> care of our pets.
④ Have you finished <u>brushing</u> your teeth?
⑤ How about <u>play</u> the violin?

**5** 다음 빈칸에 공통으로 들어갈 단어는?

- She is good at ___________.
- The singer stopped ___________ suddenly.

① sing　　　　② to sing
③ sang　　　　④ sings
⑤ singing

**6** 다음 중 어법상 옳은 것을 <u>2개</u> 고르면?

① Let's not keep make the same mistakes.
② My father is interested in collecting old coins.
③ This app is very useful for improve your English.
④ We look forward to meet you at the conference.
⑤ She expects to travel abroad next summer.

**7** 다음 대화를 읽고, 밑줄 친 우리말을 조건에 맞게 영작하세요.

*A*: I'm nervous about the test tomorrow.
*B*: <u>음악을 듣는 것은 어때?</u> It will make you feel better.
*A*: Okay, I'll give it a try.

| 조 건 | 1. How로 시작하는 의문문으로 쓸 것.<br>2. 5단어로 작성할 것.<br>3. 동명사를 사용할 것. |
| --- | --- |

➡ _______________________________________

## 8 밑줄 친 ⓐ~ⓔ 중 어법상 알맞은 것은?

Nowadays I have trouble ⓐ<u>study</u> Chinese characters. My grandmother is Chinese, so we talk in Chinese. I feel confident that I am good at speaking and ⓑ<u>listen</u> to Chinese. However, writing Chinese ⓒ<u>are</u> another story. I spend so much time ⓓ<u>learning</u> Chinese characters, but there's no progress. I hope that my Chinese writing skills will improve. If you have any ideas to help me study more efficiently, please let me ⓔ<u>knowing</u>.

① ⓐ　　② ⓑ　　③ ⓒ　　④ ⓓ　　⑤ ⓔ

## 9 주어진 문장의 밑줄 친 <u>watch</u>의 형태가 바르게 짝지어진 것은?

- What about <u>watch</u> a comedy show for some laughs?
- My dad spent time <u>watch</u> soccer on TV.

① watching – watching
② to watch – watching
③ watching – to watch
④ to watch – to watch
⑤ watching – watched

## 10 다음 빈칸에 들어갈 단어가 순서대로 바르게 짝지어진 것은?

- The noise kept me from __________.
- He spends much time __________ with his family.

① sleep　　– talk　　② sleeping – talk
③ sleep　　– talking　④ slept　　– talked
⑤ sleeping – talking

## 11 다음 문장에서 <u>틀린</u> 부분을 찾아 바르게 고치세요.

Keep go on this street, and you will get to the subway station.

__________ ➡ __________

## 12 다음 중 어법상 <u>어색한</u> 문장을 고르세요.

① I started exercising.
② They take a walk on weekends.
③ He gave up to climb a tree.
④ Mary likes talking with me.
⑤ We should drink 8 glasses of water a day.

## 13 다음 우리말과 같은 뜻이 되도록 빈칸에 들어갈 알맞은 말을 고르세요.

- 그녀는 일하던 것을 멈추고 그에게 그 소식을 말해주었다.
  = She stopped __________ and told him the news.

① work　　② working　　③ to work
④ was working ⑤ has worked

## 14 다음 글에서 어법상 <u>틀린</u> 부분을 <u>두 개</u> 골라 바르게 고쳐 쓰세요.

Paul is a disabled man. But he doesn't give up learn many things. He can play the violin and swim very well. He continues overcome his limitations.

*disabled: 장애를 가진

(1) __________ ➡ __________

(2) __________ ➡ __________

**15** 다음 빈칸 (A), (B)에 들어갈 말을 바르게 짝지은 것은?

> I sometimes dream about ______(A)______ high in the sky. I hope to go to the stars someday. So I want ______(B)______ an astronaut.

|     | (A)    | (B)      |
| --- | ------ | -------- |
| ①   | to fly | to become |
| ②   | flying | to become |
| ③   | to fly | becoming |
| ④   | flying | becoming |
| ⑤   | flying | become   |

**16** 다음 빈칸에 들어갈 말이 순서대로 짝지어진 것은?

> • He practices ___________ a baseball to get better at it.
> • Let's ___________ a helping hand to elderly people.

① throwing – giving  ② throw – give
③ throwing – give  ④ to throw – give
⑤ to throw – giving

**17** 다음 빈칸에 들어갈 말로 알맞은 것을 <u>모두</u> 고르세요.

> One of my good habits is _________________ _______________.

① to get up early in the morning
② went to school on foot
③ recycled paper, glass, and cans
④ keeping a diary every day
⑤ do enough exercise

**18** 다음 중 문법적으로 옳지 <u>않은</u> 것은?

> Saying no to others ①are difficult. It feels like you're a bad person when you refuse to do something. So, most people ②usually say yes when asked to do a favor. But sometimes, it's not easy ③to do favors for others. That's why you have to learn ④to say no. It will make your life ⑤much easier.

**19** 빈칸에 들어갈 말로 적절하지 <u>않은</u> 것은?

> M: Hey, did you hear that tomorrow is a school holiday?
> W: Yes. I can sleep until late tomorrow! Do you have any plans?
> M: No, I don't. How about you?
> W: Me neither. ___________________
> M: Sure. The movie my favorite actor appears in will be released tomorrow.
> W: Great! Let's set a time to go.

① Shall we go to a movie?
② How about going to a movie?
③ Why don't we go to a movie?
④ What do you think about watching a movie?
⑤ What would you like to do after watching the movie?

**20** 다음 중 밑줄 친 부분과 쓰임이 <u>다른</u> 것은?

> We finished <u>cleaning</u> the room.

① I stopped <u>walking</u> on the street.
② A woman is <u>carrying</u> a box.
③ My aunt loves <u>reading</u> books.
④ He spent a lot of time <u>riding</u> a bicycle.
⑤ <u>Swimming</u> is good for you.

## 21 다음 빈칸에 들어갈 말이 차례로 연결된 것은?

> In every English class, we spend a lot of time ____________ something good about ourselves. We really enjoy ____________ this because we can focus on ____________ our strengths.
>
> *strength: 장점, 강점

① writing – to do – see
② to write – doing – seeing
③ writing – doing – seeing
④ to write – to do – to see
⑤ writing – do – seeing

## 22 다음 밑줄 친 부분의 쓰임이 <u>다른</u> 하나는?

① <u>Living</u> in the mountain must be fun.
② <u>Eating</u> too much is bad for your health.
③ His dream was <u>becoming</u> a famous singer.
④ I think <u>studying</u> English only at school is not enough.
⑤ <u>Watching</u> too much TV is not good for children.

## 23 다음 두 문장의 의미가 같지 <u>않은</u> 것은?

① How about playing basketball after school?
　= Let's play basketball after school.
② My hobby is riding a bicycle.
　= I like riding a bicycle in my free time.
③ I hate to get up early.
　= I hate getting up early.
④ She likes watching soccer games on TV.
　= She likes to watch soccer games on TV.
⑤ He stopped picking up the trash.
　= He stopped to pick up the trash.

## 24 다음 대화의 밑줄 친 부분 중 어법상 바른 것을 고르세요.

> A: What does Giho ①<u>wants to do</u> this Saturday?
> B: He ②<u>want to</u> ③<u>go fishing</u>.
> A: What ④<u>does Sora going to do</u>?
> B: She is going ⑤<u>to went in-line skating</u>.

## 25 (A), (B)의 각 네모 안에서 어법상 바른 표현을 골라 쓰세요.

> Trees are useful to both nature and all human beings. They get rid of bad gas in the air and make the air cleaner. They can also keep rivers (A) from / to overflowing because they hold water and let it go little by little. If there are no trees, we will have floods. Therefore, we have to spend more time (B) to plant / planting trees.

(A) ____________________
(B) ____________________

## 26 다음 중 (a)와 (b)의 빈칸에 차례로 들어갈 말로 알맞은 것은?

> • We ________(a)________ to meet again.
> • Susan ________(b)________ dancing to her favorite music.

　　　(a)　　　　(b)
① expected – enjoys
② planned – decided
③ kept – stopped
④ hope – wants
⑤ gave up – finished

**27** 다음 밑줄 친 ⓐ～ⓔ 중 어법상 적절하지 <u>않은</u> 것은?

> W: How was your swimming lesson?
> M: It was great! But I'm not ready ⓐ <u>to swim</u> in deep water yet.
> W: Don't worry, you'll ⓑ <u>get</u> better.
> M: I just need more time ⓒ <u>to practice</u>.
> W: How about ⓓ <u>swim</u> every day?
> M: That's a good idea. I'll ask my coach for extra lessons.
> W: I'm sure he doesn't mind ⓔ <u>helping</u>.

① ⓐ   ② ⓑ   ③ ⓒ   ④ ⓓ   ⑤ ⓔ

**28** 다음 주어진 단어를 이용하여 우리말에 맞게 빈칸을 채우세요. (단, 필요시 형태를 변화시킬 것)

> • 그는 매일 운동하는 것을 포기했다.
>   (give up, exercise)

➡ He ____________________ every day.

**29** 다음 대화의 밑줄 친 ⓐ～ⓔ 중에서 쓰임이 <u>다른</u> 것 <u>두 개</u>를 고르세요.

> A: Hello. Who's ⓐ<u>calling</u>?
> B: This is Kate. Can I speak to James?
> A: Speaking. What's up?
> B: My computer is not ⓑ<u>working</u> again. Do you mind ⓒ<u>coming</u> over to fix it?
> A: Sorry, I can't. I'm ⓓ<u>doing</u> my homework now. How about tomorrow?
> B: Okay. How about ⓔ<u>meeting</u> at 3?
> A: Great. I'll see you tomorrow.

① ⓐ   ② ⓑ   ③ ⓒ   ④ ⓓ   ⑤ ⓔ

**30** 어법상 바르지 <u>않은</u> 것을 <u>두 개</u> 고르세요.

① She finished painting the walls.
② They practiced to play the guitar.
③ Sally began to walk along the beach.
④ We spent lots of time changing the rules.
⑤ Taking pictures are very interesting.

**31** 다음 중 어법상 올바른 것으로 짝지어진 것은?

> I play with my dog, Jackie, after I finish ______(A)______ my room every Sunday morning. He always wants ______(B)______ with me. And I spend lots of time ______(C)______ on Sunday afternoon.

|   | (A) | | (B) | | (C) |
|---|---|---|---|---|---|
| ① | cleaning | – | playing | – | to read |
| ② | cleaning | – | to play | – | reading |
| ③ | to clean | – | playing | – | reading |
| ④ | to clean | – | to play | – | to read |
| ⑤ | to clean | – | playing | – | to read |

**32** 다음 중 밑줄 친 부분의 쓰임이 <u>다른</u> 하나는?

① I apologize for <u>being</u> late.
② He is <u>worrying</u> about the exam.
③ <u>Making</u> cookies is a lot of fun.
④ <u>Taking</u> the stairs can be good exercise.
⑤ Are you tired of <u>eating</u> the same food every day?

# CHAPTER 9
# 분사

# PSS 1 현재분사와 과거분사의 형태와 개념

**falling** leaves

떨어지고 있는 나뭇잎

**fallen** leaves

떨어진 나뭇잎

「동사원형+-ing/-ed」의 형태로 동사를 형용사처럼 쓸 수 있게 변형한 것을 분사라고 한다.

| 현재분사(-ing) | 과거분사(-ed) |
|---|---|
| a **boring** speech 지루하게 하는 연설 (능동) | a **bored** audience 지루해진 청중 (수동) |
| a **burning** building 불에 타고 있는 건물 (진행) | a **burned** building 불에 탄 건물 (완료) |

정답 p.41

## PRACTICE 1

〈보기〉와 같이 우리말과 같은 뜻이 되도록 괄호 안의 단어를 알맞은 형태로 바꾸어 빈칸에 쓰세요.

| 보 기 | 날아가는 새<br>= a _flying_ bird (fly) |
|---|---|

**1** 죽어가는 나무들

= ＿＿＿＿＿＿＿＿ trees (die)

**2** 실종된 어린이들

= ＿＿＿＿＿＿＿＿ children (lose)

**3** 울리는 전화

= a ＿＿＿＿＿＿＿＿ telephone (ring)

**4** 잊혀진 이야기

= a ＿＿＿＿＿＿＿＿ story (forget)

**5** 잠자고 있는 고양이

= a ＿＿＿＿＿＿＿＿ cat (sleep)

**6** 이름

= a ＿＿＿＿＿＿＿＿ name (give)

**7** 갓 구워진 빵

= freshly ＿＿＿＿＿＿＿＿ bread (bake)

**8** 구르는 돌

= a ＿＿＿＿＿＿＿＿ stone (roll)

**9** 중고차

= a ＿＿＿＿＿＿＿＿ car (use)

**10** 떠오르는 태양

= the ＿＿＿＿＿＿＿＿ Sun (rise)

**11** 미소 짓는 아기

= a ＿＿＿＿＿＿＿＿ baby (smile)

**12** 깨진 창문

= a ＿＿＿＿＿＿＿＿ window (break)

# PSS 2  명사를 수식하는 현재분사와 과거분사

분사가 홀로 명사를 꾸며줄 때는 **명사 앞**에 위치하고, **구**를 이루어 명사를 꾸며줄 때는 **명사 뒤**에 위치한다. '**능동**'이나 '**진행**'의 의미일 때는 **현재분사**를 쓰고, '**수동**'이나 '**완료**'의 의미일 때는 **과거분사**를 쓴다.

| 현재분사 | 능동 | She has an **interesting book**. 그녀는 흥미로운 책을 가지고 있다. |
| | 진행 | He knows **that girl standing** at the gate. 그는 정문에 서 있는 저 소녀를 안다. |
| 과거분사 | 수동 | Jessica is **the actress loved** by a lot of people.<br>Jessica는 많은 사람들에게 사랑받는 여배우이다. |
| | 완료 | There are a lot of **closed stores**.<br>문을 닫은 상점들이 많다. |





정답 p.41

## PRACTICE 2 [1-6]

그림을 보고, 괄호 안의 단어를 알맞은 형태로 바꾸어 빈칸에 쓰세요.

1 

2 

3 

1  She carried the ________________ chair. (break)

2  Look at the kites ________________ in the sky. (fly)

3  The ________________ girl is so beautiful. (dance)

**4**  There are two candles ________________ on the table. (burn)

**5**  Tom bought a ________________ bicycle at a garage sale. (use)

**6**  I want to live in the house ________________ of red brick. (build)

정답 p.41

## PRACTICE 3

괄호 안에 주어진 단어 중 알맞은 것을 고르세요.

**1**  That (singing, sung) bird is a sparrow.

**2**  He told her the (surprising, surprised) news.

**3**  The boy (picking, picked) up trash is my son.

**4**  The money (spending, spent) for Christmas is too much.

**5**  You are like a (walking, walked) dictionary.

**6**  This is the (borrowing, borrowed) pen.

**7**  We took the (dying, died) dog to the pet hospital to save him.

**8**  This is a book (writing, written) in English.

**9**  He is the very person (bearing, born) in Europe.

**10**  Do you know the man (crossing, crossed) the street?

**11**  Water (coming, come) from factories is dirty.

**12**  She found her (losing, lost) daughter.

**13**  Look at the girl (listening, listened) to music.

**14**  Show me the picture (painting, painted) by Yumi.

**15**  Isn't it a (finishing, finished) product?

**16**  I'll keep my fingers (crossing, crossed) for you.

# PSS 3  동사의 활용에 쓰이는 현재분사와 과거분사

| | | |
|---|---|---|
| 현재분사 | 진행형 | be동사와 현재분사가 결합하여 진행형을 만든다.<br>I **am cleaning** this room. 나는 이 방을 청소하고 있다.<br>He **was writing** some letters. 그는 몇 통의 편지를 쓰고 있었다. |
| 과거분사 | 완료형 | have/has와 과거분사가 결합하여 완료형을 만든다.<br>I **have cleaned** this room. 나는 이 방을 청소했다.<br>He **has written** some letters. 그는 몇 통의 편지를 썼다. |
| | 수동태 | be동사와 과거분사가 결합하여 수동태를 만든다.<br>This room **was cleaned** by me. 이 방은 나에 의해 청소되었다.<br>Some letters **were written** by him. 몇 통의 편지가 그에 의해 쓰여졌다. |

정답 p.41

## PRACTICE 4

괄호 안에 주어진 동사를 활용하여 현재분사 또는 과거분사 중 알맞은 것으로 채우세요.

**1** The tablet PC was  broken  by my brother. (break)

**2** I have never ___________________ on an airplane. (be)

**3** We are ___________________ together. (live)

**4** Two trees were ___________________ in her garden last year. (plant)

**5** He is ___________________ lunch with his friends. (eat)

**6** I was ___________________ the piano. (practice)

**7** The street is ___________________ Chester Street. (call)

**8** Her bag was ___________________ on the bus. (steal)

**9** Has she ___________________ for this company? (work)

**10** I have ___________________ a lot of friends. (make)

**11** Some houses were ___________________ by rain. (flood)

**12** Have you ever ___________________ a horse? (ride)

**13** Children are ___________________ snowmen. (make)

**14** I have been ___________________ this work. (do)

**15** Some girls were ___________________ in the rain. (walk)

# PSS 4 현재분사와 동명사의 비교

| 현재분사 | 동명사 |
|---|---|
| 1. 「be동사+현재분사」는 '~하는 중이다'의 뜻으로 진행을 나타낸다.<br><br>She is **taking** pictures.<br>≠<br>그녀는 사진을 찍고 있는 중이다.<br><br>2. 「현재분사+명사」는 '~하고 있는'의 뜻으로 명사를 꾸며주며, 현재의 상태나 현재 진행 중인 동작을 나타낸다.<br><br>a **sleeping** baby 자고 있는 아기 | 1. 「be동사+동명사」는 '~하는 것이다'의 뜻으로 이때 동명사는 주격 보어의 역할을 한다.<br><br>Her hobby is **taking** pictures.<br>=<br>그녀의 취미는 사진을 찍는 것이다.<br><br>2. 「동명사+명사」는 명사의 용도나 목적을 나타낸다.<br><br>a **sleeping** bag 침낭<br>X |

정답 p.42

## PRACTICE 5

밑줄 친 부분이 현재분사면 '현'을 동명사면 '동'이라고 쓰세요.

1  Christmas is <u>coming</u> soon.　　　　　　　[ 　 ]

2  Take a seat in the <u>waiting</u> room.　　　　　[ 　 ]

3  They told us an <u>interesting</u> story.　　　　 [ 　 ]

4  Bring me some <u>shopping</u> bags.　　　　　 [ 　 ]

5  His job is <u>making</u> bread.　　　　　　　　[ 　 ]

6  All <u>living</u> things need air.　　　　　　　　[ 　 ]

7  My hobby is <u>collecting</u> foreign coins.　　　[ 　 ]

8  The leaves are <u>changing</u> colors.　　　　　[ 　 ]

9  My goal is <u>taking</u> nine subjects.　　　　　[ 　 ]

10 He bought a pair of <u>running</u> shoes.　　　　[ 　 ]

11 My mother was <u>waiting</u> for me.　　　　　　[ 　 ]

12 His problem is not <u>coming</u> to class on time.　[ 　 ]

# PSS 5  감정을 나타내는 분사

The game is **exciting**.

그 경기는 흥분하게 한다.

Many people are **excited** about the game.

많은 사람들이 그 경기에 대해 흥분해 있다.

| 감정을 일으키는 -ing | 감정을 느끼는 -ed |

The film was **moving**.

그 영화는 감동적이었다.

His job is **boring**.

그의 일은 지루하다.

The news was **surprising**.

그 소식은 놀라웠다.

Science is very **interesting**.

과학은 매우 흥미진진하다.

It was **disappointing** news to me.

그것은 나에게 실망스러운 소식이었다.

The movie was pretty **shocking**.

그 영화는 꽤 충격적이었다.

Many people were **moved** by the film.

많은 사람들이 그 영화에 감동 받았다.

He is **bored** with his job.

그는 그의 일에 지루해 한다.

We were **surprised** at the news.

우리는 그 소식에 놀랐다.

Ted is **interested** in science.

Ted는 과학에 흥미를 가지고 있다.

I was **disappointed** at the news.

나는 그 소식에 실망했다.

She was **shocked** by the movie.

그녀는 그 영화에 충격을 받았다.

※ **그 외 감정을 나타내는 동사의 분사형**

| | |
|---|---|
| amazing '놀라운' | amazed '놀란' |
| depressing '우울하게 하는' | depressed '우울한' |
| pleasing '기쁘게 하는' | pleased '기쁜' |
| satisfying '만족스럽게 하는' | satisfied '만족스러운' |
| tiring '지치게 하는' | tired '지친' |
| frustrating '좌절감을 주는' | frustrated '좌절감을 느끼는' |
| confusing '혼란스럽게 하는' | confused '혼란스러워 하는' |
| worrying '걱정스러운' | worried '걱정하는' |
| annoying '짜증스러운' | annoyed '짜증이 난' |

## PRACTICE 6

〈보기〉와 같이 주어진 단어를 분사 형태로 바꾸어 빈칸에 쓰세요.

| | |
|---|---|
| 보 기 | bore<br>① The TV program will be boring.<br>② He was bored with reading. |

**1** interest
① I heard some _________________ stories this morning.
② I'm _________________ in farming.

**2** please
① They will be very _________________ with the news.
② The design of this sofa is _________________.

**3** shock
① His death was _________________ to us.
② My family was _________________ at the news.

**4** move
① Kate was _________________ by his letter.
② His words are _________________.

**5** excite
① Surfing is really _________________.
② Sujin is very _________________ about this picnic.

**6** disappoint
① His novel was _________________________________.
② David was _________________________________ because he lost the game.

정답 p.42

## PRACTICE 7

그림을 보고, 괄호 안의 단어를 알맞은 형태로 바꾸어 빈칸에 쓰세요.

**1**

**2**

**3**

4　　　5　　　6

**1** He has studied all day. He feels ________________. (tire)

**2** I was very ________________ by her present. (surprise)

**3** Superman has ________________ powers. (amaze)

**4** Mary got a ________________ result. (satisfy)

**5** I'm ________________. I've lost my wallet. (depress)

**6** Her story is so ________________. (bore)

정답 p.42

## PRACTICE 8

괄호 안에 주어진 단어 중 알맞은 것을 고르세요.

**1** You can see an (interesting, interested) musical here.

**2** He always looks (tiring, tired).

**3** She did (amazed, amazing) things.

**4** Don't be (surprised, surprising) at the result.

**5** I was (moving, moved) by his behavior.

**6** How (shocked, shocking) the accident was!

**7** All of the dishes are (satisfying, satisfied).

**8** The performance was (disappointing, disappointed).

**9** I couldn't find the place because of this (confused, confusing) map.

**10** He went outside because he felt (bored, boring).

**11** My sister was (pleased, pleasing) with her new bike.

**12** This is a (frustrated, frustrating) time for Mr. Brown.

**1** 우리말과 같은 뜻이 되도록 빈칸에 들어갈 알맞은 단어를 고르세요.

> • 깨진 창문 좀 봐.
> = Look at the ___________ window.

① break　② broken　③ breaking
④ broke　⑤ breaks

**2** 다음 빈칸에 공통으로 들어갈 알맞은 말을 고르세요.

> • My cell phone is ___________.
> • I heard the phone ___________.

① ring　② rang　③ rung
④ to ring　⑤ ringing

**3** 어법상 틀린 것을 2개 고르면?

① She had her picture take at the studio.
② I heard someone singing in the room next to mine.
③ They got their car washed while they were shopping.
④ My mom made me cleaning my room before dinner.
⑤ The children watched the birds building a nest in the tree.

**4** 밑줄 친 부분의 쓰임이 나머지 넷과 다른 것은?

① Seeing is believing.
② They are talking about pop music.
③ Climbing a mountain is their favorite activity.
④ My goal is speaking English fluently.
⑤ The topic is keeping pets at home.

**5** 다음 빈칸에 들어갈 말이 순서대로 바르게 짝지어진 것은?

> • I saw a girl ___________ glasses.
> • We enjoyed ___________ at the full moon.

① to wear – looking
② wear　　 – to look
③ wearing – looking
④ wearing – to look
⑤ wear　　 – looked

**6** 다음 대화에서 밑줄 친 surprise의 알맞은 형태는?

> A: You know what? Plants like music.
> B: Really? That's very surprise.

① surprise　② surprising　③ to surprise
④ surprised　⑤ for surprising

**7** 다음 글의 빈칸에 들어갈 말이 알맞게 짝지어진 것은?

> My friends and I went camping. The weather was ___________. After setting up the tent, we saw a strange shadow. We thought it was a deer and chased after it. However, we couldn't find anything. We were ___________.

① amazed – disappointing
② amazing – disappointed
③ amazing – disappointing
④ amazed – disappointed
⑤ amaze　 – disappointed

**8** 다음 빈칸에 들어갈 단어의 알맞은 형태를 고르세요.

> She is _______________ in helping others.

① interest  ② interested  ③ interesting
④ interests  ⑤ will be interested

**9** 다음 주어진 문장의 밑줄 친 부분과 쓰임이 같은 것은?

> <u>Painting</u> brings me joy.

① Jenny is <u>riding</u> her bike.
② The dog is <u>running</u>.
③ What are you <u>doing</u>?
④ I like <u>studying</u> wild flowers.
⑤ Tom is <u>looking</u> for his book.

**10** 두 문장이 같은 뜻이 되도록 빈칸에 알맞은 단어를 쓰세요.

> • I like the boy. He's standing near the window.
>   = I like the boy _______________ near the window.

**11** 다음 중 밑줄 친 부분의 쓰임이 나머지 넷과 다른 것을 고르세요.

① <u>Eating</u> too much is bad for health.
② I enjoy <u>learning</u> different languages.
③ My hobby is <u>listening</u> to music.
④ Does he like <u>playing</u> tennis?
⑤ Look at the girls <u>dancing</u> on the stage.

**12** 다음 밑줄 친 단어를 문맥에 맞게 고쳐 쓰세요.

> She was <u>please</u> because her son won first prize in the contest.

➡ _______________

**13** (A)~(E)의 괄호 안에 주어진 단어를 활용하여 각 문장을 완성할 때, 빈칸에 들어갈 단어들로 바르게 짝 지어진 것은?

> (A) The football match had a _______________ result. (disappoint)
> (B) I got badly _______________ by the sun during the vacation. (burn)
> (C) The nights are _________ longer. (get)
> (D) She felt _______________ about the grade. (depress)
> (E) Is there any cheesecake ______? (leave)

| (A) | ⓐ disappointing | ⓑ disappointed |
| --- | --- | --- |
| (B) | ⓒ burning | ⓓ burned |
| (C) | ⓔ getting | ⓕ gotten |
| (D) | ⓖ depressing | ⓗ depressed |
| (E) | ⓘ leaving | ⓙ left |

① ⓐⓒⓔⓗⓙ  ② ⓐⓓⓕⓗⓘ
③ ⓐⓓⓔⓗⓙ  ④ ⓑⓒⓕⓗⓘ
⑤ ⓑⓓⓔⓖⓙ

**14** 다음 중 밑줄 친 부분의 쓰임이 같은 것끼리 묶인 것은?

> ⓐ What are you <u>drawing</u>?
> ⓑ <u>Drawing</u> carnations is difficult.
> ⓒ I am <u>drawing</u> a cake and candles.
> ⓓ His hobby is <u>drawing</u> cartoons.
> ⓔ She is <u>drawing</u> a dinosaur.

① (ⓐⓑ), (ⓒⓓⓔ)
② (ⓐⓔ), (ⓑⓒⓓ)
③ (ⓐⓒⓔ), (ⓑⓓ)
④ (ⓐⓒⓓ), (ⓑⓔ)
⑤ (ⓐⓑⓒⓓ), (ⓔ)

## 15 다음 빈칸에 들어갈 단어가 순서대로 바르게 짝 지어진 것은?

> • ____________ babies are so cute.
> • Look at those ____________ leaves.

① Slept – falling  ② Slept – fallen
③ Sleeping – fell  ④ Sleeping – fall
⑤ Sleeping – fallen


## 16 밑줄 친 부분의 쓰임이 다른 하나는?

① I don't like being hesitant.
② Her job is taking care of babies.
③ Susan is good at cooking spicy food.
④ Being honest is the key to a good friendship.
⑤ Those two companies are competing against each other.


## 17 괄호 안에 주어진 단어를 알맞은 형태로 바꾸어 대화를 완성하세요.

> A: What are you reading now?
> B: I'm reading a novel ____________ in English. (write)


## 18 밑줄 친 부분이 어법상 옳지 않은 것은?

(정답 2개)

① They crossed the finishing line together.
② Laura was searching the Web for interesting sites.
③ My salary is paying directly into my bank account.
④ Her childhood was spent in Singapore.
⑤ I'm still looking for the losing book.


## 19 다음 빈칸에 공통으로 들어갈 알맞은 말은?

> • I want to buy a ____________ car.
> • He has ____________ his car for 10 years.

① using  ② used  ③ use
④ be using  ⑤ be used


## 20 다음 주어진 단어를 바르게 배열하여 문장을 완성하세요.

(1) 벤치에 앉아 있는 소녀는 나의 여동생이다.

  = ____________________________________

  ____________________________________

  (my sister, sitting, the girl, is, on the bench)

(2) 나무 밑에 주차되어 있는 저 멋진 스포츠카를 봐.

  = ____________________________________

  ____________________________________

  (under, look, sports car, the tree, nice, at, that, parked)


## 21 어법상 맞는 표현으로만 짝지어진 것은?

> Jihun loves ⓐ cooking. He likes ⓑ cook for his family. One day, he invited all his family members to dinner and served them some delicious meat ⓒ roasting with garlic and onions. Everybody felt ⓓ surprising with his food. Jihun also felt ⓔ satisfied to see his family members smile.

① ⓐⓔ  ② ⓐⓒⓔ  ③ ⓐⓑⓒ
④ ⓑⓒⓓⓔ  ⑤ ⓑⓓⓔ

# CHAPTER 10
# 형용사

# PSS 1 형용사

형용사는 명사나 대명사를 꾸며주는 말로 사람이나 사물의 성질, 상태를 나타낸다. 이때 명사의 앞이나 뒤에서 꾸며주기도 하고, 주격 보어나 목적격 보어로도 쓰인다.

There is a **tall** **tree** in the field. 들판에 키가 큰 나무가 있다.

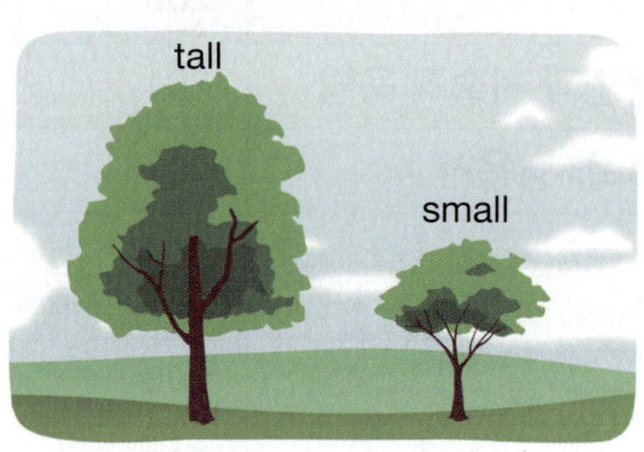


명사 수식 We help **poor** **children**. 우리는 가난한 아이들을 돕는다.

대명사 수식 There is **something strange** with the painting. 그 그림은 뭔가 이상한 점이 있다.

주격 보어 It is **cold** in winter. 겨울에는 춥다.

주격 보어 I want to be **rich** and **famous**. 나는 부유하고 유명해지고 싶다.

목적격 보어 I found **this story interesting**. 나는 이 이야기가 흥미롭다는 것을 알았다.

정답 p.44

## PRACTICE 1

〈보기〉와 같이 우리말과 같은 뜻이 되도록 괄호 안에 주어진 단어 중 알맞은 것을 고르세요.

보 기     그녀는 친절한 소녀이다.
= She is a (kind, kindness) girl.

1 그는 특별한 재능을 가지고 있다.
= He has a (special, specially) talent.

2 이 유리 조각들을 조심해라.
= Be (care, careful) with these pieces of glass.

3 그들은 멋진 시간을 보냈다.
= They had a (wonder, wonderful) time.

4 우리는 문을 열어 두었다.
= We kept the door (open, openly).

5 그것은 도움이 될 것이다.
= It's going to be (help, helpful).

6 아침 식사할 준비는 됐니?
= Are you (ready, readily) for breakfast?

7 너는 좋은 책들을 가지고 있니?
= Do you have (good, well) books?

8 배고프지, 안 그러니?
= You're (hunger, hungry), aren't you?

9 그녀는 나를 행복하게 했다.
= She made me (happy, happiness).

10 Jane은 그 편지에 대해 궁금해했다.
= Jane was (curious, curiously) about the letter.

## PSS 2  형용사의 한정적 용법과 서술적 용법

| 한정적 용법 | **형용사가 수식어로 쓰여 (대)명사 앞 또는 뒤에서 꾸며주는 경우를 가리킨다.**<br>He is a **nice boy**. 그는 다정한 소년이다.<br>We saw **something strange**. 우리는 이상한 무언가를 보았다. |
|---|---|
| 서술적 용법 | **형용사가 보어로 쓰여 주어나 목적어의 상태나 모습을 설명하는 경우를 가리킨다.**<br>**My sister** is **pretty**. 나의 여동생은 예쁘다.<br>형용사 pretty가 주어인 My sister의 상태를 설명한다.<br>The news made **me happy**. 그 소식은 나를 행복하게 만들었다.<br>형용사 happy가 목적어 me의 상태를 설명한다. |



정답 p.44

## PRACTICE 2

밑줄 친 부분의 용법이 〈보기〉의 A와 같으면 A를, B와 같으면 B를 쓰세요.

> 보 기  A. You did a <u>good</u> job!
> B. I'm not <u>good</u> at math.

**1** This subject is very <u>difficult</u>. [   ]
I like <u>difficult</u> puzzles. [   ]

**2** It is a <u>beautiful</u> necklace. [   ]
The weather is <u>beautiful</u> today. [   ]

**3** The market was very <u>crowded</u>. [   ]
I don't like <u>crowded</u> places. [   ]

**4** I'm a <u>perfect</u> person. [   ]
She didn't think he was <u>perfect</u>. [   ]

**5** I have a <u>good</u> memory. [   ]
This coffee tastes <u>good</u>. [   ]

**6** They are in <u>different</u> classes. [   ]
Minsu is <u>different</u> from his brother. [   ]

**7** The cake is so <u>sweet</u>. [   ]
He wants something <u>sweet</u>. [   ]

**8** What a <u>huge</u> place it is! [   ]
They found the palace really <u>huge</u>. [   ]

**9** She can make <u>delicious</u> food. [   ]
That sandwich looks <u>delicious</u>. [   ]

**10** This movie has nothing <u>exciting</u> in it. [   ]
The game was <u>exciting</u>. [   ]

# PSS 3  -thing, -body(one)+형용사

-thing, -body(one)로 끝나는 대명사를 꾸미는 **형용사는 항상 꾸미는 말 뒤에 위치한다.**

Let's do **something good** for others. 다른 사람들을 위해 좋은 무언가를 하자.

Do you have **anything hot** to drink? 마실 뜨거운 것이 있나요?

There was **nothing interesting** on TV. TV에는 재미있는 것이 아무것도 없었다.

There wasn't **anybody famous** at the party. 파티에는 어떤 유명한 사람도 없었다.

***cf.*** something, anything, nothing의 형태가 아닌 단독으로 thing만 쓰일 때는 형용사가 thing 앞
에 위치한다.

He learned many **new things**. 그는 많은 새로운 것들을 배웠다.

정답 p.44

## PRACTICE 3

괄호 안에 주어진 말 중 알맞은 것을 고르세요.

1  She wants (something sweet, sweet something).

2  Do you have (anything else, else anything)?

3  (Delicious everything, Everything delicious) is sold out.

4  Would you like (cold something, something cold) to drink?

5  Can you send (anything interesting, interesting anything) to me?

6  He believes that he is (nobody special, special nobody).

7  We discovered (important something, something important).

8  I don't like (anything slow, slow anything).

9  There is (wrong nothing, nothing wrong) between us.

10  They bought (everything necessary, necessary everything) for their trip.

11  He needs (useful something, something useful).

12  Have you ever met (famous anyone, anyone famous)?

13  You should not put (anything sharp, sharp anything) in your suitcase.

14  You will learn a (new thing, thing new) today.

15  The bride should wear (something old, old something) on her wedding day.

16  There was (nothing cheap, cheap nothing) in the mall.

# PSS 4 수사

## PSS 4-1 기수와 서수

기수는 '개수'를 나타내는 말이고, 서수는 '순서'를 나타내는 말이다. 대개 기수 뒤에 -th를 붙이면 서수가 된다.

(*는 주의)

| 기수 | 서수 | 기수 | 서수 |
|---|---|---|---|
| one (1) | first (1st) * | fifteen (15) | fifteenth (15th) |
| two (2) | second (2nd) * | nineteen (19) | nineteenth (19th) |
| three (3) | third (3rd) * | twenty (20) | twentieth (20th) * |
| four (4) | fourth (4th) | twenty-one (21) | twenty-first (21st) * |
| five (5) | fifth (5th) * | twenty-two (22) | twenty-second (22nd) * |
| six (6) | sixth (6th) | twenty-three (23) | twenty-third (23rd) * |
| seven (7) | seventh (7th) | thirty (30) | thirtieth (30th) * |
| eight (8) | eighth (8th) * | forty (40) | fortieth (40th) * |
| nine (9) | ninth (9th) * | ninety (90) | ninetieth (90th) * |
| ten (10) | tenth (10th) | a[one] hundred (100) | one hundredth (100th) |
| eleven (11) | eleventh (11th) | a[one] thousand (1,000) | one thousandth (1,000th) |
| twelve (12) | twelfth (12th) * | a[one] million (1,000,000) | one millionth (1,000,000th) |
| thirteen (13) | thirteenth (13th) | a[one] billion (1,000,000,000) | one billionth (1,000,000,000th) |

정답 p.44

## PRACTICE 4 [1-34]

다음 빈칸에 알맞은 말을 쓰세요.

| | 숫자 | 기수 | 서수 | | 숫자 | 기수 | 서수 |
|---|---|---|---|---|---|---|---|
| 1 | 1 | one | first | 2 | 2 | | |

| | 숫자 | 기수 | 서수 | | 숫자 | 기수 | 서수 |
|---|---|---|---|---|---|---|---|
| **3** | 3 | | | **4** | 4 | | |
| **5** | 5 | | | **6** | 6 | | |
| **7** | 7 | | | **8** | 8 | | |
| **9** | 9 | | | **10** | 10 | | |
| **11** | 11 | | | **12** | 12 | | |
| **13** | 13 | | | **14** | 14 | | |
| **15** | 15 | | | **16** | 16 | | |
| **17** | 17 | | | **18** | 18 | | |
| **19** | 19 | | | **20** | 20 | | |
| **21** | 21 | | | **22** | 22 | | |
| **23** | 30 | | | **24** | 40 | | |
| **25** | 50 | | | **26** | 55 | | |
| **27** | 60 | | | **28** | 70 | | |
| **29** | 80 | | | **30** | 90 | | |
| **31** | 100 | | | **32** | 1,000 | | |
| **33** | 1,000,000 | | | **34** | 1,000,000,000 | | |

정답 p.45

## PRACTICE 5

**괄호 안의 숫자를 서수 형태로 바꾸어 빈칸에 쓰세요.**

1   Their ＿＿＿＿＿＿＿＿ son is very clever. (2)

2   Today is my brother's ＿＿＿＿＿＿＿＿ birthday. (9)

3   This is his ＿＿＿＿＿＿＿＿ trip abroad. (12)

4   I remember the ＿＿＿＿＿＿＿＿ day of school. (1)

5   May ＿＿＿＿＿＿＿＿ is Parents' Day. (8)

6   Can you explain the ＿＿＿＿＿＿＿＿ line? (40)

7   I'm a ＿＿＿＿＿＿＿＿ grade student at middle school. (3)

8   I was born on November ＿＿＿＿＿＿＿＿. (30)

9   You are the ＿＿＿＿＿＿＿＿ person in the line. (5)

10  There were great changes in the ＿＿＿＿＿＿＿＿ century. (20)

## PSS 4-2 정수

정수는 세 자리씩 끊어서 천 단위로 읽으며, hundred 뒤의 and는 생략 가능하다.

279 ➡ two hundred (and) seventy-nine

3,000 ➡ three thousand

5,473,584 ➡ five million, four hundred (and) seventy-three thousand, five hundred (and) eighty-four

정답 p.45

## PRACTICE 6

다음 숫자를 영어로 읽을 때의 표기법을 쓰세요.

1  4,256  ➡ _______________________

2  36  ➡ _______________________

3  57,403  ➡ _______________________

4  1,052  ➡ _______________________

5  530  ➡ _______________________

6  8,826  ➡ _______________________

7  72  ➡ _______________________

8  601  ➡ _______________________

9  75,419  ➡ _______________________

10  12,000,000  ➡ _______________________

11  5,500  ➡ _______________________

12  713  ➡ _______________________

13  223,600  ➡ _______________________

14  411  ➡ _______________________

15  2,780  ➡ _______________________

16  131  ➡ _______________________

17  6,238  ➡ _______________________

18  256  ➡ _______________________

19  99  ➡ _______________________

20  302  ➡ _______________________

## PSS 4-3 전화번호

1. 전화번호는 한 자리씩 읽는데, 같은 숫자가 나란히 나오는 경우에는 double을 이용하기도 한다. 0은 o[ou]라고 읽는 것이 보통이지만, zero라고도 읽는다.

   935-7304 ➡ nine three five, seven three o four
   703-2269 ➡ seven o three, two two[double two] six nine

2. 지역번호는 area code를 붙여 읽는다. 맨 첫 자리가 0인 경우에는 주로 zero라고 읽는다.

   (02) 828-2932 ➡ **area code zero** two, eight two eight, two nine three two

3. 휴대폰 앞 자리의 경우, 주로 zero라고 읽는다.

   010-1234-5678 ➡ **zero** one **zero**, one two three four, five six seven eight

정답 p.45

## PRACTICE 7

다음 전화번호를 숫자 표기는 영어로, 영어 표기는 아라비아 숫자로 바꿔 쓰세요.

**1** 846-0236 ➡ _______________________________________

**2** 306-4400 ➡ _______________________________________

**3** (02) 428-5597 ➡ _______________________________________

**4** 319-2713 ➡ _______________________________________

**5** 018-2818-3710 ➡ _______________________________________

**6** 274-5515 ➡ _______________________________________

**7** (031) 865-8438 ➡ _______________________________________

**8** 119 ➡ _______________________________________

**9** 2060-4362 ➡ _______________________________________

**10** 963-5908 ➡ _______________________________________

**11** zero one nine, one seven nine two, o o one two ➡ _______________

**12** area code zero six four, double four o, double three one eight ➡ _______________

**13** five nine four, three three eight six ➡ _______________

**14** area code zero four two, seven five four, three eight nine two ➡ _______________

**15** two nine six, four three double o ➡ _______________

**16** one, six double seven, eight two o, double three double two ➡ _______________

**17** one one four     ➡ ______________________

**18** six four six, five nine five eight     ➡ ______________________

## PSS 4-4 분수와 소수

1. 분수 – 분자는 기수로 분모는 서수로 읽으며, 분자를 먼저 읽고 분모를 나중에 읽는다. 분자가 2 이상인 경우에는 분모에 -s를 붙인다.

    1/5 ➡ a fifth 또는 one-fifth         1/8 ➡ an eighth 또는 one-eighth

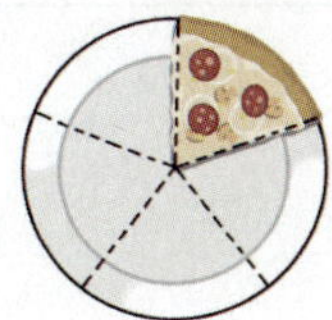 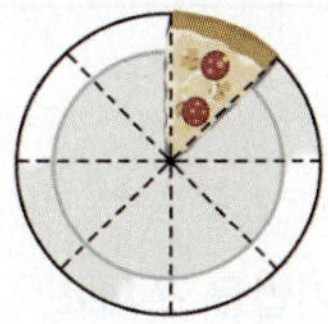

    3/8 ➡ three-eighth**s**         3 2/5 ➡ three and two-fifth**s**

    *cf.* 1/2 ➡ a half 또는 one-half         1/4 ➡ a quarter 또는 one-quarter, a fourth 또는 one-fourth

2. 소수 – 소수점까지는 기수로 읽고, 소수점은 point로, 소수점 이하는 하나씩 따로 읽는다. 소수에서는 0을 보통 zero로 읽는다.

    3.14 ➡ three **point** one four         0.01 ➡ zero **point** zero one 또는 **point** zero one

    *cf.* 소수점 앞의 수가 0인 경우에는 zero를 생략하고 point부터 읽기도 한다.

정답 p.45

## PRACTICE 8

다음 분수나 소수를 숫자 표기는 영어로, 영어 표기는 아라비아 숫자로 바꿔 쓰세요.

**1** 3/4 ➡ ______________________     **2** 1/4 ➡ ______________________

**3** 2.5 ➡ ______________________     **4** 0.31 ➡ ______________________

**5** 2.09 ➡ ______________________     **6** 20 1/3 ➡ ______________________

**7** 2/7 ➡ ______________________     **8** 2/9 ➡ ______________________

**9** 1 1/2 ➡ ______________________     **10** 5 3/10 ➡ ______________________

**11** 0.99 ➡ ______________________     **12** 1.272 ➡ ______________________

**13** seven-fifteenths ➡ ______________________     **14** four-elevenths ➡ ______________________

**15** three and six-sevenths ➡ ______________________     **16** six and one-fifth ➡ ______________________

**17** point six ➡ ______________________     **18** thirty-four point nine ➡ ______________________

**19** three point one two six ➡ ______________________     **20** five and five-sixths ➡ ______________________

## PSS 4-5 시각 I

**일반적으로 읽는 방법 – 시간과 분을 끊어서 읽는다.**

8:05 ➡ eight-(o)-five     8:07 ➡ eight-(o)-seven

8:15 ➡ eight fifteen     8:30 ➡ eight thirty

8:43 ➡ eight forty-three     8:50 ➡ eight fifty

8:55 ➡ eight fifty-five     9:00 ➡ nine (o'clock)

***cf.*** o'clock은 '～시 00분'의 의미로, 정각이 아닐 경우에는 o'clock을 쓰지 않는다.

정답 p.45

## PRACTICE 9

다음 시각을 영어로 읽을 때의 표기법을 쓰세요.

**1**   9:20  ➡ ________________     **2**   3:05  ➡ ________________

**3**   8:25  ➡ ________________     **4**   5:00  ➡ ________________

**5**   10:30  ➡ ________________     **6**   1:37  ➡ ________________

**7**   6:15  ➡ ________________     **8**   11:00  ➡ ________________

**9**   12:08  ➡ ________________     **10**   4:50  ➡ ________________

## PSS 4-6 시각 Ⅱ

'～을 지나서'를 뜻하는 after[past]와 '～ 전에'를 뜻하는 to를 사용하여 읽기도 한다. 일반적으로 past는 (a) quarter나 half와 주로 쓰이는데, (a) quarter는 '15분'을, half는 '30분'을 나타낸다.

8:05 ➡ five **after** eight     8:10 ➡ ten **after** eight

8:15 ➡ **(a) quarter after** eight 또는 **(a) quarter past** eight

8:20 ➡ twenty **after** eight     8:25 ➡ twenty-five **after** eight

8:30 ➡ **half past** eight     8:35 ➡ twenty-five **to** nine

8:40 ➡ twenty **to** nine     8:45 ➡ **(a) quarter to** nine

8:50 ➡ ten **to** nine     8:55 ➡ five **to** nine

## PRACTICE 10

다음 시각을 after[past] 또는 to를 사용하여 영어로 읽을 때의 표기법을 쓰세요.

**1**  9:45  ➡ ___________________

**2**  1:15  ➡ ___________________

**3**  11:55  ➡ ___________________

**4**  4:20  ➡ ___________________

**5**  7:15  ➡ ___________________

**6**  7:35  ➡ ___________________

**7**  8:50  ➡ ___________________

**8**  3:10  ➡ ___________________

**9**  5:45  ➡ ___________________

**10**  1:55  ➡ ___________________

**11**  3:15  ➡ ___________________

**12**  5:50  ➡ ___________________

**13**  3:30  ➡ ___________________

**14**  6:05  ➡ ___________________

**15**  2:25  ➡ ___________________

**16**  11:30  ➡ ___________________

**17**  9:10  ➡ ___________________

**18**  4:40  ➡ ___________________

**19**  10:20  ➡ ___________________

**20**  7:30  ➡ ___________________



---

# PSS 4-7 연도와 날짜

**1. 연도 – 보통 두 자리씩 끊어서 읽는다.**

1988년 ➡ nineteen eighty-eight

1700년 ➡ seventeen hundred

654년 ➡ six (hundred and) fifty-four

***cf.*** 2002년 ➡ two thousand (and) two

**2. 날짜 – 서수를 이용하여 읽는다. 연도와 날짜를 함께 읽을 때에는 월과 일을 먼저 읽고, 연도를 나중에 읽는다.**

9월 5일 ➡ September (the) fifth 또는 the fifth of September

2024년 7월 3일 ➡ July (the) third, twenty twenty-four[two thousand (and) twenty-four]
또는 the third of July, twenty twenty-four[two thousand (and) twenty-four]

***cf.*** 월을 나타내는 말

| | | | |
|---|---|---|---|
| 1월 January | 2월 February | 3월 March | 4월 April |
| 5월 May | 6월 June | 7월 July | 8월 August |
| 9월 September | 10월 October | 11월 November | 12월 December |

## PRACTICE 11

다음 연도나 날짜를 영어로 읽을 때의 표기법을 쓰세요.

1  10월 13일  ➡ __________________________________________

2  2020년  ➡ __________________________________________

3  1592년  ➡ __________________________________________

4  2월 20일  ➡ __________________________________________

5  452년  ➡ __________________________________________

6  7월 1일  ➡ __________________________________________

7  1980년  ➡ __________________________________________

8  3월 31일  ➡ __________________________________________

9  1910년  ➡ __________________________________________

10  12월 15일  ➡ __________________________________________

11  4월 8일  ➡ __________________________________________

12  9월 26일  ➡ __________________________________________

13  1999년  ➡ __________________________________________

14  5월 5일  ➡ __________________________________________

15  2000년  ➡ __________________________________________

16  11월 10일  ➡ __________________________________________

17  1238년  ➡ __________________________________________

18  6월 17일  ➡ __________________________________________

19  1600년  ➡ __________________________________________

20  1970년  ➡ __________________________________________

---

## PSS 4-8 금액

미화는 dollar와 cent를 이용하여 읽고, 원화는 won을 이용하여 읽는다.

> $7.35 ➡ seven dollars (and) thirty-five cents
>
> ₩900 ➡ nine hundred won

***cf.*** $1 = 100¢ (cents)

***cf.*** dollar나 cent는 복수일 경우 -s를 붙이지만, won은 붙이지 않는다.

## PRACTICE 12

다음 금액을 영어로 읽을 때의 표기법을 쓰세요.

**1** $1.25 ➡ _______________

**2** ₩5,200 ➡ _______________

**3** $10.10 ➡ _______________

**4** ₩12,000 ➡ _______________

**5** ₩1,850 ➡ _______________

**6** $0.75 ➡ _______________

**7** $12.30 ➡ _______________

**8** ₩400 ➡ _______________

**9** $3.50 ➡ _______________

**10** ₩4,900 ➡ _______________

# PSS 4-9 온도

**섭씨는 Celsius를 이용하여 나타내고 화씨는 Fahrenheit를 이용하여 나타낸다.**

35℃ ➡ thirty-five **degrees** Celsius

95℉ ➡ ninety-five **degrees** Fahrenheit

***cf.*** 전 세계적으로 지배적인 온도 단위는 섭씨이지만, 미국에서는 주로 화씨를 사용한다. 화씨는 1724년 독일의 물리학자 Gabriel Fahrenheit가 제안한 온도 측정 단위로 물의 어는 점이 32도, 끓는점이 212도가 되어 180단계로 구분된다. 섭씨 35도(35℃)는 화씨 95도(95℉)이다.



## PRACTICE 13 [1-10]

다음 온도를 영어로 읽을 때의 표기법을 쓰세요.

**1** 23℃ ➡ _______________

**2** 50℉ ➡ _______________

**3** 150℃ ➡ _______________

**4** 75℉ ➡ _______________

**5** 350℉ ➡ _______________

6   275℃      ➡  ______________________________________________

7   180℃      ➡  ______________________________________________

8   116.6℉    ➡  ______________________________________________

9   273.15℃   ➡  ______________________________________________

10  420℉      ➡  ______________________________________________


정답 p.46

## PRACTICE 14

우리말과 같은 뜻이 되도록 괄호 안에 주어진 동사를 알맞은 형태로 쓰고, 숫자를 영어로 바르게 바꿔 쓰세요.

1   설탕 1/4컵을 넣어라. (add)

= __________ __________ __________ of a cup of sugar.

2   세종대왕은 1443년에 한글을 발명했다. (invent)

= King Sejong __________ Hangul in __________ __________ - __________ .

3   이 셔츠는 4,900원이다. (cost)

= This shirt __________ __________ __________ __________ won.

4   그녀는 그녀의 오래된 신발을 $18.90에 팔았다. (sell)

= She __________ her old shoes for __________ __________ and __________ __________ .

5   나는 3월 1일 뉴욕에 도착하였다. (arrive)

= I __________ in New York on __________ __________ of __________ .

6   식품 가격이 80.7% 증가했다. (rise)

= Food prices __________ by __________ __________ __________ percent.

7   Elena는 총 투표수의 4/5를 받았다. (receive)

= Elena __________ __________ - __________ of the vote.

8   나는 보통 아침 7시 15분에 일어난다. (get up)

= I usually __________ __________ at a __________ __________ __________ in the morning.

9   Evelyn은 2000년 11월 4일에 태어났다. (be born)

= Evelyn __________ __________ on __________ the __________ , __________ .

10  그는 동전 4,774개를 수집했다. (collect)

= He __________ __________ __________ , __________ __________ and __________
  - __________ coins.

11  물은 100℃에서 끓기 시작한다. (start)

= Water __________ to boil at __________ __________ degrees __________ .

**12** 그의 사무실 전화번호는 (02) 767-4367이다. (be)

= His office number ___________ ___________ ___________ ___________ ___________, seven six

seven, ___________ ___________ ___________ ___________.

**13** 기온이 86℉에 도달했다. (reach)

= The air temperature ___________ ___________ ___________ - ___________ Fahrenheit.

**14** Logan의 새로운 핸드폰 번호는 010-275-9981이다. (be)

= Logan's new cell phone number ___________ ___________ ___________ ___________, two

seven five, ___________ ___________ ___________ one.

**15** 나의 할머니는 1,229,900원을 모으셨다. (save)

= My grandmother ___________ one ___________, ___________ ___________ and ___________

- ___________ ___________, ___________ ___________ won.

# PSS 5 관용적인 수사 표현



## PSS 5-1 tens[hundreds, thousands, millions] of + 복수 명사

**막연히 큰 수를 나타낼 때는 숫자의 단위를 복수형으로 쓴다.**

tens[dozens] of '수십의'/hundreds of '수백의'/thousands of '수천의'/millions of '수백만의'

I have collected **tens of** **coins**. 나는 수십 개의 동전을 수집했다.

**Thousands of** **people** watched the TV program. 수천 명의 사람들이 그 TV 프로그램을 보았다.

***cf.*** 막연한 숫자가 아니라 정해진 수를 나타낼 때는 「기수+hundred, thousand, million」을 쓴다.

**two thousand** **people** 2000명의 사람들

정답 p.47

**PRACTICE 15** [1-10]

〈보기〉와 같이 우리말과 같은 뜻이 되도록 빈칸에 알맞은 말을 쓰세요.

보 기      수백 명의 기자들이 파리에 모였다.

= _Hundreds of_ reporters gathered in Paris.

**1** 매년 우리는 수백만 그루의 나무를 벤다.

= Every year we cut down ___________ trees.

**2** 그는 수십 통의 편지를 가지고 있다.

= He has ___________ letters.

**3** 이 사원은 400년 전에 세워졌다.

= This temple was built ________________________ years ago.

**4** 수백 명의 사람들이 그 뉴스를 보고 있었다.

= ________________________ people were watching the news.

**5** 나는 500장의 우표를 수집했다.

= I've collected ________________________ stamps.

**6** 수천 명의 사람들이 그 도시에 산다.

= ________________________ people live in the city.

**7** 수백만의 어린이들이 이 책을 읽는다.

= ________________________ children read this book.

**8** 나는 어제 수십 권의 책을 기부했다.

= I donated ________________________ books yesterday.

**9** 극장에는 1000개의 좌석이 있다.

= There are ________________________ seats in the theater.

**10** 3백만 명의 노동자들이 거리로 나왔다.

= ________________________ workers went out to the street.

---

## PSS 5-2 every + 숫자

「every+기수+복수 명사」와 「every+서수+단수 명사」는 '매 ~, ~마다'의 의미를 나타낸다.

He goes to the gym **every two days**.

그는 이틀마다 체육관에 간다.

= He goes to the gym **every second day**.

I meet her **every three weeks**.

나는 그녀를 3주마다 만난다.

= I meet her **every third week**.

## PRACTICE 16

짝지어진 두 문장의 의미가 같도록 빈칸에 알맞은 말을 쓰세요.

**1** I call her every fifth day.

= I call her ________________________.

**2** I read a book every second week.

  = I read a book ___________________________.

**3** We practice soccer every third day.

  = We practice soccer ___________________________.

**4** My family eats out every four weeks.

  = My family eats out ___________________________.

**5** They change their car every tenth year.

  = They change their car ___________________________.

**6** She goes shopping every seventh day.

  = She goes shopping ___________________________.

**7** I go to the hospital every fifteenth day.

  = I go to the hospital ___________________________.

**8** The World Cup is held every fourth year.

  = The World Cup is held ___________________________.

**9** He had swimming lessons every two days.

  = He had swimming lessons ___________________________.

**10** Tony goes to the theater every nine days.

  = Tony goes to the theater ___________________________.

# PSS 6  수나 양을 나타내는 형용사



## PSS 6-1  many, much, a lot of

| | |
|---|---|
| many | 셀 수 있는 명사 앞에 쓰여 '많은, 다수의'의 의미를 나타낸다.<br>There are **many books** in the library. 도서관에 많은 책들이 있다.<br>How **many hours** did you watch TV? 너는 얼마나 많은 시간동안 TV를 봤니? |
| much | 셀 수 없는 명사 앞에 쓰여 '많은, 다량의'의 의미를 나타낸다.<br>I don't have **much money**. 나는 돈이 많지 않다.<br>How **much milk** do you drink every day? 너는 매일 얼마나 많은 우유를 마시니?<br><br>***cf.*** much는 주로 부정문과 의문문에서 쓰이지만, too much와 so much는 긍정문에도 쓰인다.<br>There was **so much** trash in the park. 공원에 아주 많은 쓰레기가 있었다. |

<table>
<tr><td>a lot of<br>[lots of]</td><td>셀 수 있는 명사와 셀 수 없는 명사 앞에 모두 쓰이며 '많은'의 의미를 나타낸다.<br>a lot of[lots of] 뒤에 복수 명사가 오면 many가, 단수 명사가 오면 much가 대신할 수 있다.<br>I saw a lot of[lots of] animals in the zoo. 나는 동물원에서 많은 동물들을 보았다.<br>= I saw many animals in the zoo.<br>We don't have a lot of[lots of] food. 우리는 많은 음식을 가지고 있지 않다.<br>= We don't have much food.</td></tr>
</table>

정답 p.47

## PRACTICE 17

〈보기〉와 같이 빈칸에 many나 much 중 알맞은 것을 쓰고, 괄호 안에 주어진 단어의 알맞은 형태를 쓰세요.

> 보 기
>
> There are <u>many stores</u> on that street. (store)
> I didn't have <u>much money</u>. (money)

**1** She has ________________________. (flower)

**2** Do you need ________________________? (water)

**3** She used ________________________. (dish)

**4** I joined ________________________. (club)

**5** I have too ________________________. (homework)

**6** I had ________________________ last night. (dream)

**7** He can make ________________________. (kite)

**8** There isn't ________________________ in the bottle. (juice)

**9** She saw ________________________. (planet)

**10** There are ________________________ in the world. (job)

**11** Do you have ________________________ in summer? (rain)

**12** He visited ________________________ in London. (place)

**13** She didn't get ________________________. (sleep)

**14** I have ________________________. (Korean friend)

**15** How ________________________ is Kate taking? (subject)

**16** Did the idea give her ________________________? (pleasure)

**17** We don't have _________________________ in winter. (snow)

**18** There are _________________________ . (sports activity)

**19** There are _________________________ . (interesting site)

**20** Do you have _________________________ in a trip to China? (interest)

**21** She doesn't have _________________________ with dogs. (experience)

**22** Thanks to his efforts, _________________________ live better lives. (people)

정답 p.47

## PRACTICE 18

빈칸에 many와 much 중 밑줄 친 부분을 대신할 수 있는 말을 쓰고, 괄호 안에 주어진 단어의 알맞은 형태를 쓰세요.

**1** I saw lots of (rock). ➡ many rocks

**2** Did you spend lots of (time) with her? ➡ _________________________

**3** We have a lot of (apple pie). ➡ _________________________

**4** There are lots of (school) here. ➡ _________________________

**5** Do you save a lot of (money)? ➡ _________________________

**6** Ted took a lot of (picture). ➡ _________________________

**7** It doesn't need a lot of (courage). ➡ _________________________

**8** There are a lot of (animal). ➡ _________________________

**9** Susan doesn't drink a lot of (coffee). ➡ _________________________

**10** He told me a lot of (thing) about you. ➡ _________________________

**11** There were lots of (insect) here. ➡ _________________________

**12** They didn't have lots of (fun). ➡ _________________________

**13** We can see lots of (child) there. ➡ _________________________

**14** A lot of (people) came to the party. ➡ _________________________

**15** The car doesn't need a lot of (oil). ➡ _________________________

**16** He asked David a lot of (question). ➡ _________________________

**17** The book doesn't have a lot of (information). ➡ _________________________

**18** People came from a lot of (different country). ➡ _________________________

**19** The players should follow lots of (rule). ➡ _________________________

**20** I didn't get lots of (sleep) last night. ➡ _________________________

# PSS 6-2 (a) few, (a) little

<table>
<tr><td>a few, few</td><td>

**셀 수 있는 명사 앞**에 쓰이며, a few는 '**약간의**', few는 '**거의 없는**'의 의미를 나타낸다.

I have **a few** candies in the bowl.   I have **few** candies in the bowl.

나는 그릇에 사탕이 몇 개 있다. (긍정적 의미)   나는 그릇에 사탕이 거의 없다. (부정적 의미)

a few   few
</td></tr>
<tr><td>a little, little</td><td>

**셀 수 없는 명사 앞**에 쓰이며, a little은 '**약간의**', little은 '**거의 없는**'의 의미를 나타낸다.

There is **a little** juice in the glass.   There is **little** juice in the glass.

유리잔에 주스가 약간 있다. (긍정적 의미)   유리잔에 주스가 거의 없다. (부정적 의미)

a little   little
</td></tr>
</table>

정답 p.47

## PRACTICE 19

우리말과 같은 뜻이 되도록 빈칸에 a few, a little, few, little 중 알맞은 것을 쓰세요.

**1** Bill은 프랑스 단어를 거의 모른다.

= Bill knows _________ French words.

**2** 남은 음식이 거의 없다.

= There is _________ food left.

**3** 몇 명의 학생들이 그것에 동의했다.

= _________ students agreed to that.

**4** 우리는 그것에 관해 거의 문제가 없었다.

= We had _________ trouble with it.

**5** 오직 몇 명의 사람들만이 그들의 음악을 좋아한다.

= Only _________ people like their music.

**6** Jane은 사촌이 거의 없다.

= Jane has _________ cousins.

**7** 타이어 안에 공기가 거의 없다.

= There is _________ air in the tire.

**8** 나는 스페인어를 조금 한다.

= I speak _________ Spanish.

**9** 남은 시간이 거의 없다.

= There is _________ time left.

**10** 몇 년 전에 나는 Milo를 만났다.

= _________ years ago, I met Milo.

## PSS 6-3 some, any

| some | 셀 수 있는 명사와 셀 수 없는 명사 앞에 모두 쓰인다. 일반적으로 긍정문에 쓰이며 '약간의'의 의미를 나타낸다.<br>He wants to buy **some** milk. 그는 약간의 우유를 사기를 원한다.<br>I have **some** clothes to donate. 나는 기부할 약간의 옷들을 가지고 있다.<br><br>*cf.* Yes의 대답을 기대하는 권유나 부탁을 나타내는 의문문에는 some을 쓴다.<br>**Would you like some** juice? 주스 좀 드실래요? |
|---|---|
| any | 셀 수 있는 명사와 셀 수 없는 명사 앞에 모두 쓰인다. 일반적으로 부정문과 의문문에 쓰이며 '약간의'의 의미를 나타낸다.<br>He **doesn't** want to buy **any** milk. 그는 약간의 우유도 사기를 원하지 않는다.<br>**Do** you have **any** clothes to donate? 너는 기부할 약간의 옷들을 가지고 있니? |

정답 p.47

### PRACTICE 20

우리말 해석과 같은 뜻이 되도록 다음 문장의 빈칸에 some이나 any 중 알맞은 것을 쓰세요.

**1** 그들은 그에게 약간의 좋은 책들을 주었다.
= They gave him _________ good books.

**2** 나는 약이 좀 필요하다.
= I need _________ medicine.

**3** 나는 지금 조금의 시간도 없다.
= I don't have _________ time now.

**4** 그녀는 어떤 사진도 찍지 않았다.
= She didn't take _________ pictures.

**5** 여기 약간의 쿠키와 주스가 있어요.
= Here are _________ cookies and juice.

**6** 나는 어떤 남자 형제들도 없다.
= I don't have _________ brothers.

**7** 너는 어떤 생각이라도 있니?
= Do you have _________ ideas?

**8** 오늘 밤을 위한 어떤 계획이라도 있니?
= Do you have _________ plans for tonight?

**9** 우리는 토요일에 어떤 수업도 없다.
= We don't have _________ classes on Saturday.

**10** 커피 좀 드시겠어요?
= Would you like _________ coffee?

**11** 나는 약간의 종이와 연필이 필요하다.
= I need _________ paper and pencils.

**12** 너는 휴식을 좀 취해야 한다.
= You should get _________ rest.

**13** 그는 오늘 돈을 하나도 쓰지 않았다.
= He didn't spend _________ money today.

**14** 이 공원에 어떤 동물이라도 있나요?
= Are there _________ animals in this park?

**15** 아이스크림을 좀 드시겠습니까?
= Would you like to have _________ ice cream?

**16** 그녀는 그녀의 지갑에 약간의 지폐를 넣었다.
= She put _________ bills in her wallet.

## PSS 6-4 not ~ any = no

**not ~ any는 no로** 바꾸어 쓸 수 있으며 **'조금도[아무(것)도] ~ 없는'**의 의미를 나타낸다.

There are**n't any** kids at the court. 코트에는 아이들이 아무도 없다.
= There are **no** kids at the court.
He does**n't** know **anything** about it. 그는 그것에 관해 조금도 모른다.
= He knows **nothing** about it.

정답 p.48

## PRACTICE 21

〈보기〉와 같이 짝지어진 두 문장의 의미가 같도록 빈칸을 채우세요.

| 보 기 | I don't have any time.<br>= I have <u>no</u> time. |
| --- | --- |

**1** There aren't any seats now.

= There are _________________ seats now.

**2** They didn't see anybody.

= They saw _________________.

**3** I don't have anything to say.

= I have _________________ to say.

**4** There isn't anyone in the room.

= There is _________________ _________________ in the room.

**5** My car isn't anywhere around here.

= My car is _________________ around here.

**6** You don't need any special ways.

= You need _________________ special ways.

**7** I couldn't see anybody in this house.

= I could see _________________ in this house.

**8** There isn't anything wrong.

= There is _________________ wrong.

**9** I cannot go anywhere without the shoes.

= I can go _________________ without the shoes.

**10** We won't have any chance to talk together.

= We will have _________________ chance to talk together.

# 중간·기말고사 대비문제 📝





**1** 다음 중 짝지어진 단어의 성격이 나머지 넷과 다른 것은?

① happiness - happy    ② beauty - beautiful
③ sadness - sad    ④ friend - friendly
⑤ pretty - prettily

**2** 다음 빈칸에 들어갈 수 없는 것은?

> Jack is a __________ boy.

① nice    ② smart
③ very    ④ handsome
⑤ famous

**3** 다음 중 서수의 철자 표기가 바르지 않은 것을 고르세요.

① ninth    ② third
③ hundredth    ④ twelveth
⑤ eighth

**4** 다음 빈칸에 들어갈 수 없는 것은?

> There are __________ grapes in the basket.

① a lot of    ② much    ③ many
④ lots of    ⑤ some

**5** 다음 밑줄 친 nice의 쓰임이 다른 하나는?

① He is a nice boy.
② We had a nice holiday.
③ That is a nice picture.
④ The man is really nice and kind.
⑤ This is a nice movie.

**6** 〈보기〉와 같이 다음 두 문장이 같은 뜻이 되도록 빈칸에 알맞은 말을 쓰세요.

> 보 기    This story is really interesting.
>      = This is a really interesting story.

• The girl is very pretty.
   = She is __________________.

**7** 다음 짝지어진 단어가 바르게 쓰이지 않은 것은?

① one – first    ② two – second
③ four – forth    ④ fifteen – fifteenth
⑤ twenty – twentieth

**8** 다음 ⓐ~ⓔ 중 밑줄 친 단어의 쓰임이 옳은 것을 있는 대로 고른 것은?

> ⓐ Don't seat on the wet grass.
> ⓑ He doesn't have many water.
> ⓒ The kids laugh happy in the park.
> ⓓ Let's put the dirty clothes in the basket.
> ⓔ She was so tired that she fell asleep on the bus.

① ⓐⓓ    ② ⓑⓓ    ③ ⓒⓔ
④ ⓒⓓⓔ    ⑤ ⓓⓔ

**9** 다음 우리말과 같은 뜻이 되도록 빈칸에 알맞은 단어를 쓰세요.

• 9월은 한 해의 아홉 번째 달이다.
   = September is the __________ month of the year.

**10** 다음 숫자를 영어로 읽은 것 중 옳지 <u>않은</u> 것은?

① 25 = twenty-five

② 345 = three hundred and forty-five

③ 1,251 = one two hundred fifty-one

④ 20,000 = twenty thousand

⑤ 32,903 = thirty-two thousand, nine hundred and three

**11** 다음 문장의 밑줄 친 부분과 바꾸어 쓸 수 있는 단어를 고르세요.

> She doesn't drink <u>a lot of</u> coffee.

① many  ② much

③ few  ④ little

⑤ a few

**12** 다음 중 시간 표현이 <u>잘못된</u> 것은?

① 9:15 = a quarter past nine

② 7:50 = seven fifty

③ 10:30 = half to eleven

④ 11:00 = eleven o'clock

⑤ 1:10 = ten to one

**13** 다음 밑줄 친 부분을 영어로 바르게 옮긴 것은?

> A: Can you come to my birthday party?
> B: Of course. When is it?
> A: It's <u>7월 23일</u>.

① July twenty-three

② July twenty-third

③ July twentieth-third

④ June twenty-three

⑤ June twenty-third

**14** 〈보기〉의 밑줄 친 round와 뜻이 같은 문장끼리 짝지어진 것은?

> 보 기 | I broke the <u>round</u> plate.

> ⓐ This <u>round</u> table looks nice.
> ⓑ He played a <u>round</u> of golf.
> ⓒ Soccer is played with a <u>round</u> ball.
> ⓓ How many <u>rounds</u> have passed?
> ⓔ We went <u>round</u> the school.
> ⓕ She won the game in the first <u>round</u>.

① ⓐ, ⓒ  ② ⓑ, ⓔ  ③ ⓑ, ⓕ

④ ⓒ, ⓔ  ⑤ ⓓ, ⓕ

**15** 다음 문장과 바꾸어 쓸 수 있는 표현을 고르세요.

> It's a quarter to eleven.

① It's ten fifteen.  ② It's eleven forty-five.

③ It's ten forty-five.  ④ It's twelve fifteen.

⑤ It's eleven fifteen.

**16** 다음 대화를 읽고 괄호 안의 말을 바르게 배열하여 마지막 문장을 완성하세요.

> A: I skipped breakfast this morning.
> B: Oh, I guess you are very hungry now.
> A: Of course.
>   (I, delicious, something, for, want, lunch)

➡ ______________________________________

**17** 주어진 우리말과 같은 뜻이 되도록 빈칸에 알맞은 말을 쓰세요.

> • 수백 명의 사람들이 그 행사에 참가했다.
>   = ______________ ______________ people
>   joined the event.

## 18 다음 두 문장이 같은 뜻이 되도록 괄호 안의 숫자를 알맞은 형태로 쓰세요.

> • It is good to go to the dentist every
>   ⓐ _____(6)_____ month.
> = It is good to go to the dentist every
>   ⓑ _____(6)_____ months.

ⓐ ________________   ⓑ ________________

## 19 다음 문장의 밑줄 친 부분과 바꾸어 쓸 수 있는 단어를 고르세요.

> You can see a lot of animals in the zoo.

① some         ② any
③ many         ④ much
⑤ one

## 20 다음 우리말과 뜻이 같도록 문장에서 틀린 부분을 찾아 바르게 고쳐 쓰세요.

> • 미국의 아버지날은 6월 세 번째 일요일이다.
> = Father's Day is the three Sunday in
>   June in America.

________________  ➡  ________________

## 21 다음 글에서 틀린 곳을 찾아 그 번호를 쓰고, 바르게 고치세요.

> We will ①make a cheesecake. So we ②need
> cheese and ③butter. But we ④don't need
> ⑤some apples.

(   ) ________________  ➡  ________________

## 22 밑줄 친 부분의 쓰임이 어법상 어색한 것은?

① She drank a lot of milk.
② There are many rules at school.
③ A lots of people go skiing in winter.
④ Can I have some chicken?
⑤ He has two tomatoes for lunch.

## 23 다음 시각을 나타내는 표현 중에서 같은 시각이 아닌 것을 고르세요.

① It is five thirty. = It is half past five.
② It is six forty-five. = It is fifteen to six.
③ It is nine fifteen. − It is a quarter past nine.
④ It is eight fifty-five. = It is five to nine.
⑤ It is three twenty. = It is twenty after three.

## 24 다음 두 문장이 같은 뜻이 되도록 빈칸에 들어갈 알맞은 단어를 쓰세요.

> • They don't have any money.
> = They have ___________ money.

## 25 다음 우리말과 같은 뜻이 되도록 빈칸에 알맞은 단어를 쓰세요.

> • 우리는 내년에 2학년이 될 것이다.
> = We'll be in the ___________ grade next
>   year.

① This soup smells delicious.
② Peter's jokes sounded silly.
③ Her apple jam tastes sweet.
④ You look lovely in that dress.
⑤ My mom's blanket feels softly.

**27** 다음 밑줄 친 부분의 쓰임이 <u>잘못된</u> 것은?

① They played <u>some</u> games.
② I want <u>some</u> more food.
③ Please give me <u>some</u> water.
④ He has <u>some</u> friends in Japan.
⑤ We don't need <u>some</u> special ideas.

**28** 다음 글의 빈칸에 들어갈 가장 알맞은 말은?

> I studied hard last night, but now I can't remember __________ .

① somebody
② nobody
③ anyone
④ nothing
⑤ anything

**29** 다음을 영어로 읽은 것 중 옳지 <u>않은</u> 것은?

① 847-6637
  = eight four seven, double six three seven
② 6시 45분
  = a quarter to seven
③ 2006년 11월 19일
  = November nineteenth, two thousand six
④ $2.39
  = two dollar and thirty-nine cent
⑤ 120℉
  = one hundred twenty degrees Fahrenheit

**30** 다음 중 분수 표현이 바른 것은?

① 1/5 = one-five
② 3/5 = third-fifths
③ 4/7 = four-sevenths
④ 5/6 = five-sixth
⑤ 3 1/8 = three and one-eight

**31** 다음 빈칸에 들어갈 알맞은 말로 짝지어진 것은?

> • Nathan was a (A) ______________ doctor before becoming a writer.
> • The party was a great (B) ______________ .

|     | (A)        |   | (B)          |
| --- | ---------- | - | ------------ |
| ①   | success    | – | successful   |
| ②   | success    | – | successfully |
| ③   | successful | – | successfully |
| ④   | successful | – | success      |
| ⑤   | succeed    | – | success      |

**32** 다음 그림을 보고 알맞은 대답을 완성하세요.

(1)

A: What time is it?
B: ________________________________
(단, quarter, past를 사용할 것.)

(2)

A: What time is it?
B: ________________________________
(단, quarter를 사용할 것.)

## 33 다음 빈칸에 들어갈 단어가 순서대로 짝지어진 것은?

> *A*: Excuse me, do you have __________ problems?
> *B*: Yes, I have __________ problems. Could you help me?

① any – any
② any – some
③ no – some
④ some – any
⑤ some – one

## 34 (A)~(D)의 빈칸 어디에도 들어갈 수 <u>없는</u> 단어는?

> (A) The math quiz was too __________ for me.
> (B) Your baby sister is so __________ when she smiles.
> (C) It's very __________ outside.
> (D) That movie was so __________ that I cried.

① cute
② sad
③ free
④ hard
⑤ sunny

## 35 다음 밑줄 친 우리말과 같은 뜻이 되도록 빈칸에 들어갈 알맞은 표현을 고르세요.

> *A*: What are you going to do this weekend?
> *B*: <u>특별한 일 없어.</u> What's up?
> *A*: I'm going to play basketball with some friends. Why don't you come?

① I don't know.
② Special nothing.
③ Nothing special.
④ I have something special.
⑤ I don't have nothing.

## 36 다음 중 어법상 <u>어색한</u> 것을 고르세요.

① He has a few friends.
② He has many friends.
③ He has a lot of friends.
④ He has a little friends.
⑤ He has lots of friends.

## 37 다음 문장의 밑줄 친 <u>sound</u>와 의미가 같은 것을 고르세요.

> The young man has a <u>sound</u> mind.

① The church bell <u>sounded</u> at eleven o'clock.
② That <u>sounds</u> very interesting.
③ The violin can make various <u>sounds</u>.
④ He is <u>sound</u> in body and spirit.
⑤ We heard a strange <u>sound</u> from the next room.

## 38 다음 중 어법상 <u>맞는</u> 문장은?

① I put a little soups in the bowl.
② I drink much coffees every day.
③ I put lots of sugar in my tea.
④ How many book do you have?
⑤ I got a little moneys from my grandmother.

## 39 두 문장의 의미가 같도록 빈칸에 알맞은 말을 쓰세요.

> • I don't have any houses.
>   = I __________ __________ __________.

 다음 빈칸에 들어갈 말이 순서대로 짝지어진 것은?

> • There are ____________ books in the library.
> • There is too ____________ sand in the playground.

① few    – many
② many – few
③ many – much
④ much – many
⑤ few    – few

**41** 다음 중 빈칸에 들어갈 말이 밑줄 친 부분과 같은 것은?

> He had to climb <u>many</u> stairs to reach the top of the slide.

① Does Jerry drink ____________ milk?
② There isn't ____________ water on this island.
③ There are ____________ cafeterias here.
④ I have so ____________ money.
⑤ People throw away too ____________ trash in the sea.

**42** 다음 ⓐ~ⓓ 중 어법상 잘못된 두 개의 문장을 골라 바르게 고쳐 쓰세요. (반드시 완전한 영어 문장으로 답하세요.)

> ⓐ There are a lot of children in the playground.
> ⓑ There are much pencils on the desk.
> ⓒ There's too many garbage in the park.
> ⓓ They don't have a lot of time to wait for you.

(1) _______________________________________

(2) _______________________________________

**43** 다음 ⓐ~ⓒ에 들어갈 말이 알맞게 짝지어진 것은?

> • I got ____________ⓐ____________ advice from him.
> • His dogs deliver ____________ⓑ____________ things to the neighborhood.
> • We have ____________ⓒ____________ snow in winter.

　　ⓐ　　　ⓑ　　　ⓒ
① some – many – few
② any    – much – little
③ some – many – little
④ any    – many – few
⑤ some – much – little

**44** 다음 글을 읽고 틀린 부분 세 가지를 찾아 바르게 고쳐 쓰세요.

> My friend Bob loves soccer. He goes to the soccer stadium every two week. He likes to watch soccer games there. Yesterday, Bob and I went to the stadium. About five hundreds people were watching the game. About three-forth of them cheered for the home team.

(1) ____________ ➡ ____________
(2) ____________ ➡ ____________
(3) ____________ ➡ ____________

# CHAPTER 11
# 부사

# PSS 1 부사의 형태

## PSS 1-1 부사의 역할과 형용사를 부사로 만드는 법

부사는 '천천히, 매우'처럼 행동이나 일의 상태, 특징을 설명하는 말이다. 부사는 명사를 제외한 동사, 형용사, 다른 부사, 문장 전체를 수식한다.

| | |
|---|---|
| 동사 수식 | The car **moved slowly**. 그 차는 느리게 움직였다. |
| 형용사 수식 | He is a **very brave** man. 그는 매우 용감한 남자이다. |
| 다른 부사 수식 | She studied **really hard**. 그녀는 정말로 열심히 공부했다. |
| 문장 전체 수식 | **Luckily, his son passed the exam**. 운 좋게도, 그의 아들은 시험에 통과했다. |

형용사를 부사로 만드는 법은 다음과 같다.

| | | |
|---|---|---|
| 대부분의 경우 | -ly | quick 빠른 – quick**ly** 빠르게<br>kind 친절한 – kind**ly** 친절하게<br>clear 맑은 – clear**ly** 맑게<br>nice 멋진, 훌륭한 – nice**ly** 멋지게, 훌륭하게 |
| 자음+y로 끝나는 경우 | y를 i로 바꾸고 -ly | easy 쉬운 – eas**ily** 쉽게<br>happy 행복한 – happ**ily** 행복하게<br>lucky 운이 좋은 – luck**ily** 운 좋게<br>angry 화난 – angr**ily** 화내어 |

정답 p.50

## PRACTICE 1

다음 밑줄 친 우리말에 유의하여 괄호 안에 들어갈 알맞은 말을 고르세요.

1 그녀는 매우 <u>친절한</u> 선생님이다.

➡ She is a very (kind / kindly) teacher.

2 우리는 <u>기쁘게</u> 우리의 선물 상자를 열었다.

➡ We (glad / gladly) opened our gift box.

3 그녀의 목소리는 매우 <u>크다</u>.

➡ Her voice is very (loud / loudly).

**4** 그는 그의 <u>새로운</u> 스마트폰을 <u>자랑스럽게</u> 보여주었다.

➡ He (proud / proudly) showed his (new / newly) smartphone.

**5** 그녀는 <u>몹시</u> 아팠다.

➡ She was (terribly / terrible) sick.

**6** 문이 <u>조용히</u> 열렸고 그녀가 들어왔다.

➡ The door opened (quiet / quietly) and she came in.

**7** <u>운 좋게도</u>, 나는 그 경기를 <u>쉽게</u> 이길 수 있었다.

➡ (Luckily / Lucky), I could win the game (easily / easy).

**8** 나는 그의 이야기를 <u>주의 깊게</u> 들었다.

➡ I listened (careful / carefully) to his story.

**9** 그것은 <u>아름다운</u> 꽃이다.

➡ That is a (beautifully / beautiful) flower.

**10** <u>갑자기</u>, 비가 <u>심하게</u> 내리기 시작했다.

➡ (Suddenly / Sudden), it started to rain (heavy / heavily).

정답 p.50

## PRACTICE 2

다음 형용사의 부사형을 쓰세요.

| | | | | |
|---|---|---|---|---|
| **1** nice | ➡ _______ | | **2** beautiful | ➡ _______ |
| **3** happy | ➡ _______ | | **4** clear | ➡ _______ |
| **5** different | ➡ _______ | | **6** kind | ➡ _______ |
| **7** careful | ➡ _______ | | **8** heavy | ➡ _______ |
| **9** usual | ➡ _______ | | **10** real | ➡ _______ |
| **11** quick | ➡ _______ | | **12** glad | ➡ _______ |
| **13** lucky | ➡ _______ | | **14** surprising | ➡ _______ |
| **15** pretty | ➡ _______ | | **16** strong | ➡ _______ |
| **17** dangerous | ➡ _______ | | **18** noisy | ➡ _______ |
| **19** loud | ➡ _______ | | **20** easy | ➡ _______ |
| **21** new | ➡ _______ | | **22** regular | ➡ _______ |
| **23** slow | ➡ _______ | | **24** sad | ➡ _______ |
| **25** brave | ➡ _______ | | **26** great | ➡ _______ |
| **27** special | ➡ _______ | | **28** quiet | ➡ _______ |
| **29** similar | ➡ _______ | | **30** bad | ➡ _______ |

## PRACTICE 3

〈보기〉와 같이 우리말과 같은 뜻이 되도록 괄호 안에 주어진 단어 중 알맞은 것을 고르세요.

| 보 기 | 너는 조심해서 길을 건너야 한다. = You should cross the streets (careful, ⓒarefully). |
| --- | --- |

1 Susan은 그 소식에 행복하지 않았다. = Susan didn't feel (happy, happily) at the news.

2 나는 대개 학교에 걸어간다. = I (usual, usually) walk to school.

3 그녀의 음식은 아주 맛있었다. = Her food tasted (great, greatly).

4 나는 너의 파티를 정말로 즐겼어. = I (real, really) enjoyed your party.

5 시험은 쉽지 않을 거야. = The test won't be (easy, easily).

6 그 선생님은 갑자기 나타나셨다. = The teacher appeared (sudden, suddenly).

7 지하철은 안전하고 빠르다. = The subway is (safe, safely) and fast.

8 차는 우리의 삶을 놀랍게 변화시켰다. = Cars changed our lives (surprising, surprisingly).

9 이것은 중요한 정보이다. = This is (important, importantly) information.

10 그는 문을 조용히 열었다. = He opened the door (quiet, quietly).

11 그는 슬프게 고개를 저었다. = He shook his head (sad, sadly).

12 군인들은 용감하게 적에 맞서 싸웠다. = The soldiers (bravely, brave) fought against the enemy.

---

## PSS 1-2 형용사와 형태가 같은 부사

1. late '늦은, 늦게'

   **형용사** I was **late** for school this morning. 나는 오늘 아침에 학교에 늦었다.

   **부사** She got up **late** this morning. 그녀는 오늘 아침에 늦게 일어났다.

2. early '이른, 일찍'

   **형용사** The **early** bird catches the worm. 일찍 일어나는 새가 벌레를 잡는다.

   **부사** He gets up **early** in the morning. 그는 아침에 일찍 일어난다.

3. hard '어려운, 열심히'

   **형용사** English is **hard** for me. 영어는 나에게 어렵다.

   **부사** I'm working **hard**. 나는 열심히 일하고 있다.

   ***cf.*** 그 외 형용사와 부사의 형태가 같은 단어들

   fast 빠른, 빨리   long 긴, 길게   low 낮은, 낮게   high 높은, 높게   daily 매일의, 매일

   pretty 귀여운, 꽤

## PRACTICE 4

밑줄 친 부분의 쓰임이 〈보기〉의 A와 같으면 A를, B와 같으면 B를 쓰세요.

| 보 기 | |
|---|---|
| | A. I don't eat <u>fast</u> food. |
| | B. The train goes very <u>fast</u>. |

**1** I'm <u>late</u> again. [ ]
Don't go out too <u>late</u>. [ ]

**2** The hospital opens <u>early</u>. [ ]
It is too <u>early</u> now. [ ]

**3** Everybody wants to live <u>long</u>. [ ]
There's a <u>long</u> line. [ ]

**4** The students studied very <u>hard</u>. [ ]
It is <u>hard</u> to work on the farm. [ ]

**5** We sell them at a <u>low</u> price. [ ]
The bird is flying <u>low</u>. [ ]

**6** He often drives <u>fast</u>. [ ]
I'm a <u>fast</u> runner. [ ]

**7** A bottle of milk comes <u>daily</u>. [ ]
It's a <u>daily</u> paper. [ ]

**8** I have a <u>high</u> fever. [ ]
The kite is flying <u>high</u>. [ ]



# PSS 2 빈도부사



## PSS 2-1 빈도부사의 종류와 의미

==빈도부사==란 어떤 일의 ==빈도, 즉 횟수나 정도를 나타내는 부사==를 말한다.

| | |
|---|---|
| **always** '항상' | **usually** '보통, 대개' **often** '자주, 종종' |
| **sometimes** '때때로' | **never** '결코 ~ 아닌' |

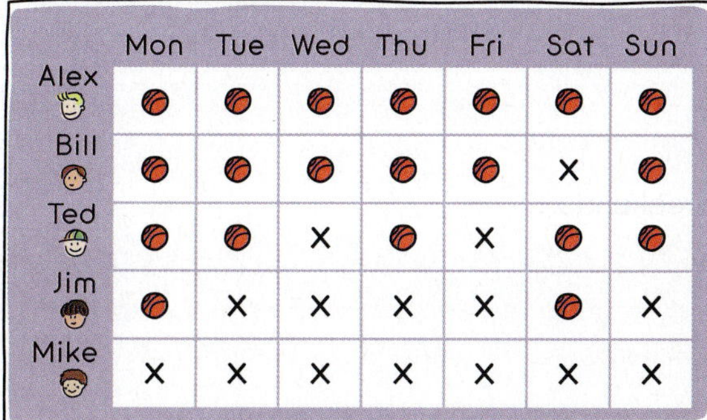


Alex **always** plays basketball.
Alex는 항상 농구를 한다.
Bill **usually** plays basketball.
Bill은 대개 농구를 한다.
Ted **often** plays basketball.
Ted는 종종 농구를 한다.
Jim **sometimes** plays basketball.
Jim은 때때로 농구를 한다.
Mike **never** plays basketball.
Mike는 결코 농구를 하지 않는다.

## PRACTICE 5

우리말과 같은 뜻이 되도록 〈보기〉에서 알맞은 빈도부사를 골라 빈칸에 쓰세요.

보 기     always   usually   often   sometimes   never

1   Paul은 절대로 아침을 먹지 않는다.
= Paul ______________ eats breakfast.

2   물은 항상 그 형태가 변한다.
= Water ______________ changes its form.

3   나는 종종 영화관에 간다.
= I ______________ go to the movies.

4   나는 네 친절을 결코 잊지 않을 것이다.
= I'll ______________ forget your kindness.

5   Jenny는 대개 하루에 다섯 번의 수업이 있다.
= Jenny ______________ has five classes a day.

6   그의 어머니는 그에게 자주 전화한다.
= His mother ______________ calls him.

7   나는 때때로 꽃을 산다.
= I ______________ buy flowers.

8   Helen은 항상 여기에 있니?
= Is Helen ______________ here?

9   그녀는 대개 매우 신중하다.
= She is ______________ very careful.

10   이곳에는 때때로 비가 내린다.
= It ______________ rains here.

11   그들은 여러 가지 방법으로 항상 나를 돕는다.
= They ______________ help me in many ways.

12   나는 태국에 한 번도 가보지 않았다.
= I've ______________ been to Thailand.

13   그는 보통 주말에 영화를 본다.
= He ______________ watches movies on weekends.

14   나는 때때로 밤에 우유를 마신다.
= I ______________ drink milk at night.

# PSS 2-2 빈도부사의 위치

## 1. be동사/조동사+빈도부사

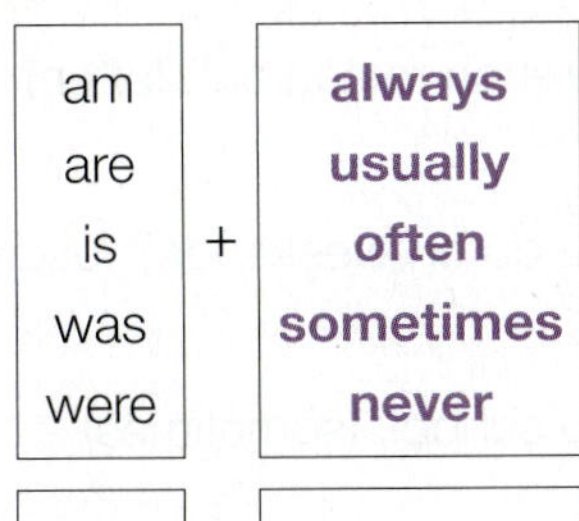

| am / are / is / was / were | + | always / usually / often / sometimes / never |

Mike **is always** kind. Mike는 항상 친절하다.
They **were usually** busy. 그들은 대개 바빴다.
Mistakes **are often** the best teachers. 실수는 종종 최고의 스승이다.
Ann **was sometimes** very sick. Ann은 때때로 매우 아팠다.
I'm **never** late for school. 나는 절대로 학교에 지각하지 않는다.

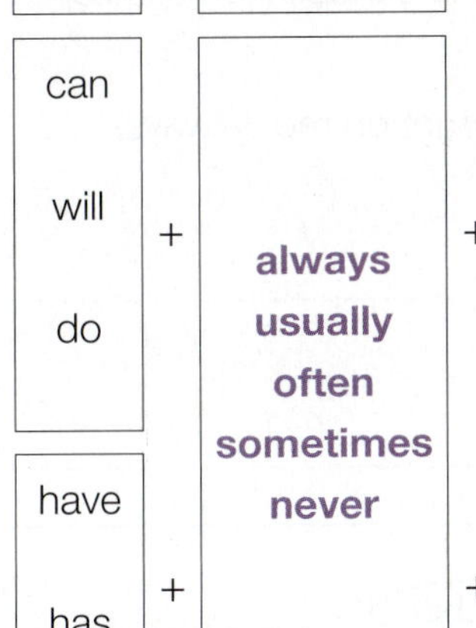

You **can always depend** on me.
너는 항상 나를 믿어도 된다.
He**'ll usually stay** there.
그는 대개 그곳에 머물 것이다.
I **don**'t **often eat** vegetables.
나는 야채를 자주 먹지 않는다.
I **have always been** a writer.
나는 항상 작가였디.
He **has never ridden** a horse.
그는 결코 말을 타본 적이 없다.

## 2. 빈도부사+일반동사

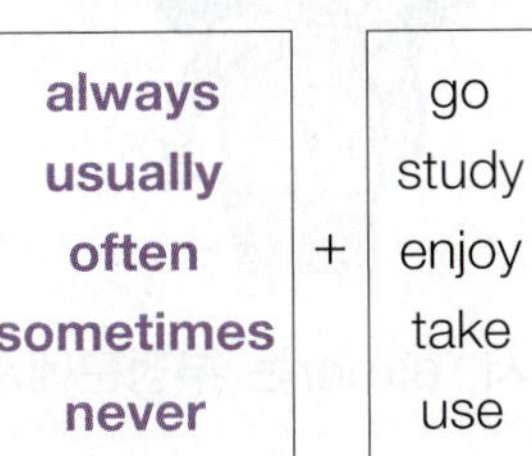

He **always goes** to bed at 10. 그는 항상 10시에 잠자리에 든다.
I **usually study** 8 hours a day. 나는 대개 하루에 8시간 공부한다.
She **often enjoys** Italian food. 그녀는 종종 이탈리아 음식을 즐겨 먹는다.
They **sometimes take** a taxi. 그들은 때때로 택시를 탄다.
We **never use** plastic bags. 우리는 절대로 비닐 봉지를 사용하지 않는다.

정답 p.51

## PRACTICE 6 [1-16]

〈보기〉와 같이 괄호 안의 빈도부사가 들어갈 알맞은 곳에 ✔로 표시 하세요.

| 보 기 | They ✔ go to church on Sundays. (always) |

**1** Mrs. Kim is kind. (always)

**2** Do you surf the Internet? (often)

**3** Shelly tries to smile. (always)

**4** I have taken an airplane. (never)

| **5** This street is crowded. (sometimes) | **6** Tom is at home after 8 o'clock. (never) |
|---|---|
| **7** It is foggy in London. (often) | **8** He has made mistakes. (often) |
| **9** He finishes his work on time. (never) | **10** I go to the French restaurant. (often) |
| **11** My school starts at 8:30. (usually) | **12** What do you do on weekends? (usually) |
| **13** She has been nice to others. (always) | **14** She walks to school. (sometimes) |
| **15** The newspaper is delivered at 7. (usually) | **16** You can count on me. (always) |

# PSS 3 too, either

too와 either는 '또한, 역시'의 뜻으로 too(= as well)는 긍정문에서, either는 부정문에서 쓰인다.

Cathy **likes** music. John **likes** music, **too**.
Cathy는 음악을 좋아한다. John도 역시 음악을 좋아한다.

Giho **doesn't like** coffee. Mary **doesn't like** coffee, **either**.
기호는 커피를 좋아하지 않는다. Mary도 역시 커피를 좋아하지 않는다.

***cf.*** '너무, 매우'의 의미를 갖는 too는 형용사나 부사 앞에 위치한다.

I have **too** **much** homework.
나는 숙제가 너무 많다.

## PRACTICE 7

다음 문장의 빈칸에 too나 either 중 알맞은 것을 쓰세요.

1   *A*: He couldn't eat any more.   *B*: I couldn't eat any more, _______________.

2   *A*: She failed her test.   *B*: I failed my test, _______________.

3   *A*: I didn't go to the meeting.   *B*: She didn't go to the meeting, _______________.

4   *A*: I studied math.   *B*: David studied math, _______________.

5   *A*: I'm thirteen years old.   *B*: I'm thirteen years old, _______________.

6   *A*: I don't have a dog.   *B*: John doesn't have a dog, _______________.

7   *A*: Mike joined the club.   *B*: I joined the club, _______________.

8   *A*: I won't stay at home.   *B*: They won't stay at home, _______________.

9   *A*: He cannot swim.   *B*: I can't swim, _______________.

10   *A*: We didn't sleep all night.   *B*: They didn't sleep all night, _______________.

11   *A*: We could find the way.   *B*: They could find the way, _______________.

12   *A*: Nice to meet you.   *B*: Nice to meet you, _______________.

13   *A*: I don't like the dish.   *B*: They don't like the dish, _______________.

14   *A*: I'm from Seoul.   *B*: I'm from Seoul, _______________.

15   *A*: I don't have a pen.   *B*: She doesn't have a pen, _______________.

16   *A*: I'm ready to go.   *B*: Your dad is ready to go, _______________.

17   *A*: I can't hear you very well.   *B*: I can't hear you very well, _______________.

18   *A*: He likes horror movies.   *B*: I like horror movies, _______________.



# PSS 4  well



**good**은 **명사를 수식하거나 보어 역할을 하는 형용사**이고, **well**은 **동사를 수식하는 부사**이다.

She is a **good swimmer**. 그녀는 훌륭한 수영 선수이다.
She **is good** at swimming. 그녀는 수영을 잘한다.
She **swims well**. 그녀는 수영을 잘한다.

*cf.* well은 '건강한, 몸이 좋은'의 의미를 갖는 형용사로도 쓰인다.
   I don't **feel well**. 나는 몸이 좋지 않다.

## PRACTICE 8

다음 문장의 빈칸에 good이나 well 중 알맞은 것을 쓰세요.

1  I couldn't sleep __________ last night.

2  It's __________ to see you.

3  Some foreigners eat gimchi __________.

4  The reading club was __________ for us.

5  I hope you get __________ soon.

6  We don't know them __________.

7  This is a __________ place to talk.

8  I'm a __________ painter.

9  His English is very __________.

10  You did __________ on the test.

11  Seho speaks French very __________.

12  My exam results were __________.

13  Your jacket looks __________ on you.

14  I can't read __________ without my glasses.

## PSS 5 「타동사 + 부사」



### PSS 5-1 「타동사 + 부사」의 종류

동사는 목적어를 필요로 하는가에 따라 자동사(목적어 불필요)와 타동사(목적어 필요)로 분류할 수 있다.

The door **opened** quickly. 그 문은 빠르게 열렸다.
주어　자동사　수식어

He **opened** the door. 그는 문을 열었다.
주어　타동사　목적어

「타동사+부사」가 만나면 원래 동사와는 다른 새로운 의미를 나타내게 된다.

turn은 '(~을) 돌리다'라는 뜻인데, turn과 on이 만나면 '(전기, TV 등을) 켜다'라는 새로운 의미가 된다.

She **turned** **on** the light. 그녀는 불을 켰다.
주어　타동사　부사　목적어

1.  turn on '켜다' ↔ turn off '끄다'

She **turned on** the light. 그녀는 불을 켰다.

He **turned off** the light. 그는 불을 껐다.

2. put on '입다[쓰다, 끼다]' ↔ take off '벗다'

Sally **put on** her glasses.

Sally는 그녀의 안경을 썼다.

Bob **took off** his jacket.

Bob은 그의 재킷을 벗었다.

3. try on '입어[신어]보다'

May I **try on** these shoes? 제가 이 신발을 신어봐도 될까요?

4. pick up '줍다, 집어 들다, ~를 (차에) 태우러 가다'

I can **pick up** food with chopsticks. 나는 젓가락으로 음식을 집어들 수 있다.

She **picked** me **up** from school. 그녀가 학교에서 나를 (차에) 태웠다.

5. throw away '버리다'

Some people **threw away** trash on the street. 몇 명의 사람들이 길거리에 쓰레기를 버렸다.

6. bring back '돌려주다'

I will **bring back** your umbrella. 나는 네 우산을 돌려줄 것이다.



정답 p.52

## PRACTICE 9

〈보기〉에서 알맞은 부사를 골라 빈칸에 쓰세요.

| 보 기 | on  off  up  away  back |
| --- | --- |

1  Put ________________ your coat to stay warm.

2  Turn ________________ your phone in the theater.

3  My brother tried ________________ his new suit.

4  I saw people throw ________________ their garbage.

5  His uncle will pick ________________ John at the station.

6  Did you bring ________________ the book to Jim?

7  You should take ________________ your shoes here.

8  Why don't you try ________________ this shirt?

9  I brought ________________ the money.

10 I turned ________________ your computer to find the file.

1. 목적어가 명사인 경우, 「타동사+부사+명사」 또는 「타동사+명사+부사」의 어순 둘 다 가능하다.

   I **turned on** the TV. = I **turned** the TV **on**. 나는 TV를 켰다.
   He **turned off** the TV. = He **turned** the TV **off**. 그는 TV를 껐다.

2. 목적어가 대명사인 경우, 「타동사+대명사+부사」의 어순만 가능하다.

   I **turned** it **on**. (○)  I **turned on** it. (×) 나는 그것을 켰다.
   He **turned** it **off**. (○)  He **turned off** it. (×) 그는 그것을 껐다.
   He **put** them **on**. (○)  He **put on** them. (×) 그는 그것들을 입었다.
   I can **pick** her **up**. (○)  I can **pick up** her. (×) 나는 그녀를 태우러 갈 수 있다.

   *cf.* 「자동사+전치사」의 경우와 혼동해서는 안 된다.
   **Listen to** this music. (○)     **Listen** this music **to**. (×) 이 음악을 들어라.
   I'm **looking for** my pen. (○) I'm **looking** my pen **for**. (×) 나는 내 펜을 찾고 있는 중이다.

정답 p.52

## PRACTICE 10

괄호 안에 주어진 말 중 알맞은 것을 고르세요.

1   Can you (turn on the radio, turn on it)?

2   Will you (try on them, try them on)?

3   Please (turn off it, turn off the alarm).

4   They (picked up Bob, picked up him).

5   Nancy (threw away her hat, threw away it).

6   Ralph (took off it, took his raincoat off).

7   Please (wait for me, wait me for) before you leave.

8   She (put on her necklace, put on it).

9   I couldn't (turn it on, turn on it).

10  Don't (throw away them, throw them away).

11  Meredith didn't (give up him, give him up).

12  The old lady couldn't even (write her name down, write down it).

13  (Look at her, Look her at), she's having so much fun!

# PSS 6 의문부사



## PSS 6 - 1 how, where, when, why

1. **방법**을 모를 때 – **how(어떻게)**로 묻는다.

   **How** does he go to the library?          – He goes to the library **by bus**.
   그는 도서관에 어떻게 가니?                        그는 버스를 타고 도서관에 가.

2. **장소**를 모를 때 – **where(어디에)**로 묻는다.

   **Where** does he go by bus?          – He goes **to the library** by bus.
   그는 버스를 타고 어디를 가니?                        그는 버스를 타고 도서관에 가.

3. **때**를 모를 때 – **when(언제)**으로 묻는다.

   **When** does he go to the library?          – He goes to the library **in the morning**.
   그는 언제 도서관에 가니?                        그는 아침에 도서관에 가.

4. **원인/이유**를 모를 때 – **why(왜)**로 묻는다.

   **Why** does he go to the library?          – **Because he wants to study in a quiet place.**
   그는 왜 도서관에 가니?                        그는 조용한 곳에서 공부하기를 원하기 때문이야.

정답 p.52

## PRACTICE 11 [1-10]

괄호 안의 단어를 바르게 배열하여 의문문을 완성하세요.

**1**  A: ________________________________          B: It's under the desk.
(my, where, bag, is)

**2**  A: ________________________________          B: I love it.
(do, food, like, how, you, this)

**3** *A*: _______________________________  *B*: December 12th.

   (her, when, birthday, is)

**4** *A*: _______________________________  *B*: Because I had a few questions.

   (call, you, why, me, did)

**5** *A*: _______________________________  *B*: It's sunny.

   (how, Seoul, the, in, is, weather)

**6** *A*: _______________________________  *B*: At about 3 o'clock.

   (did, work, finish, when, the, Minsu)

**7** *A*: _______________________________  *B*: Because it's so long.

   (book, like, the, why, he, doesn't)

**8** *A*: _______________________________  *B*: To Europe.

   (are, travel, where, going, you, to)

**9** *A*: _______________________________  *B*: At the restaurant.

   (you, did, lunch, eat, where)

**10** *A*: _______________________________  *B*: Because I was late for work.

   (why, running, you, were)

---

## PSS 6-2 How + 형용사/부사 ~?

'얼마나 ~하니?'라는 뜻으로 횟수, 기간, 거리, 나이, 금액 등의 정도를 물을 때 쓰인다.

**How often** does he come here?   – **Twice a month**.

그는 얼마나 자주 여기에 오니?   한 달에 두 번.

**How long** does it take to come here?   – It takes **about fifteen minutes**.

여기로 오는 데 얼마나 걸리니?   15분 정도 걸려.

**How far** is it from here to the station?   – It is **about three kilometers**.

여기에서 역까지는 얼마나 머니?   약 3km 정도야.

**How old** is she?   – She is **16 years old**.

그녀는 몇 살이니?   그녀는 16살이야.

**How tall** are you?   – I'm **165 centimeters**.

네 키는 얼마니?   나는 165cm야.

**How much** is this skirt?   – It is **ten dollars**.

이 스커트는 얼마인가요?   10달러예요.

**How many** sisters do you have?   – I have **two sisters**.

너는 누나가 몇 명이나 있니?   나는 누나가 두 명 있어.

## PRACTICE 12

〈보기〉와 같이 빈칸에 알맞은 단어를 넣어 대화를 완성하세요.

> 보 기  A: How _often_ do you go to the movies?
> B: About twice a year.

1  A: How ________________ will you stay in this hotel?   B: Two weeks.

2  A: How ________________ is your sister?   B: She's ten years old.

3  A: How ________________ is this notebook?   B: It's two thousand won.

4  A: How ________________ do you take the bus?   B: Every day.

5  A: How ________________ is it from here to the museum?   B: It is two blocks away.

6  A: How ________________ is that scarf?   B: It's twelve dollars.

7  A: How ________________ is your father?   B: He is 180 centimeters.

8  A: How ________________ shoes do you have?   B: I have four pairs of shoes.

9  A: How ________________ pets do you have?   B: I have a dog and a cat.

10  A: How ________________ do you play the piano a day?   B: Half an hour.

11  A: How ________________ is this table?   B: About ten years old.

12  A: How ________________ does it take to get to your home?   B: About 10 minutes on foot.

13  A: How ________________ is it from here to your school?   B: It is 2.5 kilometers.

14  A: How ________________ is this building?   B: It has 27 stories.

15  A: How ________________ do you walk to school?   B: Once a week.



## PRACTICE 13

다음 질문에 알맞은 응답을 찾아 그 기호를 쓰세요.

1  When do you leave? [     ]   ⓐ Three times a day.

2  Why can't you come here? [     ]   ⓑ It is three years old.

3  How often do you brush your teeth? [     ]   ⓒ Because I have to see a doctor.

4  Where did you find it? [     ]   ⓓ In three days.

5  How old is your dog? [     ]   ⓔ Behind the sofa.

**1** 다음 문장에서 usually가 들어갈 알맞은 위치는?

> I ① dream ② about ③ flying ④ in the sky ⑤.

**2** 다음 대화의 빈칸에 들어갈 알맞은 단어는?

> A: ___________ do you go to school?
> B: I go to school by bus.

① How　　② What　　③ When
④ Why　　⑤ Where

**3** 다음 글의 밑줄 친 Ⓐ~Ⓔ 중 어법상 옳은 것은?

> My dad is a basketball coach. When I was young, I went to the basketball court Ⓐmany time to watch a game. I think that is why I want to be a basketball player when I grow up. My friends like Ⓑplay basketball, too. After school, we often play basketball. It feels so nice to Ⓒdrink a water after we sweat a lot. However, my friend, Tom, Ⓓnever plays basketball. One day, I asked him, "Tom, do you want to play basketball with us?" He answered, "I'm sorry, but I don't Ⓔhave the time."

① Ⓐ　　② Ⓑ　　③ Ⓒ　　④ Ⓓ　　⑤ Ⓔ

**4** 다음의 빈칸에 공통으로 들어갈 알맞은 단어는?

> • He tried ___________ another shirt.
> • She showed me how to turn ___________ the light.

① by　　② at　　③ to　　④ on　　⑤ off

**5** 다음 대화의 빈칸에 들어갈 알맞은 단어는?

> A: ___________ did you go during summer vacation?
> B: I went to Paris.

① How　　② What　　③ Why
④ When　　⑤ Where

**6** 다음 빈칸에 들어갈 말이 바르게 짝지어진 것은?

> • Make sure you don't take flash photos in the museum. You should not bring any food into the museum, ___________.
> • Andy and Kate are really good dancers. They can sing well, ___________.

① too　– either　　② either – too
③ either – also　　④ also　– either
⑤ too　– also

**7** 다음 두 문장이 같은 뜻이 되도록 빈칸에 들어갈 알맞은 단어를 쓰세요.

> • My mom is a good cook.
>   = My mom cooks ___________.

**8** 다음 글의 밑줄 친 (A)를 <u>6단어</u>로 영작하세요.

My brother has trouble sleeping. So, (A) 그는 밤에 커피를 절대로 마시지 않는다.

➡ _______________________________

**9** 다음 짝지어진 두 단어의 관계가 〈보기〉와 같은 것은?

| 보 기 | nice – nicely |

① friend – friendly  ② careful – carefully
③ elder – elderly  ④ week – weekly
⑤ luck – luckily

**10** 다음 대화의 빈칸에 들어갈 알맞은 말은?

A: ___________ is this blue T-shirt?
B: It is 25 dollars.

① How old  ② How far
③ How many  ④ How much
⑤ How long

**11** 다음 빈칸에 들어갈 말이 알맞게 짝지어진 것은?

A: ________ don't we go for a bike ride this weekend?
B: Sounds great!
A: ________ are we going to ride our bikes?
B: Let's go to the Grand Park.

① How – Where  ② Where – What
③ Why – What  ④ Why – When
⑤ Why – Where

**12** 다음 빈칸에 공통으로 들어갈 알맞은 단어는?

• I turned ___________ my computer.
• He took ___________ his glasses.

① on  ② off  ③ to
④ back  ⑤ away

**13** 다음 중 어법상 <u>잘못된</u> 문장을 고르세요.

① She sometimes goes to bed early.
② Mike never works out at the gym.
③ I usually play basketball after school.
④ I often visit my grandparents on Sunday.
⑤ He always is busy in the morning.



**14** 다음 대화를 읽고, 괄호 안의 단어를 이용하여 빈칸에 의문부사로 시작하는 의문문을 쓰세요. (단, 시제에 주의하세요.)

A: Hi, good to see you again.
B: Me, too. Where have you been during summer vacation?
A: I've been to Hawaii.
B: Oh, really? (1) ________ (go, there)
A: I went there to visit my uncle.
B: I see. (2) ________ (stay, there)
A: I stayed there for a week.

(1) _______________________________

_______________________________

(2) _______________________________

_______________________________

# 15 다음 대화 중 어색한 것은?

① A: What do you think about eating pizza?
   B: I'm a big fan. I have a slice every Friday night.
② A: When did you go to bed last night?
   B: I went to bed at about 10 p.m.
③ A: I didn't bring my English homework.
   B: I didn't bring mine, too. We are in trouble.
④ A: Where do your grandparents live now?
   B: They live in Sejong now.
⑤ A: Why does Mina always drink green tea?
   B: Because she likes its taste.

# 16 다음 괄호 안에 주어진 단어를 바르게 배열해 대화를 완성하세요.

A: ________________ to the shopping mall? (often, you, how, do, go)
B: I go there three times a month.

➡ ________________

# 17 다음 글의 밑줄 친 부분 중 어법상 틀린 것은?

I got up early in the morning. Birds were singing. I ①looked around the lake. I breathed ②deeply. The fresh air ③woke me up. I finished my breakfast and packed my stuff. I ④picked a map up at the front desk and ⑤looked it at. I decided where to go and started the second day of my journey.

# 18 다음 대화 중 어색한 것은?

① A: How much are these jeans?
   B: They're 70,000 won.
② A: How long does it take to get there by plane?
   B: It is 530km.
③ A: How old is your brother?
   B: He is 19 years old.
④ A: How often do you take a shower?
   B: Twice a week.
⑤ A: How many pets do you have in your house?
   B: I have three dogs and two cats.

# 19 다음 대화의 밑줄 친 부분과 바꾸어 쓸 수 있는 단어는?

A: What time shall we meet?
B: How about seven?
A: No problem.

① Where        ② How        ③ What
④ Who          ⑤ When

# 20 다음 두 문장이 같은 뜻이 되도록 빈칸에 알맞은 단어를 쓰세요.

• My teacher also gave me some good books.
  = My teacher gave me some good books, ________________.

## 21 다음 글의 ⓐ～ⓔ 중 어법상 바른 것은?

This is my family. We love music. I play ⓐ violin and my dad plays the guitar. Mom and my sister ⓑ plays the piano. Our family ⓒ goes often to a concert. I ⓓ feel great when I am at the concert. I hope ⓔ having a concert with my family one day.

① ⓐ　　② ⓑ　　③ ⓒ　　④ ⓓ　　⑤ ⓔ

## 22 다음 빈칸에 공통으로 들어갈 의문부사를 쓰세요.

- ___________ long does it take?
  - It only takes half an hour.
- ___________ can I get there?
  - You can get there by subway.

➡ ___________________________

## 23 다음 문장들 중 어법상 옳은 것의 개수는?

ⓐ There is wrong something with my computer.
ⓑ I am knowing the answer to this question.
ⓒ They will pick up us at the station.
ⓓ They walked slowly to the park.
ⓔ He can swim very good.

① 1개　　② 2개　　③ 3개　　④ 4개　　⑤ 5개

## 24 다음 질문에 대한 대답으로 가장 알맞은 것은?

A: How can I get to Busan?
B: _______________________

① Sure, I will get you a map.
② It won't take too long.
③ Yes, you can get anything.
④ I went to Busan a month ago.
⑤ You can go there by train.

## 25 다음 밑줄 친 부분의 쓰임이 바르지 못한 것은?

① The bus arrived very lately in the morning.
② She always studies very hard.
③ Thank you so much.
④ You have to carry it carefully.
⑤ You should get up early.

## 26 다음 대화의 빈칸에 들어갈 단어로 알맞은 것은?

A: ___________ does she live?
B: She lives in New York.

① When　　② Where　　③ What
④ Which　　⑤ Why

**27** 제시된 단어를 어법에 맞게 활용하여 빈칸에 넣었을 때, ⓐ와 ⓑ의 관계가 나머지 넷과 <u>다른</u> 하나는?

| | | |
|---|---|---|
| ① | heavy | • The box is too ____ⓐ____ to lift.<br>• It rained ____ⓑ____ last night. |
| ② | happy | • She is ____ⓐ____ with her new job.<br>• They lived ____ⓑ____ ever after. |
| ③ | slow | • The turtle moves at a ____ⓐ____ speed.<br>• The baby crawled ____ⓑ____ across the floor. |
| ④ | hard | • This is a ____ⓐ____ problem to solve.<br>• The ground is very ____ⓑ____. |
| ⑤ | lucky | • He was ____ⓐ____ to find his lost wallet.<br>• ____ⓑ____, no one was injured in the accident. |

**28** 다음 대화의 빈칸에 들어갈 것이 알맞게 연결된 것은?

> A: She sings very ____(A)____.
> B: She is a ____(B)____ singer. I'm into her songs ____(C)____.

| | (A) | | (B) | | (C) |
|---|---|---|---|---|---|
| ① | good | – | famous | – | lately |
| ② | good | – | famous | – | late |
| ③ | well | – | famously | – | lately |
| ④ | well | – | famous | – | lately |
| ⑤ | well | – | famously | – | late |

**29** 다음 밑줄 친 부분이 의미하는 것은?

> A: Why do some people want to watch horror movies? I don't like watching scary things.
> B: <u>I don't, either.</u> But I've heard that some people get excited by scary movies.

① I like to watch horror movies.
② I don't like watching horror movies.
③ I understand why people watch horror movies.
④ I don't understand why people watch horror movies.
⑤ I don't like to see scary things, but I like horror movies.

**30** 다음 대화의 빈칸에 들어갈 말로 알맞게 짝지어진 것은?

> A: __________ are you so moody today?
> B: My puppy is sick. She cannot eat anything.
> A: Oh, I'm so sorry to hear that. __________ about going to a pet hospital?
> B: Yes, I already made an appointment for this afternoon.

① What – Why     ② How – What
③ Why – How     ④ What – Where
⑤ Why – Where

## 31 다음 중 어법상 틀린 문장은?

① They were shouting loudly at the concert.
② You have to think carefully before you speak.
③ He sings well, and his voice is very sweet.
④ The family lived in their new home.
⑤ I need to run fastly to catch the bus.

## 32 다음 두 문장이 같은 뜻이 되도록 빈칸에 주어진 철자로 시작하는 알맞은 단어를 쓰세요.

> • It was lucky that Mary met James on the street.
> = L____________, Mary met James on the street.

## 33 다음 빈칸 (A), (B)에 들어갈 말로 알맞게 짝지어 진 것은?

> Hi! I'm Minho. I started to learn how to play the piano recently. It's not _______(A)_______ but I'm not going to quit it. I hope I can play my favorite song _______(B)_______ by the end of this year.

|   | (A) |   | (B) |
|---|-----|---|-----|
| ① | ease | – | beautiful |
| ② | easily | – | beauty |
| ③ | easily | – | beautifully |
| ④ | easy | – | beautifully |
| ⑤ | easy | – | beauty |

## 34 다음 학생들이 학교에 가는 방법을 나타낸 표와 내용이 다른 것은?

|       | MON | TUE | WED | THU | FRI |
|-------|-----|-----|-----|-----|-----|
| James | bus | bus | bus | bus | bus |
| Susan | bike | bike | bike | bus | bike |
| Mike | subway | bus | subway | bus | subway |
| Kate | bike | subway | subway | bike | subway |
| Lucy | subway | bike | subway | bus | bike |

① James always goes to school by bus.
② Susan usually goes to school by bike.
③ Mike sometimes goes to school by bus.
④ Kate often goes to school by subway.
⑤ Lucy never goes to school by bus.

## 35 다음 정민이의 주간 계획표를 보고 각 문장에 들어가기에 적합한 단어를 〈보기〉에서 골라 쓰세요. (단, 각 단어는 반드시 한 번씩만 쓸 것.)

> *Jungmin's weekly plan*
>
> go swimming every morning
>
> eat pizza once a week
>
> play tennis three times a week
>
> go to the library five times a week
>
> go to bed before 10

| 보 기 | never, often, sometimes, always, usually |
|---|---|

(1) Jungmin ____________ plays tennis.
(2) Jungmin ____________ goes to the library.
(3) Jungmin ____________ eats pizza.
(4) Jungmin ____________ goes to bed after 10 o'clock.
(5) Jungmin ____________ goes swimming in the morning.

# CHAPTER 12
# 비교구문

# PSS 1 원급, 비교급, 최상급의 형태

## PSS 1-1 규칙 변화형 Ⅰ

원급은 형용사나 부사의 원형, 비교급은 원급에 -er을 붙인 형태, 최상급은 원급에 -est를 붙인 형태를 말한다.

| | |
|---|---|
| **대부분의 경우**<br>: 원급에 -er/-est | tall – tall**er** – tall**est** 키가 큰 – 키가 더 큰 – 키가 가장 큰<br><br>old – old**er** – old**est** 나이 든 – 더 나이 든 – 가장 나이 든<br>hard – hard**er** – hard**est** 열심히 – 더 열심히 – 가장 열심히 |
| **-e로 끝나는 경우**<br>: 원급에 -r/-st | nice – nic**er** – nic**est** 멋있는 – 더 멋있는 – 가장 멋있는<br>large – larg**er** – larg**est** 큰 – 더 큰 – 가장 큰<br>wise – wis**er** – wis**est** 현명한 – 더 현명한 – 가장 현명한 |

정답 p.55

## PRACTICE 1

다음 형용사나 부사의 비교급과 최상급을 쓰세요.

1 kind – __________ – __________

2 large – __________ – __________

3 tall – __________ – __________

4 loud – __________ – __________

5 safe – __________ – __________

6 weak – __________ – __________

7 great – __________ – __________

8 soft – __________ – __________

9 low – __________ – __________

10 huge – __________ – __________

11 smart – __________ – __________

12 cheap – __________ – __________

13 nice – __________ – __________

14 strong – __________ – __________

15 clean – __________ – __________

16 fast – __________ – __________

# PSS 1-2 규칙 변화형 Ⅱ

| 단모음+단자음으로<br>끝나는 경우<br>: 마지막 자음을<br>하나 더 쓰고<br>-er/-est | fat – fat**ter** – fat**test**<br>뚱뚱한 – 더 뚱뚱한 – 가장 뚱뚱한<br>hot – hot**ter** – hot**test**<br>더운 – 더 더운 – 가장 더운<br>big – big**ger** – big**gest**<br>큰 – 더 큰 – 가장 큰<br> |
|---|---|
| 자음+y로 끝나는 경우<br>: y를 i로 바꾸고<br>-er/-est | pretty – prett**ier** – prett**iest**<br>예쁜 – 더 예쁜 – 가장 예쁜<br>happy – happ**ier** – happ**iest**<br>행복한 – 더 행복한 – 가장 행복한<br>easy – eas**ier** – eas**iest**<br>쉬운 – 더 쉬운 – 가장 쉬운 |



정답 p.55

## PRACTICE 2

다음 형용사나 부사의 비교급과 최상급을 쓰세요.

1  hot   – __________ – __________
2  light  – __________ – __________
3  mild  – __________ – __________
4  noisy – __________ – __________
5  heavy – __________ – __________
6  fat   – __________ – __________
7  wise  – __________ – __________
8  sunny – __________ – __________
9  dirty  – __________ – __________
10 cool  – __________ – __________
11 warm  – __________ – __________
12 happy – __________ – __________
13 hungry – __________ – __________
14 big   – __________ – __________
15 wet   – __________ – __________
16 tasty – __________ – __________
17 strict – __________ – __________
18 ugly  – __________ – __________
19 pretty – __________ – __________
20 hard  – __________ – __________

**다음의 경우에는 원급 앞에 more, most를 붙여 비교급과 최상급을 만든다.**

| | |
|---|---|
| 대부분의 2음절 이상의 형용사(단, -y로 끝나는 형용사는 제외) | useful – **more** useful – **most** useful<br>유용한 – 더 유용한 – 가장 유용한<br>hopeless – **more** hopeless – **most** hopeless<br>가망 없는 – 더 가망 없는 – 가장 가망 없는<br>foolish – **more** foolish – **most** foolish<br>어리석은 – 더 어리석은 – 가장 어리석은<br>famous – **more** famous – **most** famous<br>유명한 – 더 유명한 – 가장 유명한<br>patient – **more** patient – **most** patient<br>인내심 있는 – 더 인내심 있는 – 가장 인내심 있는<br>popular – **more** popular – **most** popular<br>인기 있는 – 더 인기 있는 – 가장 인기 있는<br>difficult – **more** difficult – **most** difficult<br>어려운 – 더 어려운 – 가장 어려운<br>important – **more** important – **most** important<br>중요한 – 더 중요한 – 가장 중요한<br>expensive – **more** expensive – **most** expensive<br>비싼 – 더 비싼 – 가장 비싼<br><br>***cf.*** 음절이란 모음을 포함한 소리의 단위를 말한다.<br>useful – **u**se / f**u**l 2음절<br>important – **i**m / p**o**r / t**a**nt 3음절 |
| 분사 형태의 형용사 | interesting – **more** interesting – **most** interesting<br>흥미로운 – 더 흥미로운 – 가장 흥미로운<br>tired – **more** tired – **most** tired<br>피곤한 – 더 피곤한 – 가장 피곤한<br>excited – **more** excited – **most** excited<br>신이 난 – 더 신이 난 – 가장 신이 난 |
| 「형용사+ly」의 형태의 부사 | quickly – **more** quickly – **most** quickly<br>빨리 – 더 빨리 – 가장 빨리<br>easily – **more** easily – **most** easily<br>쉽게 – 더 쉽게 – 가장 쉽게<br>seriously – **more** seriously – **most** seriously<br>심각하게 – 더 심각하게 – 가장 심각하게 |

CH
12
비교구문

# PRACTICE 3

다음 형용사나 부사의 비교급과 최상급을 쓰세요.

1  busy – ___________ – ___________
2  interesting – ___________ – ___________
3  beautiful – ___________ – ___________
4  bright – ___________ – ___________
5  seriously – ___________ – ___________
6  careful – ___________ – ___________
7  friendly – ___________ – ___________
8  important – ___________ – ___________
9  glad – ___________ – ___________
10  expensive – ___________ – ___________
11  lovely – ___________ – ___________
12  quickly – ___________ – ___________
13  useful – ___________ – ___________
14  quiet – ___________ – ___________
15  exciting – ___________ – ___________
16  special – ___________ – ___________
17  soon – ___________ – ___________
18  difficult – ___________ – ___________
19  close – ___________ – ___________
20  helpful – ___________ – ___________
21  popular – ___________ – ___________
22  easy – ___________ – ___________
23  colorful – ___________ – ___________
24  tough – ___________ – ___________
25  curious – ___________ – ___________
26  delicious – ___________ – ___________
27  near – ___________ – ___________
28  dangerous – ___________ – ___________
29  diligent – ___________ – ___________
30  lucky – ___________ – ___________

| 원급 | | 비교급 | 최상급 |
|---|---|---|---|
| good '좋은' / well '건강한, 잘' | | better | best |
| bad '나쁜' / badly '나쁘게' / ill '병든' | | worse | worst |
| many '수가 많은'<br>much '양이 많은' | | more | most |
| little '양이 적은' | | less | least |
| old | '나이 든, 낡은' | older | oldest |
| | '연상의, 손위의' | elder | eldest |
| late | 〈시간〉 '늦은' | later | latest |
| | 〈순서〉 '나중인' | latter | last |
| far | 〈거리〉 '먼' | farther/further | farthest/furthest |
| | 〈정도〉 '더욱, 한층' | further | turthest |

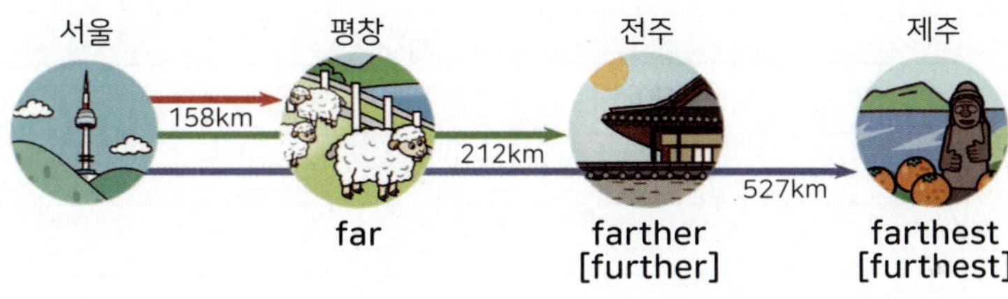


정답 p.55

## PRACTICE 4 [1-44]

다음 형용사나 부사의 비교급과 최상급을 쓰세요.

1 dark – ____________________ – ____________________

2 old(나이 든) – ____________________ – ____________________

3 boring – ____________________ – ____________________

4 slow – ____________________ – ____________________

5 terrible – ____________________ – ____________________

6 tired – ____________________ – ____________________

7 various – ____________________ – ____________________

8 small – ____________________ – ____________________

9 badly – ____________________ – ____________________

10 wonderful – ____________________ – ____________________

| | | | |
|---|---|---|---|
| **11** well | – | | |
| **12** costly | – | | |
| **13** similar | – | | |
| **14** late(늦은) | – | | |
| **15** rich | – | | |
| **16** far(더욱, 한층) | – | | |
| **17** cute | – | | |
| **18** young | – | | |
| **19** far(먼) | – | | |
| **20** famous | – | | |
| **21** thin | – | – |
| **22** faithful | – | – |
| **23** slim | – | – |
| **24** ill | – | – |
| **25** patient | – | – |
| **26** thick | – | – |
| **27** useless | – | – |
| **28** handsome | – | |
| **29** thirsty | – | |
| **30** bad | – | – |
| **31** heavily | – | – |
| **32** deep | – | – |
| **33** angry | – | – |
| **34** late(나중인) | – | – |
| **35** old(손위의) | – | – |
| **36** cold | – | – |
| **37** much | – | – |
| **38** different | – | |
| **39** foolish | – | |
| **40** little | – | |
| **41** easily | – | |
| **42** peaceful | – | |
| **43** many | – | |
| **44** generous | – | – |

# PSS 2 원급을 이용한 비교

Sena is **as tall as** Namsu.

세나는 남수만큼 키가 크다.

He isn't **as old as** her.

그는 그녀만큼 나이가 많지 않다.

1. 「as+원급+as」 '~만큼 …한'

   Sally is **as beautiful as** Ann. Sally는 Ann만큼 아름답다.

   This book is **as thick as** that one. 이 책은 저 책만큼 두껍다.

   I want to run **as fast as** lightning. 나는 번개만큼 빨리 달리고 싶다.

   I can sing **as well as** he can. 나는 그가 할 수 있는 만큼 노래를 잘할 수 있다.

   ***cf.*** 「as+원급+as」 뒤에 오는 「주어+동사」는 목적격의 형태로도 쓸 수 있다.

   I can sing **as well as he can.** = I can sing **as well as him.**

2. 「not as[so]+원급+as」 '~만큼 …하지 않은'

   Paul is**n't as[so] strong as** I am. Paul은 나만큼 강하지 않다. (→ **I'm stronger than Paul.**)

   You are**n't as[so] young as** he is. 너는 그만큼 어리지 않다. (→ **He is younger than you.**)

   His car does**n't look as[so] nice as** mine. 그의 차는 내 것만큼 멋져 보이지 않는다.

정답 p.56

## PRACTICE 5 [1-10]

우리말과 같은 뜻이 되도록 〈보기〉에서 알맞은 단어를 골라 원급 비교 문장을 완성하세요.

| 보 기 | loud   angry   cold   well   simple   interesting   tall   small   clever   slow |
|---|---|

**1** 세민이는 그의 선생님만큼이나 영어를 잘 말할 수 있다.

= Semin can speak English ___________________________________ his teacher.

**2** 극장은 나의 교실만큼이나 작았다.

= The theater was ___________________________________ my classroom.

**3** Jane은 그녀의 오빠만큼 키가 크지 않다.

= Jane is ___________________________________ her brother.

**4** 과학은 역사만큼이나 흥미롭다.

= Science is _________________________ history.

**5** 그녀는 그녀의 남편만큼 화나지는 않았다.

= She was _________________________ her husband.

**6** 개는 고양이만큼이나 영리하다.

= A dog is _________________________ a cat.

**7** 늦은 밤에 택시는 지하철만큼이나 느리지 않다.

= A taxi is _________________________ a subway late at night.

**8** 이번 겨울은 작년 겨울만큼이나 춥다.

= This winter is _________________________ last winter was.

**9** 핫도그를 만드는 것은 토스트를 만드는 것만큼이나 간단하다.

= Cooking hot dogs is _________________________ making toast.

**10** 내 목소리는 네 목소리만큼 크지 않다.

= My voice is _________________________ yours.

정답 p.56

## PRACTICE 6

〈보기〉와 같이 괄호 안의 단어와 'as ~ as' 구문을 사용하여 두 문장을 한 문장으로 연결하세요. (단, 부정문은 축약형으로 쓸 것.)

> 보 기
>
> • John is 168 cm tall. Susan is 168 cm tall, too.
>
> ➡ John <u>is as tall as</u> Susan. (tall)
>
> • This shirt is a large size. That one is an X-large size.
>
> ➡ This shirt <u>isn't as[so] large as</u> that one. (large)

**1** Nari is 13 years old. Minho is 14 years old.

➡ Nari _________________________ Minho. (old)

**2** This scarf is 30 dollars. That one is 30 dollars, too.

➡ This scarf _________________________ that one. (expensive)

**3** His pencil is 9 cm. Your pencil is 10 cm.

➡ His pencil _________________________ yours. (long)

**4** This building is ten stories high. That building is ten stories high, too.

➡ This building _________________________ that building. (high)

**5** I clean my room twice a week. Sangmin cleans his room every day.

➡ I _________________________ Sangmin. (often)

**6** This building is huge. That building is also huge.

➡ This building _________________________ that one. (huge)

**7** The train can go 120 km/h. The car can go 150 km/h.

  ➡ The train ________________________________ the car. (fast)

**8** David is honest. His father is honest, too.

  ➡ David ________________________________ his father. (honest)

**9** This book is 6cm thick. That one is 8cm thick.

  ➡ This book ________________________________ that one. (thick)

**10** This fruit doesn't look fresh. That one looks fresh.

  ➡ This fruit ________________________________ that one. (fresh)

## PSS 3 비교급을 이용한 비교



### PSS 3-1 비교급 + than

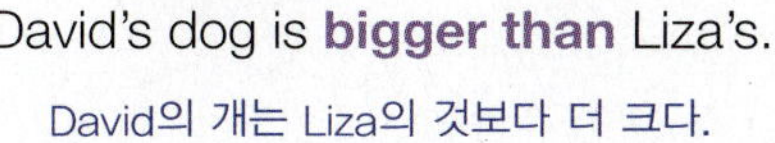

David's dog is **bigger than** Liza's.
David의 개는 Liza의 것보다 더 크다.

The blue shirt is **more expensive than** the yellow one.  파란 셔츠가 노란 셔츠보다 더 비싸다.

「-er than」 또는 「more+원급+than」 '~보다 더 …한' / 「less+원급+than」 '~보다 덜 …한'

> Nari studies math **harder than** he does. 나리는 그보다 수학을 더 열심히 공부한다.
> My mother gets up **earlier than** I do. 엄마는 나보다 더 일찍 일어나신다.
> Two heads are **better than** one. 혼자보다 두 사람의 머리가 낫다.
> This story is **more interesting than** that one. 이 이야기는 저 이야기보다 더 흥미롭다.
> Diet Coke is **less popular than** the original one. 다이어트 콜라는 일반 콜라보다 덜 인기 있다.

> *cf.* than 뒤의 「주어+동사」는 목적격의 형태로도 쓸 수 있다.
> Nari studies math harder **than he does**. = Nari studies math harder **than him**.

## PRACTICE 7

괄호 안의 단어를 사용하여 비교급 문장을 완성하세요.

1  Seoul is _______larger than_______ Busan. (large)

2  My book is _______________________ yours. (heavy)

3  His English is _______________________ hers. (good)

4  Next week will be _______________________ this week. (cool)

5  Sally is _______________________ her sister. (careful)

6  I am _______________________ Minho. (young)

7  The movie was _______________________ the play. (interesting)

8  Your garden is _______________________ Mr. Kim's. (beautiful)

9  I work _______________________ Miss Ford. (quickly)

10  It is _______________________ before. (bright)

11  Your shoes are _______________________ mine. (new)

12  This house is _______________________ that one. (modern)

13  My teacher's voice is _______________________ our voices. (high)

14  Cooking is _______________________ eating. (difficult)

15  Bees are _______________________ butterflies to humans. (useful)

16  The library is usually _______________________ the cafeteria. (quiet)

17  Pigs are _______________________ dogs. (intelligent)

18  A bad excuse is _______________________ no excuse. (bad)



## PRACTICE 8

괄호 안에 주어진 말 중 알맞은 것을 고르세요.

1  Paris is (beautiful, more beautiful) than London.

2  Andy is as (kind, kinder) as Mary.

3  China is (small, smaller) than Canada.

4  You didn't eat as (much, more) food as I did.

5  This actor is as (popular, more popular) as his father.

6  Your computer is (slow, slower) than mine.

7  My father is as (busy, busier) as my mother.

**8** Sora eats (little, less) than I do.

**9** I bought a (cheap, cheaper) jacket than Namsu's.

**10** This dog is as (cute, cuter) as mine.

**11** Mike looks (old, older) than his older brother.

**12** We traveled (far, farther) than they did.

**13** He goes to the theater as (often, more often) as I do.

**14** Today's test was (easy, easier) than yesterday's.

**15** Tim's room is (clean, cleaner) than his sister's.

**16** Sarah rode the roller coaster even though she was scared, showing she was as (brave, braver) as a knight.

**17** A cell phone can be (dirty, dirtier) than a public restroom.

## PSS 3-2 비교급 + and + 비교급

「비교급+and+비교급」 또는 「more and more+원급」은 '점점 더 ~한'의 뜻으로 주로 get, become, grow, turn과 같이 '~되다'의 의미를 갖는 동사와 함께 쓰인다.

It's getting cold. 날씨가 추워지고 있다.

→ It's getting **colder and colder**. 날씨가 점점 더 추워지고 있다.

Her grades became **better and better**. 그녀의 성적은 점점 더 향상되었다.

Companies are turning **more and more eco-friendly**.
기업들은 점점 더 친환경적으로 변하고 있다.

The sky is growing **darker and darker**. 하늘이 점점 더 어두워지고 있다.

## PRACTICE 9

〈보기〉와 같이 괄호 안의 단어를 사용하여 '비교급+and+비교급' 문장을 완성하세요.

> 보 기  It is getting <u>darker and darker</u>. (dark)

1  He became ________________________________. (poor)

2  The boy is becoming ________________________________. (handsome)

3  The leaves are turning ________________________________. (red)

4  The class is getting ________________________________. (boring)

5  Her dancing is getting ________________________________. (good)

6  Mark's sickness is getting ________________________________. (bad)

7  The hall became ________________________________. (quiet)

8  My cat is growing ________________________________. (fat)

9  It is raining ________________________________. (heavily)

10  Computers are becoming ________________________________. (cheap)

---

## PSS 3-3 비교급 강조

다음의 부사는 비교급 앞에서 '훨씬, 더욱'의 뜻으로 쓰여 비교급을 강조한다.

| 부사 | | 비교급 |
| --- | --- | --- |
| even | | larger |
| much | | bigger |
| still | + | better |
| far | | more famous |
| a lot | | more important |

This sweater is **still better** than that one.
이 스웨터는 저것보다 훨씬 더 좋다.

That camera is **much more expensive** than mine.
저 카메라는 내 것보다 훨씬 더 비싸다.

He works **a lot harder** than others. 그는 다른 사람들보다 훨씬 더 열심히 일한다.

He works **very harder** than others. (×)

*cf.* very는 '매우'의 뜻으로 형용사나 부사의 원급을 수식한다. very는 비교급을 수식할 수 없다.

We are **very close** friends. ( ○ )    We are **very closer** friends. ( × )

He sings **very well**. ( ○ )    He sings **very better**. ( × )

## PRACTICE 10

〈보기〉와 같이 괄호 안의 단어를 알맞은 형태로 바꾸어 빈칸에 쓰세요.

| 보 기 | My house is <u>much bigger</u> than yours. (much, big) |

**1** Love is _______________ than money. (far, important)

**2** Her Korean is _______________ than her sister's. (a lot, good)

**3** My school has _______________ rules than his. (much, strict)

**4** Nami studied _______________ than he did. (even, hard)

**5** My brother was _______________ to me than they were. (much, helpful)

**6** My diary is _______________ than his. (still, thin)

**7** The wind blew _______________ than it did in the morning. (even, strong)

**8** Online shopping is _______________ than going to the mall. (far, convenient)

**9** This way is _______________ than that one. (still, safe)

**10** London has _______________ rain than Rome. (a lot, much)



## PRACTICE 11

밑줄 친 부분의 쓰임이 바르면 ○표, 바르지 않으면 ✕표 하세요.

**1** This box is <u>still</u> larger than that one. [    ]

**2** She got up <u>even</u> late this morning. [    ]

**3** The hospital is <u>a lot</u> farther than the drugstore. [    ]

**4** My sister is <u>very</u> happier than I am. [    ]

**5** The women looked <u>a lot</u> weak. [    ]

**6** I have a headache. I need <u>far</u> fresher air. [    ]

**7** Ted is a <u>very</u> brave boy. [    ]

**8** The Nile is <u>much</u> longer than the Han River. [    ]

**9** They are looking for a <u>very</u> cheap desk. [    ]

**10** Going on a camping trip is <u>much</u> exciting. [    ]

**11** Dolphins are <u>very</u> cleverer than sharks. [    ]

**12** He is <u>far</u> curious about the woman. [    ]

# PSS 4  최상급을 이용한 비교

## PSS 4-1  the + 최상급

The red pencil is **the shortest of the three**.
빨간 연필이 셋 중에서 가장 짧다.

My brother is **the tallest in my family**.
나의 오빠는 우리 식구 중에서 가장 크다.

「the+최상급+(명사)+of+복수명사/시간, 기간」 '~중에서 가장 …한'

Summer is **the hottest** season **of the four**. 여름은 사계절 중 가장 더운 계절이다.

This was **the funniest** movie **of the year**. 이것은 그 해 (나온) 영화 중 가장 재미있는 영화였다.

「the+최상급+(명사)+in+장소, 범위」 '~에서 가장 …한'

Kelly is **the prettiest** girl **in her class**. Kelly는 그녀의 학급에서 가장 예쁜 소녀이다.
The dress is **the most expensive** thing **in the clothing shop**.
그 원피스는 그 옷 가게에서 가장 비싼 것이다.

***cf.*** 「the+최상급+명사」의 형태로 쓰는 것이 일반적이지만, 앞뒤 문맥상으로 그 내용을 미루어 짐작할
수 있는 경우에는 뒤의 명사를 생략할 수 있다.
Mary is **the fastest** (student) **in her class**.
Mary는 그녀의 학급에서 가장 빠르다(가장 빠른 학생이다).

## PRACTICE 12

괄호 안의 단어를 사용하여 최상급 문장을 완성하세요.

1 Today is ______*the coldest*______ day of the year. (cold)

2 He is ______________ person in the group. (important)

3 Insu is ______________ of his brothers. (young)

4 It was ______________ day of his life. (happy)

5 It was ______________ choice of my life. (bad)

6 My bag is ______________ of them all. (heavy)

7 That room is ______________ in this house. (bright)

8 We visited ______________ people in the village. (poor)

9 What is ______________ mountain in the world? (high)

10 Sujin is ______________ student in her class. (good)

11 He did ______________ work in the team. (little)

12 A cheetah is ______________ of all animals. (fast)

13 His picture is ______________ of them all. (interesting)

14 It's ______________ news. (late)

15 This is ______________ tree in the garden. (thick)

16 Monday is ______________ day of the week. (busy)

17 Soccer is ______________ sport worldwide. (popular)

18 An ant is ______________ worker of all insects. (hard)

19 The Sahara is ______________ desert on the planet. (large)

20 Yesterday was ______________ day of the trip. (exciting)

CH
**12**
비교구문

## PSS 4-2 one of the + 최상급 + 복수 명사

「one of the+최상급+복수 명사」 '가장 ~한 것들 중의 하나'로 해석하며 주어로 쓰일 경우 단수 취급한다.

**One of the brightest students** in the class **is** Emily.
반에서 가장 똑똑한 학생들 중 한 명은 Emily이다.
He **is one of the best players** in the team.
그는 그 팀에서 가장 훌륭한 선수들 중 한 명이다.
Mount Everest **is one of the most famous mountains on Earth**.
에베레스트 산은 지구상 가장 유명한 산들 중 하나이다.

정답 p.58

## PRACTICE 13

〈보기〉와 같이 괄호 안의 단어를 바꾸어 문장을 완성하세요.

| 보 기 | Soccer is <u>one of the most popular sports</u>. (popular, sport) |
| --- | --- |

1 The World Cup is ____________________________. (exciting, festival)

2 It is ____________________________ in this city. (nice, restaurant)

3 Kate got ____________________________ in her class. (high, score)

4 ____________________________ in Italy is Venice. (beautiful, city)

5 The dinosaur was ____________________________. (big, animal)

6 Andy is ____________________________ in his class. (handsome, student)

7 This is ____________________________. (pleasant, present)

8 ____________________________ is the bee. (helpful, insect)

9 Minsu is ____________________________ in his class. (strong, boy)

10 ____________________________ is the dog. (faithful, animal)

11 ____________________________ is soccer. (exciting, sport)

12 The necklace is ____________________________ in the store. (expensive, thing)

## PRACTICE 14

그림을 보고, 빈칸에 알맞은 사람의 이름을 쓰세요.

**1** _______________ is as tall as John.

**2** John is taller than _______________.

**3** Ted is not as old as _______________.

**4** _______________ is younger than Ted.

**5** _______________ is the oldest of the three.



## PRACTICE 15

괄호 안에 주어진 단어 중 알맞은 것을 고르세요.

**1** That pig is the (fatter, fattest) of them all.

**2** It is the (brighter, brightest) star in the sky.

**3** My brother is (better, best) at math than I am.

**4** This problem is as (difficult, most difficult) as that one.

**5** This drink isn't as (cool, cooler) as that one.

**6** She didn't spend as (much, more) money as her friends did.

**7** One of the tallest mountains on Earth, Mount Everest, (attracts, attract) climbers from all over.

**8** A queen bee is the (big, biggest) of all the bees.

**9** Yumi is even (quiet, quieter) than her sister.

**10** Bob was one of the happiest (men, man) at the party.

**11** The potato is very (healthy, healthiest) food.

**12** His illness became (very, even) worse than before.

**13** Snowboarding is one of the most exciting (sports, sport).

**14** She became (much, more) and more famous.

**15** One of the fastest cars in the world (are, is) on display at the auto show.

# 중간·기말고사 대비문제

**1** 빈칸 ⓐ, ⓑ에 들어갈 말이 순서대로 알맞게 짝지어진 것은?

> Let me introduce my friend, John. He is the ⓐ ___________ student in my school. He always cleans the classroom and helps his classmates and teachers. Everyone likes John. Is there anyone ⓑ ________ than John?

① most nice – nicer
② most nice – more nice
③ nicest – nicer
④ nicest – nicest
⑤ nicest – more nice

**2** 다음 중 빈칸에 알맞지 <u>않은</u> 것은?

> A is more ___________ than B.

① famous　　② funny　　③ difficult
④ useful　　⑤ interesting

**3** 다음 우리말과 같은 뜻이 되도록 빈칸에 들어갈 알맞은 단어를 고르세요.

> • 수미는 민수만큼이나 영어를 잘 구사한다.
> = Sumi speaks English as ___________ as Minsu.

① so　　② good　　③ much
④ better　　⑤ well

**4** 우리말과 같은 뜻이 되도록 괄호 안의 단어를 활용하여 빈칸을 완성하세요.

> • 역사상 가장 유명한 과학자들 중 한 명은 알버트 아인슈타인이다.
> = _________________________________
> _________________________________
> Albert Einstein. (famous, scientist, be)

**5** 다음 내용의 밑줄 친 ①~⑤ 중 어법상 <u>어색한</u> 것은?

> Cats and dogs are the ①<u>most</u> popular pets ②<u>in</u> the world. Cats are ③<u>quieter</u> than dogs. Cats like to stay inside, ④<u>but</u> dogs like to go outside. However, dogs are ⑤<u>more brave</u> than cats. Dogs can protect your house and family.

**6** 다음 우리말과 같은 뜻이 되도록 주어진 단어를 바르게 배열하여 문장을 완성하세요.

> • 개들은 곰들만큼 크지 않다.
> = _________________________________
> (dogs, big, not, as, bears, so, are)

**7** **Fill in the blanks so that each sentence has the same meaning as its translation.**

(1) 그녀는 나의 할머니만큼 나이 들었다.
= She is ____ ________ ____ my grandmother.

(2) 나는 너만큼 일찍 일어난다.
= I get up ____ ________ ____ you.

**8** 다음 문장에서 <u>틀린</u> 부분을 찾아 바르게 고쳐 쓰세요.

> The elephant is one of the heaviest animal of the world.

(1) _________________ ➡ _________________
(2) _________________ ➡ _________________

**9** 다음 우리말과 같은 뜻이 되도록 빈칸에 알맞은 말을 고르세요.

> • 그녀는 큰 집들보다 작은 집들을 더 좋아한다.
> = She likes _________________ .

① better small houses than big houses
② big houses better than small houses
③ small houses than big houses
④ small houses better than big houses
⑤ small houses better

**10** 다음 문장과 같은 의미가 되도록 주어진 단어를 알맞은 형태로 바꾸어 쓰세요.

> Playing tennis is easier than playing the piano.
> = Playing the piano is _________________ playing tennis. (difficult)

**11** **Which underlined part is <u>NOT</u> correct?**

① She is <u>the beautifulest student</u> in her class.
② My younger brother is <u>the shortest of his friends</u>.
③ It was <u>the greatest moment</u> of my life.
④ Seho is <u>the best singer</u> in my class.
⑤ Antarctica is <u>the coldest place</u> on Earth.

**12** 다음 메뉴판에 대한 설명으로 <u>틀린</u> 것은?

① The cheese burger is cheaper than the shrimp burger.
② The chicken burger is more expensive than the shrimp burger.
③ The beef burger is the most expensive of all.
④ The shrimp burger is the cheapest burger on the menu.
⑤ The shrimp burger is less expensive than the beef burger.

**13** 다음 밑줄 친 비교급의 형태가 <u>잘못된</u> 것은?

① Mike gets up <u>earlier</u> than I do.
② My dad goes to bed <u>latter</u> than I do.
③ New York is <u>bigger</u> than Seoul.
④ I play basketball <u>better</u> than soccer.
⑤ Mina reads <u>faster</u> than her sister.

**14** 우리말과 같은 뜻이 되도록 괄호 안의 단어를 활용하여 빈칸을 채우세요.

> • 낮이 점점 더 길어지고 있다.
> = The daytime is getting _________________ _________________ _________________. (long)

## 15 학생들에게 인기 있는 스포츠에 관한 조사결과에 대해 옳은 것은?

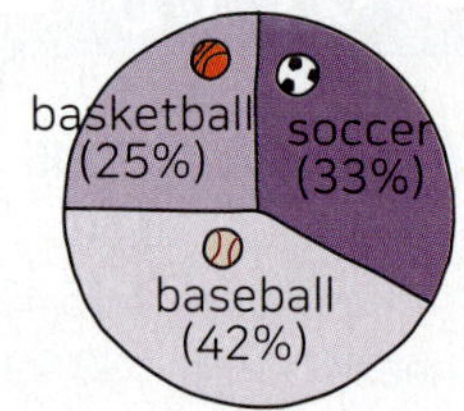


① Soccer is the least popular sport among students.
② Basketball is more popular than baseball.
③ Soccer is less popular than basketball.
④ Baseball is as popular as soccer.
⑤ Basketball is less popular than soccer.

## 16 다음 중 밑줄 친 부분이 바르게 쓰인 것을 모두 고르세요.

① Susan is very taller than Jenny.
② Korea can become a stronger country.
③ It is getting more and more dark.
④ This book is the heavier than that one.
⑤ A cheetah is still faster than a zebra.

## 17 다음 중 어법상 옳은 문장을 고르세요.

① You are the bestest at math.
② That was one of the funniest activity.
③ Sam is the most strongest of the three.
④ This test was the difficultest test of my life.
⑤ What is the most popular tourist attraction in the city?

## 18 빈칸에 들어갈 단어가 순서대로 바르게 짝지어진 것은?

> • Kate is a lot ___________ than Liza.
> • Kate is the ___________ student in our class.

① smart     – smarter
② smart     – smartest
③ smarter   – smarter
④ smarter   – smartest
⑤ smartest – smartest

## 19 우리말 뜻과 같은 뜻이 되도록 다음 괄호 안의 단어들을 알맞은 형태로 바꿔 빈칸에 쓰세요.

(1) 당신의 가방 안에서 가장 비싼 것이 무엇인가요?
= What is _____________________
thing in your bag? (expensive)

(2) 세계에서 가장 큰 나라는 무엇인가요?
= What is _______________ country in the world? (large)

(3) 이것은 모든 것들 중에서 가장 맛있는 케이크입니다.
= This is _____________________
cake of all. (delicious)

## 20 주어진 우리말과 같은 뜻이 되도록 빈칸에 알맞은 단어를 쓰세요.

> • 이 매장에서 가장 싼 것은 무엇인가요?
> = What is _________ _____________
> thing in this shop?

## 21 다음 질문에 대한 대답으로 적절하지 <u>않은</u> 것은?

> *A:* Which color do you like better, pink or blue?
>
> *B:* ______________________________

① Pink is better than blue.
② Blue is darker than pink.
③ Blue.
④ I like blue better than pink.
⑤ I like pink better.

## 22 다음 표와 일치하도록 괄호 안의 단어를 알맞은 형태로 바꿔 빈칸을 채우세요.

| 이름 | 나이 | 키 | 몸무게 |
|---|---|---|---|
| Yuri | 17 | 158cm | 47kg |
| Sangmin | 15 | 175cm | 62kg |
| Jiyeon | 16 | 170cm | 60kg |

(1) Jiyeon is ___________ than Yuri. (tall)
(2) Sangmin is ___________ than Jiyeon. (young)
(3) Yuri is ___________ of the three. (old)
(4) Sangmin is ___________
     of the three. (heavy)

## 23 다음 중 어법상 <u>옳은</u> 문장을 고르세요.

① I'll watch the most interesting movie all movies.
② Daegu is more hot than Seoul.
③ Your legs are long as mine.
④ Jack is one of the funny friends in my class.
⑤ Who sings better than you in your family?

## 24 다음 밑줄 친 부분 중 어법상 <u>어색한</u> 것을 고르세요.

> Find the hobbies you enjoy and keep practicing ⓐ <u>them</u>. It can be hard at first, but learning new things makes your life ⓑ <u>richer</u>. Remember, everyone ⓒ <u>has</u> their own pace of improvement. Be patient, because great skills take time ⓓ <u>to develop</u>. Enjoy the process, and you will feel ⓔ <u>confidenter</u> each day.

① ⓐ     ② ⓑ     ③ ⓒ     ④ ⓓ     ⑤ ⓔ

## 25 다음 표와 일치하지 <u>않는</u> 내용을 고르세요.

| | Sena | Yumi |
|---|---|---|
| Get up | 5:30 a.m. | 6:00 a.m. |
| Go to bed | 9:00 p.m. | 10:00 p.m. |

① Sena gets up earlier than Yumi.
② Sena sleeps more than Yumi.
③ Sena goes to bed earlier than Yumi.
④ Yumi sleeps longer than Sena.
⑤ Yumi goes to bed later than Sena.

## 26 우리말과 같은 뜻이 되도록 괄호 안의 단어를 알맞은 형태로 바꾸어 빈칸에 쓰세요.

(1) 너는 다음번에는 더 잘 할 것이다.
    = You will do ___________ next time. (well)
(2) 너는 어제보다 더 좋아 보인다.
    = You look ___________ than yesterday.
     (good)

## 27 다음 표에 대한 설명으로 옳은 것은?

| Supple-<br>mentary<br>battery | A | B | C |
|---|---|---|---|
| capacity | 20,000mAh | 10,000mAh | 20,000mAh |
| price | 26,000won | 11,000won | 22,000won |

① C is more expensive than A.
② B's capacity is as big as A's.
③ B is the most expensive of the three.
④ C's capacity is bigger than B's.
⑤ A is as expensive as B.

## 28 다음 문장 중 어법상 표현이 틀린 것을 모두 고르세요.

① The building is as tall as others in the city.
② Russia is the biggest country in the world.
③ The Han river is not longer than the Mississippi.
④ I get up early than my dad.
⑤ The restaurant has one of the most cheap steak in the town.

## 29 두 문장의 의미가 다른 하나는?

① I am older than my brother.
   = My brother is not older than me.
② Giraffes are taller than horses.
   = Horses are not as tall as giraffes.
③ America is smaller than Russia.
   = Russia is larger than America.
④ My fan makes cooler air than yours.
   = Your fan makes less cool air than mine.
⑤ My room is not cleaner than your room.
   = Your room is as clean as my room.

## 30 다음 글에서 틀린 곳이 몇 군데인지 고르세요.

I went to the shopping mall this afternoon with my parents. On the second floor, I went into a store and saw the most pretty skirt in the entire mall. I wanted to buy it but my mom said, "Don't you have many other prettier skirts at home?" I said, "Mom! It's on sale. It's very cheaper than other skirts in the store!"

① 1          ② 2          ③ 3          ④ 4          ⑤ 5

## 31 다음 빈칸에 들어갈 알맞은 표현은?

W: Hey, Jihoon. How's your school life these days?
M: ________________, but I'm enjoying it.
W: Oh really? What's been happening?
M: I'm preparing for the school festival and the math contest at the same time!
W: Wow, that explains why you're always in the library.

① It's busy than ever
② It's busy ever than
③ It's busier ever than
④ It's busier than ever
⑤ It's busyer ever than

## 32 어법상 옳은 문장을 고르세요.

① I believe Tom is the funniest student in our class.
② They are one of the best team this year.
③ That chair is the most comfortable than this chair.
④ His score is the highest at his friends'.
⑤ My hair is longer than you.

# CHAPTER 13
## 접속사

# PSS 1  and, but



He is old **and** unhealthy.
그는 늙고 건강하지 않다.

He is old **but** healthy.
그는 늙었지만 건강하다.

He likes her **and** she likes him. 그는 그녀를 좋아하고 그녀는 그를 좋아한다.
He likes her **but** she doesn't like him. 그는 그녀를 좋아하지만 그녀는 그를 좋아하지 않는다.

정답 p.61

## PRACTICE 1

괄호 안에 주어진 접속사 중 알맞은 것을 고르세요.

1  I have a brother (and, but) I don't have a sister.

2  There are cats (and, but) dogs in the garden.

3  She has dark brown eyes (and, but) short black hair.

4  The soup is a little cold (and, but) very tasty.

5  Jason (and, but) I live in the same house.

6  I like fish a lot (and, but) Susan doesn't like them.

7  We played games (and, but) sang songs after lunch.

8  My teacher is kind (and, but) strict.

9  They drink a lot of milk (and, but) they don't drink coffee.

10  The sky is cloudy (and, but) dark.

11  He is lazy (and, but) smart.

12  I learned speaking (and, but) reading from him.

# PSS 2  and, or

---

1. **and는 둘 다를**, **or는 둘 중 하나를** 선택하여 말할 때 쓰인다.

   He **and** I have to take care of the child. 그와 내가 그 아이를 돌보아야 한다.
   He **or** I have to take care of the child. 그 또는 내가 그 아이를 돌보아야 한다.

   I will clean my room **and** wash the dishes. 나는 내 방을 청소하고 설거지를 할 것이다.
   I will clean my room **or** wash the dishes. 나는 내 방을 청소하거나 설거지를 할 것이다.

2. and와 or가 각각 명령문 뒤에 쓰이면 **and는 앞 내용에 대해 '그러면'**의 뜻을, **or는 '그렇지 않으면'**의 뜻을 나타낸다.

   **Study harder**, **and** you'll pass the exam. 더 열심히 공부해라. 그러면 너는 시험에 합격할 것이다.
   = If you study harder, you'll pass the exam. 만약 네가 더 열심히 공부하면, 너는 시험에 합격할 것이다.

   **Hurry up**, **or** you can't get there in time. 서둘러라. 그렇지 않으면 시간 내에 거기에 도착할 수 없다.
   = If you don't hurry up, you can't get there in time.
   만약 네가 서두르지 않으면, 너는 시간 내에 거기에 도착할 수 없다.

---

정답 p.61

## PRACTICE 2

괄호 안에 주어진 접속사 중 알맞은 것을 고르세요.

1   Run fast, (and, or) you'll be late.

2   I can swim (but, or) she can't swim.

3   Work hard, (and, or) you will succeed.

4   Eat more, (and, or) you'll be hungry later.

5   Come here two (and, or) three times a month.

6   Put this coat on, (and, or) you'll get warm.

7   She will be a writer (but, or) a reporter.

8   He is playing the guitar (and, or) his brother is singing.

9   Don't watch TV too close, (and, or) your eyesight will go bad.

10  Don't throw trash (but, or) cans away.

11  Use a navigation app, (and, or) you won't be lost.

12  My mother may be in the living room (and, or) in the kitchen.

CH
13
접
속
사

## PRACTICE 3

〈보기〉와 같이 다음 문장을 괄호 안의 지시에 따라 명령문으로 바꾸어 쓰세요.

> 보 기　　　If you take a taxi, you won't be late for work.
> = <u>Take a taxi, and you won't be late for work.</u> (and 사용)
> = <u>Take a taxi, or you will be late for work.</u> (or 사용)

**1** If you turn right, you'll see the post office.

= _________________________________________________ (and 사용)

**2** If you put salt on your hamburger, it will taste good.

= _________________________________________________ (or 사용)

**3** If you call him, he will help you.

= _________________________________________________ (and 사용)

**4** If you take the medicine, you'll feel better.

= _________________________________________________ (or 사용)

**5** If you do your homework, your teacher won't be angry.

= _________________________________________________ (and 사용)

**6** If you go now, you can avoid traffic jams.

= _________________________________________________ (or 사용)

**7** If you wait a moment, I'll come and open the door.

= _________________________________________________ (and 사용)

**8** If you get up early, you will see the sunrise.

= _________________________________________________ (or 사용)

# PSS 3  SO

PROBLEM
SOLVING
SKILL

> so는 '그래서, 그러므로'라는 뜻으로 so 앞의 절은 원인을, 뒤의 절은 결과를 나타낸다.
>
> I was tired, **so** I went to bed very early. 나는 피곤해서 매우 일찍 잠자리에 들었다.
> Sumi didn't have breakfast, **so** she is hungry. 수미는 아침식사를 하지 않아서 배가 고프다.

정답 p.62

## PRACTICE 4

괄호 안에 주어진 접속사 중 알맞은 것을 고르세요.

**1** We tried hard, (but, so) we didn't win.

**2** She bought a pair of glasses, (but, or) she didn't wear them.

**3** There are no classes on Saturday (and, but) Sunday.

**4** It is summer, (but, so) the weather is hot.

**5** The box was heavy, (or, so) I asked for help.

**6** My friend (and, but) I go to the same school.

**7** She needed some help, (but, so) I helped her.

**8** Are you Japanese (and, or) Chinese?

**9** I got up late, (or, so) I had to hurry up.

**10** Are you good with computers (or, so) other machines?

# PSS 4  that

**타동사의 목적어절을 이끄는 that은 '~라는 것'으로 해석할 수 있으며 생략이 가능하다.**

I think (**that**) he is right. 나는 그가 옳다고 생각한다.

I believed (**that**) she would come. 나는 그녀가 올 거라고 믿었다.

I know (**that**) the Earth is round. 나는 지구가 둥글다는 것을 안다.

정답 p.62

## PRACTICE 5

〈보기〉와 같이 목적어절을 이끄는 접속사 that이 들어갈 자리에 ✔표 하세요.

보 기   I know ✔ she is smart.

**1** Minji believes there is a God.

**2** The doctor says I have a cold.

**3** I don't think it is a nice restaurant.

**4** They wish they weren't late.

**5** Do you believe she is kind?

**6** Kate thinks there is no one at home now.

**7** I wish I could meet your family soon.

**8** Sumi hopes she can speak English well.

**9** Did you know the dolphin is very clever?

**10** People say only the strongest man survives.

## PRACTICE 6

우리말과 일치하도록 괄호 안에 주어진 말을 바르게 배열하세요.

**1** 나는 그것이 멋진 건물이라고 생각한다.

= I think ___________________________________. (is, a nice building, that, it)

**2** 그녀는 우리가 이틀 동안 거기에 머물 거라는 것을 알고 있다.

= She knows ___________________________. (for two days, we, there, will, that, stay)

**3** 나는 날씨가 좋기를 바란다.

= I wish ___________________________________. (that, be, fine, would, the weather)

**4** Jim은 그의 반에서 Mary가 가장 예쁜 소녀라고 믿는다.

= Jim believes ___________________________ in his class. (that, is, Mary, the prettiest girl)

**5** 나는 그가 시험을 잘 볼 수 있기를 바랐다.

= I hoped ___________________________. (well, he, do, could, on his test, that)

---

## PSS 5  when, because, if



시간, 원인, 조건을 나타내는 접속사 when, because, if는 부사절을 이끄는 대표적인 접속사이다. 부사절이 주절 앞에 위치할 경우에는 부사절의 맨 뒤에 콤마(,)를 써서 주절과 부사절의 경계를 구분해 준다.

**1. when '~할 때' (시간)**

**When** it rains, I don't go out. 비가 올 때, 나는 밖에 나가지 않는다.

***cf.*** when은 '언제'라는 의미의 의문부사로도 쓰이므로 구분해야 한다.
「When+동사+주어 ~?」 '언제 ~하니?'
**When** do you go to school? 너는 언제 학교에 가니?

**2. because[since] '~때문에' (원인/이유)**

I didn't go out **because** it rained. 비가 왔기 때문에, 나는 밖에 나가지 않았다.

***cf.*** because of 다음에는 명사(구)를 쓴다.
**Because of the rain**, I didn't go to the party. 비 때문에 나는 파티에 가지 않았다.

**3. if '만약 ~라면' (조건)**

**If** it rains, I will not go out. 만약 비가 온다면, 나는 밖에 나가지 않을 것이다.

***cf.*** 부사절이 시간과 조건의 의미일 때, 현재시제가 미래시제 역할을 한다.
If I **am** late, don't wait for me. (○) 만약 내가 늦으면, 나를 기다리지 말아라.
If I will be late, don't wait for me. (×)

## PRACTICE 7

〈보기〉와 같이 괄호 안의 접속사를 사용하여 두 문장을 한 문장으로 연결하세요.

> 보 기    I feel good. I sing a song. (when)
> ➡ When I feel good, I sing a song.
> ➡ I sing a song when I feel good.

**1** It snows. We will go skiing. (if)
➡ _______________________________
➡ _______________________________

**2** She got up late. She took a taxi. (because)
➡ _______________________________
➡ _______________________________

**3** I took a walk. I met my best friend. (when)
➡ _______________________________
➡ _______________________________

**4** There are no traffic lights. This road is dangerous. (because)
➡ _______________________________
➡ _______________________________

**5** It rains hard. My uncle usually listens to music. (when)
➡ _______________________________
➡ _______________________________

**6** You go to the supermarket. Buy some milk for me. (if)
➡ _______________________________
➡ _______________________________

**7** I was tired. I went home early. (because)
➡ _______________________________
➡ _______________________________

**8** He heard the news. He cried. (when)
➡ _______________________________
➡ _______________________________

**9** You ask Ms. Han about the problem. You'll get the answer. (if)
➡ _______________________________
➡ _______________________________

**10** I didn't dress warmly. I have a cold. (because)
➡ _______________________________
➡ _______________________________

CH
13
접속사

# PSS 6  as

| as | ~처럼,<br>~대로 | Do **as** I say, not **as** I do.<br>내가 하는 대로가 아니라 말하는 대로 해라.<br>I have to work on math **as** my teacher said.<br>나는 선생님이 말씀하신 대로 수학을 열심히 해야 한다. |
|---|---|---|
| | ~함에 따라,<br>~할수록 | **As** I help poor people more often, I feel happier.<br>가난한 사람을 더 자주 도울수록, 나는 더 행복하다.<br>**As** she grew older, she became interested in arts.<br>그녀는 나이가 듦에 따라, 예술에 관심을 가지게 되었다. |
| | ~때문에 | **As** she did well on the test, she was happy.<br>그녀는 시험을 잘 봤기 때문에 기뻤다.<br>**As** he broke his arm, he was in the hospital.<br>그는 팔이 부러졌기 때문에 입원했다. |

정답 p.62

## PRACTICE 8

밑줄 친 as의 의미가 〈보기〉의 (A)와 같으면 A, (B)와 같으면 B, (C)와 같으면 C를 쓰세요.

보 기
(A) <u>As</u> the days get long, the nights get short.
(B) I wore a hat to protect myself from the sun, <u>as</u> my mom did.
(C) <u>As</u> the book was so sad, he was crying.

1   <u>As</u> time goes by, we get older.  [          ]

2   <u>As</u> he is honest, he is trusted by everyone.  [          ]

3   Do in Rome <u>as</u> the Romans do.  [          ]

4   <u>As</u> my mom is sick, I feel sad.  [          ]

5   I saved money every month, <u>as</u> my sister did, to buy a bicycle.  [          ]

6   <u>As</u> it snowed heavily, I stayed at home.  [          ]

7   She hugged her friend tightly, <u>as</u> her mom did, to show how much she cared.  [          ]

8   It became colder <u>as</u> it grew darker.  [          ]

9   <u>As</u> Tom grows up, he gets brighter.  [          ]

10  We have to hurry <u>as</u> we are late.  [          ]

# PSS 7 however, therefore, for example



접속부사는 두 개의 문장을 연결하면서, 동시에 의미 관계(역접, 인과, 예시)를 나타낸다.

**1. however** '그러나, 하지만' (역접, 대조)

David drives carefully. **However**, he had an accident this morning.

David는 주의 깊게 운전한다. 그러나 그는 오늘 아침에 사고를 당했다.

**2. therefore** '그러므로, 그리하여' (인과)

He studied hard. **Therefore**, he got a good mark in this exam.

그는 열심히 공부했다. 그리하여 그는 이번 시험에서 좋은 점수를 받았다.

**3. for example** '예를 들어' (예시)

Becky loves Italian food. **For example**, she enjoys pasta, pizza and so on.

Becky는 이탈리아 음식을 좋아한다.
예를 들어 그녀는 파스타, 피자 등을 즐긴다.

 pasta   pizza   gelato

정답 p.63

## PRACTICE 9

괄호 안에 주어진 말 중 알맞은 것을 고르세요.

1  It is sunny. (However, Therefore), it is a little cold.

2  She was very tired. (Therefore, For example), she went to bed early.

3  We didn't have any money. (Therefore, For example), we had to walk home.

4  Barbara is kind. (However, For example), she always smiles and helps her neighbors.

5  Jenny's test was difficult. (However, For example), she did very well.

6  I don't throw away used things. (However, Therefore), my room is full of old things.

7  He bought a new computer. (However, Therefore), it didn't help him with his work.

8  Many people like roses. (However, Therefore), I bought some for her.

9  You can shop on the Internet. (However, For example), you can order books and clothes on it.

10  He likes sports. (However, For example), he plays tennis, soccer, and many other sports.

11  I was very tired. (However, Therefore), I stayed up all night studying for the test.

12  I need some clothes. (However, For example), I want a white T-shirt and a blue skirt.

**1** 다음 문장에 공통으로 들어갈 단어를 고르면?

- Wake up now, _____________ you can eat breakfast.
- Eat more vegetables, _____________ you will be healthy.

① as 　② and 　③ but
④ or 　⑤ that

**2** 다음 글의 빈칸에 들어갈 알맞은 단어는?

My friends and I visited a home for the aged last Saturday. We cleaned their rooms and washed their clothes. It was hard work, _____________ we felt proud of ourselves.

① and 　② or 　③ but
④ therefore 　⑤ because

**3** 다음 빈칸에 and가 들어가기에 <u>어색한</u> 것을 고르세요.

① He studied hard _____________ got an A on the test.
② She _____________ I have to water the plants.
③ Run fast, _____________ you'll be late.
④ This is a picture of me _____________ my brother, Sean.
⑤ He is tall _____________ has curly hair.

**4** 다음 문장에서 that이 들어갈 알맞은 위치는?

I ① think ② we ③ will ④ be ⑤ very good friends.

**5** 다음 대화의 빈칸에 들어갈 접속사가 순서대로 바르게 짝지어진 것은?

A: You look tired. Let's get some rest.
B: _____________ we must hurry up. The museum closes at 5 o'clock.
A: Why don't we take a bus _____________ a taxi?
B: Yes, let's do that.

① And – so 　② And – or
③ So  – or 　④ But – or
⑤ But – so

**6** 다음 우리말과 같은 뜻이 되도록 올바르게 영작한 것은?

- 너무 더웠기 때문에 그는 재킷을 벗었다.

① He took off his jacket if it was too hot.
② He took off his jacket when it was too hot.
③ He took off his jacket as it was too hot.
④ He took off his jacket, so it was too hot.
⑤ He took off his jacket because of it was too hot.

**7** 다음 중 밑줄 친 부분이 생략 가능한 문장만을 있는 대로 고른 것은?

ⓐ I think that he is a good singer.
ⓑ That she is kind makes her popular.
ⓒ We know that the store opens at 9 a.m.
ⓓ This bag is light, but that is heavy.
ⓔ She said that she was tired.
ⓕ Is that your brother over there?

① ⓐⓒⓔ   ② ⓑⓒⓔ   ③ ⓐⓑⓕ
④ ⓐⓒⓓⓔ   ⑤ ⓑⓓⓕ

**8** 다음 빈칸에 공통으로 들어갈 알맞은 단어는?

- I respect King Sejong ___________ he invented Hangeul, the Korean alphabet.
- He is hungry ___________ he didn't have breakfast.

① so   ② but   ③ when
④ then   ⑤ because

**9** 다음 대화의 빈칸에 공통으로 들어갈 알맞은 단어는?

*A*: Why did you go to bed ___________ early yesterday?
*B*: I was feeling tired, ___________ I went to bed early.

① but   ② and   ③ so
④ very   ⑤ that

**10** 다음 중 밑줄 친 부분의 쓰임이 어색한 것은?

① Hurry up, or you'll miss the train.
② Just do your best, and you'll do better.
③ Take a taxi, and you can get there in time.
④ Get up now, or you won't be late for school.
⑤ Work hard, and you will succeed.

**11** 다음 글의 빈칸에 들어갈 알맞은 단어는?

A dirty environment is harmful to our body. ___________, we should care more about our environment.

① And   ② But   ③ Therefore
④ However   ⑤ For example

**12** 다음 밑줄 친 부분의 쓰임이 나머지와 다른 것은?

① They know that Jiho is honest.
② I think that Betty would like *gimchi*.
③ I know that boy standing under the tree.
④ Do you believe that he is telling the truth?
⑤ She hopes that she sings well in the contest.

**13** 다음 글의 빈칸에 들어갈 수 없는 것은?

We played a baseball game ___________ the Dragon team last Tuesday. We lost the game. ___________, we weren't disappointed ___________ we did our best. We know that sometimes we learn more ___________ losing than winning. We won't stop trying, ___________ will go on to win next time.

① however   ② with
③ and   ④ because of
⑤ from

## 14 다음 중 어법상 <u>어색한</u> 것은?

① I'm very tall, but my sister isn't.
② We can go there by subway or by taxi.
③ We had dinner and watched a movie.
④ She is not beautiful, but she is kindly.
⑤ I go to school, but Kate doesn't.

## 15 다음 빈칸에 들어갈 알맞은 단어를 고르세요.

British people would feel upset __________
you stick out your tongue to them because,
in England, it means "I don't respect you."

① or      ② if      ③ what
④ so      ⑤ that

## 16 다음 두 문장을 한 문장으로 연결할 때 빈칸에 들어갈 알맞은 단어를 쓰세요.

• I came back home from school. My mom
  was cooking then.
➡ My mom was cooking __________ I
  came back home from school.

## 17 다음 빈칸에 들어갈 가장 알맞은 단어를 고르세요.

The subway system in Seoul is very
well-organized, so you can go anywhere
you want. __________, visitors to Seoul
usually travel by subway.

① Therefore      ② However      ③ But
④ Anyway      ⑤ Because

## 18 다음 글의 빈칸에 들어갈 알맞은 말은?

Sumi is good at foreign languages.
__________, she can speak English,
Chinese and Japanese well.

① If      ② That
③ However      ④ For example
⑤ Then

## 19 우리말과 같은 뜻이 되도록 주어진 단어를 바르게 배열하여 문장을 완성하세요.

• 나는 그가 거짓말을 했다고 믿지 않는다.
 = __________________________________

  (lie, believe, a, I, not, do, told, he, that)

## 20 다음 표를 보고 문장을 완성하세요. (단, 빈칸 하나당 한 단어만 쓸 것.)

| likes | Minwoo | Dana |
|---|---|---|
| dogs | ☺ | ☺ |
| computer games | ☺ | ☹ |

(1) Minwoo and Dana __________ __________.
(2) Minwoo likes computer games, __________
 Dana __________ __________ computer games.

## 21 주어진 문장의 밑줄 친 <u>as</u>와 용법이 같은 것은?

Please do that <u>as</u> I asked.

① <u>As</u> time went by, she missed him more.
② <u>As</u> she grew older, she got smarter.
③ The air grows colder <u>as</u> we go up.
④ I'm talking to you <u>as</u> a friend.
⑤ When in Rome, do <u>as</u> the Romans do.

## 22 다음 빈칸에 알맞은 동사의 형태는?

> If you ___________, will you buy some food for me?

① goes shopping　　② went shopping
③ go shopping　　④ will go shopping
⑤ did go shopping

## 23 다음 빈칸에 들어갈 알맞은 접속사를 쓰세요.

> • I caught a cold, so I couldn't go camping.
>  = I couldn't go camping ___________
>    I caught a cold.

## 24 다음 빈칸 ⓐ~ⓒ에 들어갈 말이 순서대로 알맞게 짝지어진 것은?

> Exercise Club
> Do you want to enjoy more activities like baseball, soccer, ___ⓐ___ volleyball?
> Come ___ⓑ___ join us right now!
> If you have any questions, come to the school gym ___ⓒ___ e-mail us!

|  | ⓐ | | ⓑ | | ⓒ |
|---|---|---|---|---|---|
| ① | and | – | and | – | or |
| ② | but | – | or | – | and |
| ③ | or | – | or | – | and |
| ④ | and | – | or | – | and |
| ⑤ | but | – | and | – | or |

## 25 밑줄 친 when의 쓰임이 나머지 넷과 다른 것은?

① She was ill when I was young.
② I was hungry when I got home.
③ Tony, when do you usually have dinner?
④ What do you do first when you get up?
⑤ When it gets cold, people wear heavy coats.

## 26 (a)~(e) 중 문법적으로 옳은 것을 있는 대로 고른 것은?

> Sumin learns about community service at school. (a) She decides to volunteer at a local nursing home. She talks to her friends about the idea. Three of them agree to join her. (b) They are planing the visit together. (c) They are makeing a list of things to do. The day of the visit comes. (d) Sumin and her friends meet with nervous excitement. The elderly residents welcome them kindly. Sumin reads a story to a small group. Her friends play games and chat with others. The two hours pass quickly. They walk home. (e) Sumin feels proud and plan to return again soon.

① (a), (e)　　② (a), (d)　　③ (b), (c)
④ (b), (e)　　⑤ (d), (e)

## 27 다음 밑줄 친 부분과 쓰임이 다른 것은?

> Do you know that he is good at singing?

① Did you believe that he would come back?
② I hope that I will go skiing this winter.
③ I know that man in the picture.
④ She believed that it was true.
⑤ He thinks that she will do better next time.

**28** 다음 중 밑줄 친 because와 다른 의미로 사용된 것은?

> Eric was angry <u>because</u> his sister drew on his book.

① <u>Since</u> my computer didn't work, I had to borrow my friend's.
② <u>As</u> Tony speaks little Korean, I talk with him in English.
③ I climb the mountain on Sundays <u>since</u> it makes me healthy.
④ I have to work on English <u>as</u> my parents said.
⑤ <u>As</u> he always comes late, no one expects him to come early.

**29** 다음 빈칸 ⓐ~ⓒ에 들어갈 말이 알맞게 짝지어 진 것은?

> Jiho had to do a presentation about his special talent in class. _____ⓐ_____, he couldn't think of his special talent. _____ⓑ_____ he asked his classmates about their talents, they all knew about their talents. _____ⓒ_____ he thought that he didn't have any special talent, he was worried about the presentation.

|  | ⓐ | ⓑ | ⓒ |
|---|---|---|---|
| ① | However | – When | – Therefore |
| ② | Because | – As | – That |
| ③ | As | – However | – Therefore |
| ④ | However | – When | – As |
| ⑤ | Because | – However | – That |

**30** 다음 중 어법상 옳은 문장을 고르세요.

① If you will clean your room, you will feel better afterwards.
② They go on a field trip as it didn't rain.
③ He wasn't late for school because of he got up early.
④ I want to be in good shape, but I work out every morning.
⑤ Hurry up, or you'll miss the bus.

**31** because를 사용하여 다음 두 문장을 한 문장 으로 쓰세요.

> • I couldn't sleep at all. It was noisy outside.
> = ____________________________
> ____________________________
> ____________________________

**32** 다음 중 어법상 옳은 것을 〈보기〉에서 모두 고른 것은?

> 보 기
> ⓐ I'll call you when she will come back.
> ⓑ She was very ill when she was seven.
> ⓒ I think you can do it.
> ⓓ I was very sick yesterday, so I went to the hospital.
> ⓔ He was tired because he gets up early.

① ⓐ, ⓑ  　② ⓐ, ⓒ  　③ ⓑ, ⓒ
④ ⓑ, ⓒ, ⓓ  　⑤ ⓒ, ⓓ, ⓔ

# CHAPTER 14
# 전치사 & 속담

# 전치사

1. **전치사는 명사 앞에 쓰여** 그 명사와 다른 어구와의 관계를 밝혀주는 말이다.

   a cell phone **on** the desk 책상 위의 휴대폰    stay **at** home 집에 머물다

2. **전치사 뒤에는 (대)명사, 동명사**가 올 수 있다.

   I'm afraid **of bugs[them]**. 나는 벌레들을[그것들을] 두려워한다.

   I'm good **at singing**. 나는 노래 부르기를 잘한다.

3. **전치사 뒤에 오는 대명사는 주로 목적격을** 쓴다.

   I'm looking **for him**. 나는 그를 찾고 있는 중이다.

## PSS 1   시간, 때를 나타내는 전치사



### PSS 1-1 at, on, in

| | |
|---|---|
| **at** | 1. 구체적인 시각 – **at** nine 9시에<br><br>2. 특정한 시점<br><br>**at** noon 정오에 　　　　 **at** that time 그때에<br>**at** night 밤에 　　　　 **at** the end of this year 올 연말에<br>**at** midnight 자정에 　　　　 **at** this time tomorrow 내일 이맘때에<br>**at** dawn 새벽에 　　　　 **at** the beginning of the 21st century 21세기 초에<br>**at** lunchtime 점심시간에 |
| **on** | 1. 날짜 – **on** May 5th 5월 5일에　 **on** the 18th of August, 1992 1992년 8월 18일에<br>2. 요일 – **on** Monday 월요일에<br>3. 특정한 날, 특정한 날의 아침·점심·저녁<br><br>**on** my birthday 내 생일에 　　　　 **on** Thanksgiving Day 추수감사절에<br>**on** Christmas morning 크리스마스 아침에　 **on** Saturday afternoon 토요일 오후에 |
| **in** | 1. 월, 연도 – **in** November 11월에 　　　 **in** 2010 2010년에<br>2. 계절 – **in** (the) spring 봄에<br>3. 세기 – **in** the 21st century 21세기에<br>4. 아침·점심·저녁 – **in** the morning[afternoon, evening] 아침[점심, 저녁]에 |

School begins **at nine o'clock**. 학교는 9시에 시작한다.

We're going to move **at the beginning of this month**. 우리는 이번 달 초에 이사할 것이다.

There are no classes **on Saturday and Sunday**. 토요일과 일요일에는 수업이 없다.

Koreans eat *songpyeon* **on Chuseok**. 한국인들은 추석에 송편을 먹는다.

정답 p.66

## PRACTICE 1

다음 문장의 빈칸에 at, on, in 중 알맞은 전치사를 쓰세요.

1  He has breakfast __________ 7:30.

2  I'll invite them for dinner __________ Saturday.

3  I heard someone shouting __________ midnight.

4  Will you send Jiyeon a card __________ her birthday?

5  What time do you get up __________ the morning?

6  My sister graduated from college __________ 2023.

7  We eat rice-cake soup __________ New Year's Day.

8  Shall we meet here __________ this time tomorrow?

9  I was very sick __________ that time.

10  I left here __________ July 15th.

# PSS 1-2 before, after

before dinner 저녁 식사 전에

at dinner 저녁 식사 중에

after dinner 저녁 식사 후에

| before | ~ 전에 | She set up the table **before** dinner.<br>그녀는 저녁 식사 전에 상을 차렸다.<br>She set up the table **before** 7 o'clock.<br>그녀는 7시 이전에 상을 차렸다. |
| --- | --- | --- |
| after | ~ 후에 | She did her homework **after** dinner.<br>그녀는 저녁 식사 후에 숙제를 하였다.<br>She did her homework **after** 7 o'clock.<br>그녀는 7시 이후에 숙제를 하였다. |

## PRACTICE 2

〈보기〉에 주어진 표현과 before나 after를 사용하여 우리말과 같은 뜻이 되도록 문장을 완성하세요.

| 보 기 | lunch | school | the meeting | twelve | six | work |
| --- | --- | --- | --- | --- | --- | --- |

**1** 회의가 끝난 후에, 그는 휴식을 취했다.

= ________________________________________, he took a break.

**2** Jenny는 6시 전에 아침 식사를 한다.

= Jenny has breakfast ________________________________________.

**3** 점심을 먹기 전에, 미나는 바이올린을 연습한다.

= ________________________________________, Mina practices the violin.

**4** 퇴근 후에, 우리는 그 불쌍한 아이들을 돕는다.

= ________________________________________, we help the poor children.

**5** 12시 전에, 모든 것이 팔렸다.

= ________________________________________, everything was sold out.

**6** 그들은 방과 후에 배드민턴을 친다.

= They play badminton ________________________________________.

---

## PSS 1-3 for, during

| | | |
| --- | --- | --- |
| **for** | ~ 동안 | **구체적인 시간의 길이**를 나타내는 말과 함께 쓰인다.<br>We stayed there **for a month**. 우리는 한 달 동안 그곳에 머물렀다.<br>I waited **for 30 minutes** outside her house.<br>나는 30분 동안 그녀의 집 밖에서 기다렸다. |
| **during** | | **특정 기간**을 나타내는 말과 함께 쓰인다.<br>We stayed there **during** summer vacation.<br>우리는 여름방학 동안 그곳에 머물렀다.<br>Nobody spoke **during the presentation**. 그 발표 동안 아무도 말하지 않았다. |



## PRACTICE 3

다음 문장의 빈칸에 for와 during 중 알맞은 전치사를 쓰세요.

**1** She played the piano ________________ three hours.

**2** I fell asleep ________________ the meeting.

**3** My father went away _________________ a few weeks.

**4** Cathy traveled _________________ her holidays.

**5** Don't speak _________________ mealtime.

**6** Sujin took swimming lessons _________________ four years.

**7** Stay out of the sun _________________ these hours.

**8** What are you doing _________________ the winter?

<br>

## PSS 1-4 from, since

| | | |
|---|---|---|
| from | ~부터 | 시작된 시점만 나타내며 완료형 이외의 시제들과 함께 쓰인다.<br>They **stayed** there **from** yesterday.<br>그들은 어제부터 그곳에 머물렀다.<br><br>***cf.*** from A to B 'A에서 B까지'<br>They stayed there **from** yesterday **to** this morning.<br>그들은 어제부터 오늘 아침까지 그곳에 머물렀다. |
| since | ~ 이래로<br>~ 이후로 | 과거에 시작된 일이 현재까지 지속되는 것을 나타내며 **완료형 시제**<br>**와 함께** 쓰인다.<br>They **have stayed** there **since** yesterday.<br>그들은 어제 이후로 그곳에 머물고 있다. |

정답 p.66

### PRACTICE 4

괄호 안에 주어진 전치사 중 알맞은 것을 고르세요.

**1** I've studied (from, since) this morning.

**2** They have been married (from, since) 2020.

**3** The store opens (from, since) 10 o'clock.

**4** I have played tennis (from, since) last month.

**5** (From, Since) this morning, she cleaned all day.

**6** She worked for the company (from, since) last year.

## PRACTICE 5

〈보기〉와 같이 괄호 안에 주어진 단어와 'from ~ to …'를 사용하여 문장을 완성하세요.

> 보 기   He usually works <u>from Monday to Friday.</u> (Monday, Friday)

1   I study in the library ________________________________. (eight, four)

2   ________________________________, she's not at home. (morning, afternoon)

3   The building was repaired ________________________________. (March, June)

4   Lunchtime is ________________________________. (12:00, 12:40)

5   You need a jacket ________________________________. (late fall, early spring)

6   The house was built ________________________________. (2003, 2005)



## PRACTICE 6

괄호 안에 주어진 전치사 중 알맞은 것을 고르세요.

1   I don't work so late (at, on) night.

2   What do you do (in, on) Sunday afternoons?

3   (Since, After) shopping, they were tired and hungry.

4   I have been busy (since, at) last weekend.

5   (At, In) 1492, Columbus sailed west.

6   My friend called me (at, in) 9.

7   She usually takes a walk (before, since) sunset.

8   Mom has been ill (from, since) last Thursday.

9   He painted the house (during, for) a week.

10   My father sleeps from 11 p.m. (at, to) 7 a.m.

11   Lunchtime starts (at, on) twelve thirty.

12   I couldn't go to school (from, since) Tuesday to Thursday.

13   Spring begins (in, on) March.

14   The food will be served (from, since) 11 o'clock.

15   We came back home (after, at) a long trip.

# PSS 2  장소를 나타내는 전치사

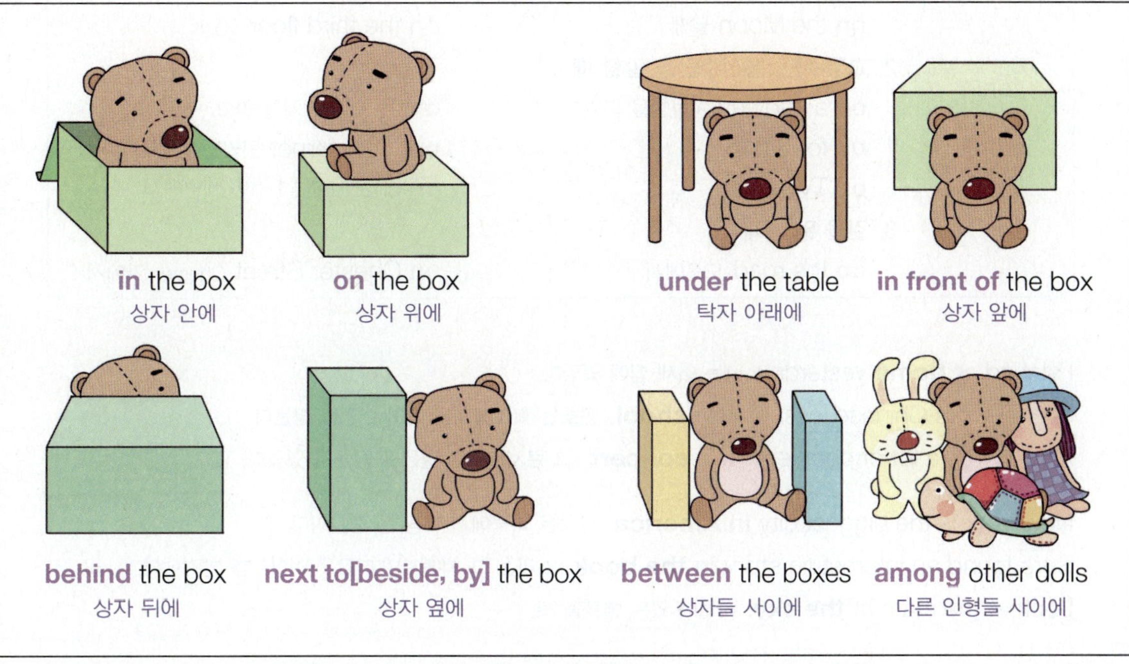



## PSS 2-1  at, in, on

| at | |
|---|---|
| **1. 하나의 지점을 나타낼 때** | |
| **at** home 집에 | **at** the bus stop 버스 정류장에 |
| **at** the corner 모퉁이에 | **at** the door 문에 |
| **2. 건물의 용도에 맞는 일을 하고 있을 때** | |
| **at** school 학교에 | **at** work 직장에 |
| **at** university 대학에 | **at** the airport 공항에 |
| **3. 행사나 모임을 말할 때** | |
| **at** sports events 스포츠 행사에 | **at** the wedding 결혼식에 |
| **at** the concert 콘서트에 | **at** the party 파티에 |

| in | |
|---|---|
| **1. 마을, 도시, 국가와 같은 비교적 넓은 장소일 때** | |
| **in** a small town 작은 마을에 | **in** Seoul 서울에 |
| **in** America 미국에 | **in** the world 세계에 |
| **2. 건물, 탈것, 용기 등의 내부를 말할 때** | |
| **in** the building 건물 안에 | **in** a car 차 안에 |
| **in** a box 상자 안에 | **in** the pocket 호주머니 안에 |
| **3. 우주, 하늘을 말할 때** | |
| **in** space 우주에 | **in** the sky 하늘에 |

<table>
<tr><td rowspan="3">on</td><td colspan="2">1. 표면상에 맞닿은 것을 말할 때</td></tr>
</table>

| on | 1. 표면상에 맞닿은 것을 말할 때 | |
|---|---|---|
| | **on** the wall 벽에 | **on** the ground 땅에 |
| | **on** an island 섬에 | **on** the Earth 지구상에 |
| | **on** the Moon 달에 | **on** the third floor 3층에 |
| | 2. 교통수단, 통신수단을 말할 때 | |
| | **on** a subway 지하철을 타고 | **on** a train 기차를 타고 |
| | **on** foot 걸어서 | **on** the Internet 인터넷상에서 |
| | **on** TV TV에서 | **on** channel 11 11번 채널에서 |
| | 3. 길을 말할 때 | |
| | **on** the road 도로에서 | **on** Chester Street Chester 가에서 |

I stayed **at home** yesterday. 나는 어제 집에 있었다.

Minho takes Chinese lessons **at school**. 민호는 학교에서 중국어 수업을 받는다.

There were a lot of people **at the concert**. 그 콘서트에는 많은 사람들이 있었다.

New York is the biggest city **in America**. 뉴욕은 미국에서 가장 큰 도시이다.

Sora found an interesting story **in the book**. 소라는 그 책에서 흥미로운 이야기를 발견했다.

Look at the stars **in the sky**. 하늘에 있는 별들을 봐.

Peter saw a beautiful picture **on the wall**. Peter는 벽에 있는 아름다운 그림을 보았다.

They came here **on the subway**. 그들은 지하철을 타고 이곳에 왔다.

There is a bank **on 5th Street**. 5번가에 은행이 하나 있다.

정답 p.66

## PRACTICE 7

다음 문장의 빈칸에 at, in, on 중 알맞은 전치사를 쓰세요.

1  You should turn right __________ the next corner.

2  There are many stores __________ the mall.

3  Did they go home __________ a train?

4  Jane stayed __________ home all day.

5  We're living __________ the Earth.

6  Paris is one of the oldest cities __________ Europe.

7  Who are you going to dance with __________ the party?

**8**  She takes a lot of lessons ___________ school.

**9**  My car won't work so I have to travel ___________ foot.

**10**  I studied hard ___________ university.

**11**  Mom listens to the news ___________ the radio.

**12**  We met foreigners ___________ the street.

**13**  Mary keeps her socks ___________ a drawer.

**14**  I dropped my cup ___________ the floor.

**15**  We have computers ___________ our classroom.

**16**  How many planets are there ___________ space?

**17**  He was talking loudly ___________ the phone ___________ the subway.

**18**  The groom sang a lovely song for his bride ___________ the wedding.

**19**  ___________ Canada, milk comes ___________ bags, not ___________ cartons.

**20**  The popular organic restaurant is ___________ Green Street.

**21**  There are offices ___________ the first and second floor.

**22**  Storm clouds are hanging low ___________ the sky.



## PSS 2-2 over, under

over '~ 위에' ↔ under '~ 아래에' – 기준이 되는 사물의 표면과 접촉해 있지 않은 상태를 나타낸다.

Birds are flying **over** the tree.
새들이 나무 위를 날아가고 있다.

Tom and Ann are standing
**under** the tree.
Tom과 Ann은 나무 아래에 서 있다.

## PRACTICE 8

그림을 보고, 빈칸에 over나 under 중 알맞은 전치사를 쓰세요.

**1**

**2**

**3**

**4**

**5**

**6**

**1** My bag is ___________ the chair.

**2** A plane is flying ___________ the city.

**3** The ball is passing ___________ his head.

**4** There is a key ___________ the sofa.

**5** There is a rainbow ___________ the mountain.

**6** A boat is passing ___________ the bridge.

---

## PSS 2-3 in front of, behind, next to

in front of '~ 앞에' / behind[in back of] '~ 뒤에' / next to[beside, by] '~ 옆에'

- There is a bus stop **in front of** the bank. 은행 앞에 버스 정류장이 있다.
- There is a department store **behind** the bank. 은행 뒤에 백화점이 있다.
  = There is a department store **in back of** the bank.
- There is a toyshop **next to** the bank. 은행 옆에 장난감 가게가 있다.
  = There is a toyshop **beside** the bank.
  = There is a toyshop **by** the bank.

*cf.* behind 대신 in back of, next to 대신 beside나
by도 같은 뜻으로 쓸 수 있다.

**in front of** the bank

**next to** the bank

## PRACTICE 9

그림을 보고, 빈칸에 알맞은 말을 쓰세요.

1 Yumi is sitting ________________ Jiyeon.

2 Yunsu is sitting next to ______________ .

3 Sangmin is sitting ________________ Inho.

4 Changho is sitting behind ______________ .

5 Jinho is sitting _______________ Sujin.

6 ________________ is sitting in front of Hana.

7 ________________ is sitting by Seho.

8 Sujin is sitting _______________ Changho.

---

## PSS 2-4 between, among

1. **between** '~ 사이에' (둘 사이)

   I was standing **between** two children.

   나는 두 아이들 사이에 서 있었다.

   **cf.** between은 between A and B의 형태로도 사용된다.

   I was standing **between** Mina **and** Inho.

   나는 미나와 인호 사이에 서 있었다.

2. **among** '~ 사이에' (셋 이상일 때)

   Kelly was standing **among** five children.

   Kelly는 다섯 명의 아이들 사이에 서 있었다.

---

## PRACTICE 10

**다음 문장의 빈칸에 between이나 among 중 알맞은 전치사를 쓰세요.**

1 There is a ten-minute break _________________ classes.

2 Do you know the difference _________________ the twins?

3 Her postcard was _________________ dozens of letters.

4 There is a house _________________ three trees.

5 You should hold chopsticks _________________ your fingers.

6 The star is shining the brightest _________________ many other stars.

7 Sumi is popular _________________ her classmates.

8 It's _________________ the bank and the hotel.



## PRACTICE 11

**괄호 안에 주어진 말 중 알맞은 것을 고르세요.**

1 Do you live (at, in) a big city?

2 There is a store (among, between) the station and the post office.

3 The bus stopped (at, on) a small village.

4 His family lives next (to, by) my house.

5 There are many plants (under, over) the sea.

6 There are five floors (in, on) the building.

7 Draw a line (at, on) the ground.

8 What time is it (at, in) Korea?

9 The cat was sitting (over, on) the roof.

10 She threw the ball (over, between) the wall.

11 There is an interesting program (at, on) channel 7.

12 The drummer is (behind, at) the singer.

13 I want to live (between, in) a nice house.

14 Jack is the most popular (between, among) the four men.

15 Let's meet (in front of, on) the station at 3.

# PSS 3 방향을 나타내는 전치사

She's walking
**into** her house.

그녀는 그녀의 집 안으로
걸어 들어가고 있다.

She's walking
**out of** her house.

그녀는 그녀의 집 밖으로
걸어 나오고 있다.

She's walking
**up** the stairs.

그녀는 계단을
오르고 있다.

She's walking
**down** the stairs.

그녀는 계단을
내려가고 있다.

She's walking
**along** the street.

그녀는 길을 따라
걷고 있다.

She's walking
**across** the street.

그녀는 길을 가로질러
걷고 있다.

She's walking
**through** the park.

그녀는 공원을 통과하여
걷고 있다.

She's walking
**around** the park.

그녀는 공원 주변을
걷고 있다.

## PSS 3-1 into, out of, up, down

1. into '~ 안으로' ↔ out of '~ 밖으로'

He put his hands **into** his pockets.
그는 손을 호주머니 안으로 넣었다.

He took his hands **out of** his pockets.
그는 손을 호주머니 밖으로 꺼냈다.

2. up '~ 위로' ↔ down '~ 아래로'

They climbed **up** a mountain.
그들은 산 위로 올라갔다.

They climbed **down** a mountain.
그들은 산 아래로 내려갔다.

정답 p.67

## PRACTICE 12

그림을 보고, 〈보기〉에서 알맞은 전치사를 골라 빈칸에 쓰세요.

1

2

3

4

5

6

| 보 기 | into   out of   up   down |
| --- | --- |

**1**  We walked ______________ the hill.

**2**  I put the card ______________ an envelope.

**3** Go ______________ the steps.

**4** A famous actress came ______________ the car.

**5** They went ______________ the gift shop.

**6** Salmon swim ______________ the stream.

## PSS 3-2 along, across, through, around

**1. along '~을 따라서', across '~을 가로질러'**

He ran **along** the road.

그는 길을 따라 달려갔다.

He ran **across** the road.

그는 길을 가로질러 달려갔다.

**2. through '~을 통하여', around '~ 주위에'**

We drove **through** the city.

우리는 그 도시를 통과하여 운전했다.

We drove **around** the city.

우리는 그 도시 주변을 운전했다.

## PRACTICE 13

그림을 보고, 〈보기〉에서 알맞은 전치사를 골라 빈칸에 쓰세요.

| 보 기 | along  across  through  around |
| --- | --- |

1  The Earth goes _______________ the Sun.

2  People go _______________ the road when the light is green.

3  The thief came into the house _______________ the window.

4  There are a lot of tall buildings _______________ the museum.

5  We took a walk _______________ the river.

6  The train is passing _______________ a tunnel.

## PSS 3-3 from, to, for

| from | ~로부터 | 출발 지점을 나타낸다.<br>Paul came **from** London. Paul은 런던에서 왔다. |
| --- | --- | --- |
| to | ~에, ~으로 | go, come 같은 동사와 함께 쓰여 도착 지점을 나타낸다.<br>Paul went **to** London. Paul은 런던으로 갔다.<br>Paul came **from** London **to** Seoul by airplane.<br>Paul은 비행기를 타고 런던에서 서울로 왔다. |
| for | ~을 향하여 | start, leave 같은 동사와 함께 쓰여 방향을 나타낸다.<br>Paul left **for** London. Paul은 런던을 향해 떠났다. |

## PRACTICE 14

**우리말 해석과 같은 뜻이 되도록 다음 문장의 빈칸에 from, to, for 중 알맞은 전치사를 쓰세요.**

1   We went _______ the town.  ➡ 우리는 시내로 갔다.

2   This bus leaves _______ Busan.  ➡ 이 버스는 부산을 향해 떠난다.

3   Can you come _______ my house tomorrow?  ➡ 너 내일 우리 집으로 올 수 있니?

4   Are those students _______ Canada?  ➡ 저 학생들은 캐나다 출신이니?

5   They started _______ Africa.  ➡ 그들은 아프리카를 향해 출발했다.

6   We moved _______ a restaurant _______ a coffee shop.  ➡ 우리는 식당에서 커피숍으로 옮겨갔다.

7   How far is your school _______ your house?  ➡ 네 학교는 네 집에서 얼마나 머니?

8   We are heading _______ the nearest river.  ➡ 우리는 가장 가까운 강으로 향하고 있다.



## PRACTICE 15

**괄호 안에 주어진 전치사 중 알맞은 것을 고르세요.**

1   A lot of foreigners come (at, to) Korea.

2   The airplane started (for, to) China.

3   We did the dishes (after, since) dinner.

4   The Moon goes (around, through) the Earth.

5   A man walked (between, into) a restaurant.

6   Tears ran (down, into) her cheeks.

7   Kitty stayed at my home (during, for) five days.

8   A boy ran (across, over) the street.

9   I was born (in, on) 2010.

10   There is a bakery (among, by) the gift shop.

11   Monkeys climbed (between, up) a tree.

12   The astronaut landed (in, on) the Moon.

13   I will meet Mike (at, on) 3:30.

14   The boat went (above, along) the river.

15   The children jumped (among, into) the water.

CH
14
전치사
&
속담

## PSS 4  도구, 수단을 나타내는 전치사

1. **도구와 함께 쓰이는 전치사 with '~을 가지고'**

   She wrote a letter **with a pencil**. 그녀는 연필을 가지고 편지를 썼다.

2. **교통수단과 함께 쓰이는 전치사 by '~을 타고'**

   Mina goes to school **by bus**. 미나는 버스를 타고 학교에 간다.

   *cf.* Giho goes to school **on foot**. 기호는 걸어서 학교에 간다.

3. **일반적 수단과 함께 쓰이는 전치사 by '~을 통해'**

   He got well **by taking the medicine**. 그는 그 약을 먹고 몸이 좋아졌다.

**with** a pencil

**by** bus

정답 p.68

### PRACTICE 16

〈보기〉에서 알맞은 전치사를 골라 빈칸에 쓰세요.

| 보 기 | with  by  on |
|---|---|

1  We can go to the Moon ______________ spacecraft.

2  It takes about ten minutes ______________ foot.

3  I cut the picture into pieces ______________ the scissors.

4  We went there ______________ plane.

5  You can improve your English ______________ writing more.

6  You can save money ______________ this coupon.

7  He makes money ______________ selling clothes.

## PSS 5  기타 주요 전치사



1. **like '~처럼, ~같이'**

   I want to be a scientist **like** my father. 나는 나의 아버지처럼 과학자가 되기를 원한다.

   She looks **like** a middle-aged woman. 그녀는 중년 여성 같이 보인다.

**2. without '~ 없이'**

People can't live **without** water. 사람들은 물 없이 살 수 없다.

He can't see **without** his glasses. 그는 그의 안경 없이 볼 수 없다.

**3. about '~에 대해'**

We learned **about** Greece. 우리는 그리스에 대해 배웠다.

Can you tell us **about** her? 그녀에 대해 말해줄 수 있니?

정답 p.68

## PRACTICE 17

다음 문장의 빈칸에 like나 without, about 중 알맞은 전치사를 쓰세요.

**1** I like coffee ________________ cream.

**2** I'll write ________________ my family.

**3** She looks ________________ a teacher.

**4** I've never seen a nice car ________________ yours.

**5** Let's talk ________________ the issue.

**6** Don't go out ________________ an umbrella.

**7** My brother can swim ________________ a fish.

**8** ________________ enough money, you can't travel.

정답 p.68

## PRACTICE 18

괄호 안에 주어진 전치사 중 알맞은 것을 고르세요.

**1** My dad goes to work (by, with) bicycle.

**2** The dog looked (like, without) a lion.

**3** Paint a picture (by, with) the brush.

**4** You can't enter (with, without) your ID card.

**5** It'll take a long time to go there (by, on) foot.

**6** I couldn't succeed (from, without) your advice.

**7** David drew a picture (by, with) his crayons.

**8** He dreams of becoming a pilot (like, about) his uncle.

**9** Tim went to the theater (by, with) subway.

**10** You can gargle (by, with) salt water.

# PSS 6 관용 표현



## PSS 6-1 형용사와 함께 쓰이는 전치사

1. **be afraid of** '~을 두려워하다'
   I**'m afraid of** the dark. 나는 어둠을 두려워한다.

2. **be absent from** '~에 결석하다'
   Mike **was absent from** school. Mike는 학교에 결석했다.

3. **be curious about** '~에 대해 궁금해하다'
   We **were curious about** the story. 우리는 그 이야기에 대해 궁금해했다.

4. **be different from** '~와 다르다'
   Middle school **is different from** elementary school. 중학교는 초등학교와 다르다.

5. **be good at** '~을 잘하다'
   She **is good at** singing. 그녀는 노래하는 것을 잘한다.

6. **be good for** '~에 좋다, 유익하다'
   This event may **be good for** children. 이 행사는 어린이들에게 유익할지도 모른다.

7. **be bad for** '~에 나쁘다, 해롭다'
   This game may **be bad for** children. 이 게임은 어린이들에게 해로울지도 모른다.

8. **be famous for** '~으로 유명하다'
   This village **is famous for** its traditional houses. 이 마을은 전통 가옥들로 유명하다.

9. **be full of** '~으로 가득하다'
   The basket **is full of** fruit. 그 바구니는 과일로 가득하다.

10. **be interested in** '~에 흥미[관심]가 있다'
    Barbara **is interested in** plants. Barbara는 식물에 관심이 있다.

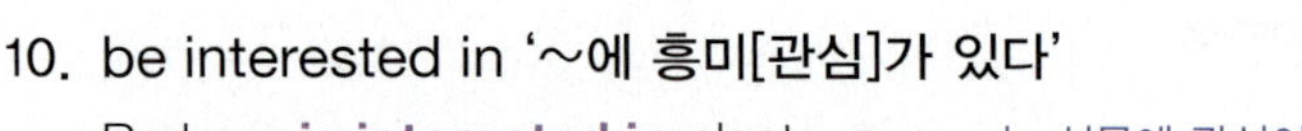

11. **be late for** '~에 늦다'
    She **is** never **late for** school. 그녀는 학교에 절대 늦지 않는다.

12. **be proud of** '~을 자랑스러워하다'
    He **is proud of** himself. 그는 그 자신을 자랑스러워한다.

13. **be ready for** '~을 위한 준비가 되다'
    We **are ready for** the test. 우리는 시험 볼 준비가 되어있다.

14. **be sorry for[about]** '~에 대해 미안해하다'
    He **was sorry for[about]** making the mistake. 그는 그 실수를 저지른 것에 대해 미안해했다.

## PRACTICE 19

다음 문장의 빈칸에 알맞은 전치사를 쓰세요.

**1** Ann is interested _______________ Korean food.

**2** Exercise is good _______________ your health.

**3** Paris is famous _______________ the Eiffel Tower.

**4** My brother is curious _______________ jazz music.

**5** Don't be late _______________ dinner.

**6** Her room is full _______________ books.

**7** My idea is different _______________ yours.

**8** He is afraid _______________ insects.

**9** My father is good _______________ cooking.

**10** Are you ready _______________ the test?

**11** I've never been absent _______________ this class.

**12** I am sorry _______________ being late.

**13** She was proud _______________ her work.

**14** Too much sugar is bad _______________ your teeth.

---

## PSS 6-2 동사와 함께 쓰이는 전치사

1. **buy … for ~** '～에게 …를 사주다'
   She wants to **buy** a hat **for** him. 그녀는 그에게 모자를 사주고 싶어한다.

2. **give … to ~** '～에게 …를 주다'
   He **gave** his old textbooks **to** his brother. 그는 그의 옛 교과서들을 그의 남동생에게 주었다.

3. **look at** '～을 보다'
   I **looked at** the bird. 나는 그 새를 보았다.

4. **look for** '～을 찾다'
   Ted is **looking for** the bus stop. Ted는 버스 정류장을 찾고 있다.

5. **thank ~ for …** '～에게 …에 대해 고맙게 여기다'
   **Thank** you **for** your help. 너의 도움에 대해 고마워. (도와줘서 고마워.)

6. **wait for** '～을 기다리다'
   We were **waiting for** the sunrise. 우리는 일출을 기다리고 있었다.

CH
**14**
전치사
&
속담



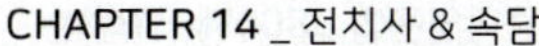

## PRACTICE 20

괄호 안에 주어진 전치사 중 알맞은 것을 고르세요.

1 Look (at, to) the beautiful birds.

2 You must wait (for, to) the green light.

3 Thank you (for, with) waiting while I finished my work.

4 His mother bought a computer (for, to) him.

5 Can you give this book (of, to) Giho?

6 The baby looked (for, on) her mother.

7 My family is now (at, on) Jeju Island.

8 He always goes skiing (at, in) winter.

9 We must not throw trash (into, out of) the river.

10 (After, In) lunch, they cleaned up their picnic area.

11 It's hard to find a Korean meal (by, without) gimchi.

12 My family took a trip (of, to) Italy.

13 I will arrive (on, in) July 8th.

14 He became popular (from, since) that time.

15 Susan took her present (into, out of) the box.

16 It rained (during, for) several days.

17 People will watch the singer (in, on) TV.

18 My sister goes to bed late (in, on) Fridays.

19 Summer comes (after, before) autumn.

20 The market opens (at, for) 10 a.m.

21 He has already left (for, to) his hometown.

22 I'm not good (at, in) math.

23 Summer vacation starts (at, in) July.

24 I couldn't find him (during, for) class.

25 She washes her hair (by, with) soap.

26 I met him (at, in) this time yesterday.

27 The room was full (with, of) treasures.

28 They went to the waterfall (by, on) boat.

29 He studies drama (at, in) New York.

30 There was no one (around, through) the beach.

# PSS 7 속담

1. **Walls have ears.**

   벽에도 귀가 있다. (낮말은 새가 듣고 밤말은 쥐가 듣는다.)

2. **No pain, no gain.**

   고통 없이는 얻는 것도 없다.

3. **Even a worm will turn.**

   벌레도 돌아설 것이다. (지렁이도 밟으면 꿈틀한다.)

4. **Look before you leap.**

   잘 보고 뛰어라. (돌다리도 두드려보고 건너라.)

5. **Every dog has his day.**

   모든 개도 그의 날이 있다. (쥐구멍에도 볕들 날 있다.)

6. **More haste, less speed.**

   급할수록 천천히. (급할수록 돌아가라.)

7. **All roads lead to Rome.**

   모든 길은 로마로 통한다. (많은 길을 통해 같은 목표에 도달한다.)

8. **Practice makes perfect.**

   훈련이 완벽을 만든다.

9. **Fine clothes make the man.**

   좋은 옷이 사람을 만든다. (옷이 날개다.)

10. **Small drops make a shower.**

    작은 물방울이 소나기를 만든다. (티끌 모아 태산이다.)

11. **Go home and kick the dog.**

    집에 가서 개를 발로 차다. (종로에서 뺨 맞고 한강 가서 눈 흘긴다.)

12. **A barking dog never bites.**

    짖는 개는 절대 물지 않는다. (빈 수레가 요란하다.)

13. **Don't cry over spilt milk.**

    엎질러진 우유 때문에 울지 마라. (이미 엎질러진 물이다.)

14. **Out of sight, out of mind.**

    눈에서 멀어지면 마음에서도 멀어진다.

**A monkey sometimes falls from the tree.**

**Don't cry over spilt milk.**

CH
**14**
전치사
&
속담

15.  Habit is (a) second nature.

습관은 제2의 천성이다. (세 살 버릇 여든까지 간다.)

16.  Honesty is the best policy.

정직이 최선의 방책이다.

17.  So many men, so many minds.

너무나 많은 사람들, 너무나 많은 생각들. (각인각색)

18.  A good medicine tastes bitter.

몸에 좋은 약은 입에 쓰다.

19.  Kill two birds with one stone.

한 개의 돌멩이로 두 마리의 새를 죽인다. (일석이조)

**Kill two birds with one stone.**

20.  Two heads are better than one.

두 사람이 한 사람보다 낫다. (백지장도 맞들면 낫다.)

21.  The early bird catches the worm.

일찍 일어나는 새가 벌레를 잡는다.

22.  Experience is the best teacher.

경험이 최고의 스승이다.

23.  There is no smoke without fire.

불 없이 연기가 날 리 없다. (아니 땐 굴뚝에 연기 나랴.)

24.  Too many cooks spoil the broth.

요리사가 너무 많으면 수프를 망친다. (사공이 많으면 배가 산으로 올라간다.)

25.  Don't judge a book by its cover.

책의 표지로 그 책을 판단하지 말라. (겉모습보다는 내면이 중요하다.)

26.  When in Rome, do as the Romans do.

로마에 있을 때는 로마인들이 하는 것처럼 해라. (로마에서는 로마법을 따르라.)

27.  A bad workman always blames his tools.

서투른 일꾼이 항상 연장을 탓한다.

28.  A monkey sometimes falls from the tree.

원숭이도 나무에서 떨어질 때가 있다.

29.  Don't put off today's work until tomorrow.

오늘의 일을 내일로 미루지 말라.

30.  A journey of 1000 miles begins with a single step.

1000마일 여행도 한 걸음으로 시작한다. (천리 길도 한 걸음부터.)

## PRACTICE 21

다음 우리말에 맞는 속담을 〈보기〉에서 골라 그 번호를 쓰고 전체 문장을 빈칸에 쓰세요.

| 보 기 | |
|---|---|
| ① | Two heads are better than one. |
| ② | Small drops make a shower. |
| ③ | A good medicine tastes bitter. |
| ④ | Even a worm will turn. |
| ⑤ | A journey of 1000 miles begins with a single step. |
| ⑥ | Don't judge a book by its cover. |
| ⑦ | Fine clothes make the man. |
| ⑧ | Too many cooks spoil the broth. |
| ⑨ | Go home and kick the dog. |
| ⑩ | Walls have ears. |

**1** 낮말은 새가 듣고 밤말은 쥐가 듣는다. ➡ [ ⑩ ] Walls have ears.

**2** 옷이 날개다. ➡ [ ] __________

**3** 겉모습보다는 내면이 중요하나. ➡ [ ] __________

**4** 종로에서 뺨 맞고 한강 가서 눈 흘긴다. ➡ [ ] __________

**5** 지렁이도 밟으면 꿈틀한다. ➡ [ ] __________

**6** 티끌 모아 태산이다. ➡ [ ] __________

**7** 몸에 좋은 약은 입에 쓰다. ➡ [ ] __________

**8** 백지장도 맞들면 낫다. ➡ [ ] __________

**9** 사공이 많으면 배가 산으로 올라간다. ➡ [ ] __________

**10** 천리 길도 한 걸음부터. ➡ [ ] __________

CH
**14**
전치사
&
속담

## PRACTICE 22

**빈칸에 알맞은 단어를 넣으세요.**

1  A bad workman always _________________________.  서투른 일꾼이 항상 연장을 탓한다.

2  Experience is _____________ teacher.  경험이 최고의 스승이다.

3  _________________________ catches the worm.  일찍 일어나는 새가 벌레를 잡는다.

4  _____________ makes _____________.  훈련이 완벽을 만든다.

5  There is no smoke _________________________.  아니 땐 굴뚝에 연기 나랴.

6  So many _____________, so many _____________.  각인각색

7  Every _____________ has his _____________.  쥐구멍에도 볕들 날 있다.

8  When in Rome, do _________________________.  로마에서는 로마법을 따르라.

9  No _____________, no _____________.  고통 없이는 얻는 것도 없다.

10  Out of _____________, out of _____________.  눈에서 멀어지면 마음에서도 멀어진다.

11  A _____________ dog never _____________.  짖는 개는 절대 물지 않는다. (빈 수레가 요란하다.)

12  Habit is a _________________________.  습관은 제2의 천성이다. (세 살 버릇 여든까지 간다.)

13  _____________ is the best _____________.  정직이 최선의 방책이다.

14  Look before you _____________.  잘 보고 뛰어라. (돌다리도 두드려보고 건너라.)

15  More _____________, less _____________.  급할수록 돌아가라.



## PRACTICE 23

**아래의 속담에 들어갈 알맞은 전치사를 〈보기〉에서 골라 쓰세요.**

| 보 기 | until   with   from   to   over |
| --- | --- |

1  A journey of 1000 miles begins _____________ a single step.

2  All roads lead _____________ Rome.

3  Don't put off today's work _____________ tomorrow.

4  Kill two birds _____________ one stone.

5  A monkey sometimes falls _____________ the tree.

6  Don't cry _____________ spilt milk.

**1** 다음 빈칸에 들어갈 알맞은 단어를 고르세요.

> Yujin plays computer games ___________ Saturdays.

① in      ② to      ③ on
④ at      ⑤ for

**2** 다음 빈칸에 들어갈 알맞은 단어를 고르세요.

> Our summer vacation begins ___________ July.

① on      ② at      ③ in
④ to      ⑤ for

**3** 다음 빈칸에 들어갈 알맞은 전치사를 쓰세요.

> A: When is your birthday?
> B: It is ___________ the 27th of September.

**4** 다음 우리말과 같은 뜻이 되도록 빈칸에 들어갈 알맞은 말을 고르세요.

> • 나는 잠시 동안 그와 이야기하기를 원했다.
>   = I wanted to talk with him ___________.

① on a minute      ② by a minute
③ at a minute      ④ for a minute
⑤ in a minute

**5** 다음 우리말과 같은 뜻이 되도록 빈칸에 들어갈 알맞은 전치사를 쓰세요.

(1) 문 뒤에 있는 저 아이는 누구니?
= Who is that child ___________ the door?

(2) 너는 대도시에서 살기를 원하니?
= Do you want to live ___________ a big city?

**6** 다음 대화의 빈칸에 들어갈 알맞은 단어는?

> A: Can you cut this apple ___________ a knife?
> B: Of course.

① to      ② at      ③ on
④ with      ⑤ by

**7** 다음 우리말과 같은 뜻이 되도록 빈칸에 들어갈 알맞은 전치사를 쓰세요.

> • Kate는 노래를 잘한다.
>   = Kate is good ___________ singing.

**8** 다음 빈칸에 공통으로 들어갈 말로 알맞은 것은?

> • It opens ___________ 9 a.m. to 6 p.m.
> • My name is Mina. I am ___________ Jinju.
> • He's going to come back ___________ France this Friday.

① to      ② at      ③ from
④ of      ⑤ on

CH **14** 전치사 & 속담

# 9
다음 우리말과 같은 뜻이 되도록 빈칸에 들어갈 알맞은 전치사를 쓰세요.

> • 어머니는 저녁 식사 후에 설거지를 하신다.
> = My mother does the dishes ______ dinner.

# 10
다음 (a)~(e) 어디에도 들어갈 수 <u>없는</u> 것은?

> Meet Jaehoon. He is a first-year middle school student. Let's see what his morning and evening are like. He wakes (a) ______ at 7:00 and washes his face. He eats breakfast, usually toast and eggs. He prepares his school bag the day before, so he just grabs his bag and leaves the house by 8:00. He walks to school (b) ______ his friend, talking about funny things they see online. (c) ______ a full day of classes, he gets home around 4 p.m. He eats snacks and then does his homework (d) ______ his desk. He helps his mom set the table for dinner around 7 p.m. After dinner, he spends time with his family watching TV and reading books together. At 9:30, he prepares his school bag (e) ______ the next day and goes to bed.

① for　　② with　　③ at　　④ from　　⑤ up

# 11
빈칸에 들어갈 단어가 순서대로 바르게 연결된 것은?

> • My uncle grows tomatoes and potatoes ______ his farm.
> • Look ______ the wonderful rocks in the picture.

① on – at　　② on – with　　③ at – on
④ with – to　　⑤ for – at

# 12
다음 빈칸에 들어갈 말이 알맞게 짝지어진 것은?

> • I was late ______ school today.
> • He went bungee jumping ______ fear.
> • He will stay at his grandparents' ______ a month.

① to – without – for
② for – without – during
③ to – on – for
④ for – without – for
⑤ to – on – during

# 13
다음 그림에 대한 설명으로 올바르지 <u>않은</u> 것은?

① There is a dog under the desk.
② There is a clock next to the desk.
③ There are backpacks beside the desk.
④ There are a few books on the desk.
⑤ There are a calendar and a picture on the wall.

# 14
빈칸에 공통으로 들어갈 알맞은 전치사를 쓰세요.

> • What's ______ channel 9 at 8 p.m.?
> • My favorite drama is now ______ TV.

**15** 다음은 학교 체험학습 관련 선생님의 공지사항이다. 글의 빈칸에 들어갈 수 <u>없는</u> 것은?

Hello, students. Are you ready _____ our school field trip tomorrow? _____ you know, we will visit Newton Science Center. It is full _____ interesting inventions. We will use our school buses for the trip. The buses will leave _____ 9 a.m. So, I expect you to be in front of the school gate _____ 8:30.

① at
② for
③ by
④ as
⑤ with

**16** 다음 우리말 해석과 일치하도록 〈보기〉의 단어를 활용하고, 어법상 필요한 단어를 추가하여 문장을 완성하세요. (필요시 단어의 형태를 바꿀 것.)

| 보 기 | feel / sorry / her |
| --- | --- |

내가 그 소식을 들었을 때, 나는 그녀에 대해 안쓰럽게 느꼈다.

= When I heard the news, _____ _____ _____ _____ _____.

**17** 빈칸에 공통으로 들어갈 알맞은 전치사는?

- The weather changes very often _____ fall.
- There are many people _____ the building.

① at
② to
③ for
④ of
⑤ in

**18** 다음 지도를 보고 빈칸에 들어갈 알맞은 말로 짝지어진 것을 고르세요.

*A*: How can I get to the bakery?
*B*: Go straight and turn right. It's _____ the post office.
*A*: Sorry, I don't understand. Could you tell me again?
*B*: Go straight and turn right. It's _____ the post office and the bank.

① next to – by
② in front of – next to
③ next to – between
④ in front of – among
⑤ next to – in front of



**19** 빈칸에 들어갈 단어가 순서대로 바르게 연결된 것은?

- A little bear was walking _____ the forest.
- My father works _____ Computer Plus Company.

① around – to
② around – on
③ across – as
④ around – for
⑤ across – on

## 20 다음 중 밑줄 친 부분이 잘못 쓰인 것은?

① There are no classes in Saturday and Sunday.
② We usually eat breakfast at 8:40.
③ Our office hours are from 9 a.m. to 5 p.m.
④ I sent him a gift on his birthday.
⑤ Where did you go during the vacation?

## 21 다음 빈칸에 들어갈 말이 알맞게 짝지어진 것은?

My parents give me 70 dollars for my monthly allowance. I've made a plan to spend my money wisely. First, I will spend 30 dollars ___________ my favorite things ___________ movies and snacks. Next, I will put 30 dollars in the bank because I will buy a new cell phone ___________ this money next year. I will also send 10 dollars to hungry children in Africa.

① on – like – in      ② in – to – for
③ on – like – with      ④ in – like – with
⑤ on – in – for

## 22 우리말과 같은 뜻이 되도록 빈칸에 들어갈 알맞은 전치사를 쓰세요.

A: Excuse me. Where is the Hanil Building?
B: It's ___________ the street from the drugstore.
(약국 길 건너편에 있어요.)

## 23 다음 빈칸에 들어갈 전치사를 순서대로 바르게 나열한 것은?

- There are a lot of shops ___________ my town.
- The first class begins ___________ 8:30 every day.
- What do Koreans usually do ___________ special holidays?

① on – at – in      ② for – at – in
③ at – in – on      ④ in – at – on
⑤ in – for – to

## 24 다음 글의 빈칸에 알맞은 속담을 고르세요.

There is a saying "___________" In my case, I had an important math exam but I wasn't really good at math. However, I wanted to get a good grade on the exam. So I didn't watch TV and hang out with my friends in order to study hard. It wasn't easy to study all day long. I really wanted to read comic books and watch TV. But I had to study hard to achieve what I wanted. As a result, I got a good grade on the math exam.

① More haste, less speed.
② No pain, no gain.
③ All roads lead to Rome.
④ Two heads are better than one.
⑤ Kill two birds with one stone.

## 25 다음 문장의 빈칸에 들어갈 알맞은 단어는?

___________ the way home, Seho came across his old friend.

① To     ② In     ③ On     ④ By     ⑤ For

**26** 다음 대화의 빈칸에 쓰일 수 <u>없는</u> 말은?

> A: Excuse me, may I ask you something?
> B: Sure, go ahead.
> A: I'm looking for Times Square. Do you know how I can get there?
> B: Oh, it's very close from here. Here, look at this map. We're here now. So, just go straight for three blocks and turn right at the bank.
> A: Is it __________ the bank?
> B: That's right.

① next to ② close to ③ in front of
④ looking for ⑤ across from

**27** 다음 빈칸에 들어갈 말이 나머지와 <u>다른</u> 것은?

① They went there __________ taxi.
② He goes to work __________ car.
③ Do you go to school __________ foot?
④ She always comes home __________ bicycle.
⑤ I go to my grandma's house __________ train.

**28** 빈칸에 들어갈 단어가 순서대로 바르게 연결된 것은?

> We sometimes go __________ the shopping mall __________ a subway.

① to – by ② to – on ③ with – for
④ for – by ⑤ on – at

**29** 다음 빈칸에 공통으로 들어갈 단어로 알맞은 것은?

> • He dreams of being a singer __________ his favorite pop star.
> • He acts __________ a comedian in class. He is funny.

① for ② like ③ from
④ on ⑤ at

**30** 다음 ①~⑤ 중 어법상 <u>옳은</u> 것은?

> Yesterday, I ①<u>take</u> a walk after dinner. I was walking ②<u>on</u> the river when I found three dogs. They were sleeping ③<u>under</u> a tree. The smallest one ④<u>between</u> them was shaking with cold. I brought them home, so they have been with me ⑤<u>from</u> yesterday.

**31** 다음 밑줄 친 단어의 뜻이 나머지 넷과 <u>다른</u> 하나는?

① The Turtle Ship looks <u>like</u> a turtle.
② How do you <u>like</u> this place?
③ Mina wants to be a famous singer <u>like</u> him.
④ Does he swim <u>like</u> a fish?
⑤ I have never seen a nice picture <u>like</u> that.

**32** 주어진 우리말과 같은 뜻이 되도록 빈칸에 공통으로 들어갈 알맞은 전치사를 쓰세요.

> • 아니 땐 굴뚝에 연기 나랴.
>   = There is no smoke _____________ fire.
> • 우리는 우주선 없이 달에 갈 수 없다.
>   = We can't go to the Moon _____________ spaceships.

**33** 〈보기〉 중 다음 글의 빈칸에 들어가는 것끼리 짝지어진 것은?

> Some good bacteria live inside some foods. For example, *gimchi* is full _____________ good bacteria. So *gimchi* is good _____________ your body.

> 보 기 │ ⓐ of  ⓑ on  ⓒ by  ⓓ about  ⓔ for

① ⓐ,ⓒ  　　② ⓒ,ⓔ  　　③ ⓑ,ⓒ
④ ⓑ,ⓓ  　　⑤ ⓐ,ⓔ

**34** 다음 문장의 빈칸과 들어갈 말이 같은 것은?

> • She read a book _____________ flowers.
> • Kids are curious _____________ everything around them.

① Look _____________ the picture on the wall.
② She is afraid _____________ bees.
③ The city is famous _____________ its buildings.
④ I am interested _____________ playing the piano.
⑤ I'm going to write _____________ animals.

**35** 우리말과 일치하도록 주어진 말을 알맞게 배열하세요.

> 우리의 관습은 너희의 것과 상당히 다르다.
> (are / yours / customs / different / our / quite / from)

➡ _______________________________________

**36** 다음 글의 밑줄 친 부분과 쓰임이 <u>다른</u> 것은?

> Take a look at this. It's a bagel. It looks <u>like</u> a doughnut. It came from Poland. However, now it is the favorite breakfast of New York.

① The paper smells <u>like</u> a flower.
② Let's make two rooms <u>like</u> this.
③ My parents treat me <u>like</u> a child.
④ They <u>like</u> riding a bicycle very much.
⑤ What's the weather <u>like</u> in your country?

**37** 다음 ①~⑤ 중 어법상 옳지 <u>않은</u> 것은?

> Amy went to Paris during winter vacation. She arrived ①<u>at</u> the hotel. The next day, she visited the Versailles Palace ②<u>by</u> car. She walked ③<u>into</u> the palace. She found that there were a lot of mirrors. She looked ④<u>on</u> those mirrors with a smile. She was answered with the same smiles ⑤<u>from</u> the mirrors.

## 38 다음 중 빈칸에 on이 들어갈 수 <u>없는</u> 것을 고르세요.

① Koreans wear *hanbok* ______ Chuseok.
② Look at the beautiful kites ______ the sky.
③ What do you do ______ Sundays?
④ We enjoyed ourselves ______ the beach.
⑤ I'm ______ a diet now.

## 39 다음 문장의 빈칸에 들어갈 알맞은 전치사를 쓰세요.

(1) I bought some flowers __________ her.

(2) Can you tell me __________ Korean history?

## 40 다음 글에 알맞은 속담을 고르세요.

In India, people eat with their right hands. So it is important to wash your hands before a meal. In France, people may think you're rude if you speak with your mouth full at table. In Italy, it is not polite to place your hands under the table during a meal. So before you go to other countries, you had better know about their etiquette.

① Don't cry over spilt milk.
② Practice makes perfect.
③ When in Rome, do as the Romans do.
④ Fine clothes make the man.
⑤ Go home and kick the dog.

## 41 빈칸에 들어갈 단어가 순서대로 바르게 연결된 것은?

• The bus stops __________ Gwanghwamun.
• She made a circle __________ her thumb and forefinger.
• There is a department store __________ 5th Street.

① at – with – on
② in – on　 – to
③ at – to　 – with
④ in – with – on
⑤ at – on　 – in

## 42 주어진 우리말과 같은 뜻이 되도록 빈칸에 들어갈 알맞은 전치사를 쓰세요.

• 나는 티셔츠를 찾고 있다.
　= I'm looking __________ a T-shirt.
• 당신은 이 사진을 보고 있나요?
　= Are you looking __________ this picture?

## 43 빈칸에 공통으로 들어갈 알맞은 전치사를 쓰세요.

• We always have lunch __________ noon.
• I'm going to Paris __________ the end of this year.

**44** 우리말과 같은 뜻이 되도록 빈칸에 알맞은 전치사를 쓰세요.

> • 나는 3개월 동안 고모 댁에 머물렀다.
> = I stayed at my aunt's ____________ 3 months.

**45** Jason의 방을 보고 엄마가 남긴 메모입니다. 그림을 보고 빈칸에 알맞은 말을 쓰세요.

Dear Jason,
Look at your room. Your pants are
(1) ____________ the table. Your sock is
(2) ____________ the table.  Look at the box.
It's (3) ____________ your bed.
Please, don't forget to clean your room!
*Mom*

**46** 빈칸에 들어갈 전치사가 순서대로 짝지어진 것은?

> Minji was absent ____________ school today. She was very sick because she got a bad cold. Her mother made her hot soup. It was good ____________ her headache and sore throat.

① at  – for
② in  – to
③ with – by
④ from – of
⑤ from – for

**47** 다음 글과 어울리는 속담을 고르세요.

> Seho wants to get a new bag, but he has no way to earn money. So, he walks to school instead of taking a bus these days. In this way, he can save about 30,000 won a month. Moreover, he decides not to spend money on fun things. By doing so, he will be able to buy a new bag in about three months.

① Every dog has his day.
② Look before you leap.
③ Too many cooks spoil the broth.
④ Small drops make a shower.
⑤ Don't put off today's work until tomorrow.

**48** 주어진 문장의 밑줄 친 for와 의미가 같은 것을 고르세요.

> What food do you want for dessert?

① He is always late for school.
② We ate steak for dinner.
③ She is looking for her bag.
④ I planned to stay here for two weeks.
⑤ Thank you for your letter.

**49** 빈칸에 공통으로 들어갈 알맞은 단어는?

> • Mr. Brown and his family live next ____________ my house.
> • How about writing a letter ____________ her?
> • You should go ____________ see a doctor.

① for
② with
③ to
④ in
⑤ by

## 50 다음 글의 주제와 어울리는 속담을 고르세요.

One day, Thomas was invited to a dinner party by his neighbor. He wore his old suit and went there. But the neighbor said that Thomas couldn't come to the party in such an old suit. Soon after, Thomas went back to the party in his new suit and the neighbor welcomed him. But Thomas didn't enter his house and gave him his new suit, saying "Enjoy your party with my new suit. You invite not me but my suit."

① A barking dog never bites.
② Honesty is the best policy.
③ Don't judge a book by its cover.
④ Even a worm will turn.
⑤ Go home and kick the dog.

## 51 ①~⑤ 중 들어갈 말이 나머지 넷과 <u>다른</u> 것은?

Many children ____①____ the world are ____②____ danger now. They are suffering ____③____ hunger and disease. They need your help. You can donate money for them. You can start from 3,000 won a month! Your small help can make a big change ____④____ their lives. Save your money for children ____⑤____ need.

## 52 다음 빈칸에 들어갈 알맞은 말을 쓰세요.

Boryeong is famous for its global Mud Festival. It is one of the most famous festivals (1)____________ Korea. It takes place at mud flat. It usually starts very early (2)____________ the morning. It lasts (3)____________ eleven days.

*mud: 진흙

## 53 다음 빈칸에 들어갈 말이 차례대로 짝지어진 것은?

• We should not sleep ____________ class.
• She exercises ____________ 30 minutes a day.

① for – to      ② to – for      ③ to – during
④ during – for      ⑤ for – during

## 54 아래의 전치사 중 필요한 것을 선택하여 다음 〈보기〉와 같이 괄호 안의 단어를 가지고 그림을 묘사하세요.

보 기 | There is a table in the room. (table)

in, on, between, over, behind, under, next to, in front of

(1) ____________________________ (books)
(2) ____________________________ (dog)

## 55 다음을 읽고 틀린 부분 세 가지를 찾아 바르게 고쳐 쓰세요.

On weekends, Maria's family goes camping. They go there by foot. They usually stay in a cabin. They like to spend time on nature. On sunny days, Maria and her sister, Anna, go in the forest to pick wild fruits.

(1) _______________  ➡  _______________

(2) _______________  ➡  _______________

(3) _______________  ➡  _______________

## 56 ⓐ~ⓒ에 들어갈 알맞은 말로 바르게 짝 지어진 것은?

### *Rock Paper Scissors*

We often play the game rock paper scissors. It is good ⓐ_________ making a fair decision. ⓑ_________ using a hand, each player forms one of three gestures. There are three possible outcomes: a win, a loss, or a draw. The earliest form of the game originated in China, and it was brought ⓒ_________ Japan in the 17th century. The Japanese version named "janken" is similar to the modern version.

|     | ⓐ   |   | ⓑ  |   | ⓒ    |
| --- | --- | --- | --- | --- | --- |
| ① | for | – | On | – | from |
| ② | at  | – | By | – | to   |
| ③ | for | – | By | – | from |
| ④ | at  | – | On | – | from |
| ⑤ | for | – | By | – | to   |

## 57 다음 빈칸에 들어갈 말과 같은 말이 들어갈 수 있는 문장을 고르세요.

The bridge has been built _________ the river.

① Can you come _________ my room in an hour?

② I picked up a strawberry and put it _________ my mouth.

③ She is _________ the Philippines.

④ The birds are flying _________ the river.

⑤ We make wonderful movies _________ our digital cameras.

## 58 다음 ⓐ~ⓒ에 들어갈 말이 알맞게 짝지어진 것은?

Jessie's family stayed _____ⓐ_____ a *hanok* guesthouse last night. She slept _____ⓑ_____ *ondol* instead of in a bed. After breakfast, they went to Gyeongbokgung _____ⓒ_____ bus. Jessie and her brother took lots of pictures with a camera.

|     | ⓐ   |   | ⓑ   |   | ⓒ   |
| --- | --- | --- | --- | --- | --- |
| ① | at | – | on | – | from |
| ② | in | – | in | – | on |
| ③ | at | – | over | – | on |
| ④ | at | – | on | – | by |
| ⑤ | on | – | on | – | by |

# 중학영문법 3800제 1학년 교과서 활용 진도표

## 🔶 동아 윤정미

| 과 | 교과서 문법 내용 | CH | PSS |
|---|---|---|---|
| 1 | be동사 현재시제 | 1 | 1-2~1-3 |
| 1 | 일반동사 현재시제 | 2 | 1-1~1-4 |
| 2 | 현재진행시제 | 2 | 4-1~4-3 |
| 2 | 조동사 can | 3 | 4-1~4-2 |
| 2 | 조동사 will | 2 | 3 |
| 3 | be동사 과거시제 | 1 | 1-2~1-3 |
| 3 | 일반동사 과거시제 | 2 | 2-1~2-5 |
| 3 | 명령문 | 1 | 1-10 |
| 4 | 동명사 | 8 | 1~2 |
| 4 | be going to | 2 | 3 |
| 5 | 비교급 | 12 | 1-1~1-4, 3-1~3-3 |
| 5 | There+be동사 | 5 | 10 |
| 6 | to부정사(명사적 용법) | 7 | 1-1~1-2 |
| 6 | 접속사 that | 13 | 4 |
| 7 | to부정사(부사적 용법) | 7 | 3 |
| 7 | 접속사 when | 13 | 5 |
| 8 | give 수여동사(4형식) | 1 | 2-3 |
| 8 | 비인칭 주어 it | 6 | 3 |

## 🔵 동아 이병민

| 과 | 교과서 문법 내용 | CH | PSS |
|---|---|---|---|
| 1 | be동사 현재시제 | 1 | 1-2~1-3 |
| 1 | 일반동사 현재시제 | 2 | 1-1~1-4 |
| 2 | 의문문(일반동사) | 1 | 1-5 |
| 2 | 명령문 | 1 | 1-10 |
| 3 | 조동사 can | 3 | 4-1~4-2 |
| 3 | 조동사 will | 2 | 3 |
| 3 | 현재진행시제 | 2 | 4-1~4-3 |
| 4 | 일반동사 과거시제 | 2 | 2-1~2-5 |
| 4 | There is/are | 5 | 10 |
| 5 | to부정사(명사적 용법) | 7 | 1-1~1-2 |
| 5 | 비인칭 주어 it | 6 | 3 |
| 6 | 감각동사+형용사(2형식) | 1 | 2-4 |
| 6 | 동사원형+-ing(동명사) | 8 | 1,2 |
| 7 | 비교급 | 12 | 1-1~1-4, 3-1~3-3 |
| 7 | 접속사 when | 13 | 5 |
| 8 | 수여동사 | 1 | 2-5 |
| 8 | 접속사 that | 13 | 4 |

## 🟢 미래엔 문영인

| 과 | 교과서 문법 내용 | CH | PSS |
|---|---|---|---|
| 1 | be동사 현재시제 | 1 | 1-2~1-3 |
| 1 | 일반동사 현재시제 | 2 | 1-1~1-4 |
| 2 | 현재진행형 | 2 | 4-1~4-3 |
| 2 | There is/are 구문 | 5 | 10 |
| 3 | 과거 시제 | 2 | 2-1~2-5 |
| 3 | 조동사 can | 3 | 4-1~4-2 |
| 4 | 명사 역할을 하는 동명사 | 8 | 1~2 |
| 4 | 조동사 will | 2 | 3 |
| 5 | 목적어가 두 개인 동사 (4형식) | 1 | 2-5 |
| 5 | 조동사 should | 3 | 4-10 |
| 6 | 동사의 목적어로 쓰이는 to 부정사 | 7 | 1-2 |
| 6 | 때를 나타내는 접속사 when | 13 | 5 |
| 7 | 비교급 | 12 | 1-1~1-4, 3-1~3-3 |
| 7 | 최상급 | 12 | 1-1~1-4, 4-1~4-2 |

## 🔵 비상 황종배

| 과 | 교과서 문법 내용 | CH | PSS |
|---|---|---|---|
| 1 | be동사 현재형 | 1 | 1-2~1-3 |
| 1 | 일반동사 현재형 | 2 | 1-1~1-4 |
| 2 | There is/are | 5 | 10 |
| 2 | 현재진행형 | 2 | 4-1~4-3 |
| 3 | be동사 과거형 | 1 | 1-2~1-3 |
| 3 | 일반동사 과거형 | 2 | 2-1~2-5 |
| 4 | 목적어가 두 개인 동사 (4형식) | 1 | 2-5 |
| 4 | 조동사 will | 2 | 3 |
| 4 | 조동사 can | 3 | 4-1~4-2 |
| 5 | 동명사 | 8 | 1~2 |
| 5 | 감각동사+형용사(2형식) | 1 | 2-4 |
| 6 | 접속사 when | 13 | 5 |
| 6 | 비교급 | 12 | 1-1~1-4, 3-1~3-3 |
| 7 | 명사처럼 쓰이는 to부정사 (to부정사의 명사적 용법) | 7 | 1-1~1-2 |
| 7 | 감탄문 | 1 | 1-13 |
| 8 | 부사처럼 쓰이는 to부정사 (to부정사의 부사적 용법) | 7 | 3 |
| 8 | 접속사 that의 쓰임 | 13 | 4 |

## 🌸 YBM 박준언

| 과 | 교과서 문법 내용 | CH | PSS |
|---|---|---|---|
| 1 | be동사의 현재형 | 1 | 1-2~1-3 |
| 1 | 일반동사의 현재형 | 2 | 1-1~1-4 |
| 2 | 현재진행형 | 2 | 4-1~4-3 |
| 2 | 조동사 will | 2 | 3 |
| 2 | 조동사 can | 3 | 4-1~4-2 |
| 3 | 과거 시제 | 2 | 2-1~2-5 |
| 3 | 명령문 | 1 | 1-10 |
| 4 | to부정사의 명사적 용법 | 7 | 1-1~1-2 |
| 4 | 시간을 나타내는 접속사 when | 13 | 5 |
| 5 | 비교급 | 12 | 1-1~1-4, 3-1~3-3 |
| 5 | 감각 동사 | 1 | 2-4 |
| 6 | 동명사 | 8 | 1~2 |
| 6 | 4형식 | 1 | 2-3 |
| 7 | 접속사 that | 13 | 4 |
| 7 | 감탄문 | 1 | 1-13 |
| 8 | 재귀대명사 | 6 | 2 |
| 8 | to부정사의 부사적 용법 | 7 | 3 |

중학영문법 3800제 1학년 **교과서 활용 진도표**

### 🐝 지학사 송미정

| 과 | 교과서 문법 내용 | CH | PSS |
|---|---|---|---|
| 1 | be동사 현재시제 | 1 | 1-2~1-3 |
| | 일반동사 현재시제 | 2 | 1-1~1-4 |
| 2 | 현재진행형 | 2 | 4-1~4-3 |
| | There+be동사 | 5 | 10 |
| 3 | 조동사 can | 3 | 4-1~4-2 |
| | 감각동사 | 1 | 2-4 |
| 4 | 동사의 과거시제 | 2 | 2-1~2-5 |
| | 조동사 will | 2 | 3 |
| 5 | 비교급 | 12 | 1-1~1-4, 3-1~3-3 |
| | 최상급 | 12 | 1-1~1-4, 4-1~4-2 |
| | 명사절 that | 13 | 4 |
| 6 | to부정사의 명사적 용법 | 7 | 1-1~1-2 |
| | 동명사 | 8 | 1~2 |
| 7 | to부정사의 부사적 용법 | 7 | 3 |
| | 접속사 when | 13 | 5 |
| 8 | 접속사 because | 13 | 5 |
| | have to/don't have to | 3 | 4-8~4-9 |

### 🐝 천재 이상기

| 과 | 교과서 문법 내용 | CH | PSS |
|---|---|---|---|
| 1 | be동사 현재형 | 1 | 1-2~1-3 |
| | 일반동사 현재형 | 2 | 1-1~1-4 |
| 2 | 현재진행형 | 2 | 4-1~4-3 |
| | 의문문 | 1 | 1-5 |
| 3 | 명령문 | 1 | 1-10 |
| | 조동사 can | 3 | 4-1~4-2 |
| | 조동사 will | 2 | 3 |
| 4 | 과거형 | 2 | 2-1~2-5 |
| | 감탄문 | 1 | 1-13 |
| 5 | There is/are | 5 | 10 |
| | 동명사 | 8 | 1~2 |
| 6 | 접속사 that | 13 | 4 |
| | to부정사의 명사적 용법 | 7 | 1-1~1-2 |
| 7 | 감각동사 | 1 | 2-4 |
| | 비교급 | 12 | 1-1~1-4, 3-1~3-3 |
| 8 | 접속사 when | 13 | 5 |
| | to부정사의 부사적 용법 | 7 | 3 |

### 🐝 천재 소영순

| 과 | 교과서 문법 내용 | CH | PSS |
|---|---|---|---|
| 1 | be동사 현재시제 | 1 | 1-2~1-3 |
| | 일반동사 현재시제 | 2 | 1-1~1-4 |
| 2 | 현재진행형 | 2 | 4-1~4-3 |
| | 조동사 will | 2 | 3 |
| | 조동사 can | 3 | 4-1~4-2 |
| 3 | 의문사 의문문 | 1 | 1-7 |
| | to부정사(명사적 용법) | 7 | 1-1~1-2 |
| 4 | 과거시제 | 2 | 2-1~2-5 |
| | 동명사 | 8 | 1~2 |
| 5 | 비교급 | 12 | 1-1~1-4, 3-1~3-3 |
| | 최상급 | 12 | 1-1~1-4, 4-1~4-2 |
| 6 | to부정사(부사적 용법) | 7 | 3 |
| | 접속사 that | 13 | 4 |
| 7 | 4형식 | 1 | 2-3 |
| | 접속사 when | 13 | 5 |

### 🐝 능률 김기택

| 과 | 교과서 문법 내용 | CH | PSS |
|---|---|---|---|
| 1 | be동사 | 1 | 1-2~1-3 |
| | 일반동사 현재시제 | 2 | 1-1~1-4 |
| 2 | 현재진행형 | 2 | 4-1~4-3 |
| | 동명사 | 8 | 1~2 |
| 3 | 일반동사 과거시제 | 2 | 2-1~2-5 |
| | 접속사 when | 13 | 5 |
| 4 | to부정사(명사적 용법) | 7 | 1-1~1-2 |
| | 조동사 should | 3 | 4-10 |
| | 조동사 will | 2 | 3 |
| 5 | 재귀대명사 | 6 | 2 |
| | to부정사(부사적 용법) | 7 | 3 |
| 6 | 감각동사+형용사(2형식) | 1 | 2-4 |
| | 접속사 becasue | 13 | 5 |
| 7 | make+목적어+형용사(5형식) | 1 | 2-3 |
| | 접속사 that | 13 | 4 |
| 8 | How 감탄문 | 1 | 1-13 |
| | What 감탄문 | 1 | 1-13 |
| | something 후치 수식 | 10 | 3 |

### 🐝 YBM 김은형

| 과 | 교과서 문법 내용 | CH | PSS |
|---|---|---|---|
| 1 | be동사의 현재형 | 1 | 1-2~1-3 |
| | 일반동사의 현재형 | 2 | 1-1~1-4 |
| 2 | be동사/일반동사의 의문문 | 1 | 1-5 |
| | 현재진행형 | 2 | 4-1~4-3 |
| 3 | be동사/일반동사의 과거형 | 2 | 2-1~2-5 |
| | 조동사 will | 2 | 3 |
| 4 | 동명사 | 8 | 1~2 |
| | There is/are ~ | 5 | 10 |
| 5 | to부정사의 명사적 용법 | 7 | 1-1~1-2 |
| | 재귀대명사 | 6 | 2 |
| 6 | 접속사 when | 13 | 5 |
| | 조동사 should | 3 | 4-10 |
| 7 | 비교급 | 12 | 1-1~1-4, 3-1~3-3 |
| | 최상급 | 12 | 1-1~1-4, 4-1~4-2 |
| 8 | 수여동사 | 1 | 2-5 |
| | to부정사의 부사적 용법 | 7 | 3 |

2026 새 교과서에 맞춘 16차 개정판

# 중학영문법 3800제 1학년

# 정답과 해설

MOTHERTONGUE
마더텅출판사
since 1999.4.1.

## PRACTICE 1

**1** it  **2** they  **3** you  **4** he  **5** they
**6** it  **7** we  **8** they  **9** he  **10** we
**11** she  **12** you  **13** they  **14** they

## PRACTICE 2

**1** was  **2** was  **3** are  **4** were
**5** are  **6** am

## PRACTICE 3

**1** is  **2** O  **3** are  **4** are
**5** O  **6** am  **7** were  **8** was

## PRACTICE 4

**2** He's  **3** I'm not
**4** She's not[She isn't]  **5** We're not[We aren't]
**6** You weren't  **7** They're
**8** It's not[It isn't]  **9** I wasn't
**10** She wasn't  **11** We weren't
**12** It wasn't  **13** He wasn't
**14** They're not[They aren't]
**15** You're not[You aren't]
**16** He's not[He isn't]

## PRACTICE 5

**2** The boy was not[wasn't] very friendly.
**3** I am not[I'm not] thirteen years old.
**4** This towel was not[wasn't] wet.
**5** You were not[weren't] afraid of dogs.
**6** The flowers are not[aren't] very pretty.
**7** She is not[She's not/She isn't] from London.
**8** We are not[We're not/We aren't] late.
**9** I was not[wasn't] in the school band.
**10** We were not[weren't] happy with the news.

## PRACTICE 6

**2** It did not[didn't] rain a lot.
**3** You do not[don't] drink coffee.
**4** I do not[don't] want a pet.
**5** We did not[didn't] buy a newspaper.
**6** It does not[doesn't] happen very often.
**7** They do not[don't] work very hard.
**8** He does not[doesn't] look like a good player.
**9** Mike did not[didn't] go to the cinema.
**10** He does not[doesn't] watch TV in the morning.

## PRACTICE 7

**2** like  **3** makes
**4** don't fight  **5** buys
**6** doesn't have  **7** love
**8** doesn't swim  **9** didn't study
**10** don't read

## PRACTICE 8

**2** Are you in this class?
**3** Does Mary like cats?
**4** Do you live near here?
**5** Did he take photographs?
**6** Was Tom's father in hospital?
**7** Do they enjoy a rock concert?
**8** Does she have big blue eyes?
**9** Were these books very interesting?
**10** Is this the Empire State Building?

> **2, 6, 9, 10** be동사가 있는 의문문의 경우 be동사를 문장의 맨 앞으로 옮겨서 「be동사+주어 ~?」의 형태로 만든다.
> **3, 4, 5, 7, 8** 일반동사가 있는 의문문의 경우 「Do[Does, Did]+주어+동사원형 ~?」의 형태로 만든다. 주어가 3인칭 단수일 경우 Does를, 문장의 시제가 과거일 경우 Did를 사용한다.

## PRACTICE 9

**1** No, he isn't.  **2** Yes, we do.
**3** Yes, he does.  **4** Yes, they were.
**5** No, it isn't.  **6** No, they didn't.
**7** No, I'm not.  **8** Yes, she was.
**9** Yes, she did.  **10** No, I don't.

## PRACTICE 10

**1** What is your name?
**2** Who is that boy?
**3** Where are you from?
**4** How was your vacation?

5   When did you buy it?

6   Why are you so happy?

7   What does she do?

8   Where is the bank?

9   How do you go to school?

10  When is the party?

## PRACTICE 11

| | | | |
|---|---|---|---|
| 1 Which, or, Milk | | 2 Who, or, Liza | |
| 3 or, dog | | 4 or, hamburger | |
| 5 or, oranges | | 6 Which, or, blue | |
| 7 Who, or, woman | | 8 Is, or, white | |

## PRACTICE 12

| | | |
|---|---|---|
| 1 can he | 2 is it | 3 aren't we |
| 4 will they | 5 does she | 6 can't they |
| 7 doesn't he | 8 don't you | 9 did she |
| 10 aren't you | | |

## PRACTICE 13

1   Wear a helmet.

2   Don't be afraid of snakes.

3   Take a bus or a taxi.

4   Don't be late again.

5   Enter my room.

6   Don't worry about the test.

7   Be careful.

8   Don't be upset.

9   Be ready to go.

10  Don't turn on the TV.

11  Be prepared for anything.

12  Don't tell her the truth.

> **2, 4, 6, 8, 10, 12** 의미가 강조된 부정명령문을 만들기 위해 Don't 대신 Never를 쓰는 것도 가능하다.

## PRACTICE 14

| | |
|---|---|
| 1 Let's keep | 2 Let's take |
| 3 Let's go | 4 Let me help |
| 5 Let's not hurry | 6 Let me tell |
| 7 Let's study | 8 Let's not open |
| 9 Let's not make | 10 Let's join |

## PRACTICE 15

| | | |
|---|---|---|
| 1 shall we | 2 will you | 3 didn't she |
| 4 will you | 5 isn't it | 6 can't you |
| 7 doesn't he | 8 shall we | 9 aren't they |
| 10 does she | 11 will you | 12 did he |

> **1, 8** Let's로 시작하는 청유문의 부가의문문은 'shall we?'로 쓴다.
> **2, 4, 11** 명령문의 부가의문문은 'will you?'로 쓴다.
> **3, 5, 6, 7, 9** 긍정문 뒤에는 부정의 부가의문문이 온다. 「주어+동사의 긍정형, be/do/조동사의 부정형+인칭대명사?」 형태로 쓴다. 3번은 문장의 시제가 과거이므로 didn't를, 7번은 주어가 3인칭 단수이므로 doesn't를 사용한다.
> **10, 12** 부정문 뒤에는 긍정의 부가의문문이 온다. 「주어+동사의 부정형, be/do/조동사의 긍정형+인칭대명사?」 형태로 쓴다. 10번은 주어가 3인칭 단수이므로 does를, 12번은 문장의 시제가 과거이므로 did를 사용한다.

## PRACTICE 16

2   How pretty she is!

3   What big eyes you have!

4   What a huge waterfall!

5   How handsome he is!

6   How fast the robots can move!

7   What a big liar you are!

8   What cute mascots those are!

9   What a high mountain!

10  What a nice museum!

11  What a small dictionary you have!

12  How happy I am!

## PRACTICE 17

| | | | |
|---|---|---|---|
| 1 부사 | 2 접속사 | 3 동사 | 4 대명사 |
| 5 형용사 | 6 명사 | 7 감탄사 | 8 전치사 |
| 9 동사 | 10 형용사 | | |

## PRACTICE 18

| | | |
|---|---|---|
| 1 dangerous | 2 amazing | 3 arrived |
| 4 information | 5 or | 6 introduce |
| 7 happy | 8 scary | 9 healthy |
| 10 busy | 11 helps | 12 heavy |
| 13 careful | | |

## PRACTICE 19

1   Her cap is red.

2   They went camping last Saturday.

3   She keeps a diary every day.

**4**  My favorite subject is music.

**5**  Tony sat on the bench.

**6**  Her family lives in Seoul.

## PRACTICE 20

**1**  some trees  **2**  his voice  **3**  them
**4**  TV  **5**  a notebook  **6**  tennis

## PRACTICE 21

**1**  Mr. Brown  **2**  cold  **3**  interesting
**4**  sing  **5**  exciting  **6**  a cook

## PRACTICE 22

**1**  so  **2**  next time
**3**  heavily tomorrow
**4**  about computer science
**5**  late  **6**  In my opinion

## PRACTICE 23

**1**  He is happy.
**2**  We love winter.
**3**  These shirts are small.
**4**  Her parents live in New York.
**5**  The teacher teaches math.
**6**  My mother washed the dishes.

## PRACTICE 24

**1**  [1형식] 주어  동사
**2**  [2형식] 주어  동사  주격 보어
**3**  [5형식] 주어  동사  목적어  목적격 보어
**4**  [3형식] 주어  동사  목적어
**5**  [4형식] 주어  동사  간접목적어  직접목적어
**6**  [3형식] 주어  동사  목적어
**7**  [5형식] 주어  동사  목적어  목적격 보어
**8**  [1형식] 주어  동사
**9**  [2형식] 주어  동사  주격 보어
**10**  [4형식] 주어  동사  간접목적어  직접목적어
**11**  [2형식] 주어  동사  주격 보어
**12**  [4형식] 주어  동사  간접목적어  직접목적어
**13**  [1형식] 주어  동사
**14**  [5형식] 주어  동사  목적어  목적격 보어
**15**  [2형식] 주어  동사  주격 보어
**16**  [1형식] 주어  동사
**17**  [5형식] 주어  동사  목적어  목적격 보어
**18**  [2형식] 동사  주어  주격 보어
**19**  [4형식] 주어  동사  간접목적어  직접목적어
**20**  [5형식] 주어  동사  목적어  목적격 보어
**21**  [1형식] 주어  동사
**22**  [4형식] 동사  간접목적어  직접목적어
**23**  [1형식] 주어  동사
**24**  [2형식] 주어  동사  주격 보어
**25**  [2형식] 주어  동사  주격 보어
**26**  [3형식] 주어  동사  목적어
**27**  [4형식] 주어  동사  간접목적어  직접목적어
**28**  [1형식] 주어  동사
**29**  [3형식] 주어  동사  목적어
**30**  [5형식] 주어  동사  목적어  목적격 보어

**1** [1형식: S는 V한다. 나무 사이로 바람이 분다.] 문장의 주어(The wind)와 동작을 나타내는 동사(blows), 수식어구(through the trees)로 이루어진 문장이므로 1형식이다.

**2** [2형식: S는 C하게 V한다. 그 남자는 강하다.] 주어(The man)의 상태를 설명해주는 형용사(strong)가 주격 보어 자리에 있으므로 2형식이다. 참고로 be동사는 1,2형식만 가능하다.

**3** [5형식: S는 O를 O.C하도록(하게) V한다. Mary는 그 기사가 흥미롭다고 생각했다.] 타동사(found) 뒤에 목적어(the article)가 나오고 그 목적어를 설명해주는 형용사(interesting)가 목적격 보어 자리에 나왔으므로 5형식이 적절하다. 5형식에서 find(found)는 '생각하다' think로 해석된다.

**4** [3형식: S는 O를 V한다. 나는 그 문을 열었다.] 타동사(opened) 뒤에 동사의 대상이 되는 명사(the door)가 나왔으므로 3형식이다.

**5** [4형식: S는 I.O에게 D.O를 V한다. 그는 그녀에게 반지를 주었다.] 타동사(gave) 뒤에 명사 her과 the ring이 나란히 나왔으므로 4형식이다. 첫 번째 명사(her)는 간접목적어(~에게), 두 번째 명사(the ring)는 직접목적어(~을,를)에 해당된다.

**6** [3형식: S는 O를 V한다. John은 남동생이 하나 있다.] 타동사 has 뒤에 동사의 대상이 되는 명사(a brother)가 목적어로 왔으므로 3형식이다.

**7** [5형식: S는 O를 O.C하도록(하게) V한다. 그 영화는 나를 슬프게 만들었다.] 동사(made)의 대상이 되는 목적어(me)와 목적어의 상태를 설명해주는 형용사(sad)가 그 뒤에 나왔으므로 5형식 문장이다.

**8** [1형식: S는 V한다. 그 아기는 크게 울었다.] 문장의 주어(The baby)와 주어의 동작을 나타내는 동사(cried), 수식어(loudly)로 이루어진 문장이므로 1형식이다.

**9** [2형식: S는 C가 V이다. 그는 기술자가 되었다.] 자동사 became이 나오고, 문장의 주어(He)와 주격 보어 자리에 나온 명사(an engineer)가 가리키는 대상이 같으므로 2형식이다.

**10** [4형식: S는 I.O에게 D.O를 V한다. 우리는 그를 크게 안아주었다.] 타동사(gave) 뒤에 명사 him과 a big hug가 나란히 나왔으므로 4형식이다. 첫 번째 명사(him)는 간접목적어(~에게), 두 번째 명사(a big hug)는 직접목적어(~을,를)에 해당된다.

**11** [2형식: S는 C하게 V한다. 나뭇잎들은 빨갛고, 노랗게 된다.] 주어(Leaves)의 상태를 설명해주는 형용사(red and yellow)가 주격 보어 자리에 나왔으므로 2형식 문장이다. 동사 turn은 자동사, 타동사 둘 다 가능하며, 2형식에서 자동사로 쓰인 경우 '~되다, ~해지다'로 해석한다.

**12** [4형식: S는 I.O에게 D.O를 V한다. 그녀는 그녀의 아기에게 새 장난감을 하나 사주었다.] 타동사(bought) 뒤에 명사 her baby와 a new toy가 나란히 나왔으므로 4형식이다. 첫 번째 명사(her baby)는 간접목적어(~에게), 두 번째 명사(a new toy)는 직접목적

**13** [1형식: S는 V한다. 나는 아침에 늦게 일어났다.] 주어(I)와 동사(woke up)만 있어도 '나는 일어났다'로 완전한 문장이다. late in the morning은 동사를 꾸며 주고 있으므로 부사구에 해당된다.

**14** [5형식: S는 O를 O.C하도록(하게) V한다. 나는 나의 방을 깨끗하게 유지했다.] 타동사(kept) 뒤에 목적어(my room)와 목적어의 상태를 보충 설명해주는 형용사(clean)가 나왔으므로 5형식 문장이다.

**15** [2형식: S는 C하게 V한다. 나는 학교 축제 후에 인기가 많아졌다.] 문장의 주어(I)와 동사(became), 그리고 주어의 상태를 나타내는 형용사(popular)가 주격 보어 자리에 있는 2형식 문장이며, 수식어구(after the school festival)는 문장의 형식에 영향을 미치지 않는다.

**16** [1형식: S는 V한다. 때때로 나는 차를 타고 일하러 간다.] 문장의 주어(I)와 동사(go)로 이루어진 1형식 문장이다. 문장에 의미를 더하는 부사인 수식어(Sometimes)와 동사를 수식하는 수식어구(to work by car)는 문장의 형식에 영향을 미치지 않는다.

**17** [5형식: S는 O를 O.C하도록(하게) V한다. 채소는 너를 건강하게 만든다.] 동사(make)의 대상이 되는 목적어(you)와 목적어의 상태를 설명해주는 형용사(healthy)가 그 뒤에 나왔으므로 5형식 문장이다.

**18** [2형식: S는 C하게 V한다. 넌 준비가 됐니?] 주어와 동사의 위치가 바뀐 의문문으로 주어(you)와 동사(are), 주어의 상태를 설명하는 형용사(ready)가 주격 보어 자리에 나온 2형식 문장이다.

**19** [4형식: S는 I.O에게 D.O를 V한다. 그녀가 네게 그 비밀을 말해주었니?] 일반 동사의 과거시제 의문문 문장으로 디동사(tell) 뒤에 명사 you와 the secret이 나란히 나온 4형식 문장이다. 첫 번째 명사(you)는 간접목적어(~에게), 두 번째 명사(the secret)는 직접목적어(~을,를)에 해당된다.

**20** [5형식: S는 O를 O.C하도록(하게) V한다. 난 그가 똑똑하다고 생각했다.] 동사(found)의 대상이 되는 목적어(him)와 목적어의 상태를 설명해주는 형용사(smart)가 그 뒤에 나왔으므로 5형식 문장이다. 5형식에서 find(found)는 '생각하다' think로 해석된다.

**21** [1형식: S는 V한다. 그녀는 내게 미소 지었다.] 주어(She)와 동사(smiled), 동사를 수식하는 수식어구(at me)로 이루어진 1형식 문장이다.

**22** [4형식: S는 I.O에게 D.O를 V한다. 소금을 내게 건네줘.] 주어가 생략된 명령문으로 타동사(Pass) 뒤에 명사 me와 the salt가 나란히 나온 4형식 문장이다. 첫 번째 명사(me)는 간접목적어(~에게), 두 번째 명사(the salt)는 직접목적어(~을,를)에 해당된다.

**23** [1형식: S는 V한다. 나는 공항에 일찍 도착했다.] 주어(I)와 동사(arrived), 동사를 수식하는 수식어구(at the airport early)로 이루어진 1형식 문장이다. 수식어(구)는 문장의 형식에 영향을 미치지 않는다.

**24** [2형식: S는 C이다. 수영하는 것은 좋은 취미이다.] 문장의 주어(Swimming)와 동사(is), 그리고 주어를 설명하는 명사구(a good hobby)가 주격 보어 자리에 있는 2형식 문장이다. 주격 보어 자리에 명사(구)가 나올 경우 주어와 동격이 된다.

**25** [2형식: S는 C하게 V한다. 그 수프는 짠 맛이 난다.] 문장의 주어(The soup)와 동사(tastes), 그리고 주어의 상태를 설명하는 형용사(salty)가 주격 보어 자리에 있는 2형식 문장이다.

**26** [3형식: S는 O를 V한다. 엄마는 첼로를 매우 잘 연주하신다.] 타동사(plays) 뒤에 동사의 대상이 되는 명사(the cello)가 목적어로 왔으므로 3형식이다. 수식어구(very well)는 동사를 수식하며 문장의 형식에 영향을 미치지 않는다.

**27** [4형식: S는 I.O에게 D.O를 V한다. 그는 내게 사과 파이 한 개를 구워주었다.] 타동사(baked) 뒤에 명사 me와 an apple pie가 나란히 나온 4형식 문장이다. 첫 번째 명사(me)는 간접목적어(~에게), 두 번째 명사(an apple pie)는 직접목적어(~을, 를)에 해당된다.

**28** [1형식: S는 V한다. 소리는 빛보다 더 느리게 이동한다.] 주어(Sound)와 동사(travels), 그리고 수식어구(more slowly than light)로 이루어진 1형식 문장이다.

**29** [3형식: S는 O를 V한다. 나는 지난 금요일에 내 장난감들을 팔았다.] 타동사(sold) 뒤에 동사의 대상이 되는 명사(my toys)가 목적어로 왔으므로 3형식이다. 수식어구(last Friday)는 문장의 형식에 영향을 미치지 않는다.

**30** [5형식: S는 O를 O.C하도록(하게) V한다. 내 부모님은 내 여동생을 Annie라고 이름 지으셨다.] 동사(named)의 대상이 되는 목적어(my sister)와 목적어와 동격이 되는 명사(Annie)가 그 뒤에 목적격 보어로 나왔으므로 5형식 문장이다.

## PRACTICE 25

| | | | | | |
|---|---|---|---|---|---|
| **1** beautiful | **2** delicious | **3** strange |
| **4** beautifully | **5** hungry | **6** ghost |
| **7** sadly | **8** terrible | **9** soft |
| **10** strangely | **11** soap | **12** softly |

**1, 2, 3, 5, 8, 9** 감각동사 look, smell, sound, feel, taste는 보어로 형용사만을 가진다. 우리말 해석이 부사처럼 되어 영어로도 부사를 쓸 것 같지만 보어로 형용사만 쓸 수 있음에 유의해야 한다.

**4** 빈칸이 없다고 가정할 때 They decorated the room.(그들은 방을 꾸몄다.)은 문장 구성 요소 중 빠진 것이 없이 완선하다. 따라서 빈칸에는 문장의 필수 구성 요소가 아닌 부사 beautifully(아름답게)가 들어가는 것이 적절하다.

**6** look like 뒤에는 명사가 오므로 ghost가 적절하다.
look like+명사: ~처럼 보이다

**7** 빈칸이 없다고 가정할 때 She shook her head.(그녀는 고개를 가로저었다.)는 문장 구성 요소 중 빠진 것이 없이 완전하다. 따라서 빈칸에는 문장의 필수 구성 요소가 아닌 부사 sadly(슬프게)가 들어가는 것이 적절하다.

**10** 빈칸이 없다고 가정할 때 She was calm while he was panicking.(그녀는 차분했고 한편 그는 겁에 질려 있었다.)은 문장 구성 요소 중 빠진 것이 없이 완전하다. 따라서 빈칸에는 문장의 필수 구성 요소가 아닌 부사 strangely(이상하게)가 들어가는 것이 적절하다.

**11** 감각동사(smell) 뒤에 전치사(like)가 나올 경우 명사가 온다.
smell like+명사: ~같은 냄새가 나다

**12** He hugged me.(그는 나를 포옹했다.) 자체로 완전한 문장이다. 따라서 빈칸에는 부사 softly(부드럽게)가 들어가는 것이 적절하다.

## PRACTICE 26

| | | | | | | | |
|---|---|---|---|---|---|---|---|
| **1** for | **2** to | **3** for | **4** to |
| **5** of | **6** to | **7** to | **8** for |
| **9** for | **10** to | | |

## PRACTICE 27

**1** Mary told the news to him.

**2** Mr. Kim teaches English to them.

**3** My mother made a pretty bag for me.

**4** Please get some water for me.

**5** Can I ask some questions of you?

**6** She often writes a letter to Shelly.

**7** He found a storybook for us.

**8** Did you buy a cake for her?

**9** Will you show your album to me?

**10** The Internet gives a lot of information to us.

**11** Please tell the real reason to me.

**12** Will you pass the salt to me?

**13** Vivien sent some flowers to me.

**14** We built a new house for the family.

**15** My dad cooked spaghetti for me.

**16** I read a newspaper to senior citizens.

**17** Can I ask a favor of you?

**18** Homework gives too much stress to us.

**19** I sent a birthday gift to you.

**20** My friend made a birthday cake for me.

**21** Will you give another chance to me?

**22** Can you get that book for me?

**23** He bought a box of chocolates for us.

**24** Olivia teaches Korean history to students.

**25** Evan built a treehouse for his children.

**26** Mom often cooks noodles for me.

**27** She often reads a fairy tale to her son.

**28** He showed his report card to his father.

**29** The police officer found the car key for me.

**30** Dominic made a big sand castle for his son.

---

## 📝 중간·기말고사 대비문제 정답  본문 _ p.31

**1** ⑤  **2** ④  **3** ③  **4** ③  **5** ② has → have

**6** ③  **7** ⑤  **8** be  **9** is, am, are, is, is  **10** ④

**11** ⑤  **12** (1) Yes, I did.  (2) No, I didn't.

**13** (1) Does, read  (2) Is my brother  (3) Did, meet

**14** ②  **15** ④  **16** What a small monkey it is!

**17** ④  **18** ③  **19** ③  **20** ②  **21** ④  **22** ⑤

**23** ②  **24** ②  **25** ④  **26** ④  **27** ③

**28** (가) knowing → know  (나) sweetly → sweet

**29** ⑤  **30** gave the salt to  **31** ④  **32** ①

**33** No, she didn't  **34** ④  **35** ②  **36** ③

**37** ③  **38** ③  **39** ②  **40** ②  **41** ②

**42** Let's  **43** ②  **44** ④  **45** ③  **46** ①

**47** ④  **48** ②,⑤  **49** ③  **50** ④  **51** ③

**52** ③

---

## 중간·기말고사 대비문제 해설

**1** (A), (B), (C), (D)에는 be동사 is[Is]가 들어가지만, (E)에는 일반동사 does[washes]가 들어간다.

**2** I amn't → I'm not, They'r → They're, This's → This is, She're → She's

**3** 긍정문(practices) 뒤에는 부정(doesn't)의 부가의문문이 와야 하며, 주어 Jack은 인칭대명사 he로 받는다.

**4** ③ taste like(~와 같은 맛이 나다) 뒤에는 명사가 오므로 어법상 적절하다. strawberry가 셀 수 있는 명사여서 like 뒤에 a strawberry[strawberries]가 와야 하는 것이 아닌가 생각할 수 있다. taste like a strawberry[strawberries]는 「딸기 '과일' 같은 맛이 나다」라는 뜻이고 taste like strawberry는 「딸기 '맛'과 같은 맛이 나다」라는 표현으로 둘 다 어법상 맞다. 주스의 맛을 표현하는 이 문장에서는 관사 없이 쓰는 것이 더 적절하다.

① Don't shy → Don't be shy

② happily → happy

④ tall boy → tall

⑤ likes → like

**5** 일반동사 현재의 부정문은 「do[does]+not+동사원형」의 어순이며, has의 동사원형은 have이다.

**6** (b) 문장의 주어가 Some ducks이므로 복수동사 are을 쓴 것은 적절하다.

(c) 문장의 주어가 a bench이므로 단수동사 is를 쓴 것은 적절하다.

(e) 주어가 I이고 현재시제이므로 일반동사 want의 부정형은 don't want로 쓴다.

(a) 문장의 주어가 a big pond and many tall trees이므로 복수동사 are을 써야 한다. (is → are)

(d) 의문사로 시작하지 않는 일반동사의 의문문을 만들 때는 「Do[Does, Did]+주어+동사원형 ~?」의 어순을 따른다. (Are → Do)

우리 가족은 우리 집 근처의 공원에 간다. 큰 연못 하나와 많은 키 큰 나무들이 있다. 몇몇 오리들은 연못에서 수영하고 있다. 연못 옆에는 벤치가 하나 있다. 나의 아빠는 나에게 "벤치에 앉고 싶니?"라고 묻는다. 벤치는 젖어 있다. 나는 그 벤치 위에 앉고 싶지 않다.

**7** ① I'd not → I don't

② Its → It's

③ I amn't → I'm not

④ Jane's not → Jane doesn't

**8** 부정명령문은 「Never+동사원형」의 어순으로 나타낼 수 있다. late는 형용사이므로 be동사와 함께 써야 하고 be동사의 원형은 be이다.

**9** 빈칸에는 be동사가 들어가야 한다. 주어가 3인칭 단수(My name, My hobby, My father)일 때는 is, 1인칭 단수(I)일 때는 am, 주어가 복수형(My favorite subjects)일 때는 are를 쓴다.

**10** ④ 창조하다(동사):창조(명사)
① 행복한(형용사):행복(명사)
② 재미있는(형용사):유머(명사)
③ 아름다운(형용사):아름다움(명사)
⑤ 강한(형용사):힘(명사)

**11** ⑤ 일반동사의 부정형:「do/does+not+동사원형」

**12** 부정의문문에 대한 대답은 질문의 형태와 관계없이 대답의 내용이 긍정이면 Yes, 부정이면 No로 답한다.

**13** (1),(3)일반동사가 있는 의문문 「Do[Does, Did]+주어+동사원형 ~?」
(2) be동사가 있는 의문문 「Be동사+주어 ~?」

**14** 감탄문의 어순 「How+형용시/부사(+주어+동사)!」 또는 「What(+a/an)+형용사+명사(+주어+동사)!」

**15** ④ help는 「주어+동사+간접목적어(사람)+직접목적어(사물)」의 어순인 4형식 동사로 쓰이지 않는다.

**16** 감탄문의 어순 「What(+a/an)+형용사+명사(+주어+동사)!」

**17** ① be동사의 부정문은 be동사 다음에 not을 쓴다. (don't → are not/aren't)
② 주어가 3인칭 단수인 일반동사의 부정문은 「does+not+동사원형」이므로 like를 쓴다. (likes → like)
③ be동사 과거의 부정문은 be동사의 과거형 다음에 not을 쓴다. (isn't → was not/wasn't)
⑤ 일반동사 과거의 부정문은 「did+not+동사원형」이므로 call을 쓴다. (called → call)

**18** (b) 주어가 The dog으로 단수이므로 단수동사 barks를 쓴 것은 적절하다.
(d) 주어가 I이므로 1인칭 be동사 am을 쓴 것은 적절하다.
(e) 주어가 The children으로 복수이므로 복수동사 run을 쓴 것은 적절하다.
(a) 주어가 Sarah and I로 복수이므로 복수동사 are을 써야 한다. (am → are)
(c) 일반동사의 부정문은 do를 활용하는데, 주어가 My little sister로 단수이므로 단수동사 doesn't

like로 써야 한다. (isn't likes → doesn't like)
(f) 주어가 Lisa and Jenny로 복수이므로 복수동사 walk를 쓴다. (walks →walk)

**19** 3형식 문장에서 buy는 간접목적어(사람) 앞에 전치사 for를 쓰며, show와 teach는 전치사 to를 쓴다.

**20** ① Did my brother <u>buy</u> any flowers?
③ <u>Do</u> you have a cell phone?
④ Do they <u>have</u> a big house?
⑤ <u>Does</u> she like movies?

**21** 인칭대명사 they로 받을 수 있는 주어는 Kevin and Jim이다.

**22** ⑤ Yes, he is. 또는 No, he isn't.

**23** ⓑ look like(~처럼 보인다) 뒤에는 명사가 오므로 어법상 적절하다.
ⓓ expensive의 첫소리가 모음으로 시작하므로 부정관사 an을 사용하는 것은 적절하며 형용사 expensive와 useful이 접속사 but으로 연결되어 있다.
ⓕ 3형식 문장에서 show는 간섭복석어(사람) 앞에 전치사 to를 사용하므로 어법상 적절하다.
ⓐ 감탄의 대상이 되는 delicious cookies가 복수형이므로 뒤의 '주어+동사' 또한 그에 맞춰 써야 한다. (this is → these are)
ⓒ 사역동사 make의 목적격 보어로 동사원형인 look이 왔으며, look은 감각동사이므로 보어로 형용사가 온다. (nicely → nice)
*cf.* nicely 멋지게(부사)
ⓔ 동사(sang)를 수식하고 있기 때문에 형용사 good이 아닌 부사 well을 써야 한다. (good → well)
ⓖ 긍정문 뒤에는 부정의 부가의문문이 오는데, 이때 시제는 앞에 나온 동사와 일치되어야 하므로 didn't를 써야 한다. (doesn't → didn't)

**24** 일반동사 과거 의문문에 대해 긍정으로 답했으므로 「Yes, 주어+did.」와 바꿔 쓸 수 있다.

**25** ㉠ 그녀가 주로 언제 일어나냐고 묻는 것이므로 의문사 When이 적절하다.
㉡ 요즘 기분이 어떻냐고 묻는 것이므로 의문사 How가 적절하다.
㉢ 그 소년들이 어젯밤 무엇을 했냐고 묻는 것이므로 의문사 What이 적절하다.
㉣ 언제 돌아올 것이냐고 묻는 것이므로 의문사 When이 적절하다.
㉤ 지금 어디를 가고 있냐고 묻는 것이므로 의문사

Where가 적절하다.

**26** ① 주어가 3인칭 단수(Tommy)이고 과학을 싫어하므로 doesn't like가 와야 한다.
② 주어가 3인칭 단수(Jane)이므로 does가 와야 한다.
③ 주어가 복수(Somi and Mark)이고 수학을 싫어하므로 don't like가 와야 한다.
⑤ 3인칭 단수(Mark)의 일반 동사 현재의 부정문은 「doesn't+동사원형」이다. 따라서 doesn't 뒤에 동사원형 like가 와야 한다.

**27** I(나)를 주어로 대답하였으므로 Do you ~?(너는 ~하니?)로 묻는 의문문이 되어야 한다.

**28** (가)「Let me+동사원형~」은 '제가 ~하도록 해주세요'의 뜻을 나타낸다. Let me know는 '알려주세요'라는 의미이다.
(나) 감각동사 sound(~하게 들리다)의 주격 보어 자리에는 형용사만 올 수 있다.

**29** ⑤ Do Kevin's parents get up early?

**30** 3형식 문장은 「주어+동사+목적어」의 형태로 쓰며, 이때 동사 give가 오면 간접목적어(사람) 앞에 전치사 to를 쓴다. 사건이 일어난 것이 어제이므로 give의 과거형 gave를 쓰는 것이 적절하다.

**31** 일반동사 현재의 부정문은 「do[does]+not+동사원형」의 어순이며, 주어(she)가 3인칭 단수이므로 does not을 쓴다.

**32** 「주어+동사+주격 보어」의 어순인 2형식 문장이므로, 빈칸에는 감각동사(feel, look, smell, sound)를 써야 한다.

**33** didn't she?로 물어봤기 때문에 시제는 과거이며, '그녀가 아파서 집에 있었다.'라고 말하고 있기 때문에 부정의 대답을 써야 한다.

**34** ④ How  ①②③⑤ What

**35** be동사 다음에는 명사, 형용사, 전치사구만 쓸 수 있다.

**36** 부정문(can't) 뒤에는 긍정(can)의 부가의문문이 와야 하며, 조동사로 묻는 의문문은 조동사로 대답한다.

**37** ⓑ 부정명령문 「Don't+동사원형」
ⓓ「look+형용사」'~하게 보이다'
　「look like+명사」'~처럼 보이다'
ⓔ make+직접목적어+for+간접목적어

**38** ③ 4형식 「주어+동사+간접목적어(사람)+직접목적어(사물)」
①②④⑤ 5형식 「주어+동사+목적어+목적격 보어」

**39** 긍정문 뒤에는 부정의 부가의문문이 오는데, 이때 시제는 앞에 나온 동사와 일치해야 하므로 didn't you?로 고쳐야 한다.

**40** ② 어떤 배낭을 원하냐고 물었으므로 원하는 배낭의 조건에 대해 말하는 것이 적절하다.
여: Brian, 뭐 하고 있니?
남: 나는 온라인으로 새 배낭을 찾아보고 있어.
여: 너는 어떤 종류의 배낭을 원하니?
남: 나는 가볍고 큰 것을 원해. 너는 이것을 어떻게 생각해?
여: 응, 그건 정말 좋아 보인다.

**41** 부정의문문에 대한 대답은 질문의 형태와 관계없이 대답의 내용이 긍정이면 Yes, 부정이면 No로 답한다. 내용상 배가 고프지만 지금 다이어트 중이라는 말이 되어야 하므로 긍정형(Yes)으로 대답해야 한다.
Yes, I am. (= Yes, I am hungry.)

**42** 「Let's+동사원형」'~하자'

**43** 3형식 문장에서 동사 give, teach, tell, show가 오면 간접목적어 앞에 전치사 to를 쓰고, make가 오면 for를 쓴다.

**44** ⓐⓑⓓⓔ was　　ⓒ were

**45** ③ Sumi likes dancing, doesn't she?

**46** ② What a wonderful gift this is!
③ What nice pants these are!
④ How smart your dog is!
⑤ What a cloudy day it is!

**47** ⓑ 명사 trip을 수식하는 형용사 fun의 쓰임은 적절하다.
ⓔ 주어 This food가 단수이므로 단수동사 tastes를 쓴 것은 적절하다.
ⓐ「make+목적어+형용사」 구조가 되어야 하므로 부사 sadly가 아닌 형용사 sad를 써야 한다.
(sadly → sad)
ⓒ seat는 '~를 앉히다'라는 뜻의 타동사이고, sit은 '앉다'라는 뜻의 자동사이다. 문장의 주어 Joanne이 스스로 앉는 것이므로 동사 sit을 쓰는 것이 적절하다. (seat → sit)
ⓓ 동사 sings를 수식하는 부사가 들어가야 한다. (perfect → perfectly)

**48** ② 감각동사(taste) 뒤에는 보어로 형용사가 온다.
(greatly → great)
⑤ 감각동사(smell) 뒤에는 보어로 형용사가 온다.
(badly → bad)

**49** ③ They made some soup for me.

**50** ① 부정명령문 「Do not[Don't]+동사원형」

② 4형식: My father gave me the guitar.

　　3형식: My father gave the guitar to me.

③ 부정문(aren't) 뒤에는 긍정(are)의 부가의문문이 와야 한다.

⑤ 주어가 3인칭 단수일 때 일반동사의 부정문은 동사원형 앞에 does not[doesn't]를 쓴다.

**51** ① 고양이가 지금 자고 있음을 나타내는 현재진행 시제이므로 동사의 -ing 형태를 사용해서 Is ~ sleeping~?으로 써야 한다. (sleep → sleeping)

② bread는 물질명사로 복수형으로 쓸 수 없다. 따라서 동사를 단수동사 is를 쓴다. (are only some breads → is only some bread)

④ 현재진행형 동사는 「am/is/are+-ing」의 형태로 쓴다. (do playing → are playing)

⑤ 현재진행형 동사가 쓰인 의문문에 대한 대답은 be동사를 활용한다. (she does → she is)

**52** (c) 주어 they가 복수이므로 복수동사 make를 쓴 것은 적절하다. 여기서 make는 5형식으로 쓰였으며 명사 writing이 목적어, 형용사 more fun이 목적격 보어로 알맞게 왔다.

(a) 일반동사의 의문문은 「의문사+do+주어+동사원형 ~?」의 어순으로 쓴다. (have you → do you have)

(b) 주어 It이 단수이므로 단수동사 grows를 써야 한다. (grow → grows)

(d) 주어 She가 단수이므로 단수동사 doesn't를 써야 한다. (don't → doesn't)

(e) Let's로 시작하는 청유문은 「Let's+동사원형」의 형태로 쓴다. (keeping → keep)

박 선생님: 학생 여러분! 여러분 집의 책상 위에는 무엇이 있나요?

재호: 작은 식물이요! 저는 그 식물을 봐요. 그것은 마치 저처럼 매일 자라요.

수민: 저는 알록달록한 펜을 많이 가지고 있어요. 저는 그것들을 사용해요. 그것들은 쓰기를 더 재미있게 만들어줘요.

Angie: 달력이요! 엄마가 그것을 저에게 주셨어요. 엄마는 제가 중요한 날짜를 잊지 않기를 바라세요.

Nick: 저는 책상 조명을 가지고 있어요. 그것은 제가 밤 늦게 공부하는 동안 제 공간을 밝혀줘요.

박 선생님: 공유해줘서 고마워요. 여러분의 책상 위에 유용한 물건들을 계속 두도록 해요.

## PRACTICE 1

| | | | |
|---|---|---|---|
| **1** stands | | **2** reaches | |
| **3** impresses | | **4** reads | |
| **5** begins | | **6** wishes | |
| **7** pushes | | **8** spends | |
| **9** sends | | **10** misses | |
| **11** wakes | | **12** meets | |
| **13** teaches | | **14** solves | |
| **15** wears | | **16** catches | |
| **17** sounds | | **18** goes | |
| **19** mixes | | **20** finds | |
| **21** passes | | **22** finishes | |
| **23** rides | | **24** watches | |
| **25** washes | | **26** sits | |
| **27** throws | | **28** burns | |
| **29** climbs | | **30** crosses | |

## PRACTICE 2

| | | | |
|---|---|---|---|
| **1** drinks | | **2** buys | |
| **3** studies | | **4** hurries | |
| **5** discusses | | **6** draws | |
| **7** lays | | **8** sells | |
| **9** has | | **10** pays | |
| **11** says | | **12** cries | |
| **13** copies | | **14** puts | |
| **15** closes | | **16** enjoys | |
| **17** touches | | **18** tries | |
| **19** believes | | **20** loses | |
| **21** tells | | **22** carries | |
| **23** repeats | | **24** grows | |
| **25** plays | | **26** makes | |
| **27** costs | | **28** judges | |
| **29** cheers | | **30** uses | |
| **31** brings | | **32** thinks | |
| **33** means | | **34** breaks | |
| **35** shows | | **36** flies | |
| **37** visits | | **38** feels | |
| **39** sings | | **40** turns | |
| **41** harms | | **42** wins | |
| **43** falls | | **44** builds | |
| **45** stays | | **46** sets | |

## PRACTICE 3 (continued)

| | | | |
|---|---|---|---|
| **47** sees | | **48** envies | |
| **49** dreams | | **50** speaks | |
| **51** eats | | **52** leaves | |
| **53** gets | | **54** understands | |
| **55** worries | | **56** keeps | |
| **57** gives | | **58** laughs | |
| **59** holds | | **60** hears | |

## PRACTICE 3

| | | | | | |
|---|---|---|---|---|---|
| **1** iz | **2** z | **3** z |
| **4** z | **5** z | **6** s |
| **7** iz | **8** s | **9** z |
| **10** s | **11** iz | **12** s |
| **13** z | **14** s | **15** iz |
| **16** z | **17** z | **18** s |
| **19** s | **20** z | **21** s |
| **22** iz | **23** iz | **24** s |
| **25** z | **26** iz | **27** s |
| **28** iz | **29** z | **30** z |
| **31** iz | **32** s | **33** iz |
| **34** iz | **35** s | **36** iz |
| **37** z | **38** iz | **39** iz |
| **40** z | **41** s | **42** z |
| **43** s | **44** iz | **45** s |

## PRACTICE 4

| | | | |
|---|---|---|---|
| **1** am | | **2** plays | |
| **3** leaves | | **4** are | |
| **5** goes | | **6** are | |
| **7** likes | | **8** is | |
| **9** look | | **10** are | |
| **11** watches | | **12** are | |
| **13** studies | | **14** is | |
| **15** rises | | **16** gets | |
| **17** has | | **18** reads | |
| **19** make | | | |

> **19** 이 문장에서 hands는 '일손, 일꾼'이란 뜻이며, '일손이 많으면 일이 수월해진다'는 문장으로 우리나라 속담 '백짓장도 맞들면 낫다' 와 비슷하다.

## PRACTICE 5

| | | | |
|---|---|---|---|
| **1** | shopped | **2** | agreed |
| **3** | called | **4** | wished |
| **5** | invented | **6** | believed |
| **7** | crossed | **8** | rained |
| **9** | saved | **10** | worked |
| **11** | started | **12** | turned |
| **13** | lived | **14** | planned |
| **15** | raised | **16** | happened |
| **17** | wanted | **18** | moved |
| **19** | improved | **20** | loved |
| **21** | walked | **22** | jumped |
| **23** | visited | **24** | arrived |
| **25** | pushed | **26** | covered |
| **27** | placed | **28** | stopped |
| **29** | learned | **30** | opened |

## PRACTICE 6

| | | | |
|---|---|---|---|
| **1** | closed | **2** | guided |
| **3** | worried | **4** | used |
| **5** | repeated | **6** | waited |
| **7** | stayed | **8** | joined |
| **9** | wondered | **10** | ended |
| **11** | studied | **12** | surprised |
| **13** | added | **14** | connected |
| **15** | dropped | **16** | played |
| **17** | tried | **18** | spoiled |
| **19** | baked | **20** | suggested |
| **21** | rolled | **22** | tied |
| **23** | collected | **24** | carried |
| **25** | entered | **26** | obeyed |
| **27** | discussed | **28** | answered |
| **29** | touched | **30** | solved |
| **31** | enjoyed | **32** | helped |
| **33** | married | **34** | served |
| **35** | listened | **36** | wasted |
| **37** | watched | **38** | sounded |
| **39** | shared | **40** | trained |
| **41** | hurried | **42** | poured |
| **43** | cheered | **44** | danced |
| **45** | returned | **46** | missed |
| **47** | locked | **48** | laughed |
| **49** | hated | **50** | typed |

| | | | |
|---|---|---|---|
| **51** | seemed | **52** | failed |
| **53** | looked | **54** | decided |
| **55** | practiced | **56** | kicked |
| **57** | guessed | **58** | changed |
| **59** | reached | **60** | swallowed |

## PRACTICE 7

| | | | | | |
|---|---|---|---|---|---|
| **1** | t | **2** | d | **3** | t |
| **4** | d | **5** | t | **6** | id |
| **7** | d | **8** | d | **9** | id |
| **10** | d | **11** | id | **12** | d |
| **13** | t | **14** | d | **15** | t |
| **16** | d | **17** | d | **18** | t |
| **19** | id | **20** | d | **21** | t |
| **22** | d | **23** | d | **24** | t |
| **25** | d | **26** | t | **27** | id |
| **28** | t | **29** | t | **30** | id |
| **31** | d | **32** | d | **33** | t |
| **34** | t | **35** | id | **36** | t |
| **37** | d | **38** | d | **39** | t |
| **40** | id | **41** | t | **42** | d |
| **43** | d | **44** | id | **45** | d |

## PRACTICE 8

| | | | |
|---|---|---|---|
| **1** | set, set | **2** | held, held |
| **3** | became, become | **4** | smelled/smelt, smelled/smelt |
| **5** | bore, borne/born | **6** | broke, broken |
| **7** | cost, cost | **8** | meant, meant |
| **9** | stayed, stayed | **10** | dreamed/dreamt, dreamed/dreamt |
| **11** | ran, run | **12** | blew, blown |
| **13** | fed, fed | **14** | drove, driven |
| **15** | put, put | **16** | understood, understood |
| **17** | came, come | **18** | chose, chosen |
| **19** | drank, drunk | **20** | drew, drawn |
| **21** | read, read | **22** | shopped, shopped |
| **23** | fought, fought | **24** | stood, stood |
| **25** | wore, worn | **26** | bit, bitten |
| **27** | sang, sung | **28** | let, let |
| **29** | won, won | **30** | hit, hit |
| **31** | told, told | **32** | wrote, written |

| | | | |
|---|---|---|---|
| **33** sold, sold | **34** slid, slid | **9** finished | **10** practices |
| **35** took, taken | **36** woke, woken | | |
| **37** flew, flown | **38** carried, carried | | |

**33** sold, sold **34** slid, slid
**35** took, taken **36** woke, woken
**37** flew, flown **38** carried, carried
**39** tried, tried **40** swam, swum
**41** felt, felt **42** showed, shown
**43** burned/burnt, **44** kept, kept
burned/burnt
**45** forgot, forgotten **46** rang, rung
**47** sent, sent **48** heard, heard
**49** built, built **50** hurt, hurt
**51** rose, risen **52** caught, caught
**53** brought, brought **54** spread, spread
**55** lent, lent **56** grew, grown
**57** began, begun **58** threw, thrown
**59** bought, bought **60** enjoyed, enjoyed
**61** sat, sat **62** was/were, been
**63** played, played **64** found, found
**65** went, gone **66** gave, given
**67** planned, planned **68** ate, eaten
**69** rode, ridden **70** knew, known
**71** spent, spent **72** closed, closed
**73** spoke, spoken **74** got, got(ten)
**75** taught, taught **76** saw, seen
**77** led, led **78** studied, studied
**79** made, made **80** had, had
**81** fell, fallen **82** said, said
**83** lost, lost **84** left, left
**85** slept, slept **86** did, done
**87** met, met **88** thought, thought
**89** laid, laid **90** paid, paid

### PRACTICE 9

**1** was **2** am
**3** wasn't **4** was
**5** were **6** were
**7** weren't **8** is
**9** are **10** weren't

### PRACTICE 10

**1** bought **2** eat
**3** went **4** wears
**5** built **6** began
**7** read **8** found

**9** finished **10** practices

### PRACTICE 11

**1** is going to pass **2** are going to go
**3** are going to get **4** is going to visit
**5** is going to make **6** are going to do

### PRACTICE 12

**1** help **2** Is
**3** will **4** went
**5** make **6** Will
**7** be **8** gets
**9** studied **10** are

### PRACTICE 13

**1** am going to paint **2** will travel
**3** is going to study **4** will have
**5** are going to buy

### PRACTICE 14

**1** living **2** leaving
**3** sleeping **4** holding
**5** drawing **6** playing
**7** carrying **8** believing
**9** writing **10** saying
**11** buying **12** spending
**13** losing **14** waking
**15** checking **16** bringing
**17** looking **18** diving
**19** joining **20** smoking
**21** doing **22** blowing
**23** making **24** choosing
**25** adding **26** selling
**27** giving **28** having
**29** taking **30** meeting

### PRACTICE 15

**1** getting **2** lying
**3** changing **4** opening
**5** parking **6** pushing
**7** reading **8** wearing
**9** putting **10** calling
**11** finding **12** biking
**13** burning **14** setting

<table>
<tr><td>15</td><td>coming</td><td>16</td><td>respecting</td></tr>
<tr><td>17</td><td>winning</td><td>18</td><td>seeing</td></tr>
<tr><td>19</td><td>closing</td><td>20</td><td>beginning</td></tr>
<tr><td>21</td><td>tying</td><td>22</td><td>growing</td></tr>
<tr><td>23</td><td>keeping</td><td>24</td><td>drinking</td></tr>
<tr><td>25</td><td>swimming</td><td>26</td><td>helping</td></tr>
<tr><td>27</td><td>climbing</td><td>28</td><td>entering</td></tr>
<tr><td>29</td><td>singing</td><td>30</td><td>going</td></tr>
<tr><td>31</td><td>jumping</td><td>32</td><td>shopping</td></tr>
<tr><td>33</td><td>lending</td><td>34</td><td>catching</td></tr>
<tr><td>35</td><td>collecting</td><td>36</td><td>sending</td></tr>
<tr><td>37</td><td>staying</td><td>38</td><td>riding</td></tr>
<tr><td>39</td><td>falling</td><td>40</td><td>flying</td></tr>
<tr><td>41</td><td>teaching</td><td>42</td><td>dreaming</td></tr>
<tr><td>43</td><td>sitting</td><td>44</td><td>driving</td></tr>
<tr><td>45</td><td>planting</td><td>46</td><td>turning</td></tr>
<tr><td>47</td><td>standing</td><td>48</td><td>starting</td></tr>
<tr><td>49</td><td>floating</td><td>50</td><td>breaking</td></tr>
<tr><td>51</td><td>telling</td><td>52</td><td>eating</td></tr>
<tr><td>53</td><td>speaking</td><td>54</td><td>running</td></tr>
<tr><td>55</td><td>arriving</td><td>56</td><td>building</td></tr>
<tr><td>57</td><td>asking</td><td>58</td><td>camping</td></tr>
<tr><td>59</td><td>cheering</td><td>60</td><td>walking</td></tr>
</table>

## PRACTICE 16

1 It is snowing.

2 I am cleaning my room.

3 Sumi is making a card.

4 He is wearing blue jeans.

5 It was flying over the tree.

6 We were enjoying the holiday.

7 They are doing their homework.

8 My grandparents were smiling at us.

9 A man was standing in front of the door.

10 I was playing basketball with my friends.

## PRACTICE 17

2 am reading a book

3 is visiting her aunt

4 are eating out with their family

5 are going to church

## PRACTICE 18

| 1 | is taking | 2 | went |
|---|---|---|---|
| 3 | am going to bake | 4 | will paint |
| 5 | was walking | | |

## PRACTICE 19

| 2 | has driven | 3 | haven't heard |
|---|---|---|---|
| 4 | Has, met | 5 | has had |
| 6 | Have, visited | 7 | haven't seen |
| 8 | has taught | 9 | Have, studied |

## PRACTICE 20

| 2 | Has she watched | 3 | haven't left |
|---|---|---|---|
| 4 | have fed | 5 | has had |
| 6 | hasn't done | 7 | has found |
| 8 | has he been | 9 | have never read |
| 10 | has grown | | |

2 현재완료시제 의문문은 「Have/Has+주어+과거분사」로 나타낸다. 동사 watch의 과거분사형은 watched이다.
3, 6 현재완료시제 부정문은 「haven't/hasn't+과거분사」로 나타낸다. leave의 과거분사형은 left, do의 과거분사형은 done이다.
4, 7, 10 현재완료시제는 「have/has+과거분사」로 나타낸다. feed의 과거분사는 fed, find의 과거분사는 found, grow의 과거분사는 grown이다.
5 세연이가 작년부터 계속 휴대전화를 가지고 있다는 의미의 문장이므로 과거시제가 아닌 현재완료시제로 나타내야 한다.
8 문장의 주어 he가 3인칭 단수이므로 has를 써서 현재완료시제를 나타낸다.
9 살아오면서 한 번도 판타지 소설을 읽은 적이 없다는 경험을 나타내고 있으므로 현재완료시제를 쓴다.

## PRACTICE 21

| 1 | Have | 2 | has lived |
|---|---|---|---|
| 3 | brushed | 4 | did |
| 5 | left | 6 | have been |
| 7 | known | 8 | played |
| 9 | met | 10 | has |
| 11 | have studied | 12 | watched |
| 13 | has worked | 14 | went |
| 15 | ended | 16 | has rained |
| 17 | had | 18 | listened |
| 19 | threw | 20 | made |
| 21 | Did | 22 | won |
| 23 | visited | 24 | has played |
| 25 | snowed | 26 | Have |
| 27 | was | | |

**1, 26** 현재완료시제의 의문문은 「Have/Has+주어+과거분사~?」 형태로 쓴다.
**2, 6, 7, 8, 10, 11, 13, 16, 18, 20, 24** 기간을 나타내는 부사(구)가 있으므로 현재완료시제를 쓴다. 'since+시점' 또는 'for+기간'과 함께 쓰여 현재완료 용법 중 '계속'을 나타낸다.
**3, 5, 9, 14, 15, 17, 22, 27** 명백한 과거 시점을 나타내는 부사(구)가 있으므로 과거시제를 쓴다.
**4, 21** 괄호 뒤에 동사원형이 쓰였으므로 현재완료시제(have[has]+과거분사)가 될 수 없다. 따라서 과거시제가 적합하며, 과거시제의 의문문은 「Did+주어+동사원형~?」 형태로 쓴다. 4번은 의문사가 포함된 의문문으로 「의문사+did[does, do]+주어+동사원형~?」 형태로 쓴다.
**12, 19, 23, 25** ago는 명백한 과거 시점을 나타내는 부사이므로 항상 과거시제와 함께 쓰인다.

## 중간·기말고사 대비문제 정답 _ 본문 _ p.66

**1** ④　**2** ③　**3** ②　**4** builded → built　**5** ⑤
**6** does　**7** ①　**8** was　**9** is leaving
**10** ⓐ goes ⓑ has ⓒ reads ⓓ ends　**11** ①,④
**12** ⑤　**13** ⑤　**14** ②　**15** ②　**16** ①　**17** ⑤
**18** ②　**19** ③,④　**20** ④　**21** ②　**22** ②
**23** Is she watering the plant?　**24** ③　**25** ⑤
**26** ②　**27** ⑤　**28** (1) She is taking a picture[pictures]. (2) They are riding bicycles.
**29** ⑤　**30** ③　**31** has lived in Busan for five years　**32** is going to go swimming (on Thursday)　**33** ④　**34** ①,④　**35** opens, has, closes　**36** ②,⑤　**37** ②　**38** get → gets, go → goes　**39** ②　**40** ③　**41** ④　**42** ①
**43** ③　**44** ⑤　**45** ⑤　**46** ate　**47** ④　**48** ①
**49** ②　**50** ②　**51** ③　**52** ③　**53** (1) are going to play the guitar  (2) is going to make spaghetti　**54** ③　**55** (1) took (2) drawing (3) read  (4) played　**56** ⑤　**57** ②,⑤
**58** ⓐ decorates → decorated  ⓑ come → came  ⓒ sing → sang

## 중간·기말고사 대비문제 해설

**1**　④ 주어가 3인칭 단수인 현재시제 문장이므로 동사는 goes가 와야 한다. (go → goes)

**2**　Isabella가 2년 전부터 현재까지 계속 한국어를 배우고 있다는 의미의 문장이므로 현재완료시제 「have/has+과거분사」로 나타내야 한다. 주어가 she로 3인칭 단수이며, 동사 study의 과거분사가 studied이므로 has studied가 적절하다.
Isabella는 케이팝과 한국 드라마에 관심이 있다. 그녀는 한국 문화를 깊이 이해하고 싶어 한다. 그래서, 그녀는 2년 전부터 한국어를 배우기 시작했다. 2년 동안 한국어를 공부해 왔기 때문에, 이제 그녀는 영어 자막 없이 한국 드라마를 볼 수 있다.

**3**　② 현재진행형(is moving)이 미래를 의미하는 부사구(next month)와 쓰여서 미래를 나타낼 수 있으므로 어법상 알맞다.
① 과거를 나타내는 부사(yesterday)가 나왔으므로 과거시제로 써야 한다. (Does → Did)
③ '그녀가 그 집을 작년부터 계속 가지고 있다.'는 의미로 기간을 나타내는 부사구(since last year)가 쓰였으므로 과거부터 현재까지 계속되는 상태를 의미하는 현재완료를 써야 한다.
(had → has had)
④ '나는 이미 나의 숙제를 끝냈다.'는 문장으로 앞에 have가 나온 것으로 보아 현재완료시제를 쓰는 것이 적절하다. (finish → finished)
⑤ 현재를 나타내는 부사 now가 쓰였으므로 과거진행형이 아닌 현재진행형이 적절하다.
(was walking → is walking)

**4**　첫 문장의 동사 liked로 보아 이 글의 시제는 과거이다. build의 과거형은 built이다.

**5**　주어진 문장의 동사(go)의 형태로 보아 3인칭 단수인 주어는 올 수 없다.
⑤ 3인칭 단수 ① 1인칭 복수 ②③④ 3인칭 복수

**6**　주어(She)가 3인칭 단수이므로 do를 does로 바꾸어 쓴다.

**7**　'~하는 중이었다/~하고 있었다'는 과거진행시제이므로 「was/were+~ing」를 써야 하는데, 주어가 We이므로 be동사는 were이 와야 한다.

**8**　주어가 3인칭 단수이고, 과거를 나타내는 부사(yesterday)가 있으므로 be동사로 was가 와야 한다.

**9**　미래를 나타내는 부사와 함께 현재진행형으로 미래를 나타낼 수 있다.

**10**　주어인 Yuri(she), School이 3인칭 단수이므로 동사의 3인칭 단수형을 쓴다.

**11**　ride-rode-ridden　　draw-drew-drawn
bear-bore-born　　begin-began-begun

**12**　⑤ 미래를 나타내는 부사구(next week)가 있으므로 be going to가 적절하다.

① next Friday는 과거가 아니므로 과거시제가 올 수 없다. (was → is)

② yesterday가 과거를 나타내므로 동사의 시제는 과거형이어야 한다. (finish → finished)

③ 미래시제는 「will+동사원형」의 형태로 나타낸다. (reviews → review)

④ 현재를 나타내는 부사(now)가 있으므로 동사의 시제를 현재시제 또는 현재진행시제로 맞춘다. (am study → study/am studying)

**13** did로 물었으므로 과거를 나타내는 부사(구)가 와야 한다. next Saturday는 미래를 나타내는 부사구이다.

**14** ⓑ 동사 am의 부정형은 not과 함께 줄여서 쓰지 않는다. (amn't → am not)

ⓒ 지금 저녁을 준비하고 있는 것이므로 현재진행시제를 써야 한다. 현재진행시제는 「am/is/are+-ing」의 형태로 쓴다.

(does cooking → is cooking)

ⓓ 동사 swim의 진행형은 swimming으로 쓴다.

(is swiming → is swimming)

**15** 의문사로 시작하는 의문문은 Yes나 No로 대답할 수 없으며, be going to로 묻는 질문에 대해 be going to로 답한 ②번이 가장 적절하다.

**16** ①「be going to+장소」'~에 가고 있다(진행시제)'

②③④⑤「be going to+동사원형」'~하려고 하다(미래시제)'

**17** 주어(he and his family와 they)가 복수이므로 have가 와야 한다.

**18** 모음+y로 끝나는 동사의 3인칭 단수형은 –s를 붙여서 나타낸다.

② She <u>plays</u> the violin with her mother.

**19** 미래를 나타내는 부사구(next weekend)가 있으므로 미래시제가 와야 한다. 또한 현재진행시제도 미래를 나타내는 부사구와 함께 가까운 미래를 나타낸다.

**20** 현재완료 표현이 쓰인 문장으로 단어를 배열하면 'I have stayed here for seven days.'가 된다.

**21** ⓒ read-read-read

ⓓ 주어가 복수(Mr. and Mrs. Cheney)이므로 be동사는 are가 적절하다.

ⓐ This is는 This's로 줄여 쓸 수 없다.

ⓑ will을 사용한 미래시제는 「will+동사원형」으로 나타낸다.

ⓔ 주어(Jane and I)가 복수이므로 be동사는 are가 적절하다.

**22** 과거를 나타내는 부사구(A few years ago)가 있으므로 과거형(made)이 와야 한다.

**23** 현재진행형의 의문문 「be동사+주어+-ing~?」

**24** ⓒ 동사 get의 진행형은 getting이다. (geting → getting)

ⓓ 동사 smile의 진행형은 smiling이다. (smileing → smiling)

**25** ⑤ 진행을 나타내는 현재진행형

①②③④ 미래를 나타내는 현재진행형

**26** ⓐⓒⓔ「be going to+동사원형」'~하려고 하다' (미래시제)

ⓑⓓ「be going to+장소」'~에 가고 있다' (진행시제)

**27** Cathy가 이 회사에서 2년째 일을 해오고 있다는 문장이 되어야 하므로 현재완료 표현(has worked)을 쓰고 two years라는 기간을 나타내기 위해서 전치사 for를 사용한다.

**28** 현재진행시제「am/is/are+-ing」'~하고 있다'

**29** ① 엄마가 지금(now) 저녁을 요리하는 중인지 묻는 문장으로 현재진행시제를 써야 하므로 cooks를 cooking으로 고쳐야 한다. (cooks → cooking)

② 현재진행시제의 부정형을 나타낼 때 not은 be동사와 ~ing 사이에 위치한다.

③ 리본을 매고 있다는 의미이므로 현재진행형을 써서 tie를 tying으로 고쳐야 한다. (tie → tying)

④ 즐거운 시간을 보내고 있는지 묻는 문장이다. 현재진행시제의 의문문이므로 Do를 Be동사인 Are로 고쳐야 한다. (Do → Are)

**30** 미래시제는「will+동사원형」으로 나타낸다.

③ She will <u>play</u> the piano.

**31** 'Susan은 5년째 부산에 살고 있다.'는 문장을 영작해야 하므로 현재완료(has lived)를 쓰고 기간을 나타내기 위한 전치사 for를 써서 문장을 완성한다.

**32** 세미는 (목요일에) 수영을 하러 갈 예정이다. 「be going to+동사원형」의 형태로 나타낸다.

**33** ④ make - made - made

**34** ① 역사적 사실을 나타낼 때는 과거시제를 쓴다.

④ 지금까지의 경험을 나타낼 때는 현재완료시제를 쓴다.

② 가까운 미래의 계획을 나타낼 때 현재진행시제를 쓸 수 있고 문장의 주어가 we이므로 동사를 are meeting으로 쓰는 것이 적절하다.

(meeting → are meeting)

③ 문장의 주어가 She로 단수이므로 동사 has를 쓰

는 것이 적절하다. (have → has)
⑤ 상태를 나타내는 동사 like는 현재진행형으로 쓰지
않는다. (am liking → like)

**35** 현재의 상태나 반복적인 일을 나타낼 때는 현재시제
를 쓴다. 문장의 주어가 It으로 단수이므로 단수동사
opens, has, closes를 쓰는 것이 적절하다.

**36** 과거를 나타내는 부사구(last week)가 있으므로 시제
를 과거로 일치시킨다.
② I went to Mt. Halla last week.
She의 소유격은 Her이다.
⑤ Her name is Sumin.

**37** last year는 과거, now는 현재, next year는 미래를
나타내는 부사구이다.

**38** 주어가 3인칭 단수인 현재시제 문장이므로 get은
gets로, go는 goes로 고쳐 쓴다.

**39** –ie로 끝나는 동사의 –ing형은 ie를 y로 바꾸고 ing를
붙여서 만든다.
② She is lying on the floor.

**40** ⓐ 주어가 3인칭 단수(Bora)이므로 was가 와야 한다.
ⓑ 두 번째 문장의 동사(saw)로 이 글의 시제가 과거
임을 알 수 있다. 따라서 시제를 일치시키기 위해
asked가 와야 한다.
ⓒ 빈칸 앞에 be동사(were)가 있어서 과거진행시제
가 되는 것이 자연스러우므로 looking이 적절하
다. be동사(were)와 일반동사(look)를 동시에 같
이 쓰는 것은 어법에 맞지 않다.

**41** be동사(am)가 있으므로 talk의 진행형인 talking을
써야 한다.

**42** ① cleanned → cleaned

**43** 미래시제는「will+동사원형」으로 나타낸다.
① I will be a good designer.
② I will do the laundry tomorrow.
④ Mr. Park will be busy tomorrow.
현재진행시제의 부정문은「be동사+not+-ing」의 어
순으로 나타낸다.
⑤ He was not playing basketball this morning.

**44** 과거시제로 묻는 질문에 과거시제로 대답한다.
무슨 일이 있었는데? – 내 아기 여동생이 밤새 울었어.

**45** 자음+y로 끝나는 동사의 3인칭 단수형은 y를 i로 바
꾸고 –es를 붙여서 나타낸다.
⑤ fly → flies

**46** 과거시제로 묻는 질문에 과거시제로 대답한다. eat의
과거형은 ate이다.

**47** Minho는 3인칭 단수 주어이므로, 동사로 goes가 온다.

**48** 미래시제는「be going to+동사원형」이므로, Mike is
going to be busy next week.로 써야 한다.

**49** ② B는 'Sunny와 그녀의 이모는 지금 막 점심식사를
끝냈다.'라는 의미로 지금은 이미 밥을 다 먹은 상태
를 나타낸다. 그러므로 '지금 점심을 먹고 있다'는
것은 적절하지 않다.
① A. 'Lisa는 2년 동안 변호사로 일해오고 있다.'
③ C. 'Kate와 미나는 아기였을 때부터 서울에서 살아
왔다.'
④ D. '지아는 그녀의 가족과 함께 호주로 갔다.'
⑤ E. '준호는 이 만화를 일곱 살 때부터 줄곧 좋아해왔
다.'

**50** ① now는 현재를 나타내므로 과거진행인「were+
-ing」와 쓸 수 없다. (were → are)
③ tomorrow는 미래를 나타내므로 과거형인
learned와 쓸 수 없다. (learned → will learn)
④ a few minutes ago는 과거를 나타내므로 미래시
제인 will과 쓸 수 없다. (will finish → finished)
⑤ last week는 과거를 나타내므로 미래를 나타내는
be going to와 쓸 수 없다.
(We're going to have → We had)

**51** 문맥으로 보아 last week에 간 소풍에 대한 이야기이
므로 시제를 과거로 맞춰야 한다.
③ makes → made

**52** 미래시제를 나타내는 의문문은「Will+주어+동사원형
~?」또는「Be동사+주어+going to+동사원형 ~?」으
로 쓴다.
③ Will you visit Paris this summer?/Are you
going to visit Paris this summer?

**53** 「be going to+동사원형」형태를 활용하여 미래에 있
을 일에 대하여 영작하는 문제이다.
(1) 주어가 3인칭 복수(Mina and Suji)이므로 be동
사도 복수형(are)으로 씀에 유의한다.
(2) 주어가 3인칭 단수(Jieun)이므로 be동사도 3인
칭 단수형(is)으로 써야 한다.

**54** ㉠ 기간을 나타내는 부사구 since last year가 쓰여,
작년부터 지금까지 지속해서 중국어를 공부하고 있
는 상황을 나타내므로, 현재완료시제를 사용한다.
(They have studied Chinese since last year.)
㉡ 과거 특정한 시점을 나타내는 부사구 last
weekend가 사용되었으므로, 과거시제를 사용한
다. (Tony visited his parents last weekend.)

ⓒ 부사구 for the past 3 years가 쓰여, 과거부터 현재까지 계속되는 상태를 나타내므로, 현재완료시제를 사용한다. (She <u>has taught</u> English in this school for the past 3 years.)

**55** (1) '사진을 찍다'에서 동사는 take를 쓴다. and 앞 절의 동사가 visited로 과거시제이므로 그에 맞춰 과거형 took을 쓴다.

(2) be good at은 '~을 잘하다'라는 뜻이고, 전치사 at 뒤에는 목적어의 역할을 할 수 있는 동명사 drawing이 와야 한다.

(3) 내가 방금 막 만화책 읽기를 끝낸 것이므로 현재완료시제를 쓴다. (read – read – read)

(4) 우리가 어제 축구를 한 것이므로 과거시제 played를 쓰는 것이 적절하다.

**56** B가 '이번 토요일에 조부모님 댁에 방문할 예정이야.'라고 대답했으므로 '이번 토요일에 무엇을 할 예정이니?'라고 물어야 한다.

① 너희 조부모님 댁에 어떻게 방문할 거니?

② 너는 매주 너희 조부모님 댁에 방문하니?

③ 너는 무엇 때문에 너희 조부모님 댁을 방문하니?

④ 너는 왜 조부모님 댁 방문을 계획했니?

**57** 지문의 밑줄 친 부분은 '나는 책 또한 읽은 적 있다.'는 뜻으로 앞에 have가 나온 것으로 보아 「have+과거분사」의 형태의 현재완료시제이다. 이때 과거분사 read는 [red]로 발음된다.

② '너는 우리 선생님으로부터 온 이메일을 읽었니?'라는 의미로 「have+주어+과거분사~?」의 현재완료 의문문 형태로 사용되었다. 이때 과거분사 read는 [red]로 발음된다.

⑤ When I was a child라는 과거를 나타내고 있기 때문에, 동사 역시 과거시제로 사용한다. 이때 과거형 read는 [red]로 발음된다.

① 「how to+동사원형」는 '~하는 법'이라는 뜻을 나타낸다. 이때 동사원형 read는 [ri : d]로 발음된다.

③ 조동사 Did로 시작하는 의문문은 주어 뒤에 동사원형이 온다. 이때 동사원형 read는 [ri : d]로 발음된다.

④ 5형식 문장은 「주어+동사+목적어+목적격 보어」의 형태로 동사 tell은 「to+동사원형」 형태의 목적격 보어를 가진다. 이때 동사원형 read는 [ri : d]로 발음된다.

**58** 어제 있었던 일로 과거시제로 통일한다. decorate의 과거형은 decorated, come의 과거형은 came, sing의 과거형은 sang이다.

## PRACTICE 1

| | | | |
|---|---|---|---|
| **1** watch | | **2** swim | |
| **3** be able to | | **4** see | |
| **5** leaves | | **6** come | |
| **7** be | | **8** wants | |
| **9** wash | | **10** have | |
| **11** writes | | **12** bite | |

> **1, 2, 4, 6, 7, 9, 10, 12** 「조동사+동사원형」 형태로 쓴다.
> **3** 조동사는 겹쳐 쓰지 않으므로 will 뒤에 can을 쓸 수 없다.
> **5, 8, 11** 주어-동사 수일치를 하여 3인칭 주어인 경우 동사에 '-(e)s'를 붙인다.

## PRACTICE 2

**1** Jane will not[won't] use your desk.

**2** You must not[mustn't] take this ball.

**3** She cannot[can't] play the guitar.

**4** He should not[shouldn't] break the promise.

**5** It might not[mightn't] be true.

**6** Minsu could not[couldn't] dance last night.

**7** I knew she would not[wouldn't] come here.

**8** You may not like the movie.

**9** You had better not['d better not] stay here.

## PRACTICE 3

**1** Will they get there by subway?

**2** Should we take a bus?

**3** Can he play the violin?

**4** Will Jenny move to London?

**5** Should I buy this shirt?

**6** Can Minsu cook Chinese food?

**7** Will the movie start at 11:20?

**8** Can this elephant draw pictures?

## PRACTICE 4

**1** Can you use chopsticks?

**2** Would you like some coffee?

**3** Should I invite Minsu to dinner?

**4** May I use your phone?

**5** Could you carry my bag?

**6** Will you go there with me?

**7** Must I recycle these bottles?

**8** May I speak to Bill?

## PRACTICE 5

**1** is able to **2** am not able to

**3** Are, able to **4** was able to

**5** were not[weren't] able to

**6** Are, able to

## PRACTICE 6

| | | | |
|---|---|---|---|
| **1** can | | **2** can't | |
| **3** can[could] | | **4** Can[Could] | |
| **5** can[could] | | **6** can't | |
| **7** Can[Could] | | **8** can't | |
| **9** Can[Could] | | **10** can | |

> **1** 목말라 보이시네요. 당신은 거기서 주스를 마셔도 됩니다. (허가)
> **2** 당신은 밤에 혼자 나가서는 안 됩니다. 그건 위험합니다. (금지)
> **3** Jane, 내가 너의 펜을 빌려도 될까? (허가)
> **4** 값을 조금만 깎아 주시겠어요? (요청)
> **5** 여보세요, Tom과 통화할 수 있을까요? (허가)
> **6** 그녀는 그를 사랑하지만, 그녀는 그와 결혼할 수 없어. (능력)
> **7** 저를 좀 도와주시겠어요? (요청)
> **8** 여기 주차해서는 안 돼요. 차를 옮겨주세요. (금지)
> **9** 나의 부탁을 들어주겠니? (요청)
> **10** 너의 숙제를 먼저 하렴. 그 다음에 TV를 봐도 돼. (허가)

## PRACTICE 7

| | | | | | |
|---|---|---|---|---|---|
| **1** 허가 | | **2** 허가 | | **3** 추측 | |
| **4** 추측 | | **5** 추측 | | **6** 허가 | |
| **7** 허가 | | **8** 추측 | | **9** 추측 | |
| **10** 추측 | | **11** 허가 | | **12** 추측 | |
| **13** 허가 | | **14** 허가 | | | |

> **1** 안녕하세요, 제가 도와드려도 괜찮을까요? (허가)
> **2** 너는 나의 연필을 써도 좋아. (허가)
> **3** 그녀는 아프지 않을지도 몰라. (추측)
> **4** 그것은 사실일지도 몰라. (추측)
> **5** 그들은 바쁠지도 몰라. (추측)
> **6** 제가 질문을 해도 될까요? (허가)
> **7** 여보세요, Smith 씨랑 통화해도 될까요? (허가)
> **8** 그녀는 우리를 보고 싶지 않을지도 몰라. (추측)
> **9** 그 버스가 5분 후에 올지도 몰라. (추측)
> **10** Jenny는 목이 마를지도 몰라. (추측)
> **11** 너는 내일까지 그것을 돌려줘도 좋아. (허가)
> **12** 그녀는 마흔 두 살일지도 몰라. (추측)
> **13** 내가 그 차를 빌려도 될까? (허가)
> **14** 너는 자리에 앉아도 좋아. (허가)

## PRACTICE 8

| | | | |
|---|---|---|---|
| **1** | may[can] | **2** | not |
| **3** | you | **4** | course |
| **5** | not | **6** | Sure[Okay] |
| **7** | may[must] | **8** | Why |

## PRACTICE 9

**1** Will you stay here?

**2** Would you help me?

**3** Would you turn down the music?

**4** Will you send me an email?

**5** Will you wake me up at 7 a.m. tomorrow?

**6** Would you tell me your phone number?

**7** Would you show me your ID card?

## PRACTICE 10

**1** would like

**2** Would, like to

**3** would like to

**4** would like to

**5** Would, like

**6** would, like to, would like to

## PRACTICE 11

| | | | |
|---|---|---|---|
| **1** | Could | **2** | could |
| **3** | Can | **4** | will |
| **5** | may | **6** | Would |
| **7** | Will | **8** | Can |

> **1** could가 허가를 나타낸다.
> **2** '문제를 풀지 못했다'고 했으므로 능력의 can을 과거시제로 맞추어 could를 써야 한다.
> **3** can이 능력을 나타낸다.
> **4** will+동사원형: ~할 것이다
> **5** may가 추측을 나타낸다.
> **6** would like+(대)명사: ~을 원하다
> **7** 'Will(Would) you ~?' 구문이 요청을 나타낸다.
> **8** can이 요청을 나타낸다.

## PRACTICE 12

| | | | |
|---|---|---|---|
| **1** | 의무 | **2** | 강한 추측 |
| **3** | 의무 | **4** | 의무 |
| **5** | 강한 추측 | **6** | 강한 추측 |
| **7** | 의무 | **8** | 의무 |
| **9** | 강한 추측 | **10** | 강한 추측 |
| **11** | 의무 | **12** | 강한 추측 |

> **1** 차들이 이 거리에서 매우 빨리 다닌다. 우리는 <u>조심해야 한다</u>. (의무)
> **2** 그녀는 하루 종일 아무것도 먹지 않았다. 그녀는 배가 고픔에 <u>틀림없다</u>. (강한 추측)
> **3** 학생들은 교복을 <u>입어야 한다</u>. 그들은 평상복을 입어서는 안 된다. (의무)
> **4** 나는 내일 시험이 있다. 나는 공부를 열심히 <u>해야 한다</u>. (의무)
> **5** 죄송합니다. 제가 전화를 잘못 건 것이 <u>분명합니다</u>. (강한 추측)
> **6** 아기가 울고 있다. 그녀는 졸림에 <u>틀림없다</u>. (강한 추측)
> **7** 그것에 대해 아무 말도 하지 마세요. 당신은 그것을 비밀로 <u>해야 합니다</u>. (의무)
> **8** 불이 났다. 우리는 소방서에 <u>전화해야 한다</u>. (의무)
> **9** 나리는 매일 핑크색 옷을 입는다. 그녀는 그 색깔을 좋아함에 <u>틀림없다</u>. (강한 추측)
> **10** 민호는 어려 보인다. 그는 학생임에 <u>틀림없다</u>. (강한 추측)
> **11** 나는 밖에 나갈 수 없다. 나는 집에서 엄마를 <u>도와드려야 한다</u>. (의무)
> **12** 그는 밤 늦게까지 공부했다. 그는 피곤함에 <u>틀림없다</u>. (강한 추측)

## PRACTICE 13

| | | | |
|---|---|---|---|
| **1** | have to | **2** | has to |
| **3** | has to | **4** | have to |
| **5** | have to | **6** | have to |

## PRACTICE 14

| | | | |
|---|---|---|---|
| **1** | had to | **2** | has to |
| **3** | have to | **4** | had to |
| **5** | have to | **6** | has to |
| **7** | had to | **8** | have to |
| **9** | had to | **10** | had to |

## PRACTICE 15

| | | | |
|---|---|---|---|
| **1** | doesn't have to | **2** | must not |
| **3** | don't have to | **4** | must not |
| **5** | must not | **6** | don't have to |

## PRACTICE 16

**1** should make

**2** had better put

**3** should not throw

**4** had better wear

**5** should not play

**6** had better not go

**7** should change

**8** had better not walk

**9** should not copy

**10** had better not stay

> **1** make a good impression: 좋은 인상을 주다
> **2** put on: ~을 입다
> **6** go outside: 밖에 나가다
> **7** change clothes: 옷을 갈아입다
> **9** copy: 베끼다, 복사하다
> **10** stay out: 밖에 나가 있다

## PRACTICE 17

**1** must

**2** don't have to

**3** cannot

**4** Would

**5** could

**6** may

**7** may, had better

**8** have to

**9** Would

**10** should not

**11** Can

**12** should

**13** must not

**14** had better

**15** Could

**16** should not

**17** had to

**18** will

> **1** must가 강한 추측을 나타낸다.
> **2** don't have to가 불필요를 나타낸다.
> **3, 5** cannot, could가 능력을 나타낸다.
> **4** 'Would you ~?'가 요청을 나타낸다.
> **6** may가 추측을 나타낸다.
> **7** may가 추측, had better가 강한 충고나 권유를 나타낸다.
> **8, 17** have to(=must), had to가 의무를 나타낸다.
> **9** would like+(대)명사: ~을 원하다
> **10, 16** should not(~하면 안 된다)이 금지를 나타낸다.
> **11** can이 허가를 나타낸다.
> **12** should가 의무를 나타낸다.
> **13** must not이 강한 금지를 나타낸다.
> **14** had better가 강한 충고나 권유를 나타낸다.
> **15** 'Could you ~?'가 요청을 나타낸다.
> **18** will not+동사원형: ~하지 않을 것이다

## 중간·기말고사 대비문제 정답 본문 _ p.92

**1** ④  **2** ①  **3** is able to  **4** ③  **5** ⑤
**6** had better   **7** (1) are → be (2) borrowing → borrow   **8** ⑤   **9** ④   **10** Do I have to go home now?   **11** are able to   **12** ④   **13** Will he meet his friends tomorrow?   **14** ④   **15** ③
**16** (1) She will not[won't] listen to pop songs. (2) Will you be quiet in the library?   **17** ③   **18** ④
**19** ①   **20** ③   **21** ①   **22** ③   **23** ③   **24** ④
**25** ⑤   **26** You must not carry a balloon here.
**27** ④   **28** ④   **29** May I swim in this river?
**30** ⑤   **31** ③   **32** ①   **33** ②   **34** ②   **35** ②
**36** ①   **37** ⑤   **38** ①   **39** ①   **40** ①   **41** ④
**42** ④   **43** You had better go to bed   **44** ②
**45** ②   **46** ③   **47** ① You may not use your phone on the bus. ② You may not bring food into the classroom. ③ You may take pictures at the festival.   **48** ②

## 중간·기말고사 대비문제 해설

**1**   ④ 조동사 may 뒤에 동사원형 be를 쓴 것은 적절하다.
① 조동사 can't 뒤에 동사원형 begin을 써야 한다. (began → begin)
② 조동사 will의 부정형은 won't로 줄여서 쓴다. (willn't → won't)
③ 조동사 could 뒤에 동사원형 dance를 써야 한다. (dances → dance)
⑤ 조동사 should 뒤에 동사원형 study를 써야 한다. (studied → study)

**2**   '~해야 한다'의 뜻을 나타내는 조동사 must는 의무를 나타내는 have/has to와 바꾸어 쓸 수 있는데, 주어가 You이므로 have to가 가장 적절하다.

**3**   능력을 나타내는 can은 be able to와 바꾸어 쓸 수 있는데, 주어가 she이므로 is able to가 와야 한다.

**4**   would like to+동사원형 '~하고 싶다'

**5**   Yes나 sure 뒤에는 긍정형이, No 뒤에는 부정형이 와야 한다. 조동사는 인칭에 관계없이 항상 형태가 같다.

**6**   had better '~하는 게 낫다'

**7**   (1) 조동사(will) 뒤에는 동사원형이 와야 한다. are의 동사원형은 be이다.

8   (2) 조동사로 시작하는 의문문 「조동사+주어+동사원형 ~?」

8   접속사 But으로 시작하는 두 번째 문장은 앞 문장과 반대의 의미를 나타내므로 조동사의 부정형 can't가 들어가야 한다. 우리는 돈으로 무엇이든 살 수 있다. 그러나 돈으로 건강을 살 수는 없다.

9   빈칸 이후 이어지는 말에 '주차금지' 표지판이 언급되었으므로 '~해서는 안 된다'는 거절의 답이 와야 한다. May I ~?에 대한 거절의 표현으로 No, you must not.을 쓸 수 있다. 제가 여기에 주차를 해도 되나요? – 아니요, 안 됩니다. '주차금지' 표지판이 있어요.

10   have to는 do[does]를 써서 의문문을 만든다.

11   능력을 나타내는 can은 be able to와 바꾸어 쓸 수 있다. 주어(Humans)가 복수이므로 are able to로 쓴다.

12   강한 추측을 나타내는 must '~임에 틀림없다'

13   '~할 것이다'라는 의미가 되려면 will 또는 be going to가 와야 한다. 조건에서 6단어로 쓰라고 했으므로 will을 쓰는 것이 적절하다.

14   ④ don't have to '~할 필요가 없다'

15   ③ don't have to '~할 필요가 없다'
①②④⑤ '~해서는 안 된다'

16   will not[won't] '~하지 않을 것이다'
Will[Would] you ~? '~해줄래요?'

17   would like to = want to '~하고 싶다'

18   should는 '~해야 한다'의 뜻이므로 너는 도서관에서 떠들어야 한다.는 어색하다.
(should → should not[shouldn't])

19   may '~일지도 모른다' 만약 창문을 열어놓은 채로 잠들면, 너는 감기에 걸릴지도 모른다.

20   ⓐⓓ 허가의 can '~해도 된다'
ⓑⓒⓔ 능력의 can '~할 수 있다'

21   Can I ~? '~해도 될까(요)?' 내가 햄버거를 좀 먹어도 될까? – 물론이지, 여기 있어.

22   • May I ~? '~해도 될까(요)?'
• must '~해야 한다' 엄마, 친구들이랑 야구해도 되나요? – 안 돼! 너는 숙제를 먼저 끝내야 해.

23   have to의 의문문 「Do[Does]+주어+have to+동사원형 ~?」

24   you로 물었으므로 I로 대답하는 것이 적절하다.
④ Yes, I can.

25   ⑤ 두 개의 조동사는 같이 쓰일 수 없다.

26   「must not+동사원형」 '~해서는 안 된다'

27   ④ 허가의 may '~해도 좋다'
①②③⑤ 추측의 may '~일지도 모른다'

28   ① 조동사에는 s를 붙이지 않는다. (cans → can)
② 조동사 뒤에는 동사원형이 온다. (speaks → speak)
③ 조동사의 부정형을 쓸 때 not은 조동사 뒤에 위치한다. (not can → cannot)
⑤ 조동사에는 s를 붙이지 않으며, 조동사 뒤에는 동사원형이 온다. (cans rides → can ride)

29   대답이 may not으로 되어 있으므로 조동사 May를 써서 질문해야 한다. 조동사가 들어간 의문문은 「조동사+주어+동사원형 ~?」의 어순을 따른다.
질문: 제가 이 강에서 수영해도 될까요?
대답: 아니요, 안 됩니다. 이 강에서 수영하는 것은 위험해요.

30   뒤에 동사원형이 나오므로 조동사가 와야 한다. 빈칸에는 의무를 나타내는 조동사가 들어가야 의미상 자연스럽다. should는 '~해야 한다'는 뜻이다.

31   조동사 may를 사용해 허가를 묻는 분상이므로 may, can/can't, should와 같은 조동사를 사용하여 승낙 또는 거절의 표현으로 대답한다. 'Yes, I would.'는 허가를 묻는 말에 대한 응답으로 보기에 어색하다.

32   숙제를 해야 하므로 함께 갈 수 없다는 거절의 표현이 와야 한다.

33   • This work may <u>be</u> easy for you.
• You <u>don't have to</u> bring your library card.
• He <u>must</u> practice English every day.

34   will의 부정형의 축약형은 won't이다.
② willn't → won't

35   ② 주어가 3인칭 단수(Mr. Brown)이므로 has to로 써야 한다.

36   could '~할 수 있었다'

37   May I ~? '~해도 될까(요)?'

38   Will you ~? '~해줄래요?'
문 좀 닫아 줄래요? – 알겠어요.

39   • would like to+동사원형: ~하고 싶다
• 조동사 shall이 포함된 의문문이므로 두 번째 빈칸에는 동사원형이 와야 한다. 「(의문사+)조동사+주어+동사원형 ~?」

40   must는 인칭에 관계없이 항상 형태가 같다.
*cf.* have[has] to는 인칭에 따라 다르게 쓰인다.
You <u>have to</u> get there before dark.
She <u>has to</u> buy a new book.

**41** had to '~해야 했다'
*cf.* 과거의 의무를 나타낼 때는 must를 쓸 수 없고 반
드시 had to로만 쓴다.

**42** should '~해야 한다'
나는 네가 치과에 가봐야 한다고 생각해.

**43** 「had better+동사원형」 '~하는 게 낫다'
너는 오늘 밤 일찍 잠자리에 드는 게 낫다.

**44** What would you like to eat for lunch?
너는 점심으로 무엇을 먹고 싶니?

**45** ② 허가의 may '~해도 좋다'
①③④⑤ 추측의 may '~일지도 모른다'

**46** ③ 너는 식사를 걸러야 한다.
(should → should not[shouldn't])

**47** ①② 허가와 의무의 의미를 가진 조동사 may의 부정
형을 활용해 금지의 의미를 나타낸다. 조동사+not
뒤에는 동사원형을 쓴다.
③ 허가의 의미를 가진 조동사 may를 활용해 가능의
의미를 나타낸다. 조동사 뒤에는 동사원형을 쓴다.

**48** must not '~해서는 안 된다'
don't have to '~할 필요가 없다'

① 너는 매일 운동해야 한다.
② 너는 정크 푸드를 먹지 말아야 한다.
④ 너는 늦게 잠자리에 들지 말아야 한다.
⑤ 너는 채소를 많이 먹어야 한다.

---

## CHAPTER 4 수동태
Passive Voice

본문 _ p.100

### PRACTICE 1

**1** ① him  ② He
**2** ① They  ② them
**3** ① Sumi  ② Sumi
**4** ① It  ② it
**5** ① We  ② us
**6** ① my family  ② My family
**7** ① I  ② me
**8** ① You  ② you
**9** ① The bird  ② the bird
**10** ① her  ② She
**11** ① Your brother  ② your brother
**12** ① Their parents  ② their parents

### PRACTICE 2

**1** threw, thrown  **2** cooked, cooked
**3** made, made  **4** brought, brought
**5** began, begun  **6** called, called
**7** invented, invented  **8** held, held
**9** wore, worn  **10** blew, blown

| | | | |
|---|---|---|---|
| **11** read, read | | **12** built, built | |
| **13** flew, flown | | **14** killed, killed | |
| **15** lost, lost | | **16** woke, woken | |
| **17** took, taken | | **18** cleaned, cleaned | |
| **19** bore, borne/born | | **20** said, said | |
| **21** answered, answered | | **22** found, found | |
| **23** caught, caught | | **24** knew, known | |
| **25** invited, invited | | **26** stole, stolen | |
| **27** thought, thought | | **28** wrote, written | |
| **29** rode, ridden | | **30** opened, opened | |
| **31** spent, spent | | **32** was/were, been | |
| **33** bought, bought | | **34** stopped, stopped | |
| **35** used, used | | **36** spoke, spoken | |
| **37** bit, bitten | | **38** put, put | |
| **39** got, got(ten) | | **40** did, done | |
| **41** collected, collected | | **42** laid, laid | |
| **43** understood, understood | | **44** drank, drunk | |
| **45** broke, broken | | **46** kept, kept | |
| **47** sold, sold | | **48** forgot, forgotten | |
| **49** carried, carried | | **50** ate, eaten | |
| **51** sent, sent | | **52** saw, seen | |
| **53** sang, sung | | **54** set, set | |
| **55** tried, tried | | **56** drew, drawn | |
| **57** gave, given | | **58** told, told | |
| **59** dropped, dropped | | **60** taught, taught | |

## PRACTICE 3

**1** A letter is written by David.

**2** An e-mail is sent by me.

**3** Eggs are laid by chickens.

**4** Foreign coins are collected by me.

**5** The steaks are cooked by my mother.

**6** They are taught by their father.

**7** The book is read by my brother.

**8** This expression is used by most people.

**9** They are called by the principal.

**10** These bags are made by her.

**11** Those pictures are painted by her.

**12** The questions are answered by the teacher.

**13** The trash in the river is picked up by Jacob.

## PRACTICE 4

**1** were opened    **2** is played

**3** were broken    **4** is used

**5** are washed    **6** was bitten

**7** is sung    **8** was invented

**9** are grown    **10** was delivered

## PRACTICE 5

**1** A lot of letters are written (by us).

**2** Groceries are bought here.

**3** Shorts are worn in summer (by you).

**4** The lost dog was found yesterday (by them).

**5** Smartphones are used every day (by us).

**6** My bicycle was stolen (by someone).

**7** The memories were forgotten.

**8** This wine was made in 1970 (by someone).

**9** Fresh fruit is sold in the store (by us).

**10** These buildings were built (by them) 20 years ago.

## PRACTICE 6

**1** The story is found interesting by some readers.

**2** He was elected president.

**3** A lion is called the king of the jungle.

**4** People are made happy by good paintings.

**5** The rabbit was found dead by Mira.

**6** I was called a princess by my parents.

5형식 문장을 수동태로 전환할 때는 능동태의 목적어와 목적격 보어가 각각 주어, 주격 보어가 된다. 능동태의 동사를 'be동사+과거분사' 형태로 바꾸고, be동사는 바뀐 주어의 인칭과 수, 원래 능동태 문장의 동사의 시제에 일치시킨다. 능동태의 주어는 'by+목적격' 형태로 행위자를 나타낸다.

Some readers find the story interesting.
주어    동사   목적어   목적격 보어

주어   be+과거분사   주격 보어    by+목적격
The story is found interesting by some readers.

1, 3 수동태의 주어가 3인칭 단수이고, 원래 문장의 시제가 현재이므로 be동사의 형태는 is가 적절하다. 3번의 people은 일반 사람을 나타내기 때문에 'by+목적격'을 생략한다.
2, 5, 6 원래 문장의 시제가 과거이고, 수동태 문장의 주어가 단수이므로 수동태 문장의 동사는 'was+과거분사' 형태가 적절하다. 2번의 we는 일반 사람을 가리키므로 'by+목적격'을 생략한다.
4 수동태의 주어 people이 복수이고, 원래 문장의 시제가 현재이므로 be동사의 형태는 are가 적절하다.

## PRACTICE 7

**1** She is respected by her children.

**2** His sister was made angry by him.

**3** We were helped by the teacher.

**4** Their village is kept clean.

**5** Those dresses were designed by a famous fashion designer.

**6** This work was finished by Ms. Smith.

**7** Many languages are spoken in Switzerland.

**8** TV programs are watched by a lot of teenagers.

**9** Mozart and Beethoven are called great musicians.

**10** The magazine was published in 2023 by the company.

3형식 문장을 수동태로 전환할 때는 능동태의 목적어가 주어가 된다. 능동태의 동사를 'be동사+과거분사' 형태로 바꾸고, be동사는 바뀐 주어의 인칭과 수, 원래 능동태 문장의 동사의 시제에 일치시킨다. 능동태의 주어는 'by+목적격' 형태로 행위자를 나타낸다. 5형식 문장의 수동태에서는 추가적으로 능동태의 목적격 보어가 주격 보어가 되며, 나머지는 3형식과 동일하다.

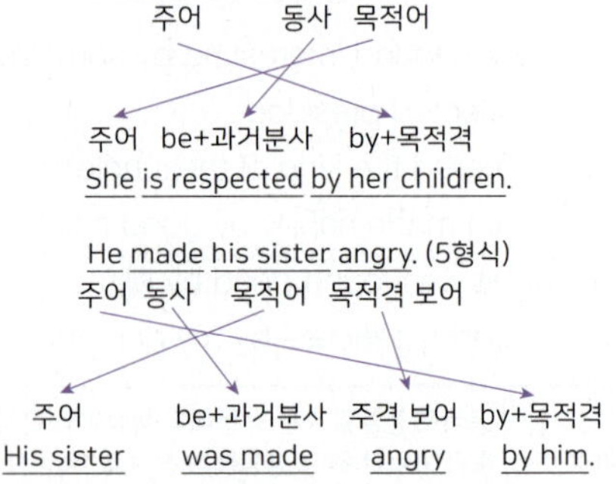


**1, 4** 수동태의 주어가 3인칭 단수이고, 원래 문장의 시제가 현재이므로 be동사의 형태는 is가 적절하다. 4번의 they처럼 행위자가 분명하지 않거나 나타낼 필요가 없을 때에는 'by+목적격'을 생략한다.
**2, 6, 10** 수동태의 주어가 3인칭 단수이고, 원래 문장의 시제가 과거이므로 be동사의 형태는 was가 적절하다.
**3, 5** 수동태의 주어가 복수이고, 원래 문장의 시제가 과거이므로 be동사의 형태는 were가 적절하다.
**7, 8, 9** 수동태의 주어가 복수이고, 원래 문장의 시제가 현재이므로 be동사의 형태는 are가 적절하다. 7번과 9번의 we는 일반 사람을 가리키므로 'by+목적격'을 생략한다.

## 📋 중간·기말고사 대비문제 정답    본문 _ p.108

**1** ③    **2** We, invited    **3** by someone    **4** ②
**5** ⑤    **6** ①    **7** (1) This room is cleaned (2) The box is kept   (3) The email is sent
**8** was written    **9** am made happy    **10** ③
**11** ①    **12** ⑤    **13** (1) English is taught by Mr. Kim.   (2) Her handbag was stolen by the thief.
**14** ④    **15** ⑤    **16** The house was built by my grandfather.    **17** is made    **18** ③
**19** ② is → was    **20** ③    **21** ③    **22** (1) was bought by Jake   (2) broke the desk

## 중간·기말고사 대비문제 해설

**1** 주어(Honey)가 동작의 대상이 되므로 「be동사+과거분사」의 형태인 수동태가 되어야 한다. 주어(Honey)가 3인칭 단수이므로 is가 온다.
*cf.* make - made - made

**2** 주어진 문장의 목적어 us가 주어 We가 되고, 수동태는 「be동사+과거분사」의 형태이므로 invite의 과거분사형인 invited를 쓴다.

**3** 행위자가 분명하지 않거나 나타낼 필요가 없을 때는 「by+목적격」을 생략할 수 있다.

**4** 주어(The World Cup)가 동작의 대상이 되므로 「be동사+과거분사」의 형태인 수동태가 되어야 한다.
*cf.* hold - held - held

**5** 능동태의 동사(broke)를 「be동사+과거분사」의 형태로 바꾼다. 동사가 과거형이므로 be동사의 과거형(was)이 와야 한다.
*cf.* break - broke - broken

**6** 주어(*gimchi*)가 동작의 대상이 되므로 「be동사+과거분사」의 형태인 수동태가 되어야 한다.

**7** 방, 상자, 이메일이 모두 그 동작을 당하는 대상이 되므로 수동태로 써야 한다. 수동태 문장은 「주어+be동사+과거분사」의 어순으로 쓴다.

**8** 주어(*Romeo and Juliet*)가 동작의 대상이 되므로 「be동사+과거분사」의 형태인 수동태가 되어야 한다. *Romeo and Juliet*은 작품명이므로 단수이고, 이미 끝난 과거의 일이므로 be동사는 was를 쓴다.
*cf.* write - wrote - written

**9** 5형식 문장의 수동태 전환은 능동태의 동사(makes)를 「be동사+과거분사」의 형태로 바꾸고, 그 뒤에 보어

(happy)를 쓴다.

**10** 수동태의 동사는 「be동사+과거분사」의 형태로 나타 낸다.
ⓔ My bicycle was fixed by Tom.

**11** • 앞에 was가 나왔으므로 과거 진행형을 써서 빈칸에 는 현재분사 holding이 들어가야 한다.
• 전시회가 '개최된' 것이므로 수동태를 써서 빈칸에 는 과거분사 held가 들어가야 한다.
• 그가 세계 기록을 보유하고 있다는 상태를 나타내 므로 빈칸에는 현재시제 동사 holds가 들어가야 한 다.
• 앞에 미래를 의미하는 조동사 will이 쓰였고, 회의는 '주최되는' 것이므로 수동태 표현을 써서 빈칸에는 be held가 들어가야 한다.

**12** ① 능동태를 수동태로 바꿀 때 동사는 「be동사+과거 분사」의 형태로 쓴다. (written → is written)
② 능동태의 시제가 현재 시제이므로 수동태로 변환 할 때 be동사의 현재 시제 is를 써야 한다.
(was → is)
③ 수동태의 주어 The plants가 복수이므로 동사 are을 쓰는 것이 적절하다. (is → are)
④ 능동태의 목적어 the dog이 수동태의 주어로 와야 한다. Max는 목적격 보어로 수동태의 주어로 쓰는 것은 적절하지 않다. (Max was named the dog → The dog was named Max)

**13** (1) English를 주어로 하는 수동태 문장으로 써야 한 다. 주어가 3인칭 단수이고 현재시제이므로 be동 사는 is를 쓴다.
(2) Her handbag을 주어로 하는 수동태 문장으로 써 야 한다. 주어가 3인칭 단수이고 과거시제이므로 be동사는 was를 쓴다.

**14** 능동태의 목적어(her)는 수동태의 주어(She)로, 동사 는 「be동사+과거분사」의 형태로 쓴다. 능동태의 동사 (call)가 현재형이므로 be동사는 is가 와야 한다.
*cf.* 능동태의 주어(People)가 일반 사람을 나타내므 로 「by+목적격」은 생략한다.

**15** ⑤ 주어진 우리말에서 주어인 거울이 '다뤄져야 한다' 고 했으므로 수동태 문장으로 영작해야 한다.
(handle → be handled)

**16** 수동태의 어순 「주어+be동사+과거분사+by+목적격」

**17** 능동태의 동사(makes)를 「be동사+과거분사」의 형태 로 바꾼다. 이때 수동태의 주어(The bed)가 단수이고, 능동태의 동사가 현재형이므로 be동사는 is를 쓴다.

**18** It은 picture를 가리키며, 이는 동작의 대상이 되므로 「be동사+과거분사」의 형태인 수동태가 되어야 한다. 지금 보는 사진의 촬영 시점은 과거일 수 밖에 없으므 로 be동사는 과거형(was)이어야 한다.

**19** 과거를 나타내는 부사구(a week ago)가 있으므로 be동사의 과거형(was)이 와야 한다.

**20** 수동태의 동사는 「be동사+과거분사」의 형태로 나타 낸다.
ⓔ He was bitten by my dog.

**21** • Some cookies were maden by her.
→ Some cookies were made by her.
• The cartoons were drawing by us.
→ The cartoons were drawn by us.

**22** (1) 문장의 목적어(the wallet)가 주어가 되었으므로 「be동사+과거분사+by 행위자」 형태의 수동태 문 장을 써야 한다.
(2) 수동태 문장의 행위자(my brother)가 주어이므 로 능동태 문장을 써야 한다.

Ch
**4**
수
동
태

## PRACTICE 1

| | | | | | |
|---|---|---|---|---|---|
| **1** ③ | | **2** ② | | **3** ⑤ | |
| **4** ④ | | **5** ② | | **6** ① | |
| **7** ⑤ | | **8** ② | | **9** ③ | |
| **10** ④ | | | | | |

> **1** coffee는 물질명사고 나머지는 보통명사다.
> **2** Becky는 고유명사고 나머지는 보통명사다.
> **3** dictionary는 보통명사고 나머지는 집합명사다.
> **4** club은 집합명사고 나머지는 고유명사다.
> **5** dish는 보통명사고 나머지는 추상명사다.
> **6** class는 집합명사고 나머지는 물질명사다.
> **7** family는 집합명사고 나머지는 추상명사다.
> **8** Mt. Halla는 고유명사고 나머지는 물질명사다.
> **9** smoke는 물질명사고 나머지는 보통명사다.
> **10** snow는 물질명사고 나머지는 추상명사다. 두 종류 다 셀 수 없
> 는 명사지만, 물질명사는 실존하는 반면 추상명사는 형태 없이 개념
> 이나 감정을 나타내는 명사다.

## PRACTICE 2

| | | | |
|---|---|---|---|
| **1** Water | | **2** a child | |
| **3** family | | **4** sugar | |
| **5** Korea | | **6** Friendship | |
| **7** class | | **8** freedom | |
| **9** Mike | | **10** a flower | |
| **11** butter | | **12** Love | |

> **1, 4, 11** water, sugar, butter는 물질명사로, 부정관사 a와 함께
> 사용할 수 없다.
> **2, 10** child, flower는 셀 수 있는 명사로, 부정관사 a와 함께 쓰는
> 것이 적절하다.
> **3, 7** family, class와 같은 명사는 해당 집합을 개개인의 모임으로
> 볼 때는 복수 취급하지만, 단일한 한 개의 집단으로 볼 때는 단수 취
> 급한다. is에 수를 일치시키려면 family, class가 적절하다.
> **5, 9** Korea, Mike는 고유명사로, 부정관사 a와 함께 사용할 수 없
> 다.
> **6, 8, 12** friendship, freedom, love는 추상명사로, 부정관사 a
> 와 함께 사용할 수 없다.

## PRACTICE 3

| | | | |
|---|---|---|---|
| **1** eggs | | **2** buses | |
| **3** addresses | | **4** stars | |
| **5** days | | **6** presents | |
| **7** photos | | **8** umbrellas | |
| **9** sports | | **10** cups | |
| **11** beaches | | **12** friends | |
| **13** cats | | **14** problems | |
| **15** tomatoes | | **16** shirts | |
| **17** boxes | | **18** maps | |
| **19** zoos | | **20** baths | |
| **21** cookies | | **22** boats | |
| **23** flowers | | **24** watches | |
| **25** radios | | **26** mosquito(e)s | |
| **27** passports | | **28** tests | |
| **29** brushes | | **30** potatoes | |

## PRACTICE 4

| | | | |
|---|---|---|---|
| **1** candies | | **2** songs | |
| **3** days | | **4** ideas | |
| **5** knives | | **6** bodies | |
| **7** cows | | **8** classes | |
| **9** shelves | | **10** factories | |
| **11** wives | | **12** ladies | |
| **13** buildings | | **14** animals | |
| **15** mistakes | | **16** doors | |
| **17** families | | **18** safes | |
| **19** pencils | | **20** stories | |
| **21** dishes | | **22** pictures | |
| **23** audios | | **24** dolls | |
| **25** toys | | **26** keys | |
| **27** wolves | | **28** foxes | |
| **29** boys | | **30** sandwiches | |
| **31** ships | | **32** videos | |
| **33** monkeys | | **34** leaves | |
| **35** letters | | **36** bananas | |
| **37** pianos | | **38** computers | |
| **39** babies | | **40** notes | |
| **41** towns | | **42** parties | |
| **43** blouses | | **44** questions | |
| **45** pigs | | **46** doughnuts | |
| **47** cards | | **48** holidays | |
| **49** cities | | **50** farmers | |
| **51** headaches | | **52** bottles | |
| **53** houses | | **54** countries | |
| **55** posters | | **56** roofs | |
| **57** blocks | | **58** diaries | |
| **59** churches | | **60** selves | |

## PRACTICE 5

| | | | |
|---|---|---|---|
| 1 | ducks | 2 | hobbies |
| 3 | oxen | 4 | festivals |
| 5 | scarves/scarfs | 6 | deer |
| 7 | rooms | 8 | students |
| 9 | sheep | 10 | men |
| 11 | candles | 12 | months |
| 13 | mice | 14 | feet |
| 15 | teams | 16 | subjects |
| 17 | snowmen | 18 | neighbors |
| 19 | geese | 20 | hours |
| 21 | fish | 22 | women |
| 23 | sweaters | 24 | bags |
| 25 | children | 26 | seats |
| 27 | benches | 28 | habits |
| 29 | teeth | 30 | thieves |

## PRACTICE 6

| | | | |
|---|---|---|---|
| 1 | knives | 2 | Mice |
| 3 | church | 4 | children |
| 5 | pencil | 6 | feet |
| 7 | leaves | 8 | fish |
| 9 | women | 10 | sheep |
| 11 | oxen | 12 | deer |
| 13 | teeth | 14 | hobbies |

## PRACTICE 7

1 glasses of milk
2 pieces of furniture
3 bottles of juice
4 pieces of chalk
5 glasses of water
6 slices of bread
7 pairs of scissors
8 pounds of sugar
9 cups of tea
10 pieces of news
11 slices of pizza
12 pairs of socks
13 pieces of paper
14 bottles of ink
15 pounds of flour

## PRACTICE 8

| | | | |
|---|---|---|---|
| 1 | pair | 2 | pair |
| 3 | piece[slice] | 4 | pieces[slices] |
| 5 | glass[bottle/cup] | 6 | cups |
| 7 | pair | 8 | slices[pounds] |
| 9 | glasses[bottles] | 10 | piece |

> 1, 2, 7 scissors, jeans, glasses와 같이 두 개의 짝으로 이루어져 복수형으로 쓰는 명사의 수량을 나타낼 때에는 단위명사 pair를 사용한다.

## PRACTICE 9

2 boys' middle school
3 Ted's birthday
4 dog's name
5 women's university
6 teachers' room
7 Mr. Kim's son
8 parents' photo album
9 people's ideas
10 children's bookstore
11 dogs' houses
12 Ana and Hailey's restaurant
13 Andy's job
14 Richard's voice

> 2, 6, 8, 11 -s로 끝나는 복수명사는 어퍼스트로피(')만을 붙여 소유격을 표현한다.
> 3, 4, 7, 13, 14 -s로 끝나지 않는 단수명사는 's를 붙여 소유격을 표현한다.
> 5, 9, 10, 12 -s로 끝나지 않는 복수명사는 's를 붙여 소유격을 표현한다.

## PRACTICE 10

2 the end of this city
3 the door of the room
4 sense of smell
5 The people of the village
6 the color of your shoes
7 the list of the classes
8 the middle of the table
9 The students of this class
10 the name of the mountain

> 2~10 무생물을 나타내는 명사는 of를 이용하여 소유격을 만든다.

Ch
5
명사와 관사

## PRACTICE 11

1 umbrella, Mira's
2 voice, my daughter's
3 puppy, her brother's
4 house, Mr. Felini's
5 books, Peter's
6 arm, a robot's
7 painting, Mr. Smith's
8 room, Yumi's
9 jacket, my friend's
10 toys, the children's

## PRACTICE 12

1 four-leaf
2 five-week
3 one hundred-page
4 three-year-old
5 ten-story
6 eight-year-old
7 two-month
8 two-meter-long
9 five-dollar
10 ten-minute

> **1** 복수형인 leaves를 단수형 leaf로 바꿔 four와 하이픈으로 연결한다.
> **5** 복수형인 stories를 단수형 story로 바꿔 ten과 하이픈으로 연결한다. 여기에서 story는 '(건물의) 층'을 의미한다.

## PRACTICE 13

| | | | | | |
|---|---|---|---|---|---|
| **1** an | **2** a | **3** an |
| **4** a | **5** a | **6** an |
| **7** an | **8** a | **9** an |
| **10** a | **11** an | **12** a |
| **13** an | **14** an | **15** a |
| **16** an | **17** a | **18** a |
| **19** a | **20** an | |

> **1, 3, 6, 7, 11, 13, 16, 20** 첫소리가 모음으로 시작하기 때문에 부정관사 an을 사용한다.
> **2, 4, 5, 10** 철자는 모음으로 시작하지만, 첫소리가 자음 '[ju]'로 시작하기 때문에 부정관사 a를 사용한다.
> **9, 14** 첫 글자인 'h'가 묵음 처리되어 첫소리가 모음이기 때문에 부정관사 an을 사용한다.
> **18** 철자는 모음으로 시작하지만, 첫소리가 자음 '[ji]'로 시작하기 때문에 부정관사 a를 사용한다.

## PRACTICE 14

| | | | | | |
|---|---|---|---|---|---|
| **1** ① | **2** ③ | **3** ② |
| **4** ① | **5** ② | **6** ③ |
| **7** ③ | **8** ① | **9** ② |

> **[보기]**
> ① 그는 아들 하나와 딸 둘이 있다. (하나의)
> ② 나는 한 달에 한 번 그를 만났다. (~에, ~마다)
> ③ 물고기는 물 없이는 살 수 없다. (종족 전체를 대표)
>
> **1** 그들은 한 시간 동안 달리고 있었다. (①하나의)
> **2** 학은 긴 다리를 가졌다. (③종족 전체를 대표)
> **3** 그녀는 일주일에 수업이 세 개밖에 없다. (②~마다)
> **4** 우리는 하나의 팀을 위해 열한 명의 선수가 필요하다. (①하나의)
> **5** 나는 주로 하루에 여덟 시간 공부한다. (②~마다)
> **6** 뱀은 겨울 동안 잠을 잔다. (③종족 전체를 대표)
> **7** 코끼리는 긴 코를 가지고 있다. (③종족 전체를 대표)
> **8** 로마는 하루아침에 이루어지지 않았다. (①하나의)
> **9** 민수는 일 년에 두 번 그의 조부모님을 방문한다. (②~마다)

## PRACTICE 15

| | | | | | |
|---|---|---|---|---|---|
| **1** ④ | **2** ⑤ | **3** ⑦ |
| **4** ③ | **5** ⑥ | **6** ① |
| **7** ② | | |

> **[보기]**의 밑줄 친 the의 용법은 다음과 같다.
> ① 앞에 나온 명사가 다시 반복될 때
> ② 문맥이나 상황으로 보아 무엇을 가리키는지 알 수 있을 때
> ③ 구나 절에 의해 수식을 받아 가리키는 대상이 분명할 때
> (the rooms in the house)
> ④ 일반적으로 유일한 것을 말할 때 (the sky)
> ⑤ 최상급 앞
> ⑥ 악기 이름 앞
> ⑦ 종족 전체를 대표
> **4** 'of France(프랑스의)'라는 구에 의해 수식을 받아 어떤 수도 (capital)인지 의미가 분명해진다.
> **7** 행인에게 길을 물어보는 상황을 고려했을 때 근처에 있는 우체국의 위치를 물어보는 점이 분명하다.

## PRACTICE 16

| | | | | | |
|---|---|---|---|---|---|
| **1** the | **2** the | **3** the |
| **4** a | **5** The | **6** A |
| **7** an | **8** the | **9** a |
| **10** The | **11** the | **12** the |
| **13** The | | |

> **1** 악기 앞에는 정관사 the를 사용한다.
> **2, 8, 12** 서수, same, last 앞에는 정관사 the를 사용한다.
> **3** '저 신호등을 봐'라는 뜻으로, 청자와 화자가 한 자리에 있어서 상황상 가리키는 대상이 분명하기 때문에 정관사 the를 사용하는 것이 적절하다.

**4** '그들은 하루에 9시간을 학교에서 보낸다'는 뜻으로, '~마다'의 의미를 가진 부정관사 a를 사용하는 것이 적절하다.
**5** 태양은 세상에서 유일한 것이기 때문에 정관사 the를 사용한다.
**6, 7, 9** '한 개'를 의미하는 부정관사 a/an을 사용하는 것이 적절하다.
**10, 11** 각각 'of the station'과 'in the door'의 수식을 받고 있기 때문에 정관사 the를 사용하는 것이 적절하다.
**13** 앞서 쓰인 명사 boy를 다시 언급하고 있으므로 정관사 the를 사용하는 것이 적절하다.

## PRACTICE 17

| | | | | | |
|---|---|---|---|---|---|
| **1** | an | **2** | X | **3** | the |
| **4** | X | **5** | X | **6** | the |
| **7** | the | **8** | a | **9** | X |
| **10** | X | **11** | the | **12** | X |
| **13** | a | **14** | X | **15** | the |

**1** 'F'의 첫소리가 모음 [e]로 시작하므로 부정관사 an을 사용한다.
**2, 5, 9, 12** 식사, 운동, 질병의 이름 앞에 관사를 사용하지 않는다.
**3** 최상급 tallest 앞에 정관사 the를 사용한다.
**4, 10** 건물이 본래의 목적으로 쓰일 때 건물을 나타내는 명사 앞에 관사를 사용하지 않는다.
**6** '내 딸을 데리러 가기 위해' 가는 것이므로 학교의 본래 목적으로 쓰이지 않았기 때문에 관사를 생략할 수 없다.
**7** 악기 이름 앞에 정관사 the를 사용한다.
**8** '하나의'의 의미를 가진 부정관사 a를 쓰는 것이 적절하다.
**11** same 앞에 정관사 the를 사용한다.
**13** '한 달에 3번'이라는 빈도를 나타내기 위해 '~마다'를 의미하는 a를 사용한다.
**14** 기구가 본래의 목적(잠을 자는 것)대로 언급되고 있기 때문에 관사를 사용하지 않는다.
**15** '문 좀 닫아줄래?'와 같은 명령문의 경우, 일반적으로 청자와 화자가 한 공간에 있어야 발화가 가능하다. 따라서 상황상 가리키는 대상이 분명하기 때문에 정관사 the를 사용할 수 있다.

## PRACTICE 18

| | | | | | |
|---|---|---|---|---|---|
| **1** | is | **2** | Are | **3** | is |
| **4** | Are | **5** | Is | **6** | are |
| **7** | are | **8** | Is | **9** | are |
| **10** | is | | | | |

**3, 8, 10** money, sugar, water는 셀 수 없는 물질명사이므로 단수 취급한다.

## PRACTICE 19

**1** there is
**2** Was there
**3** are there
**4** there weren't
**5** How many, There are

**6** Are, there are
**7** There are
**8** Is, there is
**9** How much, There is

**5** 대답이 Yes/No가 아닌 의문문은 의문사로 시작한다. 대답에 학생의 인원수가 언급되었고, student는 셀 수 있는 명사이므로 how many로 질문한다.
**9** 대답이 Yes/No가 아니고, 대답에서 구체적인 우유의 양이 언급되었으므로 의문사로 시작하는 의문문으로 질문했음을 알 수 있다. milk는 셀 수 없는 물질명사이기 때문에 how much로 질문한다.

## PRACTICE 20

| | | | | | |
|---|---|---|---|---|---|
| **1** | X | **2** | X | **3** | O |
| **4** | O | **5** | X | **6** | O |
| **7** | X | **8** | O | **9** | X |
| **10** | X | **11** | O | **12** | X |
| **13** | O | **14** | X | | |

**2** 콤마가 day를 수식하는 형용사 hot, humid, airless를 나열하기 위해 사용되었다.

### 📖 중간·기말고사 대비문제 정답  본문 _ p.132

**1** ② **2** ③ **3** ② **4** air, furniture, money, milk
**5** ② **6** ⑤ **7** ② **8** ② **9** ⓐ deer ⓑ feet
ⓒ Men **10** ① **11** (1) Jane's jacket
(2) father's building (3) my friend's **12** ④
**13** ⓐ are ⓑ Is ⓒ is **14** ③,④,⑤ **15** ⓐ, I am
playing basketball with my friends. **16** ⑤
**17** ⑤ **18** ③ **19** ④ **20** ① **21** ③ **22** ④
**23** ② **24** ① **25** ⓐ an ⓑ an ⓒ a **26** ⑤
**27** ② **28** ⑤ **29** ⑤ **30** uncle's **31** ④
**32** the Earth **33** (1) How many books are
there on the desk? (2) They are Jane's books
[Jane's]. **34** ④ **35** (1) There is a cat on the
bed. (2) There are two balls on the floor. **36** ③
**37** ① **38** ② **39** ④ **40** ③ **41** ⑤ **42** ③
**43** (1) the school → school (2) ten-minutes →
ten-minute (3) the lunch → lunch **44** ④
**45** ⑤ **46** Sungmin, the leader of our
volunteer club, is kind to everyone. **47** ②
**48** ⑤ **49** ② **50** ③ **51** ④ **52** ③

Ch **5** 명사와 관사

## 중간·기말고사 대비문제 해설

**1**  water는 셀 수 없는 명사이므로 a를 붙일 수 없다.

**2**  주어진 문장에 many가 있으므로 셀 수 있는 명사 복수형이 와야 한다. sheep은 단수형과 복수형이 같다.

**3**  umbrella의 첫소리는 모음으로 시작하므로 an을 붙인다.
*cf.* umbrella가 단수형이므로 many나 lots of는 올 수 없다.

**4**  air, money, milk: 셀 수 없는 물질명사
furniture: 물질명사의 성질을 갖는 집합명사

**5**  ② 소유격 's ①③④⑤ is의 축약형

**6**  '~가 있니?'의 뜻인 Is there ~?의 질문에 대해 Yes, there is. 또는 No, there isn't.로 대답한다.

**7**  milk는 셀 수 없는 명사이므로 five 뒤에 올 수 없다.

**8**  주어진 문장의 주어(five beds and two desks)가 복수형이므로 be동사의 수도 복수형(are)으로 맞춰야 한다.
② is → are

**9**  deer의 복수형은 'deer', foot의 복수형은 'feet', Man의 복수형은 'Men'이다.

**10**  ① hour는 철자가 자음으로 시작하지만, h가 묵음이기 때문에 발음은 모음으로 시작한다. 철자가 자음으로 시작하더라도 발음이 모음으로 시작하는 경우에는 부정관사 an을 쓴다.
② spoon은 자음으로 시작하므로, 앞에 부정관사 a를 쓴다.
③ 명사 앞에 명사를 수식하는 형용사가 있을 경우, 형용사에 맞춰 부정관사 a/an을 쓴다. interesting은 모음으로 시작하므로, 부정관사 an을 쓴다.
④ office worker는 모음으로 시작하므로, 부정관사 an을 쓴다.
⑤ uniform은 철자는 모음으로 시작하지만 u가 발음상 자음 '[ju]'로 시작하기 때문에 부정관사 a를 씀에 유의한다.

**11**  's를 이용하여 명사의 소유격(~의)이나 소유대명사(~의 것)를 표현할 수 있다.

**12**  ① Gooses → Geese
② lifes → lives
③ child → children
⑤ hobbys → hobbies
①의 make는 '만들다'가 아닌 '되다'의 의미로 쓰였다.
거위는 훌륭한 반려동물이 될 수 있다.

**13**  첫 번째 문장의 주어는 many beautiful trees(복수)이므로 ⓐ에는 복수동사 are, 두 번째 문장의 주어 (salt)와 세 번째 문장의 주어(juice)는 모두 물질명사로 단수 취급하므로 ⓑ, ⓒ에는 단수동사 is가 온다.

**14**  ③ is → are
④ women → woman
⑤ are → is

**15**  운동을 나타내는 명사 앞에는 the를 붙이지 않는다.

**16**  명사나 대명사의 동격을 나타낼 때는 그 뒤에 콤마(,)를 덧붙여 다른 명사(구)를 쓴다.

**17**  셀 수 없는 명사(juice)는 단수 취급한다.
⑤ There is a lot of juice in the bottle.

**18**  ③ one '하나의'  ①②④⑤ per '~마다'

**19**  악기 이름 앞에는 the를 쓴다.
④ He is playing the guitar.

**20**  ① is  ②③④⑤ are

**21**  useful의 첫소리는 자음 [ju:]로 시작하므로 a를, office의 첫소리는 모음으로 시작하므로 an을 쓴다.

**22**  • There are+복수 명사(some shoes)
• There are+복수 명사(jeans)
• There is+단수 명사(a clock)

**23**  child의 복수형은 children이다.
② childrens → children

**24**  ② two mouses → two mice
③ four wolfs → four wolves
④ three benchs → three benches
⑤ five foxs → five foxes

**25**  ⓐ umbrella의 첫소리는 모음으로 시작하므로 an을 쓴다.
ⓑ hour는 h로 시작하지만 h가 묵음으로 첫소리가 모음으로 시작하므로 an을 쓴다.
ⓒ university는 u로 시작하는 단어이므로 관사 an이 올 것이라 생각하기 쉽지만 첫소리가 [ju:]로 자음이므로 a를 쓴다.

**26**  ① We had a nice dinner.
② I will see you at noon.(the 삭제)
③ My father is very fat.(a 삭제)
④ Do you play the piano?

**27**  물질명사의 수량을 나타낼 때는 물질명사는 그대로 두고 단위를 나타내는 명사에 -(e)s를 붙인다.

**28**  There are+복수 명사(many old buildings)

**29**  hair는 셀 수 없는 물질명사로 단수 취급한다.
⑤ red hairs → red hair

**30**  사람을 나타내는 명사(uncle)의 소유격은 's를 붙인다.

**31** ① She likes to wear a uniform. uniform의 첫 소
리는 자음[ju]으로 시작한다.
② I am a middle school student.
③ Your father is a taxi driver.
⑤ Are you a nurse?

**32** 일반적으로 유일한 것 앞에는 the를 붙인다.

**33** (1) '~가 몇 개 있니?'의 표현으로 How many ~ are
there?를 쓴다.
(2) 's를 이용하여 명사의 소유격(~의)이나 소유대명
사(~의 것)를 표현할 수 있다.

**34** 보기와 ④ per '~마다'
① one '하나의'
② 종족 전체를 대표
③⑤ 막연한 하나

**35** There is/are는 '~가 있다'의 뜻이며, 고양이는 한 마
리이므로 There is를, 공은 두 개이므로 There are
를 써서 문장을 완성한다.

**36** 물질명사의 수량을 나타낼 때에는 물질명사는 그대로
두고 단위를 나타내는 명사를 복수형으로 나타낸다.
① pairs → pair
② glass → glasses
④ two bottle of juices → two bottles of juice
⑤ papers → paper

**37** per의 의미로 day 앞에 a를 쓰고, 서수(third) 앞에는
the를 쓴다.

**38** ① Is John a student?
③ Today is the second day of school.
④ My homeroom teacher is a math teacher.
⑤ She looks very honest. (a 삭제)

**39** 무생물의 소유격은 of로 나타낸다.
④ The color of the door is yellow.

**40** ③ 운동 이름 앞에는 관사를 쓰지 않는다.

**41** ⑤ 명사 photo의 복수형은 photos이다.
(photoes → photos)
① 뉴욕에 간 것이 지난여름이므로 과거시제 went를
쓴 것은 적절하다.
② 주어가 many famous places이므로 복수동사

werea를 쓴 것은 적절하다.
③ 형용사의 최상급 앞에는 the를 쓴다.
④ 명사 play(연극)의 복수형은 plays이다.
우리는 지난여름 뉴욕에 관광하러 갔다. 그 도시에는
방문할 만한 많은 유명한 장소가 있었다. 우리는 엠파
이어 스테이트 빌딩을 방문했다. 그것은 한때 세계에서
가장 높은 건물이었다. 우리는 브로드웨이에서 연극과
콘서트를 즐겼다. 우리는 함께 많은 사진을 찍었다.

**42** 두 개의 짝으로 이루어진 명사는 복수형으로 나타낸다.
① I'm wearing glasses.
② What kind of pants do you want?
④ Miki likes these jeans.
⑤ Did you find your scissors?

**43** (1) 건물이 본래의 목적으로 쓰일 때는 건물 앞에 관사
를 쓰지 않는다.
(2) 숫자와 명사가 하이픈(-)으로 연결되어 형용사처
럼 쓰일 때는 「숫자-단수 명사」의 형태로 쓴다.
(3) 식사 앞에 관사를 쓰지 않는다.

**44** a pair of는 jeans, shoes, scissors, glasses와 같
이 두 개의 짝으로 이루어져 항상 복수형으로 쓰는 명
사와 함께 쓸 수 있다.

**45** How much is it?의 it은 단수이므로 복수형인
tomatoes는 올 수 없다.

**46** 명사나 대명사의 동격을 나타낼 때는 그 뒤에 콤마(,)
를 덧붙여 다른 명사(구)를 쓴다.

**47** '~가 몇 개 있니?'의 표현으로 How many ~ are
there?를 쓴다. 대답으로 단수 명사(one orange)가
나왔으므로 There is가 와야 한다.

**48** ⑤ is의 축약형 's ①②③④ 명사의 소유격 's

**49** ② there '거기에' ①③④⑤ there is/are '~가 있다'

**50** 숫자와 명사가 하이픈(-)으로 연결되어 형용사처럼 쓰
일 때는 「숫자-단수 명사」의 형태가 와야 한다.

**51** advice는 셀 수 없는 명사로 단수형으로 쓴다.
④ advices → advice

**52** ③의 콤마(,)는 열거를 나타내고 ①②④⑤의 콤마(,)는
동격을 나타낸다.

## PRACTICE 1

| | | | |
|---|---|---|---|
| 1 | his | 2 | It |
| 3 | mine | 4 | theirs |
| 5 | She | 6 | hers |
| 7 | We | 8 | He |
| 9 | Its | 10 | us |
| 11 | Our | 12 | It |
| 13 | her | 14 | them[yours] |
| 15 | Their | 16 | yours |

[보기]
I don't want grapes. → I don't want them.
grapes는 복수명사이고 문장 내에서 목적어에 해당하기 때문에 목적격인 them으로 바꾸는 것이 적절하다.

**1, 3, 4, 6, 16** 빈칸에 밑줄 친 명사구를 그대로 쓸 경우, 문장 내에 같은 명사가 반복되기 때문에 소유대명사를 사용하는 것이 적절하다.

## PRACTICE 2

| | | | |
|---|---|---|---|
| 1 | your | 2 | them |
| 3 | his | 4 | me |
| 5 | his | 6 | yours |
| 7 | my | 8 | Her |
| 9 | him | 10 | ours |
| 11 | It | 12 | theirs |
| 13 | us | 14 | you |
| 15 | our | 16 | her |
| 17 | its | 18 | mine |
| 19 | hers | 20 | their |

**1, 5, 7, 8, 15, 17, 20** 명사 앞에서 명사를 꾸며주려면 소유격 인칭대명사가 와야 한다.
**2, 9** 전치사 뒤에는 목적격 인칭대명사가 오는 것이 적절하다.
**3, 10, 12, 18, 19** 주어로 쓰인 어떤 사물에 대한 설명을 보충주는 내용이 필요하므로 의미상 '~의 것'을 의미하는 소유대명사가 알맞다.
**4, 13, 14, 16** 타동사의 목적어 자리에는 목적격 인칭대명사가 오는 것이 적절하다.
**6** 전치사 뒤에 목적격 인칭대명사가 올 수 있지만, 이 문장에서는 비교 대상이 culture이므로 your culture를 의미하는 yours를 쓰는 것이 적절하다.
**11** 주어 자리에는 주격 인칭대명사를 써준다.

## PRACTICE 3

| | | | |
|---|---|---|---|
| 1 | myself | 2 | themselves |
| 3 | itself | 4 | myself |
| 5 | himself | 6 | yourself |
| 7 | himself | 8 | itself |
| 9 | herself | 10 | themselves |
| 11 | myself | 12 | yourself |
| 13 | yourself | 14 | himself |
| 15 | themselves | | |

**1, 9, 11, 15** 행위 주체와 같은 개체이며 전치사의 목적어 자리에 쓰였으므로 생략이 불가능한 재귀 용법이다.
**2, 5, 6, 8** 생략해도 완벽한 문장이 되며, 문장 구조가 변하지 않으므로 생략 가능한 강조 용법이다.
**3, 4, 14** 행위 주체와 같은 개체이며 동사의 목적어 자리에 쓰였으므로 생략이 불가능한 재귀 용법이다.
**7** think to oneself: 조용히 생각하다, 마음속으로 생각하다
전치사의 목적어 자리에 쓰였으므로 생략이 불가능한 재귀 용법이다.
**10** enjoy oneself: 즐거운 시간을 보내다
동사의 목적어 자리에 쓰였으므로 생략이 불가능한 재귀 용법이다.
**12** make oneself at home: 편히 있다
동사의 목적어 자리에 쓰였으므로 생략이 불가능한 재귀 용법이다.
**13** help oneself to: ~을 마음껏 먹다, 자유로이 먹다
동사의 목적어 자리에 쓰였으므로 생략이 불가능한 재귀 용법이다.

## PRACTICE 4

| | | | | | |
|---|---|---|---|---|---|
| 1 | O | 2 | X | 3 | X |
| 4 | O | 5 | O | 6 | O |
| 7 | X | 8 | X | 9 | O |
| 10 | X | | | | |

**1, 5, 9** 생략해도 완전한 문장이므로 강조 용법의 재귀대명사다. 문장의 맨 끝에 위치해 주어를 강조하고 있다.
**2, 3, 10** 전치사의 목적어로 쓰인 재귀 용법의 재귀대명사다. 생략 시 불완전한 문장이 되기 때문에 생략할 수 없다.
**4, 6** 생략해도 완전한 문장이므로 강조 용법의 재귀대명사다. 주어의 바로 뒤에서 주어를 강조하고 있다.
**7** 타동사의 목적어로 쓰인 재귀대명사다. 생략 시 불완전한 문장이 되기 때문에 생략할 수 없다.
**8** '역사는 스스로를 반복한다.'는 뜻으로, 역사 속에서 비슷한 일이 계속해서 일어난다는 의미이다. itself가 타동사 repeat의 목적어로 쓰였으므로 재귀 용법이고, 생략할 수 없다.

## PRACTICE 5

| | | | | | |
|---|---|---|---|---|---|
| 1 | B | 2 | A | 3 | A |
| 4 | B | 5 | A | 6 | A |
| 7 | A | 8 | A | 9 | B |
| 10 | A | 11 | A | 12 | B |
| 13 | A | 14 | B | 15 | B |
| 16 | A | | | | |

[보기]
A. <u>It</u> is Saturday. → 요일을 나타내는 비인칭 주어 it ('그것'이라고 해석하지 않는다.)
B. I'll bring <u>it</u> tomorrow. → 가리키는 것이 분명한 대명사 it ('그것'이라고 해석한다.)

1, 4, 9, 12, 14, 15 가리키는 것이 문장 내에 명시되어 있거나 그 대상을 화자-청자가 모두 알고 있어서 분명한 경우이므로 대명사 it이다.
2, 5, 13 비인칭 주어 it이 시간을 나타낸다.
3, 7 비인칭 주어 it이 계절(summer, spring)을 나타낸다.
16 비인칭 주어 it이 거리를 나타낸다.
6 비인칭 주어 it이 요일을 나타낸다.
8 비인칭 주어 it이 날씨를 나타낸다.
10 비인칭 주어 it이 날짜를 나타낸다.
11 비인칭 주어 it이 명암을 나타낸다.

1 괄호 뒤에 복수형 동사(are)가 오므로 others가 적절하다. 한편 other는 단독으로 대명사 역할을 할 수 없다.
2, 6 another+단수명사
3 여자가 많은 과일들을 갖고 있는데 그들 중 몇몇(some of them)은 오렌지이고, 나머지 것들(the others)은 사과라고 하고 있으므로 some이 적절하다.
4, 7, 9 문장의 앞에서 전체 수량이 2개임이 언급되었다. 처음 한 개는 둘 중 어느 것을 가리켜도 one으로 부를 수 있다. 첫 번째 것을 고르고 난 뒤에는 한 개만 남아 대상이 특정되므로 '나머지 하나'를 가리키는 the other를 사용한다.
5 앞서 나온 some과 짝을 이루고, courses를 꾸밀 수 있는 형용사여야 하므로 other가 적절하다.
8 드레스들 중 몇몇은 깨끗하고, 나머지 전부는 더럽다고 하는 것이므로 the others가 적절하다. 한편 other는 단독으로 대명사 역할을 할 수 없다.
10 부러진 펜 대신 다른 것을 갖고 있는지 묻는 것이므로 another가 적절하다.

## PRACTICE 6

| | | | |
|---|---|---|---|
| 1 | This | 2 | that |
| 3 | those | 4 | This |
| 5 | these | 6 | That |
| 7 | those | 8 | These |

## PRACTICE 7

| | | | |
|---|---|---|---|
| 1 | ones | 2 | it |
| 3 | one | 4 | It |
| 5 | one | 6 | ones |

1 그녀가 구매한 밀 키트와 같은 종류지만 다른 개체이기 때문에 부정대명사를 사용한다. 복수형 명사 meal kits가 언급되었기 때문에 ones를 사용한다.
2, 4 앞서 언급한 명사(paper, London)를 지칭하고 있기 때문에 대명사 it을 사용한다.
3 의문문에서 umbrella 앞에 부정관사 an을 썼으므로 특정하지 않은 아무 우산(단수)을 나타낼 수 있는 부정대명사 one을 사용하는 것이 적절하다.
5 내 가방은 이미 잃어버렸으므로 동일 개체를 가리킬 수 없다. 같은 종류(가방)의 다른 대상을 나타내는 부정대명사 one을 사용하는 것이 적절하다.
6 앞의 문장에서 노란색 장미를 언급하였는데, 화자는 그것과 같은 종류(장미)지만 다른(빨간색) 것을 구매할 것이므로 부정대명사를 사용하는 것이 적절하다. roses가 복수형이므로 ones를 사용한다.

## PRACTICE 8

| | | | |
|---|---|---|---|
| 1 | others | 2 | another |
| 3 | Some | 4 | the other |
| 5 | other | 6 | another |
| 7 | the other | 8 | the others |
| 9 | One | 10 | another |

## PRACTICE 9

| | | | |
|---|---|---|---|
| 1 | man | 2 | present |
| 3 | has | 4 | is |
| 5 | student | | |

## PRACTICE 10

| | | | | | |
|---|---|---|---|---|---|
| 1 | Whom | 2 | Who | 3 | Whose |
| 4 | Who | 5 | Whom | 6 | Whom |
| 7 | Whose | 8 | Who | 9 | Whose |
| 10 | Who | | | | |

1, 5, 6 평서문으로 바꾸면
　1 They helped _______
　5 He visited _______
　6 She talks to _______
의 형태가 되는데, 빈칸의 위치가 타동사나 전치사의 목적어 자리이므로 목적격인 whom이 적절하다. 의문문에서 whom 대신 who를 쓰는 것도 가능하다.
2, 4, 8, 10 사람의 이름이나 관계를 묻고 있으므로 who가 적절하다.
3, 9 평서문으로 바꾸면
　3 This watch is _______
　9 Those clothes are _______
의 형태가 되는데, 빈칸에 소유대명사(~의 것)를 넣어 보어로 사용하는 것이 적절하다.
7 명사 book을 앞에서 꾸며줄 수 있어야 하므로, 소유격이 적절하다.

## PRACTICE 11

| | | | | | |
|---|---|---|---|---|---|
| 1 | What | 2 | Whom | 3 | Whose |
| 4 | Who | 5 | What | 6 | Whose |
| 7 | Which | 8 | Which | 9 | Whose |
| 10 | Who | 11 | Which | 12 | What |

**1** 선택의 범위가 제한되지 않은 상태에서 사람이 아닌 것(your favorite song)에 대해 질문하려고 하므로 what이 적절하다.
**2** 평서문으로 바꾸면 He met _________ last night.가 되는데, 목적어 자리가 비게 되므로 목적격 의문대명사 whom이 적절하다.
**3, 6, 9** who와 whose 중 명사 앞에서 명사를 꾸며줄 수 있는 것은 소유격인 whose이다.
**4, 10** 사람의 이름이나 관계에 대한 질문이므로 who가 적절하다.
**5** 명사 size 앞에서 명사를 꾸며주면서, 선택의 범위가 제한되지 않은 질문을 하려면 what을 사용하는 것이 적절하다. 여기서 what은 의문형용사로 사용되어 size를 꾸며주고 있고, what size는 '어떤 사이즈'를 의미한다.
**7, 11** Canada와 Australia, of them으로 선택의 범위가 제한되어 있으므로 what이 아닌 which가 적절하다.
**8** dog과 cat으로 선택의 범위가 제한되어 있으므로 what이 아닌 which가 적절하다. 여기서 which는 pet을 꾸며주는 의문형용사로 사용되었고, which pet은 '어느 반려동물'을 의미한다.
**12** 무엇이 너를 웃게 만들었는지 묻고 있으므로 what을 쓴다.

## PRACTICE 12

| 1 | ⓓ | 2 | ⓐ | 3 | ⓒ | 4 | ⓑ |
|---|---|---|---|---|---|---|---|
| 5 | ⓕ | 6 | ⓗ | 7 | ⓔ | 8 | ⓖ |

## PRACTICE 13

**1** I don't think so.
**2** They don't look the same.
**3** He has the same opinion as you.
**4** I like bright colors such as yellow.
**5** These shoes are the same size.
**6** I believe so.
**7** He and I arrived at the same time.
**8** My sister likes sweets such as chocolate.
**9** Today's weather is the same as yesterday's.
**10** He is such a nice guy!
**11** How did you solve such problems?
**12** The flowers' colors are the same.

**1, 6** 앞서 나온 긍정의 문장을 대신하기 위해서 think, believe의 목적어 자리에 so가 와야 한다.
**2** '같아 보이다'라는 뜻과 일치하게 만들려면 look 다음에 the same을 배열해야 한다.
**3, 5, 7** '같은 의견', '사이즈가 같다', '같은 시간'이라는 뜻과 일치하게 만들기 위해서 the same이 각각 opinion, size, time을 꾸며줘야 한다.
**4** '노란색과 같은' = such as yellow
**8** '초콜릿과 같은' = such as chocolate
**9** 오늘과 어제의 날씨를 비교하는 것으로 '같다'의 의미를 가진 the same을 써야 한다.
**10** such (a/an) +형용사+명사!: 아주 좋은 것이나 놀라운 것에 대한 감탄
**11** '그러한'이라는 뜻으로 such가 problems를 꾸며준다.
**12** 꽃들의 색을 비교하는 것으로 '같다'의 의미를 가진 the same을 써야 한다.

## 📑 중간·기말고사 대비문제 **정답** 본문 _ p.154

**1** ⑤  **2** this  **3** ③  **4** (1) One  (2) the other
**5** ④  **6** ⑤  **7** Which  **8** ④  **9** What
**10** ①  **11** ③  **12** ③  **13** ②  **14** himself
**15** ③  **16** ①  **17** ④  **18** herself  **19** ③
**20** not the same as the ostrich  **21** ④
**22** This is  **23** ②  **24** ③  **25** ①  **26** ①
**27** ②  **28** Does everybody like your paintings?
**29** ④  **30** What time do you go to school
**31** ②  **32** ①  **33** ④  **34** ③,⑤  **35** ①
**36** ③  **37** ②

## 중간·기말고사 대비문제 **해설**

**1** pop songs는 복수고, 동사 like의 목적어이므로 목적격 형태인 them이 들어가야 한다.

**2** • 가까이에 있는 사람이나 사물을 가리키며 뒤의 명사를 수식하는 지시형용사 this가 쓰였다.
• 지시대명사 this는 전화상에서 전화를 건 사람과 받는 사람을 가리킬 때 쓰인다.

**3** 질문에 대한 대답이 '나의 아버지의 것이야.'이므로, '누구의'라는 의미로 명사 camera를 꾸며줄 수 있는 소유격 Whose가 적절하다. What과 Which도 명사를 꾸며줄 수 있지만, 각각 '무엇'과 '어느 것'이라는 의미이므로 여기에서는 적절하지 않다.

**4** 두 번째 문장에서 영화의 수량이 두 개임이(two different movies) 언급되었다. 두 개 중 처음 영화 한 개를 가리킬 때는 one, 한 개를 고르고 난 뒤 나머지 하나를 가리킬 때는 the other를 사용한다.

**5** 1인칭 단수를 나타내는 인칭대명사는 I이고, 나와 나의 친구들이 속한 야구팀이므로 We의 소유격인 Our를 쓴다. 단수 명사인 My uniform number는 대명사 It으로 받는다.

**6** ⓐ 부정의문문에 대한 대답은 질문의 긍정/부정 형태와 관계 없이 대답의 내용이 긍정이면 Yes, 부정이면 No로 답한다. '일기예보를 확인하지 않았니?'라는 질문에 '확인하지 않았다'고 대답하려면 No, I didn't.로 대답하는 것이 적절하다.
ⓑ 범위가 정해지지 않은 수많은 날 중 '또 다른 하루'를 지칭하는 것이므로 another를 쓰는 것이 적절하다.
ⓒ 같이 소풍을 가기로 한 친구들 중 대화를 하고 있는

두 사람을 제외한 나머지 전체를 지칭하는 것이므로 the other를 쓰는 것이 적절하다.

**7** 제한된 선택(a chocolate cake or a cheesecake)의 범위 내에서 '어느 것'인지를 물을 때 which를 쓴다.

**8** ⓐ 빨간 것이 아닌 또 다른 하나를 보여달라는 의미이므로 '또 다른 하나'라는 의미의 another를 쓰는 것이 적절하다.
ⓑ 여러 개 중 일부를 나타낼 때는 some을 쓴다.
ⓒⓓ 개가 두 마리라고 언급되었다. 둘 중 처음 하나를 가리킬 때는 one, 나머지 하나를 가리킬 때는 the other를 사용한다.

**9** • 「what+명사」의 형태로 명사를 수식하는 의문형 용사 What이 와야 한다. which도 명사를 수식하지만 선택의 범위가 제한되어 있지 않으므로 빈칸에 들어갈 수 없다.
What time is it? 몇 시니?
• What's the weather like? 날씨가 어때?

**10** the same ~ as … '…와 같은 ~'
Sora has the <u>same</u> bag as Jinhee.

**11** • 빈칸은 주격 보어의 자리이다. '이 집은 ~의 것이다'라는 뜻이 적절하므로 보어의 자리에 '~의 것'이라는 뜻을 나타내는 소유대명사 mine이나 theirs가 들어가는 것이 알맞다.
This house is <u>mine[theirs]</u>.
• 전치사 to의 목적어 자리이다. 따라서 목적어로 쓰이는 목적격 대명사 you나 us가 들어가는 것이 알맞다.
This house belongs to <u>you[us]</u>.
belong to '~의 소유물이다'
• 주어의 자리이고 동사가 own이므로 3인칭 단수 주격 대명사는 올 수 없다. 그러므로 2인칭 주격 대명사 you가 들어가는 것이 알맞다.
<u>You</u> own this house.

**12** Minjun and I(민준과 나)는 We(우리)로 쓸 수 있다.

**13** (b) 앞 문장에서 소개한 것이 벽에 걸린 세계 지도이고, 그것을 보고 다른 나라들에 대해 생각한다고 한 것으로 보아 it이 가리키는 것은 a big world map이다.

안녕하세요, 여러분! 저는 지아예요. 오늘은 여러분에게 저에 대해 조금 이야기할 차례예요. 그래서, 저는 여러분에게 저의 침실에 있는 제 좋아하는 물건들 몇 가지를 보여주고 싶어요. 먼저, 이것은 제 곰 인형의 사진이에요. 저는 잠자리에 들 때 그것을 껴안아요. 다음으로, 저는 벽에 큰 세계 지도를 가지고 있어요. 저는 그것을 보고 다른 나라들에 대해 생각해요. 저는 언젠가 그곳들에 방문하고 싶어요. 마지막으로, 저는 작은 화이트보드를 가지고 있어요. 저는 그것 위에 그림을 그려요. 또 저는 제 자신에게 재미있는 메시지를 써요. 그것들은 저를 웃게 만들어요.

**14** 문장의 주어(He)와 전치사(of)의 목적어가 같을 때 재귀대명사(himself)를 쓴다.

**15** ③ 앞에서 언급한 특정한 명사(the red one)를 가리킬 때는 it을 쓴다.

**16** 사물을 물을 때는 what을, 사람을 물을 때는 who를 쓴다.

**17** ④ It's는 It is의 줄임말이므로 명사(tail)를 꾸며줄 수 있는 It의 소유격인 Its를 써야 한다. (It's → Its)

**18** • She에 대한 재귀대명사로 herself를 쓴다. 의미상, 주어와 목적어가 같으므로 재귀 용법으로 쓰였다.
• 주어(My mom)를 강조하기 위해 문장 맨 끝에 강조 용법의 재귀대명사(herself)를 쓸 수 있다.
• 전치사의 목적어 자리이므로 재귀 용법으로 재귀대명사 herself를 쓴다.
*cf.* say to oneself '혼잣말을 하다'

**19** 보기와 ⓐⓒⓔ 비인칭 주어 it  ⓑⓓ 대명사 it

**20** A is[are] not the same as B 'A는 B와 같지 않다'

**21** its는 it의 소유격을 나타내므로 it is의 줄임말인 it's를 써야 한다. (its → it's)

**22** 전화상에서 전화를 건 사람과 받는 사람을 가리킬 때 this를 쓴다.

**23** 여러 대상 중 몇몇을 나타낼 때는 some을 사용한다. 복수 명사 people을 수식해야 하므로 복수 명사를 수식하는 other이 적절하다. Others와 The others는 대명사이므로 명사를 수식할 수 없다. Another은 단수 명사를 수식한다.

**24** 앞에서 언급한 명사(backpack)와 종류는 같지만, 다른 성질의 개체(yellow backpack)에 대해 말할 때 one을 쓴다.

**25** 사람의 직업을 물을 때 「What+do[does]+주어+do (for a living)?」 표현을 쓴다.
*cf.* What do you do? 당신은 무엇을 합니까?(당신의 직업은 무엇입니까?)

**26** 재귀대명사는 재귀 용법으로 쓰였을 때는 생략이 불가능하며, 강조 용법으로 쓰였을 때 생략이 가능하다.
①은 introduce의 목적어로 쓰인 재귀 용법이므로 생략이 불가능하다.

**27** Everyone은 '모든 사람'을 뜻하지만 단수 취급하므로 3인칭 단수 동사인 plays를 쓴다.

**28** everybody는 단수 취급하므로 「Does+주어+동사원형~?」의 의문문으로 써야 한다.

**29** ④ 대명사 it  ①②③⑤ 비인칭 주어 it

**30** What이 의문형용사로서 명사 time을 꾸며주며 '몇 시에~'라는 뜻을 나타낸다. 또한 일반동사의 의문문은 「의문사+do+주어+동사원형~?」의 어순으로 쓴다.

**31** 지하철 노선이라는 제한된 선택의 범위 내에서 '어느 것'인지를 물을 때 which를 쓴다.

**32** so는 '그렇게'라는 뜻으로 think의 목적어로 쓰여 앞에 나온 긍정의 문장을 대신한다.

**33** we의 소유대명사는 ours이다.

④ This is our car. = This car is ours.
*cf.* us는 we의 목적격 대명사이다.

**34** ③ every는 단수 명사를 수식하므로 children이 아닌 child를 써야 한다. (children → child)
⑤ Everything은 단수 취급하므로, 동사는 3인칭 단수의 형태로 looks를 써야 한다. (look → looks)

**35** One ~ the other … '하나는 ~, 다른 사람[것]은 …'

**36** ③ English and science는 복수이므로 3인칭 복수형 목적격 대명사 them으로 바꿔야 한다. (it → them)

**37** • such as ~ '~와 같은 그런'
• the same ~ '같은 ~'

---

<table><tr><td>CHAPTER</td><td>**7**</td><td># 부정사<br>Infinitives</td><td>본문 _ p.160</td></tr></table>

## PRACTICE **1**

**1** to visit a historic place
**2** It is a farmer's work
**3** to make good friends
**4** It was my plan
**5** to get enough sleep
**6** It was very dangerous

> **1~6** to부정사가 주어인 경우에는 주어 자리에 it을 쓰고 to부정사구를 뒤로 보낼 수 있다. to부정사로 시작하는 문장보다 「It~to부정사」 구문이 보다 자연스러운 문장이다. 이때 쓰인 it을 가주어라고 하고, to부정사구를 진주어라고 한다.

## PRACTICE **2**

**1** (1) to sing    (2) sing
**2** (1) to read    (2) read
**3** (1) to visit    (2) visit

> **1** (1) 보어 역할을 하는 to부정사 to sing을 쓴다.
> (2) sing이 동사로 쓰였으며 조동사 should가 있으므로 동사원형으로 쓴다.
> **2** (1) 주격 보어로 명사 역할을 하는 to부정사 to read를 쓴다.
> (2) read가 동사로 쓰인 문장이고, 주어가 I이므로 동사의 형태는 원형으로 쓴다.
> **3** (1) 주격 보어로 명사 역할을 하는 to부정사 to visit을 쓴다.
> (2) visit이 동사로 쓰였으며, 주어가 I이므로 동사의 형태는 원형으로 쓴다.

## PRACTICE **3**

**1** to start    **2** to buy
**3** to live    **4** to meet
**5** to watch    **6** to come

> plan, need, want, hope, love, would like는 to부정사를 목적어로 가질 수 있다.
>
> **1** start jogging: 조깅을 시작하다
> **2** buy a book: 책을 사다
> **3** live in+장소: ~에 살다
> **4** meet+사람: ~를 만나다
> **5** watch the stars: 별을 보다
> **6** come to dinner: 저녁 식사에 오다

## PRACTICE 4

1 began to fall
2 expected to stay
3 how to use
4 decided to meet him
5 started to grow tomatoes
6 what to buy
7 tries to keep
8 how to get

> 3 how to use: 어떻게 쓰는지, 사용하는 법
> 6 「what+to부정사」는 '무엇을 ~할지'라는 뜻을 나타낸다.
> 7 try+to부정사: ~하려고 노력하다
> 8 「how+to부정사」는 '~하는 법'이라는 뜻으로 문장 내에서 목적어 역할을 하고 있다.

## PRACTICE 5

1 homework to do
2 turn to introduce
3 place to visit
4 chance to talk
5 time to exercise
6 to write with
7 something to put on
8 time to say
9 to lie on
10 anything to read

> to부정사가 명사나 대명사를 뒤에서 꾸며주는 형용사의 역할을 할 때는 '~할, ~해야 할'로 해석된다. 형용사는 보통 수식하는 명사 앞에 쓰이지만, to부정사는 명사 뒤에서 수식한다.
>
> 1 homework to do 할 숙제
> 2 turn to introduce 소개할 차례
> 3 place to visit 방문할 곳
> 4 chance to talk 말할 기회
> 5 time to exercise 운동할 시간
> 6 pen to write with 쓸 펜
> 7 something to put on 입을 만한 무엇(어떤 것)
> 8 time to say 말할 시간
> 9 sofa to lie on 누울 소파
> 10 anything to read 읽을 만한 어떤 것

## PRACTICE 6

1 time to go back
2 something to eat
3 city to visit
4 shirt to wear
5 test to take
6 bill to pay

> to부정사의 형용사적 용법은 명사를 뒤에서 수식하며 '~할, ~해야 할'로 해석된다.
>
> 1 time to go back 돌아갈 시간
> 2 something to eat 먹을 것
> 3 city to visit 방문할 도시
> 4 shirt to wear 입을 셔츠
> 5 test to take 치를 시험
> 6 bill to pay 지불해야 할 청구서

## PRACTICE 7

1 to be a famous painter
2 to hear the bad news
3 to make cookies
4 to be 100 years old
5 to find a new cure
6 to watch with children
7 to understand without a dictionary
8 to play soccer

> 1 (결국) 유명한 화가가 되었다 (부사적 용법 중 결과)
> 2 나쁜 소식을 들어서 (부사적 용법 중 감정의 원인)
> 3 쿠키를 만들기 위해서 (부사적 용법 중 목적)
> 4 100세까지 (부사적 용법 중 결과)
> 5 새로운 치료제를 발견해서 (부사적 용법 중 감정의 원인)
> 6 아이들과 함께 보기에 (부사적 용법 중 형용사 수식)
> 7 사전 없이 이해하기에 (부사적 용법 중 형용사 수식)
> 8 축구를 하기 위해서 (부사적 용법 중 목적)

## PRACTICE 8

1 너는 무엇을 사기를 원하니?
2 목표를 설정하는 것은 중요하다.
3 학교에 갈 시간이다.
4 우리는 종이를 만들기 위해 나무를 베어 넘어뜨린다.
5 우리는 살을 빼기 위해 무엇을 할 수 있을까?
6 그의 소설은 읽기에 쉬웠다.
7 보는 것은 믿는 것이다.
8 그는 자라서 (결국) 훌륭한 아버지가 되었다.

**1, 2, 7** to부정사가 명사의 역할을 하므로 '~하는 것'으로 해석한다.
**3** to부정사가 time을 뒤에서 수식하며 형용사의 역할을 하고 있으므로 '~할'로 해석한다.
**4, 5** to부정사가 목적을 나타내는 부사의 역할을 하고 있으므로 '~하기 위해'로 해석한다.
**6** to부정사가 형용사 easy를 뒤에서 수식하며 부사의 역할을 하고 있으므로 '~하기에'로 해석한다.
**8** to부정사가 결과를 나타내는 부사의 역할을 하고 있으므로 '(결국) ~하다'로 해석한다.

## PRACTICE 9

**1** Let me hold
**2** make people feel good
**3** helps you understand people better
**4** make weeds die
**5** let me stay
**6** had my sister read books

**1** Let me+동사원형: 내가 ~하게 해 줘, 내가 ~해 줄게
**2, 4, 5, 6** 「사역동사+목적어+목적격 보어」 순서로 배열할 수 있으며 목적격 보어로 원형부정사를 사용한다.
**3** 준사역동사 help는 「help+목적어+목적격 보어」 순서로 배열할 수 있으며 목적격 보어로 원형부정사나 to부정사를 사용한다.

## PRACTICE 10

**1** to solve **2** play **3** coming **4** feed
**5** show **6** clean **7** selling **8** do
**9** calling **10** go

**1** help는 목적격 보어로 원형부정사뿐 아니라 to부정사도 사용 가능하다.
**2, 4** 지각동사 saw, watched의 목적격 보어로 원형부정사를 사용한다.
**3, 7, 9** 현재 진행 중인 상황을 강조하기 위해 지각동사 felt, saw, heard의 목적격 보어로 현재분사를 사용하기도 한다.
**5** Let me+동사원형: 내가 ~하게 해 줘, 내가 ~해 줄게
**6, 8, 10** 사역동사 made, had, let의 목적격 보어로 원형부정사를 사용한다.

## PRACTICE 11

**1** go(ing) **2** bring **3** shout(ing)
**4** wait **5** run(ning) **6** swim

**1** go out: 밖으로 나가다
**4** wait for+시간: ~동안 기다리다
**5** run after+(대)명사: ~를 뒤쫓다

## PRACTICE 12

**1** write **2** to swim **3** go **4** study

**5** wait **6** fly **7** talk **8** feel
**9** find **10** walking **11** looking **12** play

**1** Let me+동사원형: 내가 ~하게 해 줘, 내가 ~해 줄게
**2** how와 to부정사가 결합되어 '~하는 방법'이라는 뜻이다. 문장에서 동사의 목적어로 쓰였다.
**3, 4, 5, 8, 9** (준)사역동사의 목적격 보어로 원형부정사를 사용한다.
**6, 7, 12** 지각동사의 목적격 보어로 원형부정사를 사용한다.
**10, 11** 지각동사(saw, feel)의 목적격 보어로 현재분사를 사용하여 진행 중인 일을 강조할 수 있다.

### 📝 중간·기말고사 대비문제 정답 본문 _ p.169

**1** ③ **2** ② **3** ④ **4** ③ **5** homework to do **6** ⑤ **7** ① **8** inviting → to invite **9** (1) how to ride (2) how to get[go] **10** ② **11** ① **12** asked her who(m) to invite **13** ①,④ **14** ② **15** ②,⑤ **16** let Jenny use **17** ① **18** It is dangerous to walk alone at night. **19** ⑤ **20** ④ **21** ⑤ **22** ⑤ **23** ④ **24** ⓐ: It is interesting to meet new characters. ⓑ: It helps me to increase my vocabulary. **25** ③ **26** ⑤ **27** (1) to borrow a book (2) to send a letter

### 중간·기말고사 대비문제 해설

**1** and에 의해 to hear과 연결된 병렬구조이고, hope는 to부정사를 목적어로 쓰는 동사이므로 「to+동사원형」 또는 to가 생략된 동사원형의 형태가 와야 한다.
**2** ② 명사처럼 쓰이는 to부정사의 용법 중 주격 보어의 역할 (go → to go)
*cf.* 보어의 역할을 하는 동명사(going)로도 표현할 수 있다.
**3** want는 to부정사를 목적어로 쓰는 동사이므로 to buy가 뒤따라와야 하고, 의문문의 어순을 고려하여 do가 주어(they) 앞에 위치해야 한다.
**4** ③ love의 목적어로 to부정사(to go) 또는 동명사(going)가 와야 한다. (go → to go/going)
**5** 명사(homework)를 꾸미는 to부정사의 형용사적 용법으로 to do를 써야 한다.
**6** 보기와 ⑤ 가주어 it ①② 비인칭 주어 it ③④ 인칭대명사 it
**7** ⓑ to부정사가 주어로 쓰일 때 단수 취급하므로 단수

동사 is를 쓴 것은 적절하다.

(e) 그녀가 놀란 것이므로 과거분사 surprised를 썼고, 그 뒤에 to부정사구(to hear the news)가 감정의 원인을 나타내므로 적절하다.

(a) 악기 이름 앞에는 관사 the를 써야 한다.
(play guitar → play the guitar)

(c) 동사 allow 뒤에 목적어 me가 먼저 나오고, 그 뒤에 명사적 용법의 to부정사 to stay가 따라오는 것이 적절한 어순이다. allow는 to부정사를 목적격 보어로 쓰는 동사이다.
(allow to me stay → allow me to stay)

(d) to부정사(to study)가 형용사 역할을 할 때는 명사(a good place)의 뒤에 위치한다. (to study a good place → a good place to study)

(f) 사역동사 had는 목적격 보어로 동사원형을 쓴다.
(to open → open)

**8** decide는 to부정사를 목적어로 쓰는 동사이므로 「to+동사원형」의 형태가 와야 한다.

**9** 「how+to부정사」는 '~하는 방법'으로 해석된다. '~에 가다'라는 의미는 go to 외에도 get to를 써서 나타낼 수 있다.

**10** 주어진 문장의 to work는 명사 a chance를 수식하는 형용사적 용법의 to부정사이다.
② 대명사 something을 수식하는 형용사적 용법의 to부정사이다.
① 목적어로 쓰인 명사적 용법의 to부정사이다.
③ 목적을 나타내는 부사적 용법의 to부정사이다.
④ 보어로 쓰인 명사적 용법의 to부정사이다.
⑤ 주어로 쓰인 명사적 용법의 to부정사이다.

**11** 사역동사(made)는 원형부정사(paint)를 목적격 보어로 쓴다.

**12** '누구를 ~할지'는 to부정사를 활용해 「who(m) to+동사원형」의 형태로 쓸 수 있다.

**13** 지각동사(saw)는 원형부정사(swim)나 현재분사(swimming)를 목적격 보어로 쓴다.

**14** 주어진 문장과 ② 부사처럼 쓰인 to부정사의 용법 중 목적
①④ 명사(목적어)처럼 쓰인 to부정사
③ 형용사처럼 쓰인 to부정사
⑤ 명사(주어)처럼 쓰인 to부정사

**15** 목적격 보어 자리에 to부정사(to clean)가 나왔으므로 사역동사(made)와 지각동사(saw)는 빈칸에 들어갈 수 없다.

**16** 사역동사 let은 「사역동사+목적어+원형부정사」의 형태로 쓰여, 목적격 보어 위치에 원형부정사(use)를 사용한다.

**17** 주어진 문장과 ②③④⑤ 형용사처럼 쓰인 to부정사
① 명사(목적어)처럼 쓰인 to부정사

**18** 주어로 쓰인 to부정사의 길이가 길 경우 주어 자리에 가주어 It을 쓰고 to부정사를 뒤로 보낸다.

**19** 주어진 문장과 ⑤ 「to+동사원형」 to부정사
①②③④ 「to+명사」 전치사 to '~에게, ~로'
*cf.* from side to side '좌우로 (흔들리는)'

**20** 「where+to부정사」 '어디에서 ~해야 할지'
그는 어디에 머무를지 결정하지 못한다. 그는 좋은 평가를 얻은 장소를 찾기 바란다.

**21** ① 사역동사 let은 목적격 보어로 원형부정사를 쓴다. 「Let me+동사원형」 '내가 ~하게 해줘, 내가 ~해 줄게' (to show → show)
② want는 목적어로 to부정사를 쓰는 동사이다. (going → to go)
③ 지각동사 hear은 목적격 보어로 원형부정사나 현재분사를 쓴다. (to bark → bark/barking)
④ decide는 목적어로 to부정사를 쓰는 동사이다. (staying → stay)

**22** ⑤ 「to+장소」 방향을 나타내는 전치사 to '~에게, ~로'
①②③④ 「to+동사원형」 to부정사

**23** 사역동사(Let)는 원형부정사(close)를 목적격 보어로 쓴다. (closes → close)

**24** ⓐ 주어로 쓰인 to부정사의 길이가 길 경우, 「It ~ to부정사」 형태로 주어 자리에 가주어 It을 쓰고 to부정사구를 뒤로 보낼 수 있다.
새로운 캐릭터를 만나는 것은 재미있다.
ⓑ 준사역동사 help는 목적격 보어로 원형부정사 또는 to부정사를 쓸 수 있다.
그것(독서)은 내 어휘력을 늘리는 데 도움이 된다.

**25** '~하는 방법'이라는 뜻의 「how to+동사원형」은 「how+주어+should+동사원형」으로 바꿔 쓸 수 있다.

**26** 지문의 밑줄 친 부분과 ⑤ 부사처럼 쓰인 to부정사
①②④ 명사처럼 쓰인 to부정사
③ 형용사처럼 쓰인 to부정사

**27** 「to+동사원형」 형태의 to부정사가 부사적 용법으로 목적을 나타낸다. Jim은 도서관에 책을 빌리기 위해(to borrow a book) 갔으며 우체국에 편지를 부치기 위해(to send a letter) 갔다.

Ch **7** 부정사

## PRACTICE 1

| | | | |
|---|---|---|---|
| **1** | doing | **2** | keeping |
| **3** | Exercising | **4** | coming |
| **5** | playing | **6** | taking |
| **7** | drawing | **8** | joining |
| **9** | becoming | **10** | Buying |

> **1** do one's homework: 숙제를 하다
> **2** keep a diary: 일기를 쓰다
> **3** exercise regularly: 규칙적으로 운동하다
> **4** come to see: 보러 오다
> **5** play the piano: 피아노를 치다
> **6** take the subway: 지하철을 타다
> **7** draw cartoons: 만화를 그리다
> **8** join a club: 동아리에 가입하다
> **9** become a teacher: 교사가 되다
> **10** buy ~ through the Internet: 인터넷으로 ~을 사다

## PRACTICE 2

| | | | | | | | |
|---|---|---|---|---|---|---|---|
| **1** | ① | **2** | ③ | **3** | ① | **4** | ④ |
| **5** | ② | **6** | ③ | **7** | ② | **8** | ③ |
| **9** | ④ | **10** | ① | **11** | ④ | **12** | ② |

> [보기]
> ① 그와 이야기하는 것은 지루하다. (주어 역할)
> ② 우리의 목표는 상을 타는 것이다. (보어 역할)
> ③ 그녀는 보고서 쓰는 것을 끝냈다. (타동사의 목적어 역할)
> ④ 고양이들은 오르는 것을 잘한다. (전치사의 목적어 역할)
>
> **1, 3, 10** 동명사가 문장의 주어로 쓰였다.
> **2, 6, 8** 동명사가 각각 타동사 love, practice, enjoy의 목적어로 쓰였다.
> **4, 9, 11** 동명사가 각각 전치사 for, in, for의 목적어로 쓰였다.
> **5, 7, 12** 동명사가 주어에 대해 설명하는 보어로 쓰였다.

## PRACTICE 3

| | | | |
|---|---|---|---|
| **1** | travel(l)ing, to travel | **2** | opening |
| **3** | studying, to study | **4** | to watch |
| **5** | waiting | **6** | to go |
| **7** | trying | **8** | falling, to fall |
| **9** | eating | **10** | to visit |
| **11** | going | **12** | sneezing |
| **13** | to stay | **14** | to exercise |
| **15** | washing, to wash | **16** | to obey |
| **17** | seeing, to see | **18** | singing |
| **19** | playing, to play | **20** | to drive |
| **21** | wearing, to wear | **22** | to leave |

> **1, 3, 8, 15, 17, 19, 21** love, continue, start, begin, hate, like, prefer는 동명사와 to부정사 모두를 목적어로 쓰는 동사들이다.
> **2, 7, 9, 11, 12, 18** mind, give up, finish, enjoy, stop, practice는 동명사만 목적어로 쓰는 동사들이다.
> **4, 6, 10, 13, 14, 16, 20, 22** would like, decide, hope, expect, need, want, plan은 to부정사를 목적어로 쓰는 동사들이다.
> **5** 「keep+-ing」 계속해서 ~ 하다

## PRACTICE 4

| | | | |
|---|---|---|---|
| **1** | go swimming | **2** | went skating |
| **3** | go fishing | **4** | goes surfing |
| **5** | went shopping | **6** | go skiing |
| **7** | went sailing | **8** | go hiking |
| **9** | go driving | **10** | went dancing |
| **11** | go riding | **12** | went hunting |
| **13** | went jogging | | |

## PRACTICE 5

**1** How[What] about helping each other?
**2** How[What] about getting some rest?
**3** How[What] about keeping the promise?
**4** How[What] about having lunch together?
**5** How[What] about playing basketball tomorrow?
**6** How[What] about drinking a cup of coffee?
**7** How[What] about studying Spanish?
**8** How[What] about reading the newspaper?
**9** How[What] about buying some fruit?
**10** How[What] about sitting down on the bench?

## PRACTICE 6

| | | | | | |
|---|---|---|---|---|---|
| **1** | staying | **2** | visiting | **3** | taking |
| **4** | going | **5** | writing | **6** | talking |
| **7** | trying | **8** | doing | **9** | playing |
| **10** | eating | | | | |

> **1** stay at: ~에 머물다
> **2** visit+장소 명사: ~에 방문하다
> **3** take a picture: 사진을 찍다
> **4** go to the movie theater: 영화를 보러 가다
> **5** write a letter: 편지를 쓰다
> **6** talk about: ~에 대해 얘기하다
> **7** try on: ~을 입어[신어]보다

**8** do one's homework: 숙제를 하다
**9** play basketball: 농구를 하다
**10** eat ~ for lunch: 점심으로 ~을 먹다

## PRACTICE **7**

**1** stopped, from sleeping
**2** spent, buying
**3** kept, from going out
**4** is spending, talking
**5** spent, eating out
**6** keep, from leaving
**7** stopped, from fighting
**8** keep, from coming out
**9** spend, taking
**10** stopped, from biting
**11** keep, from becoming
**12** spend, using

> **1, 3, 6, 7, 8, 10, 11** 'keep/stop … from -ing'는 '… 가 ~하는 것을 막다[방지하다]'라는 의미로 쓰인다.
> **2, 4, 5, 9, 12** 'spend+시간/돈+-ing'는 '~하는 데 시간/돈을 쓰다'라는 의미로 쓰인다.

### 중간·기말고사 대비문제 정답　본문_p.182

**1** ②　**2** swimming　**3** ②　**4** ④　**5** ⑤
**6** ②,⑤　**7** How about listening to music?
**8** ④　**9** ①　**10** ⑤　**11** go → going　**12** ③
**13** ②　**14** (1) learn → learning  (2) overcome → overcoming[to overcome]　**15** ②　**16** ③
**17** ①,④　**18** ①　**19** ⑤　**20** ②　**21** ③
**22** ③　**23** ⑤　**24** ③　**25** (A) from  (B) planting
**26** ①　**27** ④　**28** gave up exercising
**29** ③,⑤　**30** ②,⑤　**31** ②　**32** ②

### 중간·기말고사 대비문제 해설

**1** ⓐ 동사 like는 to부정사와 동명사 모두 목적어로 쓸 수 있다.
　ⓑ 동사 plan은 to부정사를 목적어로 쓸 수 있다.
　ⓒ 동사 enjoy는 동명사를 목적어로 쓸 수 있다.
　　(talk → talking)
　ⓓ practice는 동명사를 목적어로 쓰는 동사이다.

(speak → speaking)
　ⓔ 등위접속사 and가 조동사(will) 뒤에서 동사원형으로 쓰인 visit과 밑줄 친 단어를 병렬 구조로 연결하므로, seeing을 see로 고쳐야 한다.
　　(seeing → see)
**2** go -ing '~하러 가다'
**3** want는 to부정사(to read)를 목적어로 쓰는 동사이다.
**4** ① 동사 keep의 뒤에 동사가 오면 -ing형으로 쓴다.
　「keep ~ing」 '계속 ~하다' (to draw → drawing)
　② 접속사가 없이 한 개의 문장에서 동사가 두 개 나올 수 없다. 따라서 밑줄 친 부분을 주어의 역할을 할 수 있는 동명사나 to부정사로 바꿔야 한다.
　　(Protect → Protecting/To protect)
　③ 전치사의 목적어로 동사가 올 때는 동명사의 형태로 쓴다. (take → taking)
　⑤ 「How about -ing?」는 '~하는 것이 어떠니?'라는 의미의 동명사를 사용한 관용표현이다.
　　(play → playing)
**5** 전치사(at)와 stop은 동명사(singing)를 목적어로 쓴다.
　*cf.* stop의 뒤에 to부정사가 올 때는 목적을 나타내는 부사적 용법이다.
　「stop+to부정사」 '~를 하기 위해 멈추다'
**6** ② be interested in '~에 관심 있는'의 의미로, 전치사 in의 목적어 역할을 할 수 있는 동명사 collecting이 온 것은 적절하다.
　⑤ expect는 to부정사를 목적어로 쓰는 동사이다.
　① 「keep+동명사」는 '~을 계속(반복)하다'라는 의미이다. (make → making)
　③ 전치사 for의 목적어 자리이므로 동명사 improving을 써야 한다. (improve → improving)
　④ 「look forward to + -ing」 '~을 고대하다'
　　(meet → meeting)
**7** 「how about+동명사~?」는 '~하는 게 어때?'라는 뜻이다.
**8** ⓐ '~하는 데 어려움을 겪다'는 뜻의 표현은 「have trouble+동명사」로 나타낸다.
　　(study → studying)
　ⓑ '~을 잘하다'는 「be good at+동명사」로 나타낸다.
　　(listen → listening)
　ⓒ 문장의 주어가 동명사일 경우 단수 취급한다.
　　(are → is)
　ⓔ 사역동사 let의 목적격 보어 자리에는 원형부정사

Ch<br>**8**<br>동명사

가 온다. (knowing → know)

**9** • What about -ing? '~하는 것이 어떠니?'
   • spend+시간+-ing '~하는 데 시간을 보내다'

**10** • keep … from ~ing '…가 ~하는 것을 막다'
   • spend … ~ing '~하는 데 …를 소비하다'

**11** 「keep+-ing」 '계속해서 ~ 하다'

**12** give up은 동명사를 목적어로 가진다.
   ③ He gave up climbing a tree.

**13** 「stop+동명사」 '~하는 것을 멈추다'(동사의 목적어)
   *cf.* 「stop+to부정사」 '~하기 위해 멈추다'
   (to부정사의 부사적 용법)

**14** (1) 첫 번째 줄 끝의 give up은 '포기하다'라는 뜻으로 동명사를 목적어로 쓴다.
   (2) 밑에서 두 번째 줄의 continue는 동명사와 to부정사 모두를 목적어로 쓸 수 있는 동사이다. 접속사 없이 동사가 연달아 나올 수 없으므로 overcome을 목적어 역할을 할 수 있는 동명사나 to부정사로 고쳐야 한다.

**15** (A) 전치사 뒤에는 동명사(flying)가 목적어로 나온다.
   (B) want는 to부정사(to become)를 목적어로 취한다.

**16** practice는 동명사를 목적어로 쓰는 동사이며 Let's는 「Let's+동사원형」의 형태로 권유나 제안을 나타낸다.

**17** 빈칸은 주격 보어의 자리이다. 동명사와 to부정사는 명사처럼 쓰여 문장 내에서 보어 역할을 한다.
   ② went → going[to go]
   ③ recycled → recycling[to recycle]
   ⑤ do → doing[to do]

**18** ① 문장의 주어가 동명사일 경우 단수 취급한다.
   (are → is)

**19** 남자가 긍정의 대답(Sure)을 하였으므로, 여자가 영화 감상에 대한 제안을 하는 것이 적절하다. ⑤는 영화 감상 이후에 무엇을 하고 싶냐는 질문이므로, 이에 Sure로 대답하는 것은 적절하지 않다.

**20** 주어진 문장과 ①③④⑤ 동명사   ② 현재분사

**21** • spend … ~ing '~하는 데 …를 소비하다'
   • enjoy는 동명사를 목적어로 쓰는 동사이다.
   • 전치사(on)의 목적어로 동명사가 와야 한다.

**22** ①②④⑤ 주어의 역할을 하는 동명사
   ③ 보어의 역할을 하는 동명사

**23** stop은 동명사를 목적어로 쓰는 동사이다. stop의 뒤에 오는 to부정사는 부사적 용법으로 목적을 나타낸다.
   「stop+동명사」 '~하는 것을 멈추다'

「stop+to부정사」 '~하기 위해 멈추다'

**24** ① 의문사가 있는 일반동사의 의문문은 「의문사+do(es)+주어+동사원형~?」의 어순으로 쓴다.
   (wants → want)
   ② 주어(He)가 3인칭 단수일 때, 일반동사의 현재형은 「동사원형+-s」로 나타낸다.
   (want → wants)
   ④ 미래 시제는 'be going to'를 사용하여 표현할 수 있다. be going to의 의문문은 「의문사+be+주어+going to+동사원형 ~?」으로 쓴다. (does → is)
   ⑤ 미래 시제를 나타내는 표현 'be going to'의 뒤에는 동사원형을 쓴다. (went → go)

**25** (A) keep … from ~ing '…가 ~하는 것을 막다'
   (B) spend … ~ing '~하는 데 …를 소비하다'

**26** (a)의 빈칸 뒤에 to부정사가 오므로, 동명사를 목적어로 쓰는 ③의 kept와 ⑤의 gave up은 올 수 없다.
   (b)의 빈칸 뒤에는 동명사가 오므로, to부정사를 목적어로 쓰는 ②의 decided와 ④의 wants는 올 수 없다.
   • We expected to meet again.
   • Susan enjoys dancing to her favorite music.

**27** ⓓ How about ~ing '~하는 게 어때?'
   (swim → swimming)
   ⓐ 형용사 ready를 수식하는 부사적 용법의 to부정사 to swim을 쓴 것은 적절하다.
   ⓑ 조동사 will 뒤에는 동사원형을 써야 한다.
   ⓒ 명사 time을 수식하는 형용사적 용법의 to부정사 to practice를 쓴 것은 적절하다.
   ⓔ mind는 동명사를 목적어로 취한다.
   여: 네 수영 수업은 어땠니?
   남: 그것은 굉장했어! 하지만 나는 아직 깊은 물에서 수영할 준비가 되지 않았어.
   여: 걱정 마, 너는 더 나아질 거야.
   남: 나는 그저 연습할 시간이 더 필요해.
   여: 매일 수영하는 게 어때?
   남: 좋은 생각이야. 나는 내 코치에게 추가 수업을 부탁해 볼게.
   여: 나는 그가 돕는 것을 꺼리지 않을 거라 확신해(기꺼이 도와주실 거야).

**28** 「give up+-ing」 '~하는 것을 포기하다'

**29** ⓒⓔ 동명사   ⓐⓑⓓ 현재분사

**30** ② practice는 동명사를 목적어로 쓰는 동사이므로 playing을 써야 한다. (to play → playing)
   ⑤ 동명사 주어는 단수 취급을 하므로 is를 써야 한다.

(are → is)

**31** (A) finish는 동명사를 목적어로 쓰는 동사이므로 cleaning이다.

(B) want는 to부정사를 목적어로 쓰는 동사이므로

to play이다.

(C) spend ⋯ ~ing '~하는 데 ⋯를 소비하다'

**32** ② 현재분사 ①③④⑤ 동명사

---

<table>
<tr><td>**CHAPTER**</td><td>**9**</td><td>**분사**<br>Participles</td><td>본문 _ p.188</td></tr>
</table>



## PRACTICE 1

| | | | |
|---|---|---|---|
| **1** | dying | **2** | lost |
| **3** | ringing | **4** | forgotten |
| **5** | sleeping | **6** | given |
| **7** | baked | **8** | rolling |
| **9** | used | **10** | rising |
| **11** | smiling | **12** | broken |

**1, 3, 5, 8, 10, 11** 빈칸 뒤의 명사와 '능동/진행'의 의미 관계를 이루므로 '동사원형+-ing' 형태인 현재분사가 알맞다.
**2, 4, 6, 7, 9, 12** 빈칸 뒤의 명사와 '수동/완료'의 의미관계를 이루므로 과거분사 형태가 알맞다. 일반적으로 과거분사는 '동사원형+-ed'의 형태이지만, lose-lost-lost, forget-forgot-forgotten, give-gave-given, break-broke-broken처럼 불규칙 동사들은 과거/과거분사 형태가 불규칙하게 변화한다.

## PRACTICE 2

| | | | |
|---|---|---|---|
| **1** | broken | **2** | flying |
| **3** | dancing | **4** | burning |
| **5** | used | **6** | built |

**1, 5, 6** 수식받는 명사와 '수동/완료'의 의미 관계를 이루므로 과거분사가 알맞다.
**2, 3, 4** 수식받는 명사와 '능동/진행'의 의미 관계를 이루므로 현재분사가 알맞다.

**1** 부서진 의자 (break-broke-broken)
**2** 하늘을 날고 있는 연
**3** 춤추고 있는 소녀
**4** 타고 있는 두 개의 초
**5** 사용된(중고) 자전거
**6** 붉은 벽돌로 지어진 집 (build-built-built)

## PRACTICE 3

| | | | |
|---|---|---|---|
| **1** | singing | **2** | surprising |
| **3** | picking | **4** | spent |
| **5** | walking | **6** | borrowed |

| | | | |
|---|---|---|---|
| **7** | dying | **8** | written |
| **9** | born | **10** | crossing |
| **11** | coming | **12** | lost |
| **13** | listening | **14** | painted |
| **15** | finished | **16** | crossed |

**1, 2, 3, 5, 7, 10, 11, 13** 수식받는 명사와 '능동/진행'의 의미 관계를 이루므로 현재분사가 알맞다.
**4, 6, 8, 9, 12, 14, 15, 16** 수식받는 명사와 '수동/완료'의 의미 관계를 이루므로 과거분사가 알맞다.

**1** 노래하는 새
**2** 놀라게 하는(놀라운) 소식
**3** 쓰레기를 줍고 있는 소년
**4** 쓰인 돈 (spend-spent-spent)
**5** 걸어 다니는 사전
*a walking dictionary: '걸어 다니는 사전'은 비유적으로 '박학다식한 사람'을 의미한다.
**6** 빌려진(빌린) 펜
**7** 죽어가는 개
**8** 영어로 써진 책 (write-wrote-written)
**9** 유럽에서 태어난 사람 (bear-bore-born/borne)
**10** 길을 건너는 남자
**11** 공장에서 나오는 물
**12** 잃어버려진(잃어버린) 딸 (lose-lost-lost)
**13** 음악을 듣고 있는 소녀
**14** 유미에 의해 그려진(유미가 그린) 그림
**15** 완성된 제품(완제품)
**16** 목적격 보어로 과거분사(crossed)를 사용하여 목적어(my fingers)가 당하는 행위나 상태를 서술한다.
*keep[have] one's fingers crossed: '행운을 빌다, 좋은 결과가 나오기를 빌다'라는 의미이다. 세 번째 손가락을 두 번째 손가락 위에 포개는 손동작을 묘사한 것으로, 이러한 손동작이 행운을 가져온다는 믿음에서 유래한 표현이다.

## PRACTICE 4

| | | | |
|---|---|---|---|
| **2** | been | **3** | living |
| **4** | planted | **5** | eating |
| **6** | practicing | **7** | called |
| **8** | stolen | **9** | worked |
| **10** | made | **11** | flooded |

**12** ridden　　　　　　**13** making

**14** doing　　　　　　**15** walking

> **1, 4, 7, 8, 11** be동사와 과거분사가 결합하여 수동태 구문을 이루
> 어야 알맞다.
> **2, 9, 10, 12** have/has와 과거분사가 결합된 완료형 구문이 알맞
> 다.
> **3, 5, 6, 13, 15** be동사와 현재분사가 결합된 진행형이 되어야 알
> 맞다.
> **14** 이 일을 (지금까지) 해 오고 있다는 의미이므로 현재완료(have
> been)에 현재분사가 결합하여 진행형이 되어야 알맞다.

## PRACTICE 5

**1** 현　　　　　　**2** 동　　　　　　**3** 현

**4** 동　　　　　　**5** 동　　　　　　**6** 현

**7** 동　　　　　　**8** 현　　　　　　**9** 동

**10** 동　　　　　　**11** 현　　　　　　**12** 동

> **1, 8, 11** '~하는 중이다/중이었다'라는 뜻으로 진행을 나타내는 현
> 재분사로 쓰였다.
> **2, 4, 10** 밑줄 친 부분이 뒤에 오는 명사의 용도나 목적을 나타내므
> 로 동명사로 쓰였다.
> **3, 6** 밑줄 친 부분이 뒤에 오는 명사를 꾸며주어 능동의 의미
> (interesting)나 현재 상태(living)를 나타내므로 현재분사로 쓰였
> 다.
> **5, 7, 9, 12** '~하는 것이다'라는 뜻으로, 밑줄 친 부분이 주격 보어
> 역할을 하므로 동명사로 쓰였다.

## PRACTICE 6

**1** ① interesting　　　② interested

**2** ① pleased　　　　② pleasing

**3** ① shocking　　　② shocked

**4** ① moved　　　　② moving

**5** ① exciting　　　　② excited

**6** ① disappointing　② disappointed

> **1** ① interesting stories: 흥미로운 이야기
> 　② be interested in: ~에 흥미를 느끼다
> **2** ① be pleased with: ~에 만족하다
> 　② pleasing: 기분 좋게 하는
> **3** ① shocking: 놀라게 하는
> 　② be shocked at: ~에 충격을 받다
> **4** ① be moved by: ~에 감동을 받다
> 　② moving: 감동을 주는
> **5** ① exciting: 흥분하게 하는
> 　② be excited about: ~에 대해 흥분하다, 들뜨다
> **6** ① disappointing: 실망스러운
> 　② be disappointed (with): (~에) 실망하다, 낙담하다

## PRACTICE 7

**1** tired　　　　　　**2** surprised

**3** amazing　　　　**4** satisfying

**5** depressed　　　**6** boring

> **1** feel tired: 피로를 느끼다
> **2** be surprised by: ~에 놀라다
> **3** amazing powers: 놀라운 힘
> **4** a satisfying result: 만족스러운 결과
> **5** be depressed: 우울해하다
> **6** boring: 지루한

## PRACTICE 8

**1** interesting　　　**2** tired

**3** amazing　　　　**4** surprised

**5** moved　　　　　**6** shocking

**7** satisfying　　　**8** disappointing

**9** confusing　　　**10** bored

**11** pleased　　　　**12** frustrating

> **1, 3, 6, 7, 8, 9, 12** 주어 또는 수식받는 명사가 감정을 일으키는
> 주체이므로 감정을 나타내는 동사의 -ing 형태가 알맞다.
> **2, 4, 5, 10, 11** 주어가 감정을 느끼는 주체이므로 감정을 나타내
> 는 동사의 -ed 형태가 알맞다.

## 중간·기말고사 대비문제 정답　본문 _ p.196

> **1** ②　**2** ⑤　**3** ①,④　**4** ②　**5** ③　**6** ②　**7** ②
> **8** ②　**9** ④　**10** standing　**11** ⑤　**12** pleased
> **13** ③　**14** ③　**15** ⑤　**16** ⑤　**17** written
> **18** ③,⑤　**19** ②　**20** (1) The girl sitting on the
> bench is my sister. (2) Look at that nice sports
> car parked under the tree.　**21** ①

## 중간·기말고사 대비문제 해설

**1**　'깨진'은 수동·완료의 의미이므로 과거분사(broken)
　가 와야 한다.

**2**　• 「be동사+현재분사」는 진행시제를 나타낸다.
　• 지각동사(heard)의 목적격 보어로 원형부정사
　(ring)나 현재분사(ringing)를 쓴다.

**3**　① 사역동사 had+목적어+p.p. (take → taken)
　④ 사역동사 make는 목적격 보어로 동사원형을 취한
　다. (cleaning → clean)

**4** ② 진행을 나타내는 현재분사
①④⑤ 보어의 역할을 하는 동명사
③ 주어 역할을 하는 동명사

**5** 명사(a girl)를 수식하는 분사로, '쓰고 있는'은 능동·진행의 의미이므로 현재분사(wearing)를 쓴다. 동사 enjoy는 동명사(looking)를 목적어로 쓴다.

**6** 식물이 음악을 좋아한다는 사실이 감정을 일으키는 주체이므로 현재분사(surprising)가 와야 한다.

**7** 두 번째 문장의 주어 The weather는 감정을 일으키는 주체이므로 현재분사(amazing)가 와야 하며, 마지막 문장의 주어 We는 감정을 느끼는 대상이므로 과거분사(disappointed)가 와야 한다.

**8** 주어 She는 감정을 느끼는 대상이므로 과거분사(interested)가 와야 한다.
*cf.* be interested in '~에 흥미가 있다'

**9** 주어진 문장과 ④ 명사의 역할을 하는 동명사
①②③⑤ 진행을 나타내는 현재분사

**10** 앞 명사 the boy를 수식하는 것으로 진행을 나타내는 현재분사(standing)가 와야 한다.

**11** ⑤ 현재분사
①②③④ 동명사

**12** 주어 She는 감정을 느끼는 대상이므로 과거분사(pleased)가 와야 한다.

**13** (A) result가 감정을 일으키는 주체이므로 현재분사(disappointing)가 와야 한다.
(B) '데인'은 수동/완료의 의미이므로 과거분사(burned)가 와야 한다.
(C) '밤이 길어지고 있다'는 능동/진행의 의미이므로 현재분사(getting)가 와야 한다.
(D) 주어 She가 감정을 느끼는 대상이므로 과거분사(depressed)가 와야 한다.
(E) '남은 치즈케이크 있나요?'라는 의미이다. 수동을 나타내는 과거분사(left)로 앞의 명사(any cheesecake)를 수식하는 것이 적절하다.

**14** ⓐⓒⓔ 현재분사
ⓑⓓ 동명사

**15** • 진행을 나타내는 현재분사(Sleeping '자고 있는')가 와야 한다.
• 명사(leaves)를 수식할 수 있는 분사가 적절하다. 진행을 나타내는 현재분사(falling '떨어지고 있는') 또는 완료를 나타내는 과거분사(fallen '떨어진')가 올 수 있다.

**16** ⑤ 현재분사
①②③④ 동명사

**17** 명사 a novel이 스스로 쓴 것이 아니라 써진 것이므로 수동 의미의 과거분사(written)가 들어간다.

**18** ③ '내 월급은 내 은행 계좌로 바로 지급된다.'는 의미가 적절하므로, 수동태로 쓰이는 「be동사+과거분사」 표현이 적절하다. (paying→ paid)
⑤ 뒤에 나온 book을 수식하며 완료의 의미를 나타내는 과거분사(lost)가 오는 것이 적절하다.
(losing → lost)
① 뒤에 오는 명사 line의 용도나 목적을 나타내는 동명사(finishing)의 사용이 적절하다.
② be동사(was)와 현재분사(searching)가 결합하여 진행형 구문을 이루는 것이 적절하다. 뒤에 나온 sites를 수식하며 능동의 의미를 나타내는 현재분사(interesting)가 오는 것이 적절하다.
④ 주어 Her childhood가 보내진 것이므로 be동사와 과거분사(spent)가 결합하여 수동태 구문을 이루는 것이 적절하나.

**19** • 뒤에 나온 명사 car를 수식하는 것으로 수동·완료의 의미를 갖는 과거분사(used)가 와야 한다.
*cf.* a used car 중고차
• 「have/has+과거분사」는 현재완료 시제를 나타낸다.

**20** (1) 현재분사(sitting)가 부사구(on the bench)의 수식을 받는 경우에는 뒤에서 명사(The girl)를 수식한다.
(2) 과거분사(parked)가 부사구(under the tree)의 수식을 받는 경우에는 뒤에서 명사(that nice sports car)를 수식한다.

**21** ⓑ 접속사 없이 동사가 연달아 나올 수 없다. 동사 cook을 목적어 역할을 할 수 있는 동명사나 to부정사로 바꿔야 한다. like는 동명사와 to부정사 모두를 목적어로 취하는 동사이다.
(cook → cooking[to cook])
ⓒ 앞에 나온 meat를 수식하는 것으로 수동·완료의 의미인 과거분사(roasted '구워진')가 와야 한다.
(roasting → roasted)
ⓓ Everybody가 감정을 느끼는 대상이므로 과거분사(surprised)가 와야 한다.
(surprising → surprised)

Ch
**9**
분사

## PRACTICE 1

| | | | |
|---|---|---|---|
| **1** special | | **2** careful | |
| **3** wonderful | | **4** open | |
| **5** helpful | | **6** ready | |
| **7** good | | **8** hungry | |
| **9** happy | | **10** curious | |

> **1, 3, 7** 명사를 앞에서 꾸며주는 자리이므로 형용사가 알맞다.
> **4** keep+목적어+형용사: 목적어가 ~한 상태로 두다
> **2, 5, 6, 8, 10** be동사 뒤에서 주어의 상태나 성질을 나타내는 주격 보어가 들어갈 자리이므로 형용사가 알맞다.
> **9** make+목적어+형용사: 목적어를 ~하게 하다

## PRACTICE 2

| | | | | | | | |
|---|---|---|---|---|---|---|---|
| **1** B, A | **2** A, B | **3** B, A | **4** A, B |
| **5** A, B | **6** A, B | **7** B, A | **8** A, B |
| **9** A, B | **10** A, B | | |

> [보기]
> A. 좋은(잘한) 일 → 명사를 앞에서 꾸며주는 한정적 용법
> B. 수학을 잘하지 못한다 → 주어의 상태나 모습을 설명하는 서술적 용법
> **1** 과목이 어렵다 (서술) / 어려운 퍼즐 (한정)
> **2** 아름다운 목걸이 (한정) / 날씨가 아름답다[좋다] (서술)
> **3** 시장이 혼잡하다 (서술) / 혼잡한 장소 (한정)
> **4** 완벽한 사람 (한정) / 그는 완벽하다 (서술)
> **5** 좋은 기억력 (한정) / 맛이 좋다 (서술)
> **6** 다른 반 (한정) / 민수는 다르다 (서술)
> **7** 케이크가 달다 (서술) / 달콤한 것 (한정)
> **8** 거대한 장소 (한정) / 궁전이 거대하다 (서술)
> **9** 맛있는 음식 (한정) / 샌드위치가 맛있게 보인다 (서술)
> **10** 전혀 흥미롭지 않은 것 (한정) / 게임이 흥미진진하다 (서술)

## PRACTICE 3

**1** something sweet
**2** anything else
**3** Everything delicious
**4** something cold
**5** anything interesting
**6** nobody special
**7** something important
**8** anything slow
**9** nothing wrong
**10** everything necessary
**11** something useful
**12** anyone famous
**13** anything sharp
**14** new thing
**15** something old
**16** nothing cheap

> **1, 2, 3, 4, 5, 7, 8, 9, 10, 11, 13, 15, 16** –thing으로 끝나는 대명사를 꾸미는 형용사는 항상 대명사 뒤에 온다.
> **6, 12** –body 또는 –one으로 끝나는 대명사를 꾸미는 형용사는 항상 대명사의 뒤에 온다.
> **14** thing이 단독으로 쓰일 때는 형용사(new)가 thing을 앞에서 꾸며준다.

## PRACTICE 4

**2** two, second
**3** three, third
**4** four, fourth
**5** five, fifth
**6** six, sixth
**7** seven, seventh
**8** eight, eighth
**9** nine, ninth
**10** ten, tenth
**11** eleven, eleventh
**12** twelve, twelfth
**13** thirteen, thirteenth
**14** fourteen, fourteenth
**15** fifteen, fifteenth
**16** sixteen, sixteenth
**17** seventeen, seventeenth
**18** eighteen, eighteenth
**19** nineteen, nineteenth
**20** twenty, twentieth
**21** twenty-one, twenty-first
**22** twenty-two, twenty-second
**23** thirty, thirtieth
**24** forty, fortieth
**25** fifty, fiftieth
**26** fifty-five, fifty-fifth
**27** sixty, sixtieth
**28** seventy, seventieth
**29** eighty, eightieth
**30** ninety, ninetieth
**31** a[one] hundred, one hundredth

**32** a[one] thousand, one thousandth

**33** a[one] million, one millionth

**34** a[one] billion, one billionth

## PRACTICE 5

| | | | |
|---|---|---|---|
| **1** | second | **2** | ninth |
| **3** | twelfth | **4** | first |
| **5** | eighth | **6** | fortieth |
| **7** | third | **8** | thirtieth |
| **9** | fifth | **10** | twentieth |

## PRACTICE 6

**1** four thousand, two hundred (and) fifty-six

**2** thirty-six

**3** fifty-seven thousand, four hundred (and) three

**4** a[one] thousand, (and) fifty-two

**5** five hundred (and) thirty

**6** eight thousand, eight hundred (and) twenty-six

**7** seventy-two

**8** six hundred (and) one

**9** seventy-five thousand, four hundred (and) nineteen

**10** twelve million

**11** five thousand, five hundred

**12** seven hundred (and) thirteen

**13** two hundred (and) twenty-three thousand, six hundred

**14** four hundred (and) eleven

**15** two thousand, seven hundred (and) eighty

**16** a[one] hundred (and) thirty-one

**17** six thousand, two hundred (and) thirty-eight

**18** two hundred (and) fifty-six

**19** ninety-nine

**20** three hundred (and) two

## PRACTICE 7

**1** eight four six, o[zero] two three six

**2** three o[zero] six, four four[double four] o[zero] o[zero][double o[zero]]

**3** area code zero two, four two eight, five five [double five] nine seven

**4** three one nine, two seven one three

**5** zero one eight, two eight one eight, three

seven one o[zero]

**6** two seven four, five five[double five] one five

**7** area code zero three one, eight six five, eight four three eight

**8** one one[double one] nine

**9** two o[zero] six o[zero], four three six two

**10** nine six three, five nine o[zero] eight

**11** 019-1792-0012

**12** (064) 440-3318

**13** 594-3386

**14** (042) 754-3892

**15** 296-4300

**16** 1-677-820-3322

**17** 114

**18** 646-5958

## PRACTICE 8

**1** three-fourths[three-quarters]

**2** a quarter[one-quarter], a fourth[one-fourth]

**3** two point five

**4** (zero) point three one

**5** two point zero nine

**6** twenty and a third[one-third]

**7** two-sevenths

**8** two-ninths

**9** one and a half[one-half]

**10** five and three-tenths

**11** (zero) point nine nine

**12** one point two seven two

**13** 7/15

**14** 4/11

**15** 3 6/7

**16** 6 1/5

**17** 0.6

**18** 34.9

**19** 3.126

**20** 5 5/6

## PRACTICE 9

**1** nine twenty

**2** three-(o)-five

**3** eight twenty-five

**4** five (o'clock)

**5**   ten thirty

**6**   one thirty-seven

**7**   six fifteen

**8**   eleven (o'clock)

**9**   twelve-(o)-eight

**10**   four fifty

## PRACTICE 10

**1**   (a) quarter to ten

**2**   (a) quarter after[past] one

**3**   five to twelve

**4**   twenty after four

**5**   (a) quarter after[past] seven

**6**   twenty-five to eight

**7**   ten to nine

**8**   ten after three

**9**   (a) quarter to six

**10**   five to two

**11**   (a) quarter after[past] three

**12**   ten to six

**13**   half past three

**14**   five after six

**15**   twenty-five after two

**16**   half past eleven

**17**   ten after nine

**18**   twenty to five

**19**   twenty after ten

**20**   half past seven

## PRACTICE 11

**1**   October (the) thirteenth[the thirteenth of October]

**2**   two thousand (and) twenty[twenty twenty]

**3**   fifteen ninety-two

**4**   February (the) twentieth[the twentieth of February]

**5**   four (hundred and) fifty-two

**6**   July (the) first[the first of July]

**7**   nineteen eighty

**8**   March (the) thirty-first[the thirty-first of March]

**9**   nineteen ten

**10**   December (the) fifteenth[the fifteenth of December]

**11**   April (the) eighth[the eighth of April]

**12**   September (the) twenty-sixth[the twenty-sixth of September]

**13**   nineteen ninety-nine

**14**   May (the) fifth[the fifth of May]

**15**   two thousand

**16**   November (the) tenth[the tenth of November]

**17**   twelve thirty-eight

**18**   June (the) seventeenth[the seventeenth of June]

**19**   sixteen hundred

**20**   nineteen seventy

## PRACTICE 12

**1**   a[one] dollar (and) twenty-five cents

**2**   five thousand two hundred won

**3**   ten dollars (and) ten cents

**4**   twelve thousand won

**5**   a[one] thousand eight hundred (and) fifty won

**6**   seventy-five cents

**7**   twelve dollars (and) thirty cents

**8**   four hundred won

**9**   three dollars (and) fifty cents

**10**   four thousand nine hundred won

## PRACTICE 13

**1**   twenty-three degrees Celsius

**2**   fifty degrees Fahrenheit

**3**   a[one] hundred (and) fifty degrees Celsius

**4**   seventy-five degrees Fahrenheit

**5**   three hundred (and) fifty degrees Fahrenheit

**6**   two hundred (and) seventy-five degrees Celsius

**7**   a[one] hundred (and) eighty degrees Celsius

**8**   a[one] hundred (and) sixteen point six degrees Fahrenheit

**9**   two hundred (and) seventy-three point one five degrees Celsius

**10**   four hundred (and) twenty degrees Fahrenheit

## PRACTICE 14

**1**   Add, a, quarter[fourth]

**2**   invented, fourteen, forty, three

**3**   costs, four, thousand, nine, hundred

**4** sold, eighteen, dollars, ninety, cents

**5** arrived, the, first, March

**6** rose, eighty, point, seven

**7** received, four, fifths

**8** get, up, quarter, after[past], seven

**9** was, born, November, fourth, two, thousand

**10** collected, four, thousand, seven, hundred, seventy, four

**11** starts, a[one], hundred, Celsius

**12** is, area, code, zero, two, four, three, six, seven

**13** reached, eighty, six, degrees

**14** is, zero, one, zero, double[nine], nine, eight

**15** saved, million, two, hundred, twenty, nine, thousand, nine, hundred

## PRACTICE 15

| | | | |
|---|---|---|---|
| **1** | millions of | **2** | tens[dozens] of |
| **3** | four hundred | **4** | Hundreds of |
| **5** | five hundred | **6** | Thousands of |
| **7** | Millions of | **8** | tens[dozens] of |
| **9** | a[one] thousand | **10** | Three million |

## PRACTICE 16

| | | | |
|---|---|---|---|
| **1** | every five days | **2** | every two weeks |
| **3** | every three days | **4** | every fourth week |
| **5** | every ten years | **6** | every seven days |
| **7** | every fifteen days | **8** | every four years |
| **9** | every second day | **10** | every ninth day |

## PRACTICE 17

| | | | |
|---|---|---|---|
| **1** | many flowers | **2** | much water |
| **3** | many dishes | **4** | many clubs |
| **5** | much homework | **6** | many dreams |
| **7** | many kites | **8** | much juice |
| **9** | many planets | **10** | many jobs |
| **11** | much rain | **12** | many places |
| **13** | much sleep | **14** | many Korean friends |
| **15** | many subjects | **16** | much pleasure |
| **17** | much snow | **18** | many sports activities |
| **19** | many interesting sites | | |
| **20** | much interest | **21** | much experience |
| **22** | many people | | |

> **1, 3, 4, 6, 7, 9, 10, 12, 14, 15, 18, 19, 22** 셀 수 있는 명사 앞에 와서 '많은, 다수의'라는 의미로 쓰이는 many가 알맞고, 이때 수식을 받는 명사는 복수 형태로 써야 한다.
> **2, 5, 8, 11, 13, 16, 17, 20, 21** 셀 수 없는 명사 앞에 와서 '많은'이라는 의미로 쓰이는 much가 알맞다.

## PRACTICE 18

| | | | |
|---|---|---|---|
| **2** | much time | **3** | many apple pies |
| **4** | many schools | **5** | much money |
| **6** | many pictures | **7** | much courage |
| **8** | many animals | **9** | much coffee |
| **10** | many things | **11** | many insects |
| **12** | much fun | **13** | many children |
| **14** | Many people | **15** | much oil |
| **16** | many questions | **17** | much information |
| **18** | many different countries | | |
| **19** | many rules | **20** | much sleep |

> **3, 4, 6, 8, 10, 11, 13, 14, 16, 18, 19** 괄호 안의 명사가 셀 수 있는 명사이므로 a lot of나 lots of 대신 many로 바꿔 쓸 수 있다. 이때 명사는 -(e)s를 붙인 복수 명사 형태가 되어야 한다.
> **2, 5, 7, 9, 12, 15, 17, 20** 괄호 안의 명사가 셀 수 없는 명사이므로 a lot of나 lots of 대신 much로 바꿔 쓸 수 있다.

## PRACTICE 19

| | | | |
|---|---|---|---|
| **1** | few | **2** | little |
| **3** | A few | **4** | little |
| **5** | a few | **6** | few |
| **7** | little | **8** | a little |
| **9** | little | **10** | A few |

> **1, 6** 셀 수 있는 명사 앞에 쓰이며 '거의 없는'이라는 의미를 나타내는 few가 알맞다.
> **2, 4, 7, 9** 셀 수 없는 명사 앞에 쓰이며 '거의 없는'이라는 의미를 나타내는 little이 알맞다.
> **3, 5, 10** 셀 수 있는 명사 앞에 쓰이며 '약간의'라는 의미를 나타내는 a few가 알맞다.
> **8** 셀 수 없는 명사 앞에 쓰이며 '약간의'라는 의미를 나타내는 a little이 알맞다.

## PRACTICE 20

| | | | |
|---|---|---|---|
| **1** | some | **2** | some |
| **3** | any | **4** | any |
| **5** | some | **6** | any |
| **7** | any | **8** | any |
| **9** | any | **10** | some |
| **11** | some | **12** | some |

**13** any    **14** any
**15** some    **16** some

> **1, 2, 5, 11, 12, 16** 셀 수 있는 명사와 셀 수 없는 명사 앞에 모두 와서 '약간의'라는 의미로 쓰이는 some이 알맞다.
> **3, 4, 6, 9, 13** 부정문에서 '약간의'라는 의미로 쓰이는 any가 알맞다.
> **7, 8, 14** 의문문에서 '어떤/약간의'라는 의미로 쓰이는 any가 알맞다.
> **10, 15** '~해주시겠어요?' 또는 '~하시겠어요?'라는 의미로 권유/부탁을 하는 의문문이므로 some이 알맞다.

## PRACTICE 21

**1** no    **2** nobody
**3** nothing    **4** no, one
**5** nowhere    **6** no
**7** nobody    **8** nothing
**9** nowhere    **10** no

## 📑 중간·기말고사 대비문제 정답   본문 _ p.221

**1** ⑤  **2** ③  **3** ④  **4** ②  **5** ④  **6** a very pretty girl  **7** ③  **8** ⑤  **9** ninth  **10** ③
**11** ②  **12** ⑤  **13** ②  **14** ①  **15** ③
**16** I want something delicious for lunch.
**17** Hundreds of  **18** ⓐ sixth ⓑ six  **19** ③
**20** three → third  **21** ⑤, some → any
**22** ③  **23** ②  **24** no  **25** second  **26** ⑤
**27** ⑤  **28** ⑤  **29** ④  **30** ③  **31** ④  **32** (1) It's a quarter past six. (2) It's a quarter to eight.
**33** ②  **34** ③  **35** ③  **36** ④  **37** ④  **38** ③
**39** have no houses  **40** ③  **41** ③
**42** (1) ⓑ There are many[a lot of/lots of] pencils on the desk. (2) ⓒ There's too much garbage in the park.  **43** ③  **44** (1) two[week] → second[weeks] (2) hundreds → hundred (3) three-forth → three-fourths

## 중간·기말고사 대비문제 해설

**1** ⑤ 형용사 - 부사
  ①②③④ 명사 - 형용사
**2** ③ '매우'라는 뜻의 부사
  ①②④⑤ 명사(boy)를 꾸며줄 수 있는 형용사
**3** ④ twelveth → twelfth

**4** much는 셀 수 없는 명사 앞에 쓰는 형용사
**5** ④ 보어로 쓰인 형용사의 서술적 용법
  ①②③⑤ 명사를 수식하는 형용사의 한정적 용법
**6** 서술적 용법의 형용사를 명사(girl)를 꾸미는 한정적 용법의 형용사로 바꾸어 쓸 수 있다.
**7** ③ four - fourth
**8** ⓐ seat은 '~을 앉히다'라는 뜻의 타동사이고 sit은 '앉다'라는 뜻의 자동사이다. 문맥상 스스로 앉는 것이므로 동사 sit을 쓰는 것이 적절하다. (seat → sit)
  ⓑ 물질명사 water는 셀 수 없으므로 양을 표현할 때 many가 아닌 much를 써야 한다. (many → much)
  ⓒ 동사 laugh를 수식하는 부사가 들어갈 자리이므로 happily로 쓰는 것이 적절하다. (happy → happily)
**9** ninth '아홉 번째'
**10** ③ 정수는 세 자리씩 끊어서 천 단위로 읽으며, hundred 뒤의 and는 생략 가능하다.
  1,251 = a[one] thousand, two hundred (and) fifty-one
**11** 셀 수 없는 명사(coffee) 앞에 '많은'의 의미로 much를 쓴다.
**12** ⑤ '~을 지나서'를 뜻하는 after[past]를 사용하여 읽는다. to는 '~전에'라는 뜻이다.
  1:10 = ten after[past] one
**13** 날짜는 서수를 이용하여 읽는다.
  *cf.* June '6월'      July '7월'
**14** <보기>의 round는 '둥근'의 의미를 가진 형용사이다.
  나는 그 둥근 접시를 깼다.
  ⓐ 이 둥근 테이블은 좋아 보인다. (형용사)
  ⓒ 축구는 둥근 공으로 경기를 한다. (형용사)
  ⓑ 그는 골프 한 판[라운드]을 했다. (명사)
  ⓓ 몇 판[라운드]이 지나갔니? (명사)
  ⓔ 우리는 학교 주변을 돌아다녔다. (부사)
  ⓕ 그녀는 첫번째 판[라운드]에서 게임을 이겼다. (명사)
**15** 11시 15분 전 = 10시 45분
  *cf.* (a) quarter '15분'    to '~ 전에'
**16** -thing으로 끝나는 대명사(something)를 꾸미는 형용사(delicious)는 항상 뒤에 위치한다.
**17** hundreds of '수백의'
  *cf.* tens[dozens] of '수십의'

thousands of '수천의' millions of '수백만의'

**18** 「every+서수+단수 명사」 = 「every+기수+복수 명사」
'매~, ~마다'

**19** 셀 수 있는 명사(animals) 앞에 '많은'의 의미로
many를 쓴다.

**20** 순서를 나타내는 서수(third)로 바꾸어야 한다.
(three → third)

**21** ⑤ 일반적으로 부정문과 의문문에서는 any를 쓴다.

**22** ③ A lots of → A lot of[Lots of]

**23** ② 6시 45분 ≠ 6시 15분 전(= 5시 45분)
(It is fifteen to six. → It is fifteen[(a) quarter]
to seven.)

**24** not ~ any는 no로 바꾸어 쓸 수 있다.

**25** 학년을 나타낼 때는 순서를 나타내는 서수(second)
를 써야 한다.

**26** ⑤ feel은 '~하게 느끼다'라는 뜻의 감각동사이므로,
보어로 형용사를 쓴다. softly는 '부드럽게'라는 뜻
의 부사이다. (softly → soft)
① smell은 '~한 냄새가 나다'라는 뜻의 감각동사이므
로, 보어로 형용사를 쓴다.
② sound는 '~하게 들리다'라는 뜻의 감각동사이므
로, 보어로 형용사를 쓴다. silly는 뒤에 -ly가 붙지
만 부사가 아닌 '어리석은'이라는 뜻의 형용사이다.
③ taste는 '~한 맛이 나다'라는 뜻의 감각동사이므
로, 보어로 형용사를 쓴다.
④ look은 '~하게 보이다'라는 뜻의 감각동사이므로,
보어로 형용사를 쓴다. lovely는 -ly가 붙지만, 부
사가 아닌 '사랑스러운'이라는 뜻의 형용사이다.

**27** 부정문에서는 일반적으로 any를 쓴다.
⑤ some → any

**28** 부정문에서는 any를 쓰며 의미상 anything이 와야
한다. 나는 지난밤에 열심히 공부했지만 지금 아무것도
기억할 수가 없다.
*cf.* anyone '누구, 아무'

**29** 미국의 화폐 단위인 dollar와 cent는 1보다 클 경우
복수형으로 쓴다.
④ $2.39 = two dollars and thirty-nine cents

**30** 분자는 기수로, 분모는 서수로 읽으며 분자를 먼저 읽
는다. 분자가 2 이상인 경우 분모에 -s를 붙인다.
① 1/5 = one-fifth[a fifth]
② 3/5 = three-fifths
④ 5/6 = five-sixths
⑤ 3 1/8 = three and one-eighth[an eighth]

**31** (A) 명사 doctor를 앞에서 수식하는 형용사
successful이 적절하다.
(B) 관사 a와 빈칸 앞에 위치한 형용사 great로 보아
빈칸에는 명사 success가 들어가는 것이 적절하
다. great가 앞에서 명사를 수식하고 있다.

**32** 시간을 읽을 때 15분은 a quarter로 표현할 수 있다.
정각을 기준으로 15분이 지난 상태이면 a quarter
past ~, 15분 전이면 a quarter to ~로 읽는다.

**33** 일반적으로 의문문에는 any를, 긍정문에는 some을
쓴다.

**34** 문맥상 (A)에 hard, (B)에 cute, (C)에 sunny, (D)에
sad가 들어가므로 어디에도 들어가지 않은 것은 free
이다.
(A) 그 수학 시험은 나에게 너무 <u>어려웠다.</u>
(B) 너의 어린 여동생은 웃을 때 정말 <u>귀엽다.</u>
(C) 밖은 아주 <u>맑다.</u>
(D) 그 영화는 너무 슬퍼서 나는 울었다.

**35** ① 밑줄 친 우리말과 같은 뜻이 아니므로 빈칸에 적절
하지 않다. 'I don't know.'는 모른다는 뜻이다.
② Nothing처럼 –thing으로 끝나는 대명사는 형용사
(special)가 뒤에서 수식한다.
④ something은 긍정문에서 '어떤 것, 무엇'이라는
뜻으로 쓰이는 부정대명사이다. 특별한 일이 없다
고 했으므로 '특별한 일이 있어'라는 뜻으로 해석되
는 ④번 보기는 적절하지 않다.
⑤ nothing은 「not ~ anything」과 바꾸어 쓸 수
있다. 이미 문장에 not이 포함되어 있으므로
nothing이 쓰이는 것은 적절하지 않다. 또한 특별
한 일이 없다고 했으므로 '특별한'이라는 뜻의 형
용사 special도 함께 써야 한다. 따라서 'I don't
have anything special'이 적절한 표현이다.

**36** ④ a little은 셀 수 없는 명사 앞에 쓴다.

**37** 그 젊은 남자는 <u>건전한</u> 정신을 가지고 있다. (형용사)
④ 그는 심신이 <u>건강하다.</u> (형용사)
① 교회 종이 11시에 울렸다. (동사)
② 그것은 매우 흥미롭게 <u>들린다.</u> (동사)
③ 바이올린은 여러 가지 <u>소리들을</u> 낼 수 있다. (명사)
⑤ 우리는 옆 방에서 이상한 <u>소리를</u> 들었다. (명사)

**38** ① soup는 셀 수 없는 명사이므로 복수형으로 쓸 수
없다. (soups → soup)
② coffee는 셀 수 없는 명사이므로 복수형으로 쓸 수
없다. (coffees → coffee)
④ many는 셀 수 있는 명사의 복수형 앞에서 명사를

수식하는 형용사이다. 따라서 셀 수 있는 명사인 book은 복수형으로 써야 한다. (book → books)

⑤ money는 셀 수 없는 명사이므로 복수형으로 쓸 수 없다. (moneys → money)

**39** not ~ any는 no로 바꾸어 쓸 수 있다.

**40** '많은'의 의미로 셀 수 있는 명사 앞에는 many를 쓰고 셀 수 없는 명사 앞에는 much를 쓴다. few는 '거의 없는'의 뜻으로 셀 수 있는 명사 앞에 쓴다.

**41** ③ many는 셀 수 있는 명사의 복수형 앞에서 명사를 수식한다. 동사(are)와 빈칸 뒤의 명사가 복수형(cafeterias)인 것으로 보아 빈칸에는 many가 들어갈 수 있다.

①②④⑤ milk, water, money, trash는 셀 수 없는 명사이다. 셀 수 없는 명사의 앞에는 much가 들어간다.

**42** ⓑ '많은'의 의미을 가지는 many[a lot of / lots of]는 셀 수 있는 명사(pencils) 앞에 쓴다.

ⓒ garbage는 셀 수 없는 명사로 앞에 many가 아닌 much를 쓴다.

**43** ⓐ 일반적으로 긍정문에 some을 쓴다.

ⓑ '많은'의 의미로 셀 수 있는 명사(things) 앞에는 many를 쓴다.

ⓒ '거의 없는'의 의미로 셀 수 없는 명사(snow) 앞에는 little을 쓴다.

**44** (1) 두 번째 줄에서 '매~, ~마다'라는 뜻으로 쓰이는 every는 「every+기수+복수명사」나 「every+서수+단수명사」로 써야 한다.

(every two week → every two weeks/every second week)

(2) 4번째 줄에서 500이라는 정수를 표현할 때는, hundred에 –s를 붙이지 않고 「기수+hundred」로 나타낸다. (hundreds → hundred)

(3) 밑에서 두 번째 줄에서 3/4라는 분수를 표현할 때는 분자가 2 이상이기 때문에 분모에 –s를 붙여야 한다. 또한 숫자 4의 서수 표현은 forth가 아닌 fourth이다. (three-forth → three-fourths)

---

## CHAPTER 11 부사
Adverbs

본문 _ p.228

## PRACTICE 1

| | | | |
|---|---|---|---|
| **1** | kind | **2** | gladly |
| **3** | loud | **4** | proudly, new |
| **5** | terribly | **6** | quietly |
| **7** | Luckily, easily | **8** | carefully |
| **9** | beautiful | **10** | Suddenly, heavily |

> **1** 명사 teacher의 앞에서 수식하는 형용사 kind가 알맞다.
> **2** 동사 opened를 수식하는 부사 gladly가 알맞다.
> **3** '(소리가) 큰'이라는 뜻의 형용사 loud가 알맞다.
> **4** 동사 showed를 수식하는 부사 proudly와 명사 smartphone을 수식하는 형용사 new가 알맞다.
> **5** 형용사 sick을 수식하는 부사 terribly가 알맞다.
> **6** 동사 opened를 수식하는 부사 quietly가 알맞다.
> **7** 문장 전체를 수식하는 부사 Luckily와 동사 win을 수식하는 부사 easily가 알맞다.
> **8** 동사 listened를 수식하는 부사 carefully가 알맞다.
> **9** 명사 flower를 수식하는 형용사 beautiful이 알맞다.
> **10** 문장 전체를 수식하는 부사 Suddenly와 동사 rain을 수식하는 부사 heavily가 알맞다.

## PRACTICE 2

| | | | |
|---|---|---|---|
| **1** | nicely | **2** | beautifully |
| **3** | happily | **4** | clearly |
| **5** | differently | **6** | kindly |
| **7** | carefully | **8** | heavily |
| **9** | usually | **10** | really |
| **11** | quickly | **12** | gladly |
| **13** | luckily | **14** | surprisingly |
| **15** | prettily | **16** | strongly |
| **17** | dangerously | **18** | noisily |
| **19** | loudly | **20** | easily |
| **21** | newly | **22** | regularly |
| **23** | slowly | **24** | sadly |
| **25** | bravely | **26** | greatly |
| **27** | specially | **28** | quietly |
| **29** | similarly | **30** | badly |

## PRACTICE 3

| | | | |
|---|---|---|---|
| **1** happy | | **2** usually | |
| **3** great | | **4** really | |
| **5** easy | | **6** suddenly | |
| **7** safe | | **8** surprisingly | |
| **9** important | | **10** quietly | |
| **11** sadly | | **12** bravely | |

> **1, 3** feel, taste와 같은 감각 동사 뒤에는 보어로 형용사가 와야 한다.
> **2, 4, 6, 8, 10, 11, 12** 의미상 동사를 수식할 수 있는 부사가 들어가는 것이 알맞다.
> **5, 7** 주어의 성질이나 상태를 나타내는 주격 보어의 자리이므로 형용사가 알맞다.
> **9** 명사를 수식하므로 형용사가 와야 한다.

## PRACTICE 4

| | | | | | |
|---|---|---|---|---|---|
| **1** A, B | | **2** B, A | | **3** B, A | |
| **4** B, A | | **5** A, B | | **6** B, A | |
| **7** B, A | | **8** A, B | | | |

> [보기]
> A. <u>fast</u> food: 빠른 음식(패스트푸드) → 형용사
> B. go very <u>fast</u>: 아주 빠르게 가다 → 부사
>
> **1** be late: 늦다, 지각하다 → 형용사
> too late: 너무 <u>늦게</u> → 부사
> **2** open early: 일찍 열다 → 부사
> be too early: 너무 이르다 → 형용사
> **3** live long: <u>오래</u> 살다 → 부사
> long line: <u>긴</u> 줄 → 형용사
> **4** study very hard: 아주 <u>열심히</u> 공부하다 → 부사
> be hard: 힘들다 → 형용사
> **5** low price: <u>낮은</u> 가격 → 형용사
> fly low: <u>낮게</u> 날다 → 부사
> **6** drive fast: <u>빠르게</u> 운전하다 → 부사
> fast runner: <u>빠른</u> 달리기 주자 → 형용사
> **7** come daily: <u>날마다</u> 오다 → 부사
> daily paper: <u>매일 나오는</u> 신문(일간지) → 형용사
> **8** high fever: <u>높은</u> 열 → 형용사
> fly high: <u>높이</u> 날다 → 부사

## PRACTICE 5

| | | | |
|---|---|---|---|
| **1** never | | **2** always | |
| **3** often | | **4** never | |
| **5** usually | | **6** often | |
| **7** sometimes | | **8** always | |
| **9** usually | | **10** sometimes | |
| **11** always | | **12** never | |
| **13** usually | | **14** sometimes | |

## PRACTICE 6

**1** Mrs. Kim is ✔ kind.
**2** Do you ✔ surf the Internet?
**3** Shelly ✔ tries to smile.
**4** I have ✔ taken an airplane.
**5** This street is ✔ crowded.
**6** Tom is ✔ at home after 8 o'clock.
**7** It is ✔ foggy in London.
**8** He has ✔ made mistakes.
**9** He ✔ finishes his work on time.
**10** I ✔ go to the French restaurant.
**11** My school ✔ starts at 8:30.
**12** What do you ✔ do on weekends?
**13** She has ✔ been nice to others.
**14** She ✔ walks to school.
**15** The newspaper is ✔ delivered at 7.
**16** You can ✔ count on me.

> **1, 5, 6, 7, 15** 빈도부사는 be동사 뒤에 온다.
> **2, 3, 9, 10, 11, 12, 14** 빈도부사는 일반동사 앞에 온다.
> **4, 8, 13, 16** 빈도부사는 have, can, will과 같은 조동사 뒤에 온다.

## PRACTICE 7

| | | | |
|---|---|---|---|
| **1** either | | **2** too | |
| **3** either | | **4** too | |
| **5** too | | **6** either | |
| **7** too | | **8** either | |
| **9** either | | **10** either | |
| **11** too | | **12** too | |
| **13** either | | **14** too | |
| **15** either | | **16** too | |
| **17** either | | **18** too | |

## PRACTICE 8

| | | | |
|---|---|---|---|
| **1** well | | **2** good | |
| **3** well | | **4** good | |
| **5** well | | **6** well | |
| **7** good | | **8** good | |
| **9** good | | **10** well | |
| **11** well | | **12** good | |
| **13** good | | **14** well | |

Ch
**11**
부
사

**1, 3, 6, 10, 11, 14** 동사를 수식하는 부사가 필요한 자리이므로 well이 알맞다.

- **1** sleep well: 잘 자다
- **3** eat well: 잘 먹다
- **6** know well: 잘 알다
- **10** do well: 잘 하다 *do well on: ~을 잘하다, 잘 보다
- **11** speak well: 잘 말하다
- **14** read well: 잘 읽다

**2, 4, 9, 12** be동사 뒤 주격 보어 자리이므로 형용사 good이 알맞다.

**5** get well은 '병이 나아지다'라는 뜻이다. 이때의 get은 '~한 상태로 변하다, ~한 상태가 되다'라는 뜻의 상태 변화를 나타내는 2형식 동사이므로 뒤에 형용사가 와야 한다. 따라서 get well의 well은 feel well에서처럼 '건강한, 몸이 좋은'이라는 뜻의 형용사로 쓰인 것이다.

**7, 8** 명사를 수식하는 형용사 자리이므로 good이 알맞다.

- **7** good place: 좋은 장소
- **8** good painter: 훌륭한 화가(그림을 잘 그리는 사람)

**13** 「감각동사 look+형용사」는 '~하게 보이다, ~처럼 보이다'라는 의미로, 형용사가 주격 보어 역할을 하므로 good이 알맞다.

* look good on: ~에게 잘 어울리다

## PRACTICE 9

| **1** on | **2** off | **3** on | **4** away |
|---|---|---|---|
| **5** up | **6** back | **7** off | **8** on |
| **9** back | **10** on | | |

**1** put on: 입다[쓰다/끼다]
**2** turn off: (전원을) 끄다
**3, 8** try on: 입어[신어]보다
**4** throw away: 버리다
**5** pick up: (차로) 데리러 가다
**6, 9** bring back: 돌려주다
**7** take off: 벗다
**10** turn on: (전원을) 켜다

## PRACTICE 10

| **1** turn on the radio | **2** try them on |
|---|---|
| **3** turn off the alarm | **4** picked up Bob |
| **5** threw away her hat | **6** took his raincoat off |
| **7** wait for me | **8** put on her necklace |
| **9** turn it on | **10** throw them away |
| **11** give him up | **12** write her name down |
| **13** Look at her | |

**1, 2, 3, 4, 5, 6, 8, 9, 10, 11, 12** turn on, try on, turn off, pick up, throw away, take off, put on, give up, write down은 모두 「타동사+부사」로 이루어진 동사구이다. 「타동사+부사」로 이루어진 동사구의 목적어로 일반명사가 올 때는 「타동사+명사+부사」와 「타동사+부사+명사」의 어순이 모두 가능하지만, 목적어가 대명사인 경우에는 반드시 「타동사+대명사+부사」 어순으로 써야 한다.

**7, 13** wait for, look at은 「자동사+전치사」 구조로 「자동사+전치사+목적어」의 어순만 가능하다.

## PRACTICE 11

**1** Where is my bag?

**2** How do you like this food?

**3** When is her birthday?

**4** Why did you call me?

**5** How is the weather in Seoul?

**6** When did Minsu finish the work?

**7** Why doesn't he like the book?

**8** Where are you going to travel?

**9** Where did you eat lunch?

**10** Why were you running?

**1, 8, 9** 장소/지역을 나타내는 표현으로 답하고 있으므로 의문부사 Where로 시작하는 의문문을 쓴다.
**2** How do you like 표현을 사용하여 '~는 어때?'라는 뜻의 질문을 한다.
**3, 6** 시간을 나타내는 표현으로 답하고 있으므로 When으로 시작하는 의문문을 쓴다.
**4, 7, 10** Because로 시작하는 '왜냐하면 ~이다'라고 답하고 있으므로 Why로 시작하는 의문문을 만든다.
**5** How is the weather 표현을 사용하여 날씨를 묻는 질문을 한다.

## PRACTICE 12

| **1** long | **2** old | **3** much |
|---|---|---|
| **4** often | **5** far | **6** much |
| **7** tall | **8** many | **9** many |
| **10** long | **11** old | **12** long |
| **13** far | **14** tall | **15** often |

**1, 10, 12** 소요 시간/기간으로 답하고 있으므로 How long(얼마나 오래)이 알맞다.
**2** 나이로 답하고 있으므로 How old(몇 살)가 알맞다.
**3, 6** 금액으로 답하고 있으므로 How much(금액이 얼마인지)가 알맞다.
**4, 15** every day(매일), once a week(일주일에 한 번) 같은 빈도 표현으로 답하고 있으므로 How often(얼마나 자주)이 알맞다.
**5, 13** 거리로 답하고 있으므로 How far(얼마나 먼)가 알맞다.
**7** 사람의 키로 답하고 있으므로 How tall(얼마나 큰)이 알맞다.
**8, 9** 셀 수 있는 명사(shoes, dog, cat)의 수량으로 답하고 있으므로 How many(얼마나 많은)가 알맞다.
**11** B: About ten years old.(약 10년 정도 되었어.)라고 답하고 있으므로 질문은 '이 탁자가 얼마나 오래 되었니?'가 되는 것이 적절하다. How old는 '얼마나 오래 되었는지'의 뜻도 가지고 있다.
**14** B: It has 27 stories.(그것은 27층이야.)라고 답하고 있으므로 질문은 '건물이 얼마나 높니?'가 되는 것이 적합하다. story는 명사로 '(건물의) 층'이라는 뜻도 갖고 있다.

## PRACTICE 13

**1** ⓓ  **2** ⓒ  **3** ⓐ  **4** ⓔ  **5** ⓑ

**1** When 의문문이므로 시점을 밝힌 응답이 알맞다. → ⓓ 3일 후에
**2** Why 의문문이므로 이유를 밝힌 응답이 알맞다. → ⓒ 병원에 가야 하기 때문에
**3** How often 의문문이므로 빈도를 제시한 응답이 알맞다. → ⓐ 하루에 세 번
**4** Where 의문문이므로 장소나 위치를 제시한 응답이 알맞다. → ⓔ 소파 뒤에
**5** How old 의문문이므로 나이를 제시한 응답이 알맞다. → ⓑ 세 살이다

## 📝 중간·기말고사 대비문제 **정답**  본문 _ p.242

**1** ①  **2** ①  **3** ④  **4** ④  **5** ⑤  **6** ②
**7** well  **8** he never drinks coffee at night
**9** ②  **10** ④  **11** ⑤  **12** ②  **13** ⑤
**14** (1) Why did you go there? (2) How long did you stay there?  **15** ③  **16** How often do you go  **17** ⑤  **18** ②  **19** ⑤  **20** too  **21** ④
**22** How  **23** ①  **24** ⑤  **25** ①  **26** ②
**27** ④  **28** ④  **29** ②  **30** ③  **31** ⑤
**32** (L)uckily  **33** ④  **34** ⑤  **35** (1) often (2) usually (3) sometimes (4) never (5) always

## 중간·기말고사 대비문제 **해설**

**1** 빈도부사는 일반동사(dream) 앞에 위치한다.
**2** 교통수단으로 대답하고 있으므로 방법/수단을 묻는 의문부사 How가 와야 한다.
**3** Ⓐ many는 셀 수 있는 명사의 복수형을 수식한다. 여기서 time은 '횟수, ~번'이라는 뜻의 셀 수 있는 명사이므로 복수형으로 쓴다. (time → times)
　Ⓑ 한 문장에서 접속사 없이 동사가 연달아 올 수 없다. 밑줄 친 부분은 동사의 목적어 자리이므로 like의 목적어가 될 수 있는 to부정사나 동명사로 써야 한다. like는 to부정사와 동명사 모두 목적어로 쓸 수 있는 동사이다. (play → to play[playing])
　Ⓒ water는 셀 수 없는 명사이다. 셀 수 없는 명사의 앞에는 부정관사를 쓰지 않는다.
　(drink a water → drink water)
　Ⓔ '시간이 있다'는 뜻은 정관사 the를 쓰지 않고 「have time」으로 쓴다.
　(have the time → have time)

**4** try on '입어보다'　　turn on '켜다'
**5** 장소로 대답하고 있으므로 장소를 묻는 의문부사 Where가 와야 한다.
**6** too와 either는 '또한, 역시'의 뜻이며, either는 부정문에, too는 긍정문에 쓴다. also도 '역시'라는 뜻이지만 부정문에 쓰지 않고, 보통 be동사와 조동사 뒤, 일반동사 앞에 온다.
**7** '잘, 훌륭하게'의 뜻을 나타내는 부사 well은 동사(cooks)를 수식한다.
**8** 빈도부사 never(절대로 ~않다)를 넣어 영작하는 문제이다. 빈도부사는 일반동사 앞에 쓴다.
**9** nice-nicely는 형용사-부사의 관계이다. '멋진-멋지게'
　② 형용사-부사: careful '주의 깊은'- carefully '주의 깊게'
　① 명사-형용사: friend '친구'- friendly '친근한'
　③ 형용사-형용사: elder '나이가 더 많은'- elderly '연세가 드신'
　④ 명사-형용사: week '주'- weekly '매주의'
　⑤ 명사-부사: luck '행운'- luckily '운 좋게'
**10** 25달러라는 가격으로 답하고 있으므로 가격을 묻는 표현 How much ~?가 적절하다.
**11** Why don't we ~?는 '~하는 게 어때?'라는 뜻으로 쓰이는 관용표현이며, 장소를 물을 때는 의문부사 Where를 쓴다.
**12** turn off '끄다'　　take off '벗다'
**13** ⑤ 빈도부사는 be동사 뒤에 위치한다.
　(always is → is always)
**14** (1) 이유를 대답하고 있으므로 이유를 묻는 의문부사 Why를 쓴다.
　(2) 머문 기간을 대답하고 있으므로 기간을 묻는 How long을 쓴다.
**15** too와 either는 '또한, 역시'라는 뜻을 가지고 있지만 too는 긍정문에서, either는 부정문에서 쓰인다.
　(too → either)
**16** 「How+부사」는 정도를 물을 때 사용되며, How often은 붙여 쓸 때 '얼마나 자주'라는 의미이다.
　A: 너는 얼마나 자주 쇼핑몰에 가니?
　B: 나는 거기에 한 달에 세 번 가.
**17** ⑤ look at은 '~를 보다'라는 뜻의 「자동사+전치사」로 이루어진 동사구이다. 전치사의 목적어는 항상 전치사의 뒤에 써야 한다.
　(looked it at → looked at it)

**18** How long ~?은 기간 또는 걸리는 시간을 묻는 표현이므로 거리를 나타내는 It is 530km.와 어울리지 않는다. 거리를 묻는 표현은 How far ~?이다.

**19** What time은 때를 묻는 의문부사 When과 바꾸어 쓸 수 있다.

**20** also는 '또한, 역시'의 뜻으로 문장의 끝에 나오는 too와 같은 의미로 쓰인다.

**21** ⓐ violin과 같은 악기명의 앞에는 정관사를 써야 한다. (violin → the violin)

ⓑ 주어(Mom and my sister)가 복수이므로 동사에 –s를 붙이지 않는다. (plays → play)

ⓒ 빈도부사는 일반동사의 앞에 쓴다.
(goes often → often goes)

ⓔ hope는 목적어로 to부정사를 쓰는 동사이다.
(having → to have)

**22** • How long은 기간이나 걸린 시간을 묻는 표현이다.
• 방법을 묻는 의문부사 How가 와야 한다.

**23** ⓓ 동사 walked를 수식하는 부사 slowly의 쓰임은 적절하다.

ⓐ something과 같이 -thing으로 끝나는 대명사를 수식할 때 형용사는 대명사 뒤에 위치한다.
(wrong something → something wrong)

ⓑ 인식의 상태를 나타내는 동사 know는 진행형으로 쓰지 않는다. (am knowing → know)

ⓒ 타동사+부사 구에서 목적어가 대명사일 때는 「동사+목적어+부사」의 어순으로 써야 한다.
(pick up us → pick us up)

ⓔ 동사 swim을 수식하고 있으므로 형용사 good이 아닌 부사 well을 써야 한다. (good → well)

**24** 의문사로 시작하는 의문문은 Yes나 No로 대답할 수 없으며, 방법/수단을 묻는 How에 어울리는 대답은 by train으로 답한 ⑤번이다.

**25** ① '아침에 버스가 매우 늦게 도착했다'라는 의미가 되어야 하므로 '늦게'라는 뜻의 부사 late를 써야 한다. lately는 '최근에'라는 뜻의 부사이다.
(lately → late)

**26** 뉴욕이라는 장소로 대답했으므로 장소를 묻는 의문부사 Where가 와야 한다.

**27** 형용사-형용사의 관계인 ④를 제외한 나머지는 형용사-부사의 관계이다.

④ • This is a ⓐhard problem to solve. 이것은 해결하기 힘든 문제이다.
• The ground is very ⓑhard. 땅이 매우 단단하다.

① • The box is too ⓐ heavy to lift. 그 상자는 들기에 너무 무겁다.
• It rained ⓑ heavily last night. 지난밤 비가 아주 많이 내렸다.

② • She is ⓐ happy with her new job. 그녀는 새 직장에 만족한다.
• They lived ⓑ happily ever after. 그들은 영원히 행복하게 살았다.

③ • The turtle moves at a ⓐ slow speed. 그 거북이는 느린 속도로 움직인다.
• The baby crawled ⓑ slowly across the floor. 그 아기는 바닥을 가로질러 천천히 기었다.

⑤ • He was ⓐ lucky to find his lost wallet. 그의 잃어버린 지갑을 찾다니 그는 운이 좋았다.
• ⓑ Luckily, no one was injured in the accident. 다행히도, 그 사고에서 아무도 다치지 않았다.

**28** (A) '그녀는 노래를 잘 부른다'의 뜻이 되려면 동사 sings를 수식하는 부사 well이 들어가야 한다.

(B) '그녀는 유명한 가수이다'의 뜻이 되려면 명사 singer를 수식하는 형용사 famous가 들어가야 한다.

(C) '나는 최근에 그녀의 노래에 빠졌다'의 뜻이 되려면 동사구 am into를 수식하는 부사 lately가 들어가야 한다.

**29** either는 부정문에 쓰여 '또한, 역시'의 뜻으로 앞 문장에 대한 동의를 나타낸다. A가 공포 영화를 보는 것을 좋아하지 않는다는 말에 B도 동의하고 있으므로 I don't, either.는 I don't like watching horror movies.를 나타낸다.

**30** • B가 기분이 안 좋은 이유(My puppy is sick.)를 말하고 있으므로 첫 번째 빈칸에는 이유를 묻는 의문부사 Why가 들어가야 한다.
• 'How about ~ing?' 표현이 쓰여서 '~하는 게 어때?'라는 의미를 나타낸다.

**31** ⑤ fast는 형용사와 부사의 형태가 같다.
(fastly → fast)

**32** lucky의 부사형은 luckily이다.

**33** (A) It's not 뒤에는 주격 보어로 명사나 형용사가 올 수 있다. 문맥상 쉽지 않다는 내용이 들어가야 하므로 형용사인 easy가 와야 한다.

(B) 문맥상 올해 말쯤 자신이 제일 좋아하는 곡을 '아름답게' 연주할 수 있기를 바란다는 내용이 와야

하므로 동사 play를 수식하는 부사 beautifully가
답이다.

**34** ⑤ Lucy는 목요일에 버스를 타고 학교에 가므로
'Lucy는 결코 학교에 버스를 타고 가지 않는다.'는
표의 내용과 다르다.

**35** 일주일에 세 번은 often(종종), 일주일에 다섯 번은
usually(대개), 일주일에 한 번은 sometimes(때때
로), 전혀 하지 않는 것은 never(결코 ~않는), 늘 하는
것은 always(항상)의 빈도부사를 쓴다.

---

## CHAPTER 12 비교구문
Comparisons

본문 _ p.249

### PRACTICE 1

| | | | |
|---|---|---|---|
| **1** | kinder, kindest | **2** | larger, largest |
| **3** | taller, tallest | **4** | louder, loudest |
| **5** | safer, safest | **6** | weaker, weakest |
| **7** | greater, greatest | **8** | softer, softest |
| **9** | lower, lowest | **10** | huger, hugest |
| **11** | smarter, smartest | **12** | cheaper, cheapest |
| **13** | nicer, nicest | **14** | stronger, strongest |
| **15** | cleaner, cleanest | **16** | faster, fastest |

### PRACTICE 2

| | | | |
|---|---|---|---|
| **1** | hotter, hottest | **2** | lighter, lightest |
| **3** | milder, mildest | **4** | noisier, noisiest |
| **5** | heavier, heaviest | **6** | fatter, fattest |
| **7** | wiser, wisest | **8** | sunnier, sunniest |
| **9** | dirtier, dirtiest | **10** | cooler, coolest |
| **11** | warmer, warmest | **12** | happier, happiest |
| **13** | hungrier, hungriest | **14** | bigger, biggest |
| **15** | wetter, wettest | **16** | tastier, tastiest |
| **17** | stricter, strictest | **18** | uglier, ugliest |
| **19** | prettier, prettiest | **20** | harder, hardest |

### PRACTICE 3

**1** busier, busiest
**2** more interesting, most interesting
**3** more beautiful, most beautiful
**4** brighter, brightest
**5** more seriously, most seriously
**6** more careful, most careful
**7** friendlier, friendliest

**8** more important, most important
**9** gladder, gladdest
**10** more expensive, most expensive
**11** lovelier, loveliest
**12** more quickly, most quickly
**13** more useful, most useful
**14** quieter, quietest
**15** more exciting, most exciting
**16** more special, most special
**17** sooner, soonest
**18** more difficult, most difficult
**19** closer, closest
**20** more helpful, most helpful
**21** more popular, most popular
**22** easier, easiest
**23** more colorful, most colorful
**24** tougher, toughest
**25** more curious, most curious
**26** more delicious, most delicious
**27** nearer, nearest
**28** more dangerous, most dangerous
**29** more diligent, most diligent
**30** luckier, luckiest

### PRACTICE 4

**1** darker, darkest
**2** older, oldest
**3** more boring, most boring
**4** slower, slowest
**5** more terrible, most terrible

**6** more tired, most tired

**7** more various, most various

**8** smaller, smallest

**9** worse, worst

**10** more wonderful, most wonderful

**11** better, best

**12** costlier, costliest

**13** more similar, most similar

**14** later, latest

**15** richer, richest

**16** further, furthest

**17** cuter, cutest

**18** younger, youngest

**19** farther/further, farthest/furthest

**20** more famous, most famous

**21** thinner, thinnest

**22** more faithful, most faithful

**23** slimmer, slimmest

**24** worse, worst

**25** more patient, most patient

**26** thicker, thickest

**27** more useless, most useless

**28** more handsome[handsomer],
most handsome[handsomest]

**29** thirstier, thirstiest

**30** worse, worst

**31** more heavily, most heavily

**32** deeper, deepest

**33** angrier, angriest

**34** latter, last

**35** elder, eldest

**36** colder, coldest

**37** more, most

**38** more different, most different

**39** more foolish, most foolish

**40** less, least

**41** more easily, most easily

**42** more peaceful, most peaceful

**43** more, most

**44** more generous, most generous

## PRACTICE 5

**1** as well as          **2** as small as

**3** not as[so] tall as          **4** as interesting as

**5** not as[so] angry as          **6** as clever as

**7** not as[so] slow as          **8** as cold as

**9** as simple as          **10** not as[so] loud as

## PRACTICE 6

**1** isn't as[so] old as

**2** is as expensive as

**3** isn't as[so] long as

**4** is as high as

**5** don't clean my room as[so] often as

**6** is as huge as

**7** can't go as[so] fast as

**8** is as honest as

**9** isn't as[so] thick as

**10** doesn't look as[so] fresh as

> **1, 3, 5, 7, 9, 10** 비교하는 두 대상의 정도에 차이가 있으므로 '~만큼 …하지 않은'이라는 뜻이 되도록 「not as[so]+원급+as」 구문을 사용한다.
> not as[so] old as: ~만큼 나이가 많지 않은
> not as[so] long as: ~만큼 길지 않은
> not as[so] often as: ~만큼 자주는 아닌
> not as[so] fast as: ~만큼 빨리는 아닌
> not as[so] thick as: ~만큼 두껍지 않은
> not as[so] fresh as: ~만큼 신선하지 않은
> **2, 4, 6, 8** 비교하는 두 대상의 정도가 같으므로 '~만큼 …한'이라는 뜻이 되도록 「as+원급+as」를 사용한다.
> as expensive as: ~만큼 비싼
> as high as: ~만큼 높은
> as huge as: ~만큼 거대한
> as honest as: ~만큼 정직한

## PRACTICE 7

**2** heavier than

**3** better than

**4** cooler than

**5** more careful than

**6** younger than

**7** more interesting than

**8** more beautiful than

**9** more quickly than

**10** brighter than

**11** newer than

**12** more modern than

**13** higher than

**14** more difficult than

**15** more useful than

**16** quieter than

**17** more intelligent than

**18** worse than

> **2** heavier than yours: 네 것보다 무거운
> **3** better than hers: 그녀의 것보다 더 나은
> (good-better-best)
> **4** cooler than this week: 이번 주보다 더 시원한
> **5** more careful than her sister: 그녀의 언니보다 더 주의 깊은
> **6** younger than Minho: 민호보다 더 어린
> **7** more interesting than the play: 그 연극보다 더 흥미로운
> **8** more beautiful than Mr. Kim's: 김 선생님의 것보다 더 아름다운
> **9** more quickly than Miss Ford: Ford 씨보다 더 빠르게
> **10** brighter than before: 이전보다 더 밝은
> **11** newer than mine: 내 것보다 더 새로운
> **12** more modern than that one: 저것보다 더 현대적인
> **13** higher than our voices: 우리의 목소리보다 더 높은
> **14** more difficult than eating: 먹는 것보다 더 어려운
> **15** more useful than butterflies: 나비보다 더 유용한
> **16** quieter than the cafeteria: 구내식당보다 더 조용한
> **17** more intelligent than dogs: 개보다 더 지적인
> **18** worse than no excuse: 변명을 안 하는 것보다 더 나쁜
> (bad-worse-worst)

## PRACTICE 8

**1** more beautiful **2** kind

**3** smaller **4** much

**5** popular **6** slower

**7** busy **8** less

**9** cheaper **10** cute

**11** older **12** farther

**13** often **14** easier

**15** cleaner **16** brave

**17** dirtier

> **1, 3, 6, 8, 9, 11, 12, 14, 15, 17** 괄호 뒤에 'than+비교 대상'이 왔으므로 「-er than」 또는 「more+원급+than」 형태의 비교급 구문이 되어야 한다. 8번의 little(little-less-least)과 12번의 far(far-farther-farthest)는 불규칙 변화하는 단어들이다.
> **2, 4, 5, 7, 10, 13, 16** 괄호 앞뒤에 as가 왔으므로 「as+원급+as」 구문이 되어야 한다. 4번의 much의 비교급은 more, 최상급은 most이다.

## PRACTICE 9

**1** poorer and poorer

**2** more and more handsome
[handsomer and handsomer]

**3** redder and redder[more and more red]

**4** more and more boring

**5** better and better

**6** worse and worse

**7** quieter and quieter

**8** fatter and fatter

**9** more and more heavily

**10** cheaper and cheaper

> **1** become poorer and poorer: 점점 더 가난해지다
> **2** become more and more handsome: 점점 더 잘생겨지다
> **3** turn redder and redder: 점점 더 빨갛게 변하다
> **4** get more and more boring: 점점 더 지루해지다
> **5** get better and better: 점점 더 나아지다
> **6** get worse and worse: 점점 더 나빠지다
> **7** become quieter and quieter: 점점 더 조용해지다
> **8** grow fatter and fatter: 점점 더 살이 찌다
> **9** rain more and more heavily: 점점 더 비가 심하게 오다
> **10** become cheaper and cheaper: 점점 더 싸지다
> *become/turn/get/grow+형용사: ~해지다, (~한 상태로) 변하다

## PRACTICE 10

**1** far more important

**2** a lot better

**3** much stricter

**4** even harder

**5** much more helpful

**6** still thinner

**7** even stronger

**8** far more convenient

**9** still safer

**10** a lot more

> **1** far more important than money: 돈보다 훨씬 더 중요한
> **2** a lot better than her sister's: 그녀의 언니의 것보다 훨씬 더 나은
> **3** much stricter rules than his: 그의 것보다 훨씬 더 엄격한 규칙
> **4** even harder than he did: 그가 했던 것보다 훨씬 더 열심히
> **5** much more helpful to me than they were: 나에게 그들보다 훨씬 더 도움이 되는
> **6** still thinner than his: 그의 것보다 훨씬 더 얇은
> **7** even stronger than it did in the morning: 아침에 그것이 그랬던 것보다 훨씬 더 세게
> **8** far more convenient than going to the mall: 쇼핑몰에 가는 것보다 훨씬 더 편리한
> **9** still safer than that one: 저것보다 훨씬 더 안전한
> **10** a lot more rain than Rome: 로마보다 훨씬 더 많은 비

## PRACTICE 11

**1** O　**2** X　**3** O　**4** X

**5** X　**6** O　**7** O　**8** O

Ch **12** 비교구문

**9** O    **10** X    **11** X    **12** X

> **2, 5, 10, 12** even, a lot, much, far 같은 부사는 비교급 앞에서 '훨씬, 더욱'의 뜻으로 쓰여 비교급을 강조한다. 따라서 밑줄 친 부분을 원급을 수식하는 very로 바꿔야 한다.
> **4, 11** very는 '매우'의 뜻으로 형용사나 부사의 원급을 수식한다. 따라서 비교급 앞에서 '훨씬'의 뜻으로 쓰여 비교급을 강조하는 even, much, still, far, a lot 같은 부사로 바꿔야 한다.

## PRACTICE 12

**2** the most important    **3** the youngest

**4** the happiest    **5** the worst

**6** the heaviest    **7** the brightest

**8** the poorest    **9** the highest

**10** the best    **11** the least

**12** the fastest    **13** the most interesting

**14** the latest    **15** the thickest

**16** the busiest    **17** the most popular

**18** the hardest    **19** the largest

**20** the most exciting

> 최상급 뒤에 in이나 of가 이끄는 전치사구가 와서 비교의 대상을 한정하는 경우가 많은데, 앞뒤 문맥상으로 그 내용을 미루어 짐작할 수 있는 경우에는 'the+최상급' 뒤에 오는 명사를 생략하기도 한다.
> **1** the coldest day of the year: 일 년 중 가장 추운 날
> **2** the most important person in the group: 그 집단에서 가장 중요한 사람
> **3** the youngest (child) of his brothers: 그의 형제들 중에서 가장 막내 (아이)
> **4** the happiest day of his life: 그의 인생에서 가장 행복한 날
> **5** the worst choice of my life: 내 인생에서 가장 나쁜 선택
> **6** the heaviest (bag) of them all: 그것들 모두 중에서 가장 무거운 (가방)
> **7** the brightest (room) in this house: 이 집에서 가장 밝은 (방)
> **8** the poorest people in the village: 그 마을에서 가장 가난한 사람들
> **9** the highest mountain in the world: 세계에서 가장 높은 산
> **10** the best student in her class: 그녀의 반에서 가장 우수한 학생
> **11** the least work in the team: 그 팀에서 가장 적은 일
> **12** the fastest (animal) of all animals: 모든 동물 중에서 가장 빠른 (동물)
> **13** the most interesting (picture) of them all: 그것들 모두 중에서 가장 흥미로운 (그림)
> **14** the latest news: 최신 뉴스(late-later-latest)
> **15** the thickest tree in the garden: 정원에서 가장 굵은 나무
> **16** the busiest day of the week: 일주일 중 가장 바쁜 날
> **17** the most popular sport worldwide: 세계적으로 가장 인기 있는 스포츠
> **18** the hardest worker of all insects: 모든 곤충 중 가장 열심히 일하는 일꾼
> **19** the largest desert on the planet: 지구상에서 가장 큰 사막
> **20** the most exciting day of the trip: 여행 중 가장 신나는 날

## PRACTICE 13

**1** one of the most exciting festivals

**2** one of the nicest restaurants

**3** one of the highest scores

**4** One of the most beautiful cities

**5** one of the biggest animals

**6** one of the most handsome[the handsomest] students

**7** one of the most pleasant[the pleasantest] presents

**8** One of the most helpful insects

**9** one of the strongest boys

**10** One of the most faithful animals

**11** One of the most exciting sports

**12** one of the most expensive things

> 「one of the+최상급」 뒤에는 복수 명사가 와서 '가장 ~한 것들 중의 하나'라는 뜻을 나타낸다.
> **1** one of the most exciting festivals: 가장 신나는 축제들 중의 하나
> **2** one of the nicest restaurants: 가장 멋진 식당들 중의 하나
> **3** one of the highest scores: 가장 높은 점수들 중의 하나
> **4** one of the most beautiful cities: 가장 아름다운 도시들 중의 하나
> **5** one of the biggest animals: 가장 큰 동물들 중의 하나
> **6** one of the most handsome students: 가장 잘생긴 학생들 중의 하나
> **7** one of the most pleasant presents: 가장 기분 좋은 선물들 중의 하나
> **8** one of the most helpful insects: 가장 유용한 곤충들 중의 하나
> **9** one of the strongest boys: 가장 강한 소년들 중의 하나
> **10** one of the most faithful animals: 가장 충직한 동물들 중의 하나
> **11** one of the most exciting sports: 가장 재미있는 운동들 중의 하나
> **12** one of the most expensive things: 가장 비싼 것들 중의 하나

## PRACTICE 14

**1** Ted    **2** Cathy    **3** John

**4** Cathy    **5** John

> **1** 원급 as tall as(~만큼 키가 큰)로 비교하고 있으므로 빈칸에는 John과 키가 같은 Ted가 알맞다.
> **2** 비교급 taller than(~보다 키가 큰)으로 비교하고 있으므로 빈칸에는 John보다 키가 작은 Cathy가 알맞다.
> **3** not as old as(~만큼 나이가 많지 않은)가 쓰였다. 즉, 'Ted는 _______만큼 나이가 많지 않다'는 뜻이므로 빈칸에는 John(15세)이 와야 한다.
> **4** 비교급 younger than(~보다 어린)으로 비교하고 있으므로 빈칸에는 Ted보다 어린 Cathy가 알맞다.
> **5** 최상급 the oldest of(~ 중에서 가장 나이가 든)를 이용해 비교하고 있으므로 빈칸에는 셋 중 나이가 가장 많은 John이 알맞다.

## PRACTICE 15

| | | | | | |
|---|---|---|---|---|---|
| **1** | fattest | **2** | brightest | **3** | better |
| **4** | difficult | **5** | cool | **6** | much |
| **7** | attracts | **8** | biggest | **9** | quieter |
| **10** | men | **11** | healthy | **12** | even |
| **13** | sports | **14** | more | **15** | is |

**1, 2, 8** the의 수식을 받으며, 뒤에 비교의 대상을 한정하는 in, of 가 이끄는 전치사구가 왔으므로 최상급이 알맞다.
the fattest of them all: 그들 모두 중에서 가장 뚱뚱한
the brightest star in the sky: 하늘에서 가장 밝은 별
the biggest of all the bees: 모든 벌들 중에서 가장 큰
**3, 9** 뒤에 비교 대상을 나타내는 than이 왔으므로 비교급이 알맞다.
better at math than I am: 나보다 수학을 더 잘하는
quieter than her sister: 그녀의 여동생보다 더 조용한
**4, 5, 6** 앞뒤에 as가 왔으므로 as ~ as …(…만큼 ~한) 구문을 이루는 원급이 알맞다.
as difficult as that one: 저것만큼 어려운
not as cool as that one: 저것만큼 시원하지 않은
not as much money as her friends did: 그녀의 친구들이 (소비)한 것만큼 많지 않은 돈
**7, 15** 「One of the+최상급+복수명사」가 주어로 쓰일 때는 단수 취급하므로 동사도 단수형으로 쓴다.
**10, 13** 「one of the+최상급」 뒤에는 복수 명사가 와서 '가장 ~한 것들 중의 하나'라는 뜻을 나타낸다.
one of the happiest men at the party: 파티에서 가장 행복한 남자들 중 하나
one of the most exciting sports: 가장 신나는 스포츠들 중 하나
**11** very는 '매우'의 뜻으로 형용사나 부사의 원급을 수식한다.
very healthy food: 매우 건강에 좋은 음식
**12** 비교급 앞에는 부사인 even, much, still, far, a lot가 와서 '훨씬, 더욱'의 뜻으로 비교급을 강조한다.
even worse than before: 이전보다 훨씬 나쁜
**14** 「비교급+and+비교급」은 get, become, grow, turn과 같은 동사들과 함께 쓰여 '점점 더 ~하다'라는 뜻을 나타낸다.
become more and more famous: 점점 더 유명해지다

### 📝 중간·기말고사 대비문제 **정답** 본문 _ p.266

**1** ③　**2** ②　**3** ⑤　**4** One of the most famous scientists in history is　**5** ⑤　**6** Dogs are not so big as bears.　**7** (1) as old as (2) as early as
**8** (1) animal → animals (2) of → in　**9** ④
**10** more difficult than　**11** ①　**12** ④　**13** ②
**14** longer and longer　**15** ⑤　**16** ②,⑤
**17** ⑤　**18** ④　**19** (1) the most expensive (2) the largest (3) the most delicious
**20** the cheapest　**21** ②　**22** (1) taller

(2) younger (3) the oldest (4) the heaviest

**23** ⑤　**24** ⑤　**25** ④　**26** (1) better (2) better
**27** ④　**28** ④,⑤　**29** ⑤　**30** ②　**31** ④
**32** ①

## 중간·기말고사 대비문제 해설

**1** ⓐ의 앞에 the가 있는 것으로 보아 ⓐ에는 최상급인 nicest가 들어가고, ⓑ의 뒤에는 than이 있으므로 ⓑ 에는 비교급인 nicer가 들어간다.

**2** funny의 비교급은 funnier이므로 more와 함께 쓸 수 없다.

**3** 「as+원급+as」 '~만큼 …한'
원급의 형태로 '잘, 훌륭하게'라는 뜻의 부사 well이 들어가야 한다.

**4** 「One of the+최상급+복수명사」 '가장 ~한 것들 중에 하나' 표현을 주어 자리에 쓰고 one에 수일치 시켜서 단수 동사 is를 쓴다. famous는 앞에 most를 붙여 최상급을 만든다.

**5** ⑤ brave의 비교급은 braver이다.
(more brave → braver)

**6** 「not so[as]+원급+as」 '~만큼 …하지 않은'

**7** 「as+원급+as」 '~만큼 …한'
*cf.* 원급은 형용사나 부사의 원형을 말한다.

**8** 「one of the+최상급+복수명사+in+장소, 범위」

**9** like A better than B 'B보다 A를 더 좋아한다'

**10** 비교급을 이용한 비교는 「비교급+than」으로 나타낸다. 2음절 이상인 difficult의 비교급은 more difficult이다.

**11** ① beautiful은 2음절 이상이므로 앞에 most를 붙여 최상급을 만든다.
(beautifulest → most beautiful)

**12** ④ Cheese burger가 $3.99로 메뉴 중에서 가장 저렴하다.

**13** ② latter: (순서가) 나중의, 후자의 (latter → later)

**14** '점점 더 ~한'은 「비교급+and+비교급」의 형태로 표현한다.

**15** ① 가장 인기가 없는 것은 농구이다.
(Soccer → Basketball)
② 야구가 농구보다 인기가 많다. (Basketball is more popular than baseball. → Baseball is more popular than basketball.)
③ 축구가 농구보다 인기가 많다. (less → more)

Ch **12** 비교구문

④ 야구는 축구보다 인기가 많다. (Baseball is as popular as soccer. → Baseball is more popular than soccer.)

**16** ① 비교급은 even/much/still/far/a lot으로 강조한다. (very → even[much/still/far/a lot])
③ '점점 더 ~한'은 「비교급+and+비교급」으로 나타내는데 dark의 비교급은 darker이다.
(more and more dark → darker and darker)
④ 비교급을 이용한 비교는 「비교급+than」으로 쓴다. 정관사는 쓰지 않는다. (the heavier → heavier)

**17** ① good의 최상급은 best이다.
(the bestest → the best)
② '가장 ~한 것들 중의 하나'라는 의미를 나타낼 때에는 「one of the+최상급+복수명사」의 문형으로 쓴다. (activity → activities)
③ strong의 최상급은 strongest이다.
(the most strongest → the strongest)
④ difficult의 최상급은 most difficult이다.
(the difficultest → the most difficult)

**18** • '~보다'의 뜻인 than이 있으므로 비교급의 형태 (smarter)가 와야 한다.
*cf.* a lot은 비교급을 강조하는 부사
• 「the+최상급+(명사)+of/in」은 '~중에서 가장 …한'의 표현으로 최상급의 형태(smartest)가 와야 한다.

**19** 「the+최상급+(명사)」 '가장 …한'

**20** cheap(싼)의 최상급은 the cheapest(가장 싼)이다.

**21** 분홍색과 파란색 중 더 좋아하는 색에 대해 물었으므로 대답도 둘 중 더 좋아하는 것으로 답해야 한다. ② 번은 파란색이 더 어둡다는 뜻이므로 대답으로 적절하지 않다.
*A: 분홍색과 파란색 중 어느 색을 더 좋아하니?*
*② 파란색이 분홍색보다 더 어둡다.*

**22** (1),(2) 비교급+than
(3),(4) the+최상급+(명사)+of+복수명사

**23** ① 최상급 뒤에 '~중에서 가장 …한'의 뜻으로 비교의 대상을 한정해 주려면 전치사 of를 사용하여 「the+최상급+(명사)+of+복수명사」의 어순으로 써야 한다. (all movies → of all movies)
② hot의 올바른 비교급은 hotter이다. 단모음+단자음으로 끝나는 1음절 단어이므로 마지막 자음을 하나 더 씀에 유의한다. (more hot → hotter)
③ 원급 비교는 「as+원급+as」의 어순으로 쓴다.

(long as → as long as)
④ '가장 ~한 것들 중의 하나'라는 의미는 「one of the+최상급+복수명사」의 어순으로 쓴다. funny의 최상급은 funniest이다. 자음+y로 끝나는 경우 y를 i로 바꾸고 -est를 붙임에 유의한다.
(funny → funniest)

**24** ⓔ 형용사 confident의 비교급은 more confident로 쓴다. (confidenter → more confident)
ⓐ hobbies를 가리키고 있으므로 복수 대명사 them으로 쓴 것은 적절하다.
ⓑ 형용사 rich의 비교급은 richer이다.
ⓒ everyone은 단수 취급하므로 단수 동사 has의 쓰임은 적절하다.
ⓓ to develop은 목적을 나타내는 부사적 용법으로 쓰였다.
네가 즐기는 취미들을 찾고 그것들을 계속 연습해라. 그것은 처음에는 어려울 수 있지만, 새로운 것들을 배우는 것은 너의 삶을 더 풍요롭게 만든다. 모든 사람은 각자의 발전 속도가 있다는 것을 기억해라. 훌륭한 기술은 발전하는 데 시간을 필요로 하므로 인내심을 가져라. 과정을 즐기면 너는 매일 더 자신 있게 느낄 것이다.

**25** Sena의 수면 시간은 8시간 30분, Yumi의 수면 시간은 8시간으로 Sena가 더 오래 잔다.
④ Sena sleeps longer than Yumi.

**26** well과 good의 비교급은 better이다.

**27** 표에 따르면 C의 용량은 20,000mAh, B의 용량은 10,000mAh이므로, 「비교급+than」을 써서 C의 용량이 더 크다는 사실을 옳게 나타낸 ④가 정답이다.

**28** ④ '~보다'의 뜻인 than이 있으므로 비교급의 형태 (earlier)가 와야 한다. (early → earlier)
⑤ 「one of the+최상급+복수명사」 '가장 ~한 것들 중의 하나'
cheap의 최상급은 cheapest로 쓴다.
(most cheap steak → cheapest steaks)

**29** ⑤ 나의 방이 너의 방보다 깨끗하지 않다고 했으므로 같은 의미의 문장은 '너의 방이 나의 방보다 더 깨끗하다'라는 뜻의 'Your room is cleaner than my room.'이 되어야 한다.
나의 방은 너의 방보다 깨끗하지 않다.
≠ 너의 방은 나의 방만큼 깨끗하다.

**30** • 세 번째 줄의 pretty는 최상급을 prettiest로 쓴다. 자음+y로 끝나는 경우 y를 i로 바꾸고 -est를 붙임

에 유의한다. (most pretty → prettiest)
- 마지막에서 두 번째 줄의 very cheaper에서, 비교급을 수식할 수 있는 것은 even, much, still, far, a lot이다. very는 형용사나 부사의 원급만을 수식한다. (very →even/much/still/far/a lot)

**31** 형용사 busy의 비교급은 busier로 쓴다. than ever는 '그 어느 때보다도'라는 뜻의 부사구로 강조의 의미를 더한다.

여: 안녕, 지훈아. 요즘 너의 학교생활은 어때?

남: 그 어느 때보다도 바쁘지만, 나는 그것을 즐기고 있어.

여: 아, 정말? 무슨 일이 있는데?

남: 나는 학교 축제와 수학 경시대회를 동시에 준비하고 있어!

여: 와, 그게 왜 네가 항상 도서관에 있는지를 설명해 주네.

**32** ② '가장 ~한 것들 중의 하나'라는 의미는 「one of the+최상급+복수명사」의 어순으로 쓴다. (team → teams)

③ 형용사의 뒤에 than이 나오므로 비교급으로 써야 한다. comfortable은 2음절 이상의 단어이므로 앞에 more을 붙여서 비교급을 만든다. 이때 정관사는 쓰지 않는다. (the most comfortable → more comfortable)

④ 최상급 뒤에 '~중에서 가장 …한'의 뜻으로 비교의 대상을 한정해 주려면 전치사 of를 사용하여 「the+최상급+(명사)+of+복수명사」의 어순으로 써야 한다. (at → of)

⑤ 비교의 대상이 My hair이므로 yours 또는 your hair로 받아야 한다. (you → yours[your hair])

---

## CHAPTER 13 접속사
Conjunctions

본문 _ p.272



## PRACTICE 1

| | | | |
|---|---|---|---|
| **1** | but | **2** | and |
| **3** | and | **4** | but |
| **5** | and | **6** | but |
| **7** | and | **8** | but |
| **9** | but | **10** | and |
| **11** | but | **12** | and |

1, 4, 6, 8, 9, 11 앞의 내용과 반대되거나 대조되는 내용을 연결할 때는 접속사 but을 사용한다.
2, 3, 5, 7, 10, 12 앞의 내용과 비슷하거나 대등한 내용을 연결할 때는 접속사 and를 사용한다.

## PRACTICE 2

| | | | |
|---|---|---|---|
| **1** | or | **2** | but |
| **3** | and | **4** | or |
| **5** | or | **6** | and |
| **7** | or | **8** | and |
| **9** | or | **10** | or |
| **11** | and | **12** | or |

1, 4, 9 명령문 다음에 접속사 or를 사용하면 '~해라, 그렇지 않으면 …'이라는 뜻을 나타낸다.
2 앞의 내용과 반대되는 내용을 연결할 때는 접속사 but을 사용한다.
3, 6, 11 명령문 다음에 접속사 and를 사용하면 '~해라, 그러면…'이라는 뜻을 나타낸다.
*succeed: 성공하다
*put on: ~을 입다
5, 7, 10, 12 '둘 중 하나'의 뜻을 표현할 때는 접속사 or를 사용한다.
8 앞의 내용과 대등한 내용을 연결할 때는 접속사 and를 사용한다.

## PRACTICE 3

**1** Turn right, and you will see the post office.

**2** Put salt on your hamburger, or it won't taste good.

**3** Call him, and he will help you.

**4** Take the medicine, or you won't feel better.

**5** Do your homework, and your teacher won't be angry.

**6** Go now, or you can't avoid traffic jams.

**7** Wait a moment, and I'll come and open the door.

**8** Get up early, or you won't see the sunrise.

> **1, 3, 5, 7** If 조건절 구문은 '만약 …한다면, ~할 것이다.'라는 뜻이기 때문에 주절의 조동사를 그대로 사용하여 '명령문, and' 구문으로 바꾸면 된다.
> **2, 4, 6, 8** '명령문+or' 구문을 사용하여 '~해라, 그렇지 않으면…'으로 표현해야 하는데, If 조건절 구문이 '만약 ~한다면, …할 것이다.'라는 뜻이기 때문에 주절의 조동사를 반대로(긍정 → 부정, 부정 → 긍정) 쓰면 된다.
>   **2** 햄버거에 소금을 넣어라, 그렇지 않으면 맛이 없을 것이다.
>   **4** 약을 먹어라, 그렇지 않으면 (몸 상태가) 더 나아지지 않을 것이다.
>   **6** 지금 가라, 그렇지 않으면 교통 체증을 피할 수 없다.
>   **8** 일찍 일어나라, 그렇지 않으면 해가 뜨는 것을 볼 수 없을 것이다.

## PRACTICE 4

**1** but  **2** but  **3** and  **4** so  **5** so
**6** and  **7** so  **8** or  **9** so  **10** or

## PRACTICE 5

**1** Minji believes ✔ there is a God.
**2** The doctor says ✔ I have a cold.
**3** I don't think ✔ it is a nice restaurant.
**4** They wish ✔ they weren't late.
**5** Do you believe ✔ she is kind?
**6** Kate thinks ✔ there is no one at home now.
**7** I wish ✔ I could meet your family soon.
**8** Sumi hopes ✔ she can speak English well.
**9** Did you know ✔ the dolphin is very clever?
**10** People say ✔ only the strongest man survives.

## PRACTICE 6

**1** that it is a nice building
**2** that we will stay there for two days
**3** that the weather would be fine
**4** that Mary is the prettiest girl
**5** that he could do well on his test

## PRACTICE 7

**1** If it snows, we will go skiing.
  We will go skiing if it snows.
**2** Because she got up late, she took a taxi.
  She took a taxi because she got up late.
**3** When I took a walk, I met my best friend.
  I met my best friend when I took a walk.
**4** Because there are no traffic lights, this road is dangerous.
  This road is dangerous because there are no traffic lights.
**5** When it rains hard, my uncle usually listens to music.
  My uncle usually listens to music when it rains hard.
**6** If you go to the supermarket, buy some milk for me.
  Buy some milk for me if you go to the supermarket.
**7** Because I was tired, I went home early.
  I went home early because I was tired.
**8** When he heard the news, he cried.
  He cried when he heard the news.
**9** If you ask Ms. Han about the problem, you'll get the answer.
  You'll get the answer if you ask Ms. Han about the problem.
**10** Because I didn't dress warmly, I have a cold.
  I have a cold because I didn't dress warmly.

## PRACTICE 8

**1** A  **2** C  **3** B  **4** C
**5** B  **6** C  **7** B  **8** A
**9** A  **10** C

> **[보기]**
> (A) As the days get long, the nights get short. (~함에 따라, ~할수록)
>   낮이 길어질수록, 밤은 짧아진다.
> (B) I wore a hat to protect myself from the sun, as my mom did. (~처럼, ~대로)
>   난 엄마가 했던 것처럼 햇빛으로부터 나 자신을 보호하기 위해 모자를 썼다.
> (C) As the book was so sad, he was crying. (~때문에)
>   책이 너무 슬펐기 때문에, 그는 울고 있었다.
>
> **1, 8, 9** 문장에서 as가 '~함에 따라, ~할수록'이라는 뜻으로 사용되었다.
>   **8** grow darker: 어두워지다
>   **9** get brighter: 똑똑해지다
> **2, 4, 6, 10** 문장에서 as가 '~때문에'라는 뜻으로 사용되었다.
>   **6** snow heavily: 눈이 많이 내리다
> **3, 5, 7** 문장에서 as가 '~처럼, ~대로'라는 뜻으로 사용되었다.
>   **3** (속담) 로마에 가면 로마법을 따르라.

## PRACTICE 9

| | | | |
|---|---|---|---|
| **1** | However | **2** | Therefore |
| **3** | Therefore | **4** | For example |
| **5** | However | **6** | Therefore |
| **7** | However | **8** | Therefore |
| **9** | For example | **10** | For example |
| **11** | However | **12** | For example |

**1** 날씨가 화창한 것(It is sunny.)과 약간 추운 것(it is a little cold)은 반대되는 내용이므로 역접, 대조를 나타낼 때 쓰는 접속부사 However가 와야 한다.

**2** 매우 피곤했기 때문에(She was very tired.) 일찍 잠자리에 든 것(she went to bed early)이므로 인과를 나타내는 접속부사 Therefore가 와야 한다.

**3** 돈이 없어서(We didn't have any money.) 집에 걸어가야 했던 것(we had to walk home)이므로 인과를 나타내는 접속부사 Therefore가 와야 한다.

**4** 그녀가 항상 미소 짓고 그녀의 이웃을 돕는다는(she always smiles and helps her neighbors) 내용은 Barbara가 친절하다(Barbara is kind.)는 말의 구체적인 사례이기 때문에 '예를 들어'를 뜻하는 접속부사 For example이 와야 한다.

**5** 시험이 어려웠지만(Jenny's test was difficult.) 그럼에도 불구하고 시험을 잘 봤다(she did very well)는 의미이므로 역접, 대조를 의미하는 접속부사 However가 와야 한다.

**6** 내가 사용된 것들을 버리지 않기 때문에(I don't throw away used things.) 내 방이 오래된 것들로 가득 찬 것(my room is full of old things)이므로 인과를 나타내는 접속부사 Therefore가 와야 한다.

**7** 그가 새로운 컴퓨터를 샀지만(He bought a new computer.) 그럼에도 불구하고 그것이 그의 일에 도움이 되지 못했다(it didn't help him with his work)는 의미이므로 역접, 대조를 의미하는 접속부사 However가 와야 한다.

**8** 많은 이들이 장미를 좋아하기 때문에(Many people like roses.) 내가 그녀에게 장미를 사준 것(I bought some for her.)이므로 인과를 나타내는 접속부사 Therefore가 와야 한다.

**9** 인터넷에서 책과 옷을 주문할 수 있다(you can order books and clothes on it)는 것은 인터넷에서 쇼핑을 할 수 있다(You can shop on the Internet.)는 말의 구체적 예시이므로 '예를 들어'를 뜻하는 접속부사 For example이 와야 한다.

**10** 그가 테니스, 축구 그리고 그 외 여러 운동들을 한다(he plays tennis, soccer, and many other sports)는 것은 그가 운동을 좋아한다(He likes sports.)는 말의 구체적 예시이므로 '예를 들어'를 뜻하는 For example이 와야 한다.

**11** 내가 매우 피곤했지만(I was very tired.) 그럼에도 불구하고 시험공부를 위해 밤새 깨어 있었다(I stayed up all night studying for the test)는 내용이므로 역접, 대조를 나타내는 However가 와야 한다.

**12** 흰 티셔츠와 파란 치마(a white T-shirt and a blue skirt)는 내가 필요로 하는 옷(I need some clothes.)의 구체적 예시이므로 '예를 들어'를 뜻하는 For example이 와야 한다.

## 📑 중간·기말고사 대비문제 정답   본문 _ p.280

| | | | | | | | | | | | | | |
|---|---|---|---|---|---|---|---|---|---|---|---|---|---|
| **1** ② | **2** ③ | **3** ③ | **4** ② | **5** ④ | **6** ③ | **7** ① |
| **8** ⑤ | **9** ③ | **10** ④ | **11** ③ | **12** ③ | **13** ④ |
| **14** ④ | **15** ② | **16** when[as] | **17** ① | **18** ④ |

**19** I do not believe that he told a lie.
**20** (1) like dogs (2) but, doesn't like   **21** ⑤
**22** ③    **23** because[as/since]    **24** ①
**25** ③    **26** ②    **27** ③    **28** ④    **29** ④
**30** ⑤    **31** I couldn't sleep at all because it was noisy outside.[Because it was noisy outside, I couldn't sleep at all.]    **32** ④

## 중간·기말고사 대비문제 해설

**1** 명령문 뒤에 and가 쓰이면 '그러면'의 뜻을 나타낸다.
 • 지금 일어나라, 그러면 너는 아침을 먹을 수 있다.
 • 채소를 더 먹어라, 그러면 너는 건강해질 것이다.

**2** 반대 혹은 대조되는 내용을 연결하는 but이 와야 한다. 그것은 힘든 일이었지만, 우리는 우리 자신을 자랑스럽게 느꼈다.

**3** ③ 빠르게 달리지 않으면 늦을 것이라는 해석이 적절하므로, 명령문 뒤에서 '그렇지 않으면'의 뜻을 나타내는 or이 들어가야 한다.
 Run fast, or you'll be late.
 빠르게 달려라, 그렇지 않으면 너는 늦을 것이다.

**4** 타동사(think) 뒤에 목적어절을 이끄는 that을 쓸 수 있다.

**5** 반대 혹은 대조되는 내용을 말할 때는 But을, 둘 중 하나를 선택하여 말할 때는 or를 쓴다.

**6** 원인이나 이유를 나타내는 접속사 as, because, since가 와야 한다.

**7** ⓐⓒⓔ 타동사의 목적어절을 이끄는 that은 생략이 가능하다.
 ⓑ 문장에서 주어 역할을 하는 명사절을 이끄는 접속사 That은 생략할 수 없다.
 ⓓ that이 앞에 나온 명사 bag과 비교되는 다른 물건을 가리키는 지시대명사로 쓰였으므로 생략할 수 없다.
 ⓕ 멀리 있는 대상을 가리키는 지시대명사 that은 생략할 수 없다.

**8** 원인이나 이유를 나타내는 because가 와야 한다.

**9** 부사 so는 '그만큼, 그렇게'의 뜻을 나타낸다.

Ch<br>**13**<br>접<br>속<br>사

*A:* 왜 너는 어제 그렇게 일찍 잠자리에 들었니?
접속사 so 앞의 절은 원인을, 뒤의 절은 결과를 나타낸다.
*B:* 나는 피곤해서 일찍 잠자리에 들었어.

**10** 명령문 뒤의 and는 '그러면', or은 '그렇지 않으면'의 뜻이다.
④ Get up now, <u>and</u> you won't be late for school. 지금 일어나. <u>그러면</u> 너는 학교에 늦지 않을 거야.

**11** 인과를 나타내는 Therefore가 와야 한다.
더러운 환경은 우리의 몸에 해롭다. 그러므로, 우리는 환경에 대해 더 관심을 가져야 한다.

**12** ③ 지시형용사 that    ①②④⑤ 접속사 that

**13** • 빈칸의 뒤에 명사구(the Dragon team)가 나오므로 '~와 함께'라는 뜻의 전치사 with을 쓰는 것이 적절하다.
• 게임에서 졌지만 실망하지 않았다는 역접의 내용이 이어지므로 접속부사 However가 들어가는 것이 적절하다.
• 빈칸의 뒤에 '최선을 다했기 때문에'라는 이유가 나오므로 이유나 원인을 나타내는 접속사 because가 들어가야 한다. 접속사 because는 뒤에 주어와 동사로 이루어진 절이 오는 반면, because of 뒤에는 명사(구)가 이어진다. 주어진 빈칸의 뒤에는 절(we did our best)이 오므로 접속사 because가 적절하다.
• '지는 것으로부터 더 배운다'는 뜻이 되어야 하고 뒤에 losing이라는 동명사가 오므로, '~부터'라는 뜻의 전치사 from이 적절하다.
• 노력하는 것을 멈추지 않을 것이라는 절과 다음에는 이길 수 있도록 계속할 것이라는 비슷한 내용의 절이 이어지므로 접속사 and가 적절하다.
우리는 지난 화요일에 Dragon 팀과 함께 야구 경기를 했다. 우리는 그 경기에서 졌다. 하지만, 우리는 우리의 최선을 다했기 때문에 실망하지 않았다. 우리는 때때로 승리에서보다 패배에서 더 많이 배운다는 것을 안다. 우리는 노력을 멈추지 않을 것이고, 다음번에 이기기 위해 계속 나아갈 것이다.

**14** ④ she is 뒤에 이어지는 자리는 주격 보어의 자리이다. 부사는 보어가 될 수 없으므로 형용사 kind가 주격 보어로 쓰여야 한다. (kindly → kind)

**15** '만약 ~라면'의 조건을 나타내는 if가 와야 한다. 만약 당신이 영국 사람들에게 혀를 내민다면 그들은 화가 날

것이다. 왜냐하면 영국에서 그것은 "나는 당신을 존경하지 않아요."를 뜻하기 때문이다.

**16** 때를 나타내는 접속사 when[as]을 써야 한다. 내가 학교에서 집으로 돌아왔을 때 엄마는 요리를 하고 계셨다.

**17** 인과를 나타내는 Therefore가 와야 한다.
서울의 지하철 체계는 매우 잘 조직되어 있어서 원하는 곳 어디든지 갈 수 있다. 그러므로 서울에 오는 방문객들은 대개 지하철을 타고 이동한다.

**18** 앞 문장에 대한 예시를 나타내므로 For example이 와야 한다. 수미는 외국어에 능하다. 예를 들어, 그녀는 영어, 중국어, 일본어를 잘 말할 수 있다.

**19** 타동사(believe) 뒤에 목적어절을 이끄는 that을 쓴다.

**20** (1) Minwoo and Dana는 복수 주어이고 둘은 모두 강아지를 좋아하므로 답은 like dogs이다. 민우와 Dana는 개를 좋아한다.
(2) 표에 따르면 Minwoo는 컴퓨터 게임을 좋아하는데, Dana는 좋아하지 않는다(doesn't like). 서로 반대되는 의미의 두 문장을 연결하기 위해 접속사 but을 쓴다. 민우는 컴퓨터 게임을 좋아하지만, Dana는 컴퓨터 게임을 좋아하지 않는다.

**21** 보기와 ⑤ '~처럼, ~대로' (접속사)
①②③ '~할수록' (접속사)
④ '~로서' (전치사)

**22** 조건을 나타내는 부사절에서는 현재시제가 미래시제를 대신하므로 미래의 의미를 나타내더라도 현재시제로 써야 한다.

**23** 이유, 원인을 나타내는 because나 as, since가 와야 한다. 나는 감기에 걸려서 캠핑을 갈 수 없었다.

**24** ⓐⓑ 대등한 내용을 연결하는 and가 적합하다.
ⓒ 둘 중 하나를 선택하여 말할 때는 or를 쓴다.
운동 동아리
야구, 축구, 배구와 같은 더 많은 활동들을 즐기고 싶나요? 지금 바로 와서 우리와 함께해요! 만약 질문이 있다면, 학교 체육관으로 오거나 메일을 보내주세요!

**25** ③ 의문사 when '언제'
①②④⑤ 접속사 when '~할 때'

**26** (a) decide는 to부정사를 목적어로 취하는 동사이므로, to volunteer의 쓰임은 적절하다.
(d) 문장의 주어가 Sumin and her friends이고 현재의 상태를 나타내고 있으므로 동사 meet의 쓰임은 적절하다.
(b) 동사 plan의 현재진행형은 planning이다.

(planing → planning)

(c) 동사 make의 현재진행형은 making이다.
(makeing → making)

(e) 문장의 주어가 Sumin이고 and 앞의 동사 feels
가 현재형이므로 그에 맞춰 plans를 쓰는 것이 적
절하다. (plan → plans)

수민은 학교에서 사회 봉사 활동에 대해 배운다. 그녀
는 지역 요양원에서 자원봉사를 하기로 결심한다. 그녀
는 그녀의 친구들에게 이 아이디어에 대해 이야기한다.
그들 중 세 명이 그녀와 함께 하기로 동의한다. 그들은
함께 방문을 계획한다. 그들은 할 것들의 목록을 만들
고 있다. 방문 당일이 다가온다. 수민과 그녀의 친구들
은 긴장되면서 설레는 마음으로 만난다. 그 노인 입소
자들은 그들을 친절하게 맞아준다. 수민은 소규모 그룹
에게 이야기를 읽어준다. 그녀의 친구들은 게임을 하고
다른 사람들과 이야기를 한다. 두 시간이 빠르게 지나
간다. 그들은 집으로 걸어간다. 수민은 뿌듯함을 느끼며
조만간 다시 가기로 계획한다.

**27** 보기와 ①②④⑤ 접속사 that
③ 지시형용사 that

**28** 보기와 ①②③⑤ '~ 때문에'
④ '~대로'

**29** ⓐ 역접, 대조를 나타내는 접속부사 However가 와야
한다. Because와 As는 원인이나 이유를 나타내는
접속사이다. 지호는 수업 중에 자신의 특별한 재능
에 대해 발표를 해야 했지만 자신의 특별한 재능을
떠올릴 수 없었다.

ⓑ 시간을 나타내고 두 절을 연결할 수 있는 접속사
When이 와야 한다. As는 '~할 때'라는 뜻으로
When과 바꾸어 쓸 수 있다. However는 두 문장
의 대조 관계를 알려주는 접속부사이다. 그가 친구

들에게 그들의 재능에 대해 물어봤을 때, 그들 모두
자신들의 재능을 알고 있었다.

ⓒ 이유를 나타내는 접속사 As가 와야 한다. That은
명사절을 이끄는 접속사이다. ⓒ 뒤에 이어지는 절
은 명사의 역할을 하고 있지 않으므로 That은 적절
하지 않다. Therefore는 두 문장의 인과관계를 나
타내는 접속부사이다. 그는 자신이 특별한 재능을
가지고 있지 않다고 생각했기 때문에, 그는 발표에
대해 걱정했다.

**30** ① 조건을 나타내는 if절에서는 미래의 의미를 나타내
더라도, 현재시제로 미래시제를 나타낸다.
(will clean → clean)

② '비가 내리지 않았기 때문에 현장학습을 갔다'는 해
석이 자연스러우므로, 주절의 시제도 부사절의 시
제에 맞게 과거시제를 쓰는 것이 적절하다.
(go → went)

③ because of는 전치사로 뒤에 명사(구)를 쓴다.
주어진 문장에서는 절(he got up early)이 이어
지므로 접속사 because를 쓰는 것이 적절하다.
(because of → because)

④ '좋은 몸 상태를 유지하고 싶어서 매일 아침 운동한
다'는 해석이 적절하므로 결과를 나타내는 접속사
so를 써야 한다. (but → so)

**31** because 다음에는 주절의 원인이나 이유가 되는 절
을 쓴다. 바깥이 시끄러웠다는 절이 원인인 것이 자연
스러우므로 해당 절을 because의 뒤에 쓴다.

**32** ⓐ 시간을 나타내는 부사절에서는 현재시제가 미래
시제를 대신한다. I'll call you when she <u>comes</u>
back.

ⓔ 부사절의 시제는 주절의 시제(was)와 맞춰야 한
다. He was tired because he <u>got</u> up early.

## PRACTICE 1

**1** at **2** on **3** at **4** on **5** in
**6** in **7** on **8** at **9** at **10** on

**1** at+구체적인 시각
**2** on+요일
**3, 8, 9** at+특정한 시점
*at this time tomorrow: 내일 이맘때에
**4, 7** on+특정한 날
*on New Year's Day: 새해 첫날
**5** in+아침
**6** in+연도
**10** on+날짜

## PRACTICE 2

**1** After the meeting **2** before six
**3** Before lunch **4** After work
**5** Before twelve **6** after school

## PRACTICE 3

**1** for **2** during **3** for
**4** during **5** during **6** for
**7** during **8** during

**1, 3, 6** for+시간의 길이를 나타내는 표현
**2, 4, 5, 7, 8** during+숫자가 없는(명사로 된) 특정 기간을 나타내는 표현

## PRACTICE 4

**1** since **2** since **3** from
**4** since **5** From **6** from

**1, 2, 4** 전치사 since는 '~이래로'라는 뜻으로 과거에 시작된 일이 현재까지 지속되는 것을 나타내며 주로 완료형 시제와 함께 쓰인다.
**3, 5, 6** 전치사 from은 '~부터'라는 뜻으로, 시작된 시점만 나타내며 완료형 이외의 시제들과 함께 쓰인다.

## PRACTICE 5

**1** from eight to four
**2** From morning to afternoon
**3** from March to June
**4** from 12:00 to 12:40
**5** from late fall to early spring
**6** from 2003 to 2005

## PRACTICE 6

**1** at **2** on
**3** After **4** since
**5** In **6** at
**7** before **8** since
**9** for **10** to
**11** at **12** from
**13** in **14** from
**15** after

**1, 6, 11** at+특정한 시점, 구체적인 시각
**2** on+특정한 날의 아침/저녁
**3, 15** '~후에'라는 뜻의 after가 적절하다.
**4, 8** 동사가 현재완료시제이므로 since가 적절하다.
**5, 13** 연도, 월 앞에는 전치사 in을 쓴다.
**7** 동사가 현재시제이므로, '~이래로'라는 뜻을 가진 since보다는 '~전에'라는 뜻의 before가 적절하다.
**9** for+숫자가 들어간 시간의 길이를 나타내는 표현
**10, 12** 'A에서 B까지'라는 뜻의 'from A to B'를 써야 한다.
**14** 동사가 미래 시제이므로, '~부터'라는 뜻의 from이 적절하다.

## PRACTICE 7

**1** at **2** in **3** on
**4** at **5** on **6** in
**7** at **8** at **9** on
**10** at **11** on **12** on
**13** in **14** on **15** in
**16** in **17** on, on[in] **18** at
**19** In, in, in **20** on **21** on
**22** in

**1, 4** at+하나의 지점
**2, 13, 15** in+건물, 탈것, 용기 등의 내부
**3, 9, 11** on+교통수단, 통신수단
  **9** on foot: 걸어서, 도보로
**5, 14, 21** 표면상에 맞닿은 것을 말할 때 전치사 on을 사용한다.
**6** in+국가, 비교적 넓은 장소
**7, 18** at+행사, 모임
**8, 10** 건물의 용도에 맞는 일을 하고 있을 때 전치사 at을 사용한다.
**12, 20** 길을 말할 때 전치사 on을 사용한다.
**16, 22** in+우주, 하늘
**17** 첫 번째 빈칸에는 통신수단과 함께 쓰이는 전치사 on을 사용한다. 두 번째 빈칸에는 교통수단과 함께 쓰이는 전치사 on이나 탈 것의 내부를 뜻하는 전치사 in을 써야 한다.
**19** 첫 번째 빈칸에는 국가와 함께 쓰이는 전치사 in을 사용한다. 두 번째와 세 번째 빈칸에는 'come in: (물품이나 상품이) 나오다'라는 표현에 쓰이는 in을 사용한다.
  * carton: (음식이나 음료를 담는) 갑, 상자

## PRACTICE 8

**1** under  **2** over  **3** over
**4** under  **5** over  **6** under

## PRACTICE 9

**1** in front of  **2** Minji
**3** behind[in back of]  **4** Yunsu
**5** next to[beside/by]  **6** Minji
**7** Nami  **8** behind[in back of]

## PRACTICE 10

**1** between  **2** between  **3** among
**4** among  **5** between  **6** among
**7** among  **8** between

## PRACTICE 11

**1** in  **2** between  **3** at
**4** to  **5** under  **6** in
**7** on  **8** in  **9** on
**10** over  **11** on  **12** behind
**13** in  **14** among  **15** in front of

> **1, 8** in+도시, 국가와 같은 비교적 넓은 장소
> **2** between: ~사이에(둘 사이)
> **3** at+하나의 지점
> **4** next to: ~ 옆에
> **5** '바다 아래에는 많은 식물들이 있다.'라는 표현이 적절하므로, '~아래에'라는 뜻의 under를 써야 한다.
> **6, 13** in+건물의 내부
> **7, 9** 표면상에 맞닿은 것을 말할 때는 전치사 on을 사용한다.
> **10** '그녀는 벽 위로 공을 던졌다.'라는 표현이 적절하므로, '~위에'라는 뜻의 over를 써야 한다.
> **11** on+통신수단
> **12** behind: ~뒤에
> **14** among: ~사이에(셋 이상)
> **15** '3시에 역 앞에서 만나자'라는 표현이 적절하므로, '~앞에'라는 뜻의 in front of를 써야 한다.

## PRACTICE 12

**1** up  **2** into  **3** down
**4** out of  **5** into  **6** up

## PRACTICE 13

**1** around  **2** across
**3** through  **4** around
**5** along  **6** through

> **1** 지구는 태양 주위를 돈다.
> **2** 사람들은 초록 불일 때 길을 가로질러 간다.
> **3** 도둑이 창문을 통하여 집으로 들어왔다.
> **4** 박물관 주위에 높은 건물들이 많이 있다.
> **5** 우리는 강을 따라서 산책했다.
> **6** 기차는 터널을 통과하여 지나가고 있다.

## PRACTICE 14

**1** to  **2** for  **3** to
**4** from  **5** for  **6** from, to
**7** from  **8** for [to]

> **8** head for [to]: ~로 향하다

## PRACTICE 15

**1** to  **2** for  **3** after
**4** around  **5** into  **6** down
**7** for  **8** across  **9** in
**10** by  **11** up  **12** on
**13** at  **14** along  **15** into

> **1** to는 '~에, ~으로'라는 뜻으로 come과 함께 쓰여 도착 지점을 나타낸다.
> **2** 전치사 for는 '~을 향하여'라는 뜻으로 start와 함께 쓰여 방향을 나타낸다.
>   *start for: ~을 향해 출발하다
> **3** '~이래로'라는 뜻의 since보다는 '~후에'라는 뜻의 after가 적절하다.
> **4** '달은 지구 주위를 돈다.'라는 표현이 적절하므로, '~을 통하여'라는 뜻의 through보다는 '~주위에'라는 뜻의 around를 써야 한다.
> **5** between(~사이에)은 뒤에 복수명사가 나와야 하므로, '~안으로'라는 뜻의 into를 써야 한다.
>   *walk into: ~로 들어가다
> **6** '눈물이 그녀의 볼 아래로 흘러내렸다.'라는 표현이 적절하므로, '~안으로'라는 뜻의 into보다는 '~아래로'라는 뜻의 down을 써야 한다.
> **7** for+숫자가 들어간 시간의 길이를 나타내는 표현
> **8** '~위에'라는 뜻의 over보다는 '~을 가로질러'라는 뜻의 across가 적절하다.
> **9** in+연도
> **10** among(~사이에)은 뒤에 복수명사가 나와야 하므로, '~옆에'라는 뜻의 by를 써야 한다.
> **11** '원숭이들이 나무 위로 올라갔다.'라는 표현이 적절하므로, '~사이에(둘 사이)'라는 뜻의 between보다는 '~위로'라는 뜻의 up을 써야 한다.
> **12** 표면상에 맞닿은 것을 말할 때는 전치사 on을 사용한다.
> **13** at+구체적인 시간
> **14** '~보다 위에'라는 뜻의 above보다는 '~을 따라서'라는 뜻의 along이 적절하다.
> **15** '아이들이 물 안으로 뛰어들었다'라는 표현이 적절하므로 '~사이에(셋 이상)'라는 뜻의 among보다는 '~안으로'라는 뜻의 into가 적절하다.

Ch<br>**14**<br>전치사<br>&<br>속담

## PRACTICE 16

| | | | | | |
|---|---|---|---|---|---|
| **1** by | | **2** on | | **3** with | |
| **4** by | | **5** by | | **6** with | |
| **7** by | | | | | |

## PRACTICE 17

| | | | | | |
|---|---|---|---|---|---|
| **1** without | | **2** about | | **3** like | |
| **4** like | | **5** about | | **6** without | |
| **7** like | | **8** Without | | | |

## PRACTICE 18

| | | | | | |
|---|---|---|---|---|---|
| **1** by | | **2** like | | **3** with | |
| **4** without | | **5** on | | **6** without | |
| **7** with | | **8** like | | **9** by | |
| **10** with | | | | | |

> 1, 9 by+교통수단: ~을 타고
> 2 look like+명사: ~처럼 보이다
> 3, 7, 10 with+도구: ~을 가지고
> 4, 6 문맥상 '~없이'라는 뜻의 전치사 without을 쓰는 것이 적절하다.
> 5 on foot: 걸어서
> 8 like: ~와 같은

## PRACTICE 19

| | | | | | |
|---|---|---|---|---|---|
| **1** in | | **2** for | | **3** for | |
| **4** about | | **5** for | | **6** of | |
| **7** from | | **8** of | | **9** at | |
| **10** for | | **11** from | | **12** for[about] | |
| **13** of | | **14** for | | | |

## PRACTICE 20

| | | | | | |
|---|---|---|---|---|---|
| **1** at | | **2** for | | **3** for | |
| **4** for | | **5** to | | **6** for | |
| **7** on | | **8** in | | **9** into | |
| **10** After | | **11** without | | **12** to | |
| **13** on | | **14** from | | **15** out of | |
| **16** for | | **17** on | | **18** on | |
| **19** before | | **20** at | | **21** for | |
| **22** at | | **23** in | | **24** during | |
| **25** with | | **26** at | | **27** of | |
| **28** by | | **29** in | | **30** around | |

> 1 look at: ~을 보다
> 2 wait for: ~을 기다리다
> 3 thank A for B: A에게 B에 대해 고맙게 여기다
> 4 buy A for B: B에게 A를 사주다
> 5 give A to B: B에게 A를 주다
> 6 look for: ~를 찾다
> 7 표면상에 맞닿은 것을 말할 때 전치사 on을 사용한다.
> 8 in+계절
> 9 throw A into B: A를 B로 던지다
> 10 '점심식사를 하고 난 후에, 그들은 소풍 장소를 청소했다.'라는 표현이 적절하므로 '~후에'라는 뜻의 after를 써야 한다.
> 11 '김치가 없는 한국 음식(식사)을 찾기는 어렵다'라는 의미이므로, '~옆에'라는 뜻의 by보다는 '~없이'라는 뜻의 without을 써야 한다.
> 12 전치사 to는 '~에', '~으로'라는 뜻으로 도착 지점을 나타낸다.
> 13 on+날짜
> 14 동사가 과거 시제이므로, from이 적절하다.
> 15 'Susan은 상자 밖으로 그녀의 선물을 꺼냈다.'라는 표현이 적절하므로, '~안으로'라는 뜻의 into보다는 '~밖으로'라는 뜻의 out of를 써야 한다.
> 16 for+시간의 길이를 나타내는 표현
> 17 on+통신수단
> 18 on+요일
> 19 여름은 가을보다 먼저 오기 때문에 '~전에'라는 뜻의 before가 적절하다.
> 20 at+구체적인 시간
> 21 leave for: ~로 떠나다
> 22 be good at: ~을 잘하다
> 23 in+월
> 24 during+숫자가 없는(명사로 된) 특정 기간을 나타내는 표현
> 25 '그녀는 비누로 그녀의 머리를 감는다.'라는 표현이 적절하므로 '~옆에'라는 뜻의 by보다는 '~을 가지고'라는 뜻의 with를 써야 한다.
> 26 at+특정한 시점
> *at this time yesterday: 어제 이 시간에
> 27 be full of: ~으로 가득 차다
> 28 교통수단은 전치사 by, on[in] 모두 사용하여 표현할 수 있는데, 'by+교통수단', 'on[in]+관사+교통수단' 형태로 써야 한다. boat 앞에 관사가 없으므로 by가 적절하다.
> 29 in+도시
> 30 '해변가 주위에 아무도 없었다.'라는 표현이 적절하므로, '~을 통하여'라는 뜻의 through보다는 '~주위에'라는 뜻의 around를 써야 한다.

## PRACTICE 21

**2** ⑦, Fine clothes make the man.

**3** ⑥, Don't judge a book by its cover.

**4** ⑨, Go home and kick the dog.

**5** ④, Even a worm will turn.

**6** ②, Small drops make a shower.

**7** ③, A good medicine tastes bitter.

**8** ①, Two heads are better than one.

**9** ⑧, Too many cooks spoil the broth.

**10** ⑤, A journey of 1000 miles begins with a single step.

## PRACTICE 22

| | | | |
|---|---|---|---|
| **1** | blames his tools | **2** | the best |
| **3** | The early bird | **4** | Practice, perfect |
| **5** | without fire | **6** | men, minds |
| **7** | dog, day | **8** | as the Romans do |
| **9** | pain, gain | **10** | sight, mind |
| **11** | barking, bites | **12** | second nature |
| **13** | Honesty, policy | **14** | leap |
| **15** | haste, speed | | |

## PRACTICE 23

| | | | | | |
|---|---|---|---|---|---|
| **1** | with | **2** | to | **3** | until |
| **4** | with | **5** | from | **6** | over |

### 📑 중간·기말고사 대비문제 정답 본문 _ p.311

**1** ③ **2** ③ **3** on **4** ④ **5** (1) behind (2) in
**6** ④ **7** at **8** ③ **9** after **10** ④ **11** ①
**12** ④ **13** ② **14** on **15** ⑤ **16** I felt sorry
for her **17** ⑤ **18** ③ **19** ④ **20** ① **21** ①
**22** across **23** ④ **24** ② **25** ③ **26** ④
**27** ③ **28** ② **29** ② **30** ③ **31** ②
**32** without **33** ⑤ **34** ⑤ **35** Our customs
are quite different from yours. **36** ④ **37** ④
**38** ② **39** (1) for (2) about **40** ③ **41** ①
**42** for, at **43** at **44** for **45** (1) on (2) under
(3) in front of **46** ⑤ **47** ④ **48** ② **49** ③
**50** ③ **51** ③ **52** (1) in (2) in (3) for **53** ④
**54** (1) There are books on the table. (2) There
is a dog under the table. **55** (1) by foot → on
foot (2) on nature → in nature (3) go in → go
into[go to] **56** ⑤ **57** ④ **58** ④

## 중간·기말고사 대비문제 해설

**1** on+요일

**2** in+월

**3** on+날짜

**4** for a minute '잠시 동안'
*cf.* wait a minute '잠깐 기다리다'
　　 in a minute '곧, 즉시'

**5** (1) behind '~ 뒤에'

---

**(2)** live in '~에 살다'
*cf.* 마을, 도시, 국가와 같은 비교적 넓은 장소 앞에 in
　 을 쓴다.

**6** 도구와 함께 쓰이는 with는 '~을 가지고'의 뜻을 나타
　 낸다. 이 사과 좀 칼로 잘라줄 수 있니?

**7** be good at '~을 잘하다'

**8** • from A to B 'A에서 B까지'
　 • be[come] from '~로부터 오다, ~ 출신이다'

**9** after '~ 후에'

**10** (a) wake up '일어나다'
　 (b) with '~와 함께'
　 (c) After '~후에'
　 (d) at '~에서'
　 (e) for '~를 위해'
재훈을 만나보자. 그는 중학교 1학년 학생이다. 그의 아
침과 저녁이 어떤지 보자. 그는 7시에 일어나 세수를
한다. 그는 보통 토스트와 계란을 아침으로 먹는다. 그
는 그의 학교 가방을 전날에 미리 준비하므로, 그는 그
냥 가방을 들고 8시까지 집을 나선다. 그는 그의 친구
와 그들이 인터넷에서 본 재미있는 것들에 대해 이야
기하며 학교로 걸어간다. 하루 종일 수업을 마친 뒤, 그
는 오후 4시쯤 집에 온다. 그는 간식을 먹고 그의 책상
에서 숙제를 한다. 그는 오후 7시쯤 그의 어머니가 저녁
식사를 위해 식탁 차리는 것을 돕는다. 저녁 식사 후,
그는 그의 가족과 함께 TV를 보고 책을 읽으며 시간을
보낸다. 9시 30분에 그는 다음 날을 위해 학교 가방을
준비하고 잠자리에 든다.

**11** • 농장의 땅에 맞닿아 작물이 자라는 것이므로 전치사
　 on이 적절하다.
　 • look at '~을 보다'

**12** • be late for '~에 늦다'
　 • without '~ 없이'
　 •「for+시간의 길이를 나타내는 표현」'~ 동안에'

**13** 시계는 책상 위에 있으므로 on을 써야 한다.
　 ② There is a clock on the desk.
　 *cf.* next to '~옆에'

**14** 통신수단을 말할 때는 on을 쓴다.
　 on channel 9 '9번 채널에서' on TV 'TV에서'

**15** • be ready for: ~을 위한 준비가 되다
　 • As가 접속사로 쓰여 '~처럼, ~대로'의 의미를 나타
　 　 낸다.
　 • be full of: ~으로 가득 차다
　 • 구체적인 시각 앞에는 전치사 at을 쓴다.

Ch
**14**
전치사
&
속담

16 feel sorry for '~를 안쓰럽게 여기다'

17 • in+계절
 • 건물의 내부를 말할 때는 in을 쓴다.

18 • 빵집은 우체국의 옆에 있으므로 '~ 옆에'라는 뜻의
 전치사 next to를 쓴다. in front of는 '~ 앞에'라는
 뜻이다.
 • 빵집은 우체국과 은행의 사이에 위치해 있다. 따라
 서 '(둘) ~ 사이에'라는 뜻의 between이 적절하다.
 among도 '~ 사이에'라는 뜻이지만 세 개 이상의 대
 상들 사이를 지칭할 때 쓴다.

19 • walk around '~ 주위를 걷다'
 • work for '~에서 일하다'

20 ① on+요일 (in → on)

21 spend ~ on … '…에 ~를 소비하다[쓰다]'
 like '~처럼, ~같이'
 with '~을 가지고'

22 across '~건너편에, 맞은편에'

23 in+마을, 도시, 국가와 같은 넓은 장소
 at+구체적인 시각
 on+특정한 날

24 수학 시험을 잘 보기 위해 하고 싶었던 일들을 참아야
 했던 내용이므로 '고통 없이는 얻는 것도 없다.'라는 뜻
 의 No pain, no gain.이 적절하다.

25 on the[one's] way home '집에 가는 길에'

26 은행을 기준으로 타임스퀘어의 위치를 나타낼 때 빈
 칸에 위치나 방향을 나타내는 전치사가 들어가야 한
 다.
 ④ looking for는 '~를 찾는'이라는 뜻으로 빈칸에 들
  어갈 수 없다.

27 ③ on foot '걸어서'
 ①②④⑤ by+교통수단 '~을 타고'

28 to는 go, come과 같은 동사와 함께 쓰여 도착 지점
 을 나타낸다.
 on a subway '지하철을 타고'
 *cf.* 교통수단 앞에 관사가 없는 경우에는 by를 쓴다.
  by subway '지하철을 타고'

29 like '~처럼, ~같이'

30 ① Yesterday라는 과거를 나타내는 부사가 쓰였으므
  로, 동사도 과거시제로 써야 한다. (take → took)
 ② '강을 따라서 걷고 있었다'라는 해석이 자연스러우
  므로, '~을 따라서'라는 뜻의 전치사 along을 써야
  한다. on은 표면상에 맞닿은 것을 말한다.

(on → along)
④ 개가 세 마리 있다고 언급되어 있으므로 '(셋 이상
 의) ~ 사이에'라는 뜻의 전치사 among을 써야 한
 다. between은 두 개의 대상 사이를 지칭한다.
 (between → among)
⑤ 완료형 시제와 함께 쓰였으므로 과거부터 시작
 한 일이 현재까지 지속되는 것을 나타내는 전치사
 since를 써야 한다. from은 완료형 이외의 시제들
 과 함께 쓰인다. (from → since)

31 ② '좋아하다' (동사)
 ①③④⑤ '~처럼, ~같이' (전치사)

32 without '~ 없이'

33 be full of '~로 가득 차다'  be good for '~에 좋다'

34 • 그녀는 꽃에 관한 책을 읽었다.
 • 아이들은 그들 주위에 있는 모든 것에 호기심을 갖는
  다.
 ⑤ write about '~에 대해 글을 쓰다'
 ① look at '~을 보다'
 ② be afraid of '~을 두려워하다'
 ③ be famous for '~으로 유명하다'
 ④ be interested in '~에 흥미[관심]가 있다'

35 be different from '~와 다르다'
 different를 수식하는 quite는 different 앞에 쓴다.

36 ④ 동사 like '좋아하다'
 ①②③⑤ 전치사 like '~처럼, ~같이'

37 ④ look at '~을 보다' (on → at)
 ① arrive at '~에 도착하다'
 ② by '~를 타고'
 ③ into '~ 안으로'
 ⑤ from '~로부터'

38 전치사 in은 우주나 하늘을 나타내는 표현과 함께 쓴
 다.
 ② Look at the beautiful kites in the sky.
 ④ '해변에서'라는 뜻은 on the beach로 나타낸다.
 ⑤ be on a diet '식이요법 중이다'

39 (1) buy … for ~ '~에게 …을 사주다'
 (2) about '~에 대해'

40 각 나라에 맞는 식사 예절을 지키라는 내용이므로
 '로마에 가면 로마의 법을 따르라.'는 뜻의 When in
 Rome, do as the Romans do.가 적절하다.

41 • 하나의 지점을 나타낼 때는 at을 쓴다.
  그 버스는 광화문에서 선다.
 • 도구와 함께 쓰이는 with는 '~을 가지고'의 뜻을 나

타낸다. 그녀는 그녀의 엄지 손가락과 검지 손가락으로 원을 만들었다.

　• 길을 말할 때는 on을 쓴다. 5번가에 백화점이 있다.

**42** look for '~을 찾다'
look at '~을 보다'

**43** 특정한 시점 앞에는 at을 쓴다.
at noon '정오에'
at the end of this year '올 연말에'

**44** for는 '~ 동안'의 의미로 구체적인 시간의 길이를 나타내는 말과 함께 쓴다.
*cf.* during은 특정 기간을 나타내는 말과 함께 쓴다.

**45** (1) 그림에서 바지는 탁자 위에 있으므로, '~위에'라는 뜻으로 표면에 맞닿아 있는 것을 나타내는 전치사 on을 사용한다.
(2) 양말은 탁자의 아래에 있으므로, '~아래에'라는 뜻의 전치사 under을 사용한다.
(3) 상자는 침대의 앞에 있으므로, '~ 앞에'라는 뜻의 전치사 in front of를 사용한다.

Jason에게. 네 방을 좀 보렴. 네 바지는 탁자 위에 있구나. 네 양말 한 짝은 탁자 아래에 있어. 상자를 보렴. 그것은 네 침대 앞에 있구나. 제발, 네 방 청소하는 걸 잊지 마라! 엄마가.

**46** be absent from '~에 결석하다'
be good for '~에 좋다, 유익하다'

**47** 세호가 적은 돈을 아껴서 원하는 물건을 사려 한다는 내용이므로 '티끌 모아 태산'이라는 뜻의 Small drops make a shower.가 적절하다.

**48** for '~으로, ~로서(속성, 자격)'
후식으로 어떤 음식을 원하니?
② for '~으로, ~로서(속성, 자격)' 우리는 저녁으로 스테이크를 먹었다.
① be late for '~에 늦다' 그는 항상 학교에 늦는다.
③ look for '~을 찾다' 그녀는 그녀의 가방을 찾고 있다.
④ for '~ 동안' 나는 2주 동안 여기에 머물기로 계획했다.
⑤ thank ~ for … '~에게 …에 대해 고맙게 여기다' 너의 편지에 대해 고마워.

**49** • next to '~ 옆에'
• write … to ~ '~에게 …을 쓰다'
• go to see a doctor '병원에 가다'

**50** Thomas의 이웃은 Thomas의 옷만 중요시 했으므로 '겉모습보단 내면이 중요하다.'라는 뜻의 속담 Don't judge a book by its cover.가 적절하다.

**51** ③ suffer from '~으로부터 고통 받다'
① in the world '세계에'
② in danger '위험에 처해서'
④ in one's life/lives '~의 삶[인생]에'
⑤ in need '어려움에 처한'

이 세상의 많은 아이들이 지금 위험에 처해 있다. 그들은 배고픔과 질병으로 고통 받고 있다. 그들은 당신의 도움이 필요하다. 당신은 그들을 위해서 돈을 기부할 수 있다. 당신은 한 달에 3000원으로 시작할 수 있다! 당신의 작은 도움이 그들의 삶에 큰 변화를 만들 수 있다. 어려움에 처한 아이들을 위해 당신의 돈을 모아라.

**52** (1) 도시, 국가와 같은 넓은 장소에는 전치사 in을 쓴다.
(2) in the morning '아침에'
(3) 구체적인 시간의 길이를 나타낼 때 전치사 for를 쓴다.

보령은 세계적인 머드(진흙) 축제로 유명하다. 그것은 한국에서 가장 유명한 축제들 중 하나다. 그것(축제)은 갯벌에서 열린다. 그것(축제)은 보통 매우 이른 아침에 시작한다. 그것(축제)은 11일간 지속된다.

**53** 「during+특정 기간」, 「for+구체적인 시간의 길이」

**54** (1) 책은 탁자의 위에 있으므로, '~위에'라는 뜻으로 표면에 맞닿은 것을 나타내는 전치사 on을 사용하는 것이 적절하다.
(2) 개는 탁자의 아래에 있으므로 '~아래에'라는 뜻의 전치사 under을 사용한다.

**55** (1) 두 번째 줄: '걸어서'라는 뜻은 전치사 on을 사용해 나타낸다.
(2) 세 번째 줄: '자연 안에서 시간을 보내는 것을 좋아한다'라는 해석이 자연스러우므로 내부를 뜻하는 전치사 in을 사용하는 것이 적절하다. on은 표면에 맞닿은 것을 나타낸다.
(3) 밑에서 두 번째 줄: '숲의 안으로 들어간다'는 뜻이 되어야 하므로 '~ 안으로'의 뜻으로 방향성을 나타내는 전치사 into[to]를 사용하는 것이 적절하다. in은 '~안에'라는 뜻으로 이미 완료된 동작을 나타낸다.

주말마다 Maria의 가족은 캠핑을 간다. 그들은 걸어서 그곳으로 간다. 그들은 대개 통나무집에서 머문다. 그들은 자연 속에서 시간 보내는 걸 좋아한다. 날씨가 맑은 날이면 Maria와 그녀의 동생 Anna는 야생 과일을 따기 위해 숲 속으로 간다.

**56** ⓐ '공정한 결론을 내리는 데에 좋다'는 의미가 적절하

Ch
**14**
전치사
&
속담

므로 '~에 좋다, 유익하다'라는 의미로 사용되는 관용 표현 be good for을 써야 한다.

ⓑ '손을 사용하는 것을 통해'라는 의미가 적절하므로 일반적 수단과 함께 쓰여 '~을 통해'라는 뜻을 나타내는 전치사 by를 써야 한다.

ⓒ '그것은 17세기에 일본에 전해졌다'라는 의미가 적절하므로 '~에, ~으로'라는 뜻으로 도착 지점을 나타내는 전치사 to를 써야 한다.

**57** <보기> 강의 위에 다리가 지어진 것이므로 '~ 위에'를 뜻하는 전치사 over이 들어간다. on은 표면에 맞닿아 있는 것을 나타내므로 여기에서는 적절하지 않다.

④ '강 위로 새들이 날아가는 중이다'라는 해석이 자연스러우므로 '~ 위에'를 뜻하는 전치사 over이 들어간다.

① 동사 come과 함께 쓰여 도착 지점을 나타낼 때는 전치사 to를 사용한다.

② 입으로 집어 넣은 것이므로 '~ 안으로'라는 뜻의 방향을 나타내는 전치사 into 또는 in을 쓸 수 있다.

③ 필리핀에서 왔다는 뜻이므로 '~부터'를 나타내는 전치사 from이 들어간다. be from은 국적이나 고향을 나타내는 관용표현이다.

⑤ 디지털 카메라로 영화를 만든다는 뜻이므로, 도구를 나타내는 전치사 with을 사용한다.

**58** ⓐ 건물의 용도에 맞는 일을 하고 있을 때 전치사 at 또는 in을 쓸 수 있다.

ⓑ 표면상에 맞닿은 것을 말할 때 전치사 on을 쓴다.

ⓒ 교통수단과 함께 쓰이는 전치사 by를 쓴다. on은 교통수단의 앞에 관사가 올 때 쓸 수 있다.

2026 새 교과서에 맞춘 16차 개정판

# 중학영문법 3800제 1학년

## 단어·표현 암기장

MOTHERTONGUE
마더텅출판사
since 1999.4.1.

# 중학영문법 3800제 단어·표현 암기장 활용법

**1** 중학영문법 3800제 단어·표현 암기장은 한 달 학습 계획(총 31일)으로 구성되어 있습니다.

**2** 오늘 외울 단어를 원어민 녹음 MP3파일을 활용하여 암기합니다.

**3** 세트로 구성된 Word Test를 스스로 또는 선생님과 함께 풀어 본 후 단어·표현 암기장을
확인하며 채점합니다. (정답표가 필요하신 경우 마더텅 홈페이지를 통해 다운로드 받으실 수
있습니다. www.toptutor.co.kr)

**4** [오늘 외울 단어]로 제공되는 단어들은 3800제 본문에서 선정된 중학 필수 영단어입니다.
빈출 단어의 경우 반복적으로 제시하여 복습이 가능하도록 하였습니다.

**5** 교재와 함께 시작하여 매일의 학습 단어를 암기해 나가면, 한 달(31일)이면 3800제
주요 단어를 모두 학습할 수 있습니다.

# 중학영문법 3800제 1학년

# 단어·표현 암기장

## Problem Solving Skill

MOTHERTONGUE
마더텅출판사
since 1999.4.1.

## Chapter 1 문장의 기초

👤 PSS & PRACTICE

☐ 001 **bicycle**
[báisikl]
명 자전거

☐ 002 **pretty**
[príti]
형 예쁜 부 꽤, 매우

☐ 003 **police officer**
[pəlíːs ɔ́(ː)fisər]
명 경찰관

☐ 004 **excited**
[iksáitid]
형 신이 난, 들뜬

☐ 005 **wonderful**
[wʌ́ndərfəl]
형 아주 멋진, 훌륭한

☐ 006 **tired**
[taiərd]
형 피곤한, 지친

☐ 007 **parents**
[pɛ́ːrənts]
명 부모

☐ 008 **angry**
[ǽŋgri]
형 화난

☐ 009 **visitor**
[vízitər]
명 방문객

☐ 010 **warm**
[wɔːrm]
형 따뜻한

☐ 011 **busy**
[bízi]
형 바쁜

☐ 012 **friendly**
[fréndli]
형 다정한

☐ 013 **be afraid of**
～을 두려워하다

☐ 014 **late**
[leit]
형 늦은

☐ 015 **rain**
[rein]
동 비가 오다

☐ 016 **drink**
[driŋk]
동 마시다

☐ 017 **newspaper**
[njúːzpèipər]
명 신문

☐ 018 **happen**
[hǽpən]
동 (일, 사건 등이) 일어나다

☐ 019 **work**
[wəːrk]
동 일하다

☐ 020 **player**
[pléiər]
명 선수, 경기자

☐ 021 **go to the cinema**
영화 보러 가다

☐ 022 **have breakfast**
아침식사를 하다

☐ 023 **hungry**
[hʌ́ŋgri]
형 배고픈

☐ 024 **near**
[niər]
전 ～의 가까이(에)
부 가까이

☐ 025 **photograph**
[fóutəgræf]
명 사진

☐ 026 **hospital**
[háspitl]
명 병원

☐ 027 **interesting**
[íntərəstiŋ]
형 흥미있는, 재미있는

☐ 028 **use the Internet**
인터넷을 이용하다

☐ 029 **married**
[mǽrid]
형 결혼한

☐ 030 **speak**
[spiːk]
동 말하다

☐ 031 **enjoy**
[indʒɔ́i]
동 즐기다

☐ 032 **draw**
[drɔː]
동 (그림을) 그리다

☐ 033 **free**
[friː]
형 한가한, 자유로운

☐ 034 **movie**
[múːvi]
명 영화

☐ 035 **go jogging**
조깅하러 가다

☐ 036 **absent**
[ǽbsnt]
형 결석한

☐ 037 **vacation**
[veikéiʃən]
명 휴가, 방학

☐ 038 **great**
[greit]
형 훌륭한

☐ 039 **buy**
[bai]
동 사다

☐ 040 **grade**
[greid]
명 성적

☐ 041 **writer**
[ráitər]
명 작가

☐ 042 **corner**
[kɔ́ːrnər]
명 모퉁이

☐ 043 **clean**
[kliːn]
동 청소하다
형 깨끗한

☐ 044 **prepared**
[pripɛ́ərd]
형 준비가 되어 있는

☐ 045 **study**
[stʌ́di]
동 공부하다

☐ 046 **swim**
[swim]
동 수영하다

☐ 047 **gym**
[dʒim]
명 체육관

☐ 048 **fast**
[fæst]
형 빠른 부 빨리

☐ 049 **sleep**
[sliːp]
동 잠자다

☐ 050 **quiet**
[kwaiət]
형 조용한

☐ 051 **classroom**
[klǽsrùːm]
명 교실

☐ 052 **make a noise**
시끄럽게 하다

☐ 053 **wear**
[wɛər]
동 (옷을) 입다, (모자 등을) 쓰다

☐ 054 **helmet**
[hélmit]
명 헬멧, 안전모

☐ 055 **enter**
[éntər]
동 들어가다

☐ 056 **worry**
[wə́ːri]
동 걱정하다

☐ 057 **careful**
[kɛ́ərfəl]
형 조심스러운

☐ 058 **upset**
[ʌpsét]
형 속상한, 마음이 상한

☐ 059 **ready**
[rédi]
형 준비가 된

☐ 060 **turn on**
켜다

☐ 061 **introduce**
[ìntrədjúːs]
동 소개하다

☐ 062 **keep in touch**
연락하고 지내다, 연락하다

☐ 063 **take a break**
휴식을 취하다

☐ 064 **hurry**
[hə́ːri]
동 서두르다

☐ 065 **from now on**
지금부터

☐ 066 **ride**
[raid]
동 (탈것에) 타다

☐ 067 **go climbing**
등산하러 가다

☐ 068 **daughter**
[dɔ́ːtər]
명 딸

☐ 069 **really**
[ríːəli]
부 정말로, 실제로

☐ 070 **amazing**
[əméiziŋ]
형 놀라운

☐ 071 **huge**
[hjuːdʒ]
형 거대한

| | | |
|---|---|---|
| ☐ 072 **waterfall** [wɔ́:tərfɔ̀:l] | 명 폭포 | |
| ☐ 073 **handsome** [hǽnsəm] | 형 잘생긴 | |
| ☐ 074 **move** [mu:v] | 동 움직이다 | |
| ☐ 075 **liar** [láiər] | 명 거짓말쟁이 | |
| ☐ 076 **mountain** [máuntn] | 명 산 | |
| ☐ 077 **museum** [mju:zí:əm] | 명 박물관 | |
| ☐ 078 **dictionary** [díkʃənèri] | 명 사전 | |
| ☐ 079 **delicious** [dilíʃəs] | 형 맛있는 | |
| ☐ 080 **paint** [peint] | 동 페인트를 칠하다 | |
| ☐ 081 **boring** [bɔ́:riŋ] | 형 지루한 | |
| ☐ 082 **favorite** [féivərit] | 형 매우 좋아하는 | |
| ☐ 083 **subject** [sʌ́bdʒikt] | 명 과목 | |
| ☐ 084 **believe** [bilí:v] | 동 믿다 | |
| ☐ 085 **keep a diary** | 일기를 쓰다 | |
| ☐ 086 **healthy** [hélθi] | 형 건강한 | |
| ☐ 087 **make a mistake** | 실수를 하다 | |
| ☐ 088 **plant** [plænt] | 동 심다 | |
| ☐ 089 **honest** [ánist] | 형 정직한, 솔직한 | |

| | | |
|---|---|---|
| ☐ 090 **exciting** [iksáitiŋ] | 형 신나는, 흥미진진한 | |
| ☐ 091 **become** [bikʌ́m] | 동 ~이 되다 | |
| ☐ 092 **cook** [kuk] | 명 요리사 | |
| ☐ 093 **wash the dishes** | 설거지하다 | |
| ☐ 094 **shine** [ʃain] | 동 빛나다 | |
| ☐ 095 **article** [á:rtikl] | 명 기사 | |
| ☐ 096 **engineer** [èndʒiníər] | 명 기술자 | |
| ☐ 097 **sweet** [swi:t] | 형 달콤한, 감미로운 | |
| ☐ 098 **strange** [streindʒ] | 형 이상한 | |
| ☐ 099 **terrible** [térəbl] | 형 끔찍한, 심한 | |
| ☐ 100 **sour** [sauər] | 형 신, 시큼한 | |
| ☐ 101 **ask** [æsk] | 동 묻다 | |
| ☐ 102 **question** [kwéstʃən] | 명 질문 | |
| ☐ 103 **secret** [sí:krit] | 명 비밀 | |
| ☐ 104 **favor** [féivər] | 명 호의 | |
| ☐ 105 **cousin** [kʌ́zn] | 명 사촌 | |
| ☐ 106 **math** [mæθ] | 명 수학 | |
| ☐ 107 **storybook** [stɔ́:ribùk] | 명 동화책 | |

| | | |
|---|---|---|
| ☐ 108 **information** [ìnfərméiʃən] | 명 정보 | ☐ 125 **evening** [íːvniŋ]   명 저녁 |
| ☐ 109 **senior citizen** [síːnjər sítəzən] | 명 노인, 고령자 | ☐ 126 **watch** [watʃ]   동 보다, 지켜보다 |
| ☐ 110 **fairy tale** [fé(ː)əri teil] | 명 동화, 옛날 이야기 | ☐ 127 **lady** [léidi]   명 숙녀, 여성 |
| ☐ 111 **report card** [ripɔ́ːrt kɑːrd] | 명 성적표 | ☐ 128 **bring** [briŋ]   동 가져오다 |
| ☐ 112 **sand castle** [sænd kǽsl] | 명 모래성 | ☐ 129 **yesterday** [jéstərdei]   부 어제 |

🚶 중간기말대비

| | | |
|---|---|---|
| ☐ 113 **television** [téləvìʒən] | 명 텔레비전 | ☐ 130 **event** [ivént]   명 행사, 사건 |
| ☐ 114 **farmer** [fɑ́ːrmər] | 명 농부 | ☐ 131 **bookstore** [búkstɔ̀ːr]   명 서점 |
| ☐ 115 **umbrella** [ʌmbrélə] | 명 우산 | ☐ 132 **badminton** [bǽdmintn]   명 배드민턴 |
| ☐ 116 **swimmer** [swímər] | 명 수영 선수 | ☐ 133 **often** [ɔ́ːfən]   부 종종, 자주 |
| ☐ 117 **classmate** [klǽsmèit] | 명 동급생, 반 친구 | ☐ 134 **office worker** [ɔ́ːfis wə́ːrkər]   명 회사원 |
| ☐ 118 **play computer games** | 컴퓨터 게임을 하다 | ☐ 135 **lazy** [léizi]   형 게으른 |
| ☐ 119 **history** [hístəri] | 명 역사 | ☐ 136 **sweater** [swétər]   명 스웨터 |
| ☐ 120 **practice** [prǽktis] | 동 연습하다 | ☐ 137 **vegetable** [védʒtəbl]   명 채소 |
| ☐ 121 **hometown** [hóumtáun] | 명 고향 | ☐ 138 **guitar** [gitɑ́ːr]   명 기타 |
| ☐ 122 **far** [fɑːr] | 형 먼 | ☐ 139 **cloudy** [kláudi]   형 (날씨가) 흐린 |
| ☐ 123 **present** [préznt] | 명 선물 | ☐ 140 **scarf** [skɑːrf]   명 스카프, 목도리 |
| ☐ 124 **beautiful** [bjúːtəfəl] | 형 아름다운 | ☐ 141 **soup** [suːp]   명 수프 |
| | | ☐ 142 **nonsense** [nánsèns]   명 허튼소리 |

## Chapter **2** 시제

🧍 PSS & PRACTICE

| | | |
|---|---|---|
| ☐ 143 **get** [get] | 통 얻다 | |
| ☐ 144 **know** [nou] | 통 알다 | |
| ☐ 145 **walk** [wɔ:k] | 통 걷다 | |
| ☐ 146 **pass** [pæs] | 통 지나가다, (시험 등을) 통과하다 | |
| ☐ 147 **mix** [miks] | 통 섞다 | |
| ☐ 148 **finish** [fíniʃ] | 통 끝내다 | |
| ☐ 149 **stand** [stænd] | 통 서다, 서 있다 | |
| ☐ 150 **reach** [ri:tʃ] | 통 도착하다 | |
| ☐ 151 **impress** [imprés] | 통 감명을 주다 | |
| ☐ 152 **sing** [siŋ] | 통 노래하다 | |
| ☐ 153 **wish** [wiʃ] | 통 바라다 | |
| ☐ 154 **push** [puʃ] | 통 밀다 | |
| ☐ 155 **spend** [spend] | 통 쓰다, 소비하다 | |
| ☐ 156 **send** [send] | 통 보내다 | |
| ☐ 157 **miss** [mis] | 통 놓치다, 그리워하다 | |
| ☐ 158 **wake** [weik] | 통 잠이 깨다 | |
| ☐ 159 **teach** [ti:tʃ] | 통 가르치다 | |

| | | |
|---|---|---|
| ☐ 160 **solve** [sɑlv] | 통 풀다, 해결하다 | |
| ☐ 161 **catch** [kætʃ] | 통 붙잡다 | |
| ☐ 162 **sound** [saund] | 통 소리가 나다 | |
| ☐ 163 **throw** [θrou] | 통 던지다 | |
| ☐ 164 **burn** [bə:rn] | 통 불타다 | |
| ☐ 165 **cross** [krɔ:s] | 통 교차하다, 건너가다 | |
| ☐ 166 **copy** [kápi] | 통 복사하다 | |
| ☐ 167 **grandmother** [grǽndmʌðər] | 명 할머니 | |
| ☐ 168 **try** [trai] | 통 노력하다, 시도하다 | |
| ☐ 169 **pay** [pei] | 통 지불하다 | |
| ☐ 170 **say** [sei] | 통 말하다 | |
| ☐ 171 **help** [help] | 통 돕다, 거들다 | |
| ☐ 172 **lay** [lei] | 통 놓다, 두다 | |
| ☐ 173 **sell** [sel] | 통 팔다 | |
| ☐ 174 **kick** [kik] | 통 발로 차다 | |
| ☐ 175 **put** [put] | 통 놓다, 두다 | |
| ☐ 176 **touch** [tʌtʃ] | 통 만지다, 접촉하다, 닿다 | |
| ☐ 177 **lose** [lu:z] | 통 잃다 | |

| □ 178 **tell** [tel] | 통 말하다 | □ 196 **stay** [stei] | 통 머무르다 |
| □ 179 **carry** [kǽri] | 통 나르다, 운반하다 | □ 197 **set** [set] | 통 놓다, 설정하다, (시계 등을) 맞추다 |
| □ 180 **repeat** [ripíːt] | 통 반복하다 | □ 198 **see** [siː] | 통 보다, 이해하다 |
| □ 181 **grow** [grou] | 통 성장하다, 기르다 | □ 199 **envy** [énvi] | 통 부러워하다 |
| □ 182 **cost** [kɔːst] | 통 비용이 들다 | □ 200 **dream** [driːm] | 통 꿈꾸다 |
| □ 183 **judge** [dʒʌdʒ] | 통 판단하다 | □ 201 **live** [liv] | 통 살다 |
| □ 184 **cheer** [tʃiər] | 통 갈채하다, 응원하다 | □ 202 **leave** [liːv] | 통 떠나다 |
| □ 105 **use** [juːz] | 통 사용하다 | □ 203 **understand** [ʌndərstǽnd] | 통 이해하다 |
| □ 186 **think** [θiŋk] | 통 생각하다 | □ 204 **keep** [kiːp] | 통 계속하다, 유지하다 |
| □ 187 **mean** [miːn] | 통 의미하다 | □ 205 **give** [giv] | 통 주다 |
| □ 188 **break** [breik] | 통 깨뜨리다 | □ 206 **laugh** [læf] | 통 웃다 |
| □ 189 **show** [ʃou] | 통 보여주다 | □ 207 **hear** [hiər] | 통 듣다 |
| □ 190 **fly** [flai] | 통 날다 | □ 208 **stop** [stɑp] | 통 멈추다 |
| □ 191 **turn** [təːrn] | 통 돌다 | □ 209 **forget** [fərgét] | 통 잊다 |
| □ 192 **harm** [hɑːrm] | 통 해치다 | □ 210 **lend** [lend] | 통 빌려주다 |
| □ 193 **win** [win] | 통 이기다 | □ 211 **hug** [hʌg] | 통 껴안다 |
| □ 194 **fall** [fɔːl] | 통 떨어지다 | □ 212 **arrive** [əráiv] | 통 도착하다 |
| □ 195 **build** [bild] | 통 (건물 등을) 짓다 | □ 213 **seem** [siːm] | 통 ~처럼 보이다 |

☐ 214 **agree** [əgríː] 통 동의하다

☐ 215 **change** [tʃeindʒ] 통 바꾸다

☐ 216 **call** [kɔːl] 통 부르다, 전화하다, 이름을 지어주다

☐ 217 **check** [tʃek] 통 확인하다

☐ 218 **decorate** [dékərèit] 통 장식하다

☐ 219 **order** [ɔ́ːrdər] 통 명령하다, 주문하다

☐ 220 **beat** [biːt] 통 이기다, 때리다

☐ 221 **attack** [ətǽk] 통 공격하다

☐ 222 **sneeze** [sniːz] 통 재채기하다

☐ 223 **suggest** [səgdʒést] 통 제안하다

☐ 224 **place** [pleis] 통 두다, 놓다

☐ 225 **guess** [ges] 통 추측하다

☐ 226 **bless** [bles] 통 축복하다

☐ 227 **escape** [iskéip] 통 달아나다, 탈출하다

☐ 228 **raise** [reiz] 통 기르다, (들어) 올리다

☐ 229 **brush** [brʌʃ] 통 솔질하다

☐ 230 **cause** [kɔːz] 통 ~을 야기시키다, 초래하다

☐ 231 **dance** [dæns] 통 춤추다 명 춤

☐ 232 **gather** [gǽðər] 통 모으다

☐ 233 **moss** [mɔːs] 명 이끼

☐ 234 **sick** [sik] 형 병든, 아픈

☐ 235 **earth** [əːrθ] 명 지구

☐ 236 **capital** [kǽpitl] 명 수도

☐ 237 **east** [iːst] 명 동쪽

☐ 238 **in the morning** 아침에, 오전에

☐ 239 **drop** [drɑp] 통 떨어지다

☐ 240 **plan** [plæn] 통 계획하다

☐ 241 **invent** [invént] 통 발명하다

☐ 242 **save** [seiv] 통 구하다, 절약하다, 저축하다

☐ 243 **improve** [imprúːv] 통 개선하다, 나아지다

☐ 244 **jump** [dʒʌmp] 통 뛰다, 뛰어넘다

☐ 245 **cover** [kʌ́vər] 통 덮다

☐ 246 **learn** [ləːrn] 통 배우다

☐ 247 **obey** [oubéi] 통 준수하다, 따르다

☐ 248 **guide** [gaid] 통 안내하다

☐ 249 **join** [dʒɔin] 통 가입하다, 합류하다

오늘 외울 단어 **35개**

| | | |
|---|---|---|
| 250 **wonder** [wʌ́ndər] | 통 궁금해 하다, ~에 놀라다 | |
| 251 **end** [end] | 통 끝내다 | |
| 252 **surprise** [sərpráiz] | 통 놀라게 하다 | |
| 253 **add** [æd] | 통 더하다 | |
| 254 **connect** [kənékt] | 통 연결하다 | |
| 255 **spoil** [spɔil] | 통 망치다 | |
| 256 **bake** [beik] | 통 (빵 등을) 굽다 | |
| 257 **roll** [roul] | 통 구르다 | |
| 258 **tie** [tai] | 통 묶다 | |
| 259 **collect** [kəlékt] | 통 모으다, 수집하다 | |
| 260 **answer** [ǽnsər] | 통 대답하다 | |
| 261 **marry** [mǽri] | 통 결혼하다 | |
| 262 **serve** [səːrv] | 통 (음식을) 차려주다, 제공하다 | |
| 263 **waste** [weist] | 통 낭비하다 | |
| 264 **share** [ʃɛər] | 통 공유하다 | |
| 265 **train** [trein] | 통 훈련하다 | |
| 266 **pour** [pɔːr] | 통 따르다, 붓다 | |
| 267 **return** [ritə́ːrn] | 통 돌아오다[가다] | |

| | | |
|---|---|---|
| 268 **lock** [lɑk] | 통 (자물쇠로) 잠그다 | |
| 269 **hate** [heit] | 통 미워하다 | |
| 270 **type** [taip] | 통 타자를 치다 | |
| 271 **fail** [feil] | 통 실패하다 | |
| 272 **decide** [disáid] | 통 결정하다 | |
| 273 **swallow** [swálou] | 통 삼키다 | |
| 274 **shout** [ʃaut] | 통 외치다 | |
| 275 **spell** [spel] | 통 철자를 말하다 | |
| 276 **hurt** [həːrt] | 통 다치다, 다치게 하다 | |
| 277 **let** [let] | 통 ~하게 하다 | |
| 278 **spread** [spred] | 통 퍼지다, 펼치다 | |
| 279 **feed** [fiːd] | 통 먹이다 명 먹이 | |
| 280 **fight** [fait] | 통 싸우다 | |
| 281 **have** [hæv] | 통 가지다, 먹다 | |
| 282 **lead** [liːd] | 통 인도하다 | |
| 283 **slide** [slaid] | 통 미끄러지다 | |
| 284 **smell** [smel] | 통 냄새 맡다, 냄새가 나다 | |

| | | | | | |
|---|---|---|---|---|---|
| ☐ 285 **bear** [bɛər] | 통 낳다 | | ☐ 301 **dive** [daiv] | 통 (물속으로) 뛰어들다 |
| ☐ 286 **bite** [bait] | 통 물다 | | ☐ 302 **have lunch** | 점심을 먹다 |
| ☐ 287 **blow** [blou] | 통 불다 | | ☐ 303 **together** [təgéðər] | 부 함께 |
| ☐ 288 **choose** [tʃuːz] | 통 선택하다 | | ☐ 304 **holiday** [hálədèi] | 명 휴가, 휴일 |
| ☐ 289 **ring** [riŋ] | 통 (종, 벨이) 울리다 | | ☐ 305 **smile** [smail] | 통 미소 짓다 |
| ☐ 290 **rise** [raiz] | 통 오르다 | | ☐ 306 **library** [láibrèri] | 명 도서관 |
| ☐ 291 **take** [teik] | 통 가지고 가다 | | ☐ 307 **eat out** | 외식하다 |
| ☐ 292 **break out** | 일어나다, 발발하다 | | ☐ 308 **ill** [il] | 형 병든 |
| ☐ 293 **restaurant** [réstərənt] | 명 식당 | | ☐ 309 **sunrise** [sʌ́nràiz] | 명 일출 |
| ☐ 294 **skip** [skip] | 통 건너뛰다 | | ☐ 310 **project** [prádʒekt] | 명 계획, 기획, 프로젝트 |
| ☐ 295 **novel** [návəl] | 명 소설 | | ☐ 311 **actor** [ǽktər] | 명 (남자)배우 |
| ☐ 296 **exam** [igzǽm] | 명 시험 | | ☐ 312 **role** [roul] | 명 역할, 배역 |
| ☐ 297 **grandparent** [grǽndpɛ̀ərənt] | 명 조부, 조모 | | ☐ 313 **heavily** [hévili] | 부 심하게, 아주 많이 |
| ☐ 298 **make dinner** | 저녁식사를 준비하다 | | ☐ 314 **snow** [snou] | 통 눈이 내리다 |
| ☐ 299 **make time** | 시간을 만들다, 시간을 내다 | | ☐ 315 **ago** [əgóu] | 부 ~ 전에 |
| ☐ 300 **during** [djúəriŋ] | 전 ~ 동안 | | ☐ 316 **midnight** [mídnàit] | 명 자정 |

# Day 10



☐ 317 **throw away** — 버리다

☐ 318 **carpet** [kάːrpit] — 몡 카펫, 깔개

🏃 중간기말대비

☐ 319 **pick** [pik] — 통 고르다, 선택하다

☐ 320 **write** [rait] — 통 쓰다, 집필하다

☐ 321 **hide** [haid] — 통 감추다, 숨기다

☐ 322 **thank** [θæŋk] — 통 고마워하다

☐ 323 **explain** [ikspléin] — 통 설명히디

☐ 324 **climb** [klaim] — 통 오르다, 등반하다

☐ 325 **table tennis** [téibl tènis] — 몡 탁구

☐ 326 **weather** [wéðər] — 몡 날씨

☐ 327 **tropical** [trάpikəl] — 형 열대의

☐ 328 **visit** [vízit] — 통 방문하다

☐ 329 **weekend** [wíːkènd] — 몡 주말

☐ 330 **kite** [kait] — 몡 연

☐ 331 **listen to** — ~을 듣다

☐ 332 **have a barbecue** — 바비큐 파티를 하다

☐ 333 **concert** [kάnsə(ː)rt] — 몡 콘서트, 음악회

☐ 334 **review** [rivjúː] — 통 복습하다

☐ 335 **take a picture** — 사진을 찍다

☐ 336 **future** [fjúːtʃər] — 몡 미래

☐ 337 **begin** [bigín] — 통 시작하다

☐ 338 **discuss** [diskʌ́s] — 통 상의하다, 논의하다

☐ 339 **last year** — 작년(에)

☐ 340 **get up** — (잠자리에서) 일어나다

☐ 341 **daily** [déili] — 형 매일 일어나는

☐ 342 **foreigner** [fɔ́(ː)rinər] — 몡 외국인

☐ 343 **designer** [dizáinər] — 몡 디자이너

☐ 344 **loudly** [láudli] — 부 큰 소리로, 시끄럽게

☐ 345 **aunt** [ænt] — 몡 이모, 고모

☐ 346 **field trip** [fíːld trìp] — 몡 현장학습

☐ 347 **these days** — 요즘에는

☐ 348 **spaghetti** [spəgéti] — 몡 스파게티

☐ 349 **play baseball** — 야구를 하다

☐ 350 **headset** [hédsèt] — 몡 헤드폰

## Chapter 3 조동사

🚶 PSS & PRACTICE

351 **something** [sʌ́mθiŋ] — 대 무엇인가, 어떤 것

352 **right** [rait] — 형 옳은, 오른쪽의

353 **match** [mætʃ] — 명 경기, 시합

354 **break off** — 꺾어버리다

355 **branch** [bræntʃ] — 명 나뭇가지

356 **promise** [prámis] — 명 약속

357 **true** [tru:] — 형 진실의, 참된

358 **bill** [bil] — 명 지폐

359 **chopstick** [tʃápstìk] — 명 젓가락

360 **invite** [inváit] — 동 초대하다

361 **recycle** [rì:sáikl] — 동 재활용하다

362 **for a while** — 잠시 동안

363 **lecture** [léktʃər] — 명 강의

364 **find** [faind] — 동 찾다, 알아내다

365 **exit** [égzit] — 명 출구

366 **make it** — 성공하다, 해내다

367 **thirsty** [θə́:rsti] — 형 목마른

368 **alone** [əlóun] — 부 홀로

369 **dangerous** [déindʒərəs] — 형 위험한

370 **minute** [mínit] — 명 (시간 단위) 분

371 **have a seat** — 앉다

372 **go out** — 외출하다, 나가다

373 **tomorrow** [təmɔ́:rou] — 부 내일

374 **phone number** [fóun nʌ̀mbər] — 명 전화번호

375 **tonight** [tənáit] — 부 오늘밤에

376 **try on** — 입어 보다

377 **problem** [prábləm] — 명 문제

378 **casual** [kǽʒuəl] — 형 평상복의

379 **clothes** [klouz] — 명 옷, 의복

380 **follow** [fálou] — 동 따르다

381 **law** [lɔ:] — 명 법

382 **outside** [áutsàid] — 부 바깥에

383 **elevator** [éləvèitər] — 명 엘리베이터

384 **stair** [stɛər] — 명 계단

385 **traffic** [trǽfik] — 명 교통

☐ 386 **dentist** [déntist] — 圆 치과 의사

☐ 387 **protect** [prətékt] — 동 보호하다

☐ 388 **tell a lie** — 거짓말하다

☐ 389 **exercise** [éksərsàiz] — 동 운동하다

☐ 390 **straight** [streit] — 부 똑바로, 일직선으로

☐ 391 **take off** — 벗다

**중간기말대비**

☐ 392 **be interested in** — ~에 관심이 있다

☐ 393 **take care of** — ~을 돌보다

☐ 394 **anything** [éniθìŋ] — 대 무엇, 아무것

☐ 395 **park** [pɑːrk] — 동 주차하다

☐ 396 **human** [hjúːmən] — 명 사람, 인간

☐ 397 **fall asleep** — 잠들다

☐ 398 **turn off** — 끄다

☐ 399 **theater** [θíːətər] — 명 극장

☐ 400 **contest** [kántest] — 명 대회, 시합

☐ 401 **post office** [póust ɔ̀ːfis] — 명 우체국

☐ 402 **succeed** [səksíːd] — 동 성공하다

☐ 403 **balloon** [bəlúːn] — 명 풍선

☐ 404 **clean up** — 청소하다

☐ 405 **matter** [mǽtər] — 명 문제

☐ 406 **toothache** [túːθèik] — 명 치통

☐ 407 **be late for school** — 학교에 지각하다

☐ 408 **squirrel** [skwə́ːrəl] — 명 다람쥐

☐ 409 **lie** [lai] — 동 거짓말하다 / 명 거짓말

## Chapter 4 수동태

**PSS & PRACTICE**

☐ 410 **foreign** [fɔ́ːrin] — 형 외국의

☐ 411 **pick up** — ~을 집다, 들어올리다

☐ 412 **expression** [ikspréʃən] — 명 표현

☐ 413 **principal** [prínsəpəl] — 명 교장 선생님

☐ 414 **president** [prézidənt] — 명 대통령, 사장

☐ 415 **deliver** [dilívər] — 동 배달하다

☐ 416 **speech** [spiːtʃ] — 명 연설

☐ 417 **kill** [kil] — 동 죽이다

☐ 418 **war** [wɔːr] — 명 전쟁

☐ 419 **once** [wʌns] 甼 한 번

☐ 420 **memory** [méməri] 몡 기억

☐ 421 **someone** [sʌ́mwʌ̀n] 団 누군가

☐ 422 **fresh** [freʃ] 휑 신선한

☐ 423 **building** [bíldiŋ] 몡 건물

☐ 424 **refrigerator** [rifrídʒərèitər] 몡 냉장고

☐ 425 **reader** [ríːdər] 몡 독자

☐ 426 **elect** [ilékt] 띵 선출하다

☐ 427 **jungle** [dʒʌ́ŋgl] 몡 밀림지대, 정글

☐ 428 **painting** [péintiŋ] 몡 그림, 회화

☐ 429 **dead** [ded] 휑 죽은

☐ 430 **princess** [prínses] 몡 공주

☐ 431 **respect** [rispékt] 띵 존경하다

☐ 432 **village** [vílidʒ] 몡 마을

☐ 433 **design** [dizáin] 띵 디자인하다

☐ 434 **language** [lǽŋgwidʒ] 몡 언어

☐ 435 **teenager** [tíːnèidʒər] 몡 10대의 청소년

☐ 436 **musician** [mjuːzíʃən] 몡 음악가

☐ 437 **publish** [pʌ́bliʃ] 띵 출판하다

☐ 438 **magazine** [mæ̀gəzíːn] 몡 잡지

**중간기말대비**

☐ 439 **bee** [biː] 몡 벌

☐ 440 **be born** 태어나다

☐ 441 **crowd** [kraud] 띵 모여들다, 붐비다

☐ 442 **fix** [fiks] 띵 고치다, 수리하다

☐ 443 **make** [meik] 띵 ~하게 하다

☐ 444 **found** [faund] 띵 설립하다, 세우다

☐ 445 **robber** [rábər] 몡 도둑, 강도

☐ 446 **steal** [stiːl] 띵 훔치다

☐ 447 **somebody** [sʌ́mbàdi] 団 어떤 사람, 누군가

## Chapter 5 명사와 관사

**PSS & PRACTICE**

☐ 448 **audience** [ɔ́ːdiəns] 몡 청중, 관중

☐ 449 **beauty** [bjúːti] 몡 아름다움, 미(美)

☐ 450 **truth** [truːθ] 몡 진실

☐ 451 **freedom** [fríːdəm] 몡 자유

☐ 452 **peace**
[piːs]
명 평화

☐ 453 **flour**
[flauər]
명 밀가루

☐ 454 **wealth**
[welθ]
명 부, 재산

☐ 455 **kindness**
[káindnis]
명 친절함

☐ 456 **pity**
[píti]
명 동정, 연민

☐ 457 **pleasure**
[pléʒər]
명 즐거움, 기쁨

☐ 458 **lesson**
[lésn]
명 수업, 교훈

☐ 459 **smoke**
[smouk]
명 연기

☐ 460 **happiness**
[hǽpinis]
명 행복

☐ 461 **form**
[fɔːrm]
명 모양, 형상

☐ 462 **friendship**
[fréndʃip]
명 우정

☐ 463 **mosquito**
[məskíːtou]
명 모기

☐ 464 **address**
[ədrés]
명 주소

☐ 465 **passport**
[pǽspɔ̀ːrt]
명 여권

☐ 466 **bath**
[bæθ]
명 목욕

☐ 467 **brush**
[brʌʃ]
명 솔

☐ 468 **shelf**
[ʃelf]
명 선반

☐ 469 **wife**
[waif]
명 부인, 아내

☐ 470 **safe**
[seif]
명 금고
형 안전한

☐ 471 **roof**
[ruːf]
명 지붕

☐ 472 **country**
[kʌ́ntri]
명 나라, 국가

☐ 473 **factory**
[fǽktəri]
명 공장

☐ 474 **idea**
[aidí(ː)ə]
명 생각, 아이디어

☐ 475 **headache**
[hédèik]
명 두통

☐ 476 **bottle**
[bátl]
명 병

☐ 477 **poster**
[póustər]
명 포스터, 전단 광고

☐ 478 **block**
[blɑk]
명 나무 조각, 구역

☐ 479 **deer**
[diər]
명 사슴

☐ 480 **sheep**
[ʃiːp]
명 양

☐ 481 **goose**
[guːs]
명 거위, 기러기

☐ 482 **mouse**
[maus]
명 생쥐

☐ 483 **ox**
[ɑks]
명 황소

☐ 484 **festival**
[féstəvəl]
명 축제

☐ 485 **candle**
[kǽndl]
명 양초

☐ 486 **month**
[mʌnθ]
명 달, 개월

☐ 487 **wagon**
[wǽgən]
명 수레, 짐마차

☐ 488 **thief** [θiːf] 명 도둑

☐ 489 **autumn** [ɔ́ːtəm] 명 가을

☐ 490 **chalk** [tʃɔːk] 명 분필, 초크

☐ 491 **advice** [ədváis] 명 충고

☐ 492 **furniture** [fə́ːrnitʃər] 명 가구

☐ 493 **university** [jùːnəvə́ːrsəti] 명 대학교

☐ 494 **famous** [féiməs] 형 유명한

☐ 495 **be known for** ~로 알려져 있다

☐ 496 **sense** [sens] 명 감각

☐ 497 **special** [spéʃəl] 형 특별한

☐ 498 **story** [stɔ́ːri] 명 (건물의) 층

☐ 499 **break** [breik] 명 잠깐의 휴식

☐ 500 **European** [jùərəpíːən] 명 유럽 사람 형 유럽의

☐ 501 **elementary** [èləméntəri] 형 초급의, 초등의

☐ 502 **downtown** [dáuntáun] 명 도심지, 상업 지구

☐ 503 **crane** [krein] 명 학, 두루미

☐ 504 **snake** [sneik] 명 뱀

☐ 505 **floor** [flɔːr] 명 마루, 층

☐ 506 **clear** [kliər] 형 맑은

☐ 507 **imagine** [imǽdʒin] 동 상상하다

☐ 508 **insect** [ínsekt] 명 곤충

☐ 509 **faithful** [féiθfəl] 형 충실한

☐ 510 **bathroom** [bǽθrù(ː)m] 명 화장실

☐ 511 **station** [stéiʃən] 명 역

☐ 512 **airplane** [έərplèin] 명 비행기

☐ 513 **cancer** [kǽnsər] 명 암

☐ 514 **same** [seim] 형 같은

☐ 515 **another** [ənʌ́ðər] 대 또 하나, 다른 것

☐ 516 **seat** [siːt] 명 좌석

☐ 517 **pocket** [pákit] 명 호주머니

☐ 518 **bowl** [boul] 명 사발

☐ 519 **armchair** [áːrmtʃὲər] 명 안락의자

☐ 520 **mug** [mʌg] 명 컵, 머그잔

☐ 521 **popular** [pápjulər] 형 인기 있는

☐ 522 **humid** [hjúmid] 형 습한

☐ 523 **airless** [έərlis] 형 숨막히는, 공기가 안 통하는

☐ 524 **turkey** [tə́:rki] — 명 칠면조

☐ 525 **recognize** [rékəgnàiz] — 동 알아보다

☐ 526 **come into** — ~에 들어가다

**중간기말대비**

☐ 527 **blackboard** [blǽkbɔ̀:rd] — 명 칠판

☐ 528 **plate** [pleit] — 명 접시, 그릇

☐ 529 **play** [plei] — 명 연극, 놀이

☐ 530 **dessert** [dizə́:rt] — 명 후식, 디저트

☐ 531 **at the end of** — ~의 끝에

☐ 532 **wolf** [wulf] — 명 늑대

☐ 533 **uncle** [ʌ́ŋkl] — 명 (외)삼촌, 이모[고모]부

☐ 534 **uniform** [júːnəfɔ̀:rm] — 명 제복, 교복

☐ 535 **in front of** — ~의 앞에

☐ 536 **several** [sévərəl] — 대 몇몇 / 형 각각의, 몇몇의

☐ 537 **useful** [júːsfəl] — 형 유용한

☐ 538 **pair** [pɛər] — 명 한 쌍[벌]

☐ 539 **slice** [slais] — 명 (음식을 얇게 썬) 조각

☐ 540 **sightseeing** [sáitsì:iŋ] — 명 관광, 구경

☐ 541 **jeans** [dʒi:nz] — 명 청바지

☐ 542 **look for** — ~을 찾다

☐ 543 **scissors** [sízərz] — 명 가위

☐ 544 **cent** [sent] — 명 (화폐 단위) 센트

☐ 545 **volunteer** [vàləntíər] — 명 지원자, 자원 봉사자

☐ 546 **necklace** [néklis] — 명 목걸이

☐ 547 **oak tree** [óuk trì:] — 명 오크나무

☐ 548 **leaf** [li:f] — 명 (나무) 잎

☐ 549 **clover** [klóuvər] — 명 클로버, 토끼풀

☐ 550 **always** [ɔ́:lweiz] — 부 항상

☐ 551 **human being** [hjúːmən bí:iŋ] — 명 인간, 사람

☐ 552 **each other** [i:tʃ ʌ́ðər] — 대 서로

## Chapter 6 대명사

**PSS & PRACTICE**

☐ 553 **bakery** [béikəri] — 명 빵집, 제과점

☐ 554 **rest** [rest] — 동 쉬다, 휴식하다

☐ 555 **tail** [teil] — 명 꼬리

☐ 556 **be full of** — ~로 가득차다

□ 557 **still** [stil] — 뿐 여전히

□ 558 **journey** [dʒə́:rni] — 명 여행, 여정

□ 559 **tough** [tʌf] — 형 힘든

□ 560 **prize** [praiz] — 명 상

□ 561 **culture** [kʌ́ltʃər] — 명 문화

□ 562 **similar** [símələr] — 형 유사한

□ 563 **important** [impɔ́:rtənt] — 형 중요한

□ 564 **textbook** [tékstbùk] — 명 교과서

□ 565 **color** [kʌ́lər] — 동 색을 칠하다 / 명 색

□ 566 **kill oneself** — 자살하다

□ 567 **pay for** — ~에 대해 돈을 지불하다

□ 568 **catch[have] a cold** — 감기에 걸리다

□ 569 **dark** [dɑ:rk] — 형 어두운

□ 570 **turtle** [tə́:rtl] — 명 거북

□ 571 **between** [bitwí:n] — 전 ~ 사이에

□ 572 **fault** [fɔ:lt] — 명 잘못, 실수

□ 573 **pine tree** [páin trì:] — 명 소나무

□ 574 **dishonest** [disɑ́nist] — 형 부정직한

□ 575 **course** [kɔ:rs] — 명 교과과정, 과목

□ 576 **example** [igzǽmpl] — 명 예, 실례

□ 577 **weigh** [wei] — 동 무게가 나가다

□ 578 **wrap** [ræp] — 동 싸다, 포장하다

□ 579 **pound** [paund] — 명 (중량의 단위) 파운드

□ 580 **science** [sáiəns] — 명 과학

□ 581 **homeroom teacher** [hóumrù:m tí:tʃər] — 명 담임 선생님

□ 582 **backpack** [bǽkpæ̀k] — 명 배낭

□ 583 **no way** — 절대로 아니다, 절대로 안 되다

**👤 중간기말대비**

□ 584 **science fiction** [sáiəns fíkʃən] — 명 공상 과학 영화 [소설]

□ 585 **horror** [hɔ́:rər] — 명 공포 영화, 공포

□ 586 **after school** — 방과 후에

□ 587 **rotten** [rátən] — 형 썩은

□ 588 **belong to** — ~에 속하다, ~의 소유이다

□ 589 **own** [oun] — 동 소유하다

□ 590 **proud** [praud] — 형 자랑스러운

□ 591 **fall** [fɔ:l] — 명 가을

| | | |
|---|---|---|
| ☐ 592 **season** [síːzən] | 명 계절 | |
| ☐ 593 **mirror** [mírər] | 명 거울 | |
| ☐ 594 **need** [niːd] | 명 필요한 것 | |
| ☐ 595 **fur** [fəːr] | 명 모피, 털 | |
| ☐ 596 **hamster** [hǽmstər] | 명 햄스터 | |
| ☐ 597 **on the Internet** | 인터넷(상)에서 | |
| ☐ 598 **musical instrument** [mjúːzikəl ínstrəmənt] | 명 악기 | |
| ☐ 600 **knife** [naif] | 명 칼 | |
| ☐ 600 **pilot** [páilət] | 명 조종사 | |
| ☐ 601 **each** [iːtʃ] | 형 각각의 | |

## Chapter 7 부정사

👤 PSS & PRACTICE

| | |
|---|---|
| ☐ 602 **easy** [íːzi] | 형 쉬운 |
| ☐ 603 **goal** [goul] | 명 목표 |
| ☐ 604 **get lost** | 행방불명이 되다 |
| ☐ 605 **simple** [símpl] | 형 간단한, 단순한 |
| ☐ 606 **historic** [histɔ́ːrik] | 형 역사상 중요한 |
| ☐ 607 **place** [pleis] | 명 장소 |

| | |
|---|---|
| ☐ 608 **helpful** [hélpfəl] | 형 도움이 되는 |
| ☐ 609 **soon** [suːn] | 부 곧, 이내 |
| ☐ 610 **expect** [ikspékt] | 동 기대하다 |
| ☐ 611 **scientist** [sáiəntist] | 명 과학자 |
| ☐ 612 **peaceful** [píːsfəl] | 형 평화로운 |
| ☐ 613 **get to** | ~에 도착하다 |
| ☐ 614 **turn** [təːrn] | 명 순번, 차례 |
| ☐ 615 **ask for** | ~을 요청하다 |
| ☐ 616 **sail** [seil] | 동 항해하다 |
| ☐ 617 **breathe** [briːð] | 동 숨쉬다 |
| ☐ 618 **go back** | 되돌아가다 |
| ☐ 619 **bill** [bil] | 명 청구서 |
| ☐ 620 **pleased** [pliːzd] | 형 기뻐하는 |
| ☐ 621 **surprised** [sərpráizd] | 형 놀란 |
| ☐ 622 **deaf** [def] | 형 귀가 먼 |
| ☐ 623 **grow up** | 자라다, 성장하다 |
| ☐ 624 **cure** [kjuər] | 명 치료 |
| ☐ 625 **lose weight** | 살을 빼다 |

☐ 626 **cut down** — 베다, 줄이다

☐ 627 **one's school days** — ~의 학창 시절

☐ 628 **plant** [plænt] — 명 식물

☐ 629 **chat** [tʃæt] — 통 잡담하다, 채팅하다

☐ 630 **chemical** [kémikəl] — 명 화학 물질

☐ 631 **weed** [wi:d] — 명 잡초

☐ 632 **whole** [houl] — 형 전체의

☐ 633 **blind** [blaind] — 형 눈이 먼, 맹인의

☐ 634 **football** [fútbɔ̀:l] — 명 미식축구

☐ 635 **storm** [stɔ:rm] — 명 폭풍

☐ 636 **run after** — 뒤쫓다

🏃 중간기말대비

☐ 637 **hear from** — ~에게서 소식을 듣다

☐ 638 **do volunteer work** — 자원봉사를 하다

☐ 639 **hobby** [hábi] — 명 취미

☐ 640 **focus on** — ~에 집중하다

☐ 641 **blouse** [blaus] — 명 블라우스

☐ 642 **pool** [pu:l] — 명 수영장

☐ 643 **close** [klouz] — 통 닫다, 막다, (눈을) 감다

☐ 644 **travel** [trævl] — 통 여행하다

☐ 645 **abroad** [əbrɔ́:d] — 부 해외에, 외국에

☐ 646 **habit** [hæbit] — 명 습관, 버릇

☐ 647 **save time** — 시간을 아끼다

☐ 648 **mascot** [mǽskat] — 명 마스코트

☐ 649 **race** [reis] — 명 경주, 경기

☐ 650 **shake** [ʃeik] — 통 흔들(리)다, 떨리다

☐ 651 **pencil case** [pénsl kèis] — 명 필통

☐ 652 **from side to side** — 좌우로 (흔들리는)

☐ 653 **campaign** [kæmpéin] — 명 캠페인

☐ 654 **painter** [péintər] — 명 화가

☐ 655 **take part in** — ~에 참가하다

☐ 656 **early** [ə́:rli] — 부 일찍

☐ 657 **see a doctor** — 의사에게 진찰을 받다

☐ 658 **take a walk** — 산책하다

☐ 659 **talk about** — ~에 대해 얘기하다

☐ 660 **nursing home** [nə́:rsiŋ houm] — 명 요양원

# Day 20

| | | |
|---|---|---|
| ☐ 661 **elderly** [éldərli] | 형 나이가 지긋한 | |

## Chapter 8 동명사

**PSS & PRACTICE**

☐ 662 **activity** [æktívəti] — 명 활동

☐ 663 **farm** [fáːrm] — 동 농사를 짓다

☐ 664 **regularly** [régjulərli] — 부 규칙적으로

☐ 665 **health** [helθ] — 명 건강

☐ 666 **mind** [maind] — 동 꺼려하다

☐ 667 **cartoon** [kɑːrtúːn] — 명 (시사 풍자) 만화

☐ 668 **through** [θru] — 전 ～을 통하여

☐ 669 **win a prize** — 상을 타다

☐ 670 **continue** [kəntínjuː] — 동 계속하다

☐ 671 **someday (= some day)** [sʌ́mdèi] — 부 언젠가, 머지않아

☐ 672 **go for a walk** — 산책하러 가다

☐ 673 **rule** [ruːl] — 명 규칙

☐ 674 **go on a picnic** — 소풍 가다

☐ 675 **take a test** — 테스트[검사]를 받다, 시험을 보다

☐ 676 **bench** [bentʃ] — 명 벤치, 긴 의자

☐ 677 **tear** [tiər] — 명 눈물

☐ 678 **come out** — 나오다

☐ 679 **anyone** [éniwʌ̀n] — 대 아무나, 누구나

**중간기말대비**

☐ 680 **thank for** — ～에 대해 감사하다

☐ 681 **nature** [néitʃər] — 명 자연

☐ 682 **be good at** — ～를 잘하다

☐ 683 **suddenly** [sʌ́dnli] — 부 갑자기, 불현듯

☐ 684 **stadium** [stéidiəm] — 명 경기장

☐ 685 **meal** [miːl] — 명 식사

☐ 686 **noise** [nɔiz] — 명 소음

☐ 687 **keep ~ from …** — ～가 …하지 못하게 하다

☐ 688 **give up** — 포기하다

☐ 689 **disabled** [diséibld] — 형 신체장애가 있는

☐ 690 **play the violin** — 바이올린 연주를 하다

☐ 691 **overcome** [òuvərkʌ́m] — 동 극복하다

☐ 692 **limitation** [lìmitéiʃən] — 명 한계

☐ 693 **astronaut** [ǽstrənɔ̀ːt] — 명 우주 비행사

□ 694 **give a hand**    도움을 주다

□ 695 **ride a bicycle**    자전거를 타다

□ 696 **be good for**    ～에 좋다, 유익하다

□ 697 **strength**    몡 힘, 기운, 강점
[streŋθ]

□ 698 **be bad for**    ～에 나쁘다

□ 699 **hold**    통 잡고 있다, 개최하다
[hould]

□ 700 **fishing**    몡 낚시, 어업
[fíʃiŋ]

□ 701 **in-line skating**    몡 인라인 스케이팅
[ínlaɪn skéitiŋ]

□ 702 **get rid of**    제거하다

□ 703 **overflow**    통 넘치다
[òuvərflóu]

□ 704 **gas**    몡 기체
[gæs]

□ 705 **little by little**    조금씩, 차츰

□ 706 **therefore**    븐 그러므로
[ðɛ́ərfɔ̀ːr]

□ 707 **avoid**    통 피하다, 막다
[əvɔ́id]

□ 708 **beach**    몡 해변
[biːtʃ]

□ 709 **apologize**    통 사과하다
[əpálədʒàiz]

□ 710 **along**    젼 ～을 따라
[əlɔ́(ː)ŋ]

□ 711 **take the stairs**    계단을 이용하다

□ 712 **be tired of**    싫증이 나다

## Chapter 9 분사

🧍 PSS & PRACTICE

□ 713 **gate**    몡 정문, (대)문
[geit]

□ 714 **actress**    몡 여배우
[ǽktris]

□ 715 **garage sale**    몡 차고 세일
[gərɑ́ːdʒ seil]

□ 716 **brick**    몡 벽돌
[brik]

□ 717 **sparrow**    몡 참새
[spǽrou]

□ 718 **trash**    몡 쓰레기
[træʃ]

□ 719 **person**    몡 사람
[pə́ːrsən]

□ 720 **remember**    통 기억하다
[rimémbər]

□ 721 **product**    몡 생산품
[prádʌkt]

□ 722 **company**    몡 회사
[kʌ́mpəni]

□ 723 **flood**    통 범람하다 / 몡 홍수
[flʌd]

□ 724 **film**    몡 영화
[film]

□ 725 **death**    몡 죽음
[deθ]

□ 726 **result**    몡 결과
[rizʌ́lt]

□ 727 **behavior**    몡 행동
[bihéivjər]

# Day 22



☐ 728 **accident** [ǽksidənt] 명 사고

☐ 729 **performance** [pərfɔ́ːrməns] 명 공연

🚶 중간기말대비

☐ 730 **look at** ~을 보다

☐ 731 **broken** [bróukən] 형 부서진, 망가진

☐ 732 **cell phone** [sel foun] 명 휴대폰

☐ 733 **enjoyable** [indʒɔ́iəbl] 형 즐길 수 있는

☐ 734 **fluently** [flúːəntli] 부 유창하게

☐ 735 **topic** [tápik] 명 주제

☐ 736 **full moon** [ful muːn] 명 보름달

☐ 737 **hesitant** [hézitənt] 형 주저하는, 망설이는

☐ 738 **set up** 세우다

☐ 739 **key** [kiː] 명 비결, 열쇠

☐ 740 **disappointed** [dìsəpɔ́intid] 형 실망한

☐ 741 **wild flower** [wáild flàuər] 명 들꽃, 야생초

☐ 742 **shocking** [ʃáːkiŋ] 형 충격적인

☐ 743 **tiring** [táiəriŋ] 형 피곤하게 만드는

☐ 744 **stage** [steidʒ] 명 무대

☐ 745 **carnation** [kɑːrnéiʃən] 명 카네이션

☐ 746 **compete** [kəmpíːt] 동 경쟁하다, ~와 겨루다

☐ 747 **situation** [sìtʃuéiʃən] 명 상황, 환경

☐ 748 **show up** 나타나다, 눈에 띄다

☐ 749 **roast** [roust] 동 (불에) 굽다

☐ 750 **garlic** [gáːrlik] 명 마늘

☐ 751 **onion** [ʌ́njən] 명 양파

☐ 752 **satisfied** [sǽtisfàid] 형 만족하는

## Chapter 10 형용사

🚶 PSS & PRACTICE

☐ 753 **field** [fiːld] 명 들판

☐ 754 **poor** [puər] 형 가난한

☐ 755 **talent** [tǽlənt] 명 재능

☐ 756 **piece** [piːs] 명 조각

☐ 757 **glass** [glæs] 명 유리

☐ 758 **danger** [déindʒər] 명 위험

☐ 759 **readily** [rédili] 부 손쉽게, 기꺼이

☐ 760 **hunger** [hʌ́ŋgər] 명 굶주림, 기아

| | | |
|---|---|---|
| □ 761 **sickness** [síknis] | 명 병 | |
| □ 762 **curious** [kjúriəs] | 형 궁금한, 호기심이 많은 | |
| □ 763 **class** [klæs] | 명 학급, 수업 | |
| □ 764 **crowded** [kráudid] | 형 붐비는 | |
| □ 765 **perfect** [pə́:rfikt] | 형 완벽한 | |
| □ 766 **palace** [pǽlis] | 명 궁전 | |
| □ 767 **else** [els] | 형 그 밖의 다른 / 부 그 밖에 달리 | |
| □ 768 **be sold out** | 품절되다 | |
| □ 769 **discover** [diskʌ́vər] | 동 발견하다 | |
| □ 770 **wrong** [rɔːŋ] | 형 틀린 | |
| □ 771 **necessary** [nésəsèri] | 형 필요한 | |
| □ 772 **clever** [klévər] | 형 영리한 | |
| □ 773 **bride** [braid] | 명 신부 | |
| □ 774 **reporter** [ripɔ́:rtər] | 명 기자 | |
| □ 775 **temple** [témpl] | 명 사원 | |
| □ 776 **planet** [plǽnit] | 명 행성 | |
| □ 777 **rock** [rɑk] | 명 바위 | |
| □ 778 **courage** [kə́:ridʒ] | 명 용기 | |

| | | |
|---|---|---|
| □ 779 **French** [frentʃ] | 형 프랑스의 명 프랑스어 | |
| □ 780 **trouble** [trʌ́bl] | 명 불편, 문제점 | |
| □ 781 **luck** [lʌk] | 명 운, 행운 | |
| □ 782 **wallet** [wálit] | 명 지갑 | |
| □ 783 **medicine** [médisn] | 명 약 | |
| □ 784 **without** [wiðáut] | 전 ~이 없이 | |
| □ 785 **chance** [tʃæns] | 명 기회 | |

**중간기말대비**

| | | |
|---|---|---|
| □ 786 **basket** [bǽskit] | 명 바구니 | |
| □ 787 **century** [séntʃəri] | 명 100년, 세기 | |
| □ 788 **past** [pæst] | 형 지난, 지나간, 이전의 | |
| □ 789 **vote** [vout] | 명 표, 투표 | |
| □ 790 **boil** [bɔil] | 동 끓다, 끓이다 | |
| □ 791 **degree** [digrí:] | 명 (온도 단위) 도 | |
| □ 792 **animal** [ǽniml] | 명 동물 | |
| □ 793 **butter** [bʌ́tər] | 명 버터 | |
| □ 794 **grade** [greid] | 명 학년 | |
| □ 795 **roommate** [rú:mmèit] | 명 룸메이트 | |

## Day 24

□ 796 **church** [tʃəːrtʃ]   명 교회

□ 797 **quarter** [kwɔːrtər]   명 4분의 1, 15분

□ 798 **nothing special**   특별한 일이 없다

□ 799 **sound** [saund]   형 건전한

□ 800 **spirit** [spírit]   명 정신

□ 801 **temperature** [témpərətʃər]   명 온도

□ 802 **sand** [sænd]   명 모래

□ 803 **playground** [pléigràund]   명 놀이터, 운동장

□ 804 **bobsled** [bábslèd]   명 봅슬레이

□ 805 **difficulty** [dífikʌlti]   명 어려움, 고난

□ 806 **cafeteria** [kæ̀fətíriə]   명 식당, 구내식당

□ 807 **experience** [ikspí(ː)əriəns]   명 경험

□ 808 **effort** [éfərt]   명 노력, 공

□ 809 **neighborhood** [néibərhùd]   명 인근, 이웃

□ 810 **half** [hæf]   명 절반, 30분

□ 811 **until** [əntíl]   전 ～까지

□ 812 **before** [bifɔ́ːr]   전 ～전에

## Chapter 11 부사

👤 PSS & PRACTICE

□ 813 **quick** [kwik]   형 빠른

□ 814 **large** [lɑːrdʒ]   형 큰, 넓은

□ 815 **lucky** [lʌ́ki]   형 운 좋은

□ 816 **wise** [waiz]   형 현명한

□ 817 **usual** [júːʒuəl]   형 보통의

□ 818 **real** [ríːəl]   형 진짜의

□ 819 **surprising** [sərpráiziŋ]   형 놀라운

□ 820 **sincere** [sinsíər]   형 진실된, 진정한, 진심어린

□ 821 **silent** [sáilənt]   형 조용한

□ 822 **noisy** [nɔ́izi]   형 시끄러운

□ 823 **loud** [laud]   형 소리가 큰

□ 824 **sudden** [sʌ́dən]   형 갑작스러운

□ 825 **regular** [régjulər]   형 정기적인

□ 826 **serious** [síəriəs]   형 심각한, 진지한

□ 827 **brave** [breiv]   형 용감한

□ 828 **various** [vέəriəs]   형 여러 가지의, 다양한

□ 829 **main** [mein]   형 주된, 주요한

| | | | |
|---|---|---|---|
| ☐ 830 **graceful** [gréisfəl] | 형 우아한 | ☐ 848 **jacket** [dʒǽkit] | 명 재킷 |
| ☐ 831 **dear** [diər] | 형 친애하는 | ☐ 849 **suit** [suːt] | 명 수트, 정장 한 벌 |
| ☐ 832 **act** [ækt] | 동 행동하다 | ☐ 850 **garbage** [gáːrbidʒ] | 명 쓰레기 |
| ☐ 833 **appear** [əpíər] | 동 나타나다 | ☐ 851 **alarm** [əláːrm] | 명 자명종 |
| ☐ 834 **worm** [wəːrm] | 명 벌레 | ☐ 852 **put on** | (옷 따위를) 입다, 쓰다 |
| ☐ 835 **everybody** [évribàdi] | 대 각자 모두, 누구든지 | ☐ 853 **twice** [twais] | 부 두 번 |
| ☐ 836 **price** [prais] | 명 가격 | ☐ 854 **behind** [biháind] | 전 ~ 뒤에 |
| ☐ 837 **fever** [fíːvər] | 명 열 | 🚶 중간기말대비 | |
| ☐ 838 **depend on** | ~에 의지하다, ~에 달려 있다 | ☐ 855 **carrot** [kǽrət] | 명 당근 |
| ☐ 839 **never** [névər] | 부 결코 ~ 않다 | ☐ 856 **work out** | 운동하다 |
| ☐ 840 **plastic bag** [plǽstik bǽg] | 명 비닐봉지 | ☐ 857 **flash** [flæʃ] | 명 플래시, 번득임, 섬광 |
| ☐ 841 **foggy** [fɔ́ːgi] | 형 안개 낀 | ☐ 858 **dancer** [dǽnsər] | 명 댄서, 무용수 |
| ☐ 842 **deliver** [dilívər] | 동 배달하다 | ☐ 859 **junk food** [dʒʌŋk fuːd] | 명 정크 푸드 |
| ☐ 843 **meeting** [míːtiŋ] | 명 회의 | ☐ 860 **quickly** [kwíkli] | 부 빨리, 빠르게 |
| ☐ 844 **dish** [diʃ] | 명 요리 | ☐ 861 **weekly** [wíːkli] | 형 매주의, 주간의 |
| ☐ 845 **count on** | ~을 믿다 | ☐ 862 **look around** | 둘러보다 |
| ☐ 846 **hope** [houp] | 동 바라다, 희망하다 | ☐ 863 **pack** [pæk] | 동 (짐을) 싸다 |
| ☐ 847 **glasses** [glǽsiːz] | 명 안경 | ☐ 864 **stuff** [stʌf] | 명 물건 |

| | | |
|---|---|---|
| 865 **lately** [léitli] | 부 최근에, 얼마 전에 |
| 866 **happily** [hǽpili] | 부 행복하게 |
| 867 **carefully** [kɛ́ərfəli] | 부 주의하여, 조심스럽게 |
| 868 **scary** [skɛ́:əri] | 형 무서운 |
| 869 **well** [wel] | 부 잘, 좋게 |

## Chapter 12 비교구문

👤 PSS & PRACTICE

| | |
|---|---|
| 870 **hard** [hɑ:rd] | 형 힘든  부 열심히 |
| 871 **weak** [wi:k] | 형 약한 |
| 872 **smart** [smɑ:rt] | 형 영리한 |
| 873 **fat** [fæt] | 형 뚱뚱한 |
| 874 **light** [lait] | 형 가벼운 |
| 875 **mild** [maild] | 형 온화한 |
| 876 **tasty** [téisti] | 형 맛좋은 |
| 877 **strict** [strikt] | 형 엄격한 |
| 878 **hopeless** [hóuplis] | 형 가망 없는, 절망적인 |
| 879 **foolish** [fú:liʃ] | 형 어리석은 |
| 880 **patient** [péiʃənt] | 형 인내심 있는 |
| 881 **bright** [brait] | 형 밝은 |
| 882 **lovely** [lʌ́vli] | 형 사랑스러운 |
| 883 **close** [klous] | 형 가까운 |
| 884 **badly** [bǽdli] | 부 나쁘게 |
| 885 **colorful** [kʌ́lərfəl] | 형 다채로운, 형형색색의 |
| 886 **diligent** [dílədʒənt] | 형 근면한 |
| 887 **costly** [kɔ́:stli] | 형 값비싼 |
| 888 **thin** [θin] | 형 가는, 야윈 |
| 889 **slim** [slim] | 형 가는, 날씬한 |
| 890 **thick** [θik] | 형 두꺼운 |
| 891 **useless** [jú:slis] | 형 쓸모없는 |
| 892 **deep** [di:p] | 형 깊은 |
| 893 **generous** [dʒénərəs] | 형 관대한 |
| 894 **comfortable** [kʌ́mfərtəbl] | 형 편안한 |
| 895 **husband** [hʌ́zbənd] | 명 남편 |
| 896 **other** [ʌ́ðər] | 형 다른  대 다른 것 |
| 897 **modern** [mádərn] | 형 현대적인 |
| 898 **butterfly** [bʌ́tərflài] | 명 나비 |

□ 899 **public** [pʌ́blik] 　형 공공의

□ 900 **air mail** [ɛər meil] 　명 항공 우편

□ 901 **drugstore** [drʌ́gstɔ̀:r] 　명 약국

□ 902 **intelligent** [intélədʒənt] 　형 지적인, 총명한

□ 903 **excuse** [ikskjúːz] 　명 변명, 이유

□ 904 **clothing** [klóuðiŋ] 　명 의류

□ 905 **choice** [tʃɔis] 　명 선택

□ 906 **cheetah** [tʃíːtə] 　명 치타

□ 907 **bridge** [bridʒ] 　명 다리, 교량

□ 908 **score** [skɔːr] 　명 점수

□ 909 **dinosaur** [dáinəsɔ̀:r] 　명 공룡

□ 910 **pleasant** [plézənt] 　형 즐거운

□ 911 **illness** [ílnis] 　명 병

👤 중간기말대비

□ 912 **moment** [móumənt] 　명 순간

□ 913 **Antarctica** [æntɑ́:rktikə] 　명 남극대륙

□ 914 **elephant** [éləfənt] 　명 코끼리

□ 915 **shrimp** [ʃrimp] 　명 새우

□ 916 **daytime** [déitàim] 　명 낮

□ 917 **zebra** [zíːbrə] 　명 얼룩말

□ 918 **opinion** [əpínjən] 　명 의견

□ 919 **entire** [intáiər] 　형 전체의

□ 920 **giraffe** [dʒərǽf] 　명 기린

## Chapter 13 접속사

👤 PSS & PRACTICE

□ 921 **subway** [sʌ́bwèi] 　명 지하철

□ 922 **unhealthy** [ʌnhélθi] 　형 건강하지 않은

□ 923 **garden** [gɑ́:rdən] 　명 정원

□ 924 **be good with** 　～에 밝다, 능숙하다

□ 925 **work on** 　～을 열심히 하다, ～에 애쓰다

□ 926 **Japanese** [dʒæpəníːz] 　명 일본어, 일본인

□ 927 **Chinese** [tʃainíːz] 　명 중국어, 중국인

□ 928 **machine** [məʃíːn] 　명 기계

□ 929 **round** [raund] 　형 둥근

□ 930 **survive** [sərváiv] 　동 살아남다

□ 931 **traffic light** [trǽfik lait] 　명 교통 신호(등)

| | | | |
|---|---|---|---|
| 932 **supermarket** [súːpərmàːrkit] | 명 슈퍼마켓 | 949 **anywhere** [énihwὲər] | 부 어디든지 |
| 933 **dress** [dres] | 동 옷을 입다 / 명 옷 | 950 **stick out** | ~를 내밀다, 눈에 띄다 |
| 934 **warmly** [wɔ́ːrmli] | 부 따뜻하게 | 951 **tongue** [tʌŋ] | 명 혀 |
| 935 **Italian** [itǽljən] | 형 이탈리아의 | 952 **organized** [ɔ́ːrgənàizd] | 형 정리된 |
| 936 **art** [ɑːrt] | 명 예술 | 953 **volleyball** [válibɔ̀ːl] | 명 배구 |
| 937 **a little** | 조금, 약간 | 954 **raincoat** [réinkout] | 명 우의, 비옷 |
| 938 **mark** [mɑːrk] | 명 점수 | 955 **go on a field trip** | 현장학습을 가다 |
| 939 **neighbor** [néibər] | 명 이웃 | 956 **shape** [ʃeip] | 명 모양 |

🚹 **중간기말대비**

| | | | |
|---|---|---|---|
| | | 957 **be in shape** | 건강한 상태다, 몸매가 좋다 |
| 940 **rest** [rest] | 명 휴식 | | |

## Chapter **14** 전치사&속담

🚹 PSS & PRACTICE

| | | | |
|---|---|---|---|
| 941 **environment** [inváirənmənt] | 명 환경 | 958 **dawn** [dɔːn] | 명 새벽 |
| 942 **curly** [kə́ːrli] | 형 머리칼이 곱슬곱슬한 | 959 **lunchtime** [lʌ́ntʃtàim] | 명 점심시간 |
| 943 **in time** | 제시간에, 늦지 않게 | 960 **move** [muːv] | 동 이사하다 |
| 944 **harmful** [hɑ́ːrmfəl] | 형 해로운 | 961 **take a rest** | 휴식을 취하다 |
| 945 **care about** | ~를 걱정하다, 신경을 쓰다 | 962 **violin** [vàiəlín] | 명 바이올린 |
| 946 **work** [wəːrk] | 동 일하다, 작동되다 | 963 **everything** [évriθìŋ] | 대 모두, 모든 것 |
| 947 **tell the truth** | 사실을 말하다 | 964 **all day** | 하루 종일 |
| 948 **presentation** [prèzəntéiʃən] | 명 발표 | | |

| | | |
|---|---|---|
| □ 965 **stay out of** | ~을 피하다 | |
| □ 966 **mealtime** [mí:ltàim] | 명 식사 시간 | |
| □ 967 **repair** [ripέər] | 통 수리하다 | |
| □ 968 **need** [ni:d] | 통 필요로 하다 | |
| □ 969 **west** [west] | 부 서쪽으로 / 명 서쪽 | |
| □ 970 **sunset** [sʌ́nsèt] | 명 일몰 | |
| □ 971 **spring** [spriŋ] | 명 봄 | |
| □ 972 **airport** [έərpɔ̀:rt] | 명 공항 | |
| □ 973 **wedding** [wédiŋ] | 명 결혼식 | |
| □ 974 **among** [əmʌ́ŋ] | 전 ~사이에 | |
| □ 975 **space** [speis] | 명 우주, 공간 | |
| □ 976 **ground** [graund] | 명 땅바닥, 지면 | |
| □ 977 **island** [áilənd] | 명 섬 | |
| □ 978 **drawer** [drɔ́:ər] | 명 서랍 | |
| □ 979 **plane** [plein] | 명 비행기 | |
| □ 980 **rainbow** [réinbòu] | 명 무지개 | |
| □ 981 **boat** [bout] | 명 보트 | |
| □ 982 **department store** [dipá:rtmənt stɔ:r] | 명 백화점 | |

| | | |
|---|---|---|
| □ 983 **toyshop** [tɔ́iʃàp] | 명 장난감 가게 | |
| □ 984 **difference** [dífərəns] | 명 차이점 | |
| □ 985 **finger** [fíŋgər] | 명 손가락 | |
| □ 986 **wall** [wɔ:l] | 명 벽 | |
| □ 987 **hill** [hil] | 명 언덕 | |
| □ 988 **envelope** [énvəlòup] | 명 봉투 | |
| □ 989 **step** [step] | 명 (발)걸음 | |
| □ 990 **gift shop** [gift ʃap] | 명 선물 가게 | |
| □ 991 **salmon** [sǽmən] | 명 연어 | |
| □ 992 **stream** [stri:m] | 명 흐름, 시내 | |
| □ 993 **river** [rívər] | 명 강 | |
| □ 994 **tunnel** [tʌ́nəl] | 명 터널 | |
| □ 995 **town** [taun] | 명 읍, (소)도시 | |
| □ 996 **dinner** [dínər] | 명 저녁식사, 정찬 | |
| □ 997 **head for** | ~로 향하다 | |
| □ 998 **land** [lænd] | 통 착륙하다, 도착하다 | |
| □ 999 **fence** [fens] | 명 울타리 | |
| □ 1000 **spacecraft** [spéiskrὰft] | 명 우주선 | |

☐ 1001 **get well** — 병이 나아지다

☐ 1002 **coupon** [kúːpɑn] — 몡 쿠폰, 할인권

☐ 1003 **enough** [inʌ́f] — 혱 충분한

☐ 1004 **ID card(= identification card)** [aidèntəfikéiʃən kɑːrd] — 몡 신분증

☐ 1005 **crayon** [kréiən] — 몡 크레용

☐ 1006 **gargle** [gáːrgl] — 됭 양치질하다

☐ 1007 **traditional** [trədíʃənl] — 혱 전통의

☐ 1008 **jazz music** [dʒæz mjúːzik] — 몡 재즈 음악

☐ 1009 **area** [ɛ́əriə] — 몡 지역, 구역

☐ 1010 **middle-aged** [mídl-éidʒid] — 혱 중년의

☐ 1011 **treasure** [tréʒər] — 몡 보물

☐ 1012 **drama** [drɑ́ːmə] — 몡 연극

☐ 1013 **leap** [liːp] — 됭 뛰어오르다, 도약하다

☐ 1014 **haste** [heist] — 몡 서두름

☐ 1015 **bark** [bɑːrk] — 됭 짖다

☐ 1016 **shower** [ʃáuər] — 몡 소나기

☐ 1017 **spill** [spil] — 됭 엎지르다, 쏟다

☐ 1018 **policy** [pɑ́ləsi] — 몡 수단, 정책

☐ 1019 **bitter** [bítər] — 혱 쓴

☐ 1020 **sight** [sait] — 몡 시야

☐ 1021 **broth** [brɔːθ] — 몡 수프, 국

☐ 1022 **lead to** — ～로 이어지다

☐ 1023 **blame** [bleim] — 됭 ～를 탓하다, 비난하다

☐ 1024 **tool** [tuːl] — 몡 연장

☐ 1025 **workman** [wə́ːrkmən] — 몡 일꾼

☐ 1026 **put off** — 미루다

**🚶 중간기말대비**

☐ 1027 **comedian** [kəmíːdiən] — 몡 코미디언, 희극배우

☐ 1028 **do the dishes** — 설거지하다

☐ 1029 **rainy** [réini] — 혱 비가 오는

☐ 1030 **for a minute** — 잠시 동안

☐ 1031 **bungee jumping** [bʌ́ndʒi dʒʌ́mpiŋ] — 몡 번지점프

☐ 1032 **calendar** [kǽlindər] — 몡 달력

☐ 1033 **turn right** — 오른쪽으로 돌다

☐ 1034 **allowance** [əláuəns] — 몡 용돈

☐ 1035 **wisely** [wáizli] — 뷔 현명하게

□ 1036 **as a result**    결과적으로

□ 1037 **hang out**    어울려 놀다

□ 1038 **achieve** [ətʃíːv]    통 달성하다, 성취하다

□ 1039 **pain** [pein]    명 고통, 아픔

□ 1040 **monthly** [mʌ́nθli]    형 매달의 부 달마다

□ 1041 **come across**    우연히 만나다

□ 1042 **throat** [θrout]    명 목, 목구멍

□ 1043 **look like**    ~처럼 생기다, ~와 닮다

□ 1044 **spaceship** [spéisʃip]    명 우주선

□ 1045 **bazaar** [bəzáːr]    명 바자회, 특매장

□ 1046 **bacteria** [bæktíːəriə]    명 박테리아

□ 1047 **custom** [kʌ́stəm]    명 관습, 풍습

□ 1048 **different from**    ~와 다른

□ 1049 **bagel** [béigəl]    명 베이글

□ 1050 **come from**    ~에서 오다, ~ 출신이다

□ 1051 **treat** [triːt]    통 대우하다

□ 1052 **on a diet**    다이어트 중인

□ 1053 **rude** [ruːd]    형 무례한

□ 1054 **polite** [pəláit]    형 예의바른, 공손한

□ 1055 **etiquette** [étikit]    명 예의, 에티켓

□ 1056 **circle** [sə́ːrkl]    명 원, 동그라미

□ 1057 **thumb** [θʌm]    명 엄지

□ 1058 **forefinger** [fɔ́ːrfiŋgər]    명 검지

□ 1059 **sore** [sɔːr]    형 아픈

□ 1060 **earn** [əːrn]    통 (돈을) 벌다

□ 1061 **about** [əbáut]    전 ~에 대한 부 약, ~쯤

□ 1062 **moreover** [mɔːróuvər]    부 게다가

□ 1063 **suffer** [sʌ́fər]    통 고통을 받다

□ 1064 **welcome** [wélkəm]    통 환영하다

□ 1065 **donate** [dóuneit]    통 기부하다

□ 1066 **in need**    어려움에 처한, 궁핍한

□ 1067 **mud flat** [mʌd flæt]    명 개펄

□ 1068 **take place**    일어나다, 발생하다

□ 1069 **last** [læst]    통 지속되다

□ 1070 **lost** [lɔːst]    형 잃어버린, 분실된

□ 1071 **guesthouse** [gésthàus]    명 관광객용 숙소

# 중학영문법 3800제 1학년

# Word Test

## Problem Solving Skill

MOTHERTONGUE
마더텅출판사
since 1999.4.1.

날짜:            학급:            이름:            점수        / 35

### ●영어를 우리말로 쓰세요.

| | | | |
|---|---|---|---|
| 01 | player | 10 | angry |
| 02 | parents | 11 | happen |
| 03 | speak | 12 | have breakfast |
| 04 | be afraid of | 13 | movie |
| 05 | newspaper | 14 | friendly |
| 06 | pretty | 15 | interesting |
| 07 | warm | 16 | draw |
| 08 | go to the cinema | 17 | wonderful |
| 09 | photograph | 18 | go jogging |

### ●우리말을 영어로 쓰세요.

| | | | |
|---|---|---|---|
| 19 | 즐기다 | 28 | 비가 오다 |
| 20 | 일하다 | 29 | 배고픈 |
| 21 | 경찰관 | 30 | 인터넷을 이용하다 |
| 22 | 늦은 | 31 | ~의 가까이(에), 가까이 |
| 23 | 결혼한 | 32 | 마시다 |
| 24 | 자전거 | 33 | 피곤한, 지친 |
| 25 | 병원 | 34 | 바쁜 |
| 26 | 한가한, 자유로운 | 35 | 방문객 |
| 27 | 신이 난, 들뜬 | | |

# Word Test 036-071 — Day 02

날짜:　　　　　학급:　　　　　이름:　　　　　점수　　/36

**●영어를 우리말로 쓰세요.**

| 01 | amazing | 10 | prepared |
|---|---|---|---|
| 02 | fast | 11 | go climbing |
| 03 | careful | 12 | grade |
| 04 | vacation | 13 | keep in touch |
| 05 | enter | 14 | really |
| 06 | sleep | 15 | great |
| 07 | take a break | 16 | make a noise |
| 08 | wear | 17 | from now on |
| 09 | turn on | 18 | ready |

**●우리말을 영어로 쓰세요.**

| 19 | 사다 | 28 | 공부하다 |
|---|---|---|---|
| 20 | 작가 | 29 | 헬멧, 안전모 |
| 21 | 조용한 | 30 | 모퉁이 |
| 22 | 딸 | 31 | (탈것에) 타다 |
| 23 | 교실 | 32 | 수영하다 |
| 24 | 속상한, 마음이 상한 | 33 | 서두르다 |
| 25 | 결석한 | 34 | 체육관 |
| 26 | 소개하다 | 35 | 청소하다, 깨끗한 |
| 27 | 거대한 | 36 | 걱정하다 |

날짜:　　　　　학급:　　　　　이름:　　　　　점수　　/36

● 영어를 우리말로 쓰세요.

01 | sweet

02 | make a mistake

03 | cook

04 | handsome

05 | ask

06 | shine

07 | delicious

08 | exciting

09 | storybook

10 | terrible

11 | believe

12 | article

13 | keep a diary

14 | strange

15 | engineer

16 | subject

17 | wash the dishes

18 | healthy

● 우리말을 영어로 쓰세요.

19 | 심다

20 | ～이 되다

21 | 신, 시큼한 (맛의)

22 | 페인트를 칠하다

23 | 거짓말쟁이

24 | 비밀

25 | 산

26 | 사촌

27 | 정직한, 솔직한

28 | 호의

29 | 지루한

30 | 질문

31 | 사전

32 | 수학

33 | 폭포

34 | 매우 좋아하는

35 | 움직이다

36 | 박물관

# Word Test 108-142 · Day 04

날짜:　　　　학급:　　　　이름:　　　　점수　　/35

## ● 영어를 우리말로 쓰세요.

| | | | |
|---|---|---|---|
| 01 | umbrella | 10 | often |
| 02 | sweater | 11 | watch |
| 03 | senior citizen | 12 | bring |
| 04 | hometown | 13 | event |
| 05 | play computer games | 14 | report card |
| 06 | practice | 15 | cloudy |
| 07 | classmate | 16 | far |
| 08 | guitar | 17 | office worker |
| 09 | present | | |

## ● 우리말을 영어로 쓰세요.

| | | | |
|---|---|---|---|
| 18 | 모래성 | 27 | 허튼소리 |
| 19 | 수프 | 28 | 텔레비전 |
| 20 | 동화, 옛날 이야기 | 29 | 숙녀, 여성 |
| 21 | 역사 | 30 | 게으른 |
| 22 | 저녁 | 31 | 배드민턴 |
| 23 | 수영 선수 | 32 | 어제 |
| 24 | 스카프, 목도리 | 33 | 정보 |
| 25 | 서점 | 34 | 농부 |
| 26 | 아름다운 | 35 | 채소 |

● 영어를 우리말로 쓰세요.

01 | lose

02 | lay

03 | send

04 | reach

05 | copy

06 | wish

07 | kick

08 | know

09 | get

10 | teach

11 | pay

12 | catch

13 | say

14 | finish

15 | push

16 | impress

17 | touch

18 | wake

● 우리말을 영어로 쓰세요.

19 | 놓치다, 그리워하다

20 | 노래하다

21 | 섞다

22 | 팔다

23 | 지나가다, (시험 등을) 통과하다

24 | 돕다, 거들다

25 | 걷다

26 | 노력하다, 시도하다

27 | 서다, 서 있다

28 | 교차하다, 건너가다

29 | 할머니

30 | 던지다

31 | 놓다, 두다

32 | 불타다

33 | 풀다, 해결하다

34 | 쓰다, 소비하다

35 | 소리가 나다

| 날짜: | 학급: | 이름: | 점수 | /36 |

## ●영어를 우리말로 쓰세요.

| 01 | understand | 10 | cost |
|----|------------|----|------|
| 02 | grow | 11 | leave |
| 03 | live | 12 | seem |
| 04 | laugh | 13 | envy |
| 05 | arrive | 14 | give |
| 06 | turn | 15 | see |
| 07 | set | 16 | tell |
| 08 | keep | 17 | hear |
| 09 | dream | 18 | think |

## ●우리말을 영어로 쓰세요.

| 19 | 해치다 | 28 | 나르다, 운반하다 |
|----|--------|----|-----------------|
| 20 | 껴안다 | 29 | 날다 |
| 21 | 머무르다 | 30 | 떨어지다 |
| 22 | 갈채하다, 응원하다 | 31 | 잊다 |
| 23 | 깨뜨리다 | 32 | 판단하다 |
| 24 | 이기다 | 33 | 멈추다 |
| 25 | 반복하다 | 34 | (건물 등을) 짓다 |
| 26 | 보여주다 | 35 | 빌려주다 |
| 27 | 의미하다 | 36 | 사용하다 |

# Word Test 214-249      Day 07

날짜:      학급:      이름:      점수   / 36

## ● 영어를 우리말로 쓰세요.

| | | | |
|---|---|---|---|
| 01 | agree | 10 | raise |
| 02 | in the morning | 11 | order |
| 03 | call | 12 | change |
| 04 | check | 13 | drop |
| 05 | dance | 14 | place |
| 06 | cover | 15 | improve |
| 07 | plan | 16 | suggest |
| 08 | guess | 17 | invent |
| 09 | guide | 18 | escape |

## ● 우리말을 영어로 쓰세요.

| | | | |
|---|---|---|---|
| 19 | 가입하다, 합류하다 | 28 | 축복하다 |
| 20 | 배우다 | 29 | 구하다, 절약하다, 저축하다 |
| 21 | 뛰다, 뛰어넘다 | 30 | ～을 야기시키다, 초래하다 |
| 22 | 준수하다, 따르다 | 31 | 모으다 |
| 23 | 동쪽 | 32 | 재채기하다 |
| 24 | 솔질하다 | 33 | 이끼 |
| 25 | 병든, 아픈 | 34 | 이기다, 때리다 |
| 26 | 공격하다 | 35 | 지구 |
| 27 | 수도 | 36 | 장식하다 |

# Word Test 250-284 — Day 08

날짜:　　　　　학급:　　　　　이름:　　　　　점수　　/ 35

●영어를 우리말로 쓰세요.

01 | shout

02 | return

03 | hurt

04 | lead

05 | smell

06 | marry

07 | collect

08 | end

09 | have

10 | let

11 | hate

12 | fight

13 | connect

14 | spread

15 | slide

16 | add

17 | train

●우리말을 영어로 쓰세요.

18 | 실패하다

19 | 삼키다

20 | 망치다

21 | 먹이다, 먹이

22 | 공유하다

23 | 결정하다

24 | 궁금해 하다, ~에 놀라다

25 | 놀라게 하다

26 | 낭비하다

27 | 구르다

28 | 따르다, 붓다

29 | (자물쇠로) 잠그다

30 | 타자를 치다

31 | 대답하다

32 | 묶다

33 | (음식을) 차려주다, 제공하다

34 | 철자를 말하다

35 | (빵 등을) 굽다

# Word Test 285-316

**Day 09**

날짜:　　　　　　학급:　　　　　　이름:　　　　　　점수　　/ 32

## ●영어를 우리말로 쓰세요.

| | | | |
|---|---|---|---|
| 01 | make dinner | 09 | ago |
| 02 | holiday | 10 | have lunch |
| 03 | actor | 11 | exam |
| 04 | take | 12 | smile |
| 05 | restaurant | 13 | heavily |
| 06 | role | 14 | rise |
| 07 | ill | 15 | choose |
| 08 | bear | 16 | during |

## ●우리말을 영어로 쓰세요.

| | | | |
|---|---|---|---|
| 17 | 시간을 만들다, 시간을 내다 | 25 | 외식하다 |
| 18 | 도서관 | 26 | 일어나다, 발발하다 |
| 19 | 불다 | 27 | 일출 |
| 20 | 소설 | 28 | 자정 |
| 21 | 눈이 내리다 | 29 | 건너뛰다 |
| 22 | (종, 벨이) 울리다 | 30 | 계획, 기획, 프로젝트 |
| 23 | 물다 | 31 | 조부, 조모 |
| 24 | 함께 | 32 | (물속으로) 뛰어들다 |

# Word Test 317 - 350   Day 10

날짜:      학급:      이름:      점수   / 34

## ●영어를 우리말로 쓰세요.

| | | | |
|---|---|---|---|
| 01 | take a picture | 10 | get up |
| 02 | visit | 11 | pick |
| 03 | begin | 12 | discuss |
| 04 | hide | 13 | listen to |
| 05 | these days | 14 | loudly |
| 06 | explain | 15 | last year |
| 07 | review | 16 | thank |
| 08 | throw away | 17 | field trip |
| 09 | climb | | |

## ●우리말을 영어로 쓰세요.

| | | | |
|---|---|---|---|
| 18 | 매일 일어나는 | 27 | 디자이너 |
| 19 | 탁구 | 28 | 카펫, 깔개 |
| 20 | 미래 | 29 | 헤드폰 |
| 21 | 스파게티 | 30 | 열대의 |
| 22 | 연 | 31 | 이모, 고모 |
| 23 | 야구를 하다 | 32 | 쓰다, 집필하다 |
| 24 | 날씨 | 33 | 주말 |
| 25 | 외국인 | 34 | 바비큐 파티를 하다 |
| 26 | 콘서트, 음악회 | | |

### ●영어를 우리말로 쓰세요.

| | | | |
|---|---|---|---|
| 01 | have a seat | 10 | go out |
| 02 | bill | 11 | lecture |
| 03 | find | 12 | stair |
| 04 | try on | 13 | match |
| 05 | alone | 14 | clothes |
| 06 | make it | 15 | exit |
| 07 | outside | 16 | for a while |
| 08 | break off | 17 | dangerous |
| 09 | casual | 18 | traffic |

### ●우리말을 영어로 쓰세요.

| | | | |
|---|---|---|---|
| 19 | 나뭇가지 | 28 | 법 |
| 20 | 전화번호 | 29 | 목마른 |
| 21 | 젓가락 | 30 | (시간 단위) 분 |
| 22 | 재활용하다 | 31 | 무엇인가, 어떤 것 |
| 23 | 따르다 | 32 | 문제 |
| 24 | 옳은, 오른쪽의 | 33 | 오늘밤에 |
| 25 | 내일 | 34 | 엘리베이터 |
| 26 | 진실의, 참된 | 35 | 약속 |
| 27 | 초대하다 | | |

# Word Test 386-418　　Day 12

날짜:　　　　학급:　　　　이름:　　　　점수　　/ 33

## ●영어를 우리말로 쓰세요.

| | | | |
|---|---|---|---|
| 01 | clean up | 09 | pick up |
| 02 | human | 10 | kill |
| 03 | speech | 11 | theater |
| 04 | be late for school | 12 | lie |
| 05 | tell a lie | 13 | matter |
| 06 | dentist | 14 | contest |
| 07 | balloon | 15 | take care of |
| 08 | protect | 16 | expression |

## ●우리말을 영어로 쓰세요.

| | | | |
|---|---|---|---|
| 17 | ~에 관심이 있다 | 26 | 다람쥐 |
| 18 | 전쟁 | 27 | 무엇, 아무것 |
| 19 | 끄다 | 28 | 교장 선생님 |
| 20 | 치통 | 29 | 잠들다 |
| 21 | 우체국 | 30 | 대통령, 사장 |
| 22 | 배달하다 | 31 | 주차하다 |
| 23 | 성공하다 | 32 | 외국의 |
| 24 | 운동하다 | 33 | 똑바로, 일직선으로 |
| 25 | 벗다 | | |

# Day 13

날짜:     학급:     이름:     점수   / 33

## ●영어를 우리말로 쓰세요.

| | | | |
|---|---|---|---|
| 01 | fresh | 09 | truth |
| 02 | found | 10 | refrigerator |
| 03 | building | 11 | painting |
| 04 | language | 12 | teenager |
| 05 | robber | 13 | princess |
| 06 | dead | 14 | beauty |
| 07 | audience | 15 | fix |
| 08 | village | 16 | someone |

## ●우리말을 영어로 쓰세요.

| | | | |
|---|---|---|---|
| 17 | 모여들다, 붐비다 | 26 | 존경하다 |
| 18 | 자유 | 27 | 한 번 |
| 19 | 디자인하다 | 28 | 훔치다 |
| 20 | 기억 | 29 | 어떤 사람, 누군가 |
| 21 | 밀림지대, 정글 | 30 | 선출하다 |
| 22 | 태어나다 | 31 | 음악가 |
| 23 | 출판하다 | 32 | 독자 |
| 24 | 벌 | 33 | ～하게 하다 |
| 25 | 잡지 | | |

날짜:     학급:     이름:     점수   /36

## ●영어를 우리말로 쓰세요.

| | | | |
|---|---|---|---|
| 01 | brush | 10 | candle |
| 02 | wealth | 11 | sheep |
| 03 | safe | 12 | kindness |
| 04 | bottle | 13 | happiness |
| 05 | wagon | 14 | country |
| 06 | bath | 15 | mouse |
| 07 | festival | 16 | pleasure |
| 08 | peace | 17 | factory |
| 09 | wife | 18 | deer |

## ●우리말을 영어로 쓰세요.

| | | | |
|---|---|---|---|
| 19 | 거위, 기러기 | 28 | 우정 |
| 20 | 두통 | 29 | 밀가루 |
| 21 | 동정, 연민 | 30 | 주소 |
| 22 | 선반 | 31 | 달, 개월 |
| 23 | 연기 | 32 | 모양, 형상 |
| 24 | 황소 | 33 | 나무 조각, 구역 |
| 25 | 지붕 | 34 | 수업, 교훈 |
| 26 | 여권 | 35 | 생각, 아이디어 |
| 27 | 포스터, 전단 광고 | 36 | 모기 |

날짜:　　　　학급:　　　　이름:　　　　점수　　/36

## ●영어를 우리말로 쓰세요.

| | |
|---|---|
| 01 | another |
| 02 | faithful |
| 03 | popular |
| 04 | station |
| 05 | floor |
| 06 | airless |
| 07 | seat |
| 08 | special |
| 09 | snake |
| 10 | thief |
| 11 | clear |
| 12 | university |
| 13 | autumn |
| 14 | same |
| 15 | bathroom |
| 16 | European |
| 17 | armchair |
| 18 | imagine |

## ●우리말을 영어로 쓰세요.

| | |
|---|---|
| 19 | 곤충 |
| 20 | 가구 |
| 21 | ~로 알려져 있다 |
| 22 | 도심지, 상업 지구 |
| 23 | (건물의) 층 |
| 24 | 충고 |
| 25 | 호주머니 |
| 26 | 습한 |
| 27 | 유명한 |
| 28 | 컵, 머그잔 |
| 29 | 학, 두루미 |
| 30 | 암 |
| 31 | 사발 |
| 32 | 분필, 초크 |
| 33 | 초급의, 초등의 |
| 34 | 감각 |
| 35 | 잠깐의 휴식 |
| 36 | 비행기 |

날짜:　　　　학급:　　　　이름:　　　　점수　　/ 33

## ●영어를 우리말로 쓰세요.

01 | each other

02 | blackboard

03 | be full of

04 | always

05 | leaf

06 | uncle

07 | in front of

08 | look for

09 | recognize

10 | volunteer

11 | clover

12 | useful

13 | at the end of

14 | pair

15 | cent

16 | several

## ●우리말을 영어로 쓰세요.

17 | (음식을 얇게 썬) 조각

18 | 청바지

19 | 꼬리

20 | 오크나무

21 | 빵집, 제과점

22 | ~에 들어가다

23 | 늑대

24 | 가위

25 | 접시, 그릇

26 | 쉬다, 휴식하다

27 | 인간, 사람

28 | 제복, 교복

29 | 관광, 구경

30 | 칠면조

31 | 후식, 디저트

32 | 연극, 놀이

33 | 목걸이

날짜:     학급:     이름:     점수 / 35

## ● 영어를 우리말로 쓰세요.

| | | | |
|---|---|---|---|
| 01 | between | 10 | belong to |
| 02 | example | 11 | journey |
| 03 | horror | 12 | weigh |
| 04 | course | 13 | tough |
| 05 | culture | 14 | science fiction |
| 06 | still | 15 | prize |
| 07 | pay for | 16 | fault |
| 08 | dark | 17 | important |
| 09 | no way | | |

## ● 우리말을 영어로 쓰세요.

| | | | |
|---|---|---|---|
| 18 | 거북 | 27 | 자살하다 |
| 19 | 소나무 | 28 | 방과 후에 |
| 20 | 담임 선생님 | 29 | 가을 |
| 21 | 유사한 | 30 | 교과서 |
| 22 | 감기에 걸리다 | 31 | 배낭 |
| 23 | 썩은 | 32 | 부정직한 |
| 24 | 과학 | 33 | 자랑스러운 |
| 25 | 소유하다 | 34 | (중량의 단위) 파운드 |
| 26 | 싸다, 포장하다 | 35 | 색을 칠하다, 색 |

# Word Test 592-625 — Day 18

날짜:     학급:     이름:     점수   /34

## ●영어를 우리말로 쓰세요.

| | | | |
|---|---|---|---|
| 01 | historic | 10 | on the Internet |
| 02 | surprised | 11 | grow up |
| 03 | each | 12 | ask for |
| 04 | soon | 13 | musical instrument |
| 05 | go back | 14 | get to |
| 06 | turn | 15 | hamster |
| 07 | place | 16 | pleased |
| 08 | easy | 17 | goal |
| 09 | expect | | |

## ●우리말을 영어로 쓰세요.

| | | | |
|---|---|---|---|
| 18 | 청구서 | 27 | 귀가 먼 |
| 19 | 필요한 것 | 28 | 항해하다 |
| 20 | 평화로운 | 29 | 행방불명이 되다 |
| 21 | 거울 | 30 | 조종사 |
| 22 | 칼 | 31 | 간단한, 단순한 |
| 23 | 치료 | 32 | 살을 빼다 |
| 24 | 숨쉬다 | 33 | 과학자 |
| 25 | 계절 | 34 | 모피, 털 |
| 26 | 도움이 되는 | | |

날짜:     학급:     이름:     점수   / 35

## ●영어를 우리말로 쓰세요.

01 | talk about

02 | hobby

03 | race

04 | early

05 | cut down

06 | storm

07 | abroad

08 | see a doctor

09 | pool

10 | travel

11 | do volunteer work

12 | chemical

13 | campaign

14 | take part in

15 | whole

16 | one's school days

17 | blind

## ●우리말을 영어로 쓰세요.

18 | ~에게서 소식을 듣다

19 | 좌우로 (흔들리는)

20 | 요양원

21 | 마스코트

22 | 흔들(리)다, 떨리다

23 | 블라우스

24 | 식물

25 | 필통

26 | 잡담하다, 채팅하다

27 | 뒤쫓다

28 | 화가

29 | 잡초

30 | 산책하다

31 | 습관, 버릇

32 | 닫다, 막다, (눈을) 감다

33 | ~에 집중하다

34 | 미식축구

35 | 시간을 아끼다

# Word Test 661-693　　　　　　　　　Day 20

날짜:　　　　　　학급:　　　　　　이름:　　　　　　점수　　　/ 33

●영어를 우리말로 쓰세요.

| | |
|---|---|
| 01 | stadium |
| 02 | take a test |
| 03 | come out |
| 04 | play the violin |
| 05 | keep ~ from … |
| 06 | disabled |
| 07 | win a prize |
| 08 | suddenly |
| 09 | continue |
| 10 | cartoon |
| 11 | bench |
| 12 | through |
| 13 | go on a picnic |
| 14 | give up |
| 15 | thank for |
| 16 | go for a walk |
| 17 | mind |

●우리말을 영어로 쓰세요.

| | |
|---|---|
| 18 | 자연 |
| 19 | 소음 |
| 20 | 우주 비행사 |
| 21 | 식사 |
| 22 | ~를 잘하다 |
| 23 | 규칙 |
| 24 | 극복하다 |
| 25 | 언젠가, 머지않아 |
| 26 | 건강 |
| 27 | 아무나, 누구나 |
| 28 | 눈물 |
| 29 | 나이가 지긋한 |
| 30 | 농사를 짓다 |
| 31 | 한계 |
| 32 | 활동 |
| 33 | 규칙적으로 |

날짜: 　　　　　학급: 　　　　　이름: 　　　　　점수 　　/ 34

---

●영어를 우리말로 쓰세요.

| | | | | |
|---|---|---|---|---|
| 01 | apologize | | 10 | gas |
| 02 | ride a bicycle | | 11 | person |
| 03 | avoid | | 12 | hold |
| 04 | overflow | | 13 | along |
| 05 | in-line skating | | 14 | be good for |
| 06 | be bad for | | 15 | remember |
| 07 | result | | 16 | little by little |
| 08 | get rid of | | 17 | trash |
| 09 | fishing | | | |

---

●우리말을 영어로 쓰세요.

| | | | | |
|---|---|---|---|---|
| 18 | 생산품 | | 27 | 계단을 이용하다 |
| 19 | 범람하다, 홍수 | | 28 | 싫증이 나다 |
| 20 | 행동 | | 29 | 도움을 주다 |
| 21 | 차고 세일 | | 30 | 해변 |
| 22 | 영화 | | 31 | 회사 |
| 23 | 벽돌 | | 32 | 여배우 |
| 24 | 힘, 기운, 강점 | | 33 | 죽음 |
| 25 | 참새 | | 34 | 그러므로 |
| 26 | 정문, (대)문 | | | |

# Word Test 728 - 760

**Day 22**

날짜:　　　　　학급:　　　　　이름:　　　　　점수　　/33

## ●영어를 우리말로 쓰세요.

01 | topic

02 | enjoyable

03 | look at

04 | disappointed

05 | show up

06 | readily

07 | key

08 | piece

09 | danger

10 | accident

11 | set up

12 | satisfied

13 | poor

14 | broken

15 | situation

16 | performance

## ●우리말을 영어로 쓰세요.

17 | 휴대폰

18 | 재능

19 | 경쟁하다, ~와 겨루다

20 | 마늘

21 | 무대

22 | 유창하게

23 | 굶주림, 기아

24 | 카네이션

25 | (불에) 굽다

26 | 양파

27 | 들꽃, 야생초

28 | 보름달

29 | 유리

30 | 피곤하게 만드는

31 | 들판

32 | 충격적인

33 | 주저하는, 망설이는

# Word Test 761 - 795      Day 23



## ● 영어를 우리말로 쓰세요.

| | | | | |
|---|---|---|---|---|
| 01 | trouble | | 10 | else |
| 02 | be sold out | | 11 | boil |
| 03 | past | | 12 | chance |
| 04 | planet | | 13 | crowded |
| 05 | grade | | 14 | luck |
| 06 | discover | | 15 | bride |
| 07 | medicine | | 16 | sickness |
| 08 | degree | | 17 | clever |
| 09 | rock | | 18 | courage |

## ● 우리말을 영어로 쓰세요.

| | | | | |
|---|---|---|---|---|
| 19 | ~이 없이 | | 28 | 버터 |
| 20 | 틀린 | | 29 | 필요한 |
| 21 | 프랑스의, 프랑스어 | | 30 | 100년, 세기 |
| 22 | 동물 | | 31 | 궁금한, 호기심이 많은 |
| 23 | 표, 투표 | | 32 | 궁전 |
| 24 | 지갑 | | 33 | 룸메이트 |
| 25 | 학급, 수업 | | 34 | 기자 |
| 26 | 바구니 | | 35 | 완벽한 |
| 27 | 사원 | | | |

날짜:    학급:    이름:    점수   / 34

● 영어를 우리말로 쓰세요.

| | | | |
|---|---|---|---|
| 01 | until | 09 | cafeteria |
| 02 | spirit | 10 | various |
| 03 | noisy | 11 | wise |
| 04 | nothing special | 12 | silent |
| 05 | regular | 13 | before |
| 06 | experience | 14 | surprising |
| 07 | difficulty | 15 | sound |
| 08 | quick | 16 | sincere |

● 우리말을 영어로 쓰세요.

| | | | |
|---|---|---|---|
| 17 | 보통의 | 26 | 주된, 주요한 |
| 18 | 용감한 | 27 | 운 좋은 |
| 19 | 절반, 30분 | 28 | 소리가 큰 |
| 20 | 큰, 넓은 | 29 | 모래 |
| 21 | 4분의 1, 15분 | 30 | 교회 |
| 22 | 진짜의 | 31 | 인근, 이웃 |
| 23 | 노력, 공 | 32 | 심각한, 진지한 |
| 24 | 갑작스러운 | 33 | 봅슬레이 |
| 25 | 놀이터, 운동장 | 34 | 온도 |

날짜:     학급:     이름:     점수   / 35

## ●영어를 우리말로 쓰세요.

| | | | |
|---|---|---|---|
| 01 | put on | 10 | meeting |
| 02 | worm | 11 | act |
| 03 | garbage | 12 | dish |
| 04 | foggy | 13 | stuff |
| 05 | quickly | 14 | hope |
| 06 | twice | 15 | appear |
| 07 | dear | 16 | never |
| 08 | depend on | 17 | graceful |
| 09 | work out | 18 | price |

## ●우리말을 영어로 쓰세요.

| | | | |
|---|---|---|---|
| 19 | 비닐봉지 | 28 | 플래시, 번득임, 섬광 |
| 20 | 댄서, 무용수 | 29 | 배달하다 |
| 21 | 안경 | 30 | 재킷 |
| 22 | 매주의, 주간의 | 31 | 열 |
| 23 | ～ 뒤에 | 32 | 자명종 |
| 24 | 각자 모두, 누구든지 | 33 | (짐을) 싸다 |
| 25 | 당근 | 34 | 수트, 정장 한 벌 |
| 26 | 둘러보다 | 35 | 정크 푸드 |
| 27 | ～을 믿다 | | |

날짜:　　　　　학급:　　　　　이름:　　　　　점수　　　/ 34

## ●영어를 우리말로 쓰세요.

01 | well

02 | useless

03 | scary

04 | mild

05 | other

06 | lately

07 | badly

08 | smart

09 | costly

10 | patient

11 | happily

12 | thin

13 | tasty

14 | hard

15 | colorful

16 | foolish

17 | light

## ●우리말을 영어로 쓰세요.

18 | 두꺼운

19 | 엄격한

20 | 깊은

21 | 주의하여, 조심스럽게

22 | 가는, 날씬한

23 | 뚱뚱한

24 | 남편

25 | 나비

26 | 근면한

27 | 밝은

28 | 편안한

29 | 가망 없는, 절망적인

30 | 사랑스러운

31 | 약한

32 | 관대한

33 | 가까운

34 | 현대적인

날짜:　　　학급:　　　이름:　　　점수　　/ 33

## ●영어를 우리말로 쓰세요.

| | | | |
|---|---|---|---|
| 01 | opinion | 10 | unhealthy |
| 02 | choice | 11 | drugstore |
| 03 | be good with | 12 | machine |
| 04 | pleasant | 13 | work on |
| 05 | survive | 14 | round |
| 06 | public | 15 | moment |
| 07 | daytime | 16 | score |
| 08 | clothing | 17 | entire |
| 09 | illness | | |

## ●우리말을 영어로 쓰세요.

| | | | |
|---|---|---|---|
| 18 | 변명, 이유 | 26 | 얼룩말 |
| 19 | 기린 | 27 | 다리, 교량 |
| 20 | 남극대륙 | 28 | 중국어, 중국인 |
| 21 | 항공 우편 | 29 | 코끼리 |
| 22 | 공룡 | 30 | 정원 |
| 23 | 교통 신호(등) | 31 | 지적인, 총명한 |
| 24 | 새우 | 32 | 지하철 |
| 25 | 치타 | 33 | 일본어, 일본인 |

날짜:　　　　　학급:　　　　　이름:　　　　　점수　　/ 33

## ●영어를 우리말로 쓰세요.

01 | take a rest

02 | care about

03 | stick out

04 | warmly

05 | dawn

06 | neighbor

07 | go on a field trip

08 | volleyball

09 | anywhere

10 | mark

11 | be in shape

12 | environment

13 | supermarket

14 | move

15 | harmful

16 | organized

17 | in time

## ●우리말을 영어로 쓰세요.

18 | 혀

19 | 이탈리아의

20 | 점심시간

21 | 일하다, 작동되다

22 | 발표

23 | 옷을 입다

24 | 우의, 비옷

25 | 하루 종일

26 | 휴식

27 | 사실을 말하다

28 | 조금, 약간

29 | 예술

30 | 바이올린

31 | 머리칼이 곱슬곱슬한

32 | 모두, 모든 것

33 | 모양

날짜:　　　　　학급:　　　　　이름:　　　　　점수　　/ 36

## ●영어를 우리말로 쓰세요.

| | | | |
|---|---|---|---|
| 01 | difference | 10 | land |
| 02 | among | 11 | drawer |
| 03 | stream | 12 | spacecraft |
| 04 | repair | 13 | stay out of |
| 05 | plane | 14 | gift shop |
| 06 | dinner | 15 | space |
| 07 | envelope | 16 | fence |
| 08 | mealtime | 17 | ground |
| 09 | step | 18 | town |

## ●우리말을 영어로 쓰세요.

| | | | |
|---|---|---|---|
| 19 | 벽 | 28 | 필요로 하다 |
| 20 | 공항 | 29 | 장난감 가게 |
| 21 | 강 | 30 | 연어 |
| 22 | 보트 | 31 | 백화점 |
| 23 | 터널 | 32 | 봄 |
| 24 | 서쪽으로, 서쪽 | 33 | 섬 |
| 25 | 언덕 | 34 | 손가락 |
| 26 | 무지개 | 35 | 일몰 |
| 27 | ～로 향하다 | 36 | 결혼식 |

날짜:　　　　학급:　　　　이름:　　　　점수　　/ 35

## ●영어를 우리말로 쓰세요.

01 | treasure

02 | wisely

03 | get well

04 | broth

05 | gargle

06 | leap

07 | enough

08 | lead to

09 | haste

10 | do the dishes

11 | ID card

12 | area

13 | tool

14 | traditional

15 | for a minute

16 | put off

17 | policy

18 | workman

## ●우리말을 영어로 쓰세요.

19 | 시야

20 | 중년의

21 | 달력

22 | 소나기

23 | ~를 탓하다, 비난하다

24 | 크레용

25 | 쓴

26 | 엎지르다, 쏟다

27 | 오른쪽으로 돌다

28 | 연극

29 | 비가 오는

30 | 짖다

31 | 코미디언, 희극배우

32 | 번지점프

33 | 쿠폰, 할인권

34 | 용돈

35 | 재즈 음악

날짜:　　　　학급:　　　　이름:　　　　점수　　/ 36

## ●영어를 우리말로 쓰세요.

01 | take place

02 | come across

03 | forefinger

04 | spaceship

05 | earn

06 | bazaar

07 | as a result

08 | sore

09 | treat

10 | donate

11 | hang out

12 | about

13 | look like

14 | welcome

15 | in need

16 | come from

17 | moreover

18 | achieve

## ●우리말을 영어로 쓰세요.

19 | 원, 동그라미

20 | 박테리아

21 | 개펄

22 | ~와 다른

23 | 지속되다

24 | 다이어트 중인

25 | 엄지

26 | 고통, 아픔

27 | 예의바른, 공손한

28 | 잃어버린, 분실된

29 | 무례한

30 | 베이글

31 | 예의, 에티켓

32 | 매달의, 달마다

33 | 관광객용 숙소

34 | 관습, 풍습

35 | 고통을 받다

36 | 목, 목구멍

# 16차 개정판 중학영문법 3800제 1학년 학습계획표

| DAY | Ch | 학습내용 | 학습날짜 | |
|---|---|---|---|---|
| DAY 1 | 1 | PSS 1-1 ~ 1-4 | 월 | 일 |
| DAY 2 | | PSS 1-5 ~ 1-9 | 월 | 일 |
| DAY 3 | | PSS 1-10 ~ 1-13 | 월 | 일 |
| DAY 4 | | PSS 2-1 ~ 2-5 | 월 | 일 |
| DAY 5 | | 중간·기말고사 대비문제 | 월 | 일 |
| DAY 6 | 2 | PSS 1-1 ~ 2-5 | 월 | 일 |
| DAY 7 | | PSS 3 ~ 4-4 | 월 | 일 |
| DAY 8 | | PSS 5-1 ~ 5-2 | 월 | 일 |
| DAY 9 | | 중간·기말고사 대비문제 | 월 | 일 |
| DAY 10 | 3 | PSS 1 ~ 4-2 | 월 | 일 |
| DAY 11 | | PSS 4-3 ~ 4-6 | 월 | 일 |
| DAY 12 | | PSS 4-7 ~ 4-10 | 월 | 일 |
| DAY 13 | | 중간·기말고사 대비문제 | 월 | 일 |
| DAY 14 | 4 | PSS 1 ~ 2 | 월 | 일 |
| DAY 15 | | PSS 3 ~ 4 | 월 | 일 |
| DAY 16 | | PSS 5 ~ 6 | 월 | 일 |
| DAY 17 | | 중간·기말고사 대비문제 | 월 | 일 |
| DAY 18 | | Chapter 1 ~ 4 Review | 월 | 일 |
| DAY 19 | 5 | PSS 1 ~ 2-3 | 월 | 일 |
| DAY 20 | | PSS 3 ~ 5 | 월 | 일 |
| DAY 21 | | PSS 6 ~ 11 | 월 | 일 |
| DAY 22 | | 중간·기말고사 대비문제 | 월 | 일 |
| DAY 23 | 6 | PSS 1 ~ 3 | 월 | 일 |
| DAY 24 | | PSS 4 ~ 5-3 | 월 | 일 |
| DAY 25 | | PSS 6-1 ~ 7 | 월 | 일 |
| DAY 26 | | 중간·기말고사 대비문제 | 월 | 일 |
| DAY 27 | 7 | PSS 1-1 ~ 1-2 | 월 | 일 |
| DAY 28 | | PSS 2 ~ 3 | 월 | 일 |
| DAY 29 | | PSS 4-1 ~ 4-2 | 월 | 일 |
| DAY 30 | | 중간·기말고사 대비문제 | 월 | 일 |

| DAY | Ch | 학습내용 | 학습날짜 | |
|---|---|---|---|---|
| DAY 31 | 8 | PSS 1 ~ 2 | 월 | 일 |
| DAY 32 | | PSS 3-1 ~ 3-3 | 월 | 일 |
| DAY 33 | | 중간·기말고사 대비문제 | 월 | 일 |
| DAY 34 | 9 | PSS 1 ~ 3 | 월 | 일 |
| DAY 35 | | PSS 4 ~ 5 | 월 | 일 |
| DAY 36 | | 중간·기말고사 대비문제 | 월 | 일 |
| DAY 37 | | Chapter 5 ~ 9 Review | 월 | 일 |
| DAY 38 | 10 | PSS 1 ~ 4-2 | 월 | 일 |
| DAY 39 | | PSS 4-3 ~ 4-9 | 월 | 일 |
| DAY 40 | | PSS 5-1 ~ 6-4 | 월 | 일 |
| DAY 41 | | 중간·기말고사 대비문제 | 월 | 일 |
| DAY 42 | 11 | PSS 1-1 ~ 2-2 | 월 | 일 |
| DAY 43 | | PSS 3 ~ 4 | 월 | 일 |
| DAY 44 | | PSS 5-1 ~ 6-2 | 월 | 일 |
| DAY 45 | | 중간·기말고사 대비문제 | 월 | 일 |
| DAY 46 | 12 | PSS 1-1 ~ 1-4 | 월 | 일 |
| DAY 47 | | PSS 2 ~ 3-3 | 월 | 일 |
| DAY 48 | | PSS 4-1 ~ 4-2 | 월 | 일 |
| DAY 49 | | 중간·기말고사 대비문제 | 월 | 일 |
| DAY 50 | 13 | PSS 1 ~ 2 | 월 | 일 |
| DAY 51 | | PSS 3 ~ 4 | 월 | 일 |
| DAY 52 | | PSS 5 ~ 7 | 월 | 일 |
| DAY 53 | | 중간·기말고사 대비문제 | 월 | 일 |
| DAY 54 | 14 | PSS 1-1 ~ 1-4 | 월 | 일 |
| DAY 55 | | PSS 2-1 ~ 2-4 | 월 | 일 |
| DAY 56 | | PSS 3-1 ~ 3-3 | 월 | 일 |
| DAY 57 | | PSS 4 ~ 6-2 | 월 | 일 |
| DAY 58 | | PSS 7 | 월 | 일 |
| DAY 59 | | 중간·기말고사 대비문제 | 월 | 일 |
| DAY 60 | | Chapter 10 ~ 14 Review | 월 | 일 |

# 2026 제6기 마더텅 중학교 학습수기 공모전 안내

대상 100 만 원
금상 20 만 원
은상 10 만 원

##  지원 자격 및 장학금

중1·중2·중3

**지원 과목** 국어 / 영어 중 1과목 이상 지원 가능
※여러 과목 지원 시 가산점이 부여됩니다.

**성적 기준** 아래 2가지 항목 중 1개 이상의 조건에 해당하면 지원 가능

① 2025년 2학기 중간·기말고사 또는 2026년 1학기 중간·기말고사 성적표

② 2025년 7월~ 2026년 6월 시행 중학생 대상 국어/영어 해당 인증시험 성적표
   책과함께 KBS한국어능력시험, J-ToKL, 전국 영어 학력경시대회, TOEIC, TOEFL, G-TELP, TOSEL

**위 조건에 해당한다면**

마더텅 중학 교재로 공부하면서 **느낀 점**과 **공부 방법, 학업 성취, 성적 변화** 등에 관한 자신만의 수기를 작성해서 마더텅으로 보내 주세요. 우수한 글을 보내 주신 분들께 **학습수기 공모 장학금**을 드립니다!

## 응모 대상  마더텅 중학 교재로 공부한 중1·중2·중3

뿌리깊은 중학국어 독해력, 중학영문법 3800제, 중학영문법 3800제 스타터, 중학영문법 3800제 중간·기말고사 대비편, 중학영문법 3800제 워크북, 중학영문법 3800제 쓰기 WRITING, 마더텅 100% 실전대비 MP3 중학영어듣기 24회 모의고사, 중학영단어 9000, 문법별/주제별로 정리한 중학 영어 독해 101 및 기타 교재 중 1권 이상 신청 가능

## 응모 방법

① 마더텅 홈페이지 커뮤니티 - 이벤트 게시판에 접속
② [2026 마더텅 중학교 학습수기 공모전 게시글] 클릭 후 [2026 마더텅 중학교 학습수기 공모전 첨부 파일]을 다운
③ [2026 마더텅 중학교 학습수기 공모전 지원서] 작성 후 메일(mothert.marketing@gmail.com)로 발송

**접수 기한** 2026년 7월 31일  **수상자 발표일** 2026년 8월 17일  **장학금 수여일** 2026년 9월 17일
※세부 일정은 당사 사정에 따라 변경될 수 있습니다.

✎ ✏ 📝 **영어의 8품사** 🔍 📖 🏫

|  |  | 예문 |
|---|---|---|
| 명사 | **사람, 사물, 동물의 이름**을 나타내는 말 → 주어, 목적어, 보어<br>예 Jane, Mr. Brown, desk, chair, computer, bag, dog, bird | This computer looks new.<br>이 컴퓨터는 새것처럼 보인다.<br>I have a dog.<br>나는 개가 한 마리 있다. |
| 대명사 | 명사를 **대신**하는 말 → 주어, 목적어, 보어<br>예 I, my, you, he, she, it, them, we, myself, yourself, ourselves | Look at the dog! It is cute.<br>개 좀 봐! 그것은 귀여워.<br>I'm proud of myself.<br>나는 내 자신이 자랑스럽다. |
| 동사 | **행위, 동작, 상태를 묘사**하며 '~다'로 해석되는 말 → 서술어<br>- 일반동사: 주로 움직임을 나타내며 '~하다'라고 해석<br>　예 walk, run, eat, study, play, make, buy, love, like<br>- be동사: 상태나 위치를 주로 묘사하며 '~이다'라고 해석<br>　예 am, are, is, was, were | We eat dinner at 7.<br>우리는 7시에 저녁을 먹는다.<br>She loves her daughter.<br>그녀는 그녀의 딸을 사랑한다.<br>I am an artist.<br>나는 예술가이다. |
| 형용사 | **명사**를 꾸미거나 보충 설명하는 말 → 수식어, 보어<br>**생김새, 색깔, 크기, 성격, 특징**을 묘사하는 말<br>예 pretty, beautiful, red, tall, big, small, nice, kind, easy,<br>　difficult | She has big eyes.<br>그녀는 큰 눈을 가지고 있다.<br>He is a kind boy.<br>그는 친절한 소년이다.<br>The book is easy.<br>그 책은 쉽다. |
| 부사 | **형용사, 동사, 다른 부사, 문장 전체**를 자세히 설명하여 문장의<br>의미를 더욱 풍부하게 하는 말 → 수식어<br>**시간, 장소, 정도, 빈도**를 묘사하는 말<br>예 now, here, very, well, always, early, really, happily, sadly | What are you doing now?<br>지금 뭐 하고 있어?<br>Your sister is very pretty.<br>네 언니는 무척 예쁘다.<br>We really enjoyed the party.<br>우리는 정말 그 파티를 즐겼다. |
| 접속사 | **단어와 단어, 구와 구, 절과 절**을 이어주는 말<br>- 등위접속사: **같은 종류**의 말을 연결<br>　예 and, but, or, so<br>- 종속접속사: **명사절, 부사절, 형용사절**을 **주절**에 연결<br>　예 because, when, as, if | She is old and wise.<br>그녀는 나이가 있고 지혜롭다.<br>I slept early, because I was tired.<br>나는 피곤했기 때문에 일찍 잤다. |
| 전치사 | 명사 앞에서 **시간, 장소, 방향, 위치**를 나타내는 말<br>예 at, on, in, before, after, under, from, to, for, with, between,<br>　in front of | I sleep at 11 p.m.<br>나는 밤 11시에 잔다.<br>Your pen is under the chair.<br>네 펜은 의자 밑에 있다.<br>Let's meet in front of the building.<br>건물 앞에서 만나자. |
| 감탄사 | **감정**을 표현하는 말<br>예 Oh, Wow, Well | Wow, you got a new phone!<br>와, 너 새로운 전화기를 샀구나! |